Beginning Mac OS X Snow Leopard Server

From Solo Install to Enterprise Integration

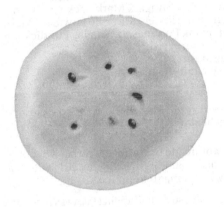

Charles S. Edge, Jr
Chris Barker
Ehren Schwiebert

Apress®

Beginning Mac OS X Snow Leopard Server: From Solo Install to Enterprise Integration

ISBN-13 (pbk): 978-1-4302-2772-4

ISBN-13 (electronic): 978-1-4302-2773-1

9 8 7 6 5 4 3 2 1

Publisher and President: Paul Manning
Lead Editor: Clay Andres
Developmental Editor: Douglas Pundick
Technical Reviewers: David A. Coyle, Joe Kissel and Brad Lees
Editorial Board: Clay Andres, Steve Anglin, Mark Beckner, Ewan Buckingham, Gary Cornell, Jonathan Gennick, Jonathan Hassell, Michelle Lowman, Matthew Moodie, Duncan Parkes, Jeffrey Pepper, Frank Pohlmann, Douglas Pundick, Ben Renow-Clarke, Dominic Shakeshaft, Matt Wade, Tom Welsh
Coordinating Editor: Kelly Moritz
Copy Editors: Kim Wimpsett and Heather Lang
Compositor: MacPS, LLC.
Indexer: John Collin
Artist: April Milne
Cover Designer: Anna Ishchenko

Distributed to the book trade worldwide by Springer-Verlag New York, Inc., 233 Spring Street, 6th Floor, New York, NY 10013. Phone 1-800-SPRINGER, fax 201-348-4505, e-mail orders-ny@springer-sbm.com, or visit www.springeronline.com.

For information on translations, please e-mail rights@apress.com, or visit www.apress.com.

Apress and friends of ED books may be purchased in bulk for academic, corporate, or promotional use. eBook versions and licenses are also available for most titles. For more information, reference our Special Bulk Sales–eBook Licensing web page at www.apress.com/info/bulksales.

To Lisa & Emerald With Love
– Charles Edge

To my loved ones
– Chris Barker

To Caroline, Luke, and Mayah
– Ehren Schwiebert

Contents at a Glance

Contents

About the Authors

Charles S. Edge, Jr is the Director of Technology at 318, the nation's largest Mac consultancy. At 318, Charles leads a team of the finest gunslingers to have been assembled for the Mac platform, working on network architecture, security, storage and deployment for various vertical and horizontal markets. Charles maintains the 318 blog at http://www.318.com/techjournal as well as a personal site at http://www.krypted.com and is the author of a number of titles on Mac OS X Server and systems administration topics. He has spoken at conferences around the world, including DefCon, Black Hat, LinuxWorld, MacWorld, MacSysAdmin and the Apple WorldWide Developers Conference. Charles is the developer of the SANS course on Mac OS X Security and the author of its best practices guide to securing Mac OS X. Charles is also the author of a number of whitepapers, including a guide on mass deploying virtualization on the Mac platform for VMware. After 10 years in Los Angeles, Charles has hung up his surfboard and fled to Minneapolis, Minnesota with his wife, Lisa and sweet little bucket of a daughter, Emerald.

Chris Barker has been helping people, schools, and businesses find better ways of accomplishing their goals for more than a decade. As an Apple Certified Systems Administrator, he currently spends his time discovering ways to best use Apple's hardware and software. When he is not at a computer, he finds ways of improving life for everybody by applying science to beer and cocktails; he writes about these and other adventures at angrydome.org.

Ehren Schwiebert is a Solutions Architect and Senior Professional Services Manager at 318, where he has worked since 2003. Prior to joining 318, he worked at Apple's technical support call centers, where he provided phone support to businesses and end users. He also served as a software developer and project manager for the Wisconsin state legislature, helping to usher in their first computerized electronic voting system. He currently lives in Los Angeles, where among other things, he enjoys theater, soccer, camping, and just hanging out with his amazing family.

About the Technical Reviewers

Dave Coyle earned his PhD in thermochronology in 1992. Research in thermal modeling and crustal evolution at the Max-Planck Institute for Nuclear Physics (Heidelberg Germany) lead to a career in software development. David has been concentrating on Apple technologies since 1997 and is a certified Apple System Administrator.

Joe Kissell is Senior Editor of TidBITS, a Web site and weekly email newsletter about the Macintosh and the Internet, and the author of numerous print and electronic books about Macintosh software, including the best-selling Take Control of Mac OS X Backups. He is also a Senior Contributor to Macworld. Joe has worked in the Mac software industry since the early 1990s, and previously managed software development for Nisus Software and Kensington Technology Group. He currently lives in Paris, France.

Brad Lees has more than 12 years of experience in application development and server management. He has specialized in creating and initiating software programs in real estate development systems and financial institutions. His professional career has been highlighted by his positions as Information Systems Manager at The Lyle Anderson Company; Product Development Manager for Smarsh; Vice President of Application Development for iNation; and Information Technology Manager at The Orcutt/Winslow Partnship, the largest architectural firm in Arizona. A graduate of Arizona State University, Brad and his wife, Natalie, reside in Phoenix with their five children.

Acknowledgments

Charles Edge

I'd like to first and foremost thank the Mac OS X community. This includes everyone from the people that design the black box to the people that dissect it and the people that help others learn how to dissect it. We truly stand on the shoulders of giants. Of those at Apple that need to be thanked specifically: Schoun Regan, Joel Rennich, Greg Smith, JD Mankovsky, Drew Tucker, Stale Bjorndal, Cawan Starks, Eric Senf, Jennifer Jones and everyone on the Mac OS X Server, Xsan and Final Cut Server development team. And of course the one and only Josh "old school game console ninja" Wisenbaker! Outside of Apple, thanks to Arek Dreyer and the other Peachpit authors for paving the way to build another series of Mac systems administration books by producing such quality. And of course, a special thanks to the late Michael Bartosh for being such an inspiration to us all to strive to understand what is going on under the hood.

The crew at 318 also deserves a lot of credit. It's their hard work that let to having the time to complete yet another book! Special thanks to JJ and to KK for holding everything together in such wild times!

And finally, a special thanks to Apress for letting us continue to write books for them. They fine tune the dribble I provide into a well-oiled machine of mature prose. This especially includes Clay Andres for getting everything in motion not only for this book but for the entire series and, of course, to Kelly Moritz for pulling it all together in the end with her amazing crack of the whhhip (yes, that's a Family Guy reference). And I'll just include the co-authors in the Apress family: Ehren and Chris, thanks for the countless hours to make the deadlines and looking forward to the next round!

Chris Barker

There is of course the community from which I learned, and my colleagues with whom I have worked, that I am much indebted for the specific knowledge and experiences I was able to convey in this book. Charles (besides creating a much more encompassing acknowledgement) has been a great help and guide in this entire writing process, and also thanks to Ehren for being a wonderful coauthor to work with, making it feel like I am not the only green thumb at this whole Author thing.

I would not be writing this if it were not for the efforts of those who gave me the opportunities earlier in my life to thrive in situations where I would have otherwise faltered.

"If I had not some strength of will I would make a first class drunkard" – Ernest Shackleton

Ehren Schwiebert

I'd like to thank my collaborators, Chris and Charles, for their hard work and prodigious output, as well as for allowing me along for the ride on this journey with them. Thanks also go out to my family and friends for putting up with my hours of isolation as I assembled my chapters for this book. I'd also like to extend my thanks and gratitude to my amazingly talented colleagues at 318, who continue to raise the bar for excellence in their field. Thanks to Kevin Klein for giving me an opportunity to work with this stellar company, and to Jonathan Jedeikin for his constant encouragement and collaboration. Thanks to all of my current and past clients who have entrusted to me the responsibility of stewardship over their business' technology. And a special thank-you goes out to Peggy Gregory, my high school journalism teacher, who not only sat me down in front of my first Mac and showed me what an amazing tool it could be, but also guided and inspired my writing, and taught me to demand the highest quality of both my writing and myself.

Chapter 1

Welcome to OS X Server

If you bought this book, then either you already have a system running Mac OS X Server or you are looking to purchase one. We agree that you've made a great choice! Mac OS X Server is a mature product that is easier to configure than most Linux systems but more cost effective than many other server solutions.

Mac OS X Server uses a healthy mixture of open source software and customized Apple versions of those open source solutions. Many open source–based servers are difficult to use, but Mac OS X Server has proven that it is fairly straightforward to configure and manage, while equally as powerful as the traditional Linux counterparts.

NOTE: This book assumes that you're running Mac OS X Server 10.6. Despite some similarities between 10.6 and previous versions of Apple's server software, you should apply the lessons and examples of this book only if you are using Mac OS X Server 10.6.

Mac OS X Server 10.6 is the latest version in a long line of the Mac OS X Server operating systems developed by Apple, dating back to 1999. The foundations of most components and services of Mac OS X Server have their origins in open source technology, which is why Apple uses the marketing phrase "Open Source Made Easy." Both the server and workstation versions of Mac OS X 10.6 include the Apache web server, Samba file server, CUPS print server, and a number of other popular open source technologies. But Mac OS X Server goes a step further than its workstation counterpart when it comes to finely grained graphical controls for the open source products underneath the hood. Mac OS X Server also comes with a number of additional open source products that are not included in the client version of Mac OS X, such as Lightweight Directory Access Protocol (LDAP) directory services, Jabber/XMPP instant messenger server, and the MySQL database server.

The server team at Apple didn't limit their product solely to integrating open source technologies. In addition to open source technologies, Apple has included a number of proprietary technologies such as Apple Filing Protocol (AFP) file sharing, Podcast Producer, Push Notification, and Xgrid. These services are likely new to recent converts to the Mac OS X platform, but the back-end concepts are probably not.

This book is for anyone not experienced with Mac OS X Server 10.6. Whether you are an enterprise administrator looking to add Mac OS X Server to your infrastructure, an experienced Mac OS X system administrator looking for an update from previous versions of Mac OS X Server, an educator in a school district who manages labs running Mac OS X Server, or a creative professional looking for new and better ways to collaborate with colleagues and clients, this book should appeal to you.

What Is a Server Anyway?

A *server* is a computer that hosts data for other computers. Any computer can act as a server if it's providing some form of service over the network. For example, a Mac OS X client that is sharing a printer is considered a print server. However, that same computer will have limitations, both in terms of granularity of the configuration of the resources that are shared and in regard to the operating system itself.

Each server is going to share at least one resource, if it is indeed a server. Each protocol used for sharing can then be considered as a *service*. In the case of a file server, different types of sharing are available. Multiple protocols, or services, can then share the same resource.

To provide shared services to other computers, a server must be placed on a network. A *network* is a collection of interconnected hosts. Notice that *hosts* here is plural. Just as you need to host a service in order to have a server, you need to have multiple hosts in order to have a network. A router interconnects two networks. A host is going to be any device connected to a network, including a firewall, router, server, or client computer. Typical modern networks are interconnected via Ethernet or 802.11 wireless networking using Transmission Control Protocol/Internet Protocol (TCP/IP).

What This Book Is

This book is a guide to help you get started with building and managing Mac OS X Server. Getting started with a server means first setting up the server, then setting up the services that will run on the server, and finally setting up client systems to connect to the server. In some cases, a fully effective setup is going to require using the command line; however, in other scenarios, this will not be necessary. Therefore, it is important to understand that although the book is predominantly going to cover the graphical user interface (GUI) tools for Mac OS X Server, the command line is not considered an advanced operation but rather an integral part of administering Mac OS X Server. So, for those of you whose experience and comfort level with systems administration ends when a Terminal window opens, welcome! As you will see in this book, command-line administration gives you a new level of control and effectiveness and can actually be quite enjoyable as well!

Although the book is going to look at the basic setup and administration of services, granular fine-tuning of each configuration will not be covered in great detail. There are a number of common scenarios for Mac OS X Server integration. But as the title suggests, this book is a beginning book. We will cover as many applicable options as possible, but we will not go into extensive detail about the specifics of advanced services management on any one service. Additional resources outlined at the end of this book can guide your search for advanced configurations.

How This Book Is Organized

Each chapter of the book is meant to get you started with managing a particular component, or service, of Mac OS X Server 10.6. This starts with planning and enabling services, then goes into more complex tasks, and concludes with showing how to connect to the services from client computers. Along the way, we will also cover the basic concepts for each service and explain how the service pertains to client interaction. While we will cover how to do tasks graphically, we will also look at doing a number of tasks programmatically, or from the command line.

This chapter is a strategic chapter, geared toward laying the foundation for subsequent chapters. In this chapter we discuss what to do before you open the box that Mac OS X Server came in!

Chapter 2 takes a look at the setup process for Mac OS X Server from the perspective of using Mac OS X Server in 30 minutes or less. This includes booting to a setup environment and the tools that are made available there, as well as the installation process and options that should be used.

Chapter 3 provides an overview of the tools that you will use with Mac OS X Server and the operating system specifics that should be configured post-installation. We'll introduce Server Preferences, Server Admin, Workgroup Manager, and Server Monitor tools, and we'll cover the typical options and even some third-party tools to make your life easier.

Chapter 4 looks at configuring a directory services server that can be used to provide a centralized repository for locating objects, storing usernames, and networking computers.

Chapter 5 looks at using Mac OS X as a traffic cop. There are two sides to this coin. The first is to set up the server to protect itself by leveraging the built-in firewall. The second is to use Mac OS X as a router so that it can provide a network for the rest of your devices.

Chapter 6 covers Dynamic Host Configuration Protocol (DHCP), which allows administrators to dynamically assign IP addresses to devices on their networks, freeing you from having to keep track of IP assignments on expansive spreadsheets or manually assigning addresses to each device. Domain Name System (DNS) allows you to assign host names to corresponding IP addresses so you can easily track and interconnect devices and services by their host name. These tools are essential for most networks to ease the burden of management, and although they are standards-based aspects of network management, their Mac OS X Server–specific implementation is covered in Chapter 6.

Chapter 7 covers taking your network and Mac OS X Server and extending it to remote users in our review of leveraging the virtual private network (VPN) server. We will also look at using Remote Authentication Dial In User Service (RADIUS) to provide usernames and passwords to other devices and application environments, such as SonicWALL, AirPort, and CommuniGate Pro.

Chapter 8 covers how to deploy Mac OS X to other systems, which allows administrators to leverage NetBoot to start up computers to a network-accessible copy of Mac OS X. We'll also explain how to use NetInstall to deploy a Mac OS X client using the NetBoot service. Finally, we'll cover the new NetRestore features, which leverage the Apple Software Restore (`asr`) command-line utility to perform mass deployment of Mac disc images. Because the Automator-like System Image Utility is the key to successfully creating and preparing images for use with these services, we will also cover it.

GroupWare is one of the most productivity-driven aspects of any modern server operating system. The GroupWare big picture consists of address books, calendars, instant messaging, and e-mail and then allowing access to all of these on mobile devices. Apple has a compelling and cost-effective strategy for delivering these services to certain environments, so over the course of Chapters 9 through 13 we will lay out how to do so.

Chapter 9 covers the Address Book Server. New in Mac OS X Server 10.6, Address Book Server is the final piece in a puzzle that was started back in the days of AppleShare IP, when Apple added Mail to AppleShare IP Server. Address Book Server leverages some of the best in open source technology, and in Chapter 9 we will explain how to set up, configure, secure, manage, and then connect to Address Book Server.

Chapter 10 covers iCal Server. iCal Server uses Calendaring Extensions to Web-based Distributed Authoring and Versioning (thankfully shortened to simply CalDAV) as the back-end protocol (through `twistedcaldav`). iCal Server provides a simplified front end to configure the server, and the iCal client is a refined and maturing product that is freely bundled with Mac OS X workstation. In Chapter 10, we'll look at how to get set up and then how to make it all work together. Yes, this includes Windows clients too!

Chapter 11 covers iChat Server. iChat Server is Apple's implementation of Extensible Messaging and Presence Protocol (XMPP), still commonly referred to by its previous official name, Jabber. In Mac OS X 10.6, the back-end solution for iChat Server received little in the way of updates, but the front-end configuration options in Server Admin did. In Chapter 11, we will show how to set up and use iChat Server, keeping a keen eye on the latest updates added in Snow Leopard.

Chapter 12 covers the mail services. There are few aspects of a technology that users simply cannot live without more than e-mail. In Chapter 12, we cover how to set up a mail server using Mac OS X Server, including the most common messaging protocols and mailbox storage, and we cover how to securely give clients access to the server.

Chapter 13 covers services for mobile devices. One of the most substantial changes in Mac OS X Server 10.6 from 10.5 is the addition of a number of features built from the ground up to provide features for the iPhone and client computers that are outside of an office. Although Address Book Server, iCal Server, and Mail Server are perfectly capable of working with the Mac OS X client (and a number of other third-party clients for that matter), they are most compelling when coupled with the new services such as Push Notification and Mobile Access.

Chapter 14 covers Apache, which is the most-used web server in the world. In Chapter 14, we'll take it from a patchy default server configuration to a fully functional, secure, enterprise-class, extensible, rock-solid solution. A wiki server has about as many uses as there are pages in Wikipedia. In Chapter 14, we'll pick some of the most common scenarios and then cover how to set up the server and implement wiki-based solutions in Snow Leopard Server.

Chapter 15 covers MySQL. When coupled with Apache and PHP, MySQL is one of the most popular web application back-end databases on the planet. Chapter 15 looks at setting up MySQL, but given that the graphical interface doesn't cover much as far as MySQL is concerned, we will quickly jump into managing MySQL beyond what comes stock with Mac OS X Server.

Chapter 16 covers Podcast Producer, which is a video blogging service that is among the best of the breed. In Chapter 16, we will look at setting up and managing Podcast Producer. A substantial update to Mac OS X Server 10.6 is Podcast Composer, an Automator-like interface that allows the fast and highly customizable configuration of Podcast Producer workflows. In Chapter 16, we will also look at leveraging Podcast Composer to build complex and really cool (yes, we said cool—because It's true) podcasting workflows.

Chapter 17 covers QuickTime Streaming Server, which is Apple's streaming media server. Built on top of the Apple-centric Darwin Streaming Server (DSS) open source project, QuickTime Streaming Server enables you to publish streaming audio and video in a manner so that it is not easily cached onto local hard drives.

Chapter 18 covers AFP and SMB. File sharing is one of the oldest services offered on any server. Mac OS X Server supports the Apple Filing Protocol (AFP), Server Message Block (SMB), File Transfer Protocol (FTP), Network File System (NFS), and Web-based Distributed Authoring and Versioning (WebDAV) protocols, of which all except the last we will cover in Chapter 18 (WebDAV is covered in Chapter 14).

Chapter 19 covers print services. This chapter will cover options for printing and serving up print jobs for clients of Mac OS X Server. The print services require that an administrator first understand how to configure a printer on the server machine. We will then cover the ins and outs of sharing that printer to the network and deploying the printer with managed preferences in Open Directory.

Chapter 20 covers backing up your Mac OS X Server. To some degree, why have a server if you aren't going to back it up? Mac OS X has a limited selection of backup applications compared to its Windows counterpart, which in some ways forces a lightly limited scope for Chapter 20. Because having an effective backup strategy doesn't just mean that you have a second copy of your data on disk or tape, it means taking a look at the whole infrastructure and determining a strategy that can be used to back up your data holistically and reliably.

Chapter 21 explains how to configure your server to provide software updates to other Mac systems on your network, in lieu of the default Apple software update servers. Setting up a Software Update server can have a dramatic impact on your company's Internet bandwidth because large patches and updates need to be downloaded through your Internet gateway only once; without this service, each system on your network would download updates individually, clogging your network with duplicative downloads. You will also learn how to control which updates are allowed to be distributed to the other systems on your network.

Before You Begin

Now that you understand the layout of this book, let's look at how best to use it. We expect that you're going to do one of two things: either you'll use the book as a guide, going through it step-by-step, or you'll use this book as a sort of cookbook when you need to complete certain tasks. We have laid out the book to be appropriate for both purposes. But before we look at installing the server and using services, we're first going to look at some preliminary steps for planning the deployment. Then, dispersed throughout Chapters 2 and 3 we're also going to sprinkle in further information about planning; however, this won't be in-depth coverage of each service but more of a look at the tools that you use to manage Mac OS X Server.

Hardware

Your intended services and applications will determine your hardware requirements, especially when you start deploying systems like Final Cut Server or Xsan. So, let your needs dictate the hardware you get, and don't buy a machine first and then figure out how to make it work. In this chapter, we'll cover some general rules for these, although for the most part if you're not sure about what hardware to get, you can lean on the Apple Business Specialists in your local Apple store, an Apple Reseller, or Apple Online for more information about a suitable solution when purchasing hardware.

When searching for the right hardware on which to install Snow Leopard Server, keep in mind that Mac OS X 10.6 is the first version of Apple's operating system that requires an Intel processor, so set aside any ideas about bringing that old Power Mac G5 into service here. But fear not: there are a number of cost-effective and affordable options available to you in Apple's current line-up of hardware offerings.

No Xserve? No Problem!

If you're a small business or home office environment, then the Mac mini with Snow Leopard Server might just be sufficient for your environment. And at around $1,000 for the machine and operating system combined, that's going to be hard to beat. The hardware specifications are modest (as the name "mini" implies): an Intel Core 2 Duo processor, a single Gigabit Ethernet port, two Serial ATA hard drives, and up to 4GB of memory. Fortunately, the Mac mini server still packs a good little punch and will help you get started with Mac OS X Server, even if it's not a towering powerhouse of processor muscle and capacious storage. However, keep in mind that the more users and services you add to your network, the more hardware performance you will require until you finally saturate what the little box can do.

For the next step up from the Mac mini, Apple offers the Mac Pro. The Mac Pro is suitable for just about any size environment that doesn't need to leverage hardware that is capable of fitting into a rack. The Mac Pro sports plenty of server-friendly features such as ample slots for memory, four hard drive bays, an optional RAID card, four- or eight-core Intel Xeon processor configurations, dual Gigabit Ethernet ports, and three PCIe expansion slots. However, although it is ideally suited to Mac OS X Server from a power and performance standpoint, the Mac Pro still lacks the redundant, hot-swappable components of many rack-mount servers. So if high availability is one of your design requirements, you should consider an Intel Xserve to run your server.

And No Problem with the Xserve Either

Beyond the Mac Pro, Apple has dedicated server-class hardware in the form of the Xserve. Like the Mac Pro, the Xserve has robust performance and hardware offerings. It sports four- or eight-core Intel Xeon processors, an optional solid-state drive (SSD), up to three Serial ATA or high-speed SAS hard drives, massive amounts of memory, dual Gigabit Ethernet ports, and two PCIe expansion slots. Most of the critical hardware components are hot-swappable and redundant, so you can quickly replace failed hardware components—in many cases without even needing to shut down the server. To top off this engineering marvel, Apple has packed all this enterprise-class server goodness into a box that consumes less than 2 inches of height (1U) in a standard server rack.

Other Hardware Options

The previous examples do not represent your only options for installing Snow Leopard. Any Mac that meets the minimum system requirements can run Mac OS X Server 10.6. In fact, for the purposes of learning and following along with the material in this book, you might just want to use an old MacBook or iMac (if running Mac OS X Server 10.6, then these would need to be Intel) system as a test server.

Get Ready!

Many of this book's readers may have used previous versions of Mac OS X Server, most notably Mac OS X Server 10.5. Although some may note that Mac OS X Server 10.6 is not an upgrade that includes a significant amount of new features, overall we're pretty impressed with how many new features there are.

Most notably, Mac OS X Server is 64-bit, netting a performance impact making it worth the price—a price, by the way, that was reduced by half of what Apple charged for Mac OS X Server 10.5. But there's more. Snow Leopard Server also sports about as many new features as every version of Mac OS X Server that it follows. These include the following:

- NetRestore has been integrated with System Image Utility to facilitate easier creation of NetRestore NetBoot sets, allowing for asr-based restores (asr has not been given a GUI, though).

- There's now an option to enable and disable directory services binding discovery on servers.

- There's now Wide Area Bonjour support in the DNS service.

- The Mobile Access service has been added, which allows you to proxy incoming connections for all the included groupware services through the server.

- The Push Notification service has been added to enhance iPhone integration with Mac OS X Server.

- The mail server now uses Dovecot, which has a GUI option in Server Admin and Server Preferences for relaying outgoing mail through a separate SMTP server.

- Podcast Producer got a pretty big overhaul in Podcast Producer 2, making workflows easier to be created and managed with an assistant and making the server much easier to set up with another assistant.

- Podcast Producer has been integrated ever so slightly with Final Cut Server workflows.

- There are new 802.1x features in networksetup.

- There is a new command, mcxrefresh, used for refreshing managed preferences on clients.

- Users now have a splash page that allows for a number of fairly self-service options including setting up easy-to-use mail rules.

- A lot of GUI logic has been added; for example, when you promote to an Open Directory master, Server Admin checks existing bindings and, if they are present, provides a different prompt; also, the toolbar in Directory Utility was cleaned up, and DHCP-supplied LDAP was removed (ostensibly for security reasons).

- You can use Server Preferences and the Server Admin/Workgroup Manager pseudo-interchangeably rather than switching between Standard, Workgroup, and Advanced (that whole idea died with 10.5).

■ The GUI iChat Server federation allows for multiple iChat servers for an organization.

The client and server updates most likely to impact server administrators more than users:

■ You can now move journaling to a dedicated drive (that is, SSD) to off-load potential I/O performance bottlenecks.

■ Directory Utility was moved to CoreServices and can now be accessed through the Accounts pane of System Preferences.

■ Hard drive spaces is now reported more accurately, changing the game in capacity planning for all those Nagios/Zenoss folks.

Looking at the difference between Server 10.5 and Server 10.6, it seems this is a similar enhancement in terms of the number of new features. Some are subtler but will allow for more agile development of features in subsequent releases.

Summary

Every new version of Mac OS X Server offers some pretty cool features to improve the performance, security, and capabilities of this innovative operating system. Mac OS X Server 10.6 is no exception. There are lots of things to learn, both old and new, so let's get started!

Chapter 2

Setting Up a Server in 30 Minutes or Less

The goal of this chapter is to walk you through the steps required to get your Snow Leopard server up and running as a basic fileserver in less than 30 minutes. For many organizations, this is the primary function and the first task assigned to a server installed on their premises. However, over time, most businesses will want to use more features than just a fileserver, so this chapter will ensure that, while accomplishing the primary task of creating a filesystem, you will be able to use other features in the future without having to start over. In the process of going through this chapter, we will touch upon many subjects that are addressed in more depth in other chapters of the book; however, we have found that it is best to provide a context for these services first before presenting the more technical and abstract components of them.

Before You Begin

Mac OS X Server 10.6 has roughly the same requirements as the Mac OS X 10.6 client. This isn't to say that the requirements are the minimum for every installation. Knowing how many users will interact with each service and whether the server can handle the load is key to building a long-term solution.

The minimum requirements for Mac OS X Server 10.6 include the following:

- Apple computer with an Intel processor
- 10GB of available hard drive space
- 2GB of RAM

The two most common systems from Apple to use as a server are the Mac Pro and the Xserve. Although it is common to recommend an Xserve for most business applications, there are circumstances (such as space limitations or cost limitations) where we would recommend a Mac Pro. It is also possible to use an iMac or even a Mac mini as a server; however, it is not recommended because of their consumer design and primarily their limitation when it comes to expandability in terms of storage and memory.

> **NOTE:** The Mac mini server is a great fit for groups of 10 to 30 users.

Although the Xserve and Mac Pro provide multiple options for storing data, whichever options you choose, you will want to account for the separation of the boot volume and the actual data storage area. Specifically, for any server, you want to have at least two volumes, one acting as the boot volume, storing the operating system and any configuration files, and the other acting as the storage or data volume, holding all the client files, share points, web sites, and other information that the server shares with other computers. The reason for this divide is simple: by backing up and documenting the relatively small amount of information pertaining to the server configuration, you can reformat and reinstall the boot partition while leaving your fileshare untouched. Or in the case of upgrading or migrating your server to a new physical machine, you only have to be concerned about moving the data volume (which could be stored on an external storage solution) instead of trying to locate it among the server's boot volume as well.

From a planning perspective, you will want to have at least 80GB available (currently the Xserve ships with a 160GB drive) just to hold the OS and any local system caches. (The Software Update server, for example, downloads to the boot drive by default, which can easily fill up your boot drive if you just used the minimum 10GB benchmark.) The data volume can be an external RAID, such as a Promise RAID, or if your server came with a hardware RAID card, you could use various RAID configurations to create a boot partition and a data partition; Apple is now offering solid-state drives to be included with an Xserve, which is a perfect place to put the boot volume while keeping the data on the larger (and less expensive) removable drives. There are many options to how you can create these two volumes, but the end result is you want to ensure that your server OS space is separated from the client access space.

Network Considerations

OS X Server does not like having its IP address changed on it after it has been set up and configured. Snow Leopard is so reliant on DNS and IP addressing working properly that it will automatically set up its own limited DNS server in order to function correctly. That is why it is essential to determine what IP address and DNS name to use before you install the OS, because once you have started configuring the server, making changes to those settings requires resorting to the command line and may lead to some service issues down the line.

> **NOTE:** DNS stands for Domain Name System and is what is used to translate your.server.com to 192.168.10.2, for example. 10.6 is very dependent on this translation process being accurate.

If you are using a standard commodity network router, you should consider what your current subnet is and how it is configured. Most consumer routers create a single class C subnet (allowing for 253 unique IP addresses to be controlled by it), and unless configured otherwise, these IP addresses will almost always start with 192.168.0.X or 192.168.1.X. You can leave your router to continue to use one of these subnets.

In the future, if you do plan to start using VPN for secure remote access to your office network, you may run into problems. Since your office would be using a very common subnet, a computer connecting over the VPN from another network may be on the same subnet (such as a user connecting from home), which makes it difficult for the computer to determine how to talk to the office network if it thinks it is already on that network. If your office network is not very complicated and this would be your first dedicated server in the office, it is safe to say you should consider changing the subnet now, because once you have two systems in place in the future, changing your subnets will be harder.

Installing Mac OS X Server 10.6

Before you even unbox the server, you will want to plan where you will put the equipment, how you will power it (do you need a battery backup?), how you will manage it (the authors have all spent too much time trying to work in a closet on folding chairs to know you will want someplace that will be marginally comfortable to be in!), and what to do with all the heat it will be generating. Along with planning the physical layout, this is also the time to collect information on the hardware serial information, the license information that came with your server software, what IP address you want to use, and what you want to name it, and then have that documented before proceeding. Thinking about these things before you start will make the installation process go much smoother.

Even if you have just unboxed and put your new Xserve (or whatever hardware you're using) into its rack enclosure, you will still want to boot from the included install DVD and reinstall the OS. This will also give you the chance to reformat and rename the internal drives and configure the built-in RAID card before proceeding with the OS install.

To get started, first boot to optical media by booting the computer while holding down the C key. Once it's booted, you'll see the language selection screen, which will allow you to, interestingly enough, select the language to use during the installation process, as you can see in Figure 2–1. Then click the right arrow icon.

You'll next be at the first screen of the installation process. Notice that you have a menu bar at the top of the screen. At this point, click the Utilities menu, and then select Disk Utility, as shown in Figure 2–2. This will open the Disk Utility screen.

Figure 2–1. *Selecting your language*

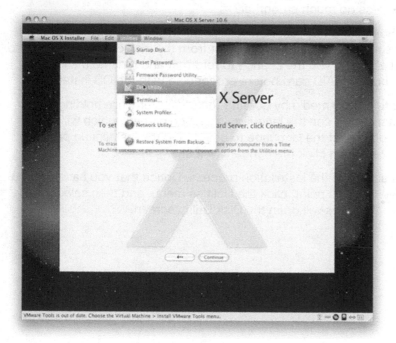

Figure 2–2. *Selecting Disk Utility from the Utilities menu will launch it for you.*

Here you can perform all the same tasks that you would typically perform with Disk Utility. Click the disk that you will be installing Mac OS X onto, and then select the number of partitions that you will be installing on the server. It's often wise to split the disk (or disks if you'll be using a RAID) you are installing the operating system on into separate partitions so the operating system is separate from the data that will be hosted. By partitioning the drive, you allow for easily replacing the operating system and keeping the shared data on the drive from filling the boot volume.

Click the disk, and then select the Partition tab. In the Volume Scheme field, select the number of partitions to be created, as shown in Figure 2–3.

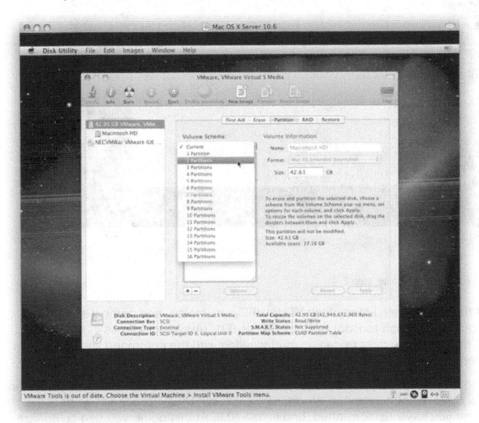

Figure 2–3. *Formatting the drive*

Once you have selected the number of partitions, click each, and provide the size that will be assigned to them, as shown in Figure 2–4.

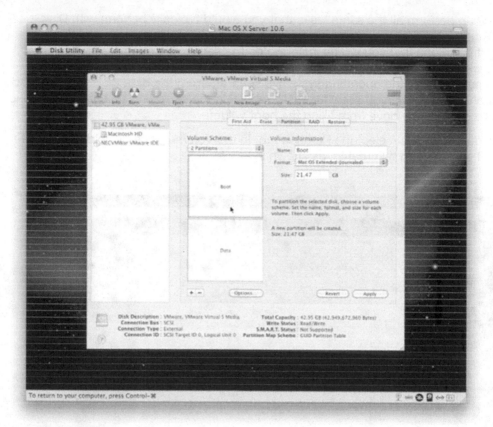

Figure 2–4. *Formatting the drive, step 2*

Reformat the drive labeled Macintosh HD to HFS+ Journaled, and name it something easier to remember such as Boot or Boot-Server-001. (Avoiding spaces in the drive name will make things easier once you start working with the command line, which you will do eventually with OS X Server.)

Ensure you have a volume labeled Data or similar, which will be for holding all your share points and other client-accessible information. Quit Disk Utility, proceed to select the boot volume you have just formatted, and install 10.6. At this point, you can customize your installation. However, with the exception of adding QuickTime 7, there isn't much to customize, and you can always add those files later if need be. Now X11 is installed by default. Once you have started the process (and the installation DVD has been verified), you will see the progress bar of your status appear, as shown in Figure 2–5.

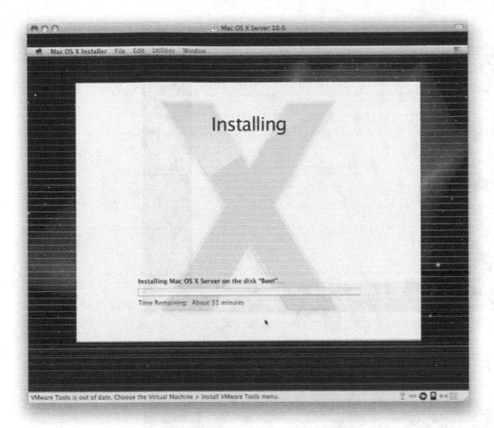

Figure 2–5. *Installation progress*

Welcome to Mac OS X Server 10.6

Once the installation process has completed, the machine will reboot and show you the new welcome screen, as shown in Figure 2–6. Unfortunately, there is no song or welcome video like there is for the 10.6 client.

After a few seconds of waiting, the Welcome screen will update to allow you to select your region (see Figure 2–7).

Figure 2–6. *Welcome screen*

Figure 2–7. *Welcome screen, with region selection*

After selecting your region, you can click Continue to move toward selecting the appropriate keyboard type.

Enter the serial number and registration information that came with your server. You will want to save this information on a .configuration document (a template is included in the appendix) for future reference in case you have to reinstall the server. Apple provides two copies of the serial number on stickers, which you can apply directly to the server if you want (see Figure 2–8).

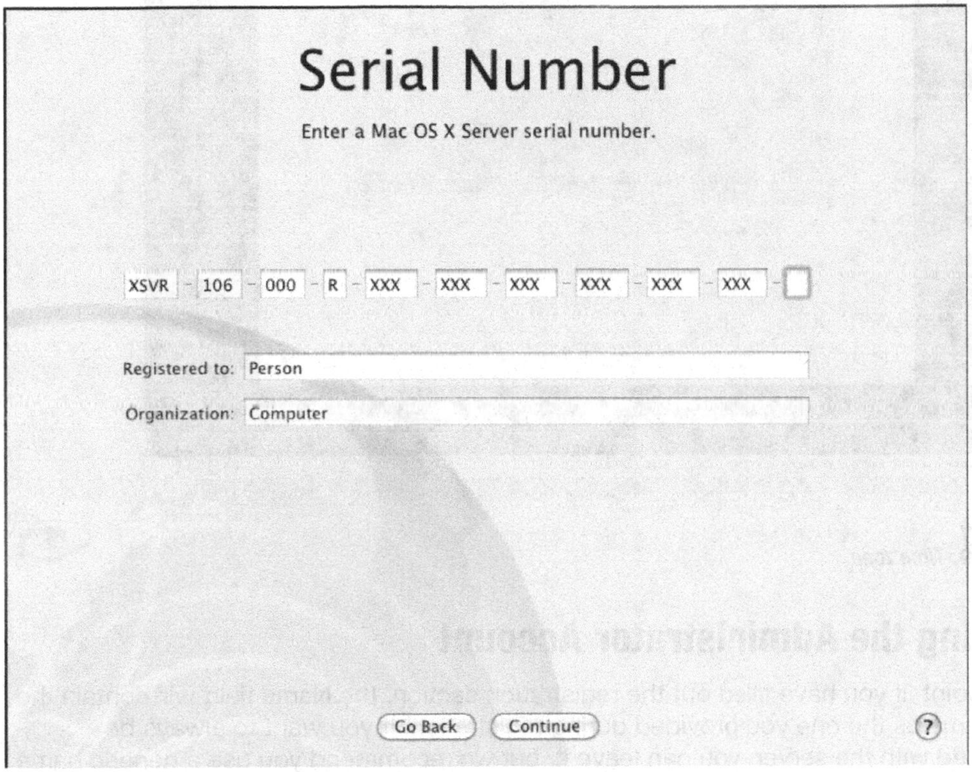

Figure 2–8. *Serial Number screen*

You will be asked to transfer information from a previous server; select "Setup a new server," and Click Continue. Rarely will you want to trust a migration for such a complicated system as your server.

Enter your registration information (Apple has not always been clear, but this can sometimes activate the warranty on your hardware). If you do not want to register, pressing Command+Q will prompt you to skip it.

Set your time zone either by clicking the map or by entering the city name in the field (the Tab key will allow you to autocomplete the entry). As you can see in Figure 2–9, the time zone is highlighted on the map for you to confirm your presence. Also ensure the Network Time Server field includes time.apple.com for now.

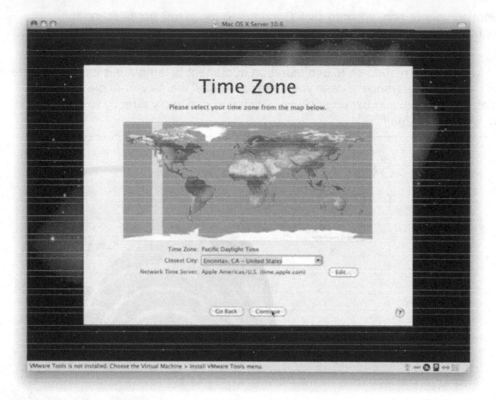

Figure 2–9. *Time zone*

Creating the Administrator Account

At this point, if you have filled out the registration section, the Name field will contain the same name as the one you provided during registration. If you want to always be associated with the server, you can leave it, but we recommend you use a generic name such as Local Admin, with the short name "ladmin" to keep things consistent among servers in the future (so even if you aren't the person registering the next server, people know that the default administrator account on the server is ladmin). You also do not want to use Administrator or Admin as a name, because those are both common names used in directory services such as Open Directory and Active Directory, which you may integrate with your server in the future. Depending on how the server is configured to check usernames and passwords, there may be confusion on where it is actually going to check to see whether the password for Admin is correct, and that can make troubleshooting difficult. So, use a local administrator account (such as "ladmin" or "localadmin") that you know won't be used in any unified user and password directory in the future in order to keep conflicts to a minimum. Figure 2–10 shows an example.

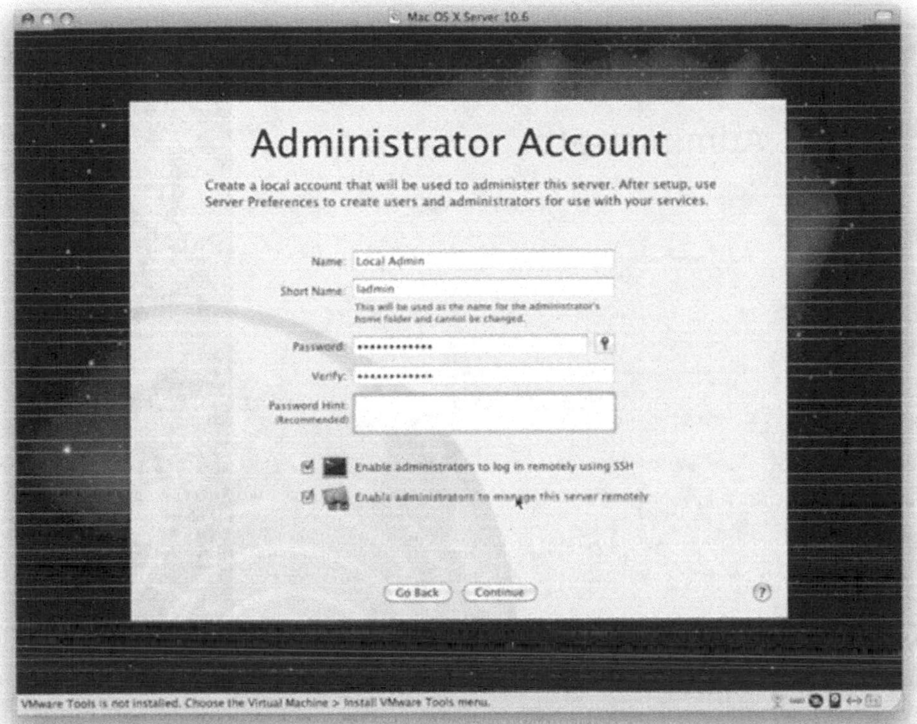

Figure 2–10. *Creating an account*

You will want to pick a secure password for your server; if you have trouble, you can click the key icon to the right of the Password field, and it will bring up the Password Assistant showing your current password strength and options to help generate a new random password for you (shown in Figure 2–11). A common practice is to use a long password of the Memorable type and replace any strange or troublesome characters (such as / \ ! @ # ' ") with simpler characters (. , ; :). Whichever password you choose, you will want to make sure it does not include spaces or common difficult characters (such as /, which is a folder divider); the reasoning behind this is OS X and its associated configuration and server tools will execute commands using the password provided to it, and in some instances things such as a space may trigger unexpected results in a script or program. Although Apple has gotten much better at ensuring consistency across the board for all the services 10.6 works with, it can still be a problem.

Figure 2–11. *Password Assistant*

Another thing to know about the password you choose is that Mac OS X Server 10.6 will create a second account as soon as you click Continue, and that is the root, or superuser, account. This account will use the same password as the one you provided for the Local Admin account, so choose wisely, because it will not be kept in sync with your Local Admin password if you choose to change it in the future. There have been specific instances of new admins creating the first administrator account with the password "password," thinking that they will change it to something more secure once they get the server up and running, only to have their servers compromised because every hacker on the planet knows to try logging onto a server with the user root and a password of "password."

Configuring the Network Interface

The next screen will load, which looks similar to the Network pane in System Preferences; here you will want to change the network interface from DHCP (the default option) to Static. You may have already picked out your IP address, but for reference, if you were using a standard small business or consumer router, that machine would by default hand out IP addresses in the range of 192.168.1.100–200, so you would want to make sure your server uses an IP outside of that range. Something such as 192.168.X.5

would be appropriate. If you already have your own internal DNS server set up (with this server added along with its associated IP address), make sure to specify that as well. If not and you are planning to follow the DNS steps later in this chapter, just add the server's IP address to the DNS field as well.

Setting Up the Network Names

On the Network Names screen, shown in Figure 2–12, you get to set the DNS name of the server. If you have already set up your internal DNS server to have an entry for your server, the first field will be completed for you, and the second field will have a short name entry there as well based on the full domain name (in other words, if your DNS entry is server-001.mycompany.lan, it will put *server-001* in the Computer Name field). If not, you will have to add the DNS entry now, which is a step that if not taken carefully may haunt you at some point in the future. One common mistake is people will use their company's current domain (mycompany.com) in this DNS field, which is perfectly acceptable if you understand some of the consequences (such as that you will have to create and manage your own DNS entries for your web sites even if they are not hosted on your server or in your office). In this case, just replace the .com with .lan (and *not* .local, no matter what your Windows administrator friend tells you).

> **NOTE:** local is what Bonjour (Apple's autodiscovery protocol) uses for its own discovery service, but it is also used by Microsoft as the default domain end under Windows Small Business Server. There is no explicit benefit to using .local, and it can cause problems with older Mac clients, so it's best to avoid it if you can.

As you can see, there will be a notice indicating that there was no DNS name found for the computer, and the server will provide its own DNS for itself (shown in Figure 2–12). Once you have finished this initial configuration, you go back and remove that custom, limited entry and create a full one instead. Because DNS is being configured locally on the server, once this installation completes, Server Admin will launch when you first log in, instead of Server Preferences (which is what would launch if DNS had been configured externally).

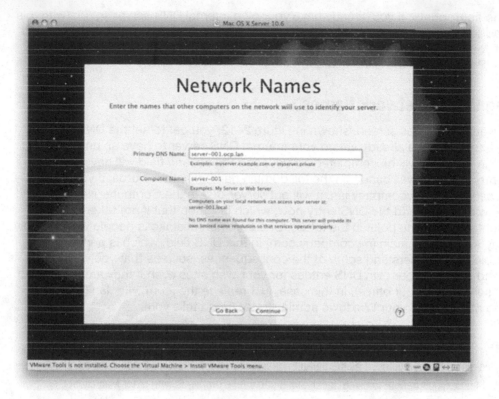

Figure 2–12. *Network Names screen explaining that it will create its own DNS server*

Wrapping Up the Server Setup

The next three stages are prompts to autoconfigure Users & Groups, connect the server to an existing directory server, and create an Open Directory master. All three of these steps are something you will want to do after running software updates and ensuring DNS is working properly. Select Configure Manually for Users & Groups, and leave the boxes unselected for the next two screens as well.

You will be given an option to review all your settings and selections before they are applied to the server, and you can export a backup of these settings to make reinstallation faster later, but for now, just click Apply.

What to Do After Server Setup Completes

Since your server has been configured with two volumes, Time Machine with cheerfully ask whether you want to use your second drive, Data, as a backup location. Select Don't Use. Although Time Machine may be an adequate backup solution for OS X clients (which can then be backed up to the server), it is still not robust enough to trust backing up your server.

Sanity Checking DNS

When Server Admin launches for the first time, you connect to the server after completing the server setup, as shown in Figure 2–13; you can see that it also enabled the DNS service for you. That is because when the Setup Assistant did not detect a full DNS name for the server, it actually configured the DNS service to run with a small entry specific to the server. It also added the DNS server 127.0.0.1 to your network interfaces in System Preferences.

Figure 2–13. *Server Admin showing DNS services running*

To see the specific DNS information that your server is using, select the DNS button and then the Zones tab; the view should be something similar to what you see in Figure 2–14. You will want to delete the current zone, which is configured to apply only to this specific server (which will be fine as long as you don't plan on using DNS for anything else ever, but you will), and you will want to create a new zone that is set up for the entire yourcompany.lan domain. To do this, select the entry with the type of primary zone, and click Remove. Do the same for the reverse zone, and then click Save.

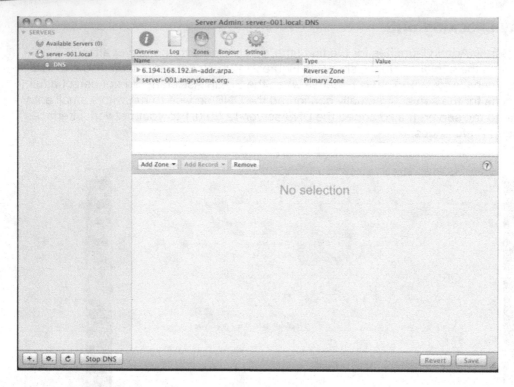

Figure 2–14. *DNS settings, with the Zones tab selected*

With the empty DNS screen, click where it says Add Zone, and select Primary Zone. For the Zone Name field, enter **mycompany.lan.** (the trailing period is important). For the admin e-mail, you can put anything you want. By default it will add "ns" as an entry in the Nameservers field, although in some cases the server name you had used from the setup will show up. Click Save.

You will now see the zone listed in the top part of the view. Select that zone, and then from the Add Record button select Machine, and enter the server name (**server-001**) without a period at the end. For the IP address, click the + sign, and add the IP address of the server. Once you click Save, you should see a second entry appear in the top pane, with the name similar to 194.168.192.in-addr.arpa. and the type reverse zone. If you click the expansion triangle, you will see your server's IP address listed there along with its IP address.

The reason for this reverse zone is to ensure the IP address tracking. Although multiple domain names can be assigned to a single IP address, only one domain name can be used for the reverse IP address; this aspect of DNS is what is used to ensure that a server is what it says it is. For Mac OS X Server 10.6, not only does there need to be a forward entry (the name you are familiar with, server-001.mycompany.lan), there has to be a reverse entry, 192.168.194.5, that points back to that full name in order for the server to use all of its services properly.

Once you have double-checked that the entries look right, you can stop and start the DNS service (using the Stop/Start DNS button in the lower-left corner of the window) just to ensure that they are refreshed properly.

Although you know that the DNS server is configured properly, you need to verify that the DNS client (the server and the rest of the operating system) is able to see those changes. First open the Terminal application in the Utilities folder (you can get there quickly by pressing the Command+Shift+U keystroke in the Finder), and enter the following command:

```
sudo changeip -checkhostname
```

You will be prompted for your administrative password, and after you have provided it and hit Enter, it should display "Success" on the last line (see Figure 2–15).

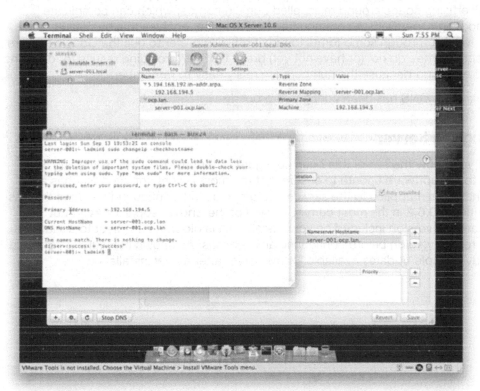

Figure 2–15. *DNS properly checked*

The changeip command checks for DNS consistency internally to your server, but you may also want to check DNS by configuring a client machine to use your new server for DNS and then use the Ping and Lookup commands in Network Utility (also located in the Utilities folder) to ensure that other machines see the server. Once you've verified them from inside the server and your network, you will want to add what are called *forwarders* to the configuration. By default, the server would try to contact the base DNS servers for a domain and do the lookups for each request you send it. The problem with this is that there are many servers out there that do this faster and better than the one sitting in your office, so you will probably not want to have your server looking up every DNS entry on its own. This becomes more of an issue down the line when all of your office machines are using the server for DNS. Adding forwarders allows your server to pass off the job of doing the DNS lookup for any name it does not explicitly have (such as google.com) to another server and then to cache the response once it comes back, speeding up the lookups for other people on the network as well.

To do so, from the DNS services view you are already in, click Settings, and under the Forwarders section, click the + sign and add the DNS forwarders of your choice. Many people prefer to use Google's DNS servers (8.8.8.8 and 8.8.4.4), since they provide extremely fast and accurate DNS information, but you can also use the ones provided by your ISP. From a technical standpoint, both should work fine, but many ISPs are now selling advertising space around misspelled domain names, which can complicate troubleshooting (OpenDNS, a common free DNS service, enables this by default, and you have to click through some forms to turn it off). We prefer to use the Google servers in part because they do not (or have not yet) break DNS by providing results for domains that don't exist and because the numbers are really easy to remember.

Congratulations, DNS has been configured properly.

Updating the Server

Now that you know the server has been configured properly and DNS is working, you will want to run software update to ensure that the most recent software patches and updates have been applied to the services before you start configuring anything this. As of this writing, 10.6.2 is the most current version of the Snow Leopard server, but chances are the version included on your install DVD is older, so it is best to update to the most recent version before configuring any services. As shown in Figure 2–16, there are already multiple updates available for the server after a new installation.

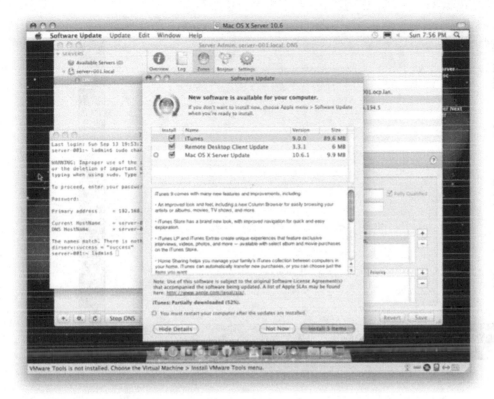

Figure 2–16. *Software Update window*

Building the Fileserver

Once you have run Software Update and rebooted your server, you will have to log back in as the local admin account. After you get to the desktop, launch the Server Admin application in the Dock (it looks like a globe on a plate; the application itself resides in the Server folder inside the Applications folder), and after a moment, it will connect you to your server.

The first steps required to get the fileserver up and running is to add two more services, AFP and Open Directory. To do this, select your server from the list on the left, click Settings, and then click Services. From there select AFP and Open Directory, and click Save (Figure 2–17).

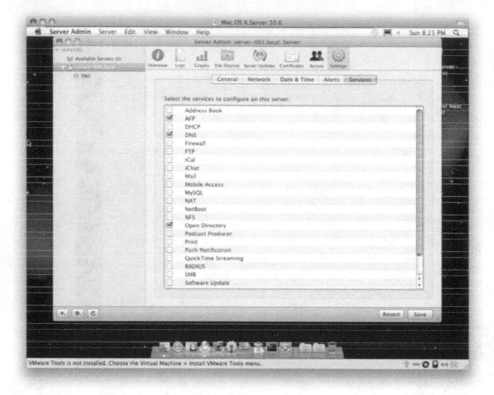

Figure 2–17. *Services list*

You may also want to click the Date & Time tab, located between the Network and Alerts tabs and ensure that the server is using a network time server (time.apple.com by default) and that the clock is correct. Again, this is not essential right now, but making sure your server has accurate time will be a larger part of integrating it with other servers and doing advanced management of your desktops.

After you have updated the services list, you will see the column on the left update to include AFP and Open Directory, both of which will have gray spheres next to them, indicating that the service is stopped (there should be a green one next to DNS). Click Open Directory, and the central pane will update to show you that the server is configured to a stand-alone directory. To create an Open Directory master (which is where the user accounts will live for the fileserver), you will need to change the role of the server; you do this by clicking the Change button to be presented with the dialog box to start that process (Figure 2–18).

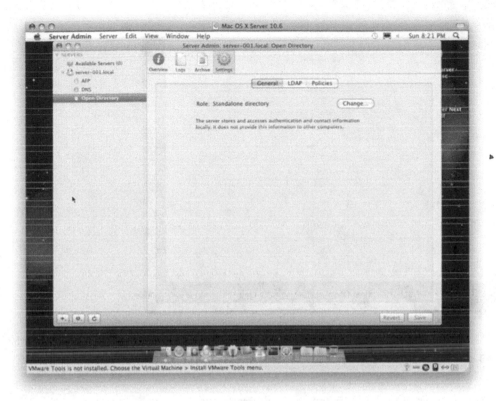

Figure 2–18. *Changing Open Directory role*

Creating the Open Directory Master

Select "Set up an Open Directory master," and click Continue (Figure 2–19). If you see an error about single sign-on not working, it means there is still a problem with DNS, and you will want to consult the advanced DNS portion of this book before continuing. If you don't have any DNS problems, you will prompted to create another user, the directory administrator (Figure 2–20). This account will be the one that can create and edit users in the Open Directory system. Although you can create other accounts and give them administrative rights as well, the directory administrator account is similar to the root account, because it is used to manage and configure other systems when they are joined to Open Directory, and you will want to ensure you use a secure password with it as well.

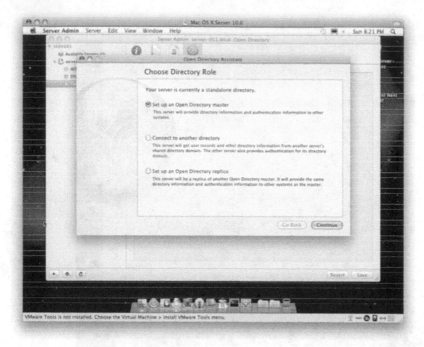

Figure 2–19. *Setting up an Open Directory master*

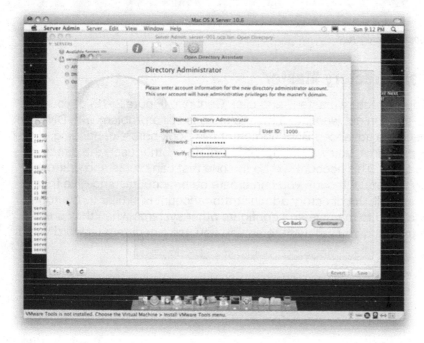

Figure 2–20. *Creating a directory administrator account*

After creating the directory administrator account, you will be prompted to name the Kerberos realm and the LDAP search base, as shown in Figure 2–21. By default these are generated from the full DNS name of the server (so SERVER-001.OCP.LAN, and so on). These are not actually tied to DNS, but the fact that they are showing up as such means that your DNS system is working as expected. You can leave them as they are, but since this information will expand to eventually include any future servers and systems, you can also just remove the prefix part, so a Kerberos realm of "SERVER-001. OCP.LAN" becomes "OCP.LAN," and the LDAP search base of "dc=server-001,dc=ocp,dc=lan" becomes "dc=ocp,dc=lan." See Figure 2–21 for an example.

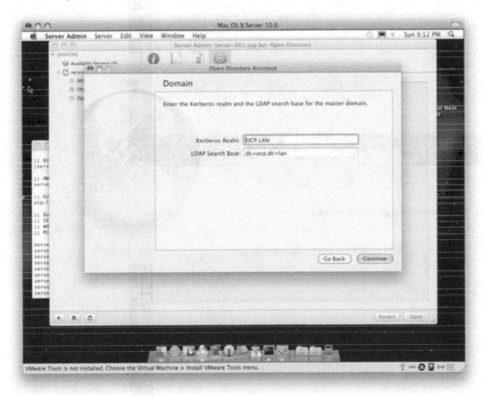

Figure 2–21. *Configuring Kerberos and LDAP names*

Clicking Continue again will allow you to review your changes before you actually take the plunge to configure the OD master (Figure 2–22). At this point, if you want to be extra cautious, you can review the process as it is happening by opening the Terminal application again and running the following command:

```
tail -f /Library/Logs/slapconfig.log
```

This will be updated in real time with the verbose status of what is going on. This is useful if for some reason your creation of the OD master goes wrong. Once the process has completed, you will be returned to the Server Admin window and see that the role has changed to Open Directory master (Figure 2–23).

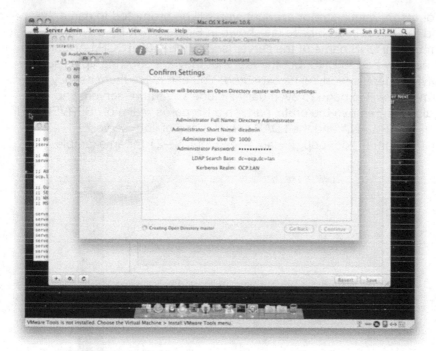

Figure 2–22. *Reviewing Open Directory settings*

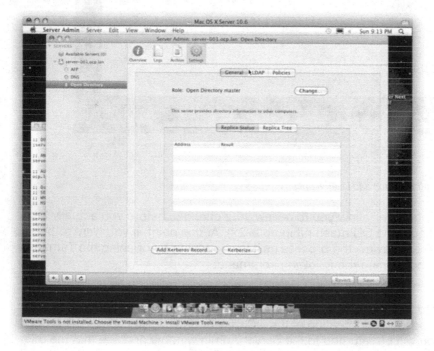

Figure 2–23. *The server is now an Open Directory master.*

Now that you have a working OD master, it is time to log into the system and start creating accounts. You can at this point use the Server Preferences tool or Workgroup Manager. Since once you start doing anything more advanced with the server, you will be doing so in the Workgroup Manager (and you can actually use Workgroup Manager from your desktop machine once you have installed it), let's start there.

Creating Users and Groups

Open Workgroup Manager, and by default it will prompt you to connect to the server. Since you just want to edit the Open Directory system, you can connect using the directory administrator account credentials you just created. In the Connect to Server dialog box, enter the full DNS name of the server (**server-001.mycompany.lan**). For the user, enter your directory administrator account name, the password, and so on. Click Connect, and you should see a window similar to Figure 2–24.

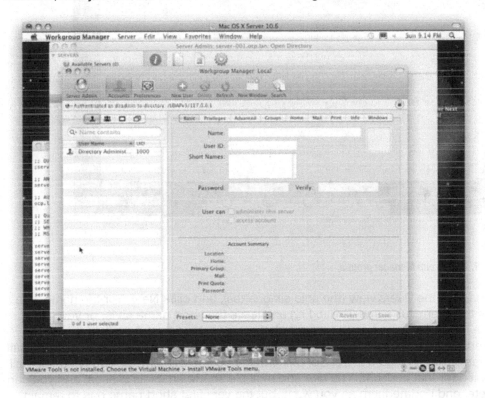

Figure 2–24. *Workgroup Manager*

Before you add users, you will want to create a group to put them in (users are by default added to the staff group, but we want a more specific group to work with, and they can be members of multiple groups anyway). Above the left pane, click the Groups icon (the one with the multiple silhouettes), and click New in the toolbar; the view should look similar to what you see in Figure 2–25. For the name, enter an appropriate office name (**OCP Research**), and leave the short name as is (it will make everything lowercase). Leave the group ID alone, and you can take care of the picture path if you want. Leave a note for yourself in the comment field of who makes up this group and why (everyone in the company), just so you don't have to remember why you created the group in the future. Then click Save.

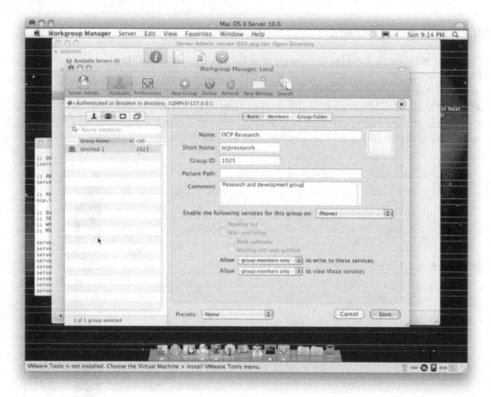

Figure 2–25. *Workgroup Manager groups*

Now go back to the Users view (the solo silhouettes), and click New. For the name, you can enter the user's full name (Phillip Fry) and leave the short name as is, or you can customize it to following a naming standard. If you decide to host e-mail on this server or on a server tied into Open Directory, by default the short name will also be their e-mail address, as shown in Figure 2–26. So, pfry would become pfry@mycompany.com if mail was enabled for that account. You can add multiple short names as aliases, and you can add, delete, and update them as you want, but the very first short name has to remain and cannot be modified easily. That is why you may want to consider a standard naming convention to be put in place now, because many companies run into the problem of initially creating accounts by first names, but then everything goes south the first day they hire their second Chris in the office.

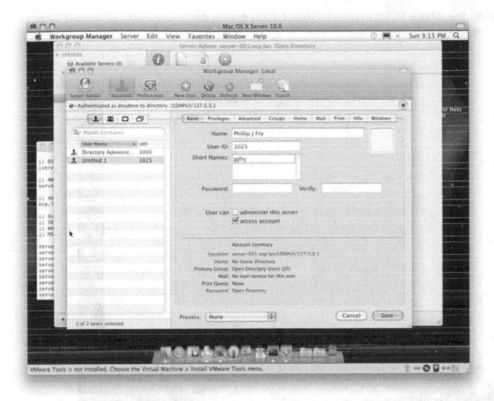

Figure 2–26. *Workgroup Manager users*

From the top of the central pane, click the Groups tab, and there you will see the current group list, which by default will just have the generic Open Directory Users container. Click the plus button to the right of the Other Groups section, and the drawer will slide out showing you the group you just created. Drag that to the Other Groups section to have it added, and click Save.

You can repeat this process for every new user you need to add, and you can continue doing that right now or later.

Creating Share Points

Now that you have your users, you need to create the share point for them to access and connect to. To do this, launch the Server Admin application (if it is not already running), ensure that you are connected to your server, and select File Sharing. By default you will see the volumes you created before installing OS X server (if you partitioned your drive or are using the Boot/Data division suggested) with the Volumes button selected, along with the List button. Click the Share Points button, and you will see three preconfigured share points. These are actually of no use to you, since they are pointing to the folders on the Boot drive, which is not where you want to keep any client files (you can see where the folder actually resides on the filesystem by the path underneath the Share Points name). Select each share, click Unshare, and then click Save to remove it from the list.

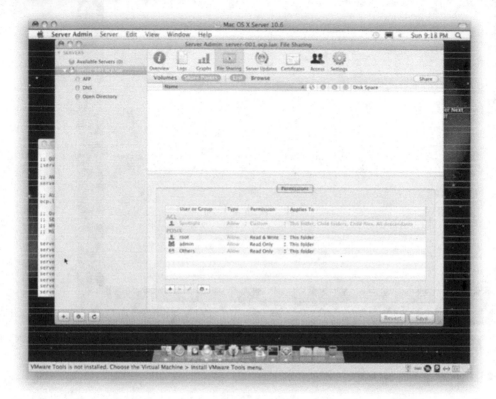

Figure 2–27. *File Sharing pane*

Once all the default shares are removed (as shown in Figure 2–27), go back to the Volumes display, and click Browse. From there, select the Data volume, and create a new folder called SharePoints. Then select SharePoints, and create another new folder called Storage, which should appear as something similar in Figure 2–28. Once you have created Storage, you can select it and click the Share button to configure it as a share point. By default it will enable the share point for Spotlight indexing. If you want, you can specify which protocols can access it, but for now the defaults (AFP for Mac, SMB for Windows enabled, and FTP and NFS turned off) are acceptable. Click Save. Now you have a share point configured, but no one in the group you just created can do anything except view it.

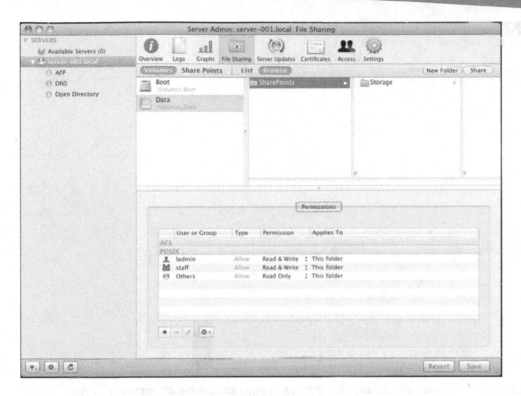

Figure 2–28. *Showing the new SharePoints folder and Storage share*

To change that, select the Permission tab, and click the plus sign. A floating window will appear with a list of users; however, you will want to select the group in this instance, so do so and then drag the group OCP Research to the field in between where it says "ACL" and "Posix" (if Spotlight is enabled, you will see an entry for Spotlight under ACL). You can also drag the OCP Research section over the POSIX field that is labeled "admin" to ensure compatibility with some applications that do not support ACLs well. The share and permissions views should look something like Figure 2–29.

Once you have updated the list of users/groups that has access to the folder, you will want to change the permissions those groups have. In the permissions column for the ACL, select Full Control, and for the Posix, select Read & Write for the OCP Research group you just added. This will allow anyone in the OCP Research group to connect to this share point and modify and update files. More importantly, with the ACL, files created by one member of the group can be edited and updated by another member without a permissions issue locking them out. The final window should look something like Figure 2–30.

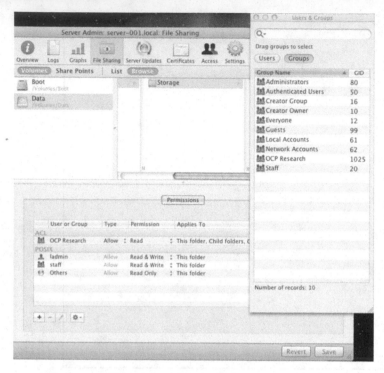

Figure 2–29. *Users & Groups selector and the OCP Research group added to the ACL section*

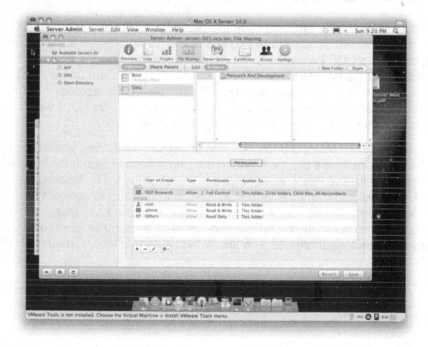

Figure 2–30. *Adding the group ACL*

Now that the permissions have been set, you can select the AFP service and click Start. The defaults for Apple File Services are adequate to get started and to test connectivity.

To test your new share point, you can go to another workstation and try to connect to the server, as shown in Figure 2–31. Unless the workstation has had its network preferences updated to use the new DNS server on your new server, you will have to connect via IP or Bonjour name or browse for it. The fastest way to test is just select Connect to Server from the Go menu (or press Command +K), enter the IP address, and click Connect.

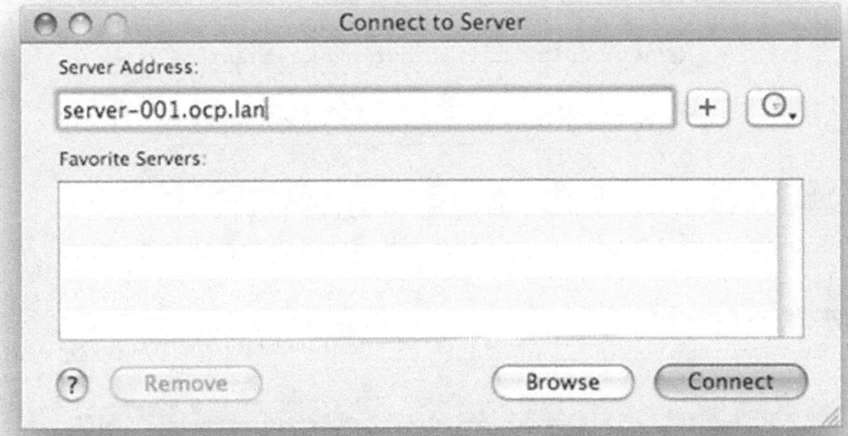

Figure 2–31. *Connecting to the server*

You should be prompted for a username and password (Figure 2–32), and by supplying the one that you added to the group in the Open Directory steps, you should see the share point open in the Finder (Figure 2–33). Once you start having multiple share points, you will instead see a window asking you to select specific shares to mount. To test, drag a file to the share, and then disconnect. Reconnect, but use a different username and password; you should still be able to open and edit the file if the permissions and groups were done successfully. If so, congratulations—you have built your first OS X Server!

Figure 2–32. *Username and password*

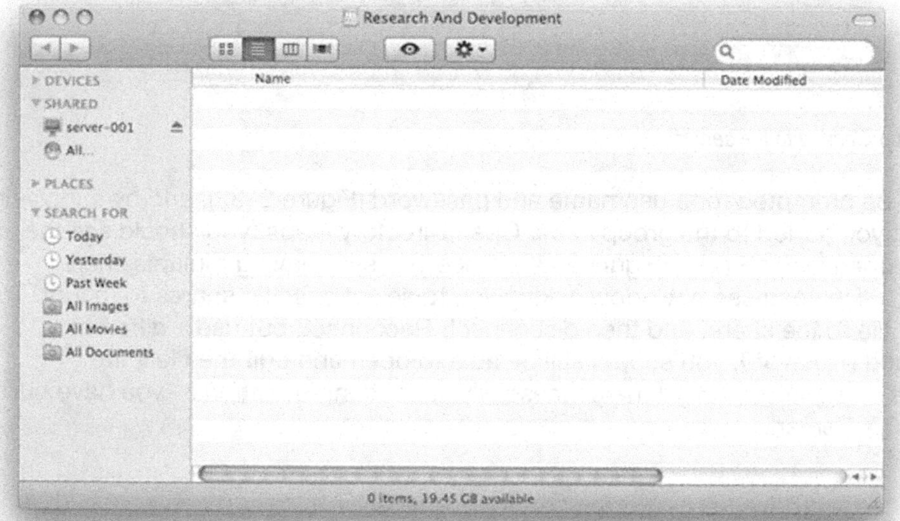

Figure 2–33. *Mounted share point: you now have a fileserver!*

Summary

You now have an Mac OS X Server 10.6 set up and configured to act as a file server for your environment. The settings and steps you have just followed are more in depth than the automatic configuration, because in part the goals are to make sure you have some understanding of what goes into creating the server and to best position you for adding to the server in the future. Through this chapter we touched on some areas of best practices (such as keeping your boot volume separate from your data volume), went through basic DNS setup, showed how to create an Open Directory master, and explained how to set up a basic file sharing service. The rest of the book will go more in depth with those features and also cover other aspects and features available in Mac OS X Server 10.6.

Chapter 3

Getting Deeper into File Sharing

We covered a lot in the previous chapter: the installation of Mac OS X Server 10.6, the initial configuration of Mac OS X Server 10.6, some rather strange things like Open Directory and DNS, and the basics of user management and file sharing management. In this chapter, we'll go deeper into file sharing, since that's one of the basic things a server does: share files to users. We'll start by covering the utilities you use to manage file sharing and users in Mac OS X Server 10.6, and then we'll cover how to use them to go beyond the basics.

In Mac OS X Server 10.6, managing file sharing is split into two parts: the file sharing services along with the individual file shares they share, and the users and groups who have access to those services and shares. In Mac OS X Server 10.6, you manage everything but users and groups in Server Admin. We'll go over Server Admin here in just a second, but first we'll show how to install it on a different Mac. The reason for this is that it's just good practice to never actually log into a server unless you have a task that can be accomplished only that way. Ideally, once you've installed and initially configured your server, it will sit at a login screen for its entire functional life. So, let's install the Mac OS X Server 10.6 administration tools.

Installing the Server Administration Tools

Installing the server administration tools is fairly straightforward. You insert the Mac OS X Server 10.6 DVD into the Mac on which you want to run the tools. When the DVD mounts, you'll see a folder called Other Installs. Inside that folder is the ServerAdministrationSoftware.mpkg installer file. (As you move along your journey as a server administrator, you'll quickly realize that the pretty filenames you see as a consumer go away. Server administrators get filenames like ServerAdministrationSoftware.mpkg.) Double-click that installer, and follow the prompts. There are no options; it's a straightforward process, and it doesn't require a restart.

When the installation is finished, you'll have a new folder in /Applications named Server. Open that folder, and you'll see the eight tools Apple gives you to manage Mac OS X Server 10.6, as shown in Figure 3–1. The tool you care about for this chapter is Server Admin, so double-click that, and you can get going.

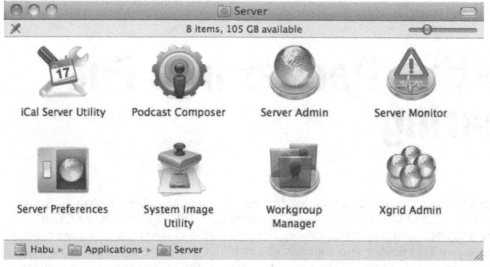

Figure 3–1. */Applications/Server/ folder*

Adding a Server to Server Admin

Before you can manage a server in Server Admin, you have to add it to Server Admin. Thanks to Server Admin's support for Bonjour, if you are on the same local network as the server, then the server will show up in the Available Servers section of Server Admin, as shown in Figure 3–2. Double-click your server in the list, enter the administrator username and password that you created in Chapter 2, and click the Connect button, as shown in Figure 3–3.

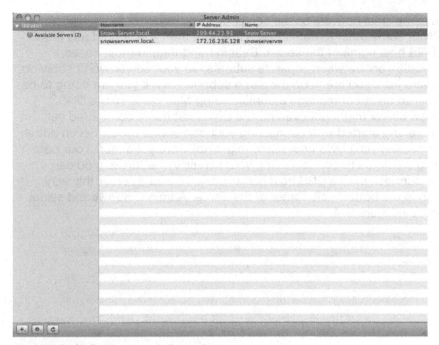

Figure 3–2. *Available servers in Server Admin*

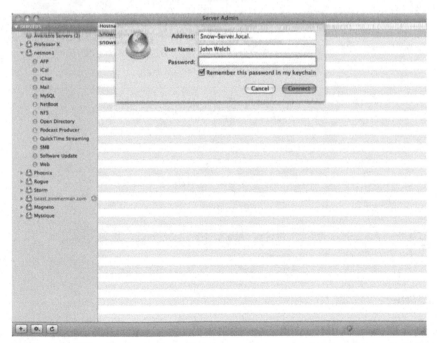

Figure 3–3. *Authenticating to the server*

If you're not on the same local network as the server or if you're going to need to access the server via a VPN or some other remote access method, then you should use the IP address or public DNS host name of the server. Bear in mind that, in most cases, Bonjour discovery won't work between separate subnets, so your server won't show up in the Available Servers list if you aren't on the same subnet. Also, if you are going to be using your new server to create or manage a domain using Mac OS X 10.6's DNS service, then your new server might not even have a DNS host name configured yet (after all, you're just getting started with configuring your server and haven't even gotten to DNS yet!), so connecting via a DNS host name might not work yet either. Your best bet for the time being would be to connect using your server's IP address (you can always change your connection to a DNS host name later). To add a server this way, click the plus (+) sign in the bottom-left corner of the Server Admin window, and select Add Server, as shown in Figure 3–4.

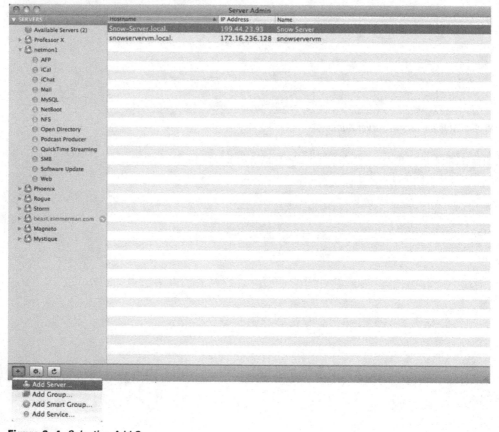

Figure 3–4. *Selecting Add Server*

Enter the IP address (or DNS host name of the server if it exists in your DNS zone), enter the administrator username and password, and click the Connect button, as shown in Figure 3–5.

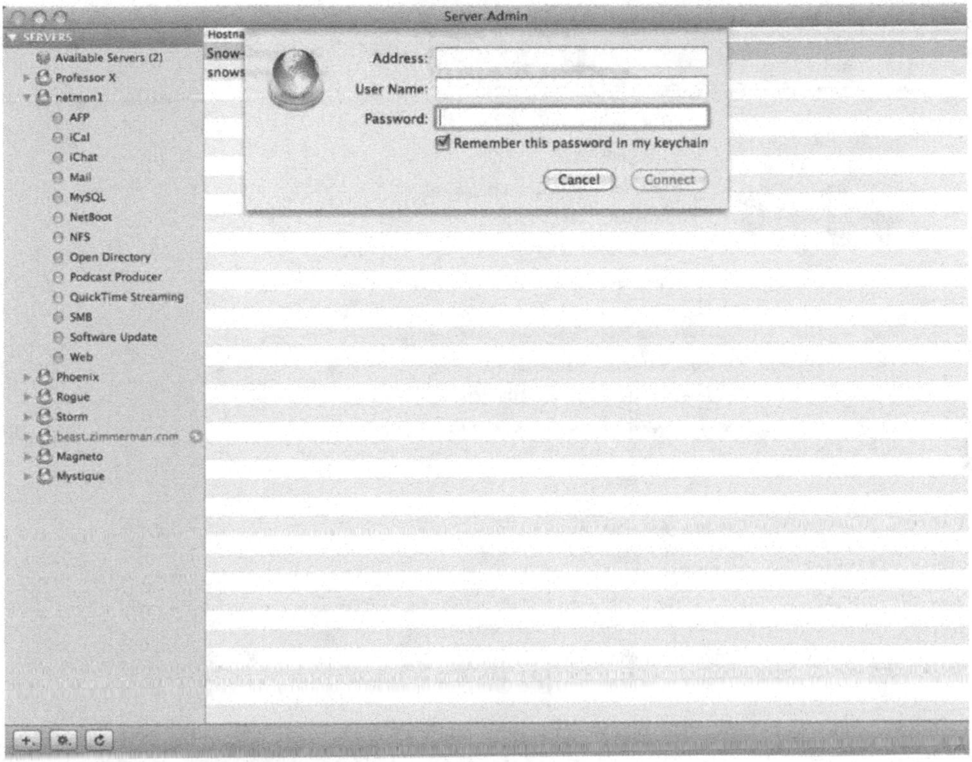

Figure 3-5. *Entering connection information to the server*

Once you connect to your server, you have a lot of options. In fact, almost all of the options for configuring and controlling your server are in Server Admin. However, since this chapter's emphasis is on file serving, you'll focus on the Server Admin features that best deal with that topic.

Server Admin Basics

Once you've added your server to Server Admin, go ahead and click it. While you're at it, click the disclosure triangle to the left of the server name. The triangle shows you the services you have enabled on that particular server. In our case, it's pretty simple right now: Apple Filing Protocol (AFP), Server Message Block (SMB), Domain Name Services (DNS), and Open Directory. If you hear someone talking about CIFS for Windows file sharing, that's a modification to SMB. They aren't *precisely* the same, but in general, both names are used interchangeably.

Looking at the main part of the Server Admin window, you see that information there too (in the Services section of the screen, along with some other useful items), as shown in Figure 3-6.

Figure 3–6. *Default Server Admin screen*

Under Hardware, you'll see an image of the server, the name of the server, the model, the CPU type and speed, the hardware serial number of the server, the amount of RAM, and the amount of disk space.

> **NOTE:** The reason why these screenshots show "unknown" for the CPU type and "Mac" for the model is because, for writing the book, we tended to install Mac OS X Server 10.6 into a virtual machine that let us run Mac OS X Server 10.6 without having to dedicate a physical computer to it. It's a handy trick, especially for testing while writing books. It's definitely lighter than lugging an Xserve to work every day.

In the Software section, you see some basic information about the OS installed on the server. Prior to Mac OS X Server 10.6, there were two versions of Mac OS X Server: a Ten-User Edition and an Unlimited Edition. With Mac OS X Server 10.6, Apple changed that to just an Unlimited version and cut the price of the Unlimited version in half. That's more functionality for less money. Along with the license type, you see the name of the boot volume, the version of the Darwin kernel, and the system version (the part most people think of when you say version).

> **NOTE:** Darwin? You may be asking yourself, "What's that?" Like most operating systems based on Unix, Mac OS X Server uses a lot of free and open source code/applications. In the earlier days of Mac OS X, Apple decided that as it released new commercial versions of Mac OS X, it'd also release an open source version, which Apple named Darwin. Darwin has all the core functionality of Mac OS X but leaves out some of the more Apple-proprietary things such as Aqua, the Finder, and so on. Since the heart of Mac OS X and Mac OS X Server, also known as the *kernel*, is part of Darwin, Apple references Darwin for the kernel version.

Since we already covered the Services section, we'll skip to the bottom section, Status. The Status section is a set of graphs that let you see what the server is doing in terms of CPU usage, network throughput, and disk usage. They're handy for an at-a-glance general status on your server.

> **FUN PRO TIP:** Although the graphs here are OK for checking on one server, if you find yourself with multiple servers, flipping between them can get tiresome. The solution? Click the Servers heading at the top of the list of servers in Server Admin. That will show you just the graphs for every server that Server Admin knows about and is much handier for checking on multiple servers at once.

At the top of the main window is a row of buttons for accessing logs, different graphs, and various settings for the server. One nice thing Apple has done is kept many of these "tabs" common throughout Server Admin. So, pretty much every file sharing–related service is going to have the same collection of buttons: Overview, Logs, Graphs, and Settings. Because these buttons exist for every file sharing service, you have to learn what they do only one time, and more important, we have to *explain* what they do only one time.

The Overview button is what you're seeing now. If it's an overview of the server, you see the current window, with its four sections. If you're in a specific service, like, say, AFP or SMB, you'll see an overview for just that service.

The second button, Logs, lets you view the logs that apply to the server as a whole. So, this pertains to the system log, the security log, the software update log, and so on. If you've ever wondered just what those know-it-alls on a mailing list or support forum are talking about when they say "What do the logs say?" well, now you know what they're talking about. In Mac OS X Server, a lot of information is recorded in various logs, both normal and error conditions. One of the best things you can do as a new sysadmin is spend some time learning how to read logs so that when something goes wrong, you can see what the server and the server software was trying to tell you about the problem. For example, if someone is having problems logging in to a server, Secure Log would show you failed login attempts on that server. Take a look at Figure 3–7, and you will see that the amount of information recorded in the logs can be extensive and exhaustive.

Figure 3–7. *Server logs in Server Admin*

The next button is Graphs, and it does what you'd think it does: it shows you graphs of various parts of the server's performance for that service, as shown in Figure 3–8.

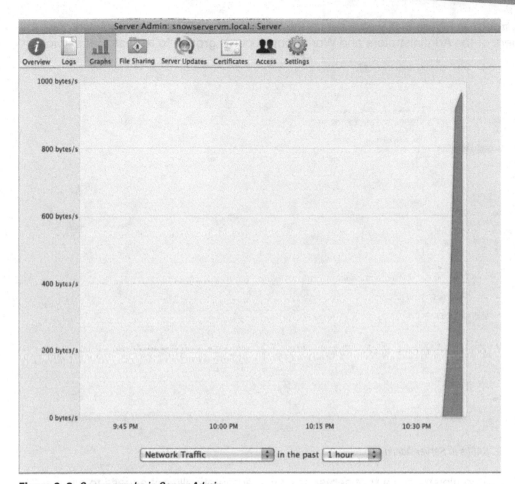

Figure 3-8. *Server graphs in Server Admin*

You already took an initial look at the File Sharing tab in Chapter 2, so we'll leave that alone for now. The next tab is the Access tab, where you want to spend a little time. Part of securing a server is limiting access to certain services. So, just like you would use file access control lists (ACLs) to control who can do what to which file and/or folder on a share, you use service ACLs (SACLs) to control who has access to a given service. Prior to Mac OS X Server 10.6, the default SACL was everyone having access to everything. With Mac OS X Server 10.6, this changed, and now the default setting is to severely limit access. This is good from a security point of view but can be a pain from an administrator's perspective (although the higher level of SACL security by default will likely save you some headaches, too!).

So, when you create new users or groups, you'll want to be sure that they have access to the services you think they should. This is a good example of why groups are important. It is far easier to create a group, set up access for that group, and then just add or remove users from that group as needed than it is to modify access controls for many services per user for many users. With SACLs, planning pays off.

For example, in Figure 3–9, we've set up the SACL for the AFP service, allowing only members of the Administrators and Workgroup security groups to access that service.

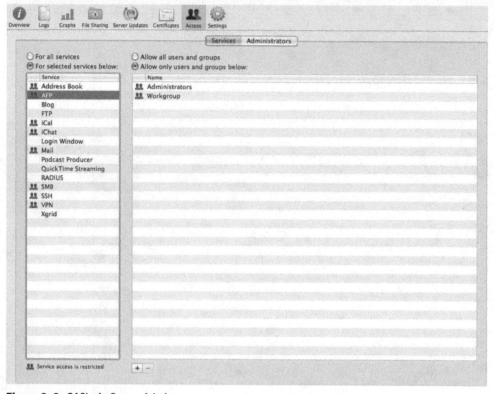

Figure 3–9. *SACLs in Server Admin*

If you're an administrator for that server, then you automatically get access to all services by default, because Mac OS X Server 10.6 has a separate set of SACLs for administrators, as shown in Figure 3–10.

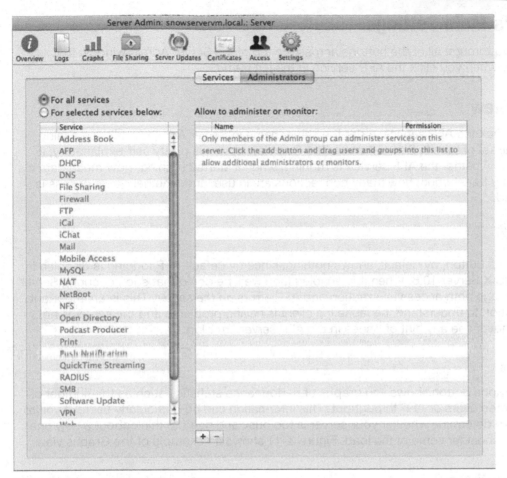

Figure 3-10. *Admin SACLs in Server Admin*

For now, there's not much in the Settings tab you need to deal with beyond what you learned in Chapter 2.

So, enough of the server and on to file sharing services!

Apple Filing Protocol (AFP)

AFP is the default file sharing protocol for Macs and for Mac OS X Server. It is a good protocol, well-designed and robust. Unfortunately, it has some of the worst press in the computing world. Some of it is because, by and large, AFP is a Mac-only protocol, and the rest is because of some technical problems that haven't existed for many years. If your server is going to be primarily serving Mac OS X end users, you will most likely be using AFP.

AFP's Main Settings

Let's go through all of the buttons across the top of the Server Admin window that appear when you click the AFP service in the left frame.

Overview

If you click the AFP service under the server name in Server Admin, you'll see a fairly familiar set of tabs in Server Admin. The Overview button is pretty self-explanatory; it tells you whether the AFP service is running, when it started running, how much data it's currently transferring, how many connections are in use, and whether guest access is enabled.

Logs

The Logs button, by default, shows nothing, since by default AFP logging is disabled in Mac OS X Server 10.6. When it is enabled (and we'll be doing that soon enough), Server Admin logs both access information and AFP errors *on the server*. This is an important distinction to understand, because if a client is having problems and the server is not, you'll never see any hint of issues in the AFP *server* error log.

Graphs

The Graphs button shows you graphs of performance statistics such as the number of connected users or AFP throughput. This information can be particularly useful if you're trying to determine whether your server is too busy and need to think about a new one to help shoulder some of the load. Figure 3–11 shows an example of the Graphs view.

Connections

The Connections tab shows you information about clients that are connected to your server via AFP. It shows the username of the person making the connection, their status, the IP address or DNS host name of the client, how long that client has been connected, and how long the client has been idle.

Those last two items are important for optimizing your server. If you have a lot of users connecting to a server, are active only for a short amount of time, but then stay connected for hours, or even days, that can eat up a server's resources just maintaining what is a wasted connection. As you'll see shortly, certain settings in Server Admin let you deal with such connections in a more proactive manner.

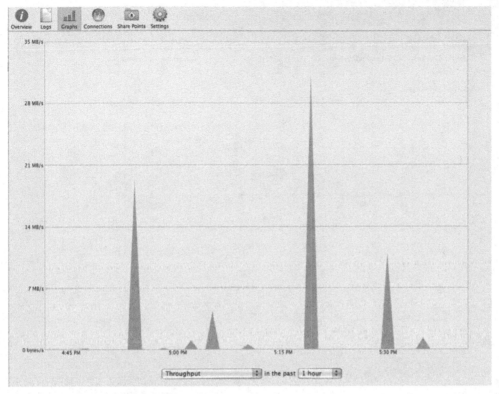

Figure 3–11. *Graph of AFP throughput*

Along the bottom of the Connections screen you have three buttons. Stop lets you shut down the AFP service. It's a bit redundant, because there's also a big Stop AFP button just below it, but the Stop button also lets you send a warning message to connected users that the AFP service is going to stop in *n* minutes (ten is the default), along with any other information you want to pass along to them, as shown in Figure 3–12. (We try to always add a reason for the shutdown, which makes life easier on everyone.) The Send Message button lets you send a message to one or more connected clients. The Disconnect button allows you to disconnect a specific user or users in *n* minutes, with a message to that user.

> **NOTE:** When you use the Stop or Disconnect button, keep in mind that the number you enter is how long the users have until the AFP service or their connection is shut down. That's not just informational; that's a functional setting, so be careful.

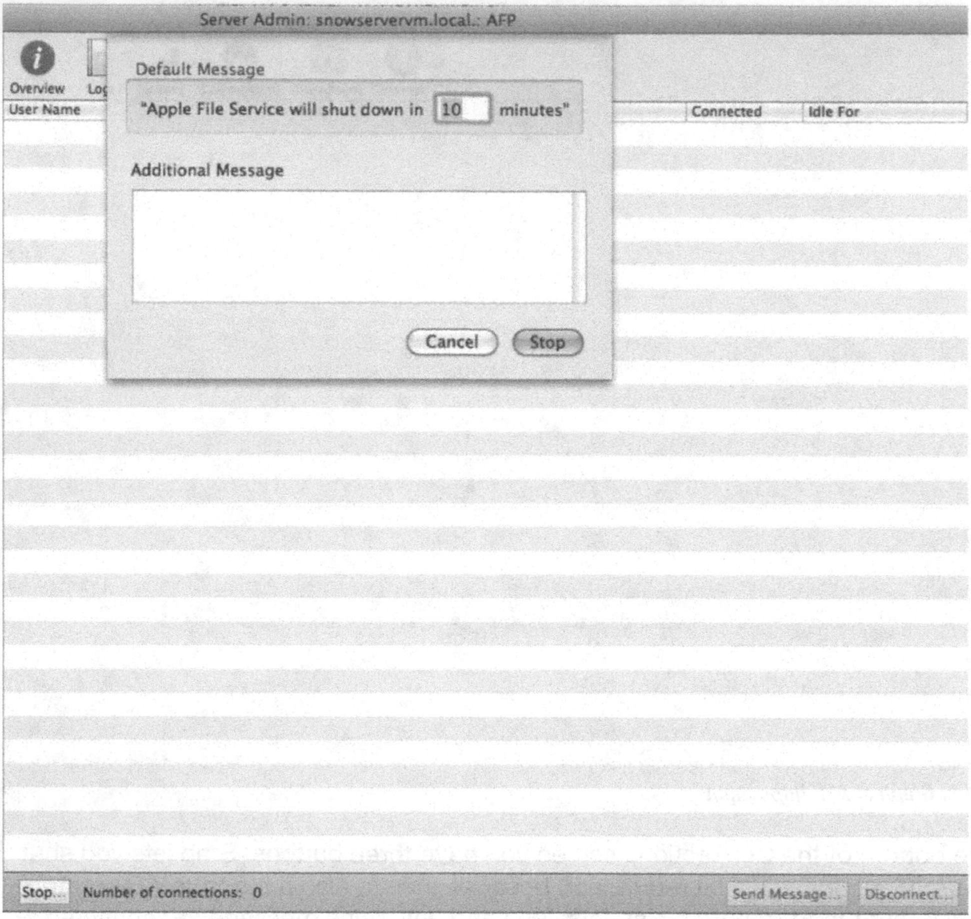

Figure 3–12. *Shutting down AFP via the Stop button*

Settings

We'll skip the Share Points button for now (don't worry, you'll be spending a lot of time there later in the chapter!) and move on to the Settings button, which has a number of subtabs within its pane. As you can see in Figure 3–13, the General tab allows you to set the text encoding for older (read: pre–Mac OS X) clients and lets you set up a greeting that will display for every client that connects to that AFP server. You can also set it so that the greeting doesn't display twice to the same user. This is handy when you have multiple shares on the same server and you don't want to bug users with the same message over and over.

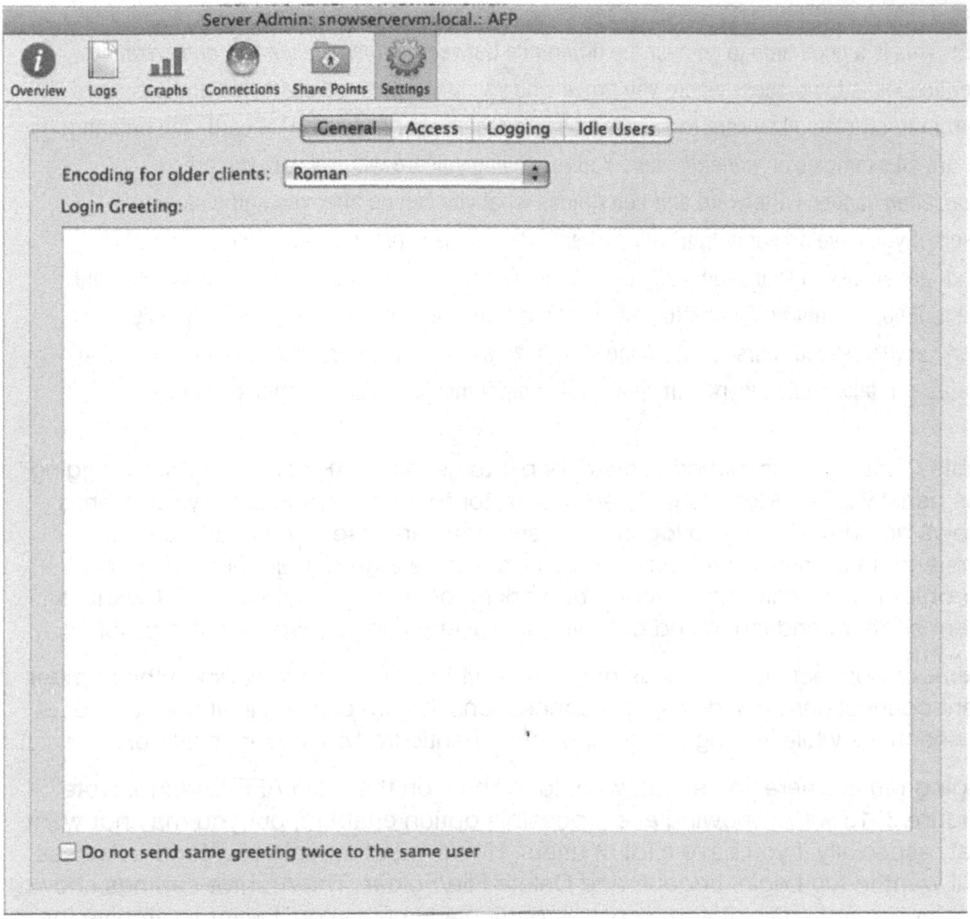

Figure 3–13. *AFP general settings*

The Access tab, as shown in Figure 3–14, controls AFP-specific access settings. These are in addition to the SACLs covered earlier. The Authentication drop-down controls the authentication method: Standard, Kerberos, or Any Method (aka all of the above). This is something you want to be careful with. If you set it to Standard, then even if you are using Kerberos on your network for single sign-on purposes, that won't work on an AFP server configured to use Standard authentication. Conversely, if you set the Authentication method to Kerberos, Kerberos will be the *only* authentication method available. This can be annoying when you're trying to troubleshoot a problem on a user's system and you need to get to a file share that they aren't authorized to have access to. In general, if you aren't sure which one to use, leave Authentication set to the default setting of Any Method.

NOTE: This is a good time to go over the difference between *authentication* and *authorization*. Authentication is the process where you prove who you are. Entering a username and password at a prompt, swiping a key card to gain access to a room, inserting your ATM card, and entering a PIN are all examples of *authentication*. You're proving you are who you say you are. *Authorization* happens afterward and determines what you can do after you authenticate yourself. If you have proper authorization, then once you have properly authenticated yourself, you can get access to shares on a server, the room door unlocks, and you can access your bank account. If you are not *authorized* to do those things, then they will still fail, even though you properly *authenticated* yourself. Wrapping your head around the differences between those two concepts can take a bit of work, but knowing the difference is critical in running a server.

The Enable Guest Access setting allows people to use your AFP server without logging in. This is usually a bad idea. "Enable administrator to masquerade as any registered user" allows an administrator to log into the server as any user by using that user's username and an administrative password. This can be a great help when a user is having problems connecting to a server or working on a server but you don't want to make them sit there and log in and out over and over while you work on the problem.

The Maximum Connections section is pretty self-evident. You can lock down the number of all client connections, including guest connections, or you can just limit the number of guest connections while leaving the number of authenticated connections alone.

The Logging tab is where you set up what logs show on the main AFP Log tab. Note that in Figure 3–15 we're showing every possible option enabled, but you may not want to do that, especially if you have a lot of users. However, at a minimum, for the Access log, you'll want to log Login, Logout, and Delete File/Folder. The Archive settings shown are the defaults, and again, if your server is particularly busy, you'll want to archive the logs more often than once a week so they don't get too long and unwieldy.

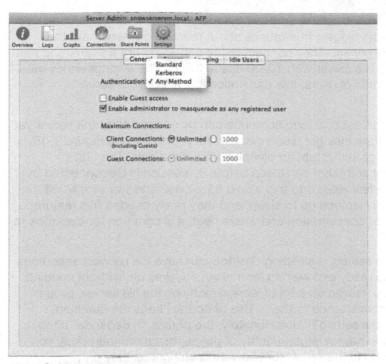

Figure 3-14. *AFP access settings*

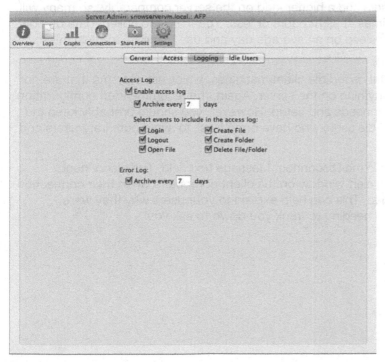

Figure 3-15. *AFP logging settings*

The options on the Idle Users tab can be some of the most important settings you'll use for AFP services. Some of the biggest frustrations about managing a server are the people who never, ever disconnect. They connect to the server, mount a share, and then leave it there forever. If this is a server with 10–20 users, this can be a minor annoyance. If this is a server with hundreds of users, this can noticeably affect your server's performance.

To help manage this, you can set how long someone can be connected to the server yet not actually do anything before they get disconnected. As you can see in Figure 3–16, there are two primary settings in this tab, for sleeping and idle clients. The first configures how long a client computer can sleep before its session is disconnected by the server. Although even a few years ago this would have been one you simply left alone (because, after all, only laptops go to sleep, and they rarely needed this feature), with the new focus on power consumption and waste heat, it is common for desktops to be set to sleep as well.

By properly configuring this setting, a sleeping desktop can have the network resources it had when it went to sleep ready and waiting for it when it wakes up, without needing to reconnect. If you have users who do a lot of work directly on the file server, proper use of this can be a huge convenience to them. This of course, begs the question, "What's the proper use of this setting?" Unfortunately, the phrase "It depends" ends up being the answer here. If you have a large quantity of users, then more than likely you will not want them connected to the server for two weeks straight as they only occasionally request small bits of data from the server. However, the authentication is both a waste of time for users and a higher load on the server comparably, so many will want to keep connection times at eight hours or less. You'll have to collect data on how long your users' Macs are asleep on an average day and use that data to base this setting on.

The second setting in this tab is for idle client machines, which are systems that are not asleep but just not doing anything on the server. Again, the recommended configuration will really depend upon your needs and setup. However, you should probably keep the disconnect exemption for "Idle users who have open files" to avoid both irate users and data loss.

You should also put a note in the Disconnect Message text field. The disconnect message will show up in an alert window on the client computers when their connection to the server has been ended. This can help explain to your users why they were disconnected, without them needing to track you down to ask you!

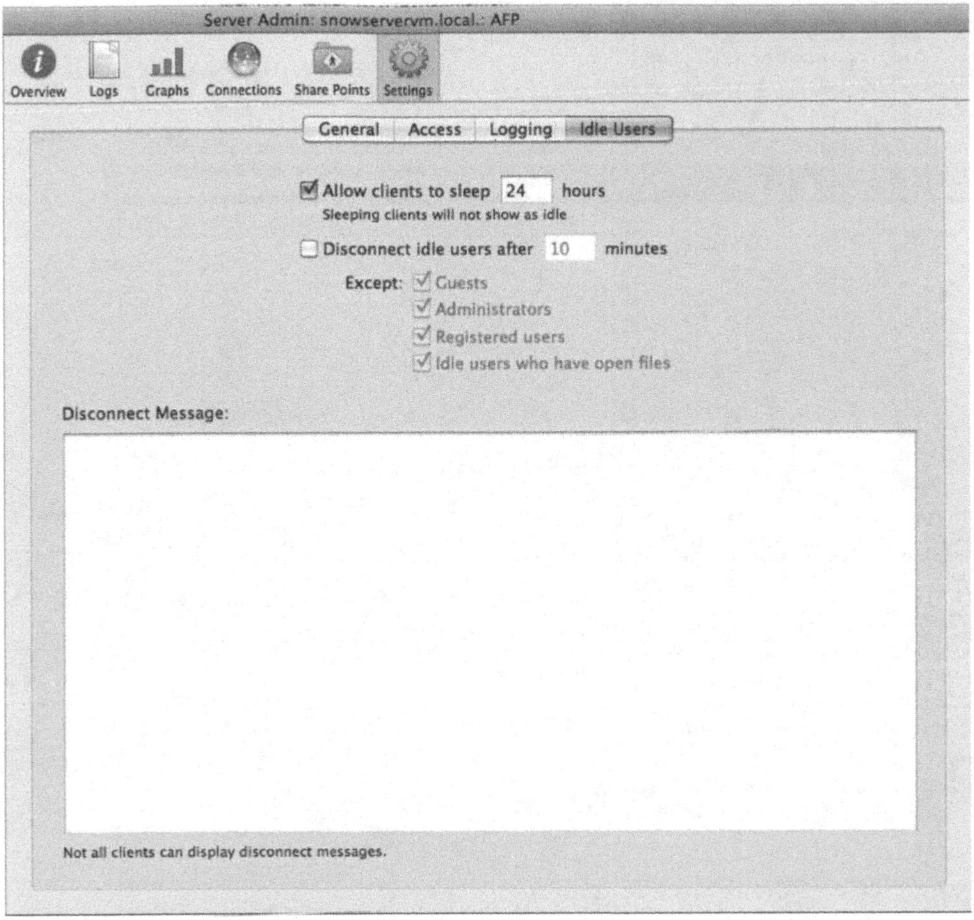

Figure 3–16. *AFP idle users settings*

Share Points

So, now that you know what the various settings are, let's take a look at the important part, which is configuring AFP shares for users. For this, you'll want to click the Share Points tab; then make sure you click Share Points and List in the area immediately under the Share Points tab.

Looking at this area, as shown in Figure 3–17, you see the three default shares created on a new install of Mac OS X Server, the disk space used by each share, and the permissions for those shares at the bottom of the screen. When you look at the space used, keep in mind that this is looking at the space available on the volume on which the share resides. If you have multiple shares on a volume, they'll all show the same space used. In our example, you can also see that the shares all have Spotlight enabled, via Spotlight's magnifying glass indicator showing in the information area for the share.

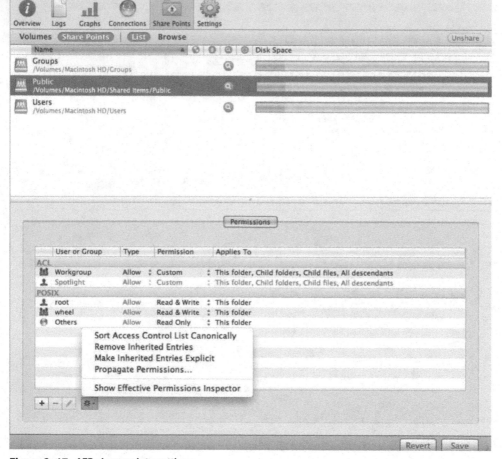

Figure 3–17. *AFP share points settings*

If you look at that area, you can see some other columns that indicate other possible settings for a share or shares. For example, if you were to enable that share as an automount (a share that is automatically mounted when a user logs in) and have Spotlight enabled, then it would look like Figure 3–18.

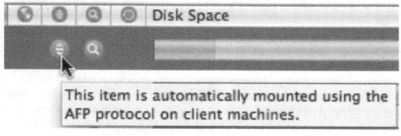

Figure 3–18. *AFP Automount and Spotlight enabled*

If you set up this share as a Time Machine destination, for client backups, then you'd see the Time Machine icon for the share like in Figure 3–19.

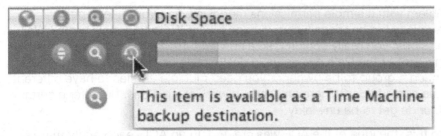

Figure 3–19. *AFP Automount, Spotlight, and Time Machine destination enabled*

Finally, if you enable guest access for this share, then you'd see an icon in the information area for that share like in Figure 3–20.

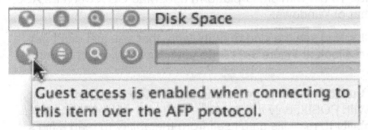

Figure 3–20. *AFP Automount, Spotlight, Time Machine destination, and guest access enabled*

Share Point Permissions and ACLs

By default, Spotlight is the only option enabled here. If you click the Permissions tab in the bottom half of the window, you see two areas: one for ACLs and one for POSIX (traditional Unix permissions).

When people first started using Unix, the security needs were simple, so simple permissions levels were all you needed. Therefore, with POSIX permissions, you have three layers of access: owner, group, and everyone else. The owner is a single user, such as root or bob. The group is a single group, such as wheel, designers, or IT. The owner doesn't have to be in the group. Finally, there's everyone else. For each of those entities, you have three kinds of permissions: Read, Write, and Execute. *Read* allows you to see the file or directory and, in the case of the file, open it and read it. Read allows you to copy a file or directory but not move it. *Write* allows you to modify or delete the file or directory. If you try to move/delete a directory but you don't have write permissions on the files in the directory, you're not going to be able to delete or move the directory. *Execute* is fairly obvious for files: it lets you run a file that is also an application. For directories, the Execute permission is a bit odd, because it is what lets you list the contents of a directory. With directories, Read access lets you see the directory is there, and you can get to files in the directory if you know the filename. If you want to list the contents of a directory, say via the ls command, then you have to have the Execute permission too. Since the Mac OS X Finder doesn't directly use the Execute permission, Server Admin shows only Read and Write permissions and assumes Execute from the other two.

However, the problem with a simple permissions model is when your needs get complex. For example, what happens when you don't want Write to equal Delete? Well, with POSIX permissions, you really couldn't, so a new feature was patched on, the *sticky bit*, which said only root or the file's owner could delete a file or directory. But then what do you do if you need a group to be owner or you need multiple entities to have different access levels to the same folder? There are ways to work around this, but after a certain point, the workarounds get to be unwieldy.

So, in response to this, the idea of the ACL was created. In an ACL, each entity that needs a specific level of access gets their own access control entity (ACE). An ACL is a list of ACEs. In addition, not only can you specifically allow specific access, but you can also *deny* specific access. ACLs are more complex to use than POSIX permissions, but they are also far more powerful. To aid with cross-platform use, Mac OS X Server's ACL implementation is similar to that of Windows.

If you look at the possible ACLs, you see the kind of granularity that you just can't get from POSIX permissions. Take a look at Figure 3–21, and you'll see how much control 10.6 Server offers.

For example, you can assign the ability to change permissions or the owner of files or folders to a user or a group. With POSIX, only the owner or root can do any of that. For Read, you can separate the ability to read file data itself from the ability to read a file's metadata (Permissions, Attributes, Extended Attributes), and you can explicitly set execute permissions for files and folders. Write is similarly granular, with the important separation of deleting a file from the ability to modify a file's contents. This isn't perfect, however. Just because someone can't completely delete a file doesn't mean they can't delete all the data within a file and leave an empty file (literally, write "nothing" to the contents of a file). ACLs also differentiate, in the case of directories, the difference between deleting the contents of the directory and the directory itself. Finally, you can decide what a specific ACE applies to: the file/directory itself, just the immediate contents of the directory, all the contents of the directory and every subdirectory of those contents, or any mix of these. (This is also known as *inheritance*.) Understanding ACLs is critical to the security of your file shares and servers. In general, you're better off leaving the POSIX permissions alone and using ACLs to control access to specific contents within a share, because ACLs win over POSIX if both are used. Also, keep in mind that ACLs are optional; POSIX permissions are always present.

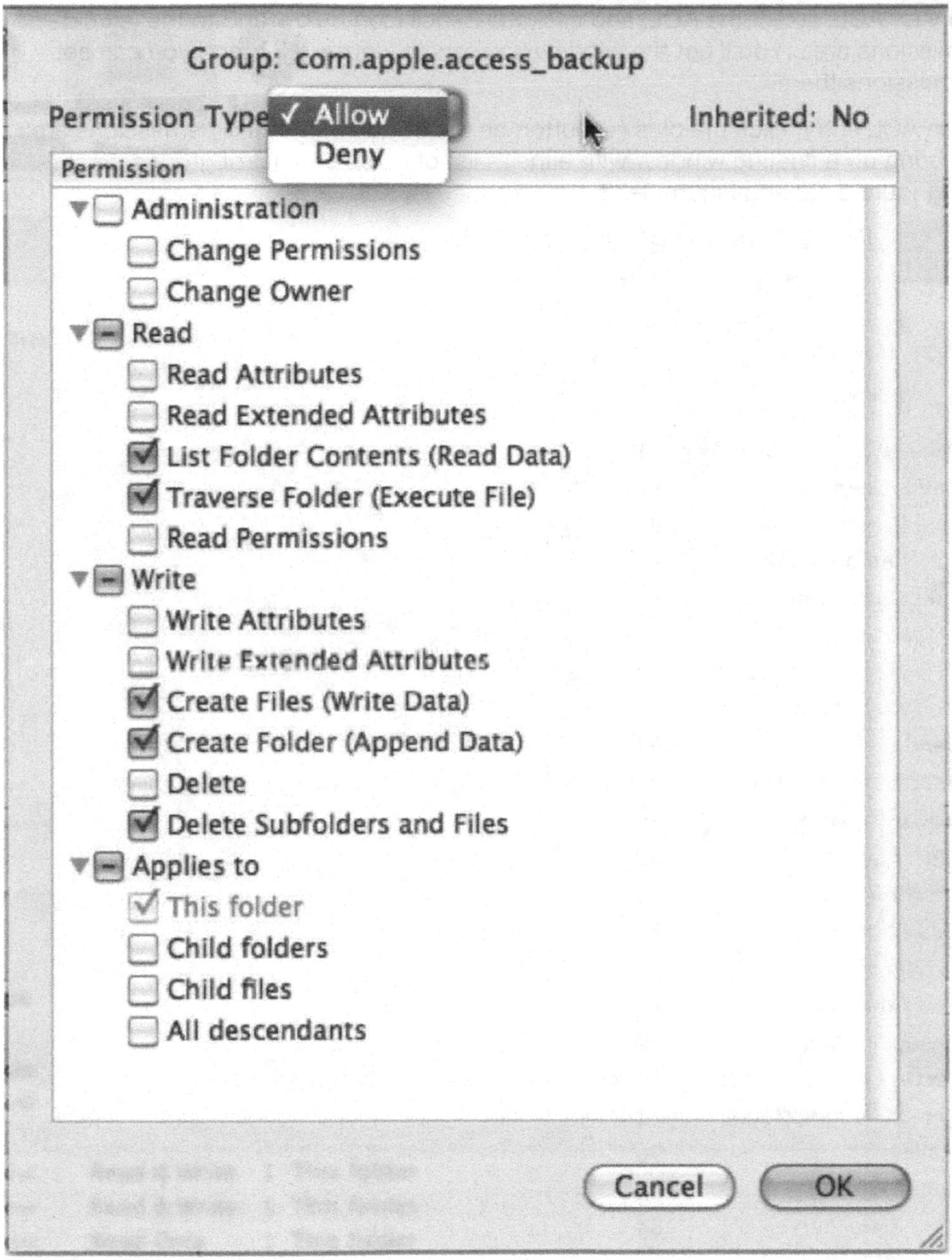

Group: com.apple.access_backup

Permission Type √ Allow   Inherited: No
                   Deny

Permission
▼ ☐ Administration
    ☐ Change Permissions
    ☐ Change Owner
▼ ⊟ Read
    ☐ Read Attributes
    ☐ Read Extended Attributes
    ☑ List Folder Contents (Read Data)
    ☑ Traverse Folder (Execute File)
    ☐ Read Permissions
▼ ⊟ Write
    ☐ Write Attributes
    ☐ Write Extended Attributes
    ☑ Create Files (Write Data)
    ☑ Create Folder (Append Data)
    ☐ Delete
    ☑ Delete Subfolders and Files
▼ ⊟ Applies to
    ☑ This folder
    ☐ Child folders
    ☐ Child files
    ☐ All descendants

(Cancel)   (OK)

Figure 3–21. *ACL settings*

TIP: for the unwary: If you set a "deny" ACL and an "allow" ACL, the deny ACL is always evaluated first and always wins any conflict with an allow ACL.

To modify an ACL, select the ACL, and click the pencil icon below and to the left side of the Permissions area. You'll get the window you saw in Figure 3–21, and you can set your permissions there.

To add an ACL entry, click the plus (+) button on the bottom left of the permissions area. This will bring up a floating window with either a list of users or a list of groups, as shown in Figure 3–22 and Figure 3–23.

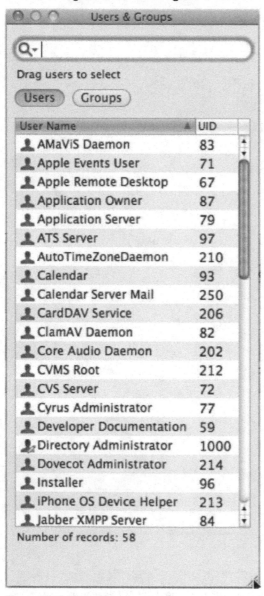

Figure 3–22. *Users list*

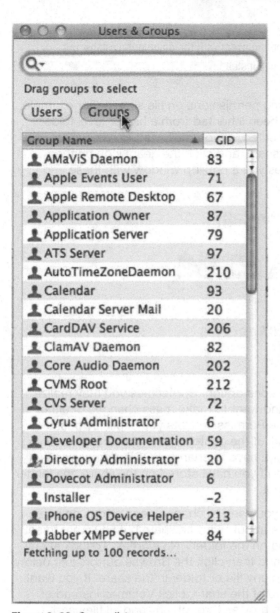

Figure 3–23. *Groups list*

Drag the users or groups for which you want to create an ACL entry to the ACL area, and close the floating window. By default, any entity you drag to the ACL area gets full Read permission that applies to the share and all contents and contents of those contents. To delete an ACL entry, select the user or group whose ACL you want to remove, and hit the minus (-) button on the bottom left of the Permissions area. To undo either an add or a remove here, click the Revert button on the bottom right of the Permissions area.

TIP: If you find yourself adding more than one or two users with the same permissions, put them in a group, and add an ACL entry for that group instead.

There are a few other useful tricks to managing permissions on file shares. For example, you may have certain permissions that have been inherited from a higher-level folder that you want to make explicit, instead of inherited, or you may want to remove the inherited ACLs in place. To do that, select a share, and click the gears icon on the bottom left of the permissions area. This gives you a pop-up window with these and other options, as shown in Figure 3–24.

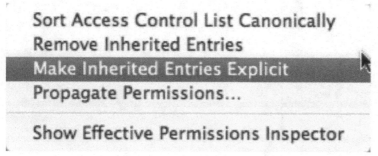

Sort Access Control List Canonically
Remove Inherited Entries
Make Inherited Entries Explicit
Propagate Permissions...

Show Effective Permissions Inspector

Figure 3–24. *ACL options*

Another option here is the Propagate Permissions option. Sometimes you may realize that you've made a muddle of permissions and want to make mass changes of either POSIX permissions, ACLs, or both. Propagate Permissions lets you explicitly push the permissions you set on the share out to the all of the contents of that share, including subfolders. This can be handy, especially if you have to change POSIX permissions en masse. However, be warned that the more stuff you have stored on the share, the longer it will take for the permissions to propagate out.

All of this control is pretty sweet, but what if you need to change permissions on some folder or file inside the share, or what if you're about to add a share but you want to set up the permissions before you enable sharing on the folder? No worries. To look at any file or folder within a share, select the share and then click the Browse button, just below the Share Points tab. You can then browse to any file or folder in the share. If you want to browse the volume(s) on the server, instead of the share, click Volumes instead of Share Points; then click Browse, and you can browse through any and all files and folders for all volumes mounted on that server.

So, you have all these great ideas for ACLs, but you also know that things can get complicated, especially with inherited permissions, deny vs. allow, and so on. Wouldn't it be great if you could somehow see what the actual results of all your ACL work would be for a user or a group? Effective Permissions Inspector to the rescue! Select the item you want; then using the gear button, just as you would for the ACL options we talked about earlier, open the Effective Permissions Inspector. Bring up the User/Group inspector window by clicking the plus (+) button, and drag a user or group onto the

Effective Permissions Inspector, as shown in Figure 3–25. This little tool is your best friend when it comes to diagnosing ACL issues.

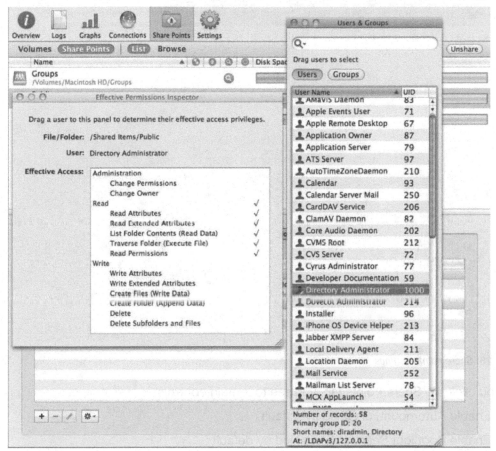

Figure 3–25. *Effective Permissions Inspector*

Wow, that was a lot of material on one subject, permissions. If you dug through it, congratulate yourself, because you've started learning about one of the biggest items that trips up a sysadmin. But what about that other tab, the one next to Permissions called Share Points?

Share Point Settings

Well, this is the tab where you do most of the nitty-gritty configuration of the share points on your server, and even though we're talking about share points in the context of AFP, the settings here apply to the other main file sharing protocols on Mac OS X Server; so, once you go through this part, you'll have picked up a lot of useful information that applies across quite a few protocols.

Click the Share Points tab, as shown in Figure 3–26.

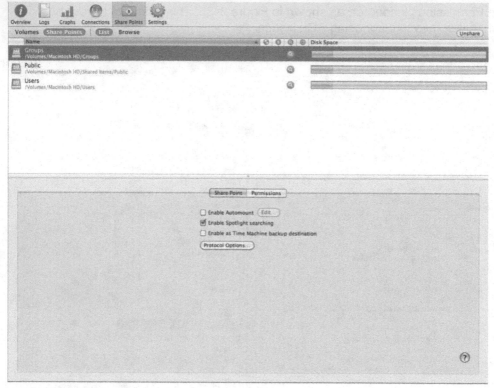

Figure 3–26. *Share points settings*

When you click the Share Points tab, you see four main controls:

- Enable Automount, disabled by default

- Enable Spotlight Searching, enabled by default

- Enable as Time Machine backup destination, disabled by default

- Protocol Options button

Enable Automount should be pretty self-explanatory. It enables a share or shares to automatically mount so that when a user logs in, they are ready to run with no work on the part of the user. When you enable an automount, you don't have to do anything on the client, such as add the share to a user's login items or create a script to mount the share point. Since automounts can apply to every client on your network, you'll only want to use them for share points that you want every user to always have available.

NOTE: Automounts are not the same kind of share point you get from the "regular" way of mounting a share point. For one, in general, there's no authentication on an automount. This makes sense, because automounts work at the computer level, not the user level. They are mounted *before* a user logs in, so there's no way to really authenticate to them. Correctly configured ACLs are very important for automounts. (There's a way around this, but you have to do some tricks with Kerberos, and Apple generally won't support you if you do.) Another difference is that although "normal" share points are mounted in /Volumes and show up on a user's desktop, automounts are normally mounted in /Network and do not show up on the user's desktop. This is true for user home folders, group folders, shared Applications folders, and Shared Library folders. You can add a custom share with a different mount point, such as an Xsan volume, but in general, automounts should live in /Network. If you need the user to see the share, you can add it to their Dock.

To set up an automount, select a share point, and select the Enable Automount check box. Since you're creating a new automount, the settings sheet will automatically open, as shown in Figure 3–27.

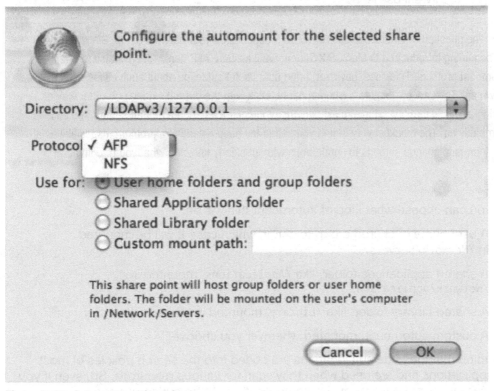

Figure 3–27. *Automount settings sheet*

The settings here are mostly straightforward, although the Directory drop-down can be the most confusing. This shows, if any, the various directory services to which your server is bound. In our case, we're only part of one, Open Directory, and since the server we're working on is also the main server for the directory system or the Open Directory master, then you see the normal form for this, /LDAPv3/127.0.0.1.

> **NOTE:** The 127.0.0.1 address is called the *loopback* address and is used when processes on a computer need to make a network connection to the same computer they're running on but don't want or need to go out onto the network and then come back. This is also useful for network testing even if you aren't on a network, because the loopback is always there.

If you were on a server that wasn't the Open Directory master, then you'd see either the IP address or the DNS name of that server in place of the 127.0.0.1.

The Protocol drop-down lets you select the file sharing protocol you want to use for the automount. Our options are AFP and NFS (Network File System is a file sharing protocol that was developed by Sun Microsystems many years ago and is mostly used by other Unix platforms). Since we're on a Mac server and going to be using automounts only for Mac clients, then we'll use AFP.

> **TIP:** The question of whether to use AFP or NFS depends on your network setup. Since this book is a beginning introduction to Mac OS X Server, we'll assume AFP here, which is also the default automount protocol. This does, however, bring up a useful guideline about such cases, also known as "The Law of Defaults": when in doubt, stick with the default settings. Another way of looking at this is that if you have to ask whether you need to change a default setting, the answer is probably no. The quickest way to find yourself in the deep weeds of a problem, especially as a beginner, is to change settings to nondefaults without clearly knowing what you're doing and why.

Finally, you can choose what kind of automount this will be:

- A user home or shared group folder, in which case it will be mounted in /Network/Servers/

- A shared applications folder, like /Applications, mounted in /Network/Applications

- A shared Library folder, like /Library, mounted in /Network/Library

- A custom automount, mounted wherever you choose

Keep in mind that these default locations are coded into the search policies of most Cocoa applications and are used when they scan for various resources. So, even if you don't necessarily want a folder of shared applications to be buried under the /Network/Applications directory, it's a good idea to just go with that location to ensure the smooth functionality of other software in use on your network.

Select your settings, click OK, click Save, and that's it. You've set up an automount. You can set up multiple automounts, but any one share can be only one automount. So, you can't have the same share be a network Library and a network home folder at the same time. Because the scope of automounts tends to span your network, you don't want to set them up willy-nilly. Some foresight and planning make a lot of sense here!

The "Enable Spotlight searching" setting is simple enough. If it's enabled, the server creates a Spotlight index for that share, usable by clients. If it's not enabled, the server doesn't create the index. If you have a really busy server, consider turning this off. Spotlight searching can be enabled only on a share that is using either AFP or SMB as the file sharing protocol; you can't use it with NFS or FTP sharing.

"Enable as Time Machine backup destination" is also pretty straightforward. If you want Mac OS X 10.5 (or newer) clients to be able to use that share as a destination for Time Machine backups, enable it. If not, don't enable it. Be aware that because of how Time Machine works, even a small number of clients can *quickly* create a *lot* of data and really bog down a server. Be sure that you actually want to enable Time Machine to a given server before you turn this on.

Finally, you have the Protocol Options button. This button covers rather a lot more than just AFP options, but we'll go through all of them here, so you don't have to keep bouncing around it later.

AFP Protocol Settings

As you can see in Figure 3–28, your options here are easy, because most of the other settings for AFP are handled on the main Settings tab for AFP in Server Admin.

Here, you can turn AFP sharing off/on, enable/disable guest access, and set the custom name for a given share on a share-by-share basis. The "Custom AFP name" setting allows you to change the name of the share to something other than the name of the folder or volume that you are sharing.

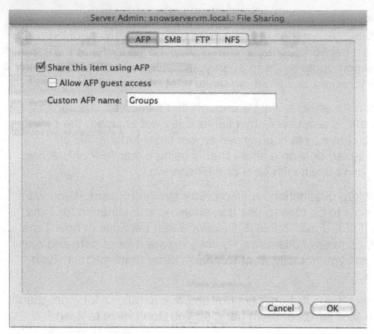

Figure 3–28. *AFP settings*

SMB Protocol Settings

There are a few more options here, as shown in Figure 3–29.

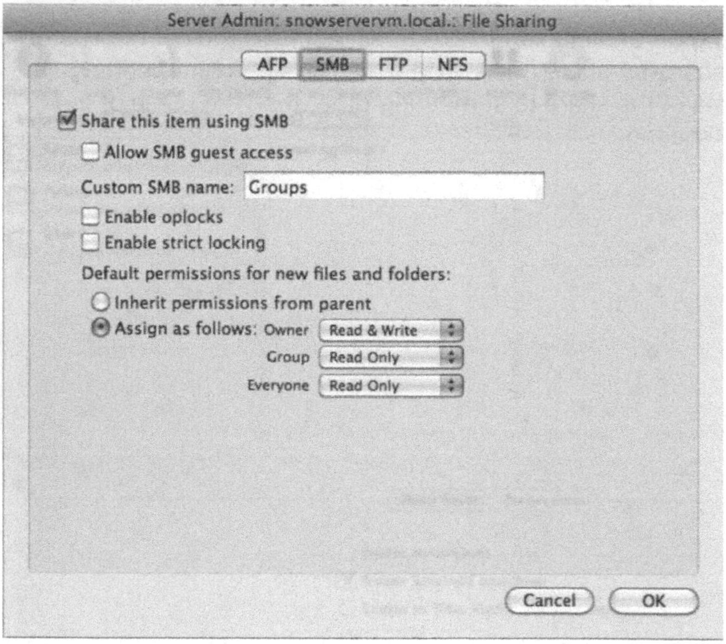

Figure 3–29. *SMB settings*

You will probably notice that you have the same three options you did for AFP, but you also have two settings for file locking.

> **NOTE:** *File locking* is the act of an application or process, when opening a file that it will need to write to, locking it so only that application or process can write to or delete that file. This can be annoying at times, but proper use of locking can really save you a lot of pain.

There are two kinds of locking for SMB shares in Mac OS X Server 10.6: strict locking and opportunistic locking (or *oplocks*). Strict locking is the simplest. With strict locking, only one client or client process can write to or modify an open file on a share. Other clients can read the file, but to modify it, they have to create a new copy of the file.

Oplocks modify strict locking a bit by allowing the client to cache changes to a locked file it didn't lock. This can improve performance, but if you are going to use oplocks, it is *very* important that you share that data out *only* via SMB. Other protocols understand strict locking, not oplocks, and if you enable oplocks when other protocols are being used, you can get yourself into a world of hurt with regard to data corruption.

The final SMB setting deals with default permissions for new files and folders, with regard to POSIX permissions. By default, new files created on an SMB share allow the owner of a file to have full, unfettered access, with the group and everyone else getting read-only access, but you can change this if you like via the drop-downs. If you want new files or folders to just take on the POSIX permissions of the directory they are in, set this to "Inherit permissions from parent."

FTP Protocol Settings

As you can see in Figure 3–30, the FTP protocol settings are the same as AFP's settings: enable/disable FTP sharing, (dis)allow guest access, and set a custom FTP name for the share point.

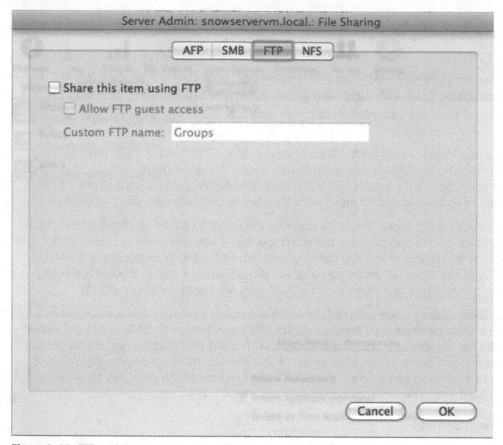

Figure 3–30. *FTP settings*

NFS Protocol Settings

NFS's settings are a little different—well a *lot* different, but then again, compared to AFP and SMB, both of which NFS predates, NFS actually *is* a lot different. NFS was developed in 1984 by Sun Microsystems (the same year the Mac was first released, with no concept of file sharing or networks at all, and many years before Microsoft even thought about Windows, much less SMB), as a way to easily share data between machines on slow, unreliable networks that could spread across a college campus. It was released to the computing world at large in 1989.

As such, it works a little differently than things like AFP do. First, at the time that NFS was developed, there was no concept of authenticating a share point, or "exporting" in NFS-ese. Either the computer you were on had access or it didn't, and if you could log into the computer, you could gain access to any available NFS shares that machine had access to.

From a security standpoint, there are obvious problems with this, so over the years, NFS implemented various security methods, but because of its roots, the way it does things is a bit different.

The first setting in NFS has to do with who can see the setting. To export an NFS share to the entire network and allow for unauthenticated access, you enable exporting the share and set the drop-down list to say World, as shown in Figure 3–31.

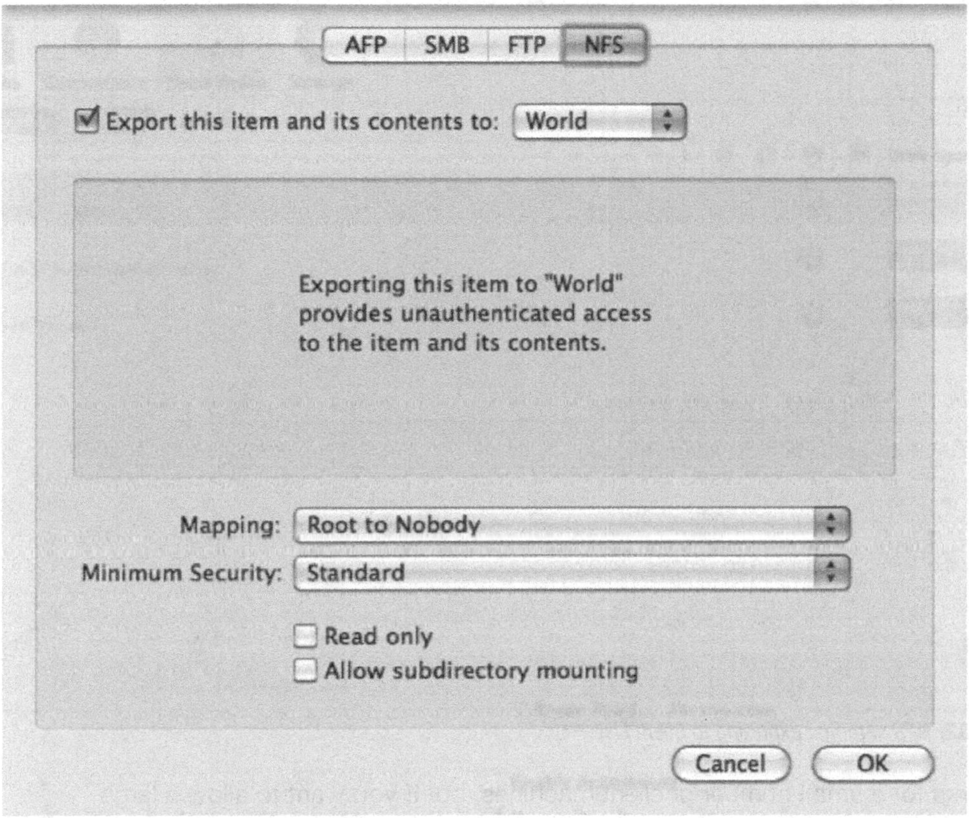

Figure 3–31. *NFS settings: exporting to World*

This makes things easy but is a very, very bad idea unless you are absolutely sure you know you need to do it. To export an NFS share to a list of clients, select Client List, and enter the IP address or DNS names of the clients you want to have access to this share, as shown in Figure 3–32.

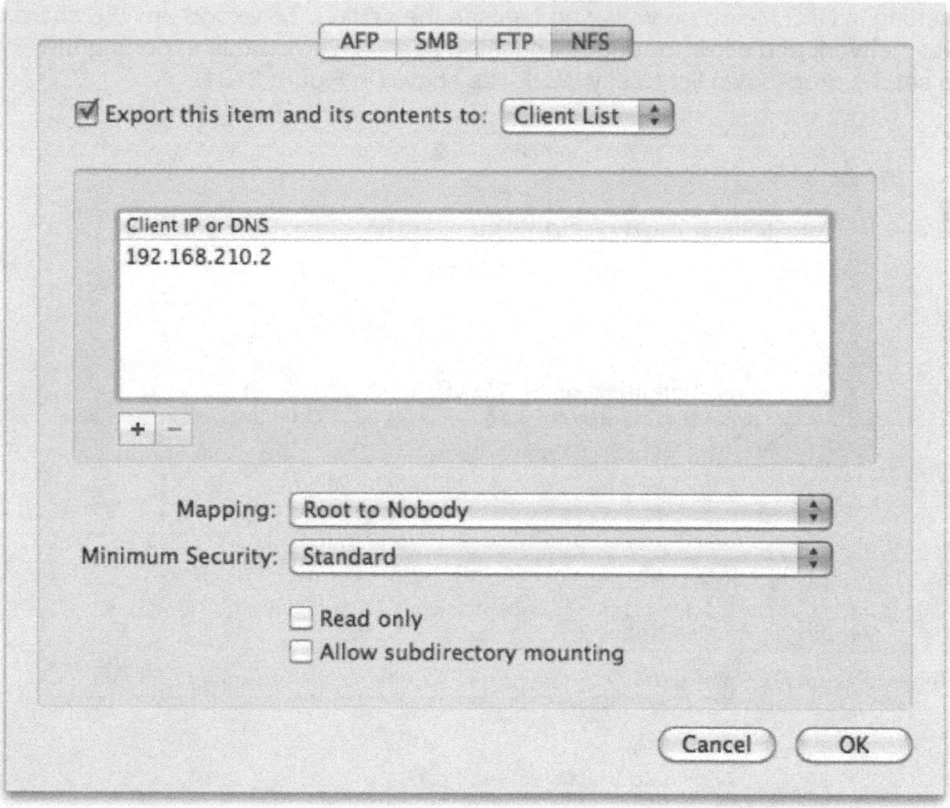

Figure 3–32. *NFS settings: exporting to Client List*

That works for a small number of client machines, but if you want to allow a large number of clients to access an export, you're better off restricting access by subnet. To do this, you set the Export drop-down to Subnet and enter the IP address and subnet mask for the subnet. For example, entering **192.168.1.0** for the IP address and **255.255.255.0** for the subnet mask would limit access to those computers with IP addresses between 192.168.1.1 and 192.168.1.254. Figure 3–33 shows an example of exporting to Subnet.

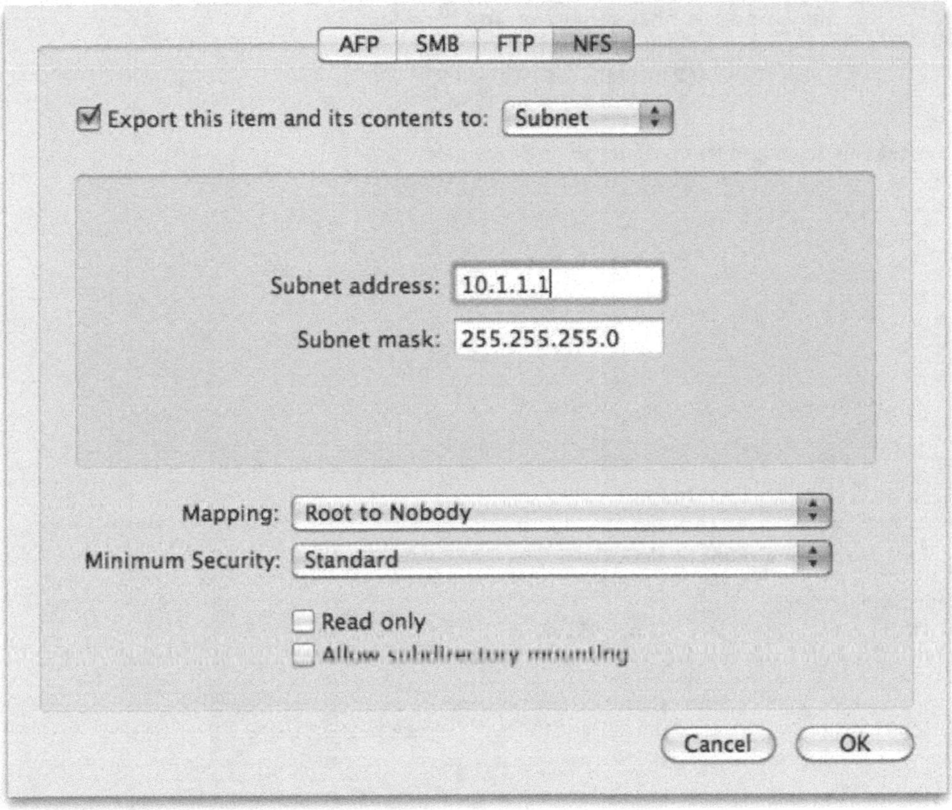

Figure 3–33. *NFS settings: exporting to Subnet*

The next setting, shown in Figure 3–34, has to do with privilege mapping. (Remember, NFS is a very old file sharing protocol, and there are some old Unix servers still out there. NFS has a large legacy client base.)

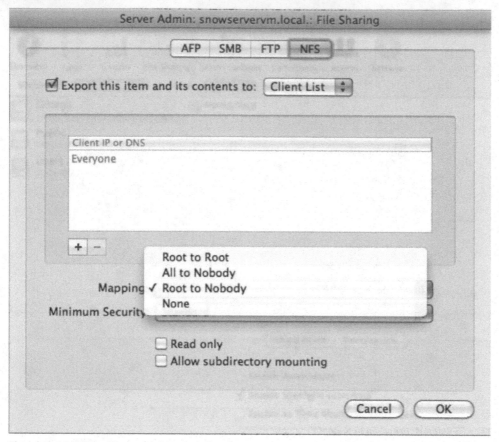

Figure 3–34. *NFS settings: privilege mapping*

You have four options here:

- *Root to Root*: This allows someone to log into a machine as the root user and have full root privileges on the NFS export. Usually this is a bad idea.

- *All to Nobody*: This severely restricts everyone's access to the NFS export to the bare minimum. It's secure but hard to work with.

- *Root to Nobody*: Only locks down someone logging in as root. Other users are unaffected.

- *None*: Don't map privileges at all; let other mechanisms handle this.

If you're going to pick a mapping setting, Root to Nobody is the first choice, with None being the second. Root to Root has a high potential for problems, and All to Nobody can make actually doing work difficult.

The next setting is for the minimum security level for the share, and you have five options here, as shown in Figure 3–35.

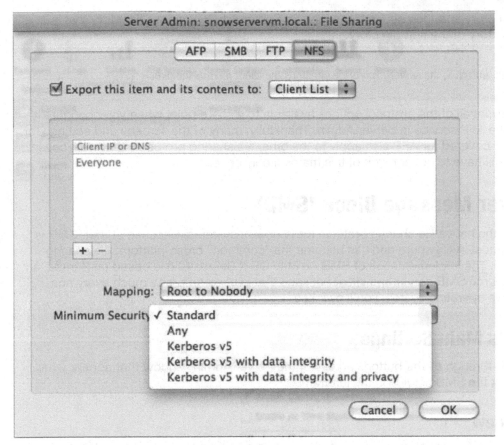

Figure 3–35. *NFS settings: minimum security levels*

- *Standard*: Don't set any level of authentication for the share.

- *Any*: Use any valid authentication mechanism for the share, good, bad, or indifferent.

- *Kerberos v5*: Only use Kerberos for authentication. There's no encryption of data, but it can be used with an single sign-on setup.

- *Kerberos v5 with data integrity*: Use Kerberos, and use checksums to validate the data during transfers.

- *Kerberos v5 with data integrity and privacy*: Use Kerberos, checksums, and encryption of data transfers.

The "Read only" check box sets the entire share and its contents to read-only access, but keep in mind that this setting applies only when the share is accessed via NFS.

The "Allow subdirectory mounting" setting allows the subdirectory of an NFS export to be directly mounted. However, if you have multiple NFS exports, then you can't export one directory and then separately export (in Server Admin) another directory that is a subdirectory of the first directory.

> **TIP:** With NFS, the server *exports* the directory; the client *mounts* the directory.

That covers all of the protocol options available to a share point when you configure it using the AFP service in Server Admin. Thankfully, many of the screens and settings for what we covered for AFP also apply to the other file sharing protocols that we'll cover, so we will have to cover much of this material only once.

Server Message Block (SMB)

SMB is the native file sharing protocol for Windows systems. Because of that, SMB is used almost everywhere and has become the "common" cross-platform file sharing protocol. The implementation of SMB on Mac OS X Server 10.6 is based on Samba, an open source SMB server and client package that is used on pretty much every non-Windows operating system you'll ever see.

SMB's Main Settings

Let's go through all the buttons across of the Server Admin window that appear when you click the SMB service in the left frame.

Overview

To get started with SMB on Mac OS X Server 10.6, start Server Admin, and click the SMB service under your server. If SMB is not showing, go into the settings for your server, click Settings, and then enable SMB on the Services tab. Looking at the SMB pane, you can see there's a lot of commonality between SMB and AFP in Mac OS X Server 10.6. This is by design, so you don't have to deal with any more differences than technically necessary. The only difference on the Overview tab, for example, is that AFP shows Current Throughput and SMB does not.

Logs

Where AFP logged access information and errors and both were off by default, SMB logs the two main processes, or *daemons*, that are used by SMB: smbd, or the SMB file service daemon, and nmbd, or the SMB Name Service daemon. The file service log shows things such as logins, logouts, and client access information. The name service log deals more with the specific function of an SMB server, and we'll dig into that in more detail here in a bit.

Graphs

Unlike AFP, SMB doesn't give you a throughput graph, only one for average connected users.

Connections

In the Connections window, you can see the username, the IP address, and the time connected. In the lower-right corner, there is a Disconnect button that lets you quickly disconnect client users from the server share. Unlike AFP, SMB only allows you to disconnect a user immediately, without the luxury of giving end users a warning and a countdown to disconnect. With SMB, there's no option to send messages to a client or clients, and there's no concept of sleeping or idle clients either.

Share Points

This tab functions just like it does for AFP, so if you want to know more about the settings here, refer to the Share Points section in within the AFP information that we covered earlier in this chapter.

Settings

This is the section where you will see most of the differences between AFP and SMB on Mac OS X Server 10.6. If you have any background in administering Windows servers and networks in the past, many of the settings here might look familiar to you. Mac OS X Server 10.6 offers basic connectivity for Windows client operating systems by emulating the behavior of older Windows servers; however, as we will discuss in a moment, Snow Leopard's Windows-friendliness does not extend to emulating modern technologies such as Active Directory. Still, for networks with a handful of Windows systems, this layer of functionality is usually more than enough for your Windows users to be able to work productively within your Mac network.

Let's dive into this section in more detail.

General Settings

This is where you set the server's role, the SMB server description, the SMB server name, and the workgroup name, as shown in Figure 3–36.

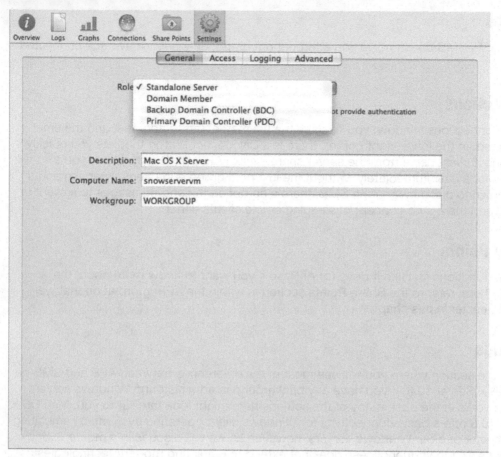

Figure 3–36. *SMB general settings*

The Role drop-down determines what the function of the SMB server is. The Standalone Server setting is just that: a server on the network sharing files via SMB. This can be a bit confusing unless you remember that this is not the role of the *physical* server, just the server provided by the SMB service on the server. A stand-alone server is just another file server on the network providing SMB access. There's nothing special about it, so let's move along. This is the most common SMB role for Mac OS X Server on a Mac network.

The second setting is Domain Member and is most often used when you have a Mac OS X Server box providing SMB services to Windows clients on a Windows network. This allows the server to participate in Windows authentication setups like Active Directory, and it can provide Windows-specific services, such as hosting user profile directories or network home directories for Windows users. If you aren't on a Windows network, you'll rarely need to use this role.

Backup Domain Controller is the third setting, and it sets up the SMB server to play a role analogous to an Open Directory replica. In fact, for Mac OS X Server 10.6 to act as a backup domain controller (BDC), it *has* to be an Open Directory replica. The BDC is an artifact of Windows networking before Active Directory and is rarely seen on Windows networks anymore. It is of limited use with modern Windows clients but can provide some basic authentication, user, and computer management in situations where you have a small number of Windows clients on a Mac network.

The final role is Primary Domain Controller and is analogous to an Open Directory master. As with the BDC role, for Mac OS X Server 10.6 to act as a primary domain controller (PDC), it has to be an Open Directory master. Although the PDC functionality can be of use where your Windows clients are small in number and have limited needs, it is not able to emulate an Active Directory network, so if you have a large number of Windows clients to manage, you really should look into implementing Active Directory.

> **NOTE:** The PDC/BDC roles are how things were done prior to Windows 2000, in the Windows NT 4 days. These functions are beyond legacy nowadays and should be almost considered relics of a bygone era, suitable only for clients that support NT4 networking, whose needs are extremely simple.

The Description and Computer Name fields should be fairly self-evident; they're where you set the name and description of the SMB server for Windows or other SMB clients.

The Workgroup name is another product of the pre–Active Directory days, but unlike the PDC/BDC, still has a useful function. In cases where you have a bunch of Windows computers on a network and no server, the Workgroup name lets them all see each other easily. It's analogous to the .local network domain used by Bonjour on Mac OS X. However, because of the age of the Windows Workgroup, the Workgroup name cannot be longer than 15 characters.

Access Settings

SMB's Access settings, as shown in Figure 3–37, are similar to AFP's Access settings.

Here you can enable guest access for the SMB server as a whole and set the number of client connections allowed. Unlike AFP, there's no differentiation between the number of authenticated connections and the number of guest connections. The major difference between SMB and AFP here is in the authentication. Because SMB has been through a few major iterations, there are three levels of authentication for SMB in Mac OS X Server 10.6:

- *NTLMv2 & Kerberos*: This is the most secure and is the one you need for single sign-on participation to work properly. NTLMv2 is an abbreviation for NT LAN Manager version 2, which was developed by Microsoft to provide stronger cryptographic features than earlier versions.

- *NTLM*: This is an earlier version of NTLM. It is not as secure as NTLMv2 but is used by older clients or by the client software on simple devices such as network scanners and printers.

■ *LAN Manager*: This is the oldest and most insecure SMB authentication method. The mechanisms for cracking Lan Manager, or LANMAN, are well understood and widely published, and there are many implementations of these cracks on the Internet. It is left turned off by default and should stay that way.

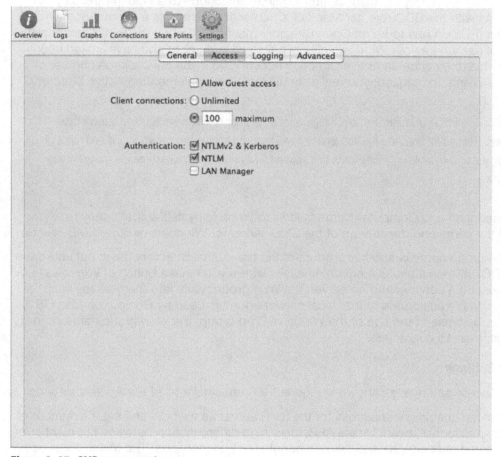

Figure 3–37. *SMB access settings*

Logging

SMB logging is always enabled if the SMB service is running. The Log Level setting, shown in Figure 3–38, allows you to set the detail level of what is logged for the SMB service. The default is Medium, and unless your server is extremely busy or you are running low on disk space, the setting can be left as is, instead of being set to Low. Setting Log Level to High should be done only when you are troubleshooting an SMB service problem and need to see *every* detail of the SMB service. A moderately busy SMB server can generate very large logs if Log Level is set to High.

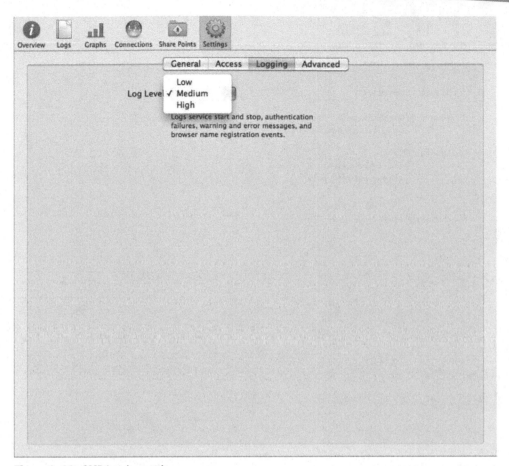

Figure 3–38. *SMB logging settings*

Advanced

This is where you set some of the more granularly detailed settings for the SMB service. As with any advanced settings (shown in Figure 3–39), change things here only when you know you need to do so.

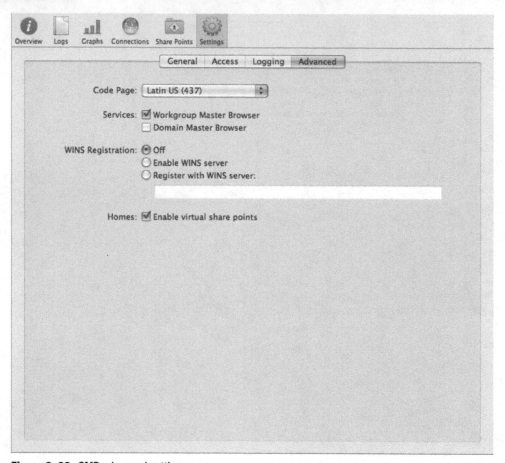

Figure 3–39. *SMB advanced settings*

The Code Page drop-down sets the character set that will be used by the SMB service. This is not the same as the *language* used. For example, English, Spanish, French, and Italian are all different languages, but all use the same basic *character set*. This setting is more for when you have to have a server that can work with Chinese, Russian, or Korean character sets.

The next two settings, Workgroup and Domain Master Browsers, are another product of the Windows NT 4 era that have been brought into the modern day. Both do the same thing, but on different scales. The job of a master browser is to control the display of network resources like file and print servers. If you have a Windows workgroup set up on a single subnet and want your server to be the master browser for that workgroup, then you would enable the Workgroup Master Browser check box. If your computer is acting as a Windows PDC and/or needs to manage network resource access across multiple subnets, then you'd use the Domain Master Browser setting. The one thing to remember is that having more than one master browser for a workgroup or a domain is a bad idea and will cause you no end of really bizarre problems.

The next setting is WINS Registration. WINS dates back to the pre–Windows 2000 days, when Windows machines used NetBIOS and NetBEUI instead of TCP/IP for file and print sharing. Those protocols handled all the needs of Windows networking, much like AppleTalk used to for the Mac. This included things such as naming and browsing. It worked well when all the computers on a network were on the same subnet.

Well, as TCP/IP took over Windows networks, Microsoft realized it needed a way to manage naming and browsing over TCP/IP, and since using DNS wasn't an option at the time, Microsoft came up with WINS, the Windows Internet Name Service, which allowed for NetBIOS name resolution over TCP/IP.

Within the SMB service, a server can have one of three options for WINS:

- *Off*: Don't use WINS at all for NetBIOS name resolution, and don't provide WINS services.

- *Enable WINS server*: This server is the WINS server for the network. Unlike the master browser, you can have multiple WINS servers, a primary WINS server, and some number of secondary WINS servers. This relationship is analogous to the DNS primary/secondary server, PDC/BDC, or Open Directory master/replica relationships.

- *Register with WINS server*: There is already a WINS server or servers on your network, and you want to use them for NetBIOS name resolution. Enter the IP address or DNS name of the server here.

If you have users who will be logging in from both Macs and Windows computers and you want their Mac network home directory to also be their Windows network home directory, then select the "Enable virtual share points" check box. To keep the Windows network home directory completely separate from the Mac network home directory, don't enable this.

That's it for SMB settings. See? We covered most of the common information already, so this was a lot less information to digest.

File Transfer Protocol (FTP)

FTP is one of the oldest file transfer protocols still in use. As the name suggests, it is a protocol for copying files between two computers, nothing more. So, unlike AFP, SMB, or NFS, you wouldn't work directly on a file that resides on an FTP share. FTP is only for copying files back and forth.

FTP's Main Settings

Let's go through all the buttons across the top of the Server Admin window that appear when you click the FTP service in the left frame.

Overview

The FTP Overview tab lets you see the current status of the service, the number of authenticated connections, the number of anonymous (guest) connections, and whether anonymous FTP is enabled on this server.

Log

FTP logging is fairly simple, as is the protocol. There's the FTP transfer log, and everything you set in the logging settings for the service is logged here.

Graphs

This tab shows only the average number of connected users over time.

Connections

Unlike AFP or SMB, there's no provision here to disconnect a client other than stopping the FTP service. For each connected client, you see the username, whether the client is connecting anonymously, the client's TCP/IP address, and what they are doing (such as listing files, getting files, putting files, and so on).

> **NOTE:** FTP is a little odd compared to "normal" file sharing services. It only transfers files between computers, lists files on the server, lists files on the client, and lets you navigate around the server or the client. To transfer a file from the client, you put the file on the server. To transfer a file to the client, you get the file from the server. To transfer directories or multiple files, you use mput and mget. Guest connections are known as *anonymous* in FTP's parlance.

Share Points

To configure share points for FTP access, refer to the section about FTP options in the AFP part of this chapter.

Settings

This is the section where you will see settings that are specific to the FTP protocol on Mac OS X Server. We'll go over each of the tabs to explain what each of them does.

General

The General settings, shown in Figure 3–40, are easy to understand. You can set the number of times a client can fail to log in before they are disconnected, with the default being 3. This is an important setting to use. FTP is an *extremely* simple protocol, and as such, an attacker can try to log in to a poorly configured FTP server thousands of times a second. Even if they don't succeed, the high levels of traffic that their requests generate can have the effect of denying legitimate users access to the FTP service and maybe even slowing the entire server down. Because FTP predates the GUI, there is often a text welcome that includes the e-mail address for the FTP administrator if there is a problem. That e-mail address goes here.

NOTE: We recommend not using the FTP service on any server that is exposed to the Internet.

For authentication, you have three options: Any Method, Standard, and Kerberos. Standard requires the client to enter a known user ID and password, Kerberos requires the client to be part of the server's Kerberos domain, and Any Method allows either.

NOTE: This refers *only* to authentication, not encryption. FTP is a plain-text protocol. Unless you encrypt it via SSH or SSL or are using Kerberos, then everything you do with FTP—every bit of data during an FTP session, including logging in—is done in clear text and trivial to sniff. If you are using FTP and aren't using Kerberos, SSL, or SSH, do not *ever* use it with administrator credentials.

When limiting access to your FTP server, you can differentiate between authenticated and anonymous or guest users. By default, anonymous access is disabled, and unless you specifically need anonymous access, it should stay that way. An FTP server with a fast connection that allows anonymous access is gravy to attackers and people trading illegal/malicious software. If you enable anonymous access, then it is imperative that you make sure you have the ACLs for the directories that will be accessible via FTP locked down as tightly as possible.

The final setting, "Enable MacBinary and disk image auto-conversion," is one that is unique to Mac OS X–based FTP servers. It's a legacy of the older "dual-fork" files that the Mac used to use. Each file normally had a data and a resource fork, but platforms other than the Mac would normally chuck the resource fork if you saved a Mac file to it. This frequently made files unreadable, especially applications. To get around this, Apple came up with a way to serialize these files, via MacBinary, so that the resource forks were preserved. It's pretty rare to run into this now, but just in case, enable this setting. To take advantage of it, a client has to add a .bin extension to the file, and when it is transferred, the FTP service will automatically convert them to MacBinary files.

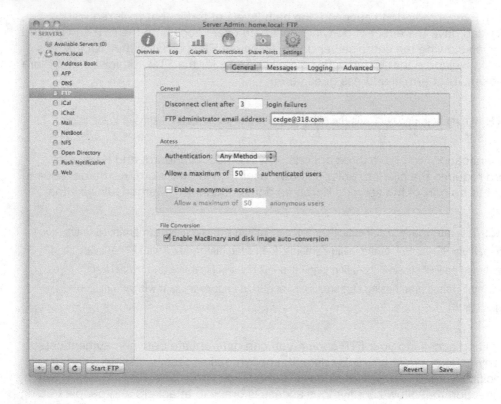

Figure 3–40. *FTP general settings*

Messages

As you can see in Figure 3–41, these are the welcome and banner messages for FTP clients logging into the FTP service. They're not required, but if you do want to use them, try to avoid inserting any information about the file server and its OS. FTP messages are frequently used by attackers to identify, or "fingerprint" the server, so they can be more targeted and efficient in their attacks. Therefore, if you plan to use a banner message for your FTP server, it is a good idea to change the default text to remove references to Mac OS X Server.

As the default sample banner states, the banner message is presented to FTP clients immediately before prompting them for a username and password. The welcome message is presented to FTP clients upon successful login to the server.

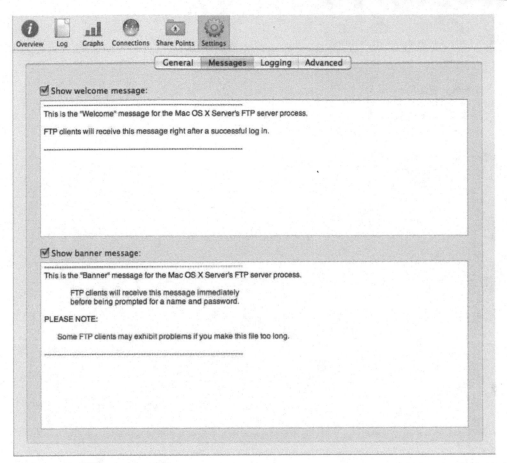

Figure 3–41. *FTP messages settings*

Logging

This is where you set the FTP logging for authenticated and anonymous users, as shown in Figure 3–42.

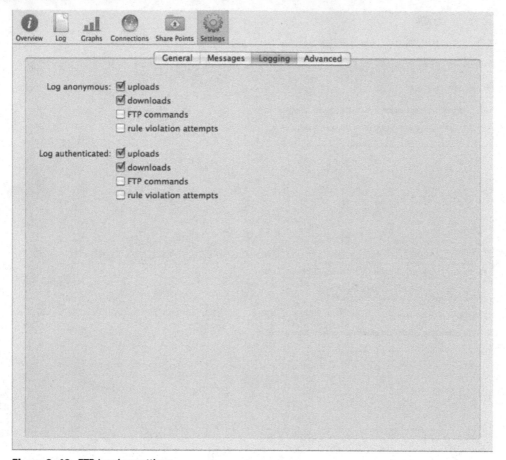

Figure 3–42. *FTP logging settings*

Each kind has four items it can log:

- *Uploads*: All put operations are logged.

- *Downloads*: All get operations are logged.

- *FTP commands*: This logs all the commands used by the client, such as ls, cd, pwd, and so on.

- *Rule violation attempts*: This logs all security violations by the client.

Advanced

The purpose of the advanced settings is to set up FTP shares beyond the share points you may have defined, as shown in Figure 3–43.

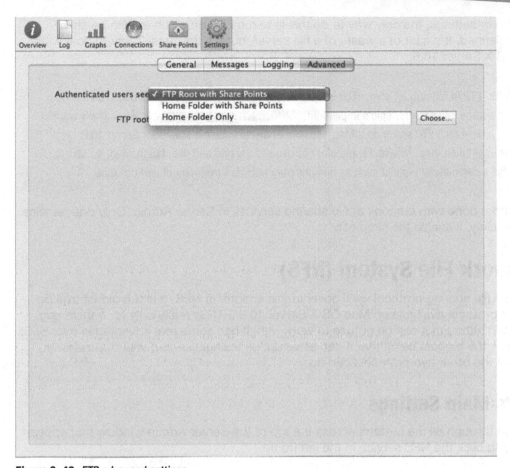

Figure 3–43. *FTP advanced settings*

These settings apply only to authenticated users. Anonymous users get only share points. There are three options here:

- *FTP Root with Share Points*: This gives users access to an FTP root directory (set in the Advanced settings as well) and any share points that have FTP enabled for them. With this enabled, when an FTP user logs in, they go to the FTP root, and within that, they see symbolic links/aliases to the share points that have FTP enabled.

- *Home Folder with Share Points*: When a user logs in, they log into their home directory on the server, and any FTP-enabled shares are seen as links/aliases in their home directory.

- *Home Folder Only*: When an authenticated user logs in, they can only see their home directory.

Looking at these three options, the obvious question is, "How do you just have an FTP root, without share points?" Unfortunately, this is where you hit a limitation of the Mac OS X Server 10.6 FTP implementation. Without doing a bit of hacking in the low-level

FTP server settings, the only way to do this is to run FTP on a server with no share points defined. It's a bit of a waste of a file server, but it's the "easy" way to do it with Mac OS X Server 10.6.

> **NOTE:** FTP in Mac OS X Server 10.6 is there as a convenience. Although it is based on a good open source FTP server, Apple's implementation is rather crippled by default. If you really want to have a top-notch FTP server on a Mac, you either have to hack the Mac OS X Server 10.6 implementation, have to install some other open source server and use that instead, or have to install a commercial product such as Rumpus from Maxum Development and use that.

Ah, almost done with our look at file sharing services in Server Admin. Only one remains: NFS. Luckily, it is also the simplest.

Network File System (NFS)

The final file sharing protocol we'll cover in this chapter is NFS. It is the oldest true file sharing protocol available on Mac OS X Server 10.6 (FTP is really only for *transferring* files), and although it can be obtuse to work with, it has some real advantages over SMB and AFP, the biggest being that it can scale up, on a single server, well beyond what either of the other two protocols can do.

NFS's Main Settings

We'll go through all the buttons across the top of the Server Admin window that appear when you click the NFS service in the left frame.

Overview

This tab shows the status of the overall NFS service and the four processes/daemons that NFS needs to function.

Connections

There is no disconnection ability with this tab (or, really, within NFS for that matter) other than stopping the NFS service. This tab shows you the username of the client, its TCP/IP address, idle time in seconds, the NFS requests used by the client, and the number of bytes read and written.

Share Points

The settings here are the same as for every other sharing protocol and were covered in the AFP section earlier in this chapter.

Settings

As you can see in Figure 3–44, it is instantly obvious that there's not a lot you can set here.

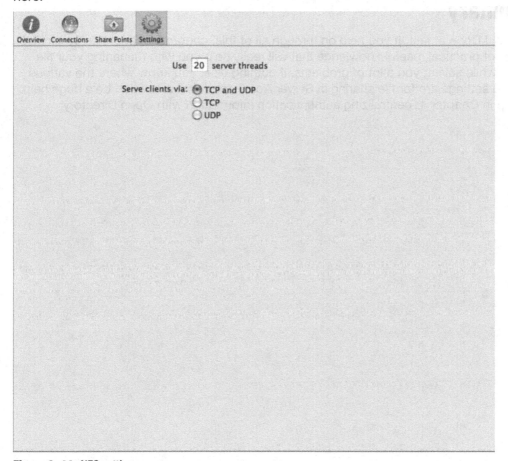

Figure 3–44. *NFS settings*

Only two options are available here (actually, you can tweak more than this with NFS, but doing so requires the command line, which is outside the scope of this chapter). The first is the number of server threads you can have running simultaneously. The more threads you have, the more clients you can have concurrently connected. If you set this too high, you can run into performance issues. If you set it too low, then clients can't connect, so be judicious in your changes here. The other setting is whether to have clients connect via TCP, UDP, or both. The default is to use both, and unless you have clear reason to change this, you should leave it there.

Note: NFS as a protocol is much older than many other protocols such as AFP and less resource intensive. In previous releases of Mac OS X Server, security concerns caused NFS to be rarely recommended. However, because NFS is mature and uses its resources wisely, it can be leveraged to provide more home folders and more consistent levels of bandwidth, namely, in server-to-server communications.

Summary

Woo-hoo! Done at last. If you held on through all of this, congratulations! You've picked up a lot of practical, useful knowledge that will really help you with managing your file servers while saving you a lot of problems. If nothing else, you know where the various logs and settings are for file sharing in Server Admin, and that alone can be a huge help. Next up in Chapter 4: centralizing authentication information with Open Directory.

Managing Directory Services

In Chapter 2, we looked at setting up a basic server to be used as, let's face it, a glorified NAS unit. But the power of Mac OS X Server is that it can grow past being a single box hosting a variety of services. By attaching it to a directory system, you can have Mail services hosted on one server and a fileserver on another, while sharing a unified directory of users and passwords hosted on a third. This division of tasks gives flexibility to your overall network infrastructure by minimizing downtime of services (now you can reboot your mail server without having to disconnect users from the fileserver), and thus increasing performance.

There are multiple directory service solutions out there, but the one we will be discussing primarily is Open Directory, which is built into OS X. It is flexible enough to be integrated into Active Directory (Microsoft's directory service) and eDirectory (Novell's solution) almost entirely or be used in a mixed environment, extending functionality locally for specific Mac OS X servers and clients while keeping eDirectory or Active Directory for global services. The latter is something commonly found in larger organizations that already have an existing directory service and possibly a smaller department of Mac OS X users that can benefit from some more specific management options by a local Open Directory server.

The majority of this chapter will be focused on setting up an independent Open Directory server that would provision and manage its own Open Directory objects. Understanding Open Directory at this basic level will help you moving forward if you decide to pursue more complicated configurations that include integrating with other directory servers (and more importantly, directory servers not under your administration).

Understanding the Components of a Directory Service

While Open Directory appears as a single service in the Server Admin application (and doesn't even appear at all in Server Preferences), it is actually composed of a handful of services including Lightweight Directory Access Protocol Server (LDAP), Kerberos, and Apple Password Server. These services work in conjunction to provide a complete directory service to clients, which can be desktop machines, other servers, services running on the same machine, or even remotely hosted web applications. The important thing to remember is that this is a composite service, so services and settings must be correct for it to function properly. There has been a huge improvement in how OS X handles and manages Open Directory over the years, but it can still be some of the most common causes of headaches for Mac administrators if it hasn't been set up properly, again because a lot of synchronization and management tasks are going on in the background.

The three major components of Open Directory are the LDAP server, the Kerberos server, and the Password server. The LDAP server provides access to the database containing all the usernames, computer records, and group roles and could be considered the place where the organizational chart of your directory system resides and from which it is retrieved. Kerberos is an advanced method of authentication to ensure that passwords are not intercepted in transit between a client service and the server it is trying to authenticate to. Finally, the Password server is used on the backend of the Open Directory system to provide a secure password repository and to serve out passwords to local services (Kerberos itself and other systems that are not Kerberos aware). While it is a server, the only clients it talks to are local, on the same system as itself.

LDAP

LDAP is a protocol developed in the early 1990s as a way to centrally manage and update information stored about users in a directory or database system. Since, in practice, it is really a way to organize and collect information on any object or attribute that one wishes, it is actually used in the core of many Directory Services, just with different templates (or schemas) for what information is available and used by the client systems.

For instance, in Open Directory, Apple used the standard LDAP attributes, where appropriate. But when there were no existing attributes for a setting that Apple wished to store the information, Apple created a schema file containing these new attributes and describing how they related to the rest of the directory system. In fact, if you took that schema file and applied to another LDAPv3-compliant server, an OS X client would think it was talking to an Open Directory server. Doing so is outside the scope of this book, but it is mentioned to illustrate how flexible and useful LDAP can be as the directory storage system, and why it is used as the basis for the majority of Directory Services in use today.

From a functional aspect, LDAP is the phonebook for your office and makes it possible for machines and services that are connected to LDAP to query and retrieve information based on records stored in it's database. Records (or *objects* as they are called in LDAP) consist of attributes, which are the individual pieces of information that makeup the record. For example, the user record Bender Rodríguez (see Figure 4–2) is actually composed of various attributes: one specifying his first name, another his last name, and others his combined name (which in some cases is a field that is calculated on the fly by combing the `firstname` and `lastname` attributes), his user ID number, his unique ID, his short name, his e-mail address, and so on. The attributes that exist for an object are defined by the schema. You can't use an attribute that doesn't exist in the collected schema of your LDAP system, but you can have attributes defined that are never used (this fact allows for Apple-specific schema additions to coexist peacefully in a Windows environment; they are separate attributes from what Windows uses for the most part).

Kerberos

Kerberos is a technology, developed by MIT Labs, to securely authenticate and authorize users and services while minimizing the risk associated with working on open networks and transferring passwords. In fact, the only time a user's password is ever sent in a Kerberos session is when a user changes that password (since it has to be updated on the server). All other times, the information sent is actually a collection of one-way encrypted and signed packets based around timestamps. A Kerberos authentication process is a multistep dialogue between the authentication service (AS), the ticket granter service (TGS), and a client workstation. The AS and TGS, in the case of Open Directory, are both running on the same server as parts of the Kerberos system, but in complex networks, they can be spread apart. The dialogue goes something like this:

The client says, "I am going to Login as Bender."

The AS server says, "OK, to prove you really are Bender, I am going to send you this package that only you can open. Inside is another package that I've timestamped and encrypted for the TGS. Once you've opened the first package, you have to reencrypt it and send it on to the TGS."

The client replies, "Well, the password I used unlocked it, so now I'll add my timestamp and the original timestamp from the AS, and I'll reencrypt this package so only the TGS can open it and send it on it's way.

The TGS server says, "I was able to decrypt the package, which I could have only been sent by a client authenticated as Bender, since it has been signed. The secret package sent to me by AS is intact. This conversation started less than five minutes ago, so I know someone could not have broken open the locks in that short a time, so I will have to trust that you are Bender. Here is your ticket-granting ticket."

Once this dialogue has completed, an abbreviated process will happen automatically whenever a client connects to a server (or service) that is configured for Kerberos, using the ticket-granting ticket (TGT) to perform the same process to ensure that the user is who they say they are. By default with Open Directory, the TGT expires after ten hours, after which a new TGT will have to be granted. In version 10.5 and higher, Apple has provided the option to allow the client to automatically renew expiring tickets for up to seven days and to allow users to save their Kerberos password in their keychains, which may be options you wish to change depending on your security needs.

As a result of the time-sensitive nature of the Kerberos process, it is important to ensure that all of the machines involved are looking at the same network time server and that their clocks are in sync. Otherwise, the authentication will fail and cause difficulty when you're trying to troubleshoot whether the problem is related to the server configuration or just something simple as the clocks being off by 12 minutes.

Password Server

While Kerberos is used for a number of authentication services, it does not actually store the passwords in the world of Open Directory. That job falls to the Password server, which along with storing the passwords, also provides authentication for services that are not compatible with Kerberos. The common example is the Mail server in OS X Server. It supports Kerberos authentication, and if every mail client was configured to use Kerberos, in theory, you would not need a Password server, because the whole dialogue would exist in the Kerberos realm. However, not all mail clients support Kerberos (including Apple's iPhone), so the Password server acts as a consolidated system to speak the various forms of password and authentication methods required for OS X Server to be able to function as a proper server in a mixed environment.

Preparing to Set Up Open Directory

Before creating your permanent Open Directory system, you will want to make sure the environment housing it will be configured properly. Most importantly, ensure that each server will have a proper forward and reverse DNS entry assigned for it's primary IP address and host name. This step is key because any new clients, servers, or systems added to the Open Directory environment after this point will contain pointers and references to that IP address and host name, and making sure you have that set exactly how you want it now will save you countless hours and headaches later on. If you have an already set up and configured a server that is not using Open Directory and populated it with users and groups, you will need to migrate those accounts and settings over to the Open Directory database, which adds another complication and potential area for issues in the future.

In Chapter 2, we covered the quick guide of checking those settings before creating the Open Directory system, using the changeip -checkhostname command from the Terminal application. Running it will report what the configured host name of the server is; the host name displayed should match your DNS. If the command reports an error, it may be because the DNS settings haven't updated yet or the cache hasn't been refreshed to show the new IP / DNS entries. If you do get an error, and the CurrentHostname seems correct, you will have to check your DNS service server settings. If the DNS host name is the one you want the server to be named after, you can use the command provided in the changeip output to make a correction. Since chances are there are minimal services running on the server at this point, this process should run quickly.

Understanding Open Directory Roles

Each OS X Server that will be participating in an Open Directory environment will have one of three roles:

- *Open Directory master:* This is the primary Open Directory server for the environment. All settings and changes about the environment are taken from this server and are replicated throughout the rest of the network. In a proper Open Directory environment, there should be only one Open Directory master.

- *Open Directory replica*: While there can be only one Open Directory master, there can be up to 32 replicas directly connected to it. Each of them contains a full copy of the Open Directory master's configuration and settings, but they primarily function to distribute load away from the Open Directory master and allow for redundancy (if the Open Directory master goes offline permanently, you can promote a replica to a master). Replicas are also useful if you have a remote office, as you can have the local workstations authenticate locally instead of having that traffic route over your office VPN or MPLS system. If you need more than 32 replicas, each replica can have 32 replicas of its own. While it is tempting to think of a replica as a backup, it is not; it will blindly replicate a deleted user, a corrupted database entry, or any other problems that may occur in Open Directory master.

- *Connected to a Directory System*: This simply means that the server is connected to the Open Directory system as a client; it does not replicate any Kerberos or LDAP databases and does not provide any central authentication services. It is dependent on the Open Directory system working properly so it can allow users to log in.

Setting Up an Open Directory Master

To set up your server as an Open Directory master, we are going to use the Server Admin tool in /Applications/Server. Once it is open and you have connected to the server you want to configure, ensure that you have enabled the Open Directory services tab and that client-side binding is unchecked in your servers settings view (If this option is checked, machines booting into 10.6 client for the first time may prompt the user to join the Open Directory environment. While a useful step, it can lead to other complications down the line if you have users who are installing or reinstalling their own machines on your network).

In the Open Directory services' Settings tab, you will want to change the role of your server from Standalone to an Open Directory master. When you do so, you will be prompted with a configuration wizard to create an Open Directory master. If you see an error about single sign on not working, there is a problem with DNS, and you will want to consult the advanced DNS portion of this book before continuing. If you don't have any DNS problems, you will prompted to create another user, the directory administrator.

This account will be the one that can create and edit users in the Open Directory system. You can create other accounts and give them administrative rights as well, but the directory administrator account is similar to the root account. It is used to manage and configure other systems when they are joined to Open Directory, and you will want to ensure you use a secure password with it.

After creating the directory administrator account, you will be prompted to name the Kerberos realm and the LDAP search base. By default, these are generated from the full DNS name of the server (for example, SERVER-001.MYCOMPANY.LAN). These are not actually tied to DNS, but the fact that they are showing up as such means that your DNS system is working as expected.

Clicking Continue will allow you to review your changes before you actually take the plunge to configure the Open Directory master (see Figure 4–1). At this point, if you want to be extra cautious, you can review the process as it is happening by opening up the Terminal application again and running the following command:

```
tail -f /Library/Logs/slapconfig.log
```

This will be updated in real time with the verbose status of what is going on and is useful if, for some reason, your creation of the Open Directory master goes wrong. Once the process has completed, you will be returned to the Server Admin window, and you'll see that the Role has changed to Open Directory master (see Figure 4–2).

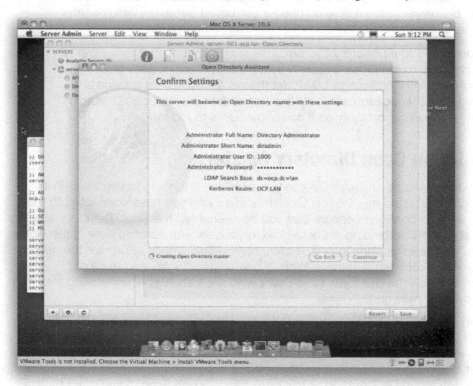

Figure 4–1. *Reviewing Open Directory settings*

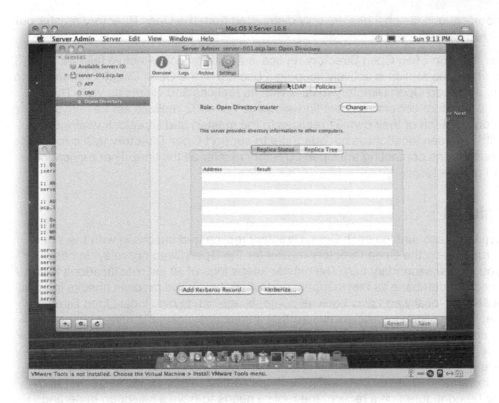

Figure 4–2. *The server is now an Open Directory master.*

NOTE: If you configured accounts during the installation of the server, that server will more than likely be running as the Open Directory master. If so, checking to make sure that Kerberos is running and that `changeip -checkhostname` passes without problems should be sufficient to ensure that your environment was set up properly.

Configuring an Open Directory Replica

An Open Directory replica can be used for one of two primary tasks. The first is as an active member to an active-passive failover scheme. In this case, the replica is configured to keep a live backup and provide authentication services to clients (who will have the IP and host name of the replicas on file) in case the Open Directory master is temporarily unavailable. If, after a period of time, you are unable to bring the Open Directory master back up, you can actually promote a replica to the master role, which will be essential when you need to start making changes to Open Directory entries (such as creating new users or disable accounts). In fact, you could have an Open Directory environment operating without a master in theory without a problem until you needed to make modifications, as changes are only distributed from the Open Directory master out to all the replicas.

The other function of an Open Directory replica is that of an active-active failover system, where the replica is actively keeping a backup of the Open Directory master and acting as a pseudo Open Directory master with its replicas and clients as well. This works well in a dual-tier environment (in which one tier of 32 replicas act as relays for the connections of each of their own 32 replicas to the master) and situations where the bandwidth between locations is not adequate to support Open Directory traffic for all the client workstations contacting the Open Directory master all the time. That replication is managed using slurpd.

Using slurpd

The slurpd process runs on each Open Directory replica and checks in with the slapd process running on the Open Directory master (or the Open Directory relay, in cases where you have a secondary tier). The master keeps logs of all the modifications to the Open Directory database as they happen, and when the slurpd process checks in, it will copy those logs locally and play back its contents against its own local Open Directory database. This replication process ensure that it keeps as close to a mirror image of the Open Directory database as possible, while also balancing the amount of time it checks in with the Open Directory master so it is not swamped with connections (remember, one of the primary goals of replication is to ensure responsiveness of services and uptime). In version 10.6, you can configure those settings in the command line. For slurpd to be configured on a replica, the replica needs to have a selection of settings pushed down to it from the Open Directory master.

> **NOTE:** You can initiate an immediate replication by using the slapconfig command along with the –replicatenow option. To see the replication interval used, you can run slapconfig along with –getmasterconfig from a replica to see what the replication interval is.

Creating an Open Directory Replica

To create your replica, you need to know the directory administrator password for your Open Directory environment and the root password (not the administrator's password, but the one first used when you configured the server, unless you changed it) for the server that will be the replica. Also, if you have configured service Access Control Lists (ACLs) that limit SSH access to the master, you will need to either include the system administrator's local group or grant all access temporarily, as the creation of the replica process requires root SSH access. You can test if you have root SSH access properly by trying to connect from the Open Directory replica to the master by using the command ssh root@odmasterhostname in terminal.app. Once you have that information and have verified that you have SSH access to the master from the Open Directory replica, you can continue with the process of creating the replica.

In Server Admin, select the server that is to be the replica, and enable Open Directory services just as you did for the Open Directory master. When changing the roles, select "Set up an Open Directory Replica" and enter in the IP address (or host name) of the Open Directory master, along with the root password, and the directory administrator's username and password again. The process is relatively automatic at this point, but you can observe the results by using the command:

```
tail -f /library/logs/slapconfig.log
```

Managing Open Directory

Once you have configured your Open Directory master and replica, it's time to focus on using Open Directory for tasks, primarily authenticating users and centralizing your access control systems to the rest of your network. But before we create users, there should be some steps taken first to ensure your Open Directory environment is secure.

Securing Open Directory

Because all of your usernames and passwords, as well as a variety of information about your environment, are stored in Open Directory, protecting that data is critical. Securing assets comes in a number of forms, but physical, network, and host security are the three main areas to focus on for this case.

First, you will want to ensure that the physical location of the server is secure. If any person can just walk right up to the server, and it was left logged in, all other security precautions would be pretty much useless.

You will want to limit network access to the Open Directory masters and replicas. If possible, they should be dedicated machines not running any other services (therefore minimizing the number of possible vulnerabilities), and you should block all but the essential network traffic going back and forth to these servers. The essential ports needed for day-to-day operation of an Open Directory master or replica follow:

- 88 and 749 (UDP and TCP) for Kerberos
- 106 and 3659 (both) for the Password server
- 389 TCP for LDAP
- 636 TCP for LDAP SSL (if you force SSL, you don't need 389)
- 311 TCP for Server Admin and Workgroup Manager
- 625 TCP for Workgroup Manager

Once you have set up your Open Directory master, you will need to immediately move to securing the infrastructure. Securing the network stack begins with making sure that only authentic users are communicating with the server, and forcing traffic that is then interchanged with the server to be signed is important. Additionally, given the fact that providing access to the directory service can provide more information than is wise to untrusted systems, it is always a good idea to allow only clients that have authenticated to the directory service to do so.

The final aspect, host security, is a complicated task. Practicing good security on a server involves limiting use to only that which is required, securing the login window and a number of other steps. For more on securing the operating system, we recommend looking into *Enterprise Mac: Mac OS X Snow Leopard Security*, also from Apress (ISBN-13: 978-1-4302-2730-4).

Configuring Binding Policies

One method of securing Open Directory is to ensure only trusted binding (or authenticated binding) is enabled. By default, Open Directory is set for untrusted binding. Since a server configured to allow untrusted binds will allow any machine to connect and get information on the network, including Open Directory information, getting the information required to spoof the Open Directory environment is easy. From a client perspective, untrusted binding does not check to see if the server really is the proper Open Directory master. Since you can manage policies and settings on workstations through Open Directory (including configuring accounts in Open Directory which have admin rights on local machines), an attacker can spoof your untrusted, bound Open Directory server and compromise clients easily.

To enforce authenticated binding, you will have to set the settings in the Open Directory Services page under Settings, in the Policies area. Make sure you have Require Authenticated Binding checked, so clients can join open directory (or talk to your LDAP server) only if they know a valid username and password for an Open Directory account. For binding, you will also want to disable clear text passwords if possible (unless you have mail clients that require otherwise) and ensure you have SSL configured by checking the boxes in the LDAP section of the Open Directory settings panel. Digitally signing all packets and blocking man-in-the-middle attacks are also additional ways to protect your Open Directory environment—not just the server but the client workstations—as a compromised client machine could act as a back door into the rest of your network. Enabling both of those options requires you have Kerberos configured and working properly for your network.

Setting Global Password Policies

By allowing users to have a single username and password to access all their information across the entire network, you have also allowed for malicious users to access all of a user's information once they have learned that password. Now, in many cases, users will use the same password for many systems, which could mean that the password that is tied to remote access to the fileserver is the same one used on a personal hobby web forum, so malicious attackers targeting your business could focus their attention on trying to retrieve passwords from the web forum instead of your server. Once they got the user's password from one, less-secure location outside of your control, they could then use that against your own servers. The way around this situation is to enforce a global security policy, which can be configured to ensure that passwords meet minimum requirements for complexity, are changed frequently, and are not the same two passwords being recycled over and over again.

The trade off from setting a password policy is that users may complain about setting these passwords and the difficulty in trying to remember them. However, this is going to be the only password they will have to remember for all their work-related computer access (remember, as part of a Directory Service, this password will be usable with any other service or server configured to talk to the Open Directory environment). So they will be able to memorize the password out of habit. Changing the password in one location will reset all other passwords; instead of a user having to change mail and fileserver passwords separately, a single change at the login window due to a report of an expired password will be reflected immediately across the network.

In the Policies section of the Open Directory settings area, you can select the Passwords tab and start modifying the password requirements. The settings shown in Figure 4–3 are common among large organizations and are considered some of the better practices for account security, even if they do mean users may have more complicated passwords.

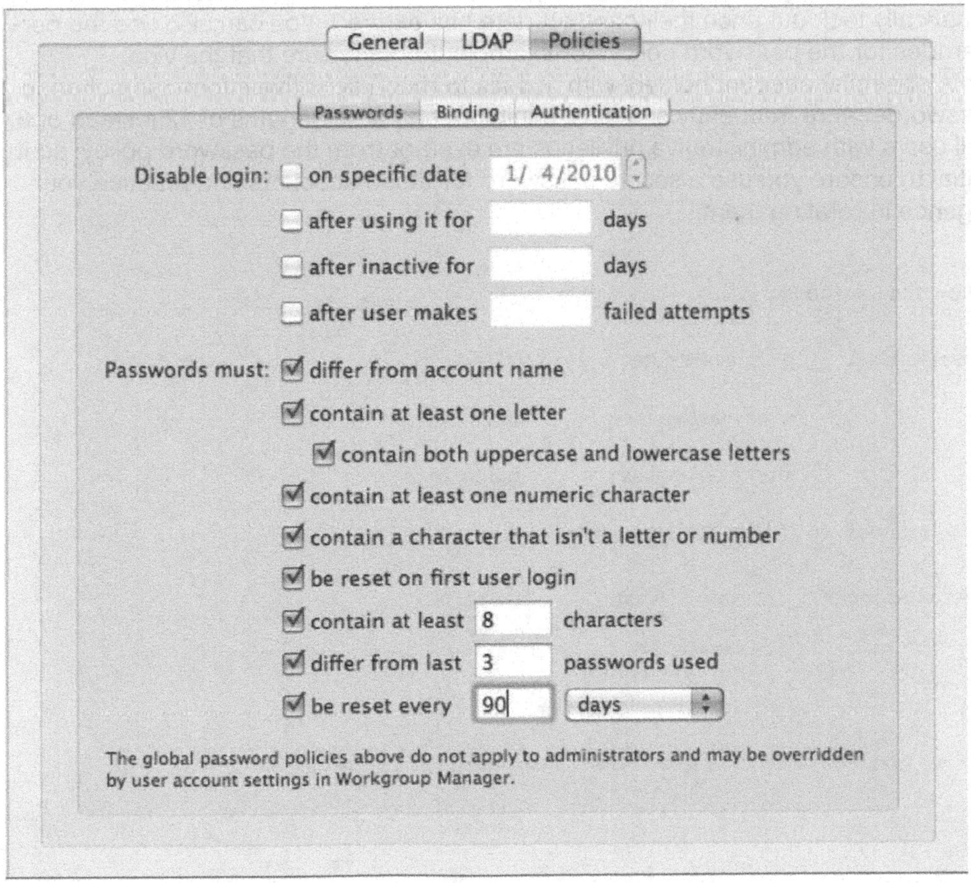

Figure 4–3. *Password policies*

There are also options to disable login. Two most common options are to disable login after a specific amount of failed login attempts (usually three or four) and for accounts inactive longer than 30 days. However, keep in mind that if you have services that do not use Kerberos and require users to save passwords in a keychain, those saved keychain entries can trigger an account lockout automatically when a user's password is changed before trying to use that service (the most notorious offender of this is FileMaker, as FileMaker Server can check passwords against Open Directory, but the client does not support Kerberos). If you think this may be a problem, you may want to train users on how to remove old entries form their keychains after their password changes, increase the number of failed login attempts allowed, or a combination of both.

Disabling inactive accounts is also important, as you do not want a legacy or temporary account you created for testing to compromise your services because you left it with a simple password and never got around to disabling it once you achieved the test goals. The options to disable the account after a specific date or number of days may not make sense as a global option, but you can also set these options (along with a few other ones) on a per user basis in Workgroup Manager (as shown in Figure 4–4). There it would make sense to set the accounts that you use for interns or contractors to be set to automatically lock out once their contract date has expired. You can also use the per-user overrides for the password policy, for example, to make sure that the vice presidents or similar account holders with access to much sensitive information change their passwords more frequently and have minimum character lengths of 12 instead of 8. Again, all users with administrative privileges are exempt from the password policy, so it is essential to ensure you use a secure password for those accounts and practice your own diligence in rotating them.

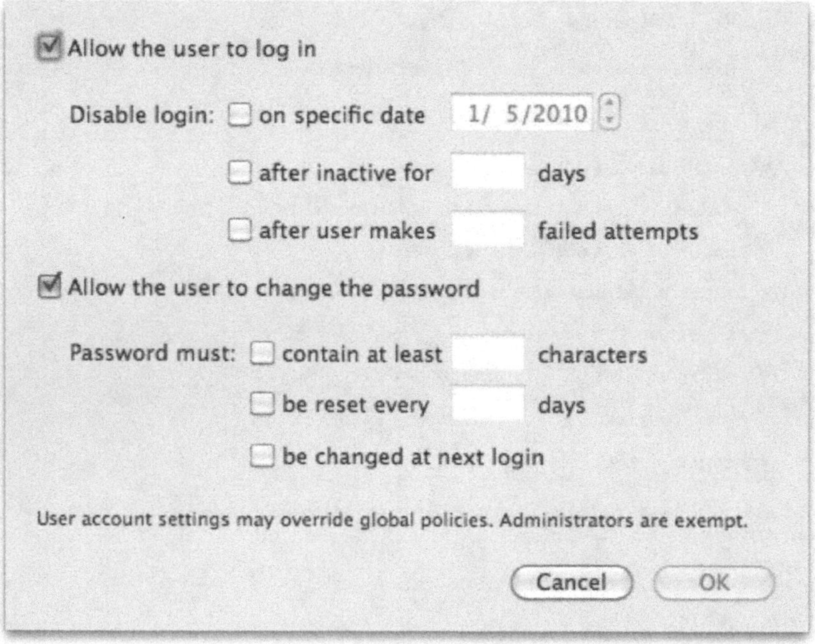

Figure 4–4. *Per-user password policy overrides*

Considering Tiered Administration

In environments with more than one administrator, or when the organization is large enough to require delegation of duties, using tiered administration means that specific groups of users can have access to modify some aspects of the Open Directory system but not the entire situation.

You can create limited administrator profiles by select an existing user in Workgroup Manager and choosing the Privileges tab. By setting the configuration options under the Limited choice in the drop-down menu, you can specify what groups or users specific limited administrators can modify and what modifications they are allowed to make. As you can see, there is no way to create limited administrators who can also create users, since that would grant too much access (in theory, they could create users with more privileges than themselves and then log in as those users). However, they can reset users' passwords, manage their preferences and update their user information (this feature alone allows for an office administrative assistant to be able to update and modify everyone's information in Open Directory without having to be a full time Open Directory administrator). They can also manage which groups a user or group of users belong to. Limited administrators do not have permission to modify accounts of full administrator users, but they can modify accounts on normal users or any user nested in an existing group. To add a user to a group, the limited administrator has to have access to a group that the user is already in (if they are not specifically listed) and access to the new group to add the user to as well; this is because modifying a user's group membership is actually modifying both the user record to contain the group membership ID and the group record to contain to user's ID.

By using these limited accounts to perform the day-to-day functions of the Open Directory environment, you are controlling the access to full administration passwords and accounts but not impeding the functionality of your directory system. Before limited administration accounts, it was not really possible to make changes to someone's home address stored in Open Directory without having to log in with full privileges. Now, an office manager can do that. Using limited accounts, you can create help desk accounts that have permission to update users' passwords or unlock accounts because users forgot their passwords and tried too many times, without giving the help desk staff access to the directory server. By combining service groups with access controls, you can even have help desk staff grant or remove end users' permissions by moving users in and out of existing groups, instead of having a full administrator modify the individual server's service access lists.

Setting Access Controls

Service access controls are also important for Open Directory (and all servers) because without them, any valid user can connect to any system attached to the Directory Service. That means a weak end user password could grant SSH or local login window access to a malicious user. While those accounts will have limited permissions, they would allow for the user to execute some commands, which could be combined with a privilege escalation to take over your servers. By using service access controls, you limit the number of users that are allowed to connect to the server to just a handful.

You can set the service access controls by using Server Admin to modify the server settings. Under Access, you can specify which services require specific users and which do not. You will want to ensure that both the Login window and SSH are limited to only the system administrators group, and possibly an Open Directory group that you use that contains the network accounts of other administrators. And you may wish to only include the local administrator account in the SSH option and just add the system administrators group when you are going to configure a replica, ensuring that you remove it afterward. This step is just to remove the possibility of a weak root password causing a remote exploitation of the server as a result.

Backing Up Open Directory

Before you start to use Open Directory, let's get it backed up. There are a number of reasons to back up Open Directory, but chief among them is the fact that users and computers, according to your configuration, may not be able to back up without Open Directory. And while an Open Directory replica is critical for fault tolerance, it does not act as a backup, much like a RAID does not provide for a true backup of the data you may be saving on your server.

Backing up Open Directory once is a fairly simple task. From Server Admin, simply click Open Directory in the SERVERS list and click the Archive icon in the Server Admin toolbar. From here, as Figure 4–5 shows, you will be able to type a path to the location on the server that you have deemed your backup location or click the Choose button to open a dialogue box for selecting the location. Then, click the Archive button, and provide a password to secure the backup.

Once the archive is complete, you will have the files to do a partial or full restoration of Open Directory if the need arises. However, the process will not yet be automated. Because setting up an automated backup for your Open Directory environment, 318 has built a package to do the whole process for you. The package is available at http://www.krypted.com/apps in the 318 Applications section of the page and provides a wizard-like interface for setting up the automated backup (i.e., the archive) of your Open Directory environment based on a few key variables that are shown in Figure 4–6.

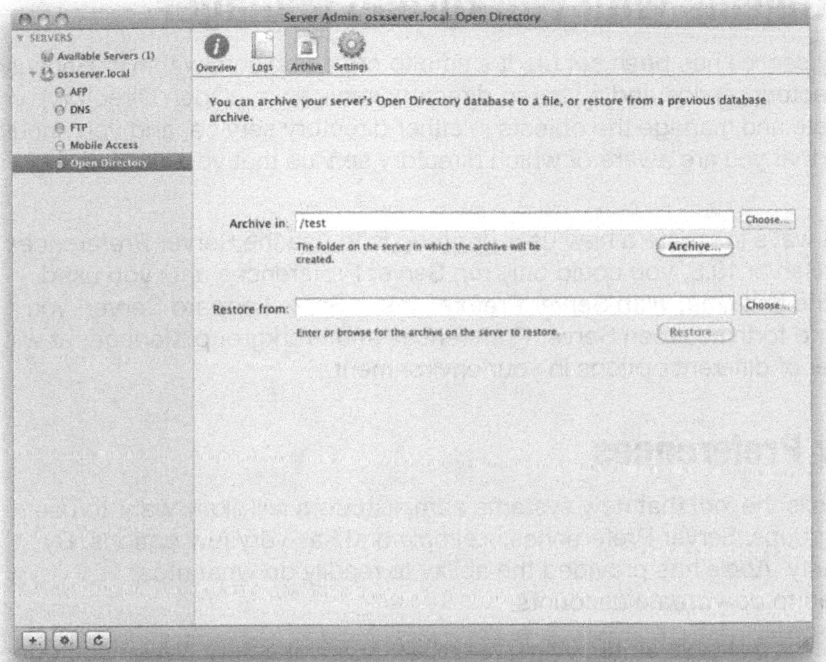

Figure 4–5. *Backing up and Restoring Open Directory*

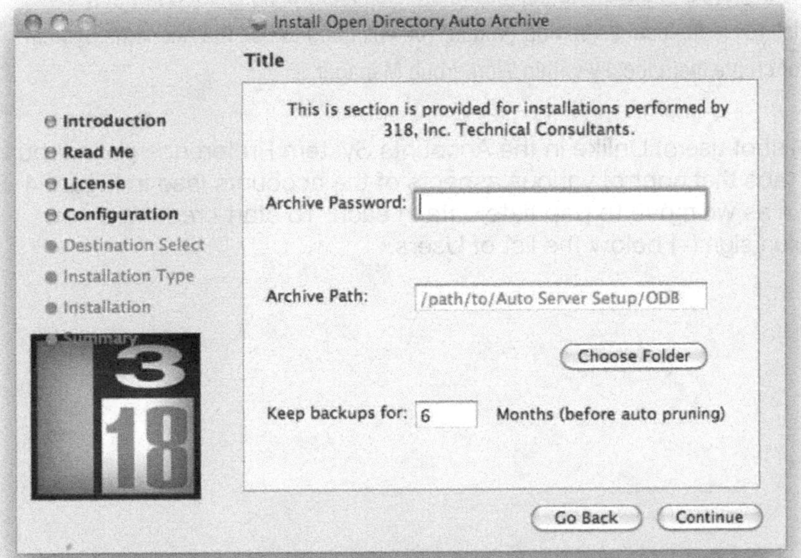

Figure 4–6. *Scheduling an Open Directory Backup*

Managing Objects with Workgroup Manager

Once the directory service has been set up, it's time to create objects within it. Because there is a local directory service and a shared directory service (i.e., Open Directory), you will be able to create and manage the objects in either directory service, and you should always make sure that you are aware of which directory service that you are creating objects within.

One of the easiest ways to create a new user or group is to use the Server Preferences tool. In Mac OS X Server 10.5, you could only run Server Preferences until you used Server Admin for the first time. With Server Preferences in Snow Leopard Server, you can switch back and forth between Server Preferences and Workgroup Manager at will, providing a number of different options in your environment.

Using Server Preferences

Server Preferences is the tool that new systems administrators will likely want to use to create users and groups. Server Preferences is simple and has very few options. By sacrificing granularity, Apple has provided the ability to readily do what most administrators need to do—create accounts.

System Preferences is available in the /Applications/Server directory. When you open Server Preferences, you will see the Users icon in the Accounts section of the screen, as shown in Figure 4–7. Click Users to start setting up an account.

> **NOTE:** All accounts that are created in the Server Preferences tool will be created in Open Directory. If you wish to create local users and groups, you will need to use the Accounts System Preferences pane or create them locally within Workgroup Manager.

You will then see a list of users. Unlike in the Accounts System Preference pane, you will notice a number of tabs that control various aspects of the accounts (see in Figure 4–8), which we will explain as we move to populate data in each. To start creating a new account, click the plus sign (+) below the list of Users.

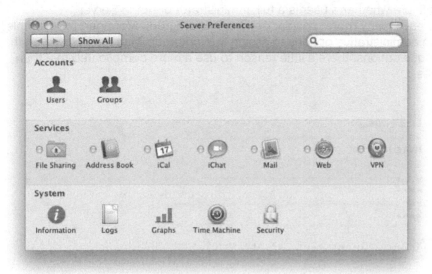

Figure 4–7. *Server Preferences*

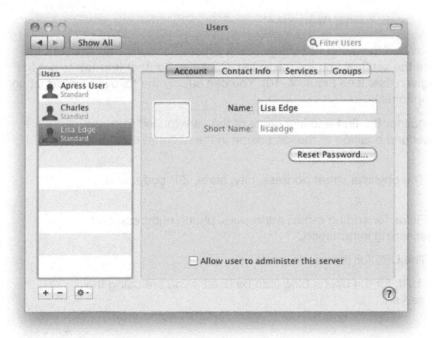

Figure 4–8. *Managing users with Server Preferences*

At the overlay account creation screen (see Figure 4–9), you will have a limited number of fields. Provide the user's full name, a short name, and a password. If you want the user to be an administrator, check the "Allow user to administer this server" check box.

You can only configure whether a user is a full administrator or not in Server Preferences. You have many more granular options in Workgroup Manager; for example, you can set which administrative options to assign in Workgroup Manager. However, if you don't need those options, there's little reason to use a more complicated tool than Server Preferences.

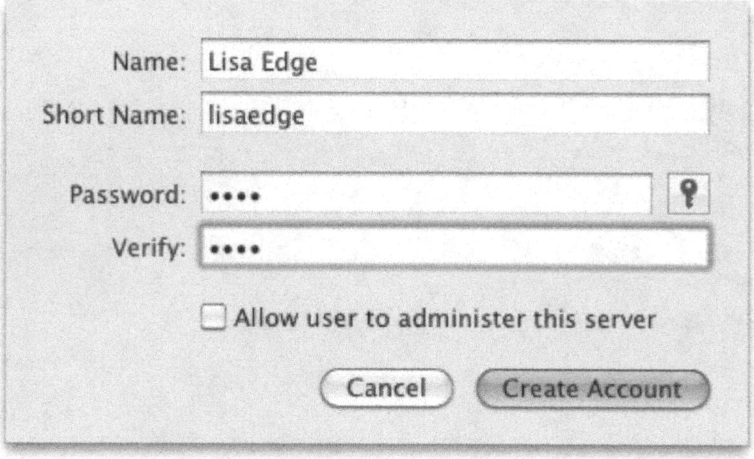

Figure 4–9. *Creating an account in Server Preferences*

Once you have provided the account settings, click Create Account. The Account tab will simply reiterate the settings you just provided. Click the Contact Info tab to set the information for a given user (see Figure 4–10). You can supply the following information, and each field is optional:

- *Name*: Fields for the first and last name of the user (pulled from the first and second position of the long name in the account creation screen)

- *Address*: The physical street address, city, state, ZIP code, and country

- *Contact*: Fields for adding e-mail addresses, phone numbers, and instant messaging information.

- *Website*: The URL for the user's web site

- *Blog*: The URL for the user's blog (can be used if you are using the blog/wiki server)

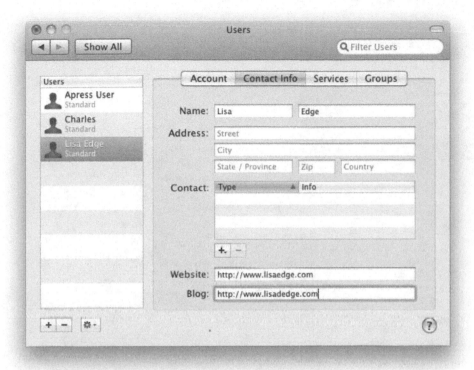

Figure 4–10. *Filling out contact information in Server Preferences*

Once you have entered all of the appropriate information, click the Services tab. As Figure 4–11 shows, you will see a list of the main services that Apple considers important. By default, all of these will be checked, meaning they are all enabled; uncheck each of the services that you do not want enabled for each user.

NOTE: If a service is not enabled, you do not necessarily need to uncheck the box for that service, although it is still a good idea to do so in case the service is enabled at a later date.

Figure 4–11. *Configuring service access controls in Server Preferences*

After you have configured the appropriate services to use for the user, click the Groups tab. Here, you will see a list of each group that the user is a member of (see Figure 4–12). If you wish to alter the list of groups, click the Edit Membership button, and uncheck each group that you do not wish the user to be a member of.

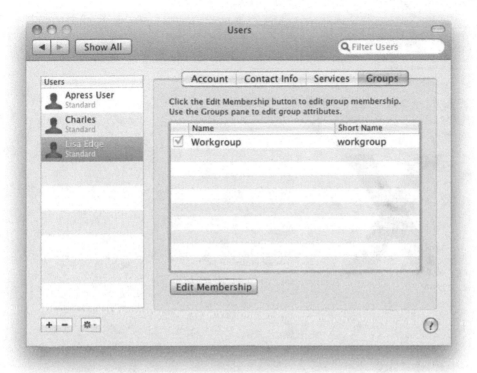

Figure 4-12. *Assigning group membership in Server Preferences*

You can then use the cog wheel in the lower left corner of the screen to send an invitation to bind a client computer to a user. If you click the cog, you will have the option to click "Send Invitation to" followed by the name of the user. If you click this setting, you will send an e-mail to the user, as shown in Figure 4-13. In this e-mail, there will be an icon to Automatically Configure My Mac.

Once you are satisfied with all of your settings, click the Show All button, or close the Server Preferences application.

NOTE: The path for the invitation is (where USERNAME is replaced with the users short name): `macosxserverinvite://USERNAME@osxserver.local`.

Once you click the Automatically Configure My Mac button, the client will automatically attempt to bind to the Open Directory environment on the server. You will be prompted for a username and password. Enter the password for the account that was just created, and click the OK button. You will then (hopefully) receive a message indicating that the client has been configured to work with the server, as in Figure 4-14. Log in as the user, and you should note that the user's Mail, iCal, and Address Book have been preconfigured to work with the server.

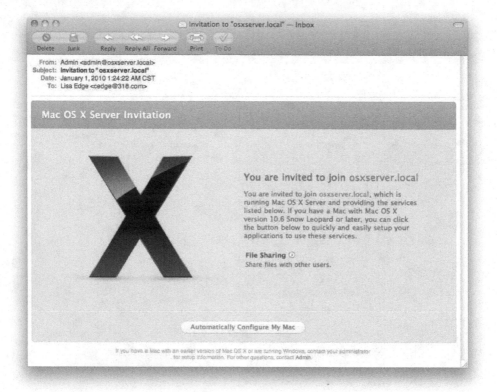

Figure 4–13. *E-mail invitations*

NOTE: You can see the changes made by clicking on the Accounts System Preference pane, clicking Login Options, and checking the Network Account Server field.

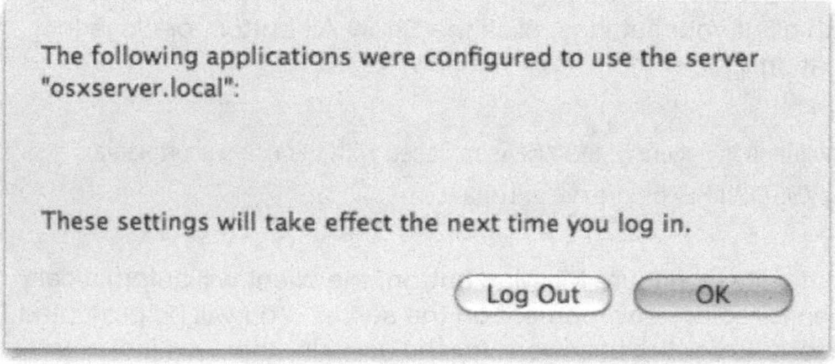

The following applications were configured to use the server "osxserver.local":

These settings will take effect the next time you log in.

Log Out   OK

Figure 4–14. *Configuration results*

Using Workgroup Manager

While Server Preferences can create accounts, Workgroup Manager is the tool that most administrators will use to create users, groups, computers, and computer lists (which are basically just groups of computers). Workgroup Manager (which can be found in /Applications/Server on any computer with the Server Admin tools installed), like many tools developed by Apple, is straightforward and easy to use, although there are a few specific things to keep in mind, which we will cover in the next few sections of this chapter.

Before you get started, note that when you open Workgroup Manager, you will not typically be able to create users in Open Directory. There is a disclosure triangle in Workgroup Manager that allows you to switch between directory domains (see Figure 4–15 in the next section). Clicking here allows you to choose /LDAPv3/127.0.0.1 (Open Directory) or the local domain if you wish to create or manage a local account rather than one in Open Directory. There is a lock on the bar where you select a directory domain. If it is in the locked position, you will need to move it to unlocked to create or augment a record within that directory domain.

Creating a User

To create a user, you will want to make sure that you are first logged into the appropriate repository (that is, directory domain). Just below the directory domain selection bar, you will notice a row of icons on the left sidebar of the screen. Click the one with just one head, to edit users. Then click the New User icon in the Workgroup manager toolbar. You will then see a new entry in the list of users called Untitled, which is shown Figure 4–15. Click in the Name field and provide a name; click in the password field and provide a password, and then choose whether or not the user should be able to administer the server. So far, this looks like the settings from Server Admin, right? Well, the similarities pretty much end here, as you may notice by looking in the Account Summary. Go ahead and click Save, and we'll then go through the other options.

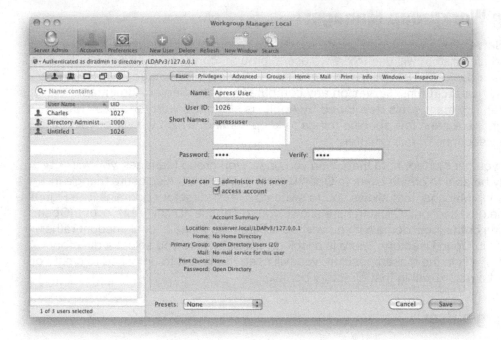

Figure 4–15. *Creating Users in Workgroup Manager*

Now that the account has been created, click the Privileges tab. Here, as Figure 4–16 shows, you can set which services a user is able to manage. The administration field has three options you can set for configuring what the user can manage:

- *None*: Create a standard user account.

- *Limited*: This allows you to set granular control. By clicking the plus sign (+), you can configure the accounts that the user can manage.

- *Full*: This allows the user to manage all user accounts.

Additionally, when using the Limited option, you can control which options a given limited administrative user has to configure on a per-account basis. To do so, you would use the check boxes below the list of users when a user is highlighted. Here, click an account, and then check (or uncheck) the appropriate options, which are shown in Figure 4–17:

- *Manage user passwords*: Change a user's password.

- *Edit managed preferences*: Change managed preference (i.e., policy) settings.

- *Edit user information*: Edit information in the Info tab.

- *Edit group membership*: Edit which groups a user is a member of.

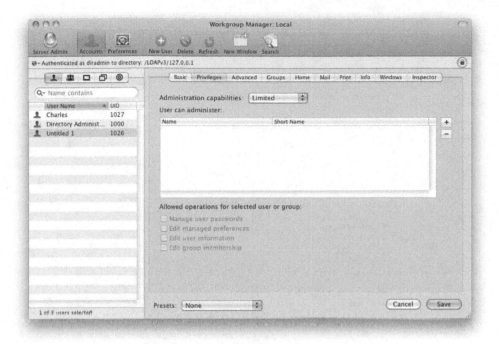

Figure 4–16. *Delegating administration in Workgroup Manager*

Granularly managing a user's ability to administer other users on a per-user basis can be pretty daunting if you have a lot of users. However, once you have the configuration as you need it, you can use account presets (templates for accounts that are accessible at the bottom of the Workgroup Manager screen) to copy these settings to other users when you are ready.

Next, click the Advanced tab. As shown in Figure 4–18, you will be able to choose whether the user is able to log in from more than one computer at a time using the "Allow simultaneous login on managed computers" option. You will also be able to use the Login Shell field to set the default shell that is used when the user opens a command prompt (Terminal), and finally, you're able to set up password policies using the Options button, as we described earlier in this chapter.

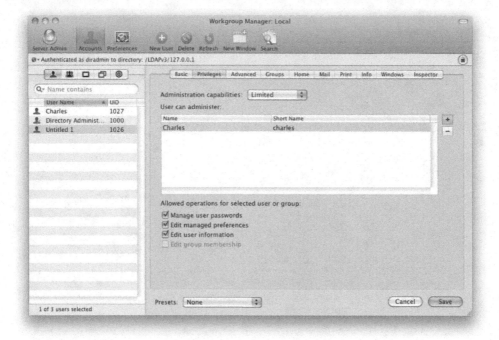

Figure 4–17. *Creating a limited administrator user*

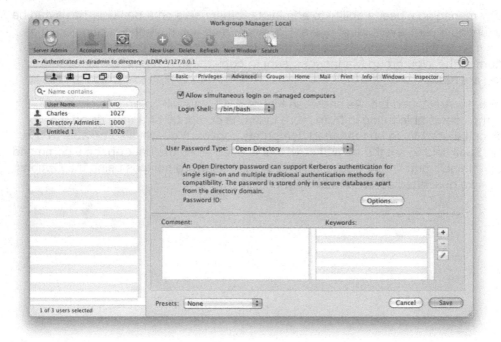

Figure 4–18. *Advanced user settings in Workgroup Manager*

Click the Groups tab. Here you will be able to configure which groups a user belongs to by clicking the plus sign (+), shown in Figure 4–19, and dragging the group into the list from the window that slides out to the side.

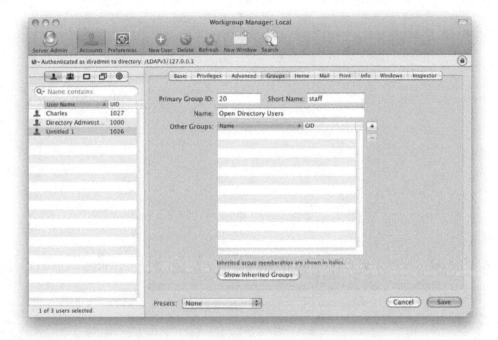

Figure 4–19. *Adding a user to groups in Workgroup Manager*

NOTE: The Home tab is covered later in this chapter. The Mail, Windows, and Print tabs are covered more fully in their respective chapters. Each of these requires those services to be enabled and, if configured, allows configuration over the users settings for those services.

Click the Info tab. As shown in Figure 4–20, you will then have many of the same options that were present when configuring information for a user in the Server Preferences tool. These settings have little impact on services (exceptions are listed in the corresponding chapters).

Finally, click the Save button to commit any changes made to the account. Any changes made to date will then be committed to the Open Directory database, and any services will be changed if need be.

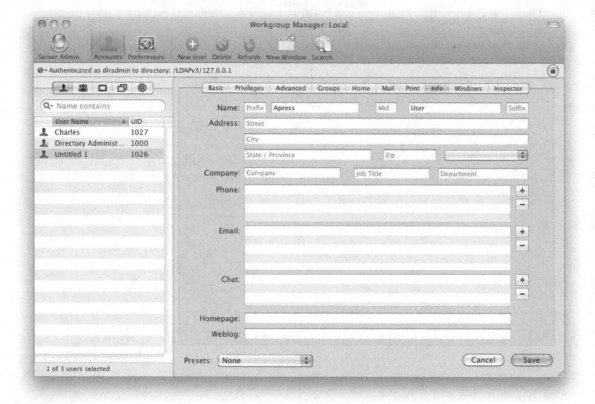

Figure 4–20. *Defining names and addresses in Workgroup Manager*

Creating a Group

Once you are done configuring users, you will likely want to group users according to your own philosophy for user management. This allows you, as an administrator, to assign permissions to data, delegate administrative access, and configure various service settings by group.

To start creating groups, click the groups icon in the Workgroup Manager sidebar. Verify that you are augmenting the appropriate directory domain, and click the New Group icon. Here, provide the following (fields are shown in Figure 4–21):

- *Name*: A friendly name for the group

- *Short Name*: The short name of the group (no spaces)

- *Group ID*: A number automatically populated (Only change this number if you are sure of why you are doing so.)

- Picture path: The path to an image that can be used for the group

- Comment: A text field for entering notes about the group, the purpose of the group, and so on

Fill in the appropriate information for the group you would like to create, and click the Save button.

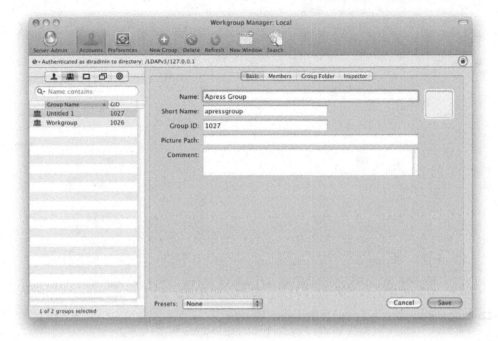

Figure 4–21. *Creating a group in Workgroup Manager*

Next, click the Members tab. This screen is similar to the Groups tab in the user account records. Click the plus sign (+) shown in Figure 4–22, and from the resulting list of users and groups, you can drag the appropriate entries into the list.

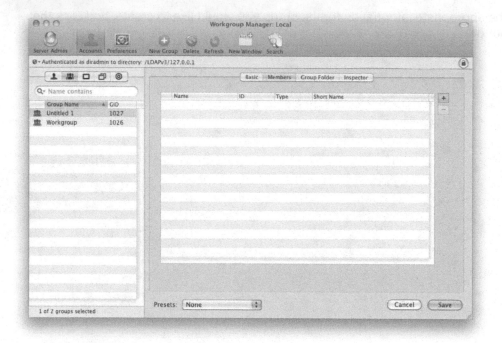

Figure 4–22. *Assigning members to a group in Workgroup Manager*

Once you have added the appropriate members to the group, click the Save button, and the members will finish being added to the group.

Creating Computer Groups

Thus far, we have looked at logically grouping users and groups. You can also logically group computers. The main reason for grouping computers in most every case ends up being to apply managed preferences to the clients, which enables policies to be set on computers. Setting policies for clients can be useful, because some (machine-specific) policies cannot be applied to a user or group, only applied to computers and computer lists.

> **NOTE:** Computers will automatically be added to the domain when bound but will not be added to a computer list.

To create a computer group, click the computers icon in the row of icons in Workgroup Manager's sidebar, and click the New Computer Group icon in the Server Admin toolbar. You will then be able to provide a Name, Short Name, Group ID, and Comment for the computer group, much as you would for a group of users (see Figure 4–23). Click the Save button to commit the change and generate the group. Initially, the group will be empty. You can add computers that have been bound to the domain by clicking the Members tab at this time.

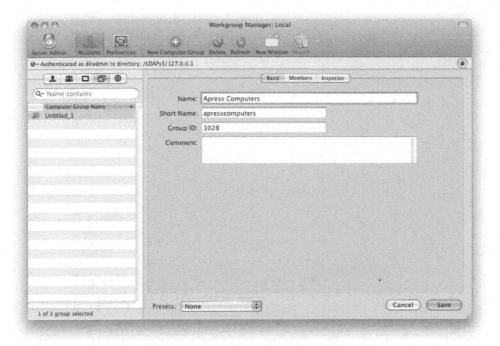

Figure 4–23. *Creating a computer group in Workgroup Manager*

You can also configure a guest account and add it to a computer group. As we've described in this chapter, a computer can be bound in a trusted or untrusted manner; because you might be allowing users to bind their own systems and have certain policies you want to be effective for all users, you can use the guest account to assign computer policies for all systems even without a computer record (which is typically generated during the trusted bind process). These are great ways to leverage the guest account, which is a placeholder for deploying, managed settings for all computers that are bound to the domain but not yet in another group. In some environments, all computers pull managed preferences from the guest, whereas in others, the guest is simply a placeholder for computers that have not yet been added to a computer group.

To create the guest account, first click computers in Workgroup Manager's sidebar. Then, click the Workgroup Manager menu, and select Create Guest Computer. After that, you can add the guest account to a computer group and assign managed preferences either directly through the guest computer account or through the computer group that the guest computer is a member of.

You can also use the ellipse button that is shown in Figure 4–24 to add computers to the group by MAC address of the adapter the client will communicate over and import lists of computers into groups (e.g., using the output of a Deploy Studio mass deployment of clients or an export from another tool you may happen to be using).

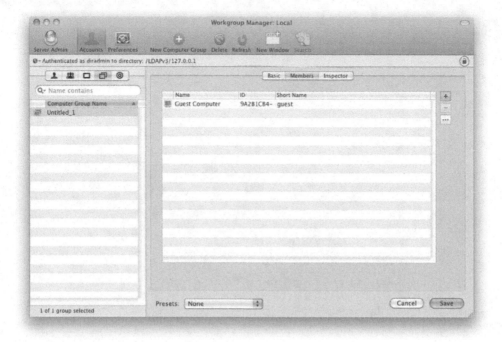

Figure 4–24. *Creating a guest computer account*

Once you are satisfied with the members for a given computer group, click the Save button in Workgroup Manager to save your changes to the group.

Configuring Policies

Users, computers, and groups that authenticate to the Open Directory domain can also leverage managed preferences. If a client is managed then it is considered a *managed client*, meaning that you have pushed various settings out to the client. While managed preferences are often considered used to lock down workstations, they can also be a very valuable to simply push settings to clients as part of an integration project, while still giving users full access to change any of the settings pushed to them.

Going through each option of each managed preference is a bit outside the scope of this book, but it is a topic covered thoroughly in the Apress title *Enterprise Mac Administrator's Guide* (ISBN-13: 978-1-4302-2443-3). In this section, instead, we'll look at a single managed preference (the location of the Dock in Mac OS X) and how to enforce it for a user. To get started, open Workgroup Manager, and authenticate to your directory domain (if you want to enforce policies on a local computer that is not bound to Open Directory, you can do so by following these steps for a local user rather than an Open Directory user).

Click the user (or group, computer, or computer group) that you would like to manage. Then click on the Preferences icon in the Workgroup Manager toolbar. Here, you will see groups of managed preferences that can be implemented, as shown in Figure 4–25.

Each of these sections will have a number of specific policies that can be applied. Click Dock to manage the dock for the object you've chosen to manage.

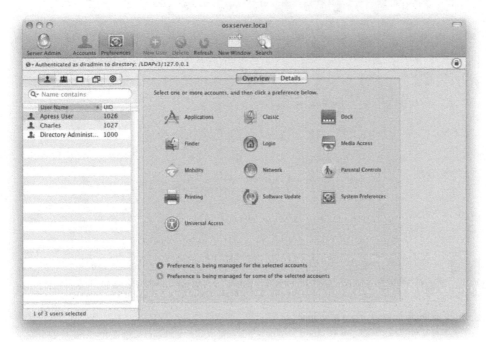

Figure 4–25. *Creating Policies in Workgroup Manager*

You will then see two options: Dock Items and Dock Display. These allow you to control which icons are in the dock and how the dock appears, respectively. As an example, click Dock Display. As shown in Figure 4–26, you will then have the option to set the Manage radio button to Never, Once, and Always. Respectively, these allow you to not manage the setting, push it to the users but allow them to change it if they want, and force your setting to be applied always. Click Always, set the "Position on screen setting" to Right, and click Apply Now when you are finished.

Now that the dock should appear on the right side of the screen, log in as the user (or if you are already logged in, log off and log back in) on the client computer. You should see the Dock on the right side of the screen instead of on the bottom (the default behavior of the Dock). If the user changes the location of the Dock, at log in, it will always go back to the right side of the screen. You can go back to Workgroup Manager and set it to Once. Then, the user will be able to change the location, and that change will be maintained.

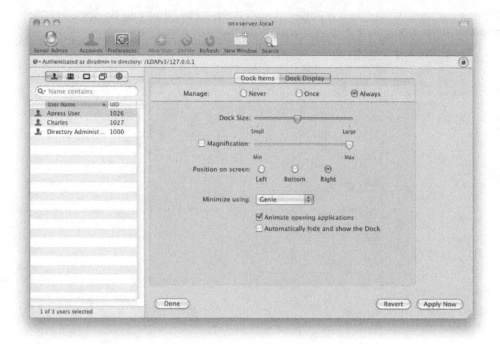

Figure 4–26. *Dock policies in Workgroup Manager*

Overall, managed preferences are a very effective way to control a variety of settings on the client computer. You can limit which applications can be opened by a user, push out new printers, force users to use the simple finder (a simplified user interface effective for guests, young students, and kiosks), create login items, limit access to resources on the computer, and provide network and mobile home directories.

Automating Client Connections with Automounts and Home Directories

Network and mobile home directories are among the most common reasons administrators choose to leverage managed preferences. The implementation of network and mobile directories in Mac OS X Server is similar to the roaming profile feature available in Active Directory. *Network home directories* allow you to put users' data on a server so that it remains there on any system they happen to log into. Certain applications do not react well to network home directories, and network home directories will not allow laptop users that leave your environment as their home folders are not stored on the laptop. Therefore, *mobile home directories* were introduced to allow synchronizing a users local home folder with a network home directory.

Getting the setup to work perfectly for your environment can be a challenge, because all environments tend to be a little different from one another. In some environments, you will have only a few megabytes of data to keep on servers or synchronize; in others, you will have several gigabytes. Each environment will have different applications that can respond poorly with data stored on servers rather than locally (i.e., Adobe CS4). Therefore, there are a number of options you can use with your home directory environment. However, everything starts with configuring an automount.

An *automount* is simply a folder that automatically mounts for a user. In the context of network home directories and mobile home directories, automounts typically mount when the user logs in. In some environments, such as servers, automounts can also mount on the server prior to login, so that if shared resources are stored on them, they can be accessed by the daemons that are sharing that resource (this is common with web environments). For the purpose of this section, we'll be keeping our blinders on just a bit and looking only at leveraging automounts for home folders.

To configure an automount to be a location to store home folders, first open Server Admin. From here, click the Share Points icon in the Server Admin toolbar, and use the Browse icon in the bar just below the Server Admin toolbar, shown in Figure 4–27, to locate the directory you would like to leverage for automounts. Click Share, and in the bottom pane, click the check box to Enable Automount. Click the Edit button after that.

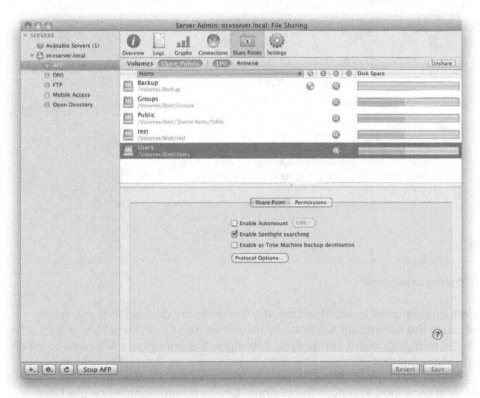

Figure 4–27. *Defining file shares in Server Admin*

As Figure 4–28 shows, you will then see an overlay that allows you to publish the automount into the directory domain of your choosing. Here, choose your Open Directory environment in the Directory field (as you can see in the figure, this is

/LDAPv3/127.0.0.1 by default). From the Protocol field, choose whether you want to use AFP, SMB, or NFS to access the automount. Then choose "User home folders and group folders" as the type of data that will be warehoused on the automount. Click OK once you are finished.

> **NOTE:** If you only have Mac OS X clients, AFP is often the best choice for your automount. If you are using AFP, you can leave all of the settings with their defaults and simply click OK here.

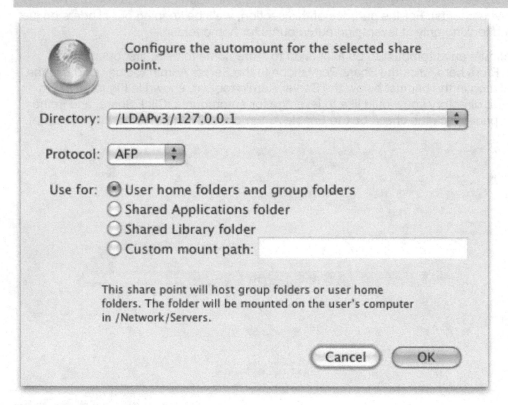

Figure 4–28. *Creating an automount*

Next, you will be prompted to authenticate into the directory domain that you have chosen, because the automount will actually be written into Open Directory and thus be made available to use for client computers. Therefore, the automount will need to be an administrative user for that domain. The default username for Open Directory is diradmin, but you may have changed it earlier in this chapter. Provide the appropriate credentials, and click the OK button to continue. Once you are done, click the Save button to commit your changes, and the automount will be generated.

Now that you have an automount that can be used, you will want to actually tell clients to use it. To do so, click a user or group, using the Accounts button in the Server Admin toolbar. Then, click the Home tab, and you should see your new automount in the list of available automounts that a home folder can be created on. Then, click the Create

Home Now button to populate the home folder with the user template (where all of the default settings are stored), and click the Save button (see Figure 4–29).

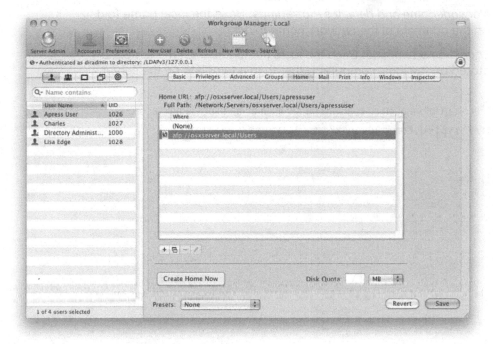

Figure 4–29. *Leveraging an automount as a home folder*

At this point, all of the user's data will be stored on the home folder located on the server at next login. The location for the local home folder will be redirected to the network home folder, and any files that are created will be stored on the server. As we said earlier in this section, this type of setup is not going to work for everyone. Therefore, you can leverage managed preferences to more granularly configure the home directory settings. To do so, open Workgroup Manager, and click the Mobility icon.

The first tab of the Mobility managed preferences is Account Creation. Account Creation references creating and potentially synchronizing data when a user logs into a client computer for the first time. As you can see in Figure 4–30, there are a number of options that allow you to do the following:

- *Create mobile account when user logs in to network account*: Automatically create a local home directory on the client computer when the user logs in.

- *Require confirmation before creating mobile account*: Prompt the user to create that account.

- *Show "Don't ask me again" check box*: Suppress further prompts.

- *Create home using*: Choose what to base the contents of the local home directory that is generated.

- *Network home and default sync settings*: Base the local home folder on the contents of the network home folder.

- *Local home template*: Base the local home folder on the template stored on the local computer rather than a template on the server.

TIP: For more information on customizing the local home folder template, see `http://krypted.com/mac-os-x/mac-os-x-user-templates-2`.

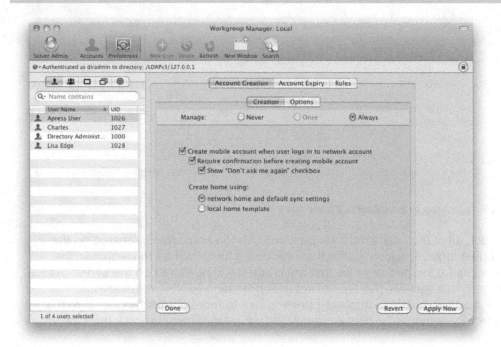

Figure 4–30. *Account creation policies in Workgroup Manager*

Once you have selected what data the new mobile home will be populated with when users log in, click the Options tab under the Account Creation tab. Here, click Always, and note the following options (see Figure 4–31); you can use these as needed:

- *Encrypt contents with FileVault*: Enable FileVault for the account that is logging in. Data on the local client will be encrypted, but data stored in the network home directory will not.

- *Use computer master password, if available*: If a master password has been enabled on the client computer, allow that password to unlock the home folder created by the network account.

- *Require computer master password*: Do not enable FileVault if there is no master password set on the client computer.

- *Restrict size*: Do not exceed the indicated size for the home folder.

- *To fixed size*: Indicate a maximum number of megabytes for the home folder.

- *To percentage of network home quota*: Use a percentage of the users quota for the directory rather than a static number of megabytes.

- *Home folder location*: Provide the location home folders are stored on the local system.

- *On startup*: Store the home folder in the /Users directory of the startup volume.

- *At path*: Set a local location other than /Users. For example, if you have a second hard drive or partition drives and want to store local home synchronizations on the local client, you can indicate that here.

- *User chooses*: Allow the end user to choose the location of the home folder when logging in for the first time (be warned that this option is somewhat dangerous, because users can put their home folders in the strangest locations).

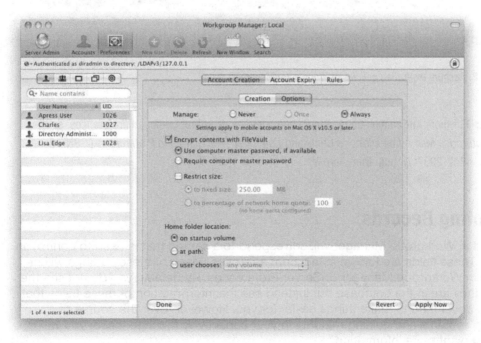

Figure 4–31. *Account creation options in Workgroup Manager*

If you have an environment where a lot of users log into various machines, you will invariably have computers whose hard drives get filled up because of stale home directory data. You can set stale data to be deleted locally after a number of days, weeks, or months of inactivity, as shown in Figure 4–32.

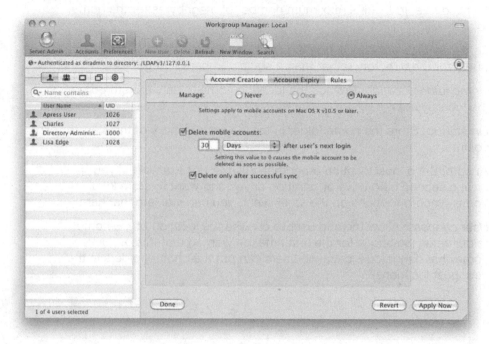

Figure 4–32. *Account expiration policies in Workgroup Manager*

> **NOTE:** For more information on managing home folders and other managed preferences, see the *Enterprise Mac Administrator's Guide* and *Enterprise Mac Managed Preferences* (ISBN-13: 978-1-4302-2937-7), both from Apress.

Inspecting Records

Each field in Workgroup Manager will correspond to a setting that is used to control an account. These fields are known as account *attributes*. Many of these settings will be exposed in Workgroup Manager or Server Preferences. By default, you do not see the fields as they are in the database but instead see the interpretation of these fields that has been developed to make things easier for you. However, over the course of managing systems and gaining maturity in your capacity to manage these, you will eventually want more information.

The Inspector is a tool that will allow you to see this data. Once enabled, the Inspector will show you a tab (which you may have noticed is in the screens throughout this chapter but that you might not yet have). Not only can you view attributes using the Inspector, but you can also alter the contents of those attributes.

To enable the Inspector, open Workgroup Manager. Then, click the Workgroup Manager menu, and click Preferences. At the Workgroup Manager Preferences screen, click the box for "Show 'All Records' tab and inspector", as shown in Figure 4–33.

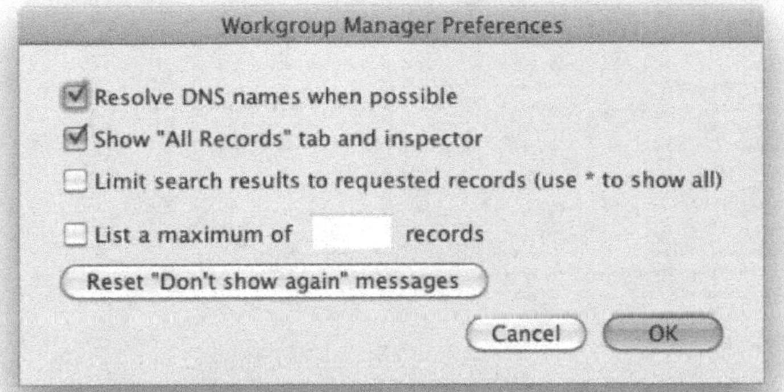

Figure 4–33. *Enabling the Inspector*

Once you enable the Inspector, you will then see the Inspector tab on users, groups, computers, and computer lists and in the tabs in the Workgroup Manager sidebar. Clicking an object will allow you to see the attributes applicable to the object by clicking that Inspector tab, as shown in Figure 4–34. Clicking the Workgroup Manager sidebar's Inspector icon (which appears as a target, or bulls-eye) will also allow you to inspect attributes for, for example, automounts.

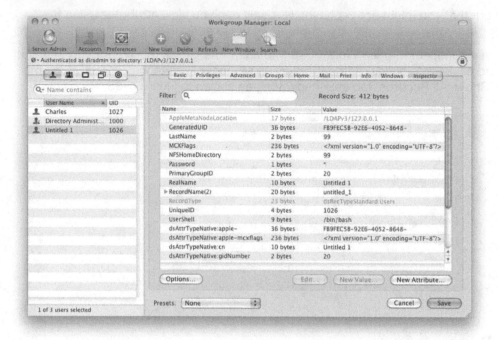

Figure 4–34. *Viewing raw attributes with the Inspector*

Binding Clients

Now that the Directory Service has been set up and this new ecosystem configured, it's time to look at putting clients into the mix.

First, you may ask yourself, "Why do I need to bind clients at all? All my users already have all their accounts configured locally on their machines, and they just save their passwords in their keychains." The answer is that when you bind your clients, you get the benefits of single-sign on (one password for all of your servers), and you can configure policies, such as locations for home folders and dock settings, as we noted earlier in this chapter. At this point, it's time to look at how the client computer is going to interact with the foundation that we have laid throughout this chapter.

There are two distinct ways to bind clients into Open Directory

- Untrusted bind
- Trusted bind

> **NOTE:** Earlier in this chapter, we looked at sending an invitation to users that allow them to bind to the server automatically. When you do so, you are doing a trusted bind.

Implementing Trusted Binding from the Accounts System Preference Pane

The easiest way to bind a computer is to simply go in System Preferences, under Accounts, and select Login Options. Once you have authenticated, you can click Join next to Network Account Server, enter in your Open Directory master information, and click OK. If you do not have a complicated network setup, this should be adequate to get a version 10.6 client connect to a version 10.6 Open Directory server. If the server requires a trusted bind (explained in the next section), you will be prompted for the credentials of an account that has access to modify the Open Directory environment.

If you are binding to a server that is also hosting Mail or other services, when you first try to connect to the server, you will be prompted to also configure the computer to use those services. You can enable them, but keep in mind that those settings and configuration details may not be correct. For example, the server may push down the local host name of the mail server but not the external Internet-accessible one, so when a user takes a bound laptop off the network, that user won't be able to retrieve mail. Therefore, when you are first starting, it is best to just bind the client and configure the services by hand. If you bind outside of the Accounts area of the System Preferences pane, the autoconfiguration of services is not available.

> **NOTE:** Using the Inspector in Workgroup Manager, you can view what services are published in LDAP servers (and their configuration) by viewing the `ClientServices` record in the `Config` container in your LDAP server.

Binding with Directory Utility

There are two ways to open Directory Utility. You can launch it from the Account window in System Preferences. When you click Join, there is an option to Open Directory Utility. Or you can just run the application from the folder `/System/Library/CoreServices/`. Once you have launched the application, the remaining steps are identical. If you are doing this from the local administration account on the workstation, you should add the directory utility to the Dock, as it can provide some useful information for troubleshooting. When you bind to Open Directory, two options are available: untrusted or trusted binds. The one you choose depends on how your server is configured and what you are looking to get out of the directory service.

Choosing Untrusted Binding

An *untrusted bind* is one that allows a machine to connect to the Open Directory server without requiring any authentication. Since, by default, the LDAP server allows anonymous connections (to query information), a client can connect and retrieve all the settings and information it needs to join an Open Directory environment without a password. In trading off some security, this option allows for easier binding of machines (and until version 10.6, you could actually have computers bind to any Open Directory server broadcast over DHCP). Untrusted binding involves opening the Directory Utility and editing the configuration for the LDAPv3 plug-in (remember, Open Directory is just customized implementation around LDAPv3 and Kerberos).

In the Directory Utility, after authenticating to unlock the settings, double-click the LDAPv3 plug-in entry, and click New to add an entry in the list. Here, you will be prompted to add the name or IP address of the Open Directory server (see Figure 4–35). If you provide that name, you would be doing a trusted bind, so for now, simply click Manual.

Figure 4–35. *Creating a new LDAP connection*

At the initial overlay screen, you will then have a new line and be able to manually add settings. Enter the fully qualified host name of the Open Directory server in the Server Name or IP Address column and a friendly name to use for accessing this account at a later date. Then, select SSL if you have enabled that on your Open Directory configuration, keep the Authentication and Contacts boxes checked, and click continue. If the server allows trusted Binding, the window will expand, allowing you to enter the machine name, an account with directory administration rights, and that account's password; you can ignore that and just click continue. Once bound, the window will update stating the configuration of the new server is complete, and Continue will change to OK (as shown in Figure 4–36).

Now that the Open Directory server has been added to the configuration list for LDAP, you can keep the default settings or change the mappings if you wish. *Mappings* are the tables of information that help an OS X client know what records it should query to get specific information. By default, Open Directory's LDAP server keeps the mapping available for the OS X clients, allowing for easy changing or updating without having to modify each client. When using other LDAPv3 servers, you may have to override or import the server-provided mappings of those systems with your own, which will be discussed later on in this chapter.

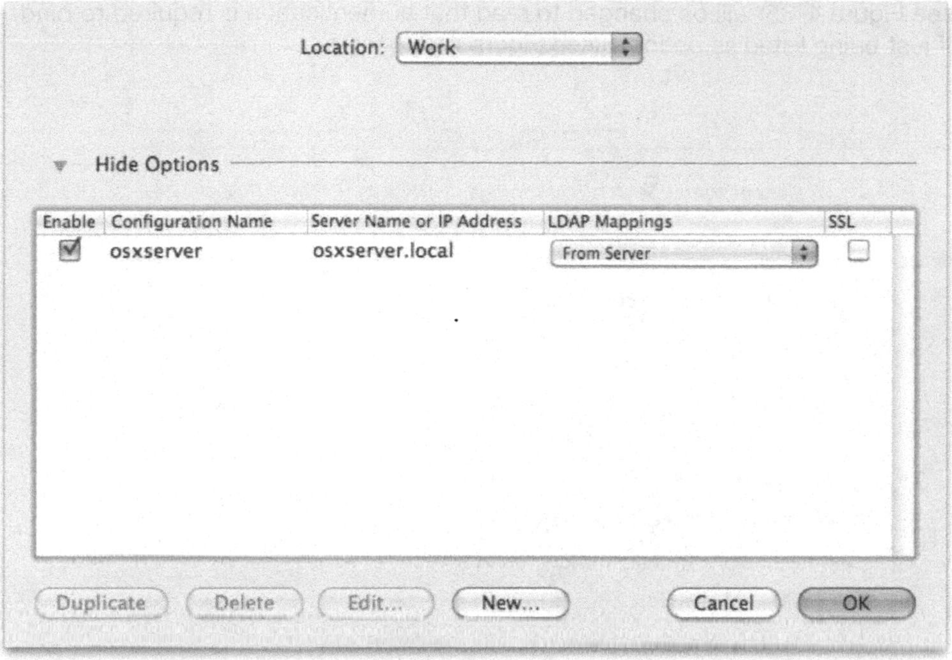

Figure 4–36. *Viewing and Creating LDAP Connections*

Once you have completed the bind, you should log out of the workstation and log in again before Directory Services will reload and start pulling down settings from Open Directory. In theory, this process may start once you've joined the Open Directory, but from experience, it is best to log out and then log back in to force a refresh.

> **NOTE:** You can also force a refresh of Open Directory settings and cached information for Directory services at the login window by logging in as the user and running >exit with no password. This will trigger a reload, causing the login window to disappear and reappear—very useful for troubleshooting.

Choosing Trusted Binding

While untrusted binding is easier, from an infrastructure standpoint, it is also inherently insecure for most environments.

By default, trusted binding follows the same steps as untrusted binding, but using a directory administrator (or in some cases, any Open Directory user) account to connect then creates a computer record in the Open Directory environment. Once that computer record is created, it gives a Kerberos shared key, which is used to encrypt and sign all communication between the client machine and the Open Directory server. In an environment where trusted binding is required, the dialogue shown in the previous section (see Figure 4–35) will be changed to read that authentication is required to bind, instead of just being listed as optional (see Figure 4–37).

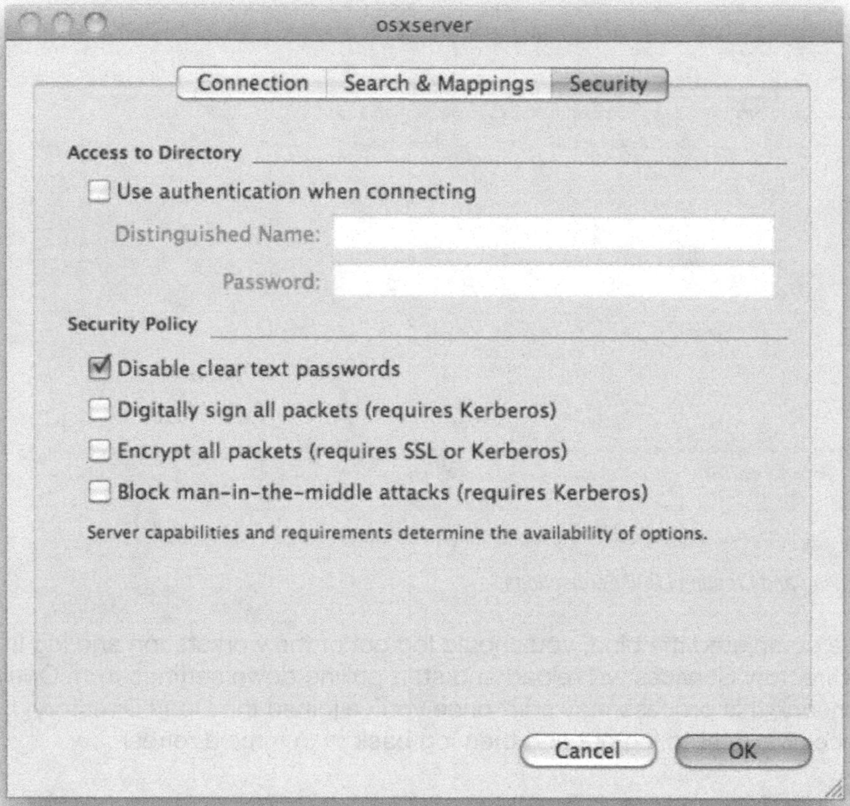

Figure 4–37. *Per-user password policy overrides*

NOTE: While any user, by default, can create a computer record in Open Directory, only administrators can delete or modify records. If you are looking to script or automate a trusted bind, you will want to use an account that has those privileges, so the bind can execute successfully if it finds an existing computer record it needs to overwrite.

Since the client will be creating a computer record, it is best to make sure that the machines sharing the name (or Bonjour name) are configured to be the same. They do not technically have to match, as Open Directory uses a unique ID to actually identify each machine, but having consistency across the board will allow for a network that's easier to manage as it grows. There is now a computer record in Workgroup Manager that matches the machine name (the dollar sign at the end indicates the record was created by a trusted bind, instead of automatically). One of the common uses of trusted binding Is to allow for scripted deployments of machines. When bound machines first boot up after being installed, they automatically rename themselves to their properly configured name (such as machinetype-assetid), bind to the Open Directory environment, and create a proper record that can then be used to enforce management policies.

On the server side, to require trusted binding, you will have to change the Open Directory settings. You will probably want to decide early on in your Open Directory environment planning whether or not you want to require trusted binding, as sometimes replicating out those environmental changes in a large network will be a problem (of course, if your are planning to use Open Directory in a large environment, you should probably use trusted binding from the beginning).

Using the Kerberos Realm

Now that the client workstation has been bound to Open Directory, it has also been configured to participate in the Open Directory's Kerberos realm. By default, the local users on a client not associated with an Open Directory user do not have any Kerberos Identitles associated with them, so at the outset, Kerberos would appear as fairly useless. However, using the Ticket Viewer application, we can add an Identity to a local account.

To do so, launch the Ticket Viewer application (located in /System/Library/CoreServices), and click the New Identity button. It will bring up a pane asking you to enter an identity (which in practical terms is just the username of an account in Open Directory) and its associated password. This will do the initial TGT process of the Kerberos authentication system, to verify that the account is correct and add the identity to that local user accounts list of Kerberos identities. Under version 10.6, your account can have multiple Kerberos identities but only one default identity. If you connect to a fileserver without specifying a user account, it will connect using your default identity. However, if you do specify a user that you also have an identity and Kerberos ticket for, you can connect as that as well, which useful if you are an administrator.

The down side of the Ticket Viewer application is that it does not give you the granularity of the previous catchall Kerberos.app application that it replaced. Specifically, it shows only your identity's initial TGT and when it will expire. To view your service tickets (the tickets specific to the fileserver you are connecting to, for example), you have to use the command line tool klist.

Search Policies

Mac OS X can be connected to a variety of different directory services, concurrently in some cases. To allow prioritization of which services to search, you can set the order in which services query for specific records. You can specify search policies for authentication (e.g., can a user log into this machine?) and contacts (e.g., what is this user's e-mail address?).

To configure the directory services search policy, you use the Directory Utility application and select Search Policy. There, you will see a list of all the services that OS X will query trying to find an answer for a lookup. It will always query locally before trying to descend the list of remote servers to find an answer. The more servers you have, the longer a query will take. Things such as a login window or a screen saver password prompt can trigger an authentication query, so keep that fact in mind before adding ten different Directory Services to your end users' machines.

If the workstation is bound to only one Open Directory server, has that server listed for authentication (and if you checked the Contacts tab, the order would be the same), and is part of a simple, single Open Directory environment, the defaults will be adequate. However, when moving to a solution that integrates with multiple Directory Services, ensuring that your search order is set properly is essential to getting the desired results.

Summary

In this chapter, we have looked at Open Directory, which is a combination of Kerberos, LDAP, and Password Server. For basic server setups, Open Directory will mostly be configured for you; very little work will need to be done from within Server Admin or the command line. However, most environments are not basic, and as soon as you get a second server, you're more than likely going to need to learn Open Directory. Therefore, we spent time looking at managing home folders, integrating services with Open Directory, and leveraging policies—all tasks that practically every Open Directory administrator will do from time to time.

What we didn't cover in this chapter was in-depth Active Directory binding and management. Active Directory is Microsoft's version of Open Directory, and it's used in a number of enterprise environments. Again, if you need more on managing Active Directory, see *Enterprise Mac Administrator's Guide*, from Apress. That book devotes an entire chapter to managing Macs in an Active Directory environment and looks at scripting and automating client functionality with Open Directory, in case you need to work with a mass deployment of Open Directory clients.

Next, we are going to look at using your Mac OS X Server to do more than just manage users and groups. We're going to start taking control of the network with routing and secure the server using the firewall in Chapter 5.

Controlling Network Traffic

Any computer—and more to the point, a Mac OS X Server—receives a barrage of traffic over the network interfaces. You can use two services in particular to control this traffic. The first is the router, and the second is the firewall. A *router* is a device on your network that chooses the paths between devices that network traffic takes; in short, a router connects networks and then manages the logic of how data is sent between them. A *firewall*, on the other hand, controls the various types of data that are allowed to communicate over those paths. In many cases, a firewall and a router are one device, although they can be two separate devices. This chapter first covers setting up the server as a router and then covers leveraging the firewall to restrict access to the server.

Before getting started, though, we'll give you a very basic overview of what TCP/IP is. Short for "Transfer Control Protocol/Internet Protocol," TCP/IP is the foundation of practically every modern network. TCP/IP is a collection of protocols that connect computers between one another in a modular (or layered) fashion. Computers each get an IP address, and each application or protocol that interconnects computers uses a unique port for communication.

Communications are then broken down into *packets*, which contain information about the sender, information about the recipient, and instructions for reassembling the original communication, in addition to the actual content of the communication, which is referred to as the packet's *payload*. Packets also contain return information if the packet is traversing a router, meaning it is destined for a location outside your local network, or local area network (LAN). This becomes the foundation for NAT, which we will describe in further detail later in this chapter.

Using Mac OS X Server as a Router

One of the services that receives little to no attention in literature on Mac OS X Server is using the server as a default gateway for your environment. This primarily is because most environments don't actually use Mac OS X Server as a router. A number of other products are more suitable to the task because they are more feature rich and come at a much lower price point than an Apple computer running Mac OS X Server.

Before you decide to use Mac OS X Server as a router, it's worth noting why you are going to do so. As a basic function, a Mac OS X Server is capable of acting as a router in order for other hosts on your local network to access systems outside your network, most notably web and mail servers on the Internet. But before you purchase Mac OS X Server as a dedicated gateway to the Internet, consider some of the tasks that a more advanced router makes more readily available:

- *Stateful packet inspection*: The inspection of packets to make sure that they conform to the standards of what should be in a packet and also do not contain any malicious content.

- *Failover*: Automated failover between multiple external network connections.

- *Logging*: Advanced logging facilities, such as a list of every connection that has been made on the device, open connections, and so on.

- *Accessible control options*: Granular control of port forwards from a graphical interface.

A number of other features are often leveraged for consumer- or prosumer-grade routing and firewalling appliances; although many environments lean on these features, if you don't need them or if you have a specific use of the routing in Mac OS X Server, then you will find the gateway services in Mac OS X Server to be suitable. If this matches your need, then read on, because we'll cover how to set up Mac OS X as a router, obtain basic functionality, and even forward a few ports.

How Network Address Translation Works

Short for "Network Address Translation," NAT is a core concept in understanding routing. NAT is the technology that hides all of your computers behind a single public IP address. Here are some basic concepts that will help you understand how NAT and routing work:

- A *subnet mask* (or netmask) on each computer instructs the network stack for that system as to what computers are on the local network. The subnet mask indicates the size of the network; anything within that subnet mask is considered local traffic, and anything outside the subnet mask is not.

- Traffic destined for computers on the local network does not traverse the *default gateway*, or router, and therefore does not use NAT. Network requests destined for IP addresses that are not on the local network use the default gateway to communicate with the computers that run those services.

- Each computer makes an outgoing request on the default gateway, which routes the traffic accordingly to its default gateway or to its own local network, with information in each packet that indicates the return path, including instructions for traversing NAT when forwarded from the gateway/router to the client systems.

There is a lot more information about NAT, but this indicates the basic functionality of how data is routed over NAT, and it will be useful for managing Mac OS X Server in the role of a router. Now that you have a better understanding of NAT, we'll cover how to set up Mac OS X Server to provide routing.

Because NAT has two connections (which we can call LAN and WAN for posterity's sake), you will need a minimum of two network connections to configure the assistant. In most environments, you will have a connection that is patched into the equipment provided by your organization's Internet service provider (ISP), which is the company you pay for your high-speed Internet access. You will also have a connection that is patched into the switch into which your computers interconnect. In other environments, your second network connection might be the AirPort interface for the system, essentially using Mac OS X Server as an Apple AirPort base station.

Using the Gateway Setup Assistant

The easiest way to enable NAT is to use the Gateway Setup Assistant. The Gateway Setup Assistant will automatically configure the server to be a router and configure the standard complement of services that are often used in routing. Throughout this chapter you'll learn about more network services than just routing; however, we will show how to set each of those up independently of using the Gateway Setup Assistant.

So, what is this Gateway Setup Assistant going to do for you? It's going to do some (or all) of the following:

- Enable NAT

- Configure the IP addresses on your network interfaces (external and internal)

- Automatically set up DHCP

- Optionally set up VPN, enable the firewall service and configure basic address groups, and finally set up a basic implementation of DNS

If that seems like a lot of acronyms to you, then don't worry; most of the heavy lifting is done by the assistant, and we'll be covering all of those services in this chapter, so you'll find plenty of information to get you up to speed on the necessary tasks to manage the gateway.

But the Gateway Setup Assistant isn't for everyone. One important thing to keep in mind is that if you enable the Gateway Setup Assistant and you have already configured some of the aforementioned services, then you might be disappointed when it completely blows away your configuration of those services and starts from scratch. Therefore, run the Gateway Setup Assistant first, or you more than likely won't be able to use it. You also won't want to use the Gateway Setup Assistant if you need to use a specific IP range, common in environments with existing networks, which, let's face it, includes most environments. But if you're setting up a new server, then the Gateway Setup Assistant can basically do all the work for you.

1. To get started, open Server Admin from /Applications/Server.

> **NOTE:** First configure the two interfaces with the addresses that they should have. Once you are able to access the Internet using the configured settings, you'll have the WAN interface configured.

2. From the Server Admin application, click Settings for the server that you will be enabling NAT for, and then click the Settings icon in the Server Admin toolbar.

3. From here, click the NAT check box, and then click the Save button.

4. You will now see an icon for NAT in the SERVERS list, under the server for which you just enabled the view. Click NAT, and then click Overview in the Server Admin toolbar.

5. Click the Gateway Setup Assistant button in the lower-right corner of the screen, as you can see in Figure 5–1.

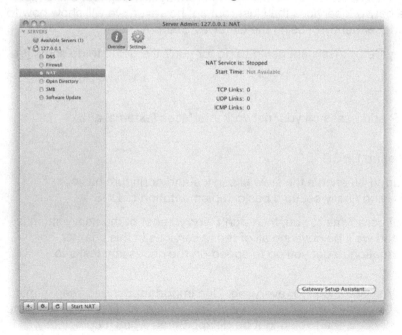

Figure 5–1. *NAT Overview screen*

6. At this point, you'll see the Gateway Setup Assistant screen warning you that existing DHCP, DNS, NAT, and VPN settings may be overwritten, as you can see in Figure 5–2. If needed, back up these services, and then click the Continue button.

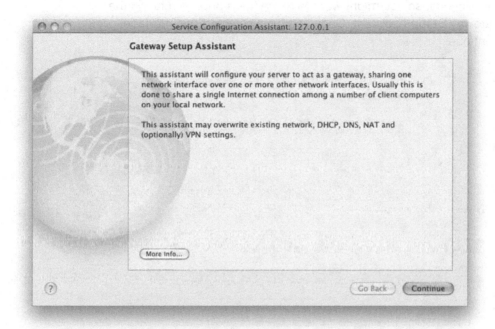

Figure 5–2. *Introduction to the Gateway Setup Assistant*

7. If DHCP has been enabled, then you will receive an error, as shown in Figure 5–3, warning you that the existing DHCP subnets will be overwritten. Click Overwrite, or back up the service settings if needed.

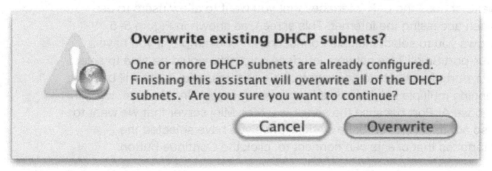

Figure 5–3. *DHCP subnets warning dialog*

8. On the Gateway: WAN Interface screen (seen in Figure 5–4), choose the network connection that is connected to your router or public network. In this case, we will choose Ethernet because it is configured to access the Internet. In many environments, you may have multiple Ethernet connections, so you might want to name them prior to running the Gateway Setup Assistant. Once you have selected the interface, click Continue.

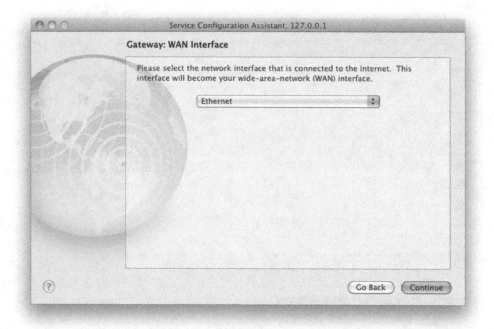

Figure 5–4. *Choosing a WAN Interface with the Gateway Setup Assistant*

9. Next, choose the LAN interfaces that you want to allow users to use when accessing the Internet. This screen, as shown in Figure 5–5, allows you to select multiple connections. For example, if you have a four-port Small Tree network interface card, you would be able to select four ports for clients to connect to. This can be useful if you will be running multiple local subnets in your environment. In this case, we will choose AirPort because the server is a Mac Mini server that we want to also act as an AirPort base station. Once you have selected the interfaces that clients can connect to, click the Continue button.

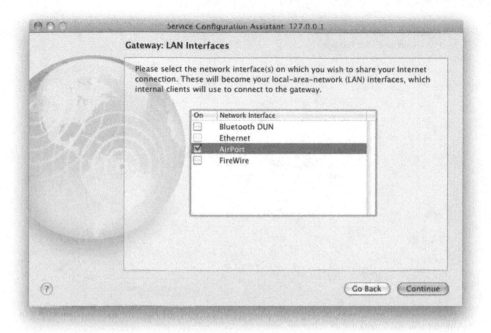

Figure 5–5. *Choosing a LAN interface with the Gateway Setup Assistant*

10. On the Gateway: VPN Settings screen, which you can see in Figure 5–6, choose whether to also enable the VPN service while setting up NAT. Here, select "Enable VPN box for this server" if you will also be setting up a VPN. If you do, the VPN service will automatically configure an L2TP-based VPN and enable port forwards as needed. Because L2TP (described further in Chapter 7) requires a shared secret as a second layer of security, enter the secret (which all users will use), and then click the Continue button. If not setting up VPN, then simply click the Continue button.

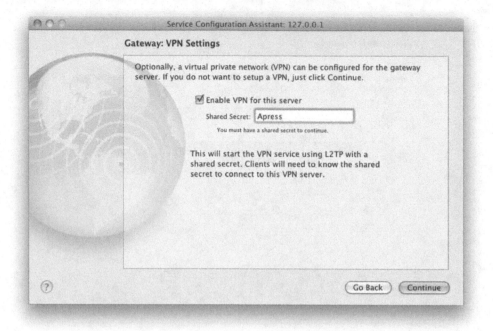

Figure 5–6. *Configuring VPN Settings using the Gateway Setup Assistant*

Next, you'll see a summary screen. Here, you'll see the settings that have been selected, the services that will be enabled, and the IP addresses that will be assigned to the LAN or internal, network interfaces. Click Continue, and the services will all be set up. Once done, DHCP will be enabled for local clients for the first 128 IP addresses of the automatically set-up subnet for the local interface, and the next 126 IP addresses will be set up for the DHCP pool for VPN clients logging in through L2TP.

Manually Enabling NAT

Many users won't need DNS, VPN, and the firewall to be enabled and may not want to use the setup assistant. Therefore, you can also enable NAT manually. To do so, click the Settings icon in the Server Admin toolbar for NAT. You will see a screen similar to Figure 5–7.

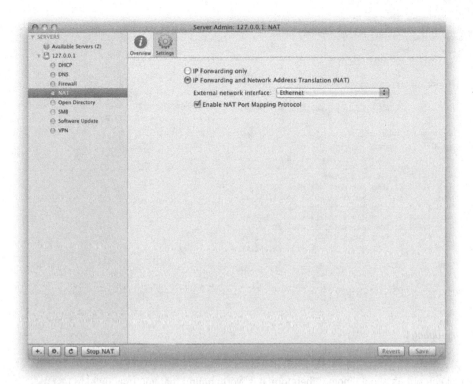

Figure 5–7. *Manually enabling NAT*

Here, you will select the Enable NAT Port Mapping Protocol box. Then choose the IP Forwarding and Network Address Translation (NAT) radio button. Once done, another field becomes available. Select the network interface that connects to your ISP or public (aka external) network interface from the "External network interface" box.

You can also use the server as a router, thus controlling network traffic, but not use NAT. This is a simpler topology but rarely used because IP addresses are becoming more and more a hot commodity. If you do want to use the server in this type of rule, use the "IP Forwarding only" radio button.

Testing NAT from a Client

To test NAT from a client, either use DHCP or use a manual IP address, with an IP that is not part of your DHCP pool. The IP address that you use should be in the same subnet as the Mac OS X Server and should have the router configured as the IP address of the server. Then, attempt to ping an IP address on the public network, such as 4.2.2.2. To ping this IP address, open Network Utility from /Applications/Utilities, and then click the Ping tab. From here, enter the IP address you want to ping in the provided field, and click the Ping button, which becomes the Stop button once the ping process has commenced, as shown in Figure 5–8.

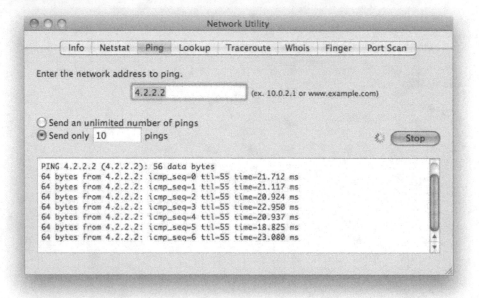

Figure 5–8. *Testing routing*

NOTE: Not all computers allow pinging; therefore, it is worth noting that you may need to test a different address and that pinging a host is not always a good test of connectivity. At times, port scanning, as explained later in this chapter, will be a better test.

Another tool in Network Utility that can be used to test connectivity is Traceroute. Traceroute will test connectivity to each hop in sequence when connecting to another computer. To test Traceroute, click the Traceroute tab, provide an address to test connectivity to, and then click the Trace button (as shown in Figure 5–9). If there is a problem with a hop in connectivity between the two points, you will see a timeout in the hop.

NOTE: You can use the Ping and Traceroute commands to perform these same functions from the command line.

Figure 5–9. *Traceroute*

Setting Up Forwarding Ports

Once NAT is enabled, the most common task that will need to be completed is forwarding ports, or taking traffic for a given port and redirecting it to a computer on the LAN. As mentioned before we started talking about the specifics of setting up NAT, it's a bit complicated to set up port forwards. Now let's look at doing so.

Previously, we discussed how NAT used a single IP address to hide other systems behind that IP. When you are using Mac OS X Server as your router, you will end up having a service running on a server or a client that needs to be accessible from outside the network. An example of this would be if you need to be able to access port 80 and you have a web server that is hosted on a server other than the Mac OS X Server acting as your router. In these cases, always use VPN where possible. If it is not possible to do so, then you'll need to forward the port or ports from the public IP address being used to the local IP address of the server. To do so, you will need to edit /etc/nat/natd.plist, which is a standard property list that allows for a key called redirect_port that contains an array of port forwards to be added. Each of these port forward entries in the array will need a number of attributes, which control the way the port forward is handled and are stored in a number of keys in the property list's array. These include the following:

- proto: The protocol being used, typically TCP or UDP

- targetIP: The IP address on the local network that the port(s) will be forwarded to

- targetPortRange: The port that is being forwarded to the targetIP

- aliasIP: The IP address on the external, or public, interface

- aliasPortRange: The port that listens on the public IP; traffic will be forwarded to the targetIP using the port indicated in the targetPortRange

Each of these keys will then consist of a corresponding string that is the value of the setting. For example, if you wanted to forward port 80 typically used for web access to 192.168.1.2 and you were using an IP address of 68.85.164.161 on the public interface, then you would add the following to /etc/nat/natd.plist:

```
<key>redirect_port</key>
        <array>
                <dict>
                        <key>proto</key>
                        <string>tcp</string>
                        <key>targetIP</key>
                        <string>192.168.1.2</string>
                        <key>targetPortRange</key>
                        <string>80</string>
                        <key>aliasIP</key>
                        <string>68.85.164.161</string>
                        <key>aliasPortRange</key>
                        <string>80</string>
                </dict>
        </array>
```

To add more port forwards, simply copy the text from the <array> to the </array> into the file again, immediately after the following entry, and then input the additional ports and IP addresses. For example, if you were to use the port forward from earlier and also add a port forward for Apple File Protocol (AFP), which uses port 548, to 192.168.1.3, then the additions in natd.plist would include the following:

```
<key>redirect_port</key>
        <array>
                <dict>
                        <key>proto</key>
                        <string>tcp</string>
                        <key>targetIP</key>
                        <string>192.168.1.2</string>
                        <key>targetPortRange</key>
                        <string>80</string>
                        <key>aliasIP</key>
                        <string>68.85.164.161</string>
```

```
                        <key>aliasPortRange</key>
                        <string>80</string>
                </dict>
        </array>
        <array>
                <dict>
                        <key>proto</key>
                        <string>tcp</string>
                        <key>targetIP</key>
                        <string>192.168.1.3</string>
                        <key>targetPortRange</key>
                        <string>548</string>
                        <key>aliasIP</key>
                        <string>68.85.164.161</string>
                        <key>aliasPortRange</key>
                        <string>548</string>
                </dict>
        </array>
```

This may seem like a fairly complicated process, but once you get the hang of it, it's actually pretty straightforward. Simply keep pasting array entries in, and set the strings as appropriate. This is similar to the process you might use on a LinkSys or SonicWall, except you're adding the step to paste in the array.

> **NOTE:** Property list files (`.plist`) need to be constructed properly and can have a variety of syntax errors that arise. To test a plist, you can use `plutil`, the property list utility included with Mac OS X. When you want `plutil` to check that a property list is correctly formatted, then you can run it with the `-lint` option and follow that with the path to the file. For example, to check that the `natd.plist` file is syntactically correct, use this:
>
> ```
> Plutil -lint /etc/nat/natd.plist
> ```

Setting the Advanced Options

You can enable a number of other advanced options for NAT, also leveraging the command line. These options are fairly dangerous for the beginner and should likely be used only if you have a good fundamental understanding of the command line. There are two commands of note to do so; the first is `serveradmin`, and the second is by manually editing the `natd.conf` file, mentioned in the "Forwarding Ports" section earlier in this chapter.

The `serveradmin` command shows a number of settings for NAT that are not exposed in a graphical interface. You can see these by using the `serveradmin` command followed by the settings verb and then nat (which is the command-line name of the service). This option is useful to see all of the settings, not just those shown in Server Admin. To see the settings, run the command as follows:

```
serveradmin settings nat
```

This will produce the following:

```
nat:reverse = no
nat:unregistered_only = yes
nat:same_ports = yes
nat:natportmap_interface = "en0"
nat:log = yes
nat:clamp_mss = yes
nat:dynamic = yes
nat:log_denied = no
nat:use_sockets = yes
nat:proxy_only = no
nat:enable_natportmap = yes
nat:interface = "en0"
nat:deny_incoming = no
```

Once you find a setting that you would like to change, you can then change it by using the serveradmin command as well. For example, you can log all traffic that the server denies. To do so, you would use the following command:

```
serveradmin settings nat:log_denied = yes
```

Using the Firewall to Control Access to the Server

A firewall is a gatekeeper. The ports that we have referenced throughout this chapter are allowed or denied by this soup-nazi-esque service. If a client requests access to a service and there is no service, then the server will by default simply respond that the service is not running.

NOTE: The firewall is a service that requires great care when configuring; you can easily end up not being able to control your own server any longer. Before you begin configuration, always perform a service backup of any service, but most important do so with the firewall service!

The ipfw (short for "IP firewall") tool is the open source project used by Mac OS X Server for a firewall. You can configure ipfw using the Server Admin tool included in /Applications/Server. You can also use the ipfw command and edit the ipfw.conf file to edit the live configuration and the startup configuration, respectively.

NOTE: The firewall used in the Mac OS X client, by default, is an application-layer firewall. This means that each application, rather than port, is used to determine what kind of access is granted. The ipfw tool set is included in the client operating system but is not enabled by default.

Setting Up the Firewall

To set up the firewall, open Server Admin from /Applications/Server, and click the name of the server in the SERVERS list. Then click Services, and select Firewall. You'll then see Firewall listed in the SERVERS list, as shown in Figure 5–10.

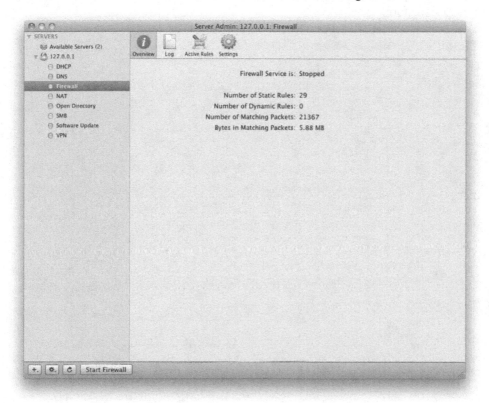

Figure 5–10. *The Firewall service*

Here, you'll see the total number of rules, the number of dynamic rules, and the number of packets that have been allowed (or denied) based on those rules. When you are trying to determine which ports to allow, you're going to want to restrict each IP address to only the traffic that is absolutely necessary in order to have a secure and reliable server. Having open ports that are not necessary will invariably lead to the risk of exploitation, whether that risk is ever realized.

Defining Address Groups

An *address group* is a group of contiguous IP addresses, defined using an IP address or an IP address and a netmask, which as we mentioned earlier in this chapter defines the size of the local network.

To define an address group, first open Server Admin. Click Settings in the Server Admin toolbar, and then click Address Groups. Here you will see a listing of all previously defined address groups. There should be a group for each IP range configured for your server and, if you used the Gateway Setup Assistant, the VPN clients that were assigned then. In Figure 5–11, you can see a good example of a number of ranges defined by the Gateway Setup Assistant.

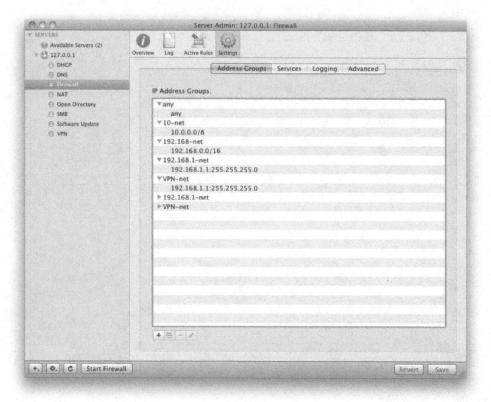

Figure 5–11. *Address groups in Server Admin*

To add an address group, click the plus sign (+) and then provide a name for the range in the "Group name" field. Then, remove "any" from the list, and use the plus sign (+) to add a new range so that it appears as shown in Figure 5–12 (obviously configured closer to your environment). You can use a single address or a range in this field. If you want to enter a range, then you will need to do so by typing the IP address followed by a slash (/) followed by the netmask. For an explanation of these numbers, see the following:

http://en.wikipedia.org/wiki/Classless_Inter-Domain_Routing

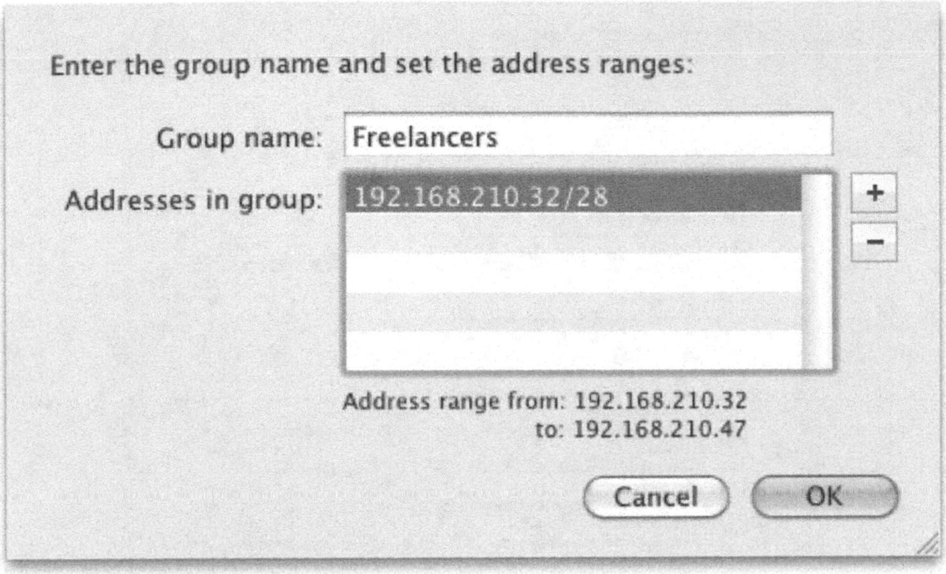

Enter the group name and set the address ranges:

Group name: Freelancers

Addresses in group: 192.168.210.32/28

Address range from: 192.168.210.32
to: 192.168.210.47

Cancel   OK

Figure 5–12. *Defining an address group*

Defining Services

Once you have configured the computers that will be able to access the servers based on groups of IP addresses, then you'll need to configure which of those address groups will be able to access each of your services. A service, in this context, is a port or range of ports, not an application bundle as with the Mac OS X client operating system. For example, one of the most common services in use in the world today, HTTP (used for web servers), uses port 80. Port 80, in the Mac OS X client, is accessible by default, provided that the application attempting to invoke port 80 is allowed to open the port. However, in Mac OS X Server, rather than limit applications from opening any port, you instead open the port, and then any application that needs to share services over that port can do so (although only one can do so at a time).

To configure service access, from Server Admin click the Firewall entry in the listing for the server name, and then click the Firewall service. From here, click the Settings icon in the Server Admin toolbar, and then click the Services tab. Here, you will see the traffic allowed for the "any" group, which is any possible IP address, whether it is in a group or not. The "any" group should have the most restrictive set of access of any group, as you can see in Figure 5–13. Let's make it even more secure by scrolling down in the list and deselecting the DNS box, which is allowed on systems set up by the Gateway Setup Assistant. Although you want to allow DNS, you will do so only for other address groups from your local network, not any of them.

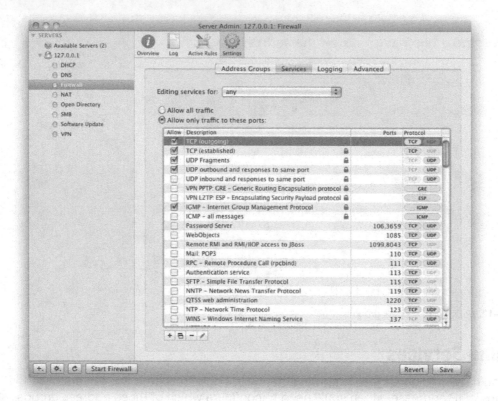

Figure 5–13. *Services for the only group*

You can use the "Editing Services for" field to switch between which address group that you are showing and configuring. Let's change it to the Freelancers group created earlier. Here, you'll notice that any new address groups allow any traffic to come into the server or leave the server, as shown in Figure 5–14.

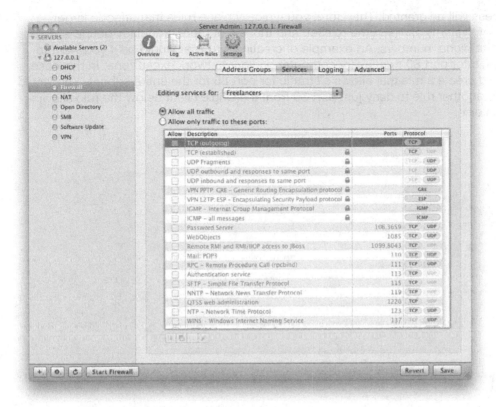

Figure 5–14. *Default behavior for new address groups*

The Freelancers group will be restricted to have only AFP access into the server. Therefore, click "Allow only traffic to these ports," scroll down to AFP, and select the Service box. You will then want to cycle through each address group, limiting access to any services per your own map of what people should be able to access.

> **NOTE:** Because the more granular configurations can be fairly complicated, it can often be a good idea to create a flow chart of who is able to access what services. OmniGraffle is a great tool for doing so.

Creating Rules

The `ipfw` service loads a configuration file that defines what can be accessed and by whom. This configuration file is comprised of a set of rules, processed in order. You can see these rules on the Advanced tab of the Firewall settings pane, as shown in Figure 5–15. Each of these rules is assigned a unique identification number and processed in order of lowest number to highest. If a lower-numbered rule blocks access to a port and a higher-numbered rule allows access, then the higher numbered rule will be enforced, and access will be granted. Therefore, you typically place rules that affect a larger number of systems earlier in the ruleset, and those that more granularly define access lower, with higher numbers. An example of creating a ruleset would be if you want to allow traffic for port 80 from every computer on your network except one. In this case, you would create a rule that allows all traffic for port 80 for the entire subnet. You would then add another rule to deny just port 80 from the single client below the rule allowing everyone else.

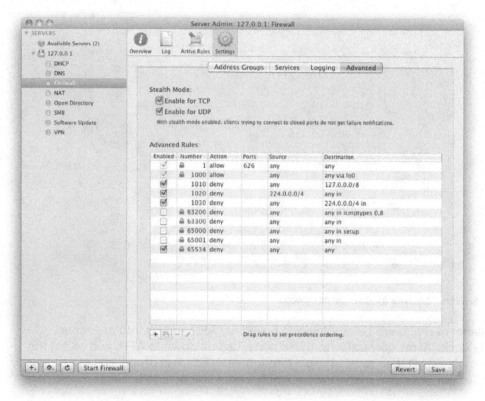

Figure 5–15. *The Firewall pane's Advanced settings*

Rules that are added in the Services pane have higher numbers by default. You can then add and remove or disable and enable rules as needed. Simply use the plus sign (+) to create rules, the minus sign (-) to remove them, and the pencil icon to augment existing rules, allowing you to control priority. You can then click the Active Rules icon in the Server Admin toolbar to see how Mac OS X Server will interpret the rules.

Preventing Intrusions

The firewall on Mac OS X Server is, by default, an aggressive little bugger. If you attempt to log on with an inappropriate password 10 times, a dynamic rule will be created blocking access from that computer for 15 minutes. After 15 minutes, the dynamic rule will be removed from the server.

Setting the Global Firewall Options

The firewall also comes with a number of global settings. These help to more granularly configure the service but are not meant to be used for service configuration and control.

As mentioned previously, the server will respond to requests for ports that it is not running any services on. This can be disabled by enabling Stealth Mode. In the case where Stealth Mode is enabled, when another computer attempts to communicate with the server using a port that is not active, rather than responding, the server will simply divert the response to a null state. This can help defeat attacks such as OS fingerprinting, which allows an attacker to learn about your setup by reading patterns derived from your response to various requests on the server and hide the server somewhat; enabling Stealth Mode is almost always a good idea. To enable Stealth Mode, open Server Admin from /Applications/Server, and then click the Firewall service under the SERVERS list. Next, click Advanced, as shown previously in Figure 5–15, and then click the Enable for TCP and Enable for UDP check boxes to enable Stealth Mode for TCP and/or UDP packets, respectively.

Configuring the Firewall from the Command Line

As with the DNS section, there are some aspects of managing the server that you will need to get into the command line to handle. For these, you will first want to be comfortable with the command line, which is beyond the scope of the book. If you are confident at the command line, then you will be happy to know that the service can be interfaced with programmatically.

To configure ipfw from the command line, you can use either the ipfw command or the serveradmin command. Most configuration of the NAT service earlier in this chapter (see the "Setting the Advanced Options" section) was done from the serveradmin command; however, for the Firewall service, you will more than likely want to use either ipfw or the ipfw.conf file for all but global settings because rule configuration from serveradmin is a bit daunting given that each field is broken out into a key within an array and becomes an entry based on such.

The ipfw command can then be used to load new rules or unload existing rules on the fly. When the server is rebooted next, then any rules added in this fashion will be forgotten; therefore, if you are adding rules that should be persistent across reboots, you should edit the ipfw.conf file in /etc/ipfilter/ipfw.conf. For a more in-depth review of ipfw, see *Foundations of Mac OS X Snow Leopard Security*, Second Edition (Apress, 2010).

NOTE: Each time a new rule is added from Server Admin, all rules are flushed and reloaded.

Testing the Firewall

Once you have disabled access to a port, verify that access is not being allowed for the port(s) in question. To do so, open Network Utility from /Applications/Utilities, and then click the Port Scan tab. From here, provide the IP address (or host name) of the computer that you have restricted access to. Then click the "Only test ports between" field, and provide a range of ports to be scanned. Click the Scan button, as you can see in Figure 5–16. If the scan does not net any results, then you have successfully blocked access.

In the example, we are testing the port from within the same network that the server is in. You can additionally check traffic from outside your network. One way to achieve this would be to simply attempt to access the server from home in much the same way. Or you could use one of a number of port scanners. For example, http://www.t1shopper.com/tools/port-scan has a list of common ports and allows you to specify a range of ports in much the same way that you can do in Network Utility.

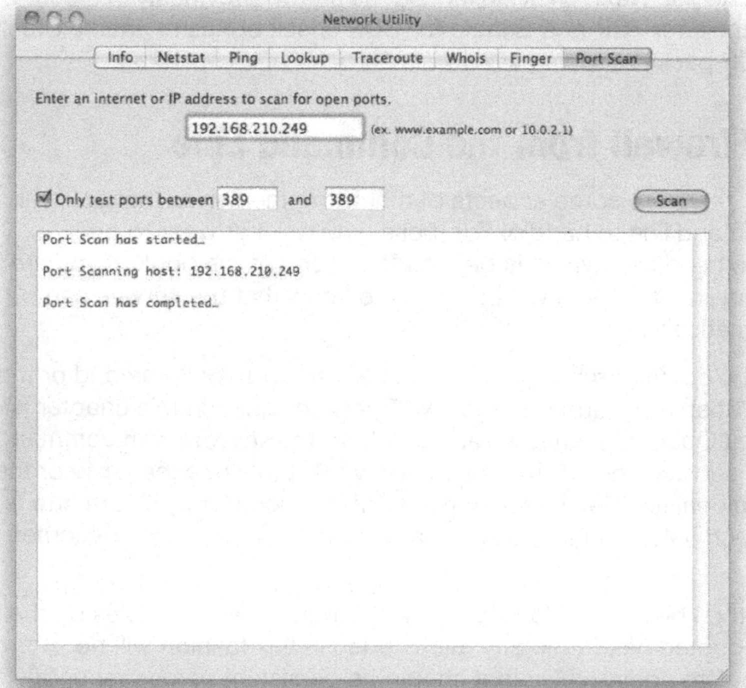

Figure 5–16. *Closed port in Network Utility*

If the port is open or if you're trying to test opening the port, then you should be able to see it listed as open when you scan, as shown in Figure 5–17.

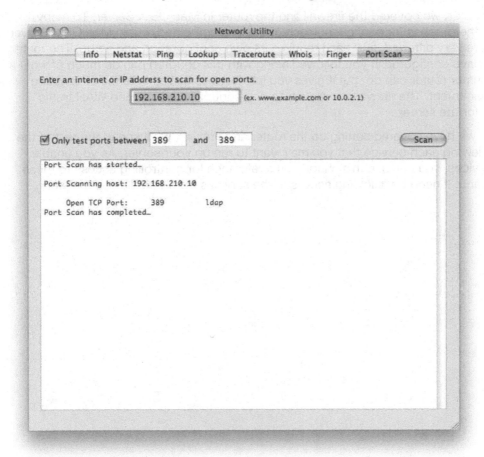

Figure 5–17. *Open port in Network Utility*

> **NOTE:** The Port Scan option in Network Utility uses the `stroke` command, located in `/Applications/Utilities/Network Utility.app/Contents/Resources`. You can use stroke directly rather than relying on the graphical application, which is much faster.

Summary

The biggest challenge in getting through a chapter like this (whether reading it or writing it) is all of the terminology, acronyms, and theory. But understanding those provides you with a good fundamental knowledge of many of the topics that will come up in future chapters. For example, if you want your web server accessible to the world, then you will need to know how to direct traffic to it.

In this chapter, we covered the firewall and the router in Mac OS X Server. To many vendors, the process for configuring each of these is combined, but in Mac OS X Server, the two are very different, and each requires its own configuration and setup. The router that you have configured (if you followed along with this chapter) can do much of what a $60 prosumer router can do, but it gives you infinite possibilities in terms of scripting and management. The firewall can then help you control both local and WAN traffic destined for the server.

Now that we have covered setting up the router and firewall, we'll spend the rest of the book reviewing each service that you may want to run on your server. As you enable those services, you can use this chapter as a reference for controlling access to those services and, if need be, allowing access to the services from outside your network.

Chapter 6

Centralizing Network Services

Now that you understand how to control access to network traffic, we'll cover how to centralize the management of the network settings on your client systems. Beyond the physical network, including switches and routers, *centralization* (in this context) means handing out IP addresses and controlling how computers find one another on the network.

In Chapter 5, we covered configuring the server to provide Internet access to client systems. Each computer will need an IP address in order to effectively communicate with other computers. The process of assigning those IP addresses can be daunting in larger environments but can be automated with DHCP, a service that allows you to control which IP address your client computers receive automatically. Environments that do not use DHCP will often have administrators statically assigning each computer a unique IP address. Assigning these IP addresses can be time-consuming and error-prone, so allowing the server to dole addresses out as needed is preferable when possible.

Once we have covered using DHCP, we'll move on to DNS. Each IP address can have a name associated with it. The combination of DHCP and DNS then allows administrators to automatically set up client systems for IP addressing and to direct those clients to various names in use in each environment. The DHCP server can hand out addresses for name servers and IP addresses. These name servers help reduce the perceived complexity of your environment, making it easier for users to access the resources they need.

DHCP

DHCP is short for "Dynamic Host Configuration Protocol." As mentioned in Chapter 1, DHCP is the service that hands out IP addresses to client computers. DHCP can be configured automatically by a number of other services when you are using setup assistants; however, for the purpose of this chapter, we will assume that DHCP has not yet been set up.

Before we cover how to configure the DHCP service, we'll explain how DHCP works. When a computer is first turned on, if there is not a static (also called *manual*) IP address assigned to it, then the computer will send out a DHCP broadcast on the network. If there is a DHCP server, then the client will receive a lease offer for an IP address from the server, which is valid for a certain period of time. The lease offer contains an IP address, a subnet mask, and a number of options including DNS and how long the computer can use the IP address. If the client can utilize the information in the offer, then it will accept it by sending an IP request. Each client can receive multiple offers, so the IP request informs the server that the client will accept the offer and that the IP address should not be handed out to another client computer for the duration of the lease. The server then responds with an acknowledgment that the lease was accepted.

NOTE: If clients will not receive leases, then a good troubleshooting step is to reduce the number of options being offered in the lease. Invalid options can cause certain DHCP clients to reject a lease offer.

Although the DHCP request that we discussed in the previous paragraph may seem like a number of steps, it is typically processed very quickly. The lease of an IP address is then refreshed routinely (using the interval contained in the lease time). Each time the lease expires, the computer will repeat the process and go get a new IP address.

DHCP also has a built-in function for dealing with multiple lease offers. This is because networks can have multiple DHCP servers. If you have multiple ones, then make sure that each of those servers is not sharing overlapping IP addresses from the pool of addresses that will be handed out (known as the *DHCP pool*). For example, if your network uses IP addresses from 192.168.1.1 through 192.168.1.254 and you have a DHCP server handing out IP addresses from 192.168.1.100 to 192.168.1.200, then do not have another pool of addresses handing out any of the addresses in the range of 192.168.1.100 to 192.168.1.200, even if your other DHCP pool is hosted on a network appliance, such as a firewall. For the purpose of our overview of the DHCP service, we will assume that you are not currently running DHCP services on any other devices in the environment.

If no DHCP server can be contacted, then you will receive an Automatic Private IP Addressing (APIPA) address. In this case, the address will be in the range of 169.254.0.1 to 169.254.255.254 with a subnet mask of 255.255.0.0 and have no options assigned. If you are receiving an IP address automatically that is not in the APIPA pool or in your configured DHCP subnets, then it is possible that you have a rogue DHCP server (or an unplanned DHCP server) in your environment or that you are not joined to the proper network. If this is a frequent occurrence and causes outages (as DHCP issues often do), then consider purchasing a switch that is capable of detecting rogue DHCP servers.

DHCP may seem daunting at first, but in reality it is one of the easier services to configure in Mac OS X Server. To get started, open Server Admin, and click the server you will be enabling DHCP on in the SERVERS list.

Next, click the Settings button in the Server Admin toolbar, as you can see in Figure 6–1. Here, select the DHCP box, and then click Save, which results in DHCP being added below the server in the SERVERS list, as shown in Figure 6–2. (Notice that Open Directory is also selected, which has no impact on the DHCP service and is selected only because, as you may have noticed in Chapters 2 and 3, it is often enabled during the setup process of a server.)

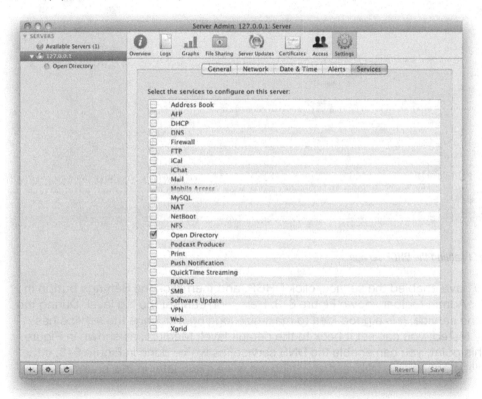

Figure 6–1. *Before enabling the DHCP service*

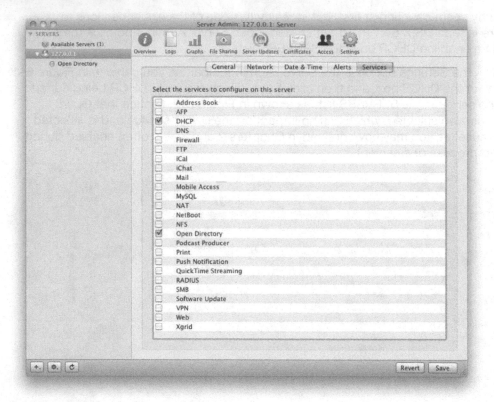

Figure 6–2. *Enabling the DHCP service*

Once you have enabled the service, click DHCP, and then click the Settings button in the Server Admin toolbar shown Figure 6–3. Here, you can set the log level. During the setup of the service, it is a good idea to maximize logging, but once the service has been fully tested, you can set it back to the default level, Medium, as shown in Figure 6–3. At this point, you can enable the DNS service, as we've done in Figure 6–3, if the server will be acting as a DNS server, which we will explain later in this chapter.

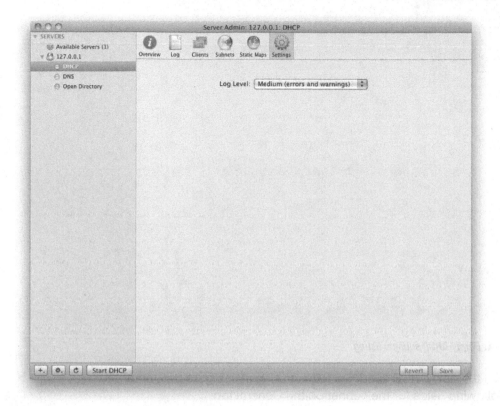

Figure 6–3. *Setting the DHCP logging level*

The service will not function without a range of IP addresses, which Mac OS X Server references as a subnet. Once you have configured the DHCP service to meet your needs, it is time to configure a subnet.

Creating a Subnet

There can be multiple DHCP servers, but each DHCP server can also share multiple pools of addresses. Again, make sure that IP addresses in each pool do not overlap and therefore that each client receives a unique IP address. Setting up the subnet is the first step to setting up a DHCP server. To do so, use the DHCP screen that you prepared in the previous section.

1. In Server Admin, click the DHCP service in the SERVERS list, and then click the Subnets button in the Server Admin toolbar. By default, the list of subnets (which is synonymous with *DHCP pools* in other DHCP servers) should be empty, as you can see in Figure 6–4. Click the plus (+) sign to enable another subnet.

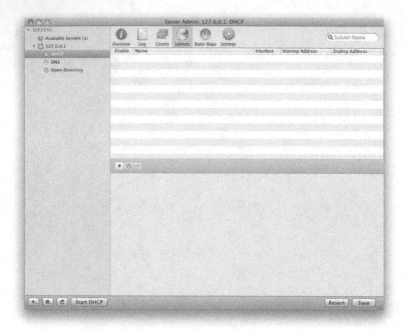

Figure 6–4. *Empty DHCP subnets listing*

2. On the new DHCP subnet screen, as shown in Figure 6–5, enter the following fields for the subnet on the General tab:

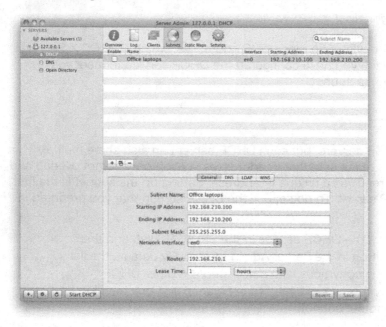

Figure 6–5. *New DHCP subnet: General tab*

- *Subnet Name*: A name that can be used by administrators to keep track of subnets in use.

- *Starting IP Address*: The first IP address being provided by the DHCP pool.

- *Ending IP Address*: The last IP address being provided by the DHCP pool.

- *Subnet Mask*: The subnet mask to be provided to client systems receiving IP addresses from the DHCP server.

- *Network Interface*: The NIC from which the subnet will be served.

- *Router*: The default gateway for your environment.

- *Lease Time*: The amount of time that the lease is good for. Increasing the lease time can lessen downtime in the event of issues with the DHCP server, and decreasing the lease time can allow for pushing out updates through DHCP more quickly. The default is one hour, but it is up to your organization whether you increase or decrease this variable.

3. Once you are satisfied with your entry, click the DNS tab, where you will provide the DNS information for your environment (correlate this information with that entered on the DNS tab of the network interface's Advanced screen in the Network pane of System Preferences). At this point, the server that we are configuring is not running the DNS service; however, if you're going to configure DNS using the steps in this chapter, you can save yourself a little time by entering the IP address of the server as the DNS now.

4. Here, enter the IP addresses of each name server as you would enter them in the DNS tab, as you can see in Figure 6–6. Also enter the domain names to which names that aren't fully qualified will be appended. For example, if your search domains are krypted.com, then if you attempt to visit www, you will find yourself visiting www.krypted.com.

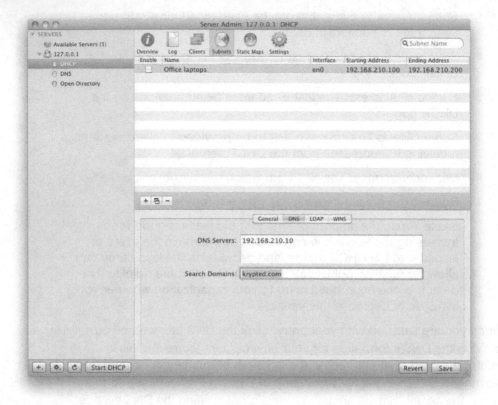

Figure 6–6. *New DHCP subnet: DNS tab*

5. Here, you will be able to specify the following, as you can see in Figure 6–7:

    ■   *Server Name*: The IP address or host name of the Open Directory master (or third-party LDAP server).

    ■   *Search Base*: The starting point in the LDAP hierarchy running on the server specified in the Server Name field. If you are unsure as to what search base to use, look in the Open Directory service, which you can find on the Overview screen.

    ■   *Port*: If you will not be using the default ports for LDAP (ports 389 and 636 for standard and SSL, respectively).

    ■   *LDAP over SSL*: Enables SSL for the LDAP connection (does not also provide the SSL certificate to the client, which would need to be done in order for this option to function as intended). We explain certificates and certificate management in further detail in Chapter 4.

    ■   *URL*: Automatically filled in based on the contents of the Server Name, Search Base, and LDAP over SSL fields.

NOTE: You will often have the opportunity to use a host name or an IP address in a field, like in the Server Name field. In these cases, you should always use a host name where possible. However, if you don't have one, you can use an IP address instead.

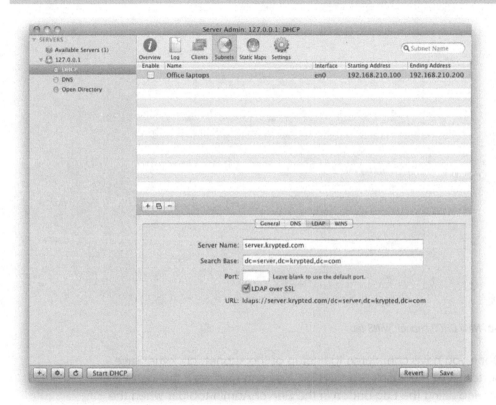

Figure 6–7. *New DHCP subnet: LDAP tab*

6. Next, click the WINS tab. Here you can configure the WINS server that is provided to clients through DHCP. Windows clients can use WINS to locate host names of other Windows systems (or systems emulating the behavior from Windows). WINS is explained fully in Chapter 4. But for now, if you will be installing the SMB role for serving data to Windows clients on any servers, then consider providing the address of that server as the WINS server in DHCP; at a minimum, this would entail entering that address in the WINS Primary Server field or entering the IP address or host name of a WINS server in your environment, as you can see in Figure 6–8.

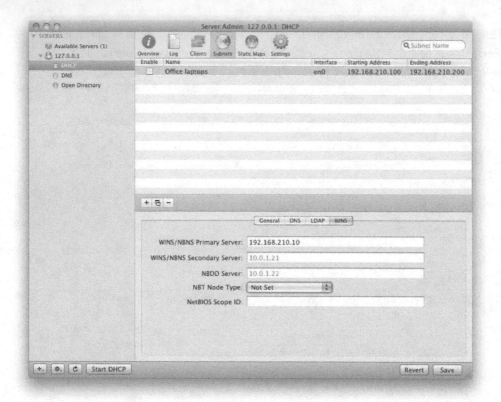

Figure 6–8. *New DHCP subnet: WINS tab*

7. Once you have completed the setup of the subnet, click the Save button, and then click Start DHCP. You can now view the logs for the service using the Log button in the Server Admin toolbar when the DHCP service is highlighted. As you can see in Figure 6–9, you can view the DHCP discovery, the offer, the request, and the acknowledgment (ACK). These options become helpful when troubleshooting connectivity.

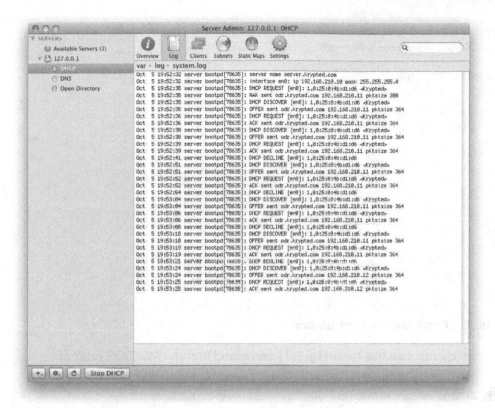

Figure 6–9. *Reviewing DHCP logs*

Finally, you get to the client—the reason you went through all of this setup. On the Mac you can look at the DHCP lease data offered on the client by opening the Network pane of System Preferences and then clicking the TCP/IP tab of any network interface, as shown in Figure 6–10. You can also click through the provided tabs to see the available options and verify that they have been supplied to the client.

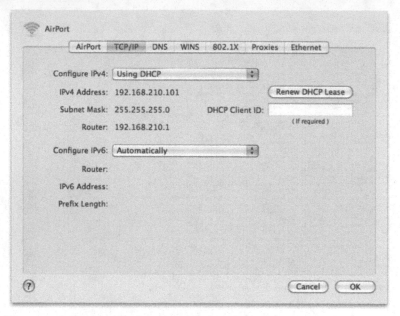

Figure 6–10. *TCP/IP settings for a network interface*

For Windows clients, use the `ipconfig /all` command from an MS-DOS prompt.

> **NOTE:** In some versions of Mac OS X, you may need to view the contents of the `/etc/resolv.conf` file to see what DNS servers are being used because the used DNS servers are not exposed in the GUI. You can also view the addresses in the Network pane of System Preferences in Mac OS X 10.6.

Reserving IP Addresses

Although DHCP allows you to assign IP addresses automatically, it can also be leveraged to provide the same IP address to a client (or clients) every time the client restarts. This is done in the form of a DHCP reservation, which the DHCP service will use to assign the same IP address to a MAC address each time the server receives a DHCP discovery. Reserving IP addresses is useful for servers, network appliances, video equipment, and other types of devices that you want a consistent IP to access or for which you want to provide a name. Any computer accessing the server using the MAC address entered into the reservation will be given only the IP address indicated in the reservation, and that IP address is no longer in the pool, so it cannot be provided to other clients.

To add a DHCP reservation, which Apple refers to as a *static map*, first open Server Admin, and then click the disclosure triangle for the server running your DHCP service in the SERVERS list. Next, click the Static Maps button in the Server Admin toolbar. Here, you will see the static maps that you may have entered, although by default the list is empty, as you can see in Figure 6–11.

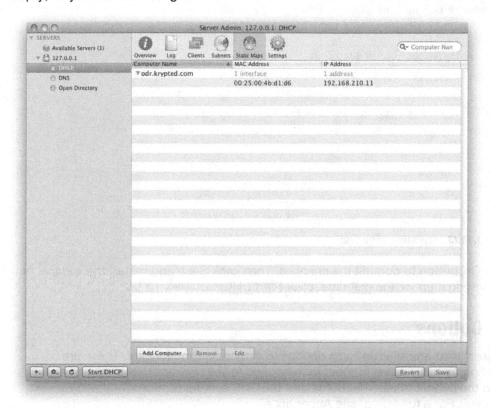

Figure 6–11. *DHCP reservation screen*

Click the Add Computer button. Here, you can provide a computer name, which does not need to match and is not connected to any other host naming fields or variables. Then provide a MAC address and an IP address in the fields for each, similar to what is shown in Figure 6–12. If the computer has multiple network interfaces (and most modern Apple computers do, especially if you include AirPort), you can use the plus (+) sign to provide multiple IP addresses to the client.

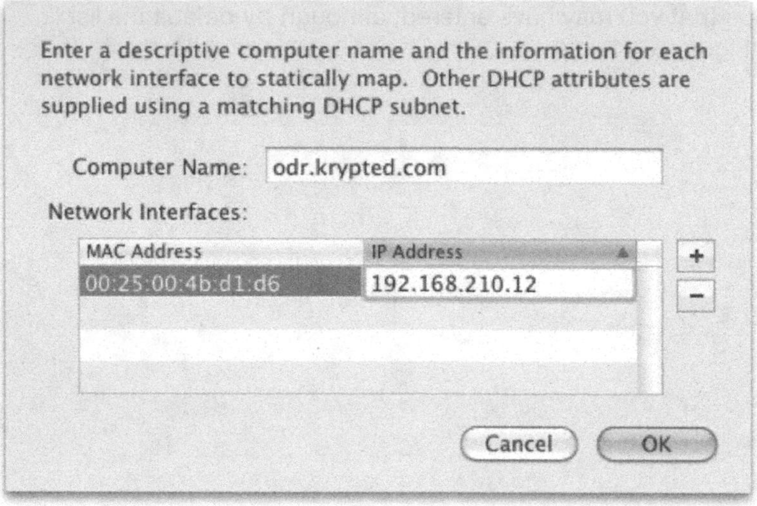

> Enter a descriptive computer name and the information for each
> network interface to statically map. Other DHCP attributes are
> supplied using a matching DHCP subnet.
>
> Computer Name: odr.krypted.com
>
> Network Interfaces:
>
> | MAC Address | IP Address ▲ |
> |---|---|
> | 00:25:00:4b:d1:d6 | 192.168.210.12 |
>
> +
> −
>
> (Cancel)   (OK)

Figure 6–12. *DHCP reservation entry field*

Click the OK button to commit the changes. Then click Save and restart the service; or if
you are setting it up for the first time, click Start DHCP.

DHCP Options

DHCP uses what are referred to as *options* to extend its functionality. These are
identified numerically. Each number corresponds to the services that they provide,
including the subnet mask, the router, and the DNS servers (options 1, 3, and 5,
respectively). For a full listing, see Appendix A.

Once you know the options that you want to enable, then you will insert them into the
/etc/bootpd.plist file, which can be done using the Property List Editor included with
Mac OS X or using your favorite text editor.

To get started, open the /etc/bootpd.plist file with your favorite text editor. Before you
do, make a copy of the file. Here we use the cp command to do so, followed first by the
name of the file and second by the name we're assigning to the backup of the file.

```
cp /etc/bootpd.plist /etc/bootpd.plist.bak
```

To do so, insert a string of dhcp_option_ followed by the option number that you will be
providing and then a key to indicate the data that is provided in the option, as follows:

```
<string>dhcp_option_OPTIONNUMBER</string>
<data>
My_Option_Payload
</data>
```

> **NOTE:** You will need to have the appropriate permissions to edit the `/etc/bootpd.plist` file. For more on file permissions, see Chapter 18.

For example, to provide Finger services to clients over DHCP, you can enable option 73. The following example sets the Finger server to hand out to 192.168.210.7. To do so, add the following to your `/etc/bootpd.plist` file and then restart the DHCP service:

```
<string>dhcp_option_73</string>
<data>
192.168.210.7
</data>
```

> **NOTE:** If you notice, a number of the options that can be provided by DHCP already have fields available in Server Admin. If an option you need has a field available, then you should not touch these in the previously mentioned property lists. These include `dhcp_time_offset` (option 2), `dhcp_router` (option 3) `dhcp_domain_name_server` (option 6), `dhcp_domain_name` (option 15), `dhcp_network_time_protocol_servers` (option 42), `dhcp_nb_over_tcpip_name_server` (option 44), `dhcp_nb__over_tcpip_dgram_dist_server` (option 45), `dhcp_nb_over_tcpip_node_type` (option 46), `dhcp_nb_over_tcpip_scope` (option 47), `dhcp_smtp_server` (option 69), `dhcp_pop3_server` (option 70), `dhcp_nntp_server` (option 71), `dhcp_ldap_url` (option 95), `dhcp_netinfo_server_address` (option 112), `dhcp_netinfo_server_tag` (option 113), `dhcp_url` (option 114), `dhcp_domain_search` (option 119), and `dhcp_proxy_auto_discovery_url` (option 252).

Enabling DHCP Relay

In a number of environments, you may have a subnet being served up that is located on the other side of a router. Because DHCP uses broadcast traffic, the DHCP service is not exactly friendly to the idea of providing DHCP services to devices on the other side of a router. But never fear, DHCP relay is here. Enabling DHCP relaying will require a little bit of command-line work, but it's pretty straightforward.

To get started, first let's use the `cp` command to back up the file again:

```
cp /etc/bootpd.plist /etc/bootpd.plist.bak
```

Then open the `/etc/bootp.plist` file with your favorite text editor. For simplicity's sake, we'll use `pico` here. Type the following command:

```
pico /etc/bootpd.plist
```

Now browse toward the end of the file using the arrow key to where you see two keys, indicated by a `<key>` field in the property list. The keys you are looking for will read as follows:

```
<key>relay_enabled</key>
<false/>
<key>relay_ip_list</key>
<array/>
```

Now let's change the contents. The following example allows an IP address of the DHCP server (in this case we will use 192.168.210.1 as that server) to relay DHCP traffic to subnets outside the local subnet, so you'll specify that IP address in your relay_ip_list key's array. You'll also be changing the relay_enabled field to read true rather than false:

```
<key>relay_enabled</key>
<true/>
<key>relay_ip_list</key>
<array>
        <string>192.168.210.1</string>
</array>
```

Now that you are finished, press Control+X to close the file, and choose to save it by pressing the Y key. When asked for a name, simply hit the Enter key to overwrite the file.

> **NOTE:** In the previous example, the array consisted of only one item; however, you could have duplicated the line with the `<string>` in order to grant relay access to multiple other IP addresses.

Now that the DHCP service is configured, we'll cover the Domain Name Service (DNS) so that you can refine how your users will access data on the server.

DNS

As indicated earlier in this chapter, DNS is the service that connects names to IP addresses (and vice versa). The DNS service is integral to many environments, and when DNS is unavailable, end users often cannot access e-mail, the Internet, and a number of internal services to your environment including Open Directory, which can cause computers to not be able to log in. Overall, if you choose to run DNS (and most Mac OS X Server environments will need to have control over their own DNS), then make sure to be well educated about what you will be doing from both the load and security standpoints, and make sure to run a secondary DNS server for the zones that are important.

In addition to the DNS that runs on your network, there's also the DNS that manages your organization's Internet-facing domain name. Because a number of outsourced services include DNS services, it's common to leave your Internet-facing DNS presence there, and for the purpose of this chapter, we will assume that the Internet DNS name that you use is indeed hosted elsewhere.

Zones and Records

A *domain* is a unique name that can be used to access your resources. For example, the domain name for Amazon is amazon.com. All the servers for Amazon can live within this domain name and then be accessed based on *records*, which are the fields separated by a dot (.) from the domain name. Each domain that your DNS server hosts is called a *zone*. Each domain has a dedicated zone file for the domain. Each subnet that your DNS hosts names for is also defined in a zone file. Each of the zone files in turn contains a number of DNS records. To complicate things, there are two types of zone files: those that you should edit and those that you shouldn't, which we'll cover more later in the "Editing Zone Files" section of this chapter.

The most commonly used types of DNS records include the following:

- *@*: Root record, assigns a name or IP address to

- *A*: Address record, assigns an IP address to a name

- *AAAA*: Same as an A record but used for IPv6

- *CNAME*: Cononical name, alias names to other names

- *DNAME*: Delegation name record, delegates part of a domain tree to a server

- *MX*: Mail exchange record, maps domain names to mail servers

- *NS*: Name server, used to delegate DNS servers to use for various domains

- *PTR*: Pointer record, used to assign a name to an IP address

- *SOA*: Start of authority record, used to track authoritative information about a domain

- *SPF*: Sender Policy Framework record, used for fighting spam; you can also use a TXT record to indicate SPF records

- *SRV*: Service locator record, used for locating services

- *TXT*: Text record, used for machine readable data

Setting Up DNS

To enable DNS, open Server Admin, and click the name of your server. Then click the Settings button in the Server Admin toolbar. You'll then see a listing of all the services that can be displayed in Server Admin. Check the box for DNS, and then click the Save button, which will result in DNS being listed under the name of the server, as you can see in Figure 6–13.

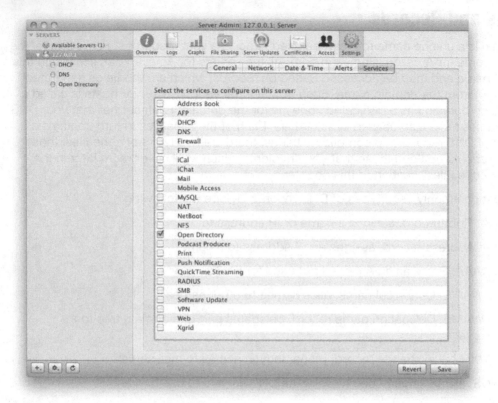

Figure 6–13. *Enabling DNS in the Server Admin view*

Once enabled, click the resultant DNS service under the name of the server. Here, you can configure the settings for the domain by clicking Services in the Server Admin toolbar. On this screen, as you can see in Figure 6–14, you can change the logging level, which is helpful in troubleshooting, and you can assign IP address ranges that are allowed to perform recursive queries and forwarders.

DNS recursion is name resolution, or the act of resolving a name to an IP address (and vice versa). Therefore, in the "Accept recursive queries from the following networks" field, you can enter IP address ranges in the form of an IP address with a corresponding netmask. If your server is only hosting DNS records for other computers that are included in the local subnet, you will not need to make any changes in this field. However, if you have other subnets in your environment, then you may need to enter other subnets in the field. For example, if you want to allow an IP range of 192.168.55.1 through 192.168.55.254, you can enter **192.168.55.1/24** in this field. For a more in-depth review of which netmask to enter given the size of a subnet, see the subnet calculator made available at `http://www.subnet-calculator` or `http://krypted.com/utilities`.

IP addresses to forward DNS requests that the server does not have cached are known as *forwarders*. If you do not specify any forwarders, then requests will instead go to the servers defined as root hints. You should define a forwarder in cases where your Internet service provider (ISP) has DNS servers that resolve names quickly and do not cache names for an unusual amount of time. In these cases, defining a forwarder can speed up name resolution. In cases where you enter a forwarder, you will want to confirm with your ISP that these servers accept what are known as *zone transfers*.

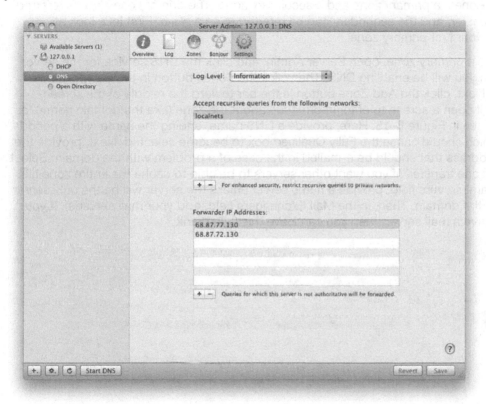

Figure 6–14. *Global DNS settings*

When you are satisfied with the global changes you have made thus far, click the Save button. If you are using DNS only to reduce network traffic over the WAN (as a caching-only server), then there is nothing left to do except click the Start DNS button to begin the service and then test everything.

> **NOTE:** Mac OS X Server and the .local namespace do not necessarily get along very well. It is widely accepted that although you can run .local namespaces with no problems on most platforms, you should not do so on Mac OS X.

Adding a Zone

Now that you understand what a zone is, it's time to add your first zone. There are two types of zones: a primary zone and a secondary zone. The primary can also be referred to as a *master*, and the secondary can be referred to as a *slave*. First let's look at creating your first primary zone.

To create a primary zone, open Server Admin, and click the DNS service for the server for which you will be enabling DNS. Then click the Zones button in the Server Admin toolbar. Next, click the Add Zone button in the bar toward the middle of the screen, which will open a screen to enter information about the zone (aka the domain name), as you can see in Figure 6–15. Here, provide a DNS name, ending the name with a period (*dot*), which should cause the Fully Qualified box to become selected. Next, provide the e-mail address that should be e-mailed in the case of a problem with the domain. Select "Allows zone transfer" if you want other servers to be able to cache the entire zone file. In the Nameservers field, provide a name server unless the server will be the only server used for the domain. Then, in the Mail Exchangers field, add your mail server(s). If you do not have a mail server, then you can leave this field blank.

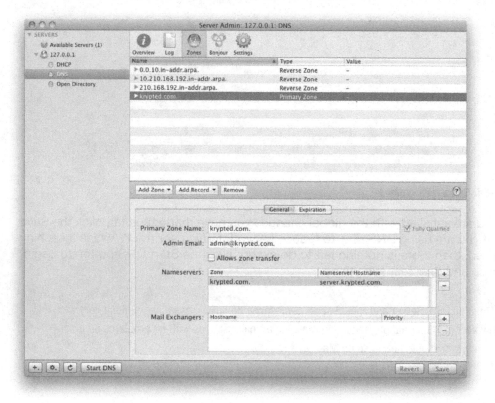

Figure 6–15. *Adding a primary zone*

NOTE: Figure 6–15 also shows the zones that are automatically generated for ranges of IP addresses. These will contain IP address that the server provides reverse lookups on, meaning that if you query the DNS server for the IP address, then you will receive a name in response.

Once you have provided the required information, click the Save button. You will still need to create records for the domain.

Creating Records

Once a zone has been added, you'll need to add records for the zone. For primary zones, these are tracked using the disclosure triangle for each domain in Server Admin, as you can see in Figure 6–16. To create a machine record, click the domain (zone) for which you want to create a record. Then click the Add Record button, and select the type of record you will create from the provided list, which allows only for the following:

- Alias (CNAME)
- Machine (A)
- Service (SRV)

When you create records, the PTR records are automatically generated for each A record or CNAME, and while you're at it, the subnet for the PTR is created as well. Each of these files can be seen in the /var/named directory and the /var/named/zones directory. Records created and managed through Server Admin will be found in the /var/named/zones directory and should only ever be edited in Server Admin.

You can also add other types of records, but when doing so, you will need to edit the configuration files. If you find that you need to work with the configuration files, don't be overly concerned; it's actually a very straightforward process that we cover later in this chapter!

NOTE: If you configured accounts during the installation of the server, then it will more than likely be running as an Open Directory master. For more on Open Directory and Open Directory masters, see Chapter 4.

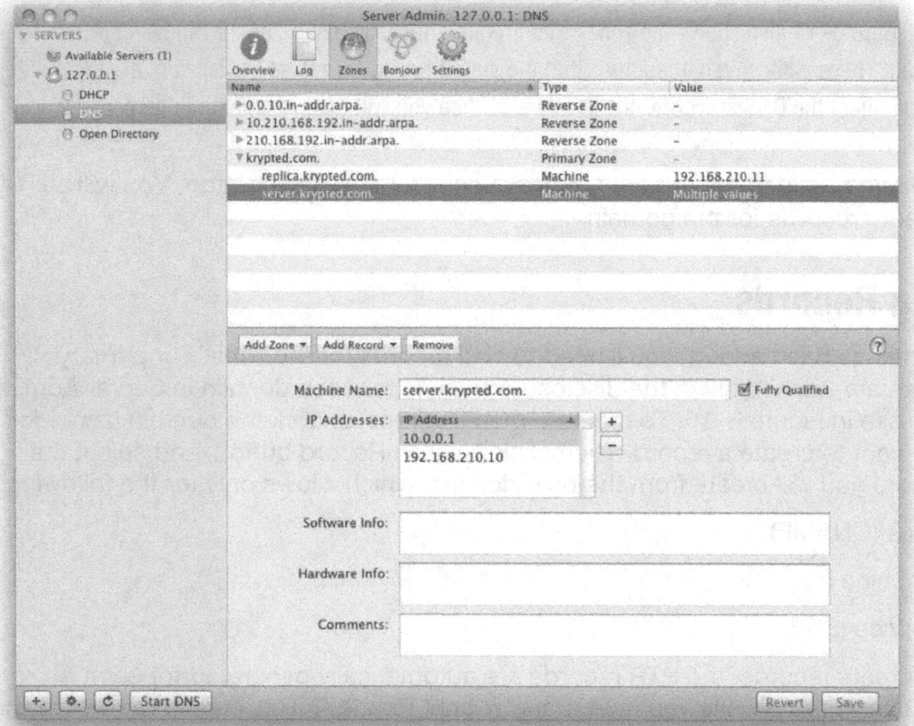

Figure 6–16. *Adding machine records*

Setting Up Wide-Area Bonjour

Once you have configured your global settings for the DNS service, you can choose whether to use automatic Bonjour browsing. Mac OS X and a number of third-party devices that support Bonjour can broadcast and/or discover services on local networks using Bonjour, which is why sometimes you plug a printer in and your Mac "automagically" sees it on the network. Bonjour is supposed to provide zero-configuration networking; however, anyone who has been charged with managing networks will likely have run into plenty of limitations to zero-configuration protocols, including Apple's Bonjour.

But fear not, you can centralize the management of these zero-configuration protocols to a degree and then provide them to computers that are not on the local subnet, known as *wide-area Bonjour browsing*. You can designate a domain that is set up as a zone (as we will show you how to do in the next section) for Bonjour browsing. You then add SRV records to the specified domain for each service type. To get started, open Server Admin, click the DNS service for the server you will be enabling wide-area Bonjour services on, and then click the Bonjour button in the Server Admin toolbar. From here, select the "Enable automatic client Bonjour browsing for domain" box, type the domain name for the zone that you will be setting up wide-area Bonjour to create service records in, and click Save (as you can see in Figure 6–17).

These services appear on computers that have the Bonjour browsing domain entered as a search domain in the Network pane of System Preferences. You can add the designated Bonjour browsing domain to the search domain of each computer manually or through DHCP.

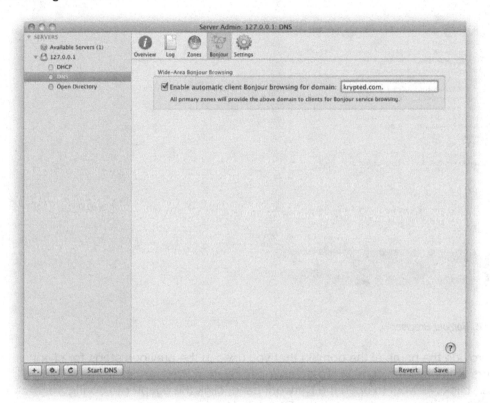

Figure 6–17. *Wide-area Bonjour*

Once added, you will then need to also create service records for each device used. The easiest way to create the service records is to find data using Bonjour Browser (or a similar tool), as you can see in Figure 6–18.

Figure 6–18. *Bonjour Browser*

Finally, provide the name of the domain that you used in the previous steps for client computers as the search domain. To do so, open System Preferences from a client computer, click Network to open the Network pane, click the adapter to configure, click the Advanced button, and then click the DNS tab. Here, enter the name, as you can see in Figure 6–19.

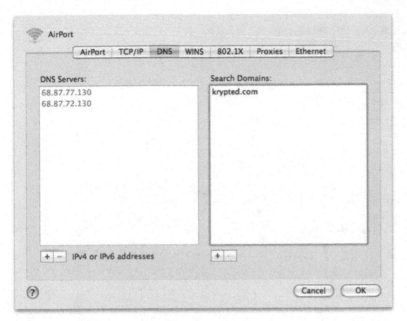

Figure 6-19. *Entering the search domain*

NOTE: Bonjour records should start with an underscore (_).

Configuring Secondary Zones

A secondary zone is a slave domain that is used to provide backup name services. The server that hosts a secondary zone will cache the information for the primary zones that the slave is keeping track of and then share the naming resources for those zones with clients. Because the data is cached, if the primary DNS server becomes unavailable, then the secondary will still be able to function until the primary is able to come back online.

To add a secondary zone, open Server Admin, click the server that you will be configuring to be the secondary DNS server, and then click the Zones button in the Server Admin toolbar. Next, click the Add Zone button and then click Add Secondary Zone (Slave). Here, enter the name of the zone that you will be caching information for; then click the plus (+) sign in the Primary DNS Servers list. Type the IP address of each primary DNS server, as you can see in Figure 6–20.

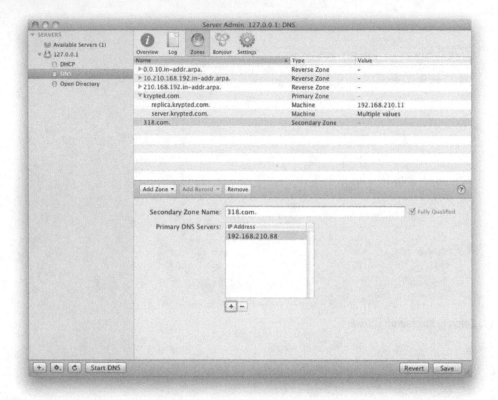

Figure 6–20. *Creating a secondary zone*

Click Save to complete the addition. A new file will then be added to the /var/named directory called bak followed by a . and then followed by the name of the domain. In other words, if the domain name is 318.com as in Figure 5.20, then the name of the file would become bak.318.com. The file is not generated until the records for the zone are cached, and therefore the existence of the file should indicate success in creating a secondary server for the domain.

> **NOTE:** The .bak file that is generated cannot also be used to restore DNS records. If you want to back up DNS records so they are restorable, use the Service Settings button in the Server menu, and make a copy of all of the files located in /etc/dns and /var/named.

Editing Configuration Files

In DNS, recursion references the process where a name server will make DNS queries to other name servers on behalf of client systems. For example, if you attempt to access www.krypted.com, then your DNS server will ask the DNS server that is authoritative for that domain what the IP address is for the www record of the domain (97.74.215.39) and respond to your request with that information. Most name servers are simply DNS clients that cache information for a specified amount of time. Recursion is disabled by default on most name servers. In Mac OS X, recursion is enabled for subnets local to the server only.

In environments where you want to provide recursive queries, you can enable recursion by opening Server Admin, clicking the disclosure triangle for the server you will be configuring, and then clicking the DNS service. From here, click the Settings button in the Server Admin toolbar, and then in the "Accept recursive queries from the following networks" section you would click the plus (+) sign. In this field, provide the IP address and netmask for which you want to enable recursion. For example, if you're enabling recursion for all computers on the 192.168.0.0 subnet and the subnet mask for those clients is 255.255.255.0, then you would enter the following:

```
192.168.0.0/24
```

This will allow recursion for those clients by updating the /etc/dns/options.conf.apple file. Alternatively, you can edit the setting by hand, but don't do so using the /etc/dns/options.conf.apple file, or you could introduce instability into the DNS service and Server Admin could overwrite your settings. Rather, edit the /etc/named.conf file. In named.conf, add the following line in the options section:

```
allow-recursion {192.168.0.0/24;};
```

Overall, this is a fairly straightforward technical note, but there is an underlying theme that Apple is doing a really good job of leveraging an include methodology with regard to configuration files. Inside the /etc/named.conf, also in the options section, you'll notice that there is a line that begins with include and specifies the path of the server-managed file, which uses the word apple at the end of it. This is mirrored in zone files as well. Although not all open source services use this method for allowing different configurations in the GUI and the command line, we hope they all will at some point.

Editing Zone Files

The flat text files that make up zone configuration files are called db followed by a dot and then followed by the name of the domain. Here, open the file that houses the zone you would like to edit in your favorite text editor, which should bring up text that looks similar to the following:

```
;THE FOLLOWING INCLUDE WAS ADDED BY SERVER ADMIN. PLEASE DO NOT REMOVE.
$INCLUDE /var/named/zones/db.krypted.com.zone.apple
```

Next, let's enter a line that creates an A record, or a record that references an IP address:

```
Server.krypted.com. IN A 192.168.210.10
```

Now let's say that you actually have two physical servers that will operate in that same namespace. Enter two IP addresses and round-robin the traffic between them:

```
Server.krypted.com. IN A 192.168.210.10
Server.krypted.com. IN A 192.168.210.11
```

Now each subsequent attempt to access the server will net the next available server. You could add another line with 192.168.210.12, and so on.

OpenDNS Web Content Filtering

OpenDNS is a great tool that allows you to freely use community-managed web content filtration. We see this used more with education customers than corporate customers, but essentially you point your DNS at them (or your DNS servers as the case may be), and they filter out different kinds of content.

Not everyone is going to want to run their own Mac OS X Server for DNS. In these cases, you can get some modicum of control without having to stand up a full naming infrastructure of your own. As is often the case with free apps, you're not going to get all the features you might get with some other applications, but OpenDNS is a great start, especially if you're not currently doing any kind of filtering.

Integrating OpenDNS is very straightforward: sign up for a free account, and define the address for your network in their dashboard. Then, point your DNS settings on clients (or DNS servers that serve your clients, as is often the case given directory services and other needs) to the 208.67.222.222 and 208.67.220.220 IP addresses, and configure the level of filtration. Most of the complaints we hear about OpenDNS is that the filter doesn't catch anything, which typically means the level of the filter isn't set properly.

By default, the filter is set to block phishing attacks (sites) only, so you'll need to increase it to block anything else. You can customize the various settings (low, moderate, and high) to block more and more types of content, eventually including even politics and social networking if you so choose. Beyond strict category-based blocking, you can choose to white-list or black-list sites as well. You can also choose to filter by type of network, although this is typically going to use a WAN IP to display the various types of networks.

Overall, it is usually possible to set up an entire web content filtering solution with no cost and be up and running within a couple of hours. We also usually like to whip up a graphic with the organization's logo explaining that a site was blocked and whom to call to get it unblocked (if it should be unblocked), as shown in Figure 6–21 (which is described in the OpenDNS tutorials).

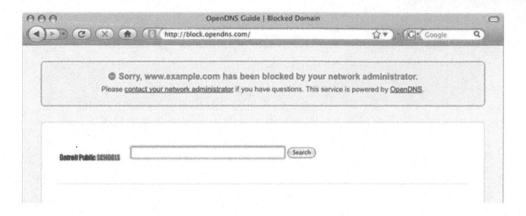

Figure 6–21. *OpenDNS*

In the future, we expect OpenDNS to have an API that will be integrated into consumer and prosumer firewalls, but for now it's a great tool to have in your IT tool belt if you don't have the budget to spring for WebSense or another more costly alternative.

Summary

In this chapter, we covered setting up and managing the DHCP and DNS services in Mac OS X Server. These services are fairly mature, because they have been included with Mac OS X Server since its inception. The reason for the historical significance is that these services are the bedrock for many a well-managed network environment: DHCP provides a centralized control of IP addresses, and DNS provides a simple means of accessing resources by names.

Although many environments will have an existing appliance for one (or both) of these services, it is still important to understand both what they do and how they can help you. Additionally, both DHCP and DNS are critical services. If either becomes dysfunctional, then the perception of many an end user will be that "the network is down." This is because if DHCP is not functional, then users will not receive IP addresses and so will not be able to interact with other computers on their networks; if DNS is not functional, then users will not be able to access resources on servers using the methods that you have shown them for accessing those resources.

Because of the critical nature of each of these services, make sure to back up both services using the process in Chapter 3 for backing up a service's settings.

Chapter 7

Configuring Network Services for Security

In Chapter 6 we reviewed leveraging DHCP and DNS to make your life easier in ways that are often a luxury for smaller environments but a necessity for larger sites. In addition to automating the setup of hosts and locating services, though, you can also use network services to provide a more robust security environment with little effort thanks to Mac OS X Server. The two main services that we'll cover in order to do so are VPN and RADIUS.

Although Mac OS X Server does make it easy to deploy your own VPN and RADIUS servers, it's not going to be entirely plug-and-play for many network environments. A virtual private network (VPN) may sound complicated, but that's only if you've never used the VPN service that comes in Mac OS X Server. In a Mac OS X Server–based environment, you can often be up and running with a VPN in only a few minutes, which brings up a very valid question: why might you need a VPN? For many system administrators, a VPN allows them to provide access to remote users as though they were on the local network. The access is only as fast as the links and so typically slower, but from a security standpoint, remote users can be treated as local users when using a VPN.

As we discussed in Chapter 5, when we were covering setting up routing and firewalling, you want to keep the ports coming into your network at a minimum. The VPN service allows you to open up very few ports because users will communicate with services inside your network as though they were on it, using an encrypted tunnel. Because the VPN service is so useful, it is one of the most common network services that is used to secure an environment, so we will review setting up a VPN server and managing it in this chapter.

A VPN is traditionally used to connect remote users into your environment securely. RADIUS, on the other hand, is meant to be a bridge between existing devices. Remote Authentication Dial In User Service (RADIUS) can help take the security of your wireless network to the next level beyond standard WPA authentication. Prior to Leopard RADIUS, communications could be obtained using Elektron or OpenRADIUS running on OS X, but in Leopard, no third-party software is required beyond Mac OS X Server.

You will likely look to RADIUS if your environment has third-party solutions that can leverage RADIUS for centralizing usernames and passwords. This may seem similar to the Open Directory service covered in Chapter 4, but Open Directory is meant for clients, whereas RADIUS is meant more for providing accounts from the directory service to be used on appliances, such as VPN appliances, wireless access points (such as the Apple AirPort), and telephony devices.

Implementing a VPN or RADIUS server will require you to open specific ports on your firewall if you'll be accessing the services remotely. Therefore, while we are covering each service, we'll also talk about which ports need to be opened on your firewall as well as any gotchas with regard to specific configuration settings you may want to use where it is appropriate to do so.

Virtual Private Networking

Earlier we described a VPN as a way to connect remote users to your office. We also mentioned that the VPN creates a tunnel that allows for the exchange of encrypted data between the remote client and the server. A number of network appliances such as the SonicWALL and Cisco devices have VPN functionality built into them. If you have an appliance that is working for you, Mac OS X Server will likely provide less functionality, but for many it will provide exactly the functionality they need.

Before you configure the VPN service, there are two main aspects to consider in a Mac OS X Server–based solution. The first is the protocol that you will be using to provide connectivity to client computers, and the second is the pool of IP addresses that the service will use to connect client computers.

There are two very different protocols to be used for serving and connecting to the VPN. The first is PPTP, and the second is L2TP. When possible, you should use L2TP. It is simply a more secure protocol. If it's more secure, then why are you still able to use PPTP? Well, PPTP is easier to set up because there is one less box to have to fill in on the client (or certificate to configure or token to use, according to which options you will use in your deployment), and it is more universally supported. However, L2TP is more secure and should therefore be chosen over PPTP whenever technically possible.

When you're setting up the services, they will each ask for a pool of IP addresses and a collection of other settings. The IP addresses are a dedicated DHCP range for that service and should not in any way overlap the IP address space supplied by other DHCP scopes. For example, let's say you will be installing a server for about 40 people. Of those 40, 8 people will need to access the network from a remote location. In addition, the organization has six other servers, and there are six printers. If you have a pool of IP addresses from 192.168.210.1 to 192.168.210.254, you will want to carve out different parts of that range to use for different purposes. As an example, you can use 192.168.210.2 through 192.168.210.10 for servers, use 192.168.210.11 through 192.168.210.20 for printers, use 192.168.210.21 through 192.168.210.30 for IP addresses to be handed out by L2TP, and then use a pool of 192.168.210.100 through 192.168.210.200 for the standard DHCP pool.

The more structured the approach, the less long-term hassle you will have. In this regard, it is wise to front-load a certain amount of future proofing so that you don't have to reconfigure services once you've put them into production. In the previous example, we have a couple of spare IP addresses to be handed off by the VPN service and about twice the size of the required IP addresses for the overall DHCP pool. We also have extra space for printers, and then there are a lot of IP addresses to still be provided to Voice over IP (VoIP) solutions and other devices that need IP addresses. Once could double most of these and still not fully saturate the available IP addresses for a network environment like the one mentioned earlier.

Once you have decided how large you want to make your DHCP pool, it's time to set up the server. Before setting up your VPN, first make sure that you have a functional Open Directory environment for VPN to use, as described in Chapter 4. Assuming that your Open Directory is fully functional, next open Server Admin from /Applications/Server, and click the name or IP address of the server that you will be installing the VPN service onto, as indicated in Figure 7–1.

Figure 7–1. *Enabling the VPN service*

Next, click the check box for the VPN service, and then click the Save button, which will result in the VPN service appearing under the name of the server in the SERVERS list.

Setting Up a PPTP Server

You can now configure the VPN server. If you choose to install and use PPTP, despite our recommendation to use L2TP instead, then let's look at how to do so first, since that is the simpler of the two to manage.

Before you set up the server, first consider the topology, and make the required changes to the network ports. PPTP uses port 1723 (UDP and TCP). With the exception of services that need to be public-facing, such as authoritative DNS, public web servers, and mail servers, many environments will need no ports open other than 1723. If you, like many businesses, have your web site with some web host (let's call it Fabrihost), then the host will more than likely also be happy to manage (if it's not already) your publicly facing DNS presence. Fabrihost, or another vendor, may even already also host your mail. In that case, if there is nothing that the general public needs from within your network environment, then you should be able to have VPN ports and only VPN ports open into your environment, leveraging those ports to gain access to other services rather than exposing all of those other services to the public.

Once you've decided what IP addresses to use, then open Server Admin, and click the VPN service for the server you will be setting up the VPN service to run on. From here, click the Settings icon in the Server Admin toolbar, and then click the PPTP tab. Next, select the Enable PPTP check box, as you can see in Figure 7–2.

Next, fill in the IP address range that will be handed out by the PPTP server. Enter the first IP address in the range of addresses to be provided in the "Starting IP address" field and the last contiguous IP address in the range to be provided into the "Ending IP address" field. The server will then provide IP addresses in the range by providing DHCP services to computers that log into the service.

Once you have configured the address range, you can choose which encryption levels to be provided to clients. If the client supports 128-bit encryption, then the server and client will negotiate a 128-bit encrypted tunnel. However, if the client does not support 128-bit encryption, then the server will negotiate a lower encryption algorithm (40-bit). You enable this option by selecting "Allow 40-bit encryption keys in addition to 128-bit." You should enable the 40-bit option only when absolutely required because it greatly reduces the encryption levels supported for PPTP clients.

Finally, it's time to configure the PPP authentication method to be used. The options are to use the directory service or to use RADIUS. If your server is running as an Open Directory master or is Kerberized against a directory services domain that supports Kerberos, then you can choose Directory Service in the PPP Authentication settings and then choose Kerberos from the Authentication field. (Kerberos is a protocol used for encrypting authentication; for more on Kerberos, see Chapter 4.) If the server has not joined a Kerberos realm and you will be pulling directory service information, use MS-CHAPv2. You can also choose RADIUS if you have a server's IP address and a shared secret, which would be entered into their corresponding fields.

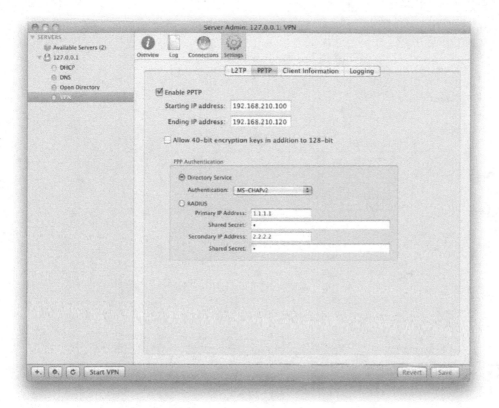

Figure 7-2. *Configuring PPTP settings*

To commit your changes to the PPTP service, click the Save button when you are finished with the configuration, and then click the Client Information tab. Here, you can choose the DNS servers that are provided to the client computers as part of their DHCP lease. You can also enter a search domain as you would in the Network pane in System Preferences for each adapter, as you would for standard client computers.

The final setting before you save your changes again and start the service is the Network Routing Definition setting (shown in Figure 7-3). Here, you can choose which traffic will be routed through the VPN and which will be routed through the default gateway for the default network interface of client systems. Here, use the plus (+) sign to provide an IP address, mask, and type for traffic. For example, if you wanted all traffic destined for 192.168.211.x IP addresses to be routed through the private network and that was a class C, then you would use 192.168.211.0 as the IP address and 255.255.255.0 as the mask. Then choose Private so traffic is routed over the tunnel, and click the OK button.

When you are satisfied with all of your PPTP settings, click Save, and then click the Start VPN button in the bottom toolbar of the screen.

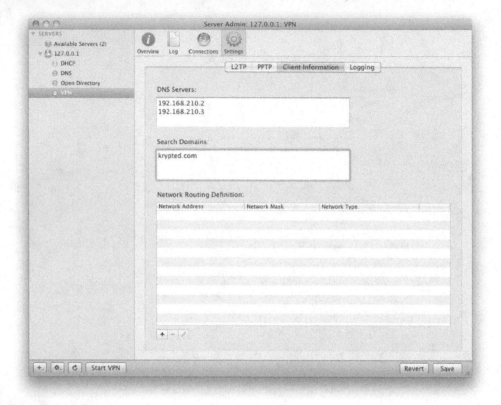

Figure 7–3. *VPN client information*

L2TP Servers

The L2TP server is similar to configuring PPTP except that there is an additional parameter of a key, which is used to establish trust with a host prior to sending a password over the connection to the server. This key can be a simple password, an SSL certificate, or even a physical hardware token such as an RSA token.

> **NOTE:** When using both PPTP and L2TP, they should have unique addresses that do not overlap with one another.

Although many of the settings are the same, you also have the option to enable load balancing and can choose an authentication mechanism for IPSec. Load balancing enables you to build a cluster of servers (multiple servers acting as one server) to distribute the resources required to manage traffic. You would use load balancing if you have enough clients to cause the VPN processes to adversely affect server performance during peak load times. IPSec authentication allows you to choose whether clients will use an SSL certificate or a simple password to authenticate to the server. SSL certificates (which are covered more fully later in this chapter) are going to be the more secure of the two choices. However, if you use an SSL certificate, then you will need to distribute the certificate to clients when configuring them (also covered later in this chapter).

Once the VPN service has been enabled, to configure it to serve L2TP, click the VPN service in Server Admin for the server you will be setting up, and then click the Settings icon in the Server Admin toolbar. From here, click the Enable L2TP over IPSec check box, and provide a beginning and ending IP address for clients, as you did previously in the "Setting Up a PPTP Server" section of this chapter. For example, in Figure 7–4 we configured a starting IP address of 192.168.1.128 and an ending IP address of 192.168.1.254, which provides us with half of a class C of IP addresses for clients to use with the L2TP service.

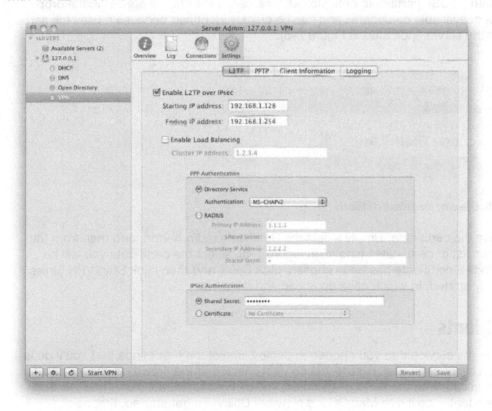

Figure 7–4. *Configuring L2TP*

Next, choose whether to configure two L2TP servers. If you select the Enable Load Balancing check box, then you will be able to have a second server. Each server should reference the other in the "Cluster IP address" field.

Now it's time to set up how authentication will work on your server. First, configure the PPP authentication settings as described in the "Setting Up a PPTP Server" section of this chapter. In addition to the standard PPP authentication, you will also need to set up IPSec authentication. To do so, you can just use a shared secret, which is simply a password used as a preshared key. The server will need the client to submit its shared secret prior to accepting a username and password to authenticate into the VPN.

> **NOTE:** If you are using a shared secret, then all of the clients will need the same secret typed in that the server is using.

You can alternatively use a certificate, which leverages SSL. The SSL certificate should be installed on the server prior to enabling this feature (as is described in Chapter 3). You can install the service now and then configure the SSL certificate later, but it is best to configure the certificate first when possible (keep in mind that Mac OS X Server comes with an SSL certificate preinstalled). The certificate should appear in the drop-down list of available certificates and can be quickly identified because it uses the same name as the server (indicated in Figure 7–5).

Figure 7–5. *Choosing the default certificate*

To choose the certificate, simply select the Certificate radio button, and then from the drop-down list of certificates (shown in Figure 7–5), select the certificate you will be using. Once a certificate has been chosen, click Save, and then click Start VPN (unless it's already started, in which case go ahead and restart it).

VPN Clients

No matter the service that you choose to deploy, one of the first things that you'll do is connect a client computer. Before you do, first check that the firewall is allowing traffic to communicate with the service. To do so, you can use a standard port scanner such as the one that is built into Mac OS X's Network Utility. To get started, first open Network Utility from /Applications/Utilities, and click the Port Scan tab. Here, click in the "Enter an internet or IP address to scan for open ports" field. In the field, provide the host name or IP address of the server (as shown in Figure 7–6).

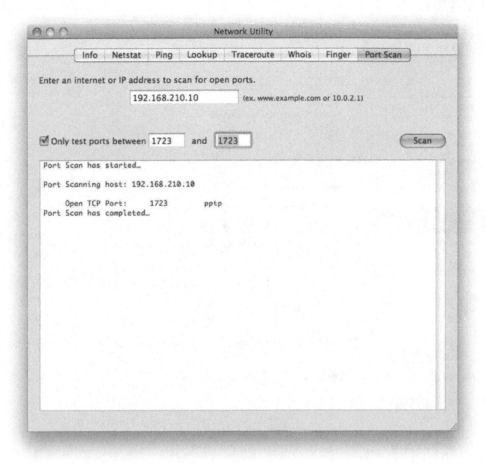

Figure 7–6. *Port scanning*

Once you have provided the IP address or host name to scan, click the "Only test ports between" check box, and enter **1723** for PPTP. When you are satisfied, click the Scan button, and you should see the port listed as Open TCP Port, provided it is running. If it is not running, then after a timeout interval, the scan will not list any entries.

Setting up a Mac OS X client to communicate over PPTP to a Mac OS X Server (or a third-party PPTP client for that matter) is built into the Network pane of System Preferences. To configure PPTP, open System Preferences, and authenticate to the service if the lock on the screen is in the locked position. Then click Network. From here, click the plus (+) sign below the list of services, as shown in Figure 7–7.

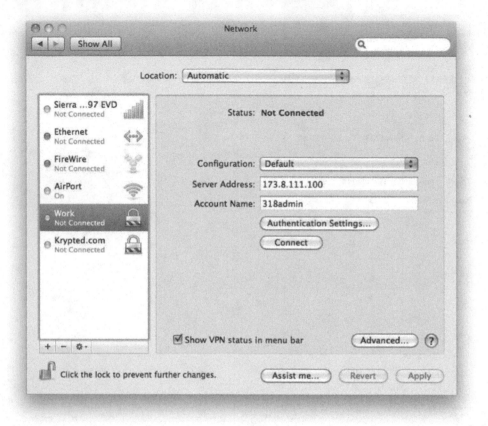

Figure 7–7. *The Network pane*

The resultant dialog will start with a field for the interface that you will be configuring, as you can see in Figure 7–8. Clicking in this field will open a number of options. Click VPN.

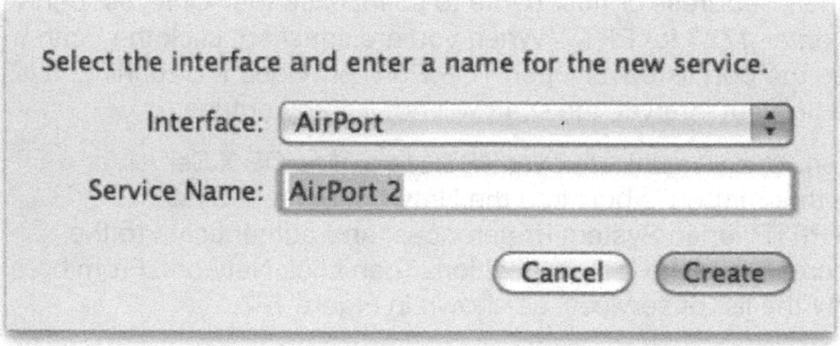

Figure 7–8. *Adding a new network interface*

Clicking VPN will add a field called VPN Type, as shown in Figure 7–9.

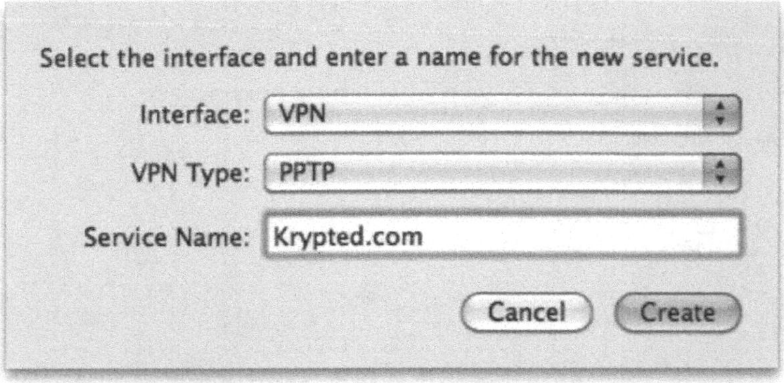

Select the interface and enter a name for the new service.

Interface: [VPN   ◆]

VPN Type: [PPTP   ◆]

Service Name: [Krypted.com   ]

(Cancel)   (Create)

Figure 7–9. *Adding a new VPN interface*

As you can see in Figure 7 10, the options available under the VPN Type field are L2TP over IPSec, PPTP, and Cisco IPSec. The first two are used to connect to your Mac OS X Server, and the third is used to connect to a Cisco-based VPN. Choose the option that maps to the service that you configured in the previous section (either L2TP or PPTP).

✓ L2TP over IPSec

PPTP

Cisco IPSec

Figure 7–10. *Choosing a VPN type*

Whichever VPN type you select, the next screen will look the same. Here, provide an address for the VPN server (the WAN address for users tapping in from outside your network), an account name (the username in your server), and an encryption level, as shown in Figure 7–11.

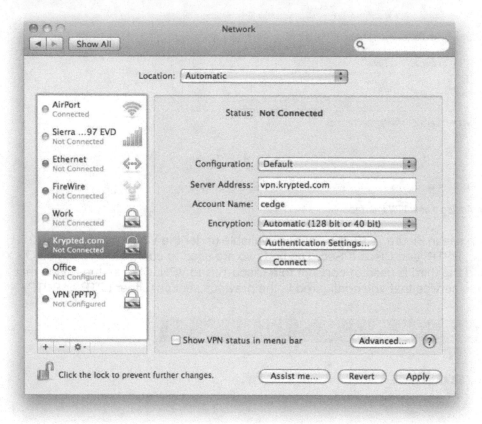

Figure 7–11. *VPN settings*

Next, click the Authentication Settings button. You can now see the main difference between the PPTP and L2TP configurations as they're implemented in Mac OS X client. Figure 7–12 shows the L2TP screen; the PPTP screen is identical with the exception that it doesn't have the Machine Authentication and Group Name sections. If you are using PPTP, then you will just enter the password for the account previously defined in the Password field (unless you will be using another form of authentication). If you are using L2TP, you will also need to enter the shared secret or select the SSL certificate, which would then need to be imported prior to it appearing in the list of available certificates.

NOTE: If the certificate is installed correctly, then it will have the same name in Keychain Utility that you saw in the Server Admin VPN service screen when you enabled the certificate.

User Authentication:

- ● Password: [   ]
- ○ RSA SecurID
- ○ Certificate (Select...)
- ○ Kerberos
- ○ CryptoCard

Machine Authentication:

- ● Shared Secret: [   ]
- ○ Certificate   (Select...)

Group Name: [   ]

(Optional)

(Cancel) (OK)

Figure 7–12. *Configuring the shared secret or certificate*

Click OK when you are satisfied with your authentication settings, and then click the Advanced button, which will open a dialog box similar to the Advanced Settings for a standard network interface, with the exception that the first two tabs provide VPN-specific settings. The Options tab allows you to configure global settings for the connection, including the following (as shown in Figure 7–13):

- *Disconnect when switching user accounts*: Terminates the VPN connection when you log out of the client or use fast user switching.

- *Disconnect when user logs out*: Terminates the VPN connection when you log out of the client.

- *Send all traffic over VPN connection*: Ignores the order that network adapters are installed and sends all traffic over the VPN tunnel

- *Disconnect if idle for*: Sets a timeout for VPN connections. If no network traffic is sent over the tunnel before the time expires, then the connection will be terminated.

- *Use verbose logging*: Log more than is logged by default.

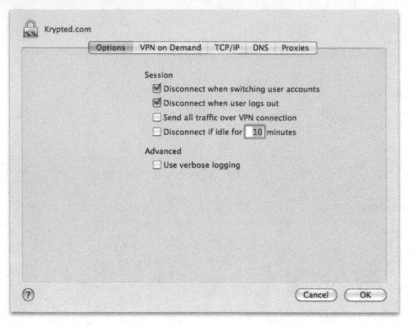

Figure 7–13. *VPN options*

The VPN on Demand tab will allow you to configure automatic connections when the client computer attempts to connect to one of the domains in the Domain list, which you can see in Figure 7–14.

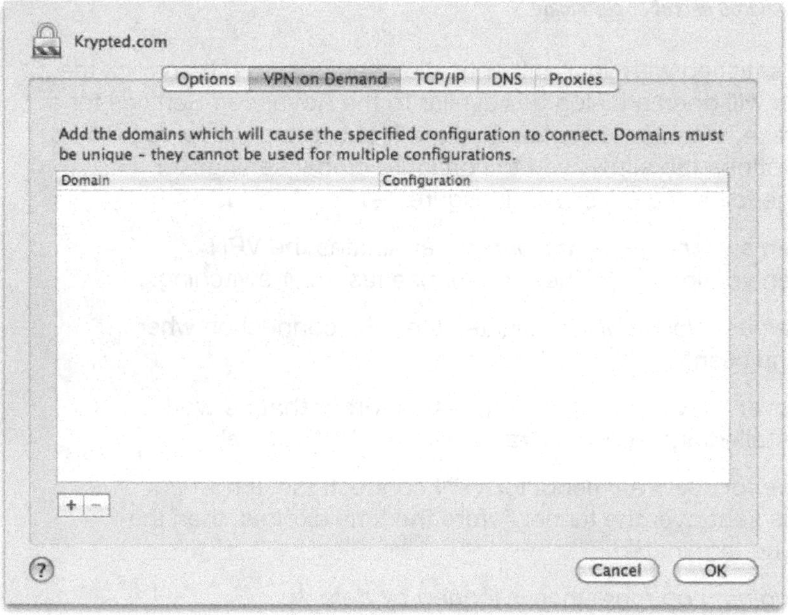

Figure 7–14. *VPN on Demand*

NOTE: The remaining tabs are TCP/IP, DNS, and Proxies and are similar to the advanced networking tabs for any other adapter.

Once all of your settings are as needed, provided you set up the menu bar icon for the VPN connections, you can use it to connect. Simply click the VPN icon in the menu bar, and the VPN contextual menu item will appear. Here, any VPN connections that have been configured for the computer will appear with the word *Connect* in front of them, as you can see in Figure 7–15. Click one to test it.

Figure 7–15. *Connecting to the VPN using the menu item*

Once you have configured and tested a VPN connection, you can then export so that it can be imported into other computers. This makes deploying the VPN connection to a large number of computers a trivial process. To export the configuration, click it from the Network pane of System Preferences, and then click the cogwheel icon below the list. This will open a listing of options where you can choose Export Configurations, as shown in Figure 7–16.

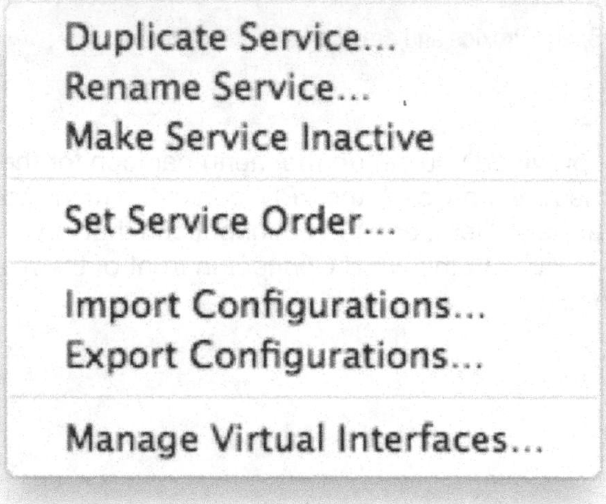

> Duplicate Service...
> Rename Service...
> Make Service Inactive
>
> Set Service Order...
>
> Import Configurations...
> Export Configurations...
>
> Manage Virtual Interfaces...

Figure 7–16. *Network service options*

Here you can choose a location to which to back up the configuration, whether you want to back up user-based configurations or the default configuration, and whether you want to export the connected items from the keychain. As you can see in Figure 7–17, if you choose to export certificates, then they will not be secure from the time they are exported until they are imported into the Keychain on the client computer. Therefore, transporting the certificates only to trusted parties will help keep your environment secure. However, including the certificate will ease your deployment of the VPN client. Where possible, distribute the certificate in your system image (more on imaging in Chapter 8), and deploy user configurations of the VPN settings separately.

Once they're exported, you can then import VPN configurations on other client computers. To do so, copy the resultant VPN configuration file (indicated by) to a client, and click the cogwheel icon from another client. Here, you can select Import Configurations, browsing to the file that was generated before importing.

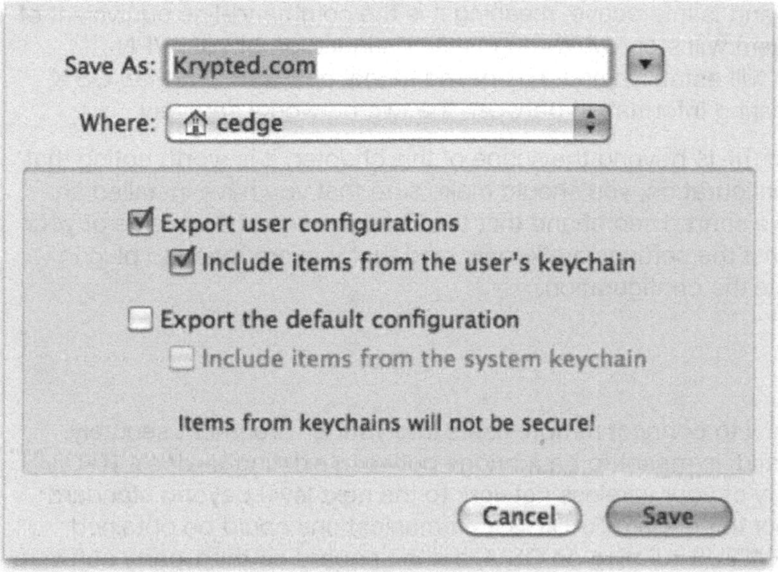

Figure 7-17. *Exporting VPN configurations*

Configuring the VPN from the Command Line

The serveradmin command is used for most VPN-oriented configurations of Mac OS X Server from the command line. To get started, first use the serveradmin command along with the status verb, which will show you whether the VPN is currently running:

Serveradmin status vpn

Next, query the server for its fullstatus, which will show a number of settings and the status:

Serveradmin fullstatus vpn

Finally, use the settings verb. In its most basic form, the settings verb will display a listing of settings for the VPN service:

Serveradmin settings vpn

Overall, this type of management exposes a number of settings not exposed within Server Admin but without altering any configuration files that can cause the service from Server Admin to overwrite your configuration files.

S2SVPN

In addition to a VPN that a client computer will connect to, you will also often have a second site. This site may have multiple employees, therefore making it inefficient to have each client connect to the VPN. So, you can use Mac OS X as a bridge between two physical networks, perhaps in different cities, by leveraging the s2svpnadmin command.

The s2svpnadmin command is interactive, meaning it is the command-line equivalent of a wizard. The menu system will step you through the configuration of your VPN environment. This setup will establish an L2TP-based tunnel between two Mac OS X Servers and allow for sharing information between the two networks securely.

Although using s2svpnadmin is beyond the scope of this chapter, it is worth noting that before you attempt a configuration, you should make sure that you have installed an SSL certificate to act as a shared secret and that the IP addresses of each side of your VPN tunnel are online, that the settings are known, and that you are ready to plug in information and complete the configuration.

RADIUS

A VPN is traditionally used to connect remote users into your environment securely. RADIUS, on the other hand, is meant to be a bridge between existing devices. RADIUS can help take the security of your wireless network to the next level beyond standard WPA authentication. Prior to Leopard RADIUS, communications could be obtained using Elektron or OpenRADIUS running on OS X, but in Leopard no third-party software is required beyond Leopard Server.

Setting Up the RADIUS Service

The first step to using RADIUS is to enable it. To do so, open Server Admin, click the name of the server in the SERVERS list, and click the Services tab. Find RADIUS in the services list, and place a check mark in the box to the left of it. When you click Save, then you should see RADIUS in the SERVERS list, as shown in Figure 7–18.

Once the RADIUS service has been enabled, select a certificate (and you should be using a certificate with this service even if you are not using one for any other services). For our purposes, we are going to use the default certificate that comes with Mac OS X Server. Click RADIUS under the SERVERS list, and then click the Settings button to see the screen shown in Figure 7–19. Click the RADIUS Certificate drop-down menu, and select the default certificate.

> **NOTE:** Click the Edit Allowed Users button to invoke the screen mentioned later in this chapter in the "Limiting Access to the VPN and RADIUS Services" section.

From here, click RADIUS, and then click the Start RADIUS button in the bottom-left corner of the screen. RADIUS is now ready to accept authentication. The next step is to configure a third-party device to work with RADIUS. In the next section we'll cover how to leverage RADIUS with the Apple AirPort base station.

Figure 7–18. *Enabling the RADIUS service*

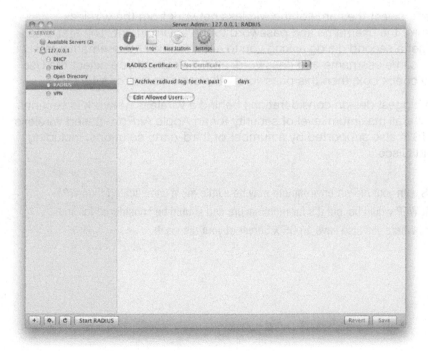

Figure 7–19. *Configuring the RADIUS service*

> **NOTE:** Although the default certificate will work for clients, things are often easier from a deployment and interoperability perspective if you purchase a certificate from a certificate authority such as Thawte. You can find more on certificates in Chapter 3.

Setting Up the Apple AirPort

Once you have configured the RADIUS server, you'll likely want to leverage it to provide centralized authentication services to other devices (otherwise why install it in the first place other than possibly for academic interests?). One of the best examples of using RADIUS in a Mac OS X–based environment is to use WPA 2 Enterprise rather than WPA 2 Personal because they're implemented on the AirPort base station, Apple's proprietary 802.11 solution. The WPA 2 Personal uses only a password as an authenticator. However, WPA 2 Enterprise can use both a username and a password if you have a RADIUS server to tie the AirPort base station into.

To configure an Apple AirPort to leverage the RADIUS server in Mac OS X Server, click the Base Stations button in the toolbar at the top of the RADIUS screen in Server Admin. Then click Browse and then select the first base station of your new wireless environment from the list of found base stations. Enter the password for the AirPort in the Base station password field (which you can see in Figure 7–20), and then click Save. Wait for the AirPort to complete its restart, and then you should be able to log in from a client.

To log in from a client, select the name of the wireless network from the wireless networks list, and enter the username and password to the environment. The first time you do so, you will get a second dialog asking you to enter the 802.1x username and password. Enter the same username and password, and click OK. If you select the Use this Password Once check box, then this password will not be saved for future use.

Because one of the biggest design considerations behind a wireless network is security, RADIUS offers the overall maximum level of security for an Apple AirPort–based wireless solution. But RADIUS is also supported by a number of third-party solutions, including HP, SonicWALL, and Cisco.

> **TIP:** Using RADIUS with your AirPort environment may be a little more complicated than WPA-Personal or 128-bit WEP would be, but it's far more secure and should be considered for any AirPort environment where you also have an OS X Server at your disposal.

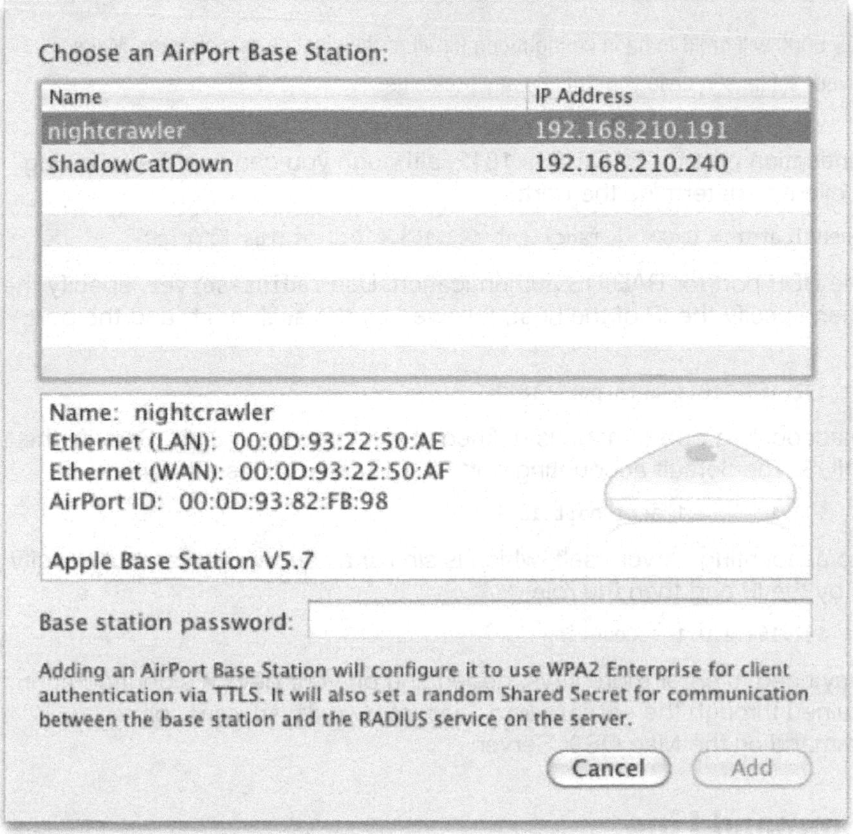

Figure 7-20. *Adding an AirPort*

Connecting to Cisco

Mac OS X Server has a RADIUS service. The Cisco MDS 9000 is becoming a pretty common Fibre Channel switch to use in Xsan environments, which often have an Open Directory server running. If you enable the RADIUS service, you can then have the MDS 9000 authenticate administrative and monitoring users over RADIUS so that you continue to centralize your authentication services. To get started, first put the MDS into config mode using the `config` command with a t option:

```
config t
```

The following command specifies the preshared key for the selected RADIUS server. This should be the same as the preshared key you use in your Mac OS X Server's RADIUS configuration, specified using the `radius-server` key command. Here, the host is 192.168.210.1, and the key isKrYpTeD (although in your case it would be the same as the one you used to configure AirPort if using WPA2 Enterprise, for example).

```
radius-server host 192.168.210.1 key KrYpTeD
```

NOTE: Your MDS 9000 will need to be in config mode for all of the steps in this chapter. Make sure to back up your settings in case you run into any problems.

The default authentication port for RADIUS is 1812, although you can use the following command from a client to determine the port:

```
echo "Message-Authenticator = 0x00" | radclient 192.168.210.1 status KrYpTeD
```

Next, configure the UDP port for RADIUS authentication. Use `radius-server`, specify the host again, and then specify the IP of the host, followed by the `auth-port` and the port number:

```
radius-server host 192.168.210.1 auth-port 1812
```

Next, provide the accounting port (if none is defined, it will try to use 1813). Specify the UDP port for RADIUS. The default accounting port is 1813, so we'll use that here:

```
radius-server host 192.168.210.1 acct-port 1813
```

Next configure the accounting server itself, which is similar as shown earlier, but specify the host followed by the IP and then the role:

```
radius-server host 192.168.210.1 accounting
```

Next, test. You may need to enter more keys, depending on your device's configuration, which can be obtained through the `serveradmin`, `eap.conf/radiusd.conf`, or `radiusconfig` command on the Mac OS X Server.

From the Command Line

Mac OS X comes with a set of tools that can be used to configure RADIUS. The first, as with many services, is the `serveradmin` command.

Apple also includes a tool specific to managing RADIUS. The `radiusconfig` tool, located in the `/usr/sbin` directory, can be used to access some of the RADIUS options not otherwise accessed in Server Admin or `serveradmin`. You can also edit many of these settings directly in the RADIUS configuration files: `/etc/raddb/eap.conf` or `/etc/raddb/radiusd.conf`. If you will be using `radiusconfig`, the following indicates what various options will do:

- -addclient: Allows you to add clients
- -appleversion: Displays the version number
- -enable-tls: Enables SSL
- -disable-tls: Disables SSL
- -getconfig: Shows information from the `radiusd.conf` and `eap.conf`
- -getconfigxml: Shows information from the `radiusd.conf` and `eap.conf` in XML

- -importclients: Allows you to import clients

- -nascount: Shows the number of clients connected through RADIUS

- -naslist: Shows the clients connected through RADIUS

- -naslistxml: Shows the clients connected through RADIUS in XML

- -removeclient: Allows you to remove connected clients

- -setgroup: Allows you to change the SACL information (more on SACLs later in this chapter)

- -ver: Shows the version number

- -help: Shows the help screen

- -q: Runs quietly, suppressing prompts

Limiting Access to the VPN and RADIUS Services

By default, all users have access to the VPN and RADIUS services. But in many environments, only a select number of users will need to access the VPN service or the RADIUS service (or devices interconnected to the directory service by virtue of the RADIUS service).

To limit access to either service, configure a service access control list for the service. To do so, open Server Admin, and then click the name of the server running the service (VPN or RADIUS). Next, click the Access button in the Server Admin toolbar. Here, click the "For Selected Services below" radio button. Then click RADIUS in the Service list. Click Allow Only Users and Groups Below, and then click the plus (+) sign. Now drag the users and groups into the Name list from the Users and Groups window. Once all users who should have access to your new wireless environment have been enabled, click the Save button.

HINT: When possible, do not manage individual users here, or they will become a nightmare to keep track of. Instead, create groups of users, and use those whenever possible.

Summary

VPN is one of the most critical services for the road warriors in your organization. The VPN service in Mac OS X Server is easily integrated into all of the other services that are hosted on that server, including the database of usernames and passwords stored in Open Directory. Although the VPN server can provide services using either the PPTP or L2TP protocol, L2TP is more secure and so should be used when possible. But VPN is not the only service that Mac OS X Server can provide to help secure the network infrastructure; you can also leverage RADIUS.

Although RADIUS is currently not deployed with the frequency that VPN is, it is important to keep in mind that whether it is a switch, a router, a third-party VPN service, or wireless networking equipment, RADIUS can help bring the same level of security to your internal network that VPN brings to the perimeter network. The number of devices that support RADIUS is growing rapidly, and although the RADIUS service in Mac OS X Server is compliant with the protocol, with new protocols there are always a number of potential interpretations. So, if you are working with a third-party service, you may have a bit of manual (in other words, command-line) configuration that you will need to do. Therefore, we covered how to use RADIUS to provide usernames and passwords from Open Directory for your Cisco devices.

Now that you have a functional and secure server and network environment, it's time to focus on setting up the computers that will then access these services. To automate much of the process of setting up workstations in your environment, we will cover deployment technologies in Chapter 8, looking at the NetBoot service and its cousins NetInstall and NetRestore. These three solutions give administrators a way to deploy a few to a few thousand computers based on two Apple technologies that have been around for a long time, maturing with each iteration: asr and NetBoot.

Managing Client Computers with NetBoot, NetInstall, and NetRestore

Mac OS X Server's NetBoot service provides systems administrators with the tools for quickly creating and managing systems and user environments for computers on the network. As a result, you have an unprecedented amount of control over the end user experience, since many of the processes and tasks that are typically associated with desktop administration can now be consolidated into the realm of the server admin.

Many Mac administrators begin their first foray into configuring and deploying multiple computers by simply duplicating one preconfigured master system to another computer over FireWire using Apple's Disk Utility or other disk duplication tools such as Carbon Copy Cloner. Other systems administrators might have created a disk image, or DMG file, from that master system and then cloned multiple systems from that image file, again using a FireWire or USB drive. Although this technique can eliminate the time required for installing the operating system and all of the supporting applications and settings on each individual system, it still does not scale well beyond a handful of computers. What does a sysadmin do when confronted with hundreds or thousands of systems that need to be booted, configured, installed, or imaged at the same time? Enter Mac OS X Server's NetBoot service.

NetBoot uses three different methods to provide you with this control over network systems: NetBoot, NetInstall, and NetRestore. It is important to understand the differences between these different functions:

■   With NetBoot, you are creating an image that will be hosted on the
    server and booted up by other systems on the network. In this
    configuration, systems will use the hosted disk image as their
    operating system. This is an ideal solution for managing a lab of
    computers that requires a uniform collection of applications and
    system settings. Because all the systems are booting from the disk
    image hosted on the central server, it is simple and easy to manage
    the client systems, since you are maintaining and hosting only a single
    system image instead of the entire network of workstations. If you
    need to make configuration changes such as software updates or
    additional applications, you can simply modify the original system and
    share the changed image with NetBoot.

■   With NetInstall, you are creating a bootable disk image from an
    installation CD or DVD in order to install the operating system onto one
    or more network clients. In its simplest form, NetInstall can be used as
    a substitute for inserting the installation disc into a system, allowing
    you to install the operating system interactively just as you would
    when booting up from the CD or DVD. If you create a network disk
    image of the installation media with the NetInstall Image option, then
    you can also create an installer that will be automated. This allows you
    to select preset options such as creating user accounts, setting the
    computer name, installing custom packages, and other steps.

■   With NetRestore, you are using Mac OS X Server to duplicate the
    contents of a hard disk image file to client systems on the network.
    NetRestore is a fantastic solution for quickly duplicating a master
    image to large numbers of computers. NetRestore uses NetBoot to
    transparently provide a thin boot environment for each so that the
    client computer's internal disk can be reimaged with the contents of
    the disk image. With this method, you will be able to repartition and
    restore images block by block, which is a faster means of transferring
    data than file by file.

All of these features are provided using a combination of System Image Utility to build
images and the NetBoot service to share them. In this chapter, we will start off with
creating images of various types in System Image Utility. We will then move on to
serving those images on the server and connecting to them from Mac OS X computers.

In this chapter, we will also look into some limited automations that can be used during
deployment. As your environment grows, automation is key to keeping the amount of
time required to install each computer at a minimum. Automator, the popular tool
included in Mac OS X, serves as a building block for these automations. Additionally, as
we will show, you can also use scripting languages to further automate processes, thus
getting as few human interactions as possible with the systems being imaged, which is
critical when deploying large numbers of computers.

We'll also explain how to set up a network restore workflow using Apple Software
Restore, or asr, Apple's robust terminal command that can use multicast streaming to

deploy images to much larger collections of computers than the unicast-only NetRestore function. We'll hit this in more detail later in the chapter.

Before you start trying to build an image, you will need a computer or a Mac OS X 10.6 disk to base the image on. You will also need to determine an appropriate strategy to use for imaging, so we'll cover that before we show how to create any images.

Developing an Imaging Strategy

In Mac OS X (and most operating systems), there are varying degrees of complexity you can take with your imaging strategy. It's easiest to introduce these strategies by looking at how imaging often matures. Most environments will start off imaging simply by copying a perfectly prepared and installed computer to other computers over portable media. For the purpose of this chapter, we will call this process *local imaging*, because this is done on local computers rather than over a network. The next step is often to take the concept and cast those images over a network, which we will call *network imaging*.

Those large images served over a network will typically be prepared with all of the software that needs to be installed. Little is automated in this type of imaging environment, but hey, at least you're not walking around and sitting down at 30 computers a day. If you are restoring an entire disk to a client, then this is known as *monolithic imaging*.

The problem with monolithic imaging is primarily with updates. Each time an update comes out, if you want to put that update on the image, you will then need to create an entirely new image, which can take hours. Therefore, many will break the image down into its various components. These components will invariably include a bare metal image, which is an image that installs only the operating system, uniquely adapted to each computer. In addition, each piece of software will typically be installed separately. This process is known as *package-based imaging*, because the Mac OS X installers are packages. By breaking down each piece of software into a separate package installer, you can then allocate software based on users, groups, and other attributes. You can also take those packages and install them for computers that have already been imaged using Apple Remote Desktop or third-party products such as the Casper Suite from JAMF Software. Package-based imaging is typically the most mature of the imaging environments, and therefore it will demand a higher degree of acumen and experience to set up and maintain this imaging strategy.

Which is best for you? The best one is the one that offers the most mature approach while still giving you the tools that you need and still being manageable. If the methodology is too complex, then you are likely to abandon it, so our suggestion is to read through this entire chapter before you install a single thing. Given how much data is on a modern operating system, it can take a long time to generate images and test them. It can also be disastrous if you push out a bad image to 200 or 20,000 computers. Therefore, more than any other service in Mac OS X Server, we recommend that you "measure twice, cut once" even more carefully with system imaging.

Activating the NetBoot Service

The first step to setting up the NetBoot service is to enable the service in Server Admin. To do so, first open Server Admin from /Applications/Server. After authenticating, click the name of the server where you will be installing the service onto, and open the server's base settings. Here, click the Settings button in the Server Admin toolbar to open the services selection screen, where you can configure which services will run on the server (although simply enabling them in this screen will not start them), as shown in Figure 8–1.

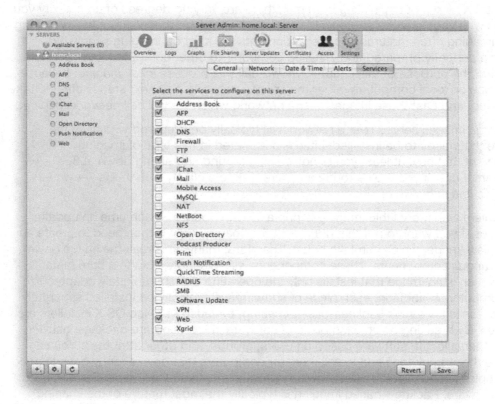

Figure 8–1. *Enabling the NetBoot service*

Select the NetBoot service, and then click the Save button. You should then see the service appear in the SERVERS list when you click the disclosure triangle to show the active services on the server. Click the Settings icon in the Server Admin toolbar to open the settings that Apple has provided for that service. You cannot actually start the service until you have prepared an image to share over clients. Therefore, at this point, we will move on to doing so with System Image Utility.

Using System Image Utility

Once you have enabled the NetBoot service, it is time to create your first image. You will need to open the /Applications/Server directory and launch System Image Utility. System Image Utility is the application that you can use to set up an image, configure automations for your images, and prepare your images to be served to client computers.

When you open System Image Utility, the application will scan for any volumes of your computer that are valid sources from which to create images. Valid sources can include a computer whose volume you have prepared to be your monolithic image (by installing all the needed software for your environment), the installation media for Mac OS X, or a mounted disk image. If System Image Utility does not find any valid images, then you will simply see an error that no valid sources for creating an image were found, as shown in Figure 8–2.

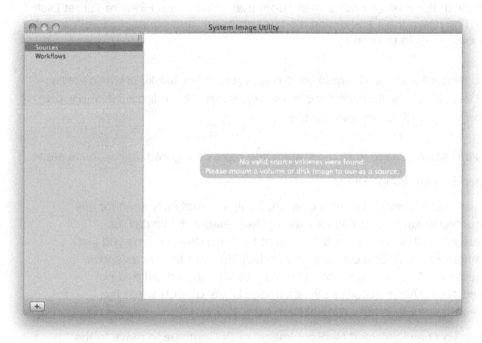

Figure 8–2. *System Image Utility with no valid sources*

At this point, we will show how to connect a volume with an appropriate configuration into the computer so you can evaluate your options for setting up NetBoot.

Creating a NetBoot Image

As discussed earlier in the chapter, NetBoot allows other systems on the network to boot from a system image file hosted on your server. This is an effective means of setting up kiosk computers, providing bootable repair utilities, and pointing client computers at an image to boot from, such as in a lab environment. With NetBoot, you can create a uniform operating environment for network systems to start up from, without necessarily needing to install it onto the client systems' internal drives. In fact, your client systems can use a NetBoot server without having any internal hard drives of their own!

A NetBoot image is one of the easiest to create. This is because NetBoot images typically do not require the custom automations that are inherent with NetInstall, and NetBoot images also do not have many requirements outside the NetBoot service itself, unlike NetRestore. Before getting started, prepare a volume on a computer with the operating system, software, and any settings that you would like computers to have when they boot to the image that you will be creating. In short, create a system environment of settings, applications, folders, and so on, that you would like your users to use when they boot up and log in. For example, you might prepare a system with Mac OS X 10.6, iWork, and Microsoft Office. When you are satisfied that the system has been configured with the desired environment, boot that volume into FireWire Target Disk Mode (holding down the T key during the boot process), and connect a FireWire cable from that computer to the server.

> **NOTE:** There are a number of ways to get an image onto a server that do not involve directly connecting the server to the client; however, for the purposes of this chapter, this is going to be the most straightforward mechanism to do so.

To create a NetBoot image from the system you have configured, follow these steps:

1. Open System Image Utility.

2. When System Image Utility is opened, it will automatically scan for any mounted volumes that can be used for NetRestore, NetInstall, or NetBoot. In this case, click the name of the hard drive volume you just configured under Sources, and then select NetBoot Image, as shown in Figure 8–3. Note that the option for NetInstall is grayed out and not selectable. This is because System Image Utility detected that the selected volume is not an installation disc.

3. Once you have selected NetBoot Image, click Continue to move to the next step.

4. Next you will provide a name and a description for your image. Enter the name in the Network Disk field and an informative description in the Description field. As you can see in Figure 8–4, the Description field can contain any information about the image that you don't necessarily want to be stored in the name itself.

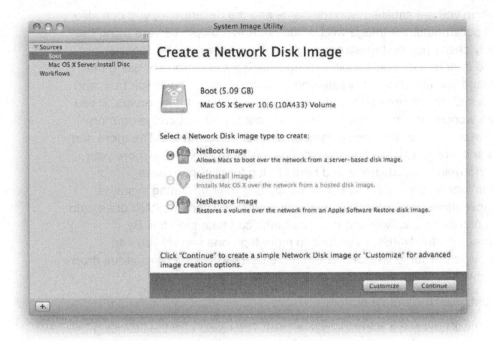

Figure 8–3. *Choosing an image type*

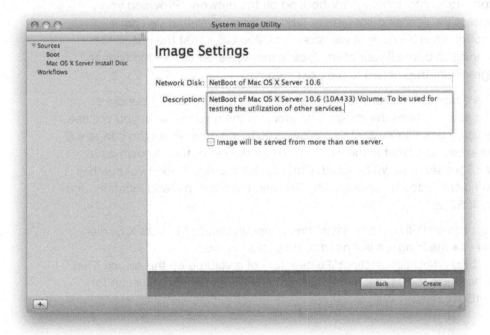

Figure 8–4. *Image settings in System Image Utility*

5. When you are satisfied with the name and the description, you can also select whether the image will be hosted from multiple servers using the only check box on this screen. If you will have 2 or 20 NetBoot servers and if more than one will be hosting a NetBoot environment using the image you are about to create, then you can enable the check box, and the system will prepare the image for hosting on multiple servers. If you are wondering why you would want to host a NetBoot image on more than one server, the answer is quite simple: performance. The more end user systems you are booting from the NetBoot server, the more your performance will degrade and begin to lag for all those users. Remember, your client systems are loading their operating systems, applications, and even their user space from the server's hard drive, and all of that disk activity and network traffic can take their toll. By spreading the NetBoot services to more than one server, you can provide the same environment to more users without a precipitous drop in overall system performance.

6. Next, click the Create button.

7. You will now see a licensing agreement. The reason for the licensing agreement is that you are accepting the licensing agreement for your NetBoot clients, because they will use the operating system you are converting into an image for booting off the network. Provided you accept the licensing agreement (and thereby affirm that you have enough valid licenses of the version of Mac OS X that the image is running to boot all your clients), click the Agree button for the license agreement to proceed to the next step.

8. The name of the image is not the same as the name of the bundle of files that contains the image. Therefore, at the next window, you will see a dialog box (Figure 8–5) that allows you to indicate where the image will be saved and what name will be used for the set of files, known as a *NetBoot set*, that will be used. Confirm that the destination volume has sufficient space to store the image. Then enter a name and location, and click Save.

9. You can save the image anywhere, although before Mac OS X Server will use the image, it will need to be copied to the /Library/NetBoot/NetBootSP0 directory of a volume on the server. That directory is the default location that the NetBoot service will scan for NetBoot sets.

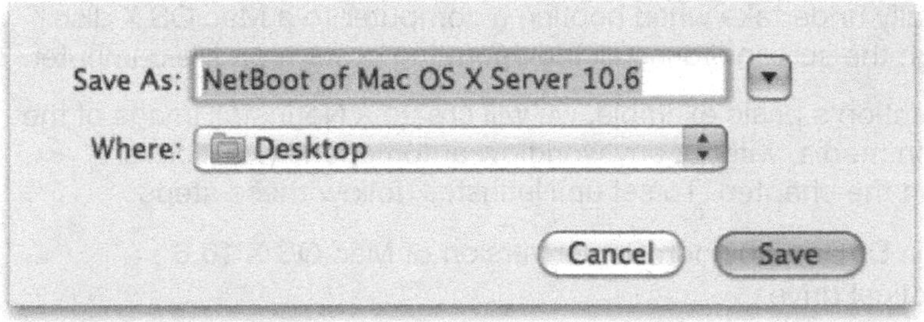

Figure 8–5. *Choosing a location for your image*

10. Because System Image Utility will need root-level access to the volume from which you are generating your image, you will then need to authenticate as an administrator. Provide the username and password, as shown in Figure 8–6, and then click the OK button.

Figure 8-6

Figure 8–6. *Authenticating for imaging*

11. At this point, be prepared to wait for quite some time while the disk image is created. Depending on how large your NetBoot image is, you may need to wait only 30 minutes. However, for larger images, you can be waiting for upwards of a few hours. Once your image is created, you will then be able to complete setting up the NetBoot service, which requires an image to start.

Creating a NetInstall Image

As discussed earlier in the chapter, NetInstall is the component of the NetBoot service that automates the installation process of Mac OS X to other computers on your network. You can prepare and deploy a standard disk image of a Mac OS X DVD for a handful or thousands of computers. Think of NetInstall as a means of streamlining the process you would normally undertake when booting a computer to a Mac OS X disc and then stepping through the screens to install the operating system on the computer.

For the purpose of this section's basic example, we will create a NetInstall image of the Mac OS X DVD installation media, without any workflow automations (we'll cover automations a little later in the chapter). To set up NetInstall, follow these steps:

1. Insert an installation DVD for the non-Server version of Mac OS X 10.6 into the server's optical drive.

2. Open System Image Utility, select NetInstall Image (as shown in Figure 8–7), and then click the Continue button.

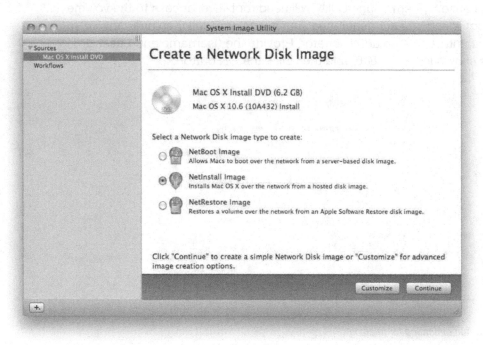

Figure 8–7. *Choosing NetInstall Image*

3. At the Image Settings screen that appears, provide a name that the installation media will have when extracted, and provide a description of the media (for example, enter **My NetInstall disk for Mac OS X 10.6.3**). You can also choose the option "Image will be served from more than one server," which will prepare the image assuming that you will have multiple Mac OS X Servers sharing this same image over the network. As mentioned earlier, you will realize better overall performance if you have more than one server providing the image to your network client systems. So, you will use this option only if you plan to have multiple Mac OS X Servers specifically running the image you are creating.

4. Once you have entered the image settings, click the Create button (Figure 8–8), and then click the Agree button to accept the Mac OS X license agreement on behalf of all the computers you will image from the disk image.

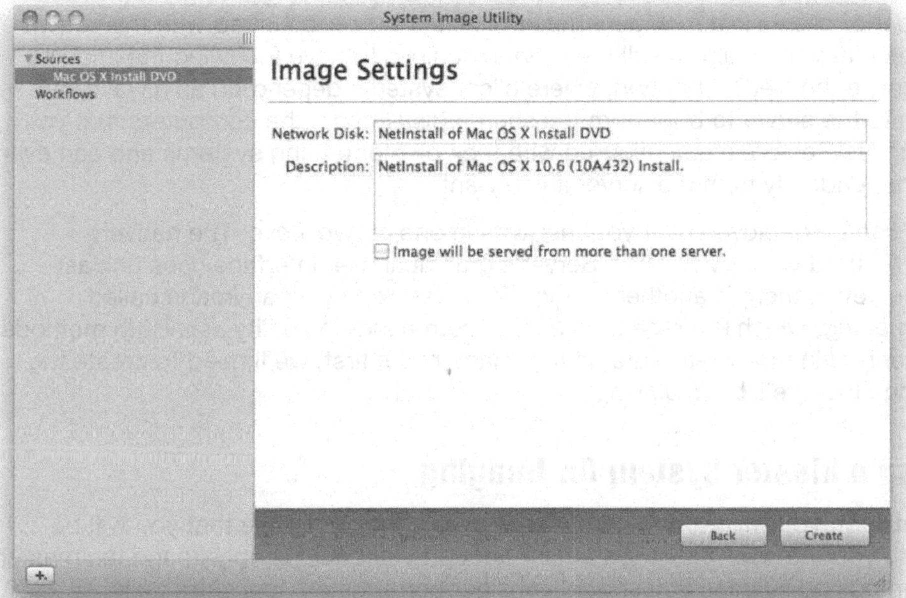

Figure 8–8. *NetInstall Image settings*

NOTE: By default there is an alphanumeric string in the description of the media, which refers to the build version of the installer. Each operating system version has a unique build version, which can be obtained using the `sw_vers` command.

5. You will then be prompted for a location and a name to give the resulting disk image file. As with the NetBoot option, the default location from which your server will share NetInstall disk images is /Library/NetBoot/NetBootSP0. So, if you are planning to share the NetInstall image from the current server you are using, locate that folder to your image. Make sure that you have enough space to save the disk image in the target directory, and then click Create.

Your image will take a while to create. Mac OS X Server is generating a disk image with all of the contents of the installation media at this point. Once complete, the image will be located in the directory you specified and will be ready for serving up to network clients.

Creating a NetRestore Image

You can also create a *NetRestore image*. This allows you to deploy a master disk image, with all the configuration settings, software, and even local user accounts that you need, directly to network client computers' internal hard drives. This is often used in a *monolithic* imaging environment, or one where you are deploying a single image to a large number of clients in a manner where the image is prepopulated with the software and settings that you would like all the client machines to have following the imaging process. Unlike the NetBoot option, where client systems depend on an always-on connection to the server to boot from the shared disk image, the computers that you create using NetRestore are configured with their own operating systems and can even operate independently from the server if you want.

The image can be deployed over your network in one of two ways. The natively supported method within Mac OS X Server's graphical user interface uses unicast imaging. However, there is another method for mass deploying an image called *multicast imaging*, which leverages the built-in command-line utility asr. Both methods will be described in more detail later in the chapter. But first, we'll need to create the master image that we'll be deploying.

Preparing a Master System for Imaging

As with NetBoot, you will want to carefully prepare a master image that you will be deploying to your network client systems. Although you could simply image the master from an unmodified system, you should consider performing a few extra tasks on your master system before imaging it. Here are some recommended tips to ensure that the master image is well prepared for optimal deployment speeds and easy maintenance and management once the imaging process is complete.

- Create an administrator account and give it full Apple Remote Desktop access. This will allow you to connect to it using ARD (assuming you have purchased this essential utility), as well as log in locally as an admin for troubleshooting and ad hoc installations.

- For all software, use a volume license wherever possible, since some software packages have duplicate serial number detection and will shut down the software if they detect another copy of the same software.

The following cannot be performed on a volume that is running an active operating system, so you will need to boot your system into FireWire Target Disk Mode first.

- Delete the contents of the cache's folders, log files, and Spotlight indexes at the following locations, substituting the name of your master system's boot volume for VolumeName:

```
sudo rm -rf /Volumes/VolumeName/Library/Caches/*
sudo rm -rf /Volumes/VolumeName/System/Library/Caches/*
sudo rm -rf /Volumes/VolumeName/System/Library/Extensions/Caches/*
sudo rm -rf /Volumes/VolumeName/private/etc/ssh_host*
```

```
sudo rm -rf /Volumes/VolumeName/var/db/Spotlight/*
sudo rm -rf /Volumes/VolumeName/var/log/*
sudo rm -rf /Volumes/VolumeName/var/vm/*
```

Configuring a NetRestore Image for Deployment

Follow these steps to complete creating the image:

1. Boot the master system into FireWire target disk mode, and connect it to your server with a FireWire cable.

2. Open System Image Utility from /Applications/Server. Provided that valid installation media is present, you will see a Create a Network Disk Image screen, as shown in Figure 8–9.

3. Click NetRestore Image, and then click the Continue button.

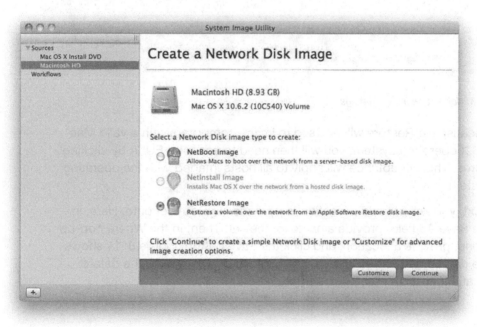

Figure 8–9. *Choosing a NetRestore image*

4. At the Image Settings screen (shown in Figure 8–10), you will be able to provide a name for the volume that will be mounted, as well as a description like with other types of images. You can also select the check box if you plan to serve this image from more than one NetBoot server.

5. When you have completed entering your image settings, click Create.

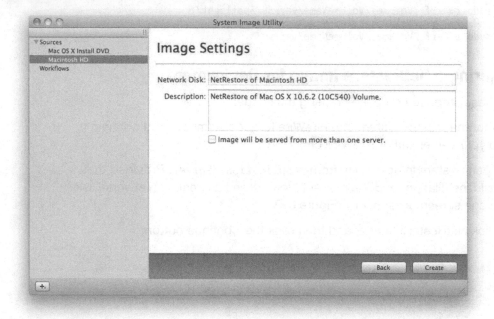

Figure 8–10. *NetRestore image settings*

6. Because NetRestore will be used to image computers with a valid Mac OS X operating system, you will then need to accept a EULA by clicking Agree. This acceptance will apply to all hosts imaged with the operating system.

7. Next, you will provide a location to save the NetBoot set onto. Here, in the Save As field, provide a name for the set. Then, in the Where pop-up menu, provide a location, and click the Save button. Figure 8–11 shows the default name, NetRestore of Macintosh HD, as well as the default location, /Library/NetBoot/NetBootSP0.

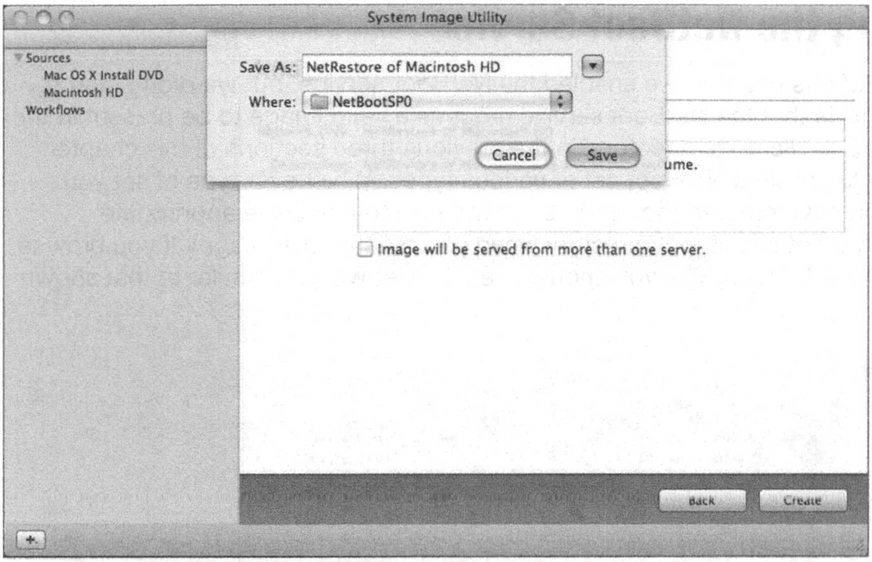

Figure 8–11. *NetRestore target location*

8. The NetBoot set will then be generated; as with the other image types, it
    will likely take a long time to complete. You can follow along with the
    progress in the window shown in Figure 8–12. Click the Done button to
    complete the process.

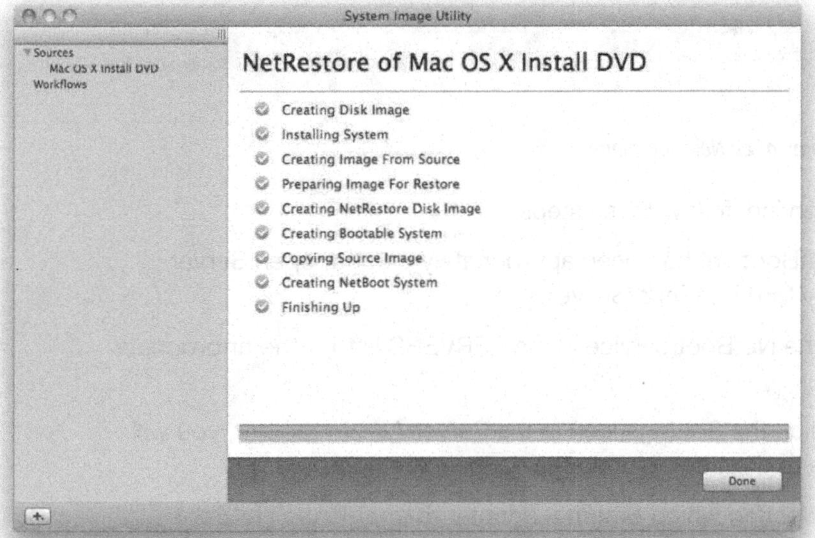

Figure 8–12. *NetRestore summary in System Image Utility*

Configuring the NetBoot Service

In the beginning of this chapter, we enabled the NetBoot service, but we didn't start it. The reason for this is that the NetBoot service requires a valid image to be present in the /Library/NetBoot/NetBootSP0 directory. In the previous three sections of this chapter, we covered how to create a NetBoot set of various types. Whichever type of set you created, once you have created the set, you will then place it into the appropriate directory (if you did not select that directory when you created the image). If you browse to /Library/NetBoot/NetBootSP0, you should see a Finder window similar to that shown in Figure 8–13.

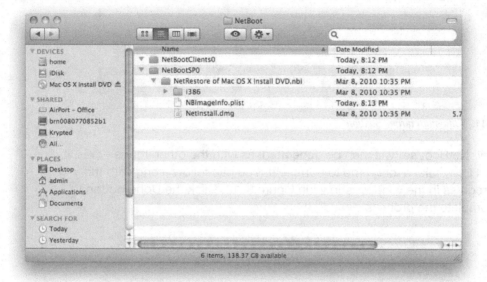

Figure 8–13. *The anatomy of an NetBoot image*

To configure the service, follow these steps:

1. Once the NetBoot set has been appropriately placed, open Server Admin from /Applications/Server.

2. Then, click the NetBoot service in the SERVERS list for the appropriate server.

3. When you click the Settings icon in the Server Admin toolbar, you will then be able to start configuring the various settings.

4. Start with selecting which Ethernet adapter to enable the NetBoot service for. Using the General tab, you will see a list of adapters (or one adapter if you have only one) available for such a task, as shown in Figure 8–14.

5. Select the most appropriate one, and then you can move on to selecting the appropriate volume.

6. Next, select the appropriate volume on the NetBoot server that houses the NetBoot set that you have placed into the /Library/NetBoot/NetBootSP0 directory. You can simply select the Images and Client Data boxes as well. You can use different volumes for each if you need more capacity than is available on one volume.

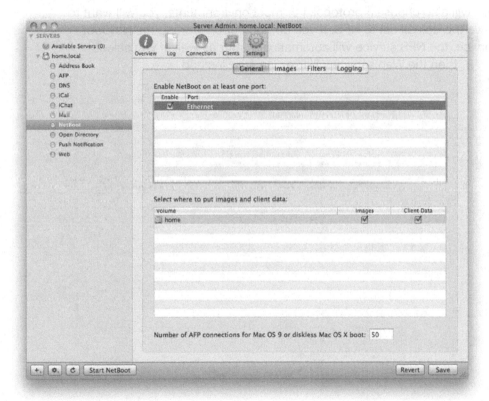

Figure 8–14. *NetBoot General settings*

7. Next, click the Images tab to open the screen shown in Figure 8–15.

8. Here, you will configure which NetBoot set will be your default for clients booting to the NetBoot server. Bear in mind that there can be only one image defined as the default. The selected default image will be automatically booted by all client workstations that start up with the N key pressed on their keyboards, regardless of whether it is a NetBoot, NetInstall, or NetRestore workflow.

9. Here, select the Enable box for the NetBoot set that you copied into the appropriate directory, and verify that the Default option is selected for the NetBoot set that you will be using.

> **NOTE:** The implication here is that you can boot to multiple NetBoot sets. This is the case, and we will explain how later in this chapter.

10. You will also choose a protocol. For most environments, you will want to leave the default set to NFS. If you do, then upon starting the NetBoot service, the NFS service will automatically start as well. If you select HTTP, then the Web service will likewise start instead.

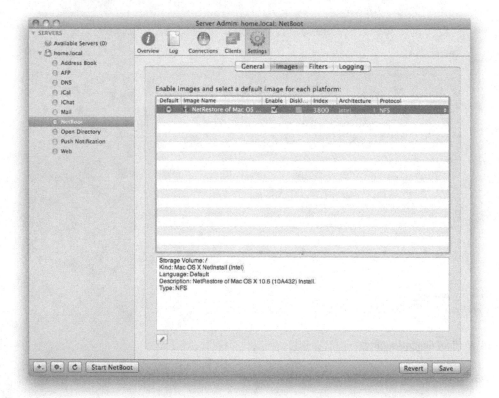

Figure 8–15. *NetBoot image settings*

Logging can be incredibly helpful in troubleshooting issues with your imaging environment. Click the Logging tab, and then click High (all events) for Log Level, as shown in Figure 8–16. This will maximize the logs that are provided to you. In the event that your server encounters issues with imaging, these options will be handy.

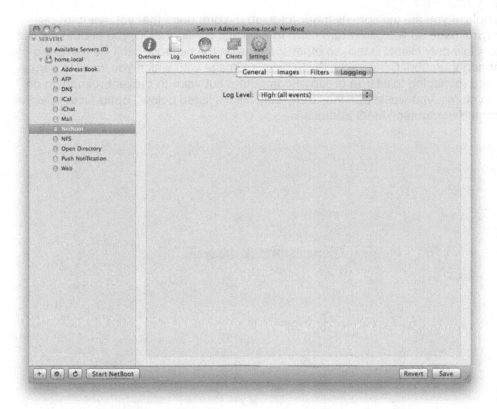

Figure 8–16. *Configuring NetBoot logs*

Finally, you can set up filters. A *filter* allows you to define which systems are allowed to connect to your NetBoot server by entering their unique MAC addresses. In doing so, you will be limiting the NetBoot service to a known set of computers or denying the NetBoot service to any unknown computers. This can be handy if you want to avoid accidental (or mischievously intentional) reimaging of systems that may be on your network but are not necessarily in the group of computers that you want running that image.

When you enable the filters, you will have two options (as shown in Figure 8–17):

- *Allow only clients listed below*: Acts as a whitelist, where only MAC addresses that have been provided can leverage the NetBoot service

- *Deny only clients listed below*: Acts as a blacklist, where all clients except those explicitly denied access can boot using the NetBoot service

If you need to add a MAC address, you can do so by manually entering it, or you can use the Find Hardware Address options to attempt to locate a valid MAC address on the network. If you have a list of MAC addresses in a tab-delimited text or RTF file, you can or import the list as well.

For example, if you are the administrator for a lab of computers that you want to frequently reimage so you can return them to a default configuration, you should set up a filter to allow only clients listed, so other systems on the network can't be reimaged with that configuration. Conversely, if you have an image with which you want to permit widespread reimaging to a large group of computers but want to prevent reimaging on specific systems, you would use the "Deny only clients listed below" option and specify the protected computers' MAC addresses.

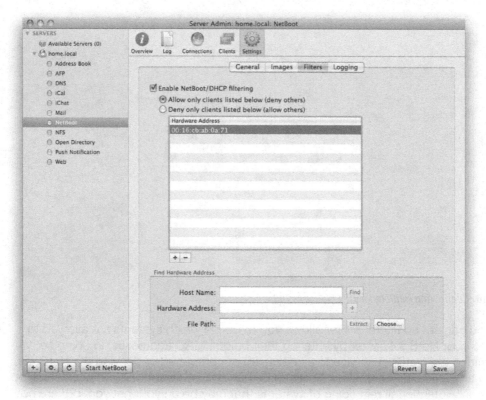

Figure 8–17. *Limiting access to NetBoot*

If you need to manually add a MAC address, then click the plus (+) sign, and you will see a dialog box for entering MAC addresses (Figure 8–18). Here, enter one address per line, and then click the OK button when you are done.

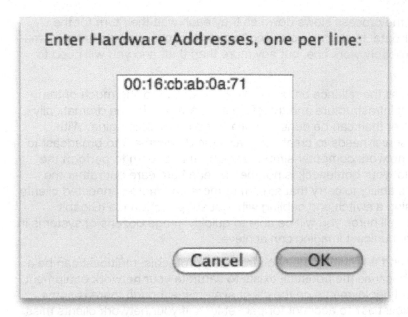

Figure 8-18. *Defining a MAC address*

Once the NetBoot service has been appropriately configured, click the Start button in Server Admin with the service highlighted to start it.

Apple Software Restore and Multicast Imaging: a NetRestore Alternative

Earlier in this chapter, we explained that NetRestore is the method you should use to replicate a master image over the network to client computers. Because these master images can frequently be quite large (dozens of gigabytes in size if you include things such as multimedia files, GarageBand elements, and large application installations such as Adobe Creative Suite and Final Cut Studio), deploying these master images requires specialized tools to accommodate their large size. Enter Apple Software Restore, or `asr`, and multicast imaging.

The steps involved in using `asr` and multicast imaging are similar to NetRestore: you create media to boot a computer, and from that media, you start imaging the systems. But before we dive into the details, let's discuss the differences between unicast and multicast so you can understand the advantages of the latter approach over the former.

Unicast imaging involves using a source disk image housed on a share point (AFP, NFS, or WebDAV). With unicast imaging, each network system that connects to your NetBoot server will demand an individual stream of data from the server. As more systems simultaneously connect to begin the imaging process, the server must create additional individual data streams to accommodate those systems' imaging processes. There comes a point when the server can't keep up with all the concurrent network stream requests, and therefore performance becomes compromised. The client systems will continue to image, but the process slows down as they each wait their turn for the server to get them their data. In short, if you need to simultaneously image ten systems or fewer, unicast will probably work fine, but any more than that, and you will need to look to multicast imaging.

Multicast imaging reduces the reliance on processing power by moving much of the workload to the network infrastructure and therefore allows you to image dramatically more computers far faster than can be done with file-based unicast imaging. With multicast imaging, the server needs to create only a single data stream to broadcast to the network, and each network computer simply picks up that stream to perform the imaging. In this scenario, your bottleneck is not the server's hardware but rather the networking equipment's ability to carry that stream to more and more connected clients. Therefore, if you are using a switch and cabling with decent performance (Gigabit Ethernet will serve you well here), you will be able to quickly image dozens of systems in a fraction of the time that unicast imaging can achieve.

In terms of configuring and fine-tuning the two streaming protocols, multicast can be a little more challenging because the potential exists to saturate your network equipment, which can result in failed deployments on the client systems; although there is some error correction in multicast asr to account for packet loss, if your network clients miss too many bits of data on the stream, the image will fail to copy correctly. So if you choose multicast imaging, you may need to throttle the speed at which the image stream is served to network clients. This will be covered later in this chapter, and we have provided a handy utility that performs this configuration automatically.

Ironically, this most powerful and high-performance method to mass-deploy images to your network is actually included in every version of Mac OS X, even the non-Server edition of the operating system. Still, its ability to provide a dramatic improvement in performance over Mac OS X Server's built-in NetBoot service warranted inclusion in this book.

Creating an Image for asr

The multicast stream will stream an asr-prepared image to your network. This image is generated using Disk Utility. To create a disk image, follow these steps:

1. Open Disk Utility from /Applications/Utilities, and then click the volume that you would like to create an image of. In this case, it will be the computer you preconfigured and connected to your server in FireWire Target Disk Mode.

2. From there, click the File menu and then select New ➤ Disk Image from "*Volume*" as shown in Figure 8–19.

Figure 8–19. *Creating an Image in Disk Utility*

3. On the next screen, provide a name for the disk image (which will be saved as a DMG file) in the Save As field. Also, select a directory (or volume) to save the disk image to (again, make sure your destination volume has enough room for your image!).

4. Then select read-only for the Image Format (as shown in Figure 8–20), and click the Save button.

Figure 8–20. *Choosing a location for your Image*

The image will then be created in the target location. This can take some time, so be patient!

Configuring asr for Multicast Imaging

The first step to configuring asr is to host an image somewhere. Since the image is to be streamed over multicast, then this will mean initiating the asr daemon to stream the image over the network. Doing so typically requires some knowledge of the command line. However, for the purposes of writing this chapter, the authors of this book decided to write a tool called ASRSetup, which will help you generate the asr stream using a graphical interface.

You can find the tool at http://asrsetup.sourceforge.net. Download the utility to the system that will be performing the streaming, and launch it. Follow these steps to configure the utility:

1. When you launch ASRSetup, it will do just as the opening dialog box (Figure 8–21) indicates: start a multicast asr stream based on a DMG disk image. Click OK to continue to the next screen.

Figure 8–21. *mASR configuration tool*

2. As the next dialog box informs you (Figure 8–22), the tool will then create a property list at /tmp/asr.plist. This configuration file will be used to start the stream and can be copied to other machines and used to start streams using the asr command. This dialog box is strictly informative, so you can click the OK button to move on to the next screen.

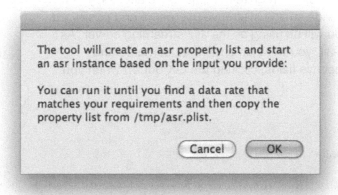

The tool will create an asr property list and start an asr instance based on the input you provide:

You can run it until you find a data rate that matches your requirements and then copy the property list from /tmp/asr.plist.

Cancel   OK

Figure 8–22. *What the mASR configuration tool does*

3.   The next screen allows you to set a data rate. The lower the speed of streams, the more resilient to packlet loss the stream will be. Because of packet loss and the fact that there is no error correction on multicast streaming, network speeds can vary greatly. At the "Enter your desired data rate" screen, you will have the option to configure the speed of the stream, as calculated in bits per second. Although this is prepopulated with a speed that is satisfactory in most environments (6 megabits per second), you can tune the rate at your discretion, as shown in Figure 8–23. Simply increase the number to get faster throughput, or reduce it if you encounter errors. Because multicast traffic relies on the switching infrastructure, the perfect combination of speed and error-free restores will vary with each environment. You can always run the tool a few times until you find the right combination. For the purpose of this example, we will leave the speed at the default setting, and click the OK button.

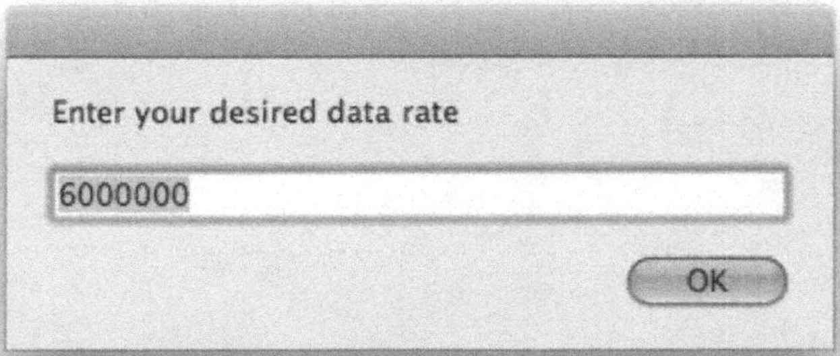

Enter your desired data rate

6000000

OK

Figure 8–23. *Setting a desired data rate*

4. Because the imaging process will require administrative access, you will then be prompted to provide an administrative username and password for the computer that you will be using as the asr streaming server. As you can see in Figure 8–24, you will then enter the username and password into their respective fields, clicking the OK button when you are done.

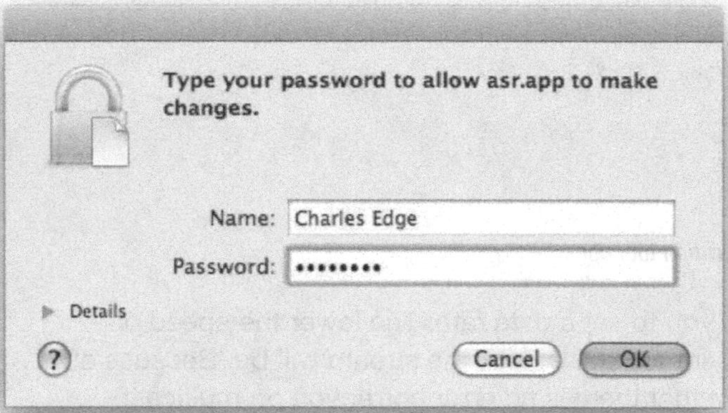

Type your password to allow asr.app to make changes.

Name: Charles Edge

Password: ••••••••

► Details

Cancel   OK

Figure 8–24. *Authenticating for starting an asr stream*

5. Because multicast network traffic requires a dedicated IP address, you will next provide the address for the stream to use. Because of the impact that multicast traffic will have on the network, this is something you will need to obtain from your network administrator. Or, if you don't have other devices that utilize multicast addresses, you can simply leave the default (which as shown in Figure 8–25 is set to 239.255.100.100), an address typically valid in many environments.

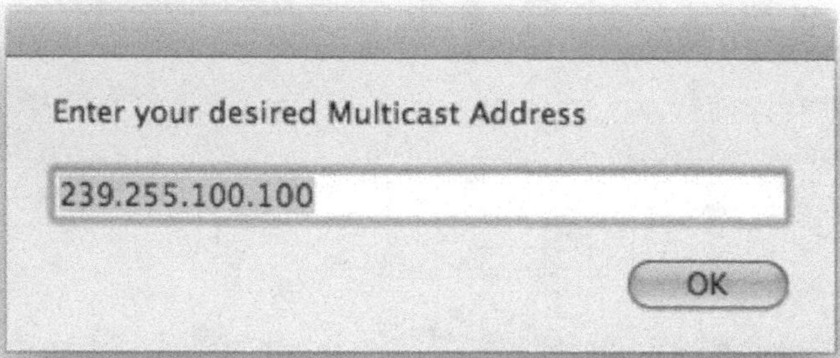

Enter your desired Multicast Address

239.255.100.100

OK

Figure 8–25. *Setting the multicast address for the stream*

6. Next, browse to the image that you created earlier in the "Creating an Image" section of this chapter. As you can see in Figure 8–26, this involves simply browsing to the DMG file that you created, clicking it, and then clicking the Choose button in the Choose a File dialog box.

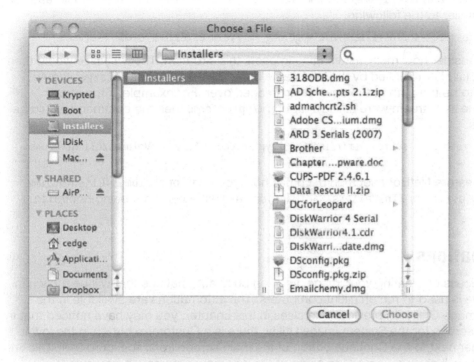

Figure 8–26. *Choosing what file to use for the stream*

7. Once you have selected the image file for streaming, then the `asr` stream should start. You can then move on to installing a client using `asr` or installing a client using NetRestore.

Imaging a Client over asr

Once you have an `asr` stream running, you can use the command line to run an installation to a target over `asr`. It is helpful to understand what is happening under the hood. The most important aspect of the `asr` command here is the `restore` verb, which restores an image from a source to a target or a file.

The most logical use of `asr` is to restore one volume over to another. In the case where you have two mounted volumes, with the one containing the image called ImageSource and the one containing the volume you will be restoring onto called ClientVolume, the command to restore would simply be `asr` followed by the verb, which is then followed by paths to the `--source` and `--target`. Here's an example:

```
sudo asr restore --source /Volumes/ImageSource --target /Volumes/ClientVolume
```

Using the previous command would require you to have the source volume always available. However, most will choose to restore from a file. Therefore, you can also use the -s option to use an image, such as the one you created earlier in this chapter. If that image is stored in the /Installers/MacImage.dmg file, then the command would end up looking similar to the following:

```
sudo asr restore -s /Installers/MacImage.dmg -t /Volumes/ClientVolume --erase
```

Finally, consider how multicast imaging impacts this situation. The --source would then be a URL (asr:// followed by the host name of the server), and the --target would continue to be the path to the drive being imaged over. For example, if the server running the asr stream were called imaging.krypted.com, then the command would be as follows:

```
 sudo asr restore --source asr://imaging.krypted.com --target /Volumes/ClientVolume --
erase
```

The NetRestore NetBoot set then becomes how you can get /Volumes/ClientVolume and either asr:// or /Installers/MacImage.dmg available while not being booted to either.

Automations

In the process of creating your image, you can build automations that will be run when that image is used to run on client computers. The automations are available in the System Image Utility. In previous exercises in this chapter, you may have noticed that in the main screen for the System Image Utility, there is a Customize button in the lower-right corner next to the Continue button of the main screen (refer to Figure 8–9). Clicking Customize will give you access to some of the workflow automation framework.

When you begin a custom setup, you will be given a basic workflow window with some default actions that you can drag and drop to rearrange and customize the workflow to suit your specific needs, as shown in Figure 8–27.

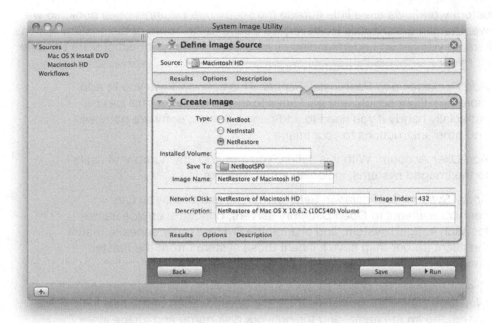

Figure 8–27. *The default System Image Utility custom workflow window*

You will also be given a collection Automator Library workflow elements, as shown in Figure 8–28.

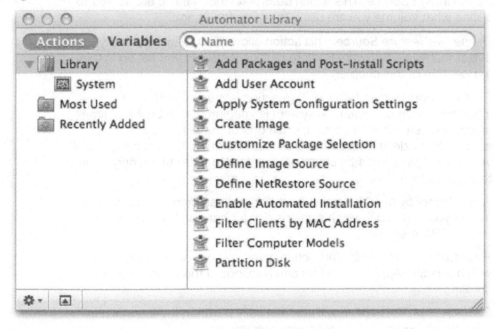

Figure 8–28. *The Automator Library pane of System Image Utility actions*

These custom workflows are a little outside the scope of a beginner-level book, so we won't cover them in great detail. However, we'll summarize some of the custom options for you here so you get an understanding of what these Automator actions are capable of doing for you:

- *Add Packages and Post-Install Scripts*: This action allows you to add more postflight scripts and packages to the disk image. This can be especially handy if you need to add printer drivers, software patches, and other instructions to your image.

- *Add User Account*: With this action, you can add any number of users to the imaged systems, including administrators.

- *Apply System Configuration Settings*: With this option, you can connect systems to Open Directory servers, configure unique names for each imaged system, and change the ByHost preferences to match the client (rather than have it inherit those systems from the master image).

- *Create Image*: This action allows you to determine the type of image (NetBoot, NetInstall, or NetRestore), the save location of the new image, the Image name, and the network disk name and image index.

- *Customize Package Selection*: This option, applicable only to NetInstall images, lets you specify which packages from the OS installation are installed.

- *Define Image Source*: This action does just what it says: allows you to define what volume you are using to create the image.

- *Define NetRestore Source*: This action allows you to automatically select the Apple Software Restore multicast stream you set up in the asr section of this chapter.

- *Enable Automated Installation*: This action lets you bypass the interactive prompts when the system is imaging. It can be a real time-saver, but use this with caution, since one of the settings will automatically delete the contents of the hard drive. It's not a big deal if you are imaging, but if an unwitting user NetBoots to the wrong image, they could lose data!

- *Filter Clients by MAC Address*: As described earlier in the chapter, this allows you to specify which systems can (or cannot) be imaged with your NetBoot server.

- *Filter Computer Models*: This action gives you the power to specify which specific Apple computers can NetBoot to the image you are creating.

- *Partition Disk*: This action will automatically partition the internal hard drive to whatever configuration you specify.

These automations can be in the form of shell scripts or packages (or even packages that only contain shell scripts). You can use automations that are in scripts. For example, if you were to create a new file called `enablefirewall.sh` and paste the following command into it, then you would enable the firewall when the script were run:

```
defaults write /Library/Preferences/com.apple.alf globalstate -int 1
```

> **NOTE:** Scripting is a bit beyond the context of this, but if you're interested, refer to `http://krypted.com/mac-os-x/` `command-line-alf-redux`.

Practically every task that you can do in Mac OS X can be scripted, whether through AppleScript or a shell script. By leveraging scripts, you can greatly reduce the amount of time required to install a system. In addition to scripts, a number of other automations are built into the Automator-style System Image Utility. We recommend looking at each of these individually and beginning there, leveraging scripts to fill in the gaps of workflow with imaging environments.

NetBooting Client Systems

You have spent most of this chapter creating images and preparing them to be deployed to network systems. There are several ways you can instruct your network computers to begin using your NetBoot server. One important point to keep in mind is that NetBoot requires an Ethernet connection; it is not possible to boot to a hosted image over wireless.

Here are the ways you can boot up your client systems to a NetBoot startup volume:

First, if you defined a default image for your network or have only a single image being hosted by your server, you can instruct your network systems to boot from your server by holding down the N key on the keyboard while they boot up. You'll know it's booting from a network source when you see a spinning globe replace the Apple logo on the gray startup screen.

Second, you can open the System Preferences on the client systems and select the Startup Disk pane. From that window, you can select your NetBoot image to boot up from and click Restart. At this point, you'll be confronted with a warning about potential data loss when booting up from a network source configured with Automator actions, which we touched on earlier. If you are sure that this is the correct disk, proceed with rebooting.

Third, you can use Apple Remote Desktop to tell a group of computers on your network to boot up from the hosted NetBoot image. In the Bonjour scanner window (or in the computer list you have built), select all of the systems you want to reboot from the NetBoot image. From the Manage menu, select Set Startup Disk. In the dialog box that appears, you should see your NetBoot image in the list of eligible volumes. Click the network volume, and then click the Set button.

Summary

Installing even a few computers can be a tricky and time-consuming endeavor. But performing a mass deployment and automating as much of the installation can be a time-saving science. Throughout this chapter we described the basics for implementing NetBoot, NetInstall, and NetRestore. These three products are all based on the NetBoot service, which simply allows a computer to boot to a shared volume. Once booted, either you can then let users work in that environment, the original design of the NetBoot service, or you can leverage the fact that you are not booted off the hard drive of that computer to perform a variety of tasks on the volume, such as restoring an operating system to it or duplicating the entire contents of a prebuilt DMG file. We also covered using the asr command to perform a multicast restore, which offers much higher performance and throughput than unicast.

Although we covered some light automation, with regard to mass deployment, it's worth pointing out that the automation is not required. The larger the environment, the less clicking in dialog boxes that you'll want. In fact, for really big installations, you'll more than likely want to get to the point where you have a one-touch (assuming a touch is a single mouse click or keyboard stroke) or even a zero-touch deployment.

A number of resources are at your disposal to help you with those automations. This includes consultants (such as 318, the organization that the authors of this book work for), mailing lists, and other books (such as the *Enterprise Mac Administrator's Guide*, also from Apress). There are also a number of third-party applications that have niche followings, such as the Casper Suite from JAMF Software; Absolute Manage from Absolute Software; and DeployStudio, a robust tool that is available for download free of charge at deploystudio.com.

But the most important aspect of deployments, and especially large ones, is to get educated about what you will be doing. Reading this chapter is a great start. Following along with the examples, although potentially time-consuming, is also a great step in the right direction. But just because we ran out of pages, don't stop here. Keep reading, testing, and researching the best options because this is what will enable you to get to a great place where you can spend more time learning and less time clicking boxes repeatedly!

Chapter 9

Configuring Address Book Server

Mac OS X Server 10.6 introduces the ability for users to store their address books on a central server using the Address Book service. Additionally, the Address Book service enables you to integrate a bridge to the LDAP contacts available in Mac OS X Server 10.6, meaning that you can perform a lookup of all the accounts on your server as though they were addresses, and with a little third-party software you can even leverage the Address Book service as a shared address book (which you could also do with the use of a shared account).

The shared Address Book services cobbled together in previous versions of Mac OS X Server were simple LDAP lookups; however, in Mac OS X Server 10.6, Apple has integrated CardDAV, similar to the CalDAV extension leveraged by the iCal services explored further in Chapter 10. One of the biggest benefits of CardDAV is that the contacts are synchronized to the local computer when offline, meaning that contacts are available to users even when they are not on the network (or any network for that matter). Mac OS X Server 10.6 also maintains the LDAP functionality, although in 10.5 you had a tool called Directory that could be used to augment the contacts that is no longer available. Not having Directory means that you will need to look to third-party products if you want to use Mac OS X Server's Address Book services as a shared contact repository.

In this chapter, we will cover the setup and configuration of Mac OS X Server 10.6's new Address Book service. We will also show how to configure the Address Book client application to communicate with its server counterpart and how to help users collaborate by sharing address information with other users. We'll cover some of the basics of administering the server and the ever-important task of backing up the data reliably. We'll touch on some command-line pointers, as well as cover a few alternatives to Apple's Address Book service that may be worth considering.

Address Book Services

The Address Book service is new in Mac OS X Server 10.6 and is based on the emerging CardDAV standard, a specification that defines the exchange of vCard information via the WebDAV protocol. Based on the same back end, the Address Book service setup and configuration will be much the same as with iCal: you can use Server Preferences to get the job done easily, you can use Server Admin if you require more options, or you can use the command line for optimal granularity. The Address Book service maintains its own data store but also allows you to search Open Directory for user or contact information.

The data store for the Address Book service stores records in the vCard format (.vcf). CardDAV serves and synchronizes these vCards. When you drag a contact out of the Address Book program, the resultant file is a vCard. The .vcf files that correspond to each contact in a user's address book are served over extensions to WebDAV that make up CardDAV and are therefore stored nested inside the /Library/AddressBookServer/Documents/addressbooks/__uuids__ directory. Each user and group has a folder there, and nested further in that directory are the .vcf files, each named with a prefix of the unique identifier of the contact followed by -ABSPlugin.vcf. The root of the shared directory can be moved, but the structure following that root will need to remain unaltered.

Mac OS X Server 10.6 represents a fundamental change (from LDAP to CardDAV) in how address books are served in Mac OS X Server. Because it's a first release version of software, it lacks the maturity that you are likely to see from iCal. However, Snow Leopard Server shows the fundamental aspects that iCal showed in previous versions and at a minimum allows users to store their contacts on a server, cache them offline, and therefore be able to access them from multiple computers. Furthermore, the LDAP integration allows you to bridge the global address list that is so commonly required in environments while also offering a foundation for building a more feature-rich contact aspect of the Mac OS X Server groupware offering in future releases of the product.

Setting Up Address Book Server

To configure the Address Book service, you can use the Server Preferences application or the Server Admin application.

Configuring with Server Preferences

To set up the Address Book service on Mac OS X Server with the Server Preferences application, follow these steps:

1. Open the Server Preferences application from /Applications/Server. Here, you will see the Address Book service, with a gray indicator light meaning that it is not yet running, as you will notice in Figure 9–1.

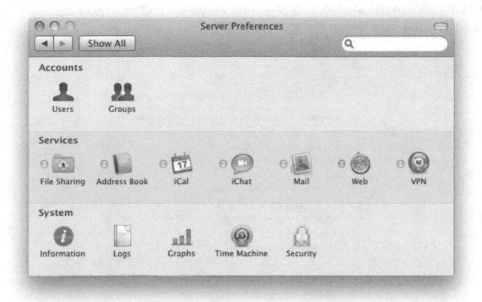

Figure 9–1. *Server Preferences*

2. Click the button for Address Book.

3. When it opens, deselect the option to limit each user's total book size if you'd like to disable user Address Book quotas, as shown in Figure 9–2.

Figure 9–2. *Address Book pane of Server Preferences*

4. Next, move the slider from the OFF to the ON position, and wait for the service to complete installation and fire up.

5. Once the service has started, click the Show All button (Figure 9–3) to get back to the main Server Preferences screen.

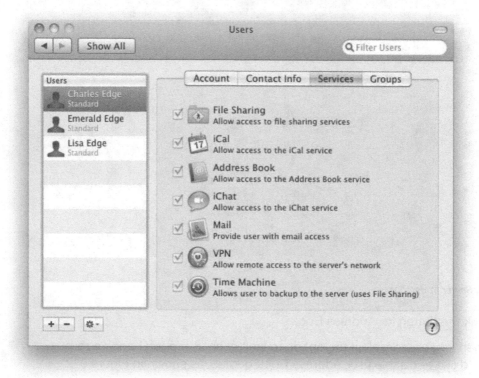

Figure 9–3. *Users pane of Server Preferences*

6. Click Users, and then select the Address Book box for each user who you would like to enable the service.

Configuring with Server Admin

As with the iCal Server service covered in Chapter 10, you can also use Server Admin, located in /Applications/Server, to more granularly configure the Address Book Server service. To enable the service to be configured, follow these steps:

1. To configure Address Book server, you will first need to configure it to be displayed in Server Admin. To do so, open Server Admin, and click the name of the server that you are configuring.

2. Then click the Settings icon and the Services tab for Settings. Here, you will see a checklist of services that can be enabled.

3. As shown in Figure 9–4, select the Address Book box, and then click the Save button to display the service in the SERVERS list, under the name of the server you are configuring to run the Address Book service.

Figure 9–4. *Enabling the Address Book service*

4. When you click the Address Book entry for your Address Book service in Server Admin, you'll see the screen in Figure 9–5. Here you can configure General (global service options) and Authentication (settings that deal with authentication and security options) settings.

■ *Data Store*: This is the path to the Address Book database.

■ *User Quotas*: This is the maximum size per user for the Address Book database in megabytes.

■ *Log Level*: This allows configuration of the verbosity of logs.

- *Directory Gateway*: This enables LDAP bridging between the Address Book service and your directory service.

  - *Search for user accounts:* Allows for searches against the address book server to optionally query Open Directory for LDAP-based users (cn=users,dc=myco,dc=com) and/or public contacts (cn=people,dc=myco,dc=com) using the All Directories option in Address Book.

  - *Search for shared contacts:* Allows for searches against the address book server to optionally query for shared contacts.

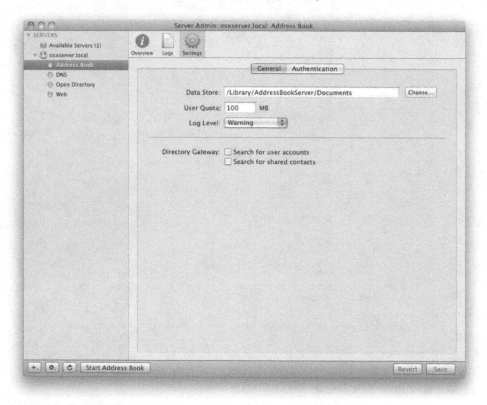

Figure 9–5. *Configuring the Address Book service in Server Admin*

5. Now click the Authentication tab. You have the following options (which you can see in Figure 9–6):

- *Type*: This allows you to configure how clients will authenticate. Options include Digest, Kerberos, and Any Method, which allows for both. Unless you are using Mobile Access, as described in Chapter 13, it is recommended that you use Any Method for the authentication type.

- *Host Name*: By default, this value is dynamically generated based on the determined host name of the server; it can also be overridden.

- *Port*: The port that the CardDAV HTTP service will listen on for Address Book traffic.

- *SSL*: By Default, SSL is set to Don't Use; however, you should set SSL to Use to enable SSL (requires a certificate to be accepted). The SSL certificates are populated from the list of available keychains in Keychain Access or on the Certificates screen when you click the name of the server in Server Admin.

- *SSL Port*: If SSL is enabled, this option allows for the customization of the port that the listener will run on.

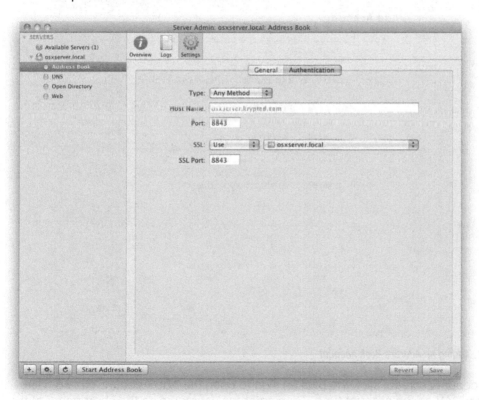

Figure 9–6. *Configuring Address Book authentication in Server Admin*

With all services, if SSL is an option, it is strongly recommended that you use it. The stock configuration of Mac OS X Server comes with a self-signed SSL certificate, and it is a fairly straightforward task to use it to secure your services. Alternately, you can obtain a certificate from a third-party certificate authority (CA), because those are often easier to deploy. If your organization has an internal certificate authority, you can use its services to sign certificates for your OS X host.

Once you are satisfied with your settings, click the Save button in the lower-right corner of the screen, and then restart the service using the Server Admin utility or the command line.

Connecting to the Address Book Server

Once your server has been configured optimally for your environment, it's time to configure your clients to connect to it. To do so, open the Address Book application from /Applications (it's also one of the icons that are placed in the Dock by default in Mac OS X), click the Address Book menu, and then click Preferences to see a list of the accounts currently on the local computer (Figure 9–7). Click the Accounts icon on the System Preferences screen.

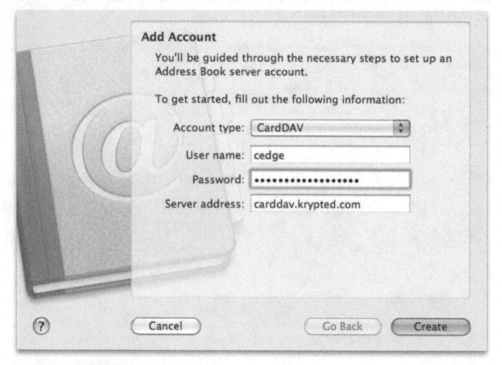

Figure 9–7. *Adding an Address Book account*

On the Accounts screen, click the plus (+) sign to open the Add Account Wizard. Here, select CardDAV as the account type. Then enter the username as the short name of the user who you are configuring Address Book services for, and supply a password for the user. Finally, provide an address for the server that is running Address Book services for your organization, and then click the Create button (see Figure 9–8).

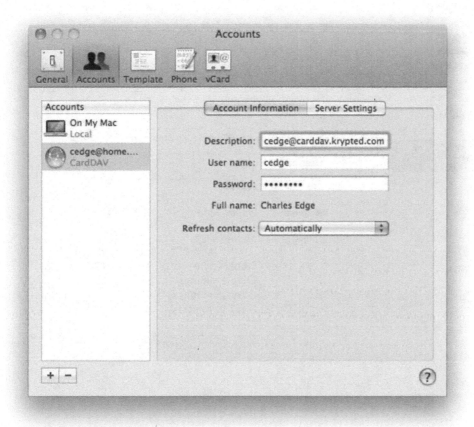

Figure 9–8. *Address Book account information*

The account will then enumerate the settings and be added to the accounts list. Once you are back on the Accounts screen, you can view the settings for the account that was just added. To do so, click the account. As you will notice in Figure 9–9, the Account Information screen will show you the settings that you provided earlier and also allow you to configure the rate with which contacts refresh. Automatically is the default setting for refresh rate, although you can set the client to query for updates on the server anywhere from every minute to once an hour.

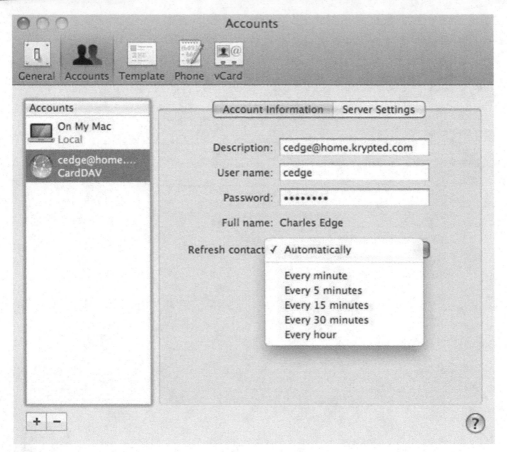

Figure 9–9. *Setting the refresh rate for contacts*

Next, click Server Settings. Here, as you can see in Figure 9–10, you will see the address and the relative path to the address that the client will use to locate vCards. The port number can be customized here, and you can enable SSL for the communications between the client and the server using the Use SSL check box.

Figure 9–10. *Enabling SSL for Address Book service accounts*

> **TIP:** Mac OS X 10.5 users will use the Directory application in the
> /Applications/Utilities directory to view and edit directory-based contacts in the
> Address Book. However, CardDAV and therefore 10.6 Address Book Server is supported only by
> Address Book in 10.6. For 10.5 support, a third-party client will be needed.

Using the Client

Once you have completed configuring the Address Book client, close the preferences
screen to see the main Address Book screen. Here, you will see a list of each repository
of contacts that you have access to. Although this chapter is not going to be sufficient to
explain every feature of Address Book, we'll spend a little time in this section looking at
the features that are specific to the Address Book service from Mac OS X Server.

When you log into the Address Book application, you will see each repository of
contacts listed in the Group column of Address Book. One of these will be the server

account that was added in the previous section. Clicking it will display the contacts that your account has installed, which you can see in Figure 9–11. From there you can use Address Book in much the same way that you would if you were connected to a server running the Address Book service.

Figure 9–11. *Viewing contacts from the Address Book*

You can't easily view a list of contacts in the shared address list from LDAP. You can also view shared contacts from the directory service (likely Open Directory) by searching for a contact. As you can see in Figure 9–12, click the disclosure triangle for All Directories, and you will see the account that you just installed. Click the address list for the name of your account, and then enter a username in the search field in the upper-right corner of the screen. Provided that the LDAP search is functioning properly, you should see any contacts from the directory populated in the list.

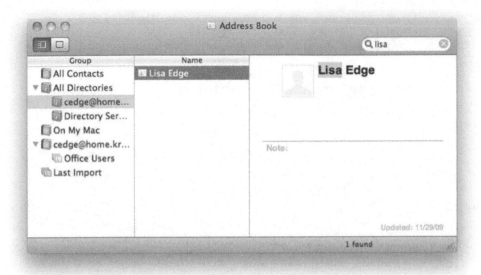

Figure 9–12. *Finding contacts in LDAP*

NOTE: Once you verify that you can search for a contact that is stored in the directory service, then you should be able to see the contact in new email messages as part of the autocomplete for accounts; however, there may be a slight delay for the autocomplete to complete, according to how many contacts and the latency between the computer that you are using and the directory server that hosts your LDAP environment.

Controlling Access

The Address Book services for your organization might not be for everybody, though. And if they are not, then you will be able to control a service access control list (SACL) to limit which users can access the Address Book services.

To configure the SACL for Address Book services, open Server Admin, and then click the name of the server that is running your Address Book services. In the Server Admin toolbar, you will see an icon for Access. Click it, and then you will see the Services tab. On the Services tab, you will have the ability to configure SACLs to be identical for all services or to be granularly configured for each service on the server. Use the "For all services" or "For selected services below" to set this option (Figure 9–13).

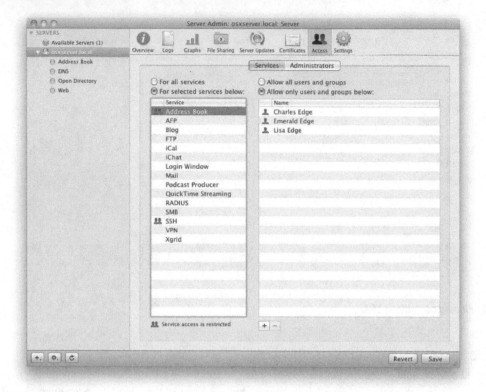

Figure 9–13. *Defining SACLs*

If you do not configure any controls, then all users will have access to all services. If you choose to granularly configure services per service, then by default the "Allow all users and groups" option will be selected. This option allows any user to access the service, provided they have an account on the server. If you want to configure a SACL for each service, then click the "Allow only users and groups below" option. Once you do, use the plus sign to bring up a list of users and groups, and then drag the users and groups that you would like to grant access to into the list on the Server Admin screen. Once you have enabled the service for all appropriate users and groups, click the Save button.

NOTE: Each service that has been configured will then have an icon indicated it has been secured.

Backing Up Address Books

Backing up the Address Book Server data store is similar to backing up the Address Book Server information store. You can find the path to the database through Server Admin by looking at the Data Store field for the Address Book service or by using the following command:

```
serveradmin settings addressbook:DocumentRoot
```

Once you know the path, you can back up the data store as you would most other directory structures. The service runs with the _calendar username as the default owner, although the root account will provide access as well. The default location to the information store is /Library/AddressBook/. Additionally, you will need to make sure that the directory server is being backed up appropriately, a process described in more detail in Chapter 4.

Leveraging the Command Line

The serveradmin command is one of the only ways that the Address Book service should be interacted with from the command line. As with other services, you can use serveradmin in conjunction with the stop, start, status, or settings options in order to stop the service, start the service, obtain information about the service, and obtain settings/change settings for the service. For example, to restart the service from the command line, you can use the following two commands in sequence, which stop and then start the service, respectively:

```
serveradmin stop addressbook
serveradmin start addressbook
```

If you need more granularity for your Address Book server configuration, you can also use the serveradmin command with the settings option to view all the settings that can be changed:

```
serveradmin settings addressbook
```

This would result in the following list:

```
addressbook:SudoersFile = ""
addressbook:DirectoryService:params:restrictEnabledRecords = no
addressbook:DirectoryService:params:cacheTimeout = 30
addressbook:DirectoryService:params:restrictToGroup = ""
addressbook:DirectoryService:params:node = "/Search"
addressbook:DirectoryService:type =
"twistedcaldav.directory.appleopendirectory.OpenDirectoryService"
addressbook:BindSSLPorts = _empty_array
addressbook:EnablePrincipalListings = no
addressbook:DocumentRoot = "/Library/AddressBookServer/Documents"
addressbook:SSLPrivateKey = ""
addressbook:ServerStatsFile = "/var/run/carddavd/stats.plist"
addressbook:ProcessType = "Combined"
addressbook:UserName = "_calendar"
addressbook:BindHTTPPorts = _empty_array
addressbook:EnableAnonymousReadRoot = no
addressbook:DefaultLogLevel = "info"
addressbook:HTTPPort = 8800
addressbook:ServerHostName = ""
addressbook:PIDFile = "/var/run/carddavd.pid"
addressbook:ReadPrincipals = _empty_array
addressbook:UserQuota = 104857600
addressbook:MultiProcess:ProcessCount = 0
addressbook:EnableProxyPrincipals = no
```

```
addressbook:Authentication:Digest:Algorithm = "md5"
addressbook:Authentication:Digest:Qop = ""
addressbook:Authentication:Digest:Enabled = yes
addressbook:Authentication:Kerberos:ServicePrincipal = ""
addressbook:Authentication:Kerberos:Enabled = yes
addressbook:Authentication:Basic:Enabled = no
addressbook:MaxAddressBookMultigetHrefs = 5000
addressbook:ErrorLogFile = "/var/log/carddavd/error.log"
addressbook:SSLCertificate = ""
addressbook:EnableSACLs = yes
addressbook:AB_EnabledGroups = _empty_array
addressbook:EnableAnonymousReadNav = no
addressbook:DataRoot = "/var/run/carddavd"
addressbook:BindAddresses = _empty_array
addressbook:AdminPrincipals = _empty_array
addressbook:MaxAddressBookQueryResults = 1000
addressbook:RedirectHTTPToHTTPS = no
addressbook:EnableSearchAddressBook = yes
addressbook:DirectoryAddressBook:params:queryUserRecords = yes
addressbook:DirectoryAddressBook:params:liveQuery = yes
addressbook:DirectoryAddressBook:params:cacheQuery = no
addressbook:DirectoryAddressBook:params:peopleNode = "/Search/Contacts"
addressbook:DirectoryAddressBook:params:fakeETag = yes
addressbook:DirectoryAddressBook:params:ignoreSystemRecords = yes
addressbook:DirectoryAddressBook:params:queryPeopleRecords = yes
addressbook:DirectoryAddressBook:params:dsLocalCacheTimeout = 30
addressbook:DirectoryAddressBook:params:queryAllAttributes = no
addressbook:DirectoryAddressBook:params:userNode = "/Search"
addressbook:DirectoryAddressBook:params:cacheTimeout = 30
addressbook:DirectoryAddressBook:params:maxDSQueryRecords = 150
addressbook:DirectoryAddressBook:type =
"twistedcaldav.directory.opendirectorybacker.OpenDirectoryBackingService"
addressbook:RotateAccessLog = no
addressbook:AnonymousDirectoryAddressBookAccess = no
addressbook:GroupName = "_calendar"
addressbook:AccessLogFile = "/var/log/carddavd/access.log"
addressbook:ResponseCompression = yes
```

There are also a couple of files that will be used by the Address Book service, which you will want to back up with your backup software (more on backups in Chapter 20). These include /etc/carddavd/carddavd.plist, which is the main configuration file for the Address Book service (the service can also be called carddavd, by the way). Although you can edit the property list (*plist*) directly, it is wise to just use serveradmin to do so unless you have a good understanding of what you're doing. Another file that should be backed up is /var/log/carddavd/access.log, the primary log file of the service. You can view the contents while data is being written to the file using the tail command along with the -f option. For example:

```
tail -f /var/log/carddavd/access.log
```

At the beginning of the chapter, you looked at the vCard files themselves. These can be viewed from the command line. Simply cd into the appropriate directory, and then use the cat command to view the contents of a .vcf file, which should appear similar to the following:

BEGIN:VCARD

VERSION:3.0

N:Smith;Zack;;;

FN:Zack Smith

ORG:318;

CATEGORIES:My Contacts

X-ABUID:F49B4804-6B5A-49D9–ABA8-C67F7FDEAF2D\:ABPerson

UID:A652C0F5-45E3-4D13-9789–FF964551AFB9–ABSPlugin

REV:2009–11-30T05:51:20Z

END:VCARD

> **NOTE:** You can also look up LDAP contacts from the command line. To do so, you can use the
> `dscl` command, which is a front-end tool for the directory services daemon in Mac OS X.

Alternatives to Apple's Address Book Server

Despite the power and flexibility it offers, Address Book services aren't the only game in town for managing and serving address books, nor are they perfect for everyone; therefore, Address Book services on Mac OS X Server are not the only methods for sharing address books that we will cover in this chapter. You see, Address Book server has some serious limitations, and if your Address Book service is to be a full-featured groupware solution, then you're going to need to address these shortcomings (no pun intended). Let's take a step back and look strategically at how Apple perceives contact sharing to work. The following is a list of solutions, indicating the preferred solution for a given environment:

- *MobileMe:* This is for sharing contacts between a very limited number of users. For example, if you have a family pack for MobileMe (or two stand-alone accounts), you can share contacts between two MobileMe users. You can also synchronize your own contacts between your local computer and MobileMe, which then has the capability of sharing those contacts to other computers that you own (this method of sharing, though, is not meant to be multiuser).

- *Microsoft Exchange:* For environments with an Exchange server, Microsoft Exchange (likely Exchange 2007 given the seamless integration sported by Mac OS X 10.6) will act as the shared contact repository. We will not be covering Exchange further in this book, although it is covered in detail in the Apress book *Enterprise Mac Administrator's Guide*.

- *Address Book Server:* This third-party product predates the inclusion of address book services management in Mac OS X Server and is why we shy away from calling the Address Book services in Mac OS X Server *Address Book Server*. Address Book Server, from http://www.addressbookserver.com, allows you to publish your contacts to a server, synchronize them to that server, and then have them accessible from any account with access to that server, a feature known to Microsoft Exchange as a *global address list* (GAL).

- *LDAP:* Contacts are looked up based on LDAP. LDAP itself is described further in Chapter 4, although for the purposes of this chapter we will actually spend some time publishing contacts in LDAP and subscribing to them on a client computer. Once we have covered MobileMe and the Mac OS X Address Book services, we will cover leveraging LDAP to provide a global address list of sorts for all users.

Summary

Mac OS X Server is all about collaboration, and until version 10.6 was released, it lacked a robust means of storing and sharing address and contact information. The Address Book service does nicely to fulfill this need, and although it may not yet be as robust as other options available, it suffices nicely for many environments. This chapter explained its features and limitations, so you can now deploy it with confidence.

Chapter 10

Working with iCal Server

Mac OS X Server can act as a centralized server to allow your users to communicate with one another, sharing calendars among users. The ability to act as a calendaring server is paramount in providing a fully featured groupware solution. In Mac OS X Server 10.6, iCal Server is in its second iteration and now a mature solution capable of serving data for even the most complicated needs.

In this chapter, we're going to install iCal Server on Mac OS X Server, so we'll also need to set up CalDAV. CalDAV is an extension of the WebDAV protocol, a protocol long supported by Mac OS X Server. CalDAV is a well-defined open standard, so developing around it is in no way a black box. However, it is not as widely dispersed as Microsoft Exchange, so fewer tools integrate with it.

Still, nothing is likely to work better with iCal Server than the iCal client itself, included by default with all Mac OS X installations. Therefore, we will cover the client software and how to integrate with Mac OS X Server seamlessly as well in this chapter, providing an overview of the typical settings to use and some of the gotchas that many administrators face. Alternative clients include open source programs like Mozilla Sunbird and the Mulberry e-mail and calendaring application. Additionally, several third-party Microsoft Outlook plug-ins are available, such as ZideOne and Mulberry, though they tend to perform less reliably.

Getting Ready to Install iCal Server

There are a number of tasks that you will need to accomplish before you move into the installation and configuration of your iCal server. First and foremost is to have a properly configured DNS. This includes both forward and reverse lookups of the host name of the server on which you are configuring the iCal services. You can use the changeip command with the –checkhostname option to verify the DNS on the server prior to starting up the services, for example:

```
changeip -checkhostname
```

Additionally, the server is going to need to be either running as an Open Directory master or configured to be a part of an Open Directory environment. In versions of Mac OS X

Server previous to 10.6, you either needed to run iCal services on an Open Directory master or leverage augmented records, a needless complication. However, now, you can now run iCal services on a Mac OS X Server connected to your Open Directory services (as was covered in Chapter 4) without first setting up augmented records.

Finally, other services can interact with the iCal service, namely, the Mail and Web services that provide e-mail notifications of calendar events and a web portal with which users are able to view these events. If you wish to use these features with iCal services, make sure they are configured and running.

> **NOTE:** While Open Directory is definitely easier to use other directory services with the iCal service, if you are running a different directory service, such as Active Directory, all is not lost. You can use iCal Server along with your directory service, but you will need to leverage augmented records to do so.

Configuring iCal Server

To get started with iCal Server, first install the service. On a freshly installed Mac OS X Server that is either running as a directory server or already bound to one, open the Server Preferences application. Server Preferences can be found at /Applications/Server and when opened looks far less intimidating than Server Admin (see Figure 10–1);Server Preferences can be considered to be like a simplified version of Server Admin.

To enable the iCal service:

1. Click the orb just to the left of the iCal icon.

2. As shown in Figure 10–2, click the "Limit each calendar event's size to" field and provide a number (in megabytes for the maximum size of a calendar event, keeping in mind that calendar events can contain attachments). Next, click the "Limit each user's total calendar size to" field and provide a maximum per user. If you will not be using attachments, you can use a number around one megabyte or smaller, at which point storage becomes a minimal issue.

3. Move the slider to the On position, and the service will start up.

Figure 10–1. *The Server Preferences application*

Figure 10–2. *Enabling iCal service using Server Preferences*

4. At this point, you might be saying to yourself, "That can't be all there is." Well, you're right. You can also set up iCal to show the service in Server Admin. To do so, first open Server Admin from /Applications/Server. After authenticating, click the name of the server where you will be installing the iCal service to bring up the servers base settings. Here, click the Settings icon in the toolbar to bring up the services selection screen, where you can configure which services will run on the server (although simply enabling them in this screen will not start them), as shown in Figure 10–3.

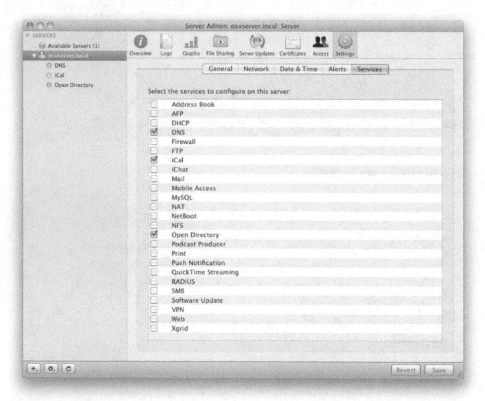

Figure 10–3. *Enabling the iCal Service*

5. Check the box for iCal, and click the Save button. You should then see the iCal service appear in the SERVERS list when you drop down the disclosure triangle to show the active services on the server. Here, click the Settings icon in the Server Admin toolbar to bring up the settings that Apple has provided you for iCal.

6. Click the iCal server entry and you will see a number of options, including these (see Figure 10–4):

- *Data Store:* Set the location on the server's file system for the iCal database.

- *Maximum Attachment Size:* Establish the maximum size of a given attachment (and therefore the maximum size of a given event).

- *User Quota:* Establish the maximum size of a user's calendar.

- *Log Level:* Set the verbosity with which you want the iCal server to trap event logs.

- *Push Notification Server:* By default, this will list the current server, but it can be used to select another host in high-volume environments. The Push Notification Server option enables the most seamless interaction between iPhone and Mac OS X Server's groupware services offerings. We'll cover more on Push notification later in this chapter.

- *Wiki Server:* This is the name or IP address of the server that will be used to provide web integration between calendars and wikis. If the wiki services will be running on the server that also runs the iCal services, leave 127.0.0.1 in this field; otherwise, provide the name or IP address for the server you are using for wiki integration services.

- *Use SSL:* Signal whether to use Secure Sockets Layer (SSL) to protect communications between the iCal service and the web server when Wiki integration has been enabled.

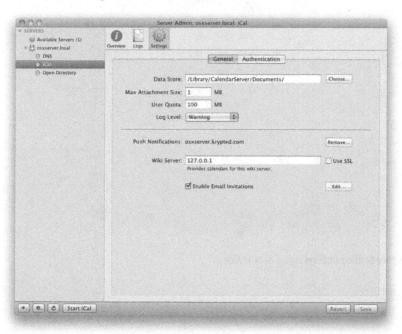

Figure 10–4. *Configuring the iCal service using Server Admin*

7. Configure the authentication settings as appropriate for your environment, as shown in Figure 10–5:

■ *Type:* Select the authentication method used—Digest, Kerberos, or Any Method. Forcing the use of Kerberos or digest authentication can be useful in troubleshooting or to enforce encryption policies.

■ *Host Name:* Provide the DNS name of the server (or service if you have multiple records pointing to the host).

■ *Port:* Set the port that the iCal service runs on.

■ *SSL:* Select a certificate that has been installed on the host. Even if you are using a self-assigned certificate on the Mac OS X Server, you should use SSL when possible.

■ *SSL Port:* Identify the port that the iCal service runs on when used with SSL.

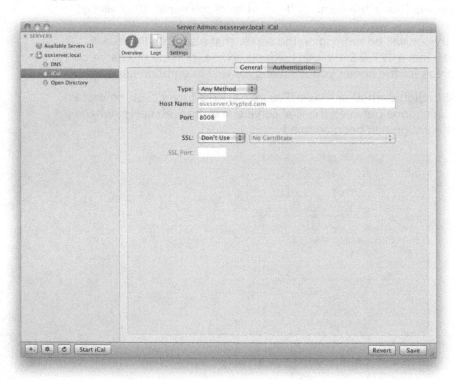

Figure 10–5. *Configuring authentication options using Server Admin*

8. Click the Save button.

9. You can now click the Start iCal button to start the iCal service. Once
    started you will note that the iCal Service will indicate that it is running in
    the Overview screen of Server Admin and that the Start iCal button will
    change to Stop iCal (Figure 10–6).

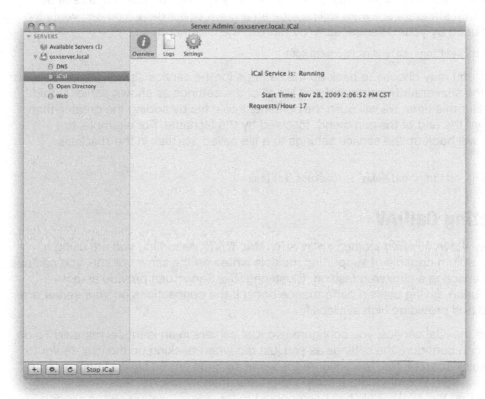

Figure 10–6. *Checking the iCal Server Status*

NOTE: iCal services can be proxied quickly and easily for remote users using the Mobile Access
service; see Chapter 13 for more information on leveraging this service.

Managing the iCal Server

In this section, we're going to look at some of the basic tasks that you will likely need to
perform when managing an iCal Server. We'll start with one of the most important
aspects of any computer (whether a server or client)—backing it up. We will also look at
clustering and integrating iCal Server with other services within Mac OS X Server, such
as Mail (for e-mailing updates) and the wiki (so that you can see your calendar from a
web page). We will then move on to enabling calendars for users in the next section of
this chapter.

Backing Up Calendars

The calendar file itself is located by default in the `/Library/CalendarServer/Documents` directory. You can customize this folder, so when you're going to back it up, be careful that no one has changed the default location. Simply backing up the contents of this directory with standard software will provide an archive of the data. You can verify the directory used by your Calendar store by running the command:

```
serveradmin settings calendar:DocumentRoot
```

However, you may choose to back up the settings for the service as well. To do so, you can use the `serveradmin` command and list all of the settings as shown earlier in this chapter. But this time, we will push the contents into a file by adding the greater-than symbol(>)at the end of the command, followed by the filename. For example, the following will back up the service settings to a file called `icalbak` in the `/backups` directory:

```
serveradmin settings calendar > /backups/icalbak
```

Clustering CalDAV

In Chapter 4, we covered storage options for Mac OS X. Assuming you are using a storage medium capable of supporting multiple writes on the same volume, you can use the iCal service in a clustered fashion. Clustering iCal Server can provide an active-active solution, giving users a performance boost if the connections on your server are saturated and providing high availability.

To cluster the iCal service, you configure two iCal servers in an identical manner. To do this, you can configure the settings as you just did when backing up the iCal server to the `/backups/icalbak` file. To configure the same settings on the second host, use the same `serveradmin` command but swap the greater-than symbol for less-than (<), assuming that the `icalbak` file has been copied to the same location on the second server:

```
Serveradmin settings calendar < /backups/icalbak
```

After running this, update the SSL settings on the second host to ensure a proper SSL certification is specified. Next, we'll move the calendar files to the server in a shared directory location. In this case, we'll copy the `/Library/CalendarServer` directory to the `/volumes/Xsan/` volume we previously created. Then, we'll point the directories for the calendar server at our shared storage:

```
serveradmin settings calendar:DocumentRoot = "/Volumes/Xsan/CalendarServer/Documents/"
serveradmin settings calendar:DataRoot = "/Volumes/Xsan/CalendarServer/Data/"
```

When you are comfortable with the settings, stop and start the iCal service:

```
serveradmin stop calendar
serveradmin start calendar
```

Now, it is up to you how to distribute the load across the two servers. Load balancers are the most obvious choice in many environments, but operating in a shared namespace and using round robin DNS will work as well, likely incurring no additional hardware costs for your setup (beyond, of course, having two or more copies of the Mac OS X Server software).

Integrating with a Wiki

Users are also able to view and manage calendars through the web portal provided as part of the wiki services in Mac OS X Server. Prior to configuring the calendar integration for the web portal, see Chapter 14 for configuring the web server.

Once configured, use the Wiki Server option from the "Configuring iCAl Server" section earlier in this chapter to define the server that will run the web interface (it should be 127.0.0.1 if the web interface is running on the same system as the iCal service or the host name or IP address of the server running the web services).

Next, click the web service in Server Admin for the Mac OS X Server that will be running the web front end for the iCal service. Then, click the site that you wish to configure access to the calendar for, and click the Web Services tab for that site, as shown in Figure 10–7. Check the box for Calendar, and click the Save button. If the service has not yet been started, use the Start Web button to begin running it.

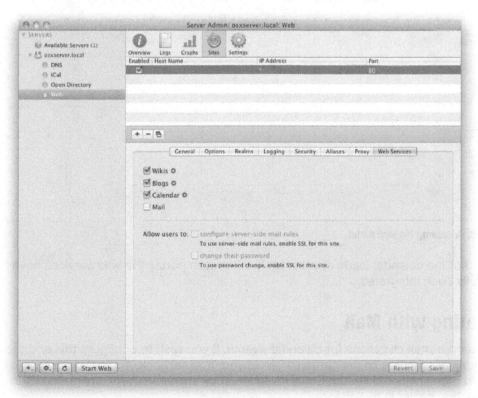

Figure 10–7. *Configuring Web Services Integration*

Once the web services have been configured and started, you can then log into the web portal from a client computer or from the server. To do so, open Safari from a client computer, and enter the address of the web server followed by /ical. For example, if the server is caldav.krypted.com, the address to use to connect to the calendars, enter http://caldav.krypted.com/ical into Safari's address bar. When the page loads, you will be prompted to authenticate. Enter a username and password for a user who has calendars configured (configuring calendars for specific users is explained in further detail later in this chapter), and click the OK button. The calendar will then load and should appear similar the one shown in Figure 10–8.

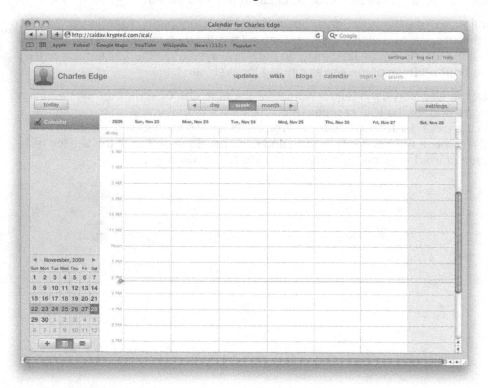

Figure 10–8. *Accessing the web portal*

Provided that the calendar loads appropriately in the web portal, the wiki services have successfully been integrated.

Integrating with Mail

iCal can send e-mail invitations for calendar events. If you wish to configure this and the mail services are running on the same server as your iCal services, you will have little more to do than check the Enable Email Invitations box shown in the "Configuring iCal Server" section earlier in this chapter.

Because not all environments are so simple, Apple has provided the ability to more granularly configure the connection between calendar and mail servers. From Server Admin, click the iCal service in the SERVERS list for the server that is running the iCal service, and click the Settings icon in the Server Admin toolbar. From the General tab, click the Edit button for Enable Email Invitations to bring up the Email Invitations settings overlay screen. Here, you can configure settings to be used for incoming mail and outgoing mail (incoming mail is used to receive invitations, whereas outgoing mail is used to send them). The settings include the following:

- *Mail Server Type*: Set the type of mail server that you will be receiving mail through. Options are IMAP(the default setting)and POP.

- *Email Address*: Provide an e-mail address that incoming invitations and responses to invitations will use.

- *Incoming Mail Server*: Identify the server IP address or host name that runs the Mail service for your environment.

    - *Port:* Provide the port number used by the Incoming mail service indicated in Mail Server Type.

    - *Use SSL:* Indicate whether to use SSL certificates to protect communications between the mail server and the calendar server.

    - *User Name:* Supply the username to use for authenticating to the incoming mail server.

    - *Password:* Set the password to use for authenticating to the incoming mail server.

- *Outgoing Mail Server (SMTP)*: Indicate the user who will be sending mail from the calendaring service.

    - *Port:* Specify the port number that SMTP uses to send mail through your organizations mail server.

    - *Use SSL:* Enable SSL for SMTP communications with the mail server indicated in the Outgoing Mail Server field.

    - *Server requires authentication:* Indicate whether the outgoing server allows for anyone to send mail, whether they have a valid password for the server or not. If not, check the box, and provide a username and password in the following two fields.

    - *User Name:* Provide the username from which you will be sending mail.

    - *Password:* Set the password used to authenticate for the user indicated in the above User Name field.

> **NOTE:** If you are using the same server for mail that you use for iCal, the default settings should work with no problem. If you do need to customize these settings, do so carefully.

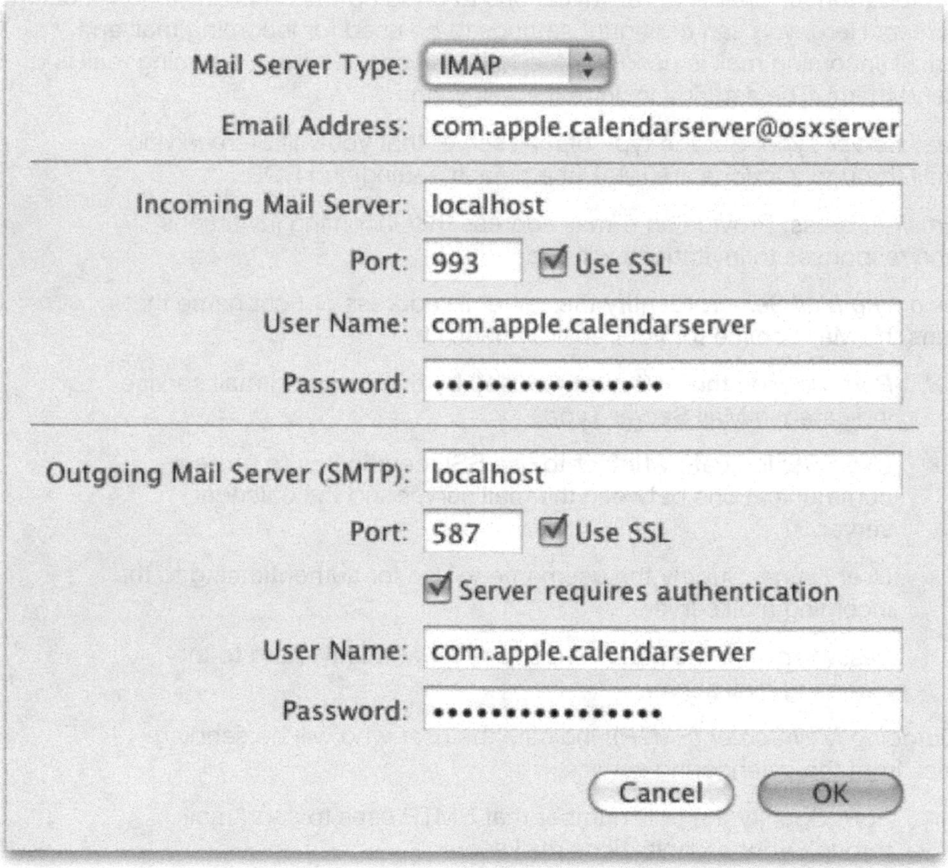

Mail Server Type: IMAP

Email Address: com.apple.calendarserver@osxserver

Incoming Mail Server: localhost

Port: 993   ☑ Use SSL

User Name: com.apple.calendarserver

Password: ●●●●●●●●●●●●●●●●

Outgoing Mail Server (SMTP): localhost

Port: 587   ☑ Use SSL

☑ Server requires authentication

User Name: com.apple.calendarserver

Password: ●●●●●●●●●●●●●●●●

(Cancel)   (OK)

Figure 10–9. *Configuring mail integration*

Once you have configured your mail connection settings, click the OK button, and use the Save button to commit your changes. If you have altered the settings, restart the service, and test that your invitations and acceptances function (these are explained further later in this chapter).

Enabling Calendars for Users

Once you have enabled the iCal service, you will want to provide access to calendars for your users. To do so, you can enable the service for an account, again using the Server Preferences tool. Simply open Server Preferences, and click the name of a user you'd like to configure, and you'll see a listing of services the user can access on the right side of the screen as in Figure 10–10.

Figure 10–10. *Enabling services for users*

Configuring iCal Clients

The next step is to set up iCal on the user's workstation. To get started, open iCal from the Dock (or if it's not in the Dock any longer, from /Application directory). Then click the iCal menu, selecting the preference option (or use the Command + comma keystroke). Next, click the Accounts icon in the application preferences toolbar to bring up the list of accounts, which you can see in Figure 10–11. Click the plus (+) sign to add an account.

Figure 10–11. *Creating an iCal account*

You will see the Add an Account screen, where you can fill in the name, e-mail address, and password of the user whose account you are setting up (see Figure 10–12). Enter the user's e-mail address and password, and click the Create button when you are finished.

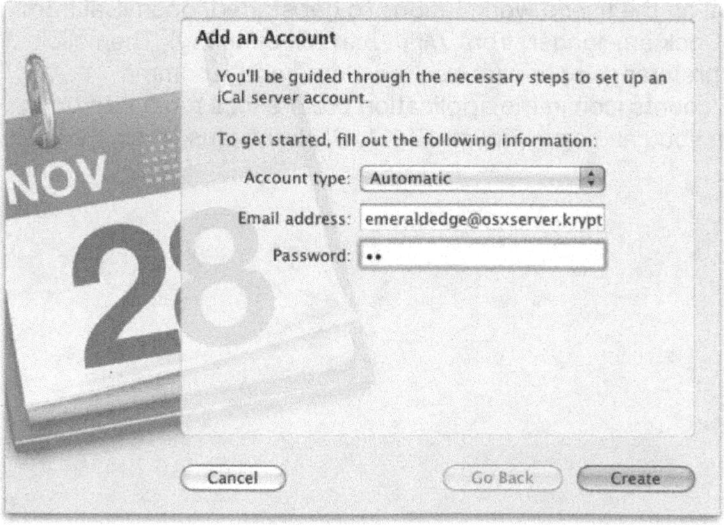

Figure 10–12. *Creating an iCal account*

If the client doesn't automatically enumerate the account information for the user, you can enter the account credentials and server information manually, selecting CalDAV as the Account Type, as shown in Figure 10–13.

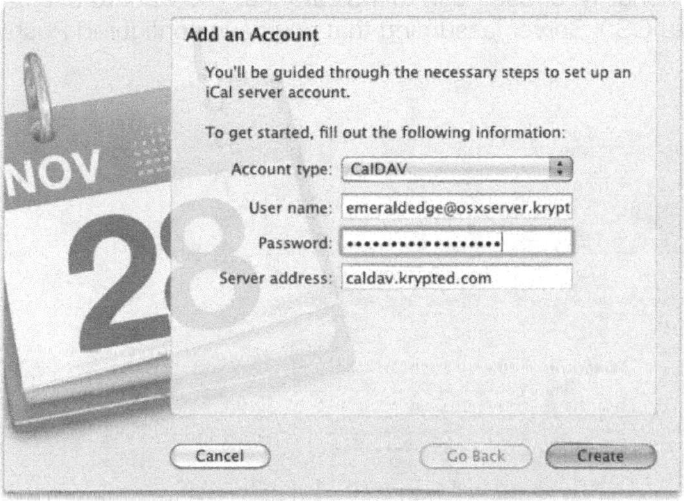

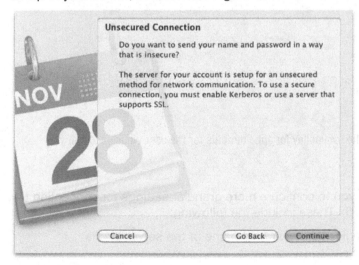

Add an Account

You'll be guided through the necessary steps to set up an iCal server account.

To get started, fill out the following information:

Account type: CalDAV

User name: emeraldedge@osxserver.krypt

Password: ••••••••••••••••

Server address: caldav.krypted.com

Cancel   Go Back   Create

Figure 10–13 *iCal account creation connection information*

> **NOTE:** If you are using Mobile Access to remotely access the iCal service from client systems, those systems will invariably not be using Kerberos for connectivity.

If you don't enable Kerberos or SSL, you will be prompted as to whether you want to use an unsecured connection. Now, you can click the Continue button to complete the setup of your server, as shown in Figure 10–14.

Unsecured Connection

Do you want to send your name and password in a way that is insecure?

The server for your account is setup for an unsecured method for network communication. To use a secure connection, you must enable Kerberos or use a server that supports SSL.

Cancel   Go Back   Continue

Figure 10–14. *iCal account creation security confirmation*

Once you have set up the client, you can set up iCal to communicate using Push or configure the frequency that the client communicates with the server. Use the "Refresh calendars" drop-down list (shown in Figure 10–15) to select that frequency in terms of minutes, set the refresh rate to Manually, or use Push to indicate that you want to use Push Notification services in Mac OS X Server (assuming that you have configured Push Notification services).

Figure 10–15. *iCal account information*

NOTE: You can also configure the availability for appointments for the user whose account you are configuring here.

The Server Settings tab allows you to configure more granular settings for connecting to the iCal server (see Figure 10–16). These include the following:

- *Server address:* Set the IP address or host name of the server that is hosting the iCal service.

- Server path: Allow customizing of the connection path, which is useful when troubleshooting, given that CalDAV runs as extensions to WebDAV and, therefore, should be able to be browsed from a web browser.

- Port: Provide the port number that the iCal server is using.

- Use SSL: Enable SSL for the connection.

- Use Kerberos v5 for authentication: Locally, Kerberos will allow for single-sign on (and therefore a more automated mass deployment). However, Kerberos will not be supported if you are running the Mobile Access service to allow remote clients to connect to the server.

Figure 10–16. *iCal Server Settings*

Delegation means allowing other users to access your calendar. Clicking the Delegation tab in the Accounts settings for the account that you are configuring will pull a list of the users who have been given delegate access to the calendar. By default, as shown in Figure 10–17, the list is empty. Click the Edit button to add a delegate.

Figure 10–17. *iCal Account Delegation*

At the Manage Account Access screen (which is shown in Figure 10–18), you will be able to add the users who have delegate access to your calendar. Click the plus sign (+) to add a user, and type the username. Provided that the address resolves properly, you can also click the Allow Write check box to provide edit access, in addition to read access, to the calendar.

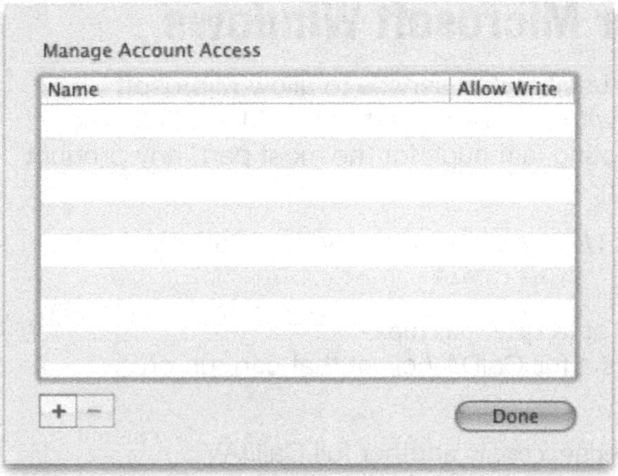

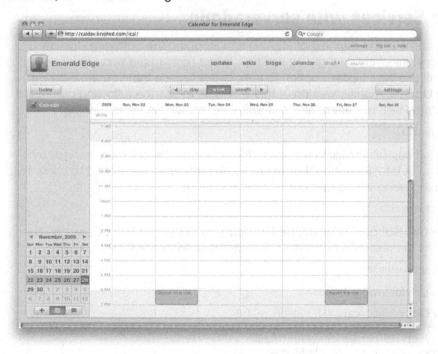

Figure 10–18. *Adding iCal Delegates*

Finally, you can also log into the account using the web portal. To do so, open Safari from a client computer, and enter the address of the server into the address bar followed by /ical in the address. For example, if the web server that is hosting the wiki service is caldav.krypted.com, the address in the address bar should be http://caldav.krypted.com/ical. You will then be prompted to authenticate into the server. Provided that the authentication is successful, you should see the users calendar, as indicated in Figure 10–19.

Figure 10–19. *The iCal wiki interface*

Setting Up iCal Clients for Microsoft Windows

iCal isn't just for Mac OS X. You can also use the iCal service to allow Microsoft Windows–based clients to communicate with the clients that run on Mac OS X. The following CalDAV connectors are worth noting (although for the most part, any product that supports CalDAV should be sufficient):

- *OpenConnector*, available at http://openconnector.org, is a CalDAV plug-in for Microsoft Outlook.

- *PostBox with Lightning*, available at http://postbox-inc.com/extensions/lightning, is a full CalDAV client that can run on Mac and Windows.

- *ZideOne*, available at http://zideone.com, is another full CalDAV client.

Using the Command Line for iCal Services

The command line options for the iCal services are fairly mature compared to some of the other services in Mac OS X Server. In addition to controlling the state of the service itself, you can also configure settings and perform a variety of troubleshooting steps, as we'll explore throughout the following sections.

Configuring Services with serveradmin

The serveradmin command is capable of starting and stopping the Software Update service and of more granularly configuring settings. When running the serveradmin command, you will use the swupdate option to specify the service that you are working with as Software Update. A basic version of this would be to use the following command, which uses the status verb to determine if the Software Update Server is running:

```
serveradmin status iCal
```

In addition, you can use serveradmin to look at the critical settings for the service by running it with the fullstatus option. For example, the following command to show that the server is running along with a number of critical settings:

```
serveradmin fullstatus iCal
```

In addition to the two GUI panels developed by Apple, a host of other options can be accessed using the serveradmin command. To see the available settings, use this:

```
Serveradmin settings calendar
```

You will then see the following items:

```
calendar:SudoersFile = "/etc/caldavd/sudoers.plist"
calendar:DirectoryService:params:restrictEnabledRecords = no
calendar:DirectoryService:params:restrictToGroup = ""
calendar:DirectoryService:params:cacheTimeout = 30
calendar:DirectoryService:params:node = "/Search"
```

```
calendar:DirectoryService:type = "twistedcaldav.directory.~CCC
appleopendirectory.OpenDirectoryService"
calendar:Aliases = _empty_dictionary
calendar:BindSSLPorts = _empty_array
calendar:EnablePrincipalListings = no
calendar:DocumentRoot = "/Library/CalendarServer/Documents/"
calendar:EnableDropBox = yes
calendar:SSLPrivateKey = ""
calendar:ServerStatsFile = "/var/run/caldavd/stats.plist"
calendar:ProcessType = "Combined"
calendar:UserName = "calendar"
calendar:BindHTTPPorts = _empty_array
calendar:EnableAnonymousReadRoot = yes
calendar:HTTPPort = 8008
calendar:ServerHostName = ""
calendar:PIDFile = "/var/run/caldavd.pid"
calendar:Authentication:Digest:Algorithm = "md5"
calendar:Authentication:Digest:Qop = ""
calendar:Authentication:Digest:Enabled = yes
calendar:Authentication:Kerberos:ServicePrincipal = ""
calendar:Authentication:Kerberos:Enabled = yes
calendar:Authentication:Wiki:Enabled = yes
calendar:Authentication:Basic:Enabled = no
calendar:ReadPrincipals = _empty_array
calendar:EnableTimezoneService = yes
calendar:FreeBusyURL:AnonymousAccess = no
calendar:FreeBusyURL:Enabled = yes
calendar:FreeBusyURL:TimePeriod = 14
calendar:UserQuota = 104857600
calendar:MaximumAttachmentSize = 1048576
calendar:MultiProcess:ProcessCount = 0
calendar:EnableProxyPrincipals = yes
calendar:DefaultLogLevel = "warn"
calendar:EnableMonolithicCalendars = yes
calendar:ErrorLogFile = "/var/log/caldavd/error.log"
calendar:SSLCertificate = ""
calendar:EnableSACLs = no
calendar:Notifications:CoalesceSeconds = 10
calendar:Notifications:Services:XMPPNotifier:Host = "snowleopardserver.krypted.com"
calendar:Notifications:Services:XMPPNotifier:JID = "com.apple.notificationuser~CCC
@snowleopardserver.krypted.com"
calendar:Notifications:Services:XMPPNotifier:Enabled = yes
calendar:Notifications:Services:XMPPNotifier:Service = "twistedcaldav.notify.~CCC
XMPPNotifierService"
calendar:Notifications:Services:XMPPNotifier:Port = 5222
calendar:Notifications:Services:XMPPNotifier:ServiceAddress = "pubsub.~CCC
snowleopardserver.krypted.com"
calendar:EnableAnonymousReadNav = no
calendar:DataRoot = "/Library/CalendarServer/Data/"
calendar:BindAddresses = _empty_array
calendar:AdminPrincipals = _empty_array
calendar:RedirectHTTPToHTTPS = no
calendar:RotateAccessLog = no
calendar:GroupName = "calendar"
calendar:EnablePrivateEvents = yes
calendar:AccessLogFile = "/var/log/caldavd/access.log"
calendar:Scheduling:CalDAV:EmailDomain = ""
```

```
calendar:Scheduling:CalDAV:HTTPDomain = ""
calendar:Scheduling:CalDAV:AddressPatterns = _empty_array
calendar:Scheduling:iSchedule:Servers = "/etc/caldavd/servertoserver.xml"
calendar:Scheduling:iSchedule:Enabled = no
calendar:Scheduling:iSchedule:AddressPatterns = _empty_array
calendar:Scheduling:iMIP:Receiving:Server = ""
calendar:Scheduling:iMIP:Receiving:UseSSL = yes
calendar:Scheduling:iMIP:Receiving:PollingSeconds = 30
calendar:Scheduling:iMIP:Receiving:Username = ""
calendar:Scheduling:iMIP:Receiving:Type = ""
calendar:Scheduling:iMIP:Receiving:Password = ""
calendar:Scheduling:iMIP:Receiving:Port = 995
calendar:Scheduling:iMIP:MailGatewayServer = "localhost"
calendar:Scheduling:iMIP:Enabled = no
calendar:Scheduling:iMIP:MailGatewayPort = 62310
calendar:Scheduling:iMIP:AddressPatterns = _empty_array
calendar:Scheduling:iMIP:Sending:Server = ""
calendar:Scheduling:iMIP:Sending:Username = ""
calendar:Scheduling:iMIP:Sending:Address = ""
calendar:Scheduling:iMIP:Sending:UseSSL = yes
calendar:Scheduling:iMIP:Sending:Password = ""
calendar:Scheduling:iMIP:Sending:Port = 587
```

Many of these settings appear cryptic, but you'll find they allow for the most granular configuration of the services. You can customize these items by using the same command and but pasting the particular setting on to the end of it, along with the desired value. For example, if you want to force all users who can authenticate into the iCal service to have an account in the directory services, you would use the following command:

```
Serveradmin settings calendar:DirectoryService:params:restrictEnabledRecords = yes
```

> **TIP:** You can further reduce the maximum attachment size to the bytes level using the
> `calendar:MaximumAttachmentSize` setting.

Each of the preceding settings can be altered using the `serveradmin` command with the `settings` option, followed by the string with the new content. For example, to change the path of the service log to the same folder on a different drive called LOGS, you would use the following command:

```
serveradmin settings
```

Serveradmin primarily gives you the ability to configure the service from the perspective of Mac OS X Server. However, keep in mind that the iCal service is actually leveraging Jabber, which is an open source package. Therefore, you can also edit the Jabber configuration files directly or edit the /etc directory, which we will cover in the next section of this chapter.

> **NOTE:** You can also just run `serveradmin` settings iCal for a full listing of all settings, but as
> the output includes information on each update it is far too verbose to include here.

Troubleshooting iCal Server

Now that you have installed your new server you may at times have a few problems. Let's take a look at the common issues and a few simple fixes for them.

Getting the iCal Service to Start

One common issue is that iCal Server will not start and shows log entries that say it is unable to create a virtual host. In this scenario, first check your server's host name. iCal Server needs the host name to be correct in order to start. Use `scutil --get HostName`, and make sure that the host name listed in the iCal Server settings is identical to this value.

Resolving Nil Errors

Another common issue is that you set up a user, check the box in Workgroup Manager for Enable Calendaring, and then save your settings, but you get the following error in your logs:

```
Oct 12 15:51:26 cedge Workgroup Manager[2282]: +[WPUser userWithGUID::] returned nil!
```

This error is likely caused by the fact that you are enabling a calendar for a local user. Try using an Open Directory–based user, and see if you get the same error.

Getting Uncooperative Clients to Connect

Perhaps you got everything started and the account was created for the user, but when you add an account in iCal, it fails to connect.

In this case, make sure that the iCal Server port is located at the tail end of the host name for the iCal Server. Unless you are using managed accounts, iCal Server is not likely going to append the port number for you.

Also verify that you can connect to the remote server, and remember that you can always use the URL of the server followed by a colon (:) and the port number to get a login prompt. If you can authenticate to this as the user whose calendar you are trying to set up, so you can use the information in this screen to determine ACL information and other security settings that could be keeping calendars from working. Then too, keep in mind that while your general default port might be set to 8008, your default port if you are using SSL is actually 8443.

Once you get this far, you should be able to create an event and see data listed in the Overview tab for iCal. If so, you should be able to do just about anything you want in iCal Server.

If you prefer to use the `serveradmin` command to control your services, you can also use the `serveradmin settings calendar:ServerHostName = "SomeHostName"` variable to change your host name. You can also use `calendar:HTTPPort` to change the port number you are using for connectivity.

Finding Errant Log Files

A number of users have been reporting an error that "The selected logfile does not exist." If you see this error, first verify that the /var/log/caldavd directory is present on the system. If not, use the mkdir command to create it:

```
mkdir /var/log/caldavd
```

Next, restart the service, and see if access.log and error.log are created in this folder. If not, run the following:

```
touch /var/log/caldavd/access.log
touch /var/log/caldavd/error.log
```

And for good measure, set appropriate permissions on those files:

```
chmod 640 access.log
chmod 640 error.log
```

How did I know where those logs go? I ran these commands:

```
serveradmin settings calendar:ErrorLogFile
serveradmin settings calendar:AccessLogFile
```

Similarly, it's possible to actually decide you'd rather your iCal Server logs to be stored in some random location, such as /foo/logs as follows:

```
serveradmin settings calendar:ErrorLogFile="/foo/logs/error.log"
serveradmin settings calendar:AccessLogFile="/foo/logs/access.log"
```

And of course, make sure there are some files in those paths to catch the logs, which brings up an interesting point—you can also use a path to a network location as the destination.

Overall, there are a number of options for troubleshooting the iCal service, and a definitive methodology has not yet surfaced other than checking your logs and troubleshooting accordingly. Good luck with your iCal services and stay tuned to the Apple Knowledge Base (http://www.apple.com/support), Charles's site (http://www.krypted.com) and the 318 company site (http://www.318.com/techjournal) for more troubleshooting tips on the iCal service.

Summary

Many an environment will already have a calendaring solution. But if you are dissatisfied with your calendaring solution or just want more than what a typical MobileMe account can give, iCal Server provides an awesome alternative. The second release of iCal Server (Mac OS X Server 10.5 was the first) is a stable, solid calendaring solution.

As we've shown in this chapter, iCal Server doesn't just synchronize your calendar to a server. iCal Server is a collaborative solution, allowing you to share calendars and use your calendar on multiple devices. You can also integrate iCal Server with other services: it can e-mail you invitations, and you can interact with it through the web services built into Mac OS X Server. The steps laid out in this chapter can be used to accomplish all of this!

In Chapter 11, we move from calendaring to another form of collaboration—instant messaging. Using the steps in the next chapter, you will be able to set up a private instant messaging server that allows you to communicate with peers without exposing your network to services such as AOL Instant Messenger.

iChat Server

Mac OS X Server can act as a centralized chat server to allow your users to communicate with one another in real time. This can take several forms, including text-based instant messages, file transfers, audio chat sessions, and video conferences. The iChat service gives users powerful and innovative ways to communicate and interact, opening up new possibilities for collaboration and productivity.

Many longtime Mac users probably associate the term *iChat* with the free instant messenger application that has been included in every version of Mac OS X since version 10.2. Since its introduction, users of MobileMe (formerly .Mac) have used iChat to connect to each other and to the AOL Instant Messenger (AIM) network. However, while the iChat name is the same, the iChat service in Mac OS X Server is slightly different, in that it offers centralized management and control over how your users connect to one another and to users and servers outside of your organization, including those on the Internet at large. This centralized management allows you to prevent the use of a third-party service, such as AIM, and allows you more control over instant messaging in your environment.

Snow Leopard server's iChat service is Apple's implementation of a protocol called Jabber, more officially known as the Extensible Messaging and Presence Protocol (XMPP). Like many technologies integrated into Mac OS X, Jabber is an open standard, so anybody can develop solutions for it and communicate with it. And because it is based on XML, it is highly extensible and flexible, allowing servers that utilize the Jabber protocol to connect to one another through a process called *federation*. This means that your iChat server can connect not only with other Mac servers running the iChat service but with *any* XMPP-compliant server that is configured to accept connections from federated servers.

In a Mac OS X environment, end users can use the iChat application to connect to an iChat server, although any Jabber-compliant client application will work. The fact that any Jabber-compliant application can connect to Mac OS X Server opens up connectivity across any platform and even federation to other services, such as Google Talk.

Setting Up iChat Server

There are two ways to set up a Mac OS X Server to be an iChat Server. The first is using the Server Preferences tool, located in /Applications/Server. A basic setup can easily be done through Server Preferences and will likely not require you to open up Server Admin. As your needs become more complex, you can revert to using Server Admin for administration rather than Server Preferences, offering a flexible approach to iChat Server administration.

Setting Up iChat Server Using Server Preferences

The most straightforward way to get iChat Server up and running is to use Server Preferences. This tool allows for the configuration of only a couple of options, but those are all you need in most environments. To get started, open Server Preferences from /Applications/Server. Once its open, you will see a list of the services on the server, which you will notice in Figure 11–1. Here, click iChat.

Figure 11–1. *Server Preferences*

At the iChat screen, you will have three options. The first is "Log and archive all chats," which is disabled by default. Check this box if you wish the server to save a centralized transcript, of every instant message sent through the iChat Server; the transcript is searchable through Spotlight (the powerful search tool built into Mac OS X). The second option is "Enable server-to-server communication," which, again, is known as *federation* in this context. If you will be federating the server as we described in the introduction of this chapter, leave this box checked (it is enabled by default); otherwise, uncheck the box to help keep your server as secure as possible. Once you are satisfied with these two settings, use the slider in the lower left corner of the screen to set the Service to On (as shown in Figure 11–2), thus enabling the service.

Figure 11–2. *Enabling the iChat service using Server Preferences*

Setting Up iChat Server Using Server Admin

The first step to setting up using Server Admin is to enable the iChat in the utility. To do this, open Server Admin from /Applications/Server. After authenticating, click the name of the server where you will be enabling the iChat service to bring up the server's base settings. Here, click the Settings icon in the toolbar to open the Services selection screen, where you can configure which services will run on the server, as shown in Figure 11–3. However, simply enabling services in this screen will not start them.

Check the box for iChat, and click the Save button. You should then see the iChat service appear in the SERVERS list when you drop down the disclosure triangle to show the active services on the server. Here, click the Settings icon in the Server Admin toolbar to bring up the settings that Apple has provided you for iChat.

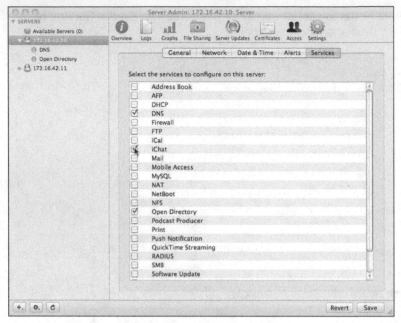

Figure 11–3. *Enabling the iChat service using Server Admin*

Configuring Advanced Features

Now that you have enabled the service, you will want to configure and start it up. By default, the Settings page for iChat looks similar to Figure 11–4.

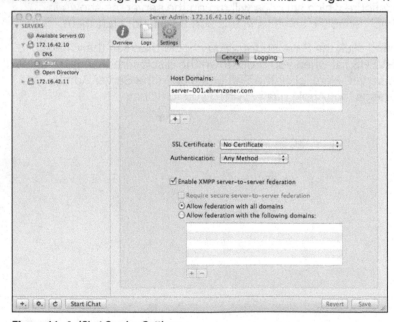

Figure 11–4. *iChat Service Settings*

For most environments, the default settings will suffice, but if you choose to customize settings, you can use the following options:

- *Host Domains*: In this field, you can specify the domains for which the iChat service will host Jabber services. Since Jabber IDs are constructed in a `username@domain.com` format, this field will form the part of the iChat user's username that follows the at symbol. By default, the Mac OS X Server that is hosting the iChat service will be the first entry in this field, but you can add and delete more if your server will be hosting Jabber services for more than one host domain.

- *SSL Certificate*: In this drop-down, you will specify which SSL certificate (if any) that the iChat service will use to encrypt communication between itself and the Jabber client systems. With any service that transmits and receives potentially sensitive information, we strongly recommend that you employ an SSL certificate, although you may elect not to if you wish. IChat can use your server's self-signed certificate, or you may opt to get a certificate that is issued by a trusted root certificate authority (CA). You can find more information about SSL and managing certificates in Chapter 3.

- *Authentication*: This determines which level of security is required of users logging into your iChat server. If all of your users are operating in a Kerberized, single sign-on environment, you will want to select Kerberos as the authentication method. However, if all of your users will be operating from a location where they cannot be granted a Kerberos ticket, you should select Password. If you have a mix of users operating in a single sign-on (SSO) environment as well as remote users, select Any from the drop-down menu, which allows non-Kerberized connectivity.

- *Enable XMPP server-to-server federation*: When this box is checked, your server can communicate with other Jabber-compliant servers in a server-to-server (S2S) relationship. This extends the reach of the authenticated users on your iChat server to communicate beyond your own domain; any Jabber server with similar trust settings will allow its users to connect with yours.

- *Require secure server-to-server federation*: If you have selected an SSL certificate to use for encrypting iChat traffic between your server and users, this option becomes available. If not, this option is grayed out. As noted before, securing your traffic is essential if your users need to protect their communications from being intercepted by third parties. By requiring secure federation, you are extending that level of security beyond your own servers and requiring that all other servers that you communicate with to use encryption as well.

- *Allow federation with all domains*: When this box is checked, your server will communicate with other Jabber servers in any domain. Any Jabber server that attempts to connect to yours will be accepted, and your server will attempt to connect to any Jabber server (whether those servers accept your server's attempts to federate will, of course, depend on the configuration choices that *their* systems administrator has made!)

- *Allow federation with the following domains*: If you want to limit the domains that your users can communicate with, you can explicitly list the specific ones allowed by checking this box and adding domains into the box below it.

Once you are satisfied with your settings, click the Start iChat button at the bottom of the Server Admin screen, and the service should start up. You can now start setting up users and clients.

Setting Up Users

By default, users created in Server Preferences will automatically have accounts in your iChat Server. Accounts created in Workgroup Manager will work similarly, provided that you have not created a Service Access Control list (as described in Chapter 3) to limit access to the iChat service.

To verify, open Server Preferences, and click the user you would like to configure. Next, click the Services tab, and locate the iChat check box, which is shown in Figure 11–5. Checking this box allows you to see the configuration screen where you will set up the iChat Server.

Figure 11-5. *Users in Server Preferences*

Connecting Remotely

Chances are that in the modern workplace not everyone is in the same physical space. But whether you're part of a two-person office or a two-thousand–person office, the connection options will be the same. If you have a site-to-site virtual private network (VPN) configured between your locations, you can more than likely connect to the server when you are a remote user without much fanfare. However, if you are going to have users remotely communicating with the server, chances are you'll need to open some TCP/IP ports on your external firewall or gateway to facilitate this communication.

In order for the iChat client to communicate with the outside world, you will need to make sure that ports 5060, 5190, 5297, 5298, 5678, and 16384 through 16403 are open.

> **NOTE:** For clients running Mac OS X 10.4 or later, also open ports 5220, 5222, and 5223.

In order for clients to remotely connect to the server, you will want to verify that ports 5222 and 5223 are open for incoming traffic. However, if you find you need to do troubleshooting due to connectivity issues, we recommend that you attempt opening the other ports (5220, 5222, 5223, etc.) as well. Finally, if you are using federation, you will also want to open port 5269.

> **NOTE:** You will also need to open port 88 and possibly port 749 if you will be using Kerberos for iChat Server authentication.

Prepopulating Buddy Lists

You can set up iChat in Mac OS X Server to facilitate the population of lists of iChat buddies. If you want to enable the automatic population of buddy lists for users of your iChat server, use the following command in Terminal:

```
serveradmin settings jabber:enableAutoBuddy = yes
```

If you have a lot of users and this causes performance issues, consider disabling this feature again by using the following command:

```
serveradmin settings jabber:enableAutoBuddy = no
```

Once you are finished setting up your AutoBuddy options, restart the iChat Server services.

Customizing the Welcome Message

Customizing the welcome message to new users of your iChat server is a fairly simple task. For this, we'll look into the Jabber configuration (because Jabber is the open source package that iChat Server is built on).

When you first setup Jabber the /etc/jabber directory will be created. Inside this folder will be a file called jabber.xml. If you open this file and look at it, anything between welcome and /welcome will be the information shown in a welcome screen when a new user signs onto the iChat server.

Before you edit the /etc/jaber/jabber.xml file make sure to back it up.

For this example, we will have all new users receive a message that says *Welcome to the 318 iChat Server*. To do this, delete or comment out the information between the existing welcome tags and add the following information:

```
"welcome"
"subject"318 iChat Server"/subject"
"body"Welcome to the 318 iChat Server"/body"
"/welcome"
```

Save the jabber.xml file, and you've now customized the welcome message for your iChat server.

Federating iChat

XMPP is used by Jabber and the Google Talk service. You can configure your iChat server to communicate to other XMPP-compliant servers. Since Google Talk leverages XMPP, it can be communicated with given only a few minutes worth of work, but you're going to need to jump into the command line again.

To get started, first open Server Admin. From here, click the iChat service for the server you wish to configure in the SERVERS list. Then, click the Settings icon in the toolbar. From the General tab, find the "Enable XMPP server-to-server federation" option. Check this box, and choose the "Allow federation with the following domains" radio button. You can now use the plus sign to provide another iChat Server, a Jabber server, or the Google Talk address, which is 216.239.45.22. The third option is used in Figure 11–6.

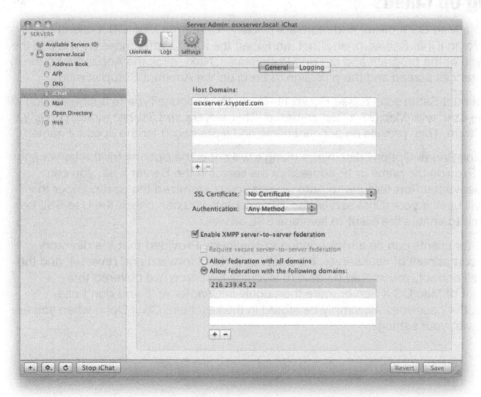

Figure 11–6. *Federating iChat*

Once you click Save, the service will need to be restarted. Upon restart, the s2s.xml file will have the new server written into it. This file can be found at /etc/jabberd and will contain any federation options that you employ.

NOTE: At the time of this writing, federation is not working in Server Admin. To configure federation at this time, you need to use the command line.

Configuring the Mac OS X Client

One of the first things you'll want to do to a newly installed iChat Server is configure a client to connect to it. Testing any service is vital, as is making sure that all settings are known so you can deploy or configure it as needed.

Setting Up Clients

To set up a Mac OS X client (and more specifically, iChat on a Mac OS X client) to connect to an iChat Server, open iChat, and open the iChat Preferences by clicking the iChat menu of the program and clicking Preferences. Next, click the Accounts button in the Preferences screen and the plus sign to bring up the Account Setup screen.

At the Account Setup screen (see Figure 11–7), set the Account Type to Jabber, which will always be used with Mac OS X Server–based iChat servers and Jabber running on any other platform. Then provide an account name and a password for the account name.

Clicking the Server Options disclosure triangle will show the options for the server and the port. Provide the name or IP address of the server in the Server field; you can typically leave the Port field set to Auto (unless you customized the port number that Jabber will use). If your iChat server has SSL enabled, you can check the Use SSL box at this time to enable the client to leverage SSL as well.

Kerberos for clients can be a tricky option to configure. Provided that the directory services component of your server, the host name (both forward and reverse), and the time are all correct, you should be able to leverage Kerberos (we covered this component of Mac OS X Server more thoroughly in Chapter 4). If you don't use Kerberos, the password will simply be stored in the keychain. Click Done when you are satisfied with your settings.

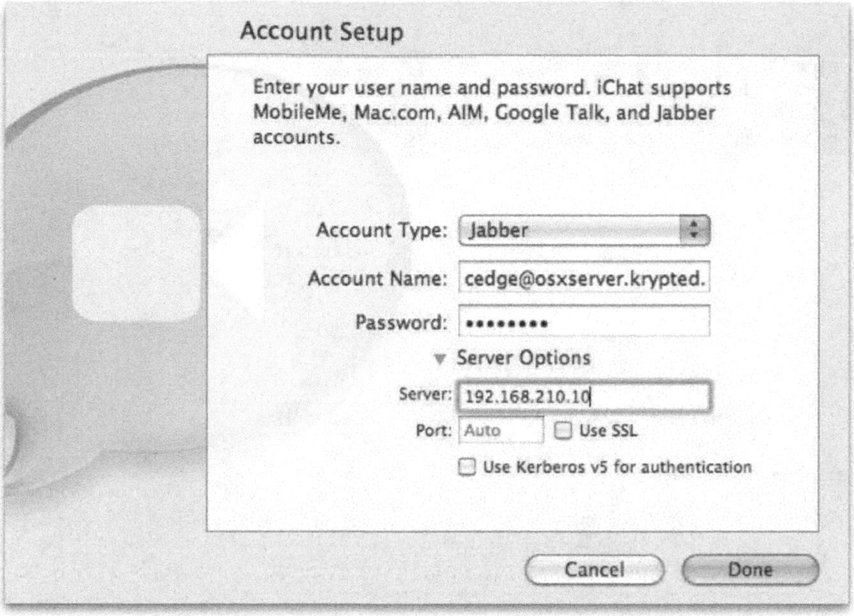

Figure 11–7. *IChat client setup*

When the Account Setup wizard is completed, the Jabber List screen will show the server that you are connected to. The user in question should now be able to communicate with other Jabber users.

> **NOTE:** The Account Name that is requested during the Account Setup wizard of the iChat client should contain a full username, which includes the user and the domain name of the account that you are logging into.

Saving iChat Transcripts

Many environments will want to save all those iChats for users. You can configure the server to do so, but the iChat client can also perform this task.

To enable transcripts, open iChat, and click the iChat menu followed by Preferences. Next, click Messages, check the box for Automatically Save Chat Transcripts, and select the location (see Figure 11–8). Then, close the Preferences dialog. That's it.

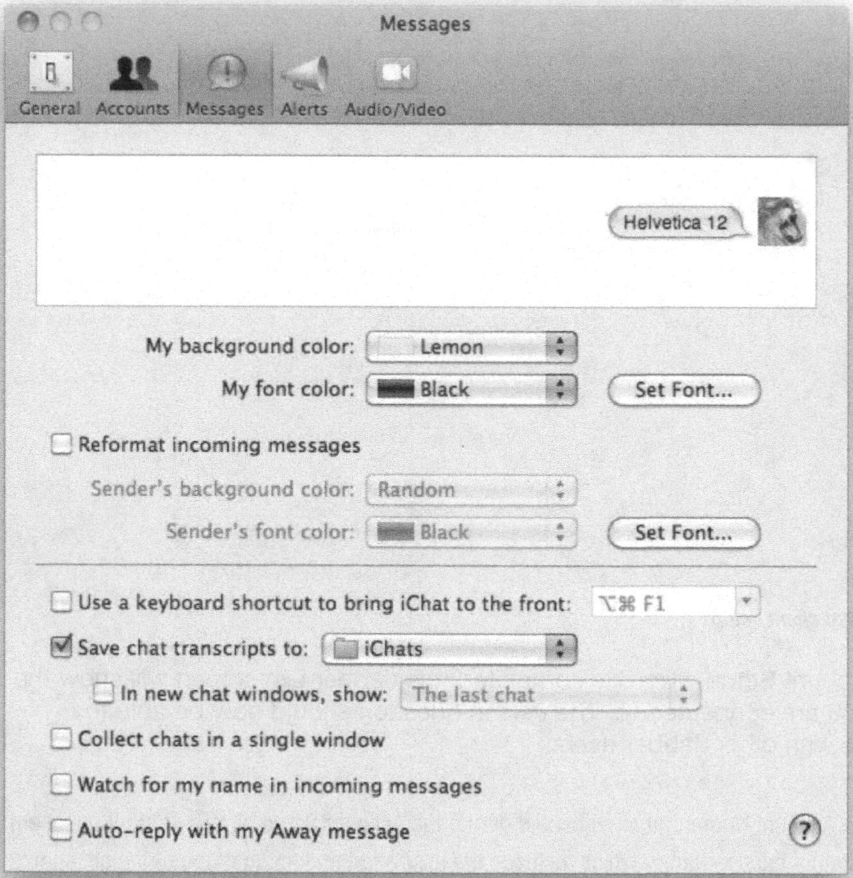

Figure 11–8. *Saving iChat transcripts*

NOTE: Enabling transcripts will save not only the transcripts of sessions for the Jabber client but also transcripts for any instant messaging session that uses the iChat client.

Using the Command Line

The command line options for iChat Server services are fairly rudimentary compared to some of the other services in Mac OS X Server. However, you can also configure the iChat Server service using the configuration files for the Jabber service, on which iChat Server is based.

Using serveradmin

The `serveradmin` command is capable of starting and stopping the iChat Server service and of granularly configuring settings. When running the `serveradmin` command, you will use the `ichat` option to specify the service that you are working with as iChat Server. A basic version of this would be to use the following command, which uses the `status` verb to determine if the iChat Service is running:

```
serveradmin status ichat
```

In addition, you can use `serveradmin` to look at the critical settings for the service by running it with the `fullstatus` option. For example, take the following command:

```
serveradmin fullstatus ichat
```

Querying for a `fullstatus` would show that the server is running, along with a number of critical settings.

> **NOTE:** You can also just run `serveradmin settings ichat` for a full listing of all settings, but as the output includes information on each update, it is far too verbose to include here.

Each of the settings in this section can then be altered using the `serveradmin` command with the `settings` option, followed by the string with the new content. For example, to set the logging level to the maximum available, you could use the following command:

```
serveradmin settings jabber:logLevel = "ALL"
```

The `serveradmin` command primarily gives you the ability to configure the service from the perspective of Mac OS X Server. However, keep in mind that the iChat service is actually leveraging Jabber, which is an open source package. Therefore, you can also edit the Jabber configuration files directly or edit the `/etc` directory, as we will explain in the next section of this chapter.

Storing Jabber Configuration Files

Jabber stores its configuration files in the `/etc/jabberd` directory. Here, you will find several files. For most readers, you will have an XML or CFG file and a corresponding bak file. For the XML file you can typically run a `man` command to determine exactly what it does. The bak file is a file that allows you to revert to the default from, before any customizations, if you need to.

These are the most common files in `/etc/jabberd`:

- `C2s.xml`
- `C2s.xml.bak`
- `C2s.xml.dist`
- `Jabberd.cfg`
- `Jabberd.cfg.bak`
- `Jabberd.cfg.dist`

- Muc-jcr.xml
- Muc-jcr.xml.bak
- Resolver.xml
- Resolver.xml.dist
- Router-filter.apple.xml
- Router-filter.xml.bak
- Router-filter.xml.dist
- Router-users.xml
- Router-users.xml.dist
- Router.xml
- Router.xml.bak
- Router.xml.dist
- S2s.xml
- S2s.xml.bak
- S2s.xml.dist
- Sm.xml
- Sm.xml.bak
- Sm.xml.dist

The `templates` directory in /etc/jabberd also stores two files—roster.xml and roster.xml.dist, which can be enabled in the `sm.xml file` and supply a given set of users to each user that joins the iChat server automatically.

> **NOTE:** When you make any changes to these files, you will need to go into the Server Admin or Server Preferences tools and restart the iChat service. Making changes with Server Admin may then overwrite these changes.

Summary

In this chapter, we took a dive into iChat Server. Whether you're looking to have internal-only messaging, chat sessions that you can track by saving transcripts, or just an intercom system for your Macs, iChat Server is a stable and mature component of Mac OS X Server that can fill the bill. And with the ability to federate to other servers and a standards-compliant core in Jabber, the iChat server that you integrate into your environment for Mac OS X clients can also be used for site-to-site communications and for a variety of platforms.

Now that we've discussed iChat Server, we will move on to another form of messaging in Chapter 12, where we cover the mail server that is built into Mac OS X Server.

Chapter 12

Setting Up Mail Services

Today, e-mail is an essential part of any business, and being able to enable accounts for the existing users on your Snow Leopard Server can be as simple as selecting a box in their account settings once the mail services have been configured and once you have your server configured. By using Mac OS X's built-in mail server, you can consolidate your management resources by ensuring that a user's single password to log into the fileserver will also provide access to their e-mail. In Snow Leopard Server, Apple has introduced the options to allow better integration with the iPhone and more robust mail storage than what was available in Leopard Server.

However, running a mail server can be one of the most difficult aspects of managing a server, because it has to integrate with the rest of the Internet as a whole. If your server is not behaving properly and respecting common mail protocols, it will be shunned like your Doritos-stained teenage self at the high-school prom. In other words, your server's ability to send and receive e-mail can be affected by how it behaves with other servers. If you aren't careful, it can end up on blacklists, and your crucial e-mails may go unread and unloved.

In this chapter, we'll cover the components that make up Mac OS X Server's built-in mail service, and then we'll go through the steps needed to have your server configured as a functional mail service. The configuration process for the server extends past the software just on your server, so we will be touching on areas such as public DNS records and configurations of your firewall.

Understanding Mac OS X Server's Mail Components

Mac OS X Server consists of a number of open source projects that have earned it the "Open Source Made Easy" moniker within Apple. For the beginner, this means you can do most of what a basic messaging administrator will need to do from within the comfort of graphical tools. But it helps to understand what is going on under the covers. This starts with protocols.

Protocols

There are three main protocols that every mail administrator should understand in varying degrees. The first is Simple Mail Transfer Protocol (SMTP), which is the primary protocol that is used to send electronic mail between servers, across the Internet. SMTP is also the protocol used by client computers to send, or *relay*, mail through their mail server.

Internet Message Access Protocol (IMAP) is one of the two most common ways you can access e-mail stored on a mail server. The other is Post Office Protocol (POP). The primary difference is that POP will download messages from your inbox to your local mail client, while IMAP will maintain a synchronization between mailboxes (often presented as folders) stored on the server (not just your inbox, but your outbox, trash, spam, and any other folders you want to create). Therefore, by using IMAP, when you check and reply to a message from webmail, the sent e-mail is put into the same sent folder that your iPhone checks, so you can easily review from the road later. In short, if you are going to be checking your mail in more than one way, IMAP is the protocol option to use. One downside of IMAP is that all the users' mail will live on the server, so it will use up more server resources, and if you are supporting many users, you will want to implement mail quotas, set up archiving policies, and most importantly set expectations among your users that they cannot keep an infinite amount of mail on the server. This may sound like something you will not want to address with them, but it is easier to inform them of the limitations before you start the process than realize that everyone is going to have to archive and throw out 10GB of mail in order for the server to function properly two years from now.

POP was the common mail service used when people had only one computer and dial-up Internet connections. The job of POP3 was to hold all your mail until you were able to connect to the Internet and download the messages with your mail client and organize them how you saw fit. The biggest drawback of using POP3 to retrieve your messages is that once one client had downloaded the messages, you might not be able to retrieve them from another computer (or iPhone), depending on how each client was configured. Although useful, we always recommend clients use IMAP to access their mail accounts, because IMAP allows for mobility between workstations and a way to centrally store and back up messages, which is useful when you don't want to have to worry about a salesperson losing an important e-mail because of a POP3 download issue.

Dovecot

Dovecot is the open source project that is used to store mail in Mac OS X Server. In Server 10.6, Apple replaced a different open source project, Cyrus, with IMAP and POP3, which are the underpinnings of the mail services with Dovecot. Although Cyrus is a more than adequate system for handling the mail loads of a small to medium-size business, it also needs some maintenance and custom configuration once installed in order to ensure its continual operation. So although it was a great mail server, it did not provide a great Apple experience in some customers' eyes. Dovecot is a relatively new (in Unix terms, it was first released in 2002) IMAP and POP3 server, and it was designed with IMAP specifically in mind.

Dovecot is not the only open source project used in the Mac OS X Server mail services. In fact, when it comes to sending and receiving messages for users, that task is performed by another program entirely, called Postfix. Postfix is a mail transport agent, and its job is to accept (or deny) e-mail sent to your mail server and to track down the appropriate address to deliver an e-mail to when you send it from your own server. When an e-mail is sent to you on your mail server, Postfix will first process it and determine whether it is valid (this is the stage where spam filtering and virus scanning is performed), before passing the message to Dovecot, which then files it away in the appropriate folder for your mail client to then pick up. Postfix drives the mail truck, and Dovecot is the mail room clerk that sorts the messages to the appropriate individuals.

Preparing for a Mail Server

Now that you understand the components that go into running a mail server and the architecture of the Mac OS X Server 10.6 mail service, let's look at what you need to do before you set that server up. This journey in prepping your environment and domain for warehousing a mail server is going to start with your DNS (we describe the basics of DNS in Chapter 6) and your network, which is mostly going to be properly configuring your firewall (if you are using the Mac OS X Server NAT and firewall services, then these are described further in Chapter 5).

DNS

Before you enable Mail for your office, you will want to ensure that you are comfortable editing the DNS entries for your domain to ensure that it contains all the appropriate information so other servers' message transfer agents (the programs that send outgoing mail to accounts that don't exist on the server itself) can find your server to deliver mail destined for your office from the other parts of the Internet. A mail exchange (MX) record is an entry in your public, world-readable DNS entries that lists which servers to contact when trying to deliver mail to your domain. So if your MX record for company.com was mail.company.com, MTAs would try to contact mail.company.com to deliver the mail. An in-depth discussion about the role of MX in mail delivery is outside the scope of this book, but needless to say, you will need to have your OS X server configured as the primary MX record to receive mail for your server, and if you want to use a backup MX service, those servers are configured with a higher MX number (your server should be 10, the backup server should be 20, and so on) and be configured to deliver messages to your server.

Before you actually commit that change on your records, you will want to test that your mail server is operating properly on your internal network first, because you will receive no mail until you have gotten the new server up and running if you change the entries prior to this. To help with the transition to the new mail server, before you actually make the final changes to the DNS, you will want to shorten the Time To Live (TTL) value (which you can think of as the rate that your DNS entries are refreshed) for the DNS entries. That way, once you do change over to using your own mail server, the transition will go quickly. Also, if there are other problems you do not discover until after the changeover, the short TTL will let you go backward just as quickly.

Firewalls

You will want to make sure that at a minimum port 25 is configured on your firewall to allow access to the OS X Server hosting mail services. If you want to use webmail, IMAP, and so on, you will want to make sure those ports are open as well. OS X Server's built-in firewall offers a list of the ports needed for each of those services and is a handy tool to use for reference, even if you are not using the firewall. You will want to test external connectivity with the server before making any official transition to it.

> **NOTE:** Before you start, you will also want to know your ISP's SMTP server. Since small business and residential Internet connections are commonly used by spammers to send e-mail, there is an increased likelihood that your legitimately configured mail server will be tagged as a spam server. By relaying through your ISP, you can avoid these blacklists. If you would like even more level of control, there are third-party services such as MXLogic and Postini that will filter and relay outbound messages for you, also helping prevent your server from being blacklisted (and if you use their inbound filter, also provide extremely robust spam filtering).

Enabling Mail Services

You have multiple options for setting up the mail services in Mac OS X Server. The first and most attractive to many beginners is the Server Preferences application, which we've covered in this book in a number of chapters. The second is through the Server Admin utility, which is likely preferred in most cases. Finally, there is the command line, because there are still some power-user features available in the Dovecot and associated mail software that are not available in the GUI. One example is that management and disabling of the graylisting feature is something that can only be done from the command line (and is discussed later in this chapter).

Server Preferences

Although some consider it to be overly simplistic (for one, if you enable services, it assumes that everything is already set up and just starts running, instead of prompting you for configuration options), the Server Preferences tool does act as a starting point, even if only with regard to conceptualizing the various aspects of managing Mac OS X Server as a mail server.

As shown in Figure 12–1, there are three options when you are configuring a server using Server Preferences, which configure relaying (for outgoing messages), blacklisting (for incoming mail), and your spam threshold (how suspicious an e-mail can be before it is marked as spam). If you server's domain is identical to your MX record, you can just enable the mail service here and be done. However, if you set up the server like we did earlier in the book, your server's domain will not match your public domain, and you will need to run the configuration wizard provided by Server Admin.

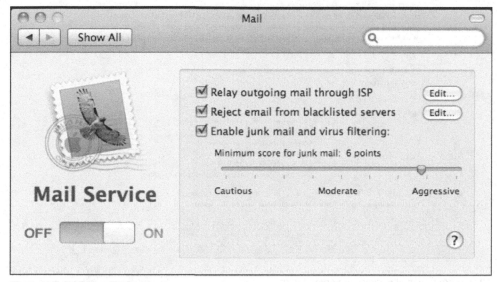

Figure 12–1. *Server Preferences*

Server Admin

Although it is tempting to enable mail using Server Preferences, it does a lot of tasks automatically and without prompting you in case of any discrepancies. Since a misconfigured mail server can lead to lost e-mail or being unable to send mail at all if your server gets blacklisted (so no one will accept the e-mails), we recommend using Server Admin, which has a full walk-through configuration wizard to ensure that you don't miss anything critical to properly configuring a basic mail server.

First, make sure you have added the Mail service to your services list, along with having Open Directory running and healthy. If you have already successfully completed Chapter 2, you can just focus on enabling the Mail service. If not, you may want to revisit Chapter 2 and possibly review Chapter 4, on Open Directory, in order to ensure you have the right environment for the user accounts to be created in, before going any further. No user accounts = no mailboxes for mail to be delivered to.

From the Mail service in Server Admin, select Overview, and then click the Configure Mail services button to open the Service Configuration Assistant, shown in Figure 12–2.

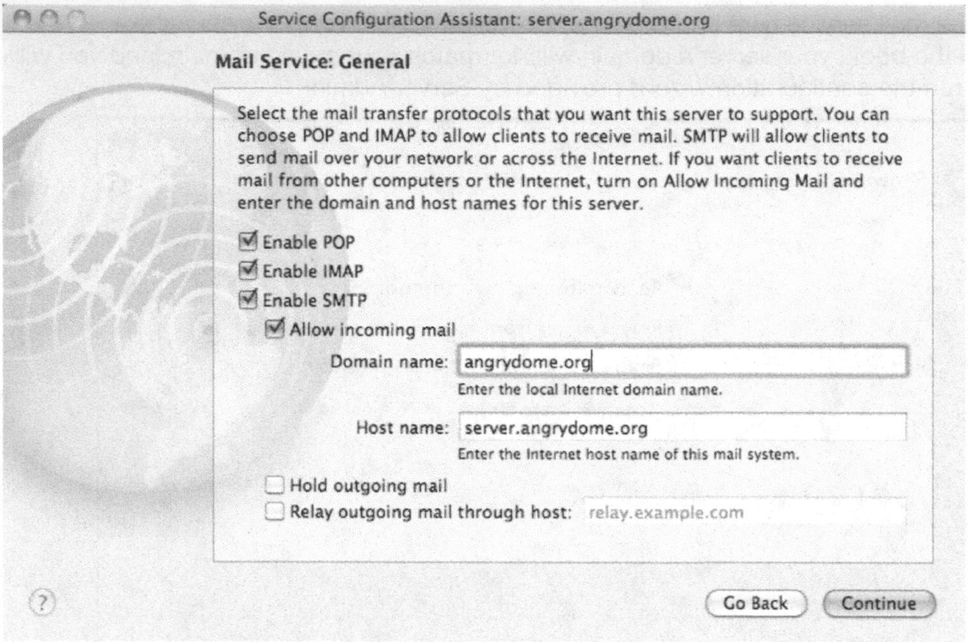

Figure 12–2. *Configuring mail services in Server Admin*

You will want to enable IMAP and SMTP at the minimum, along with accepting e-mail for the domain name. This would be your publicly facing domain, such as company.com, and not the internal domain such as company.lan. The external domain name for your server can be different from the internal name, so although internally the server maybe known as server-001.company.lan, you can use a DNS CNAME record to call your server mail.company.com to make it easier for clients and other mail servers to find it. If you are just going to use IMAP, you can disable POP entirely at this step by deselecting the box. You will be able to enable later if you need it, but depending on how your users will be configuring their clients to connect to the mail server, you might want to disable it to ensure that they connect using IMAP (a somewhat not uncommon occurrence is a user configuring one of their accounts as POP, which then downloads all the mail from the inbox and deletes it, making their e-mail disappear on every other device using IMAP). Once you have reviewed the settings on this panel, click Continue to advance to the next step.

Basic Message Hygiene

A common problem for many small businesses hosting their e-mail internally is that those easy-to-get residential DSL and cable lines are used by spammers to send bulk e-mails. This could also be home users whose computers have been infected with a Windows virus, which are then sending out spam. Given the modern rules for message hygiene, there is a higher likelihood for your e-mail to be flagged falsely as spam and not make it to its proper destination when you are using a residential class of service. Setting up a proper reverse DNS entry (as described earlier in this chapter) with your ISP is one step in the right direction, but you may also want to consider relaying your mail through your ISP's or another hosted service that maintains a large volume of redundant servers; as a service, they ensure your mail gets through. If you are going to relay mail through your ISP or one of these other mail service providers, select the "Relay outgoing messages through host" option.

You can also use a relaying mail service such as MX logic to scan incoming mail for spam. If you use such a service, then you will mostly likely want to disable spam filtering in Mac OS X Server to prevent false positives or falsely doubling the spam hits of a message. To do so, select the "Scan e-mail for junk mail" option, and set the hit threshold; the higher the hit number, the more likely spam will get through (see Figure 12–3). However, the lower the number, the easier it is to generate false positives and lose important messages. As of this writing, the current build of Server 10.6 requires some command-line modification to disable graylisting, which is a powerful spam repellent, but its current shipping state in Server 10.6 may cause you to never receive mail from some hosts, including Gmail.com and Me.com. See the "Disabling Graylisting" section later in this chapter once you have configured your mail services.

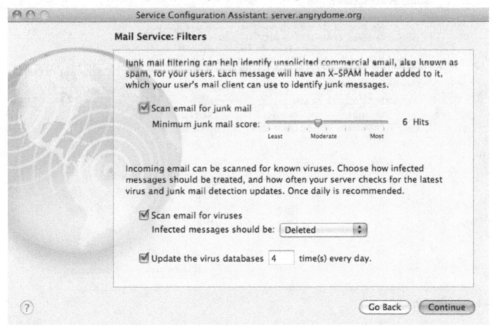

Figure 12–3. *Spam and virus detection settings*

Enabling virus checking and updates is suggested, but depending on the number of users in your office and the amount of e-mails that need to be processed, it can slow down the time for an e-mail to arrive. You will still want to have some form of protection. (By scanning e-mails at the server level, it will help you prevent viruses from spreading, and although there are few if any Mac viruses in the wild, it is best to be a good Internet citizen by preventing the spread of any Windows viruses through your machines as well.) Virus scanning is only as good as the database of viruses it checks for, so you will want to enable updating the virus database and set it to run once a day at minimum. After reviewing this panel to ensure it has settings you want, click Continue (you can change these settings later as well).

Choosing Security Protocols

The list of protocols is in descending order based on level of security, with Kerberos being the most secure (but also the most intensive to configure). If you are planning to configure desktop machines to have network accounts and be joined to Open Directory (and making Open Directory available to the Internet), you may want to consider enabling Kerberos. Besides CRAM-MD5, the other password services all have known flaws that would make it possible for a malicious Internet user to recover or crack the passwords if they were intercepted in that format. If you can configure all your clients to use CRAM-MD5 (as shown in Figure 12–4), it is the best option.

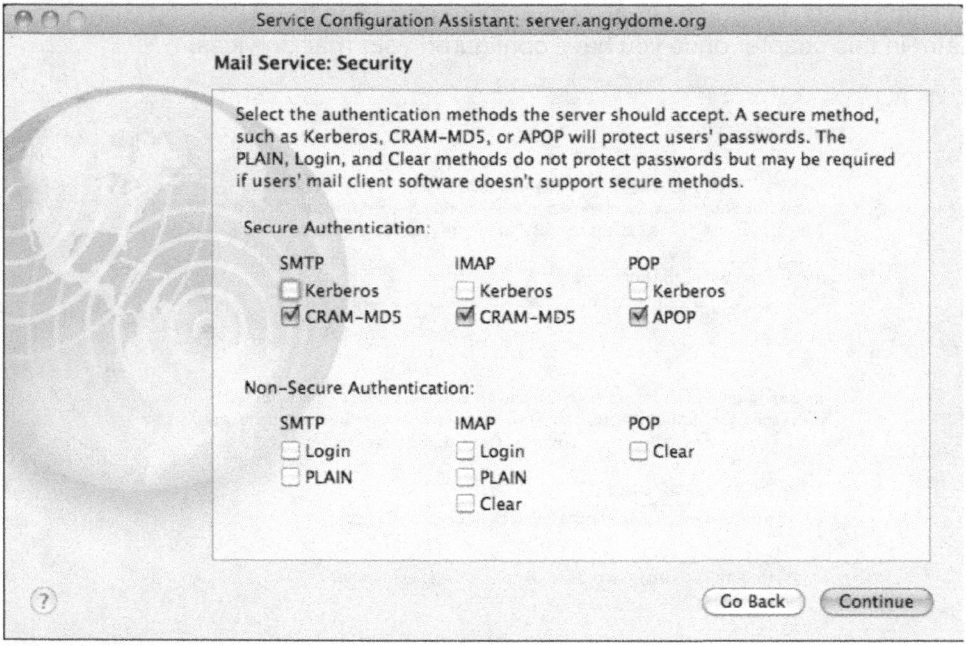

Figure 12–4. *Security settings*

Storage

Mac OS X Server 10.6 has now introduced the feature *at mail configuration time* to let you store mail on an external location instead of just internally on your boot drive. This is where you would want to move the mail location to a data partition or similar to ensure that it is protected independently of the OS X server boot drive. Also, since this could be a rapidly growing folder and data set, moving it allows you to prevent your system from grinding to a halt in case the relatively small boot partition is filled with mail. Remember, if you are planning to use IMAP for all your users' mail, all e-mail is kept on the server and is synchronized to the clients, so the mail store may become the largest collection of files on the entire server over time.

Now that Mail is configured, you will want to do some general settings change just to make life easier as you are testing and getting the service ready for prime time. The primary one is being able to change the logging levels for mail services from Critical to Informative. You will want to change these back eventually, but it will make testing your mail configuration for the first time a lot easier.

> **NOTE:** The general configuration section is a bit misleading in that it gives an option for simultaneous IMAP connections as 1,000. Although this is technically true, what you are actually configuring is the number of instances of Dovecot's IMAP process, which is the simultaneous number divided by 5. So, with 1,000 connections set, you are allowing for 200 instances of Dovecot.

Configuring SMTP

When you are enabling SMTP and you want to relay all your outgoing mail through your ISP or a hosted mail service, you will want to select the "Relay outgoing mail through host" option. On the Relay tab (Figure 12–5), you can add specific network ranges and IP addresses of machines that can send messages to other servers through your mail server, without needing any authentication. If you do decide to add any networks to this host, you will want to make sure it is only a range of addresses for computers and devices that you trust. (Localhost, or 127.0.0.1/8, is configured by default and just means that any subprocess on the server can send mail to any domain, including those hosted on other servers.) Allowing anyone to send e-mail through your server means you can quickly be blacklisted, and this can also affect your service's overall performance because you are now relaying thousands of messages for other people. For example, you would want to enable SMTP relay if you had a network device that you wanted to be able to send out emergency notifications but the device supports only the most basic SMTP services so you couldn't give it a username and password to connect to the mail server with.

By adding an IP address or network range to "Refuse to all messages from these hosts and networks," any messages from servers matching that criteria will not be accepted. Although it is tempted to try to manage your own static blacklist, chances are spammers are going to be changing their IPs so quickly and moving from so many systems that by the time you identify a single server or range of IPs to block, those servers may have already been stopped. It is easier to use the next option to add a real-time blacklist server that dynamically manages those lists of IPs and networks that are known bad hosts. By enabling the real-time blacklist option, your server will submit the incoming mail server's IP to those servers, and if they identify it as spam, your server will reject the message. This may slow down the mail delivery time if you have a slower Internet connection in your office, so if you are experiencing a huge performance hit from the blacklist process, you may want to consider migrating to using an incoming SMTP filter service. Such services will accept all mail for you and filter it before sending it to your mail server for final delivery.

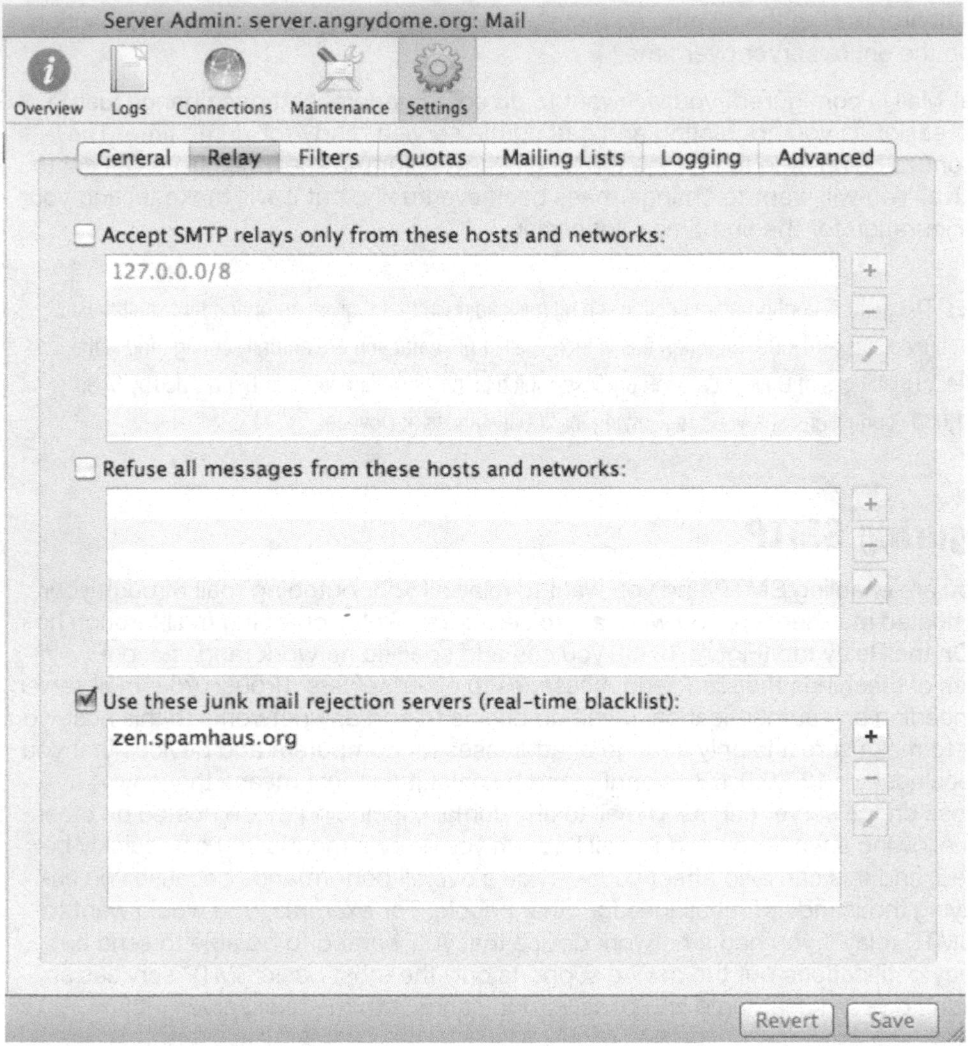

Figure 12–5. *Relay settings*

Securing Mail Services

At this point, you will want to ensure you are using the proper SSL certificate for your server to keep your mail (and more importantly your passwords) secure when communicating with the mail server. By setting the IMAP/POP SSL option to Require, you will ensure that only clients configured to use the SSL ports of your mail server can connect. Again, this allows you to let your users configure their own mail clients if they want, and by setting the standards on the server, you can be confident knowing that they will connect using approved methods only. (You can also use self-signed certificates, but your users will get an error prompt about security, and although technically the protocol is no less secure, getting your users into the habit of dismissing SSL error notifications is, because it allows for a third-party to impersonate your server, and then your end users would get the same SSL error prompt when they connected to the fake server.)

Configuring a Mail Client

Various clients are available for accessing your mail server. Besides the built-in Mail, on Mac OS X there are some common alternatives, such as Entourage, Thunderbird, Mulberry, and Eudora. Showing how to configure each one of these clients would be another book in and of itself (and that is just the OS X clients). However, we'll cover the common settings and information you will need to get basic connectivity working.

We recommend you use the external domain name of the mail server for your settings, not the internal IP address or domain name. Technically if you are inside the network, you can use the mail server's IP address. However, since we are talking about your ideal setup, using the external DNS name allows for a configured client to move from inside your network to the outside and still be able to use mail. Even if the user you are setting up right now has a desktop machine, in the future if you migrate that user to a laptop, their e-mail settings will continue to work without issue.

If you are intending to use IMAP on your clients, you will want to ensure that you choose the account type of IMAP. If SSL is enabled on the server side (and you either have a signed SSL certificate or have decided to save the self-signed certificate on the client's machines), you will want to make sure that port 993 is available on the server from the Internet. Conversely, if you are using POP and SSL, the ports required is 995. For the non-SSL versions of the services, you will want to ensure that ports 143 and 110 are available, respectively.

For clients to be able to send outgoing messages, besides port 25 on the server being accessible from the Internet, you will want to ensure that ports 587 and 465 are enabled. Because of steps taken by ISPs to control spam, the default SMTP port has been blocked, making it difficult for your end users to relay messages through your server. However, you can configure and use the SMTP SSL service on port 465. In Mail, this is as simple as selecting the Use Secure Socket Layers option, and in fact, when you are first configuring Mail, it will attempt to connect over SSL first before falling back to the less secure protocols.

NOTE: It may be useful to create a service configuration list, something you can easily distribute to your end users to allow them to configure their mail services. It can be as simple as the following:

Mail server name: mail.angrydome.org

IMAP port (SSL): 993

SMTP port (SSL): 465

Username: Your fileserver login

E-mail address: yourusername@angrydome.org

Webmail access: https://mail.angrydome.org

Webmail and Mail Rules

Webmail is a convenient way to ensure that your mail services and logins are working, because you are talking directly to the server instead of trying to connect and configure a mail client just to see whether e-mails are getting through to the mail account you just created. It is also useful for users who you do want to allow to have their own personal machines configured at home to check mail.

To enable webmail, you will want to make sure you have your SSL certificate installed and working. If you are already using collaboration services, you may want to make a different site using your server's external domain name, so you can assign it your SSL certificate and so it is just providing your users the webmail services. After creating the site, follow the instructions in Chapter 14, select the SSL certificate from the Security tab, and then select Mail on the Web tab (Figure 12–6). Click Save, and then you will be able to select the Change Password and Mail Rules boxes. Both of these options will allow your users to change their password from the site you have just created (which is useful if you decide to use a 90-day password expiration policy and they need to change it from the road) and also configure server-side mail rules. The arrows next to "configure server-side mail rules" and "change their password" will take you directly to the those web sites as well.

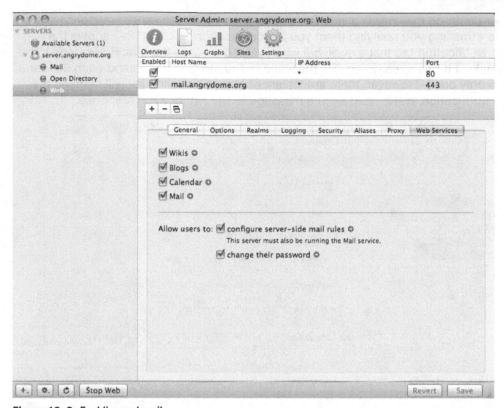

Figure 12–6. *Enabling webmail*

For webmail itself, it is using SquirrelMail, and the interface is a bit dated. However, if you want to spend some time customizing it, Squirrelmail.org provides great tips and tricks on how to do so.

Mail rules are a useful feature because they allow your server to sort incoming messages before any of your mail clients actually see them. Although you can use your mail client to sort messages for you, the problem is you need that mail client running and checking your inbox all the time to keep it organized. Having the server process the messages first solves the not so uncommon problem of users having to leave their work machines running all the time so their iPhone doesn't get flooded with useless mail when they are out of the office. When you configure mail rules, you have the option to sort messages by who they are from, who they are destined for, and what the subject of the message is (or a combination of all three). One common utility of a mail rule is when you combine it with an account alias. For example, you could create a registration alias for your own account, called *bob-register*, and whenever you need to register for a product activation, you would use bob-register@angrydome.com. Messages sent to that address would go to Bob's inbox, but now you can create a mail rule that moves any message sent to *bob-register* to a folder called Registrations as soon as a message is delivered, keeping it out of your inbox but still letting you know when a new product update is available when you feel like looking in your Registrations folder.

The other common mail rule is a vacation notification, which will send a response to someone e-mailing you notifying them you are on vacation. (Figure 12–7 shows the Vacation Notification tab that's available when you connect to the Mail Rules page.) The server tracks if it has already sent the message to the user, so it will send each sender a message only once. However, there are instances where a mailing list will confuse the vacation notification system and send a message to the list for each response.

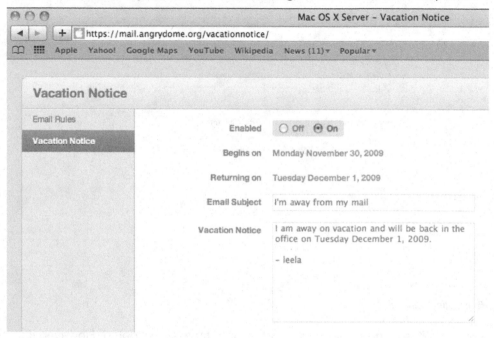

Figure 12–7. *Vacation notification*

Creating Accounts

To enable a mail account, the user first has to exist in Open Directory on your server. Once the account has been created, you will just need to select the Mail tab and choose Enabled. If you have only one domain and one mail server, that may be all the configuration that you will need. If you have enabled service ACLs on your mail services, you will also need to ensure that this user is specifically added to the list or has been added to a group that is already on the service list for mail.

In the Shortname field, you can also add mail aliases. These accept mail for that account and route it to the appropriate mailbox, so a user can have both fullname@company.com and nickname@company.com where you have provided both in the form of multiple short names. It is considered best practice for any system logins or invitations for scheduling to still be sent using their proper original login name (which is the first in the list of short names).

Setting Up Mailing Lists

There are two mailing list type of features in Server 10.6: *group lists*, which are preconfigured mailing lists generated based on members in a group (so if you had a Sales group, then sales@company.com could be a mailing list that automatically contains everyone from that group) and *standard mailman mailing lists*. To set up the server group lists, you just need to enable the check box in the Mail configuration pane and set the time to update the list membership based on who is already in the group (if you are not changing group memberships frequently, the defaults are adequate).

Mailman is an open source mailing list management tool that allows for more granular control and moderation of mailing lists than just a group option. You can consider a group list as just a shorthand for mailing everyone in a department, while a mailing list could be considered a moderated forum for participants, including people who do not have an account on your mail server. The benefit of both a group lists and mailman is that you can send a message to a mailing list without having to know each individual user's e-mail address, and they will still receive the message.

To enable mailing lists, select the box in the same Mail pane, and enter the master password (which should be extremely secure, because you do not want to make it easy for people to harvest mailing list members' e-mail addresses by logging into the administrative web interface) along with the e-mail address of a user who will be the administrator and moderator. For mailman, there are two levels of administrative control: an *administrator*, who has the abilities to change how the list itself operates, and a *moderator*, who can remove messages from the queue and approve messages to be sent to the list. Depending on how you want to have your mailing list configured, you can make it so only members of the mailing list can e-mail each other without issue, but someone off the list sending a message will have it rejected or go into a queue to allow for a moderator to review it before passing it onto the full list.

Once you have created your basic mailman list, you can easily add users by clicking the + button in the same view (Figure 12–8) and adding users' e-mail addresses. By when a new user is added to the mailing list, they will be sent a welcome message that will give them the information they need to modify their mailing list options or to remove themselves from the list. You can edit the look and feel of this message using the mailman admin web interface on the server by going to /mailman/admin/*listname* and logging in with your master password.

From the administrator perspective, the two most useful options in the Server Admin panel will be adding/removing users and being able to revoke a user's posting rights. By removing their posting rights, they are allowed to receive messages sent out to the list, but they can't respond to any messages or submit new ones. Being able to revoke someone's posting privileges may come up if a user has a rogue vacation notification setting that is continuously sending messages to the list or if a user needs a timeout for improper actions on the list. There are many different reasons to revoke someone's posting privileges, but needless to say, the option is there if you need it.

Mailman is a free open source utility; if you are interested in doing more advanced configuration of it, you can find more information at Mailman.org.

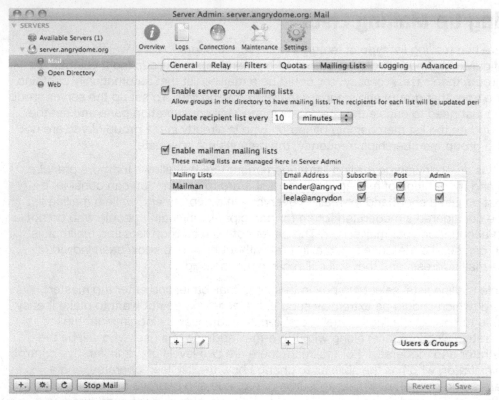

Figure 12–8. *Mailing list management*

Troubleshooting

A number of tasks are common in mail administration, such as cleaning up messages, working with databases, and performing configuration changes on servers and services.

Disabling Graylisting

If you notice that mail originating from the Internet is taking a long time to show up in your inbox, chances are graylisting is configured and running without a whitelist. As of this writing, graylisting is enabled by default in 10.6.2 when you enable the spam filter. Graylisting works on the assumption that a server sending a legitimate message will be more patient than one trying to deliver spam, so it will reject the incoming connection the first time, record that connection's IP address, and then accept it the second time it tries. This works fine in circumstances where the mail system that is attempting to deliver the message uses only one server, but many large ISPs (include MobileMe and Google Mail) use a rotating list of mail servers.

The end result is that these larger mail services will pass the message back to the "to be delivered" queue, and the next free server will pick it up and try to deliver it five minutes later. Since your server has never seen this particular server before, it will reject it, and the process starts over again. After about 24 hours, the server trying to deliver the message may return the mail to the original sender with an error message. Graylisting is a great antispam measure, but to compensate for this major limitation (who doesn't receive mail from someone with a Gmail or Me.com address?), they have implemented a whitelist, which is a list of common servers that have trouble delivering messages to hosts using graylist but are in fact legitimate mail servers.

> **NOTE:** If you want to use graylisting and are comfortable installing third-party open source projects and modifying your configuration files in depth, there are examples of advanced whitelisting systems that include web GUIs for management and monitoring at graylist.org.

If you do not want to work on implementing a manual whitelist, you can just disable graylisting entirely by doing the following steps from the Terminal (in /Applications/Utilities) as root (first run sudo -s and enter your password when prompted):

1. First, back up the Postfix configuration:

```
cp /etc/postfix/main.cf /etc/postfix/main.cf.bak
```

2. Then open the editor in a text editor (you can use vi or nano from the command line without having to worry about file permissions):

```
nano /etc/postfix/main.cf
```

3. Remove check_policy_service unix:private/policy from line 667, so this:

```
smtpd_recipient_restrictions = permit_sasl_authenticated permit_mynetworks
reject_unauth_destination check_policy_service unix:private/policy permit
```

   looks like this:

```
smtpd_recipient_restrictions = permit_sasl_authenticated permit_mynetworks
reject_unauth_destination permit
```

4. Save the file and then use the command postfix reload to update the running Postfix service without having to restart.

Troubleshooting Connectivity

The very first thing to determine when troubleshooting mail services is which protocols are affected and for whom. Is it just one user? All users? Can they log into the server's other services? Is their mail just not being delivered? These are questions you will want to ask yourself to help determine the best approach to take.

Outside connectivity is straightforward to test. Can you access the services from within your network, or are problems related only to laptop users or remote offices? If so, you may want to check your firewall and external DNS configurations, and make sure those machines are using the external DNS name for your server to contact, not your internal one.

Can you log in as an affected user through webmail? Then the user's client or computer may have connectivity issues to the mail server.

SMTP is, at the heart of it all, the easiest and least complex of all that is mail server oriented. Its role is to deliver messages to a variety of different types of mail servers on different networks and available over varying qualities of Internet connection. SMTP has a fairly limited number of commands, and it's fairly straightforward to communicate directly with an SMTP server using the `telnet` command available through OS X's Terminal:

```
telnet mail.angrydome.org 25
```

Now you should see a prompt; otherwise, the host might only accept mail from a mail server that meets a specified criteria, so just because you don't get a prompt, don't assume SMTP is busted. Here, you're going say *helo* (or *ehlo* in some cases). HELO (or EHLO) is the SMTP command to initiate a session with the host. In most cases, you'll also need to include a host name or IP as well:

```
EHLO mail.krypted.com
```

You should receive a response that begins with 250, which always means the command completed. Next you'll tell the target mail server who you are. This is done using the `MAIL FROM:` command, which tells the target server who on `mail.krypted.com` is sending the message:

```
MAIL FROM: charles@krypted.com
```

Provided you again see a 250 message, you can go ahead and tell the target mail server who the recipient is. For this, you'll use the `RCPT TO:` command followed by the target e-mail address:

```
RCPT TO: cbarker@angrydome.org
```

You should now see yet another 250, provided the address exists. In some cases, you'll see a 250 even if the address doesn't exist. It's according to the type of mail server being run and the rules in place on it. If you are allowed to route mail to an e-mail address that doesn't exist on the server and isn't in a domain on the server, then you might be looking at an open relay (which means that unless you take other methods, including setting the relay options shown earlier in Figure 12–5, your server may be used to send spam for other people). Either way, the next required part of a message is the contents, or in SMTP-speak, the DATA. DATA requires no other parameters; simply type the following:

```
DATA
```

Now you should see a message code of 354, which means that you can enter (in this case type) the contents of the message. You can start with the subject by beginning with a line that says `Subject:`, as shown here:

```
SUBJECT: test e-mail
```

Now type the text of your e-mail, and when you're done (at the bottom), simply have a line that only contains a period (.). If the server accepts the message, then you'll get another 250 code saying that the message has been queued for delivery to the mailbox in question, along with a unique ID that can be used to track the message through the queue. Provided you don't have any further messages to send, simply type QUIT to close the SMTP session.

Identifying and Recovering from Blacklisting

Although we hope that by taking some of the preventative steps mentioned in this chapter, you will not end being blacklisted, there are times where even an experienced systems administrator has to deal with a blacklisting of a server. Be it from a user's password being compromised, a client workstation being infected with the latest malware, or a long-forgotten setting being enabled for troubleshooting that allows an open relay from a specific IP range, it can happen in many environments.

The first step to getting removed from blacklist web sites it to find out which ones you have made your way onto. Then you will want to find out why, resolve the issue, and ultimately request that your domain be removed from the listing. In many cases, it can take 48 hours from the time you submit for removal for the actual removal to occur.

Websites such as Mxtoolbox.com include searches that will check your server's IP address against multiple blacklists and give you links and information on the processes to get your IP address removed from the list. Each blacklist has its own policy and program to go through to get your IP removed. You will also want to identify that your server still isn't sending messages that may be getting your IP flagged as spam.

If you have any mailing lists configured, check the lists and the Mailman admin interface. If you have any doubt that users' credentials have been compromised, you may want to reset their passwords. On the Mail services tab in Server Admin, you should check your mail queue (select Maintenance and then Mail Queue, as shown in Figure 12–9) to see whether there are a flood of messages waiting to be sent. This is usually a symptom that your mail server is sending spam on someone else's behalf. The queue view will allow you to see message, who it is supposedly from, and who it is destined for. Also, by checking your logs, you can see whether there is any suspicious activity for your server. (You may want to change your log settings to Informative under Settings, but remember to set them back when you are done troubleshooting, because they can grow rapidly for a server with a large volume of mail.) The two areas to focus on again are the SMTP and Mailing List areas, the two most vulnerable areas that will get your server flagged as malicious.

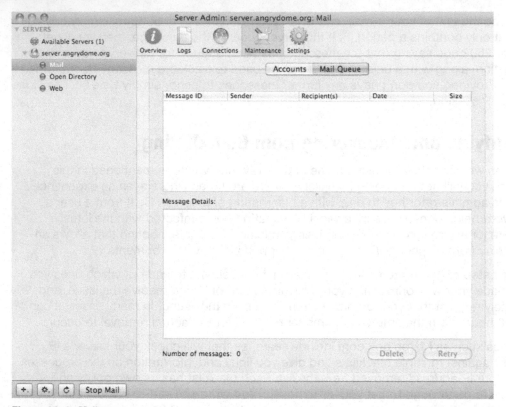

Figure 12–9. *Mail queue*

If after checking all of these settings your server and IP are still getting blacklisted, it may be because of your IP range and that your messages are coming from a bad corner of the Internet. Many small businesses can become targets for spammers. In fact, some organizations have taken very aggressive filtering standards for IPs typically assigned to residential and small business DSL and cable lines. One alternative is to use an inbound and outbound SMTP relay service. They have been mentioned throughout this chapter because we have found that for most small and medium-size businesses with in-house e-mail services, having a larger, organization dedicated to relaying and filtering your mail makes the rest of the administrative duties of a mail server much easier. One key benefit of using such a service is by letting them filter your outbound messages, they can notify you of a potentially compromised client or account before your server ends up on a blacklist.

Summary

Mail services under OS X Server are the result of the integration of many existing mail services and applications to provide an organization with a mail server. As you've read, besides the initial settings, there are a lot of possible ways to customize and optimize the experience, depending on how deeply you want to delve into the configuration. Keep in mind that OS X Server's mail is built from open source tools, and as such, there is already a significant amount of resources available on the Internet on how to work with those individual components.

Also, although Mac OS X's mail server is included with OS X Server, that does not mean it is the only mail server available for OS X. If you are looking for more advanced webmail options, specific features such as being able to remote wipe an iPhone or having a closer integration into your calendaring and address books, Kerio Connect has been a very adaptive and stable mail server for OS X.

Chapter 13

Setting Up Services for Mobile Devices

Mac OS X Server can act as a centralized server to allow your users to communicate with one another when they are not in the office. This includes two services. The first is Mobile Access, which allows a Mac OS X Server acting as a proxy to be placed into a demilitarized zone in your network environment. This device would then be exposed to potential threats from the outside world while also acting as a single point of contact for clients to access your collaborative servers when they are outside your network environment. The demilitarized zone is then the only point of contact with the outside world, and you can granularly configure controls between the hosts in your demilitarized zone and those on your internal network.

The second remote connectivity feature is Push Notification. Push Notification is new in Mac OS X Server 10.6 and comes with a number of design requirements as of this writing, which we will cover in this chapter. Push Notification was specifically designed for the iPhone, although until the next release (4.0) of the iPhone software, the Push Notification service is not that useful because push services are not able to be leveraged.

Installing Mobile Access and Push Notification

The first step to setting up either Mobile Access or Push Notification is to show the service in Server Admin. To do so, open Server Admin from /Applications/Server. After authenticating, click the name of the server where you will be installing the service, and open the server's base settings. Here, click the Settings icon in the toolbar to open the service selection screen, where you can configure which services will run on the server (simply enabling them in this screen will not start them), as shown in Figure 13–1.

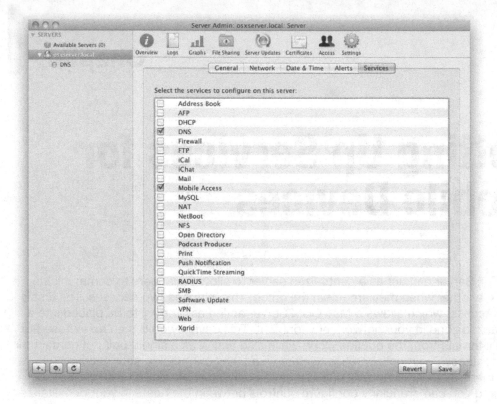

Figure 13–1. *Enabling the services*

Select the box for the appropriate service (either Push Notification or Mobile Access—or both), and then click the Save button. You should then see the service appear in the SERVERS list when you click the disclosure triangle. Click the Settings icon in the Server Admin toolbar to open the settings that Apple has provided for that service.

Setting Up Mobile Access

Now that you have enabled the services, you will want to start and configure the services that you need. The first service that we'll cover is Mobile Access. Mobile Access provides reverse proxy functionality for the Mac OS X collaborative services. This includes Mail, iCal, iChat, and web services (sadly, Mobile Access does not cover the built-in Mac OS X Wikis service).

By proxying connections, you have fewer hosts to secure, and you can place the server proxying those connections into a demilitarized zone and therefore allow as small a footprint of items exposed outside your network as possible. To properly leverage the Mobile Access server, though, you're going to need a demilitarized zone. Figure 13–2 shows the layout of this.

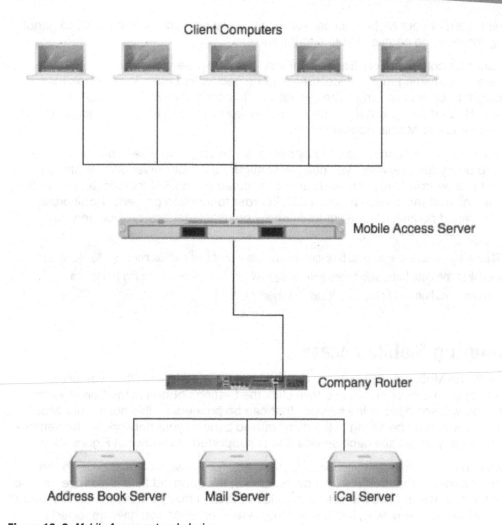

Figure 13–2. *Mobile Access network design*

You'll also need to plan for some technical design considerations when setting up DNS and SSL and deciding how to authenticate the services that are proxied.

Design Considerations

You need to consider a number of factors with regard to how remote users will interface with your systems. These include DNS, SSL, authentication mechanisms, and the layout of the services in your network environment.

The DNS configuration for the environment is pretty straightforward. The clients on the internal network need to access the servers that run each service. The remote clients need to access the Mobile Access server by the same name. If you are using an external DNS service for your public-facing DNS service, then you will be able to take the names and point them at your Mobile Access server while allowing your internal DNS to handle pointing those same names at your internal servers.

SSL is another consideration. Each server that hosts your services will need to use a certificate for providing that service. (See their respective chapters in this book for more on getting that up and running.) The easiest way to configure SSL is to simply use a wildcard SSL certificate. But if you cannot do so, you will need to import each of those certificates into the Mobile Access server.

The authentication mechanisms used by services can vary. But when you use Mobile Access to proxy mail services, you need to configure the mail server and clients to use plain-text passwords. The passwords are still secured by the SSL certificate, one of the main reasons that the service requires SSL in order to function properly. Additionally, Kerberos-based passwords will not traditionally be usable for any proxied service.

> **NOTE:** Many consider a proxy to be synonymous with a host that caches content. Mobile Access does not cache data but instead uses a reverse proxy that helps keep incoming traffic in a centralized location and helps keep it easy for users to access.

Configuring Mobile Access

By default, the Mobile Access service doesn't proxy any services. When you click Mobile Access in Server Admin and then click the Settings button in the Server Admin toolbar, you will see a list of the services that can be proxied. At this point, your Mobile Access server should be sitting in the demilitarized zone of your network. In the settings for the service, you will see each service that is supported, as shown in Figure 13–3.

To enable the proxy for each service, select the box for the service, and provide the name or IP address that traffic will be destined to in the supplied field. If you are using a wildcard certificate and it is the default certificate, then in many environments the default settings will suffice. However, if this is not the case, then once you have imported the certificate for a server, click the Advanced button for each service to select it.

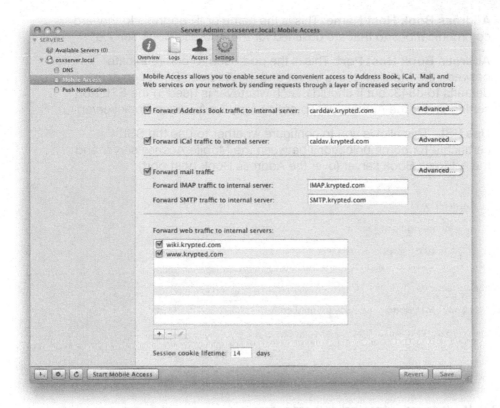

Figure 13–3. *Mobile Access service settings*

Configuring the Address Book Proxy

On the Advanced screen for the Address Book service, you can define granular options for accessing the Address Book service remotely. Before you configure the service, first import the SSL certificate from your Address Book server using Keychain Access. To do so, open Keychain Access from /Applications/Utilities on your Address Book server. Then locate the certificate for that server, and drag it to the desktop. Next copy the certificate to the Mobile Access server, and drag it into Keychain Access on the target.

Once the SSL certificate is installed, in the Mobile Access service settings, click Advanced. You will notice a number of settings that you can use. These include the following, as shown in Figure 13–4:

- **Incoming Port**: This is the port the client computers outside your network will use to access the service (it defaults to 8843).

- **SSL Certificate**: Provided that the certificate from the Address Book server was imported properly, you should see it listed in this drop-down menu.

- **Address Book Host Name**: This is the name or IP address to forward communications to that are destined for the Address Book service.

- **Address Book Host Port**: This is the port used to communicate between the Mobile Access server and the Address Book server (it defaults to 8843, but it should match whatever is used in the SSL Port setting under the Authentication option for your Address Book server).

- **Use SSL**: This allows you to configure whether to use the SSL certificate for communications between the Mobile Access server and the Address Book server (over the Address Book host port).

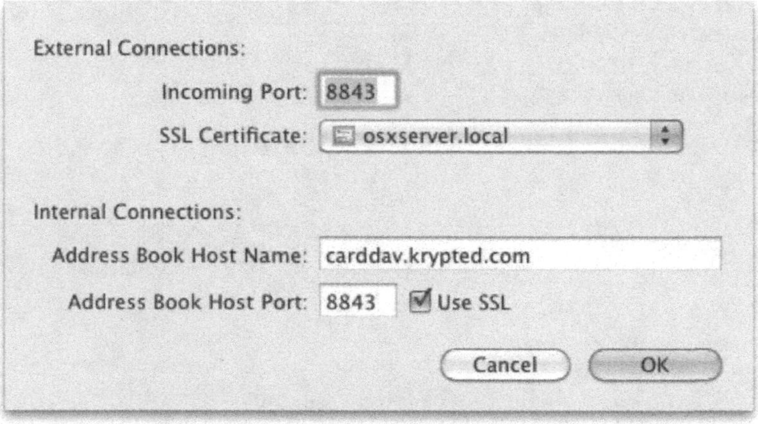

Figure 13–4. *Mobile Access Address Book advanced settings*

Configuring the iCal Proxy

Just as you configured an SSL certificate to proxy Address Book communications in the previous section, you will need to do so for iCal communications as well. The options for configuring an iCal proxy are similar to those used to configure an Address Book proxy; however, you will use the calendar server and the ports that are appropriate for these communications, as noted here and as shown in Figure 13–5:

- **Incoming Port**: This is the port the client computers outside your network will use to access the service (defaults to 8443).

- **SSL Certificate**: Provided that the certificate from the iCal server was imported properly, you should see it listed in this drop-down menu.

- **iCal Host Name**: This is the name or IP address to forward communications to that are destined for the iCal service.

- **iCal Host Port**: This is the port used to communicate between the Mobile Access server and the iCal server (it defaults to 8443 but should be set to the same as the SSL port that is specified under Authentication in the Server Admin settings for the iCal service on your iCal server).

■ **Use SSL**: This allows you to configure whether to use the SSL certificate for communications between the Mobile Access server and the iCal server (over the iCal host port).

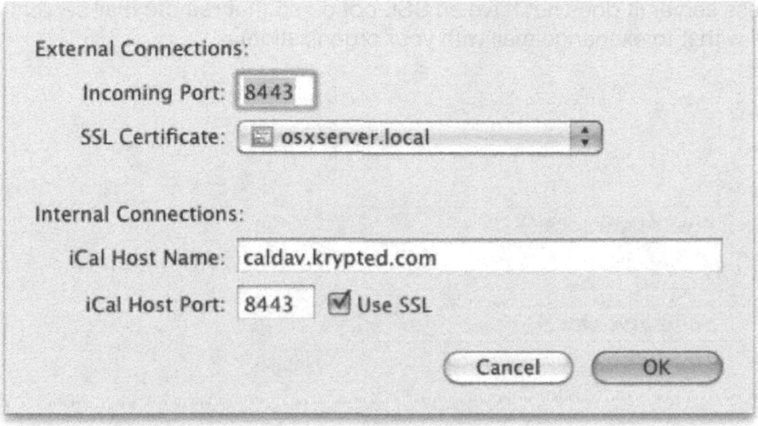

External Connections:

Incoming Port: 8443

SSL Certificate: osxserver.local

Internal Connections:

iCal Host Name: caldav.krypted.com

iCal Host Port: 8443 ☑ Use SSL

Cancel   OK

Figure 13–5. *Mobile Access iCal advanced settings*

Configuring the Mail Proxy

Prior to configuring the mail options in Mobile Access, make sure you have installed the SSL certificates for your mail service, as covered in the "Configuring the Address Book Proxy" section earlier in this chapter. On the Advanced screen for the mail proxy, you will see settings that are different from the previously configured iCal and Address Book proxies. Namely, this is because you are proxying two ports. Here, you will be able to configure ports and SSL options as you did previously. The settings include the following, as shown in Figure 13–6:

■ **Incoming IMAP Port**: This is the port that clients will use when accessing the IMAP service from outside your environment.

■ **IMAP SSL Certificate**: Select the certificate that you imported from your IMAP server.

■ **Incoming SMTP Port**: This is the port that clients will use when accessing the SMTP service from outside your environment.

■ **SMTP SSL Certificate**: Select the certificate that you previously imported for your SMTP server.

■ **IMAP Host Name**: This is the name or IP address of the internal IMAP server on your local area network.

■ **IMAP Host Port**: This is the port that IMAP will be running on the mail server.

■ **Use SSL**: Enable SSL for communications between your internal IMAP server and the Mobile Access server.

- **SMTP Host Name**: This is the name or IP address of the internal SMTP server.

SMTP Host Port: This is the port that will be used to communicate between the local SMTP service and the Mobile Access server (it does not have an SSL option so that remote mail servers will be able to communicate with it to exchange mail with your organization).

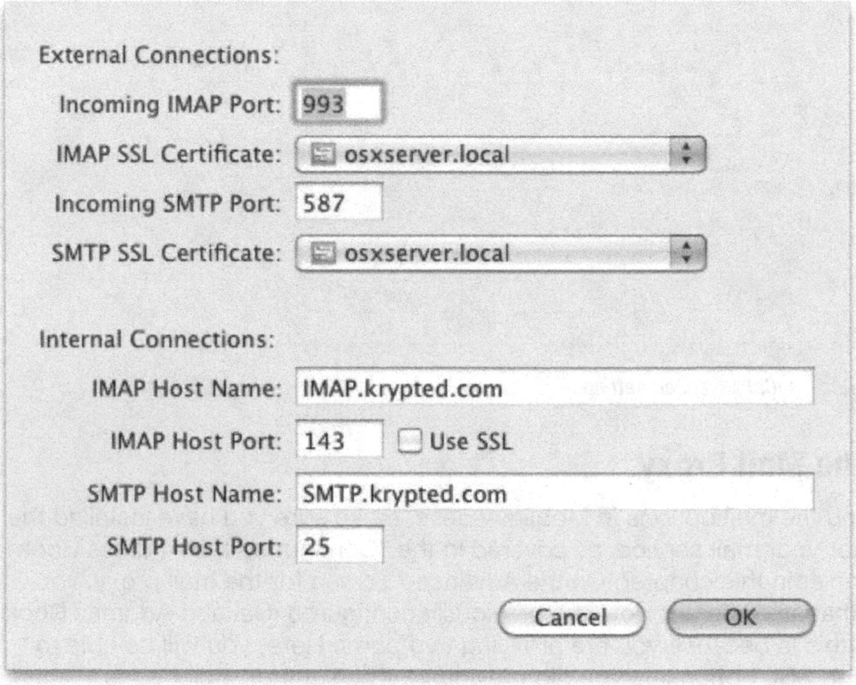

External Connections:

Incoming IMAP Port: `993`

IMAP SSL Certificate: `osxserver.local`

Incoming SMTP Port: `587`

SMTP SSL Certificate: `osxserver.local`

Internal Connections:

IMAP Host Name: `IMAP.krypted.com`

IMAP Host Port: `143` ☐ Use SSL

SMTP Host Name: `SMTP.krypted.com`

SMTP Host Port: `25`

Cancel   OK

Figure 13–6. Defining Mobile Access ports and hosts

Configuring Web Proxy Entries

Many organizations will have a number of web servers. For example, you can host a web server for your environment's web site(s), another for the webmail functionality in Mac OS X Server's Mail service, another for accessing the iCal service over a web browser, and finally one for your blog and wiki. Mobile Access for web proxying is not supported with the Mac OS X Wikis service. However, it does function for a number of other services. Because you can have multiple servers, you can also define multiple entries in Mobile Access for web proxies, with each referred to as a *web proxy entry*. You can add the entries by clicking the plus sign in the "Forward web traffic to internal servers" field in the Mobile Access Settings pane of Server Admin.

On the Edit screen for each web proxy entry, you will be able to configure more granular options for the entry. To do so, click the entry on the Server Admin Settings screen, and then click the pencil icon for that entry. The resultant screen will provide options for configuring the entry, as shown in Figure 13–7. These entries will allow you to configure the following:

- **Enable this web proxy entry**: This allows you to have unused proxies for testing purposes.

- **Incoming Port**: This is the port that traffic destined from the Internet will use.

- **Web Host Name**: This is the name or IP address of the internal web server used for the web proxy entry.

- **Web Host Port**: This is the port used to communicate between the internal web server and the Mobile Access service.

- **Use SSL**: Not all web sites will use SSL. Select this option if you require an SSL certificate for the site in question.

Figure 13–7. *Enabling the Mobile Access web proxy*

NOTE: Virtual hosts that leverage SSL and have been created based on names are not compatible (by default) with the Mobile Access service.

Starting the Service and Checking the Status

Once you are satisfied with your settings, click the Start Mobile Access button toward the bottom of the Server Admin screen. The service will then start, and you will be able to click the Overview button in the Server Admin toolbar. On the Overview screen, you will see which proxies are configured and which hosts that traffic is being forwarded to for each proxied service, as shown in Figure 13–8.

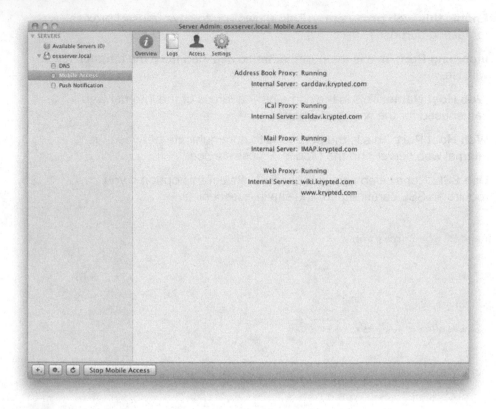

Figure 13–8. *Statuses for Mobile Access proxied services*

Controlling Access

When you enable the Mobile Access service, you will be enabling access for all users of the server. However, in many environments, not all users will be allowed to access collaborative services remotely. Therefore, you can use the Access option to limit who is able to log into the server over each service. This Access option is similar to a service access control list (SACL). However, rather than configure the SACL option for the server, you configure these access controls in the service.

To configure access controls, open Server Admin, and click Mobile Access for your Mobile Access server. Then click the Access icon in the Server Admin toolbar. By default, the "Allow access to Address Book, iCal, Mail and Web proxies for everyone" option will be selected, meaning that all users with accounts on the server will be able to access all the services proxied using Mobile Access. Click "Allow access to the selected proxies for these users and groups" to limit which users will be able to authenticate to these services. At this point, no users will be able to access the services. Next, click the plus sign, and drag a user who you would like to grant access to the list of users and groups.

Once you have dragged a user into the list, you will notice there is a check box for each of the services that Mobile Access can currently act as a proxy for, as shown in Figure 13–9. Next, select the box for each of the services (that is, Address, iCal, Mail, and Web) that the selected user should be able to access. Drag each user into the list, and select the appropriate boxes per user. Then click Save to commit your changes, and test that the authentication is allowed as intended.

NOTE: The user list that is provided will by default be empty unless the server is connected to a directory service. Therefore, you may need to provide access to the Mobile Access server that sits in the demilitarized zone to your internal directory service.

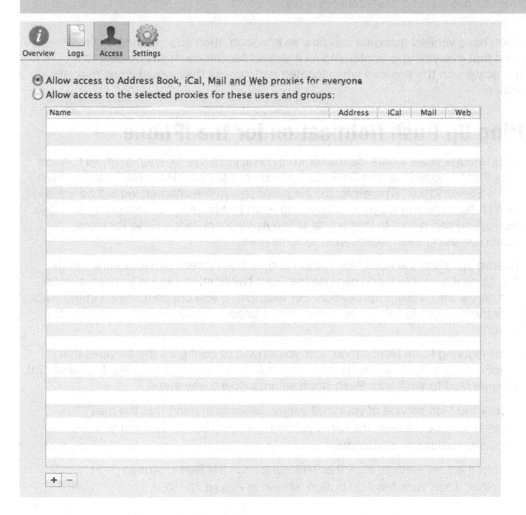

Figure 13–9. *Limiting access to Mobile Access Server*

Connecting Clients

Once you have configured each service, you'll want to make sure your firewall is configured properly. To do so, make sure that incoming traffic for the Mobile Access server is allowed into your demilitarized zone. Provided that it is, then check to make sure that the required ports (and ideally only the required ports) between your Mobile Access server and your proxied services inside your network are allowed as well.

> **NOTE:** Port scanning will not always be possible for one reason or another. See the following article for more on testing connectivity when using SSL: `http://krypted.com/mac-os-x/using-openssl-to-test-connectivity`.

Once you have verified that data can flow as intended, then you can test a client. Provided that everything is configured as it should be, the client will be able to communicate with the services when located remotely as they would when they are in your office!

Setting Up Push Notification for the iPhone

In the Knowledge Base article located at `http://support.apple.com/kb/HT3947`, Apple indicates that "iPhone Mail and Calendar apps do not support Push Notifications from Mac OS X Server v10.6." Therefore, for the purposes of this chapter, we will be limiting the Push Notification coverage to configuring Push Notification to function for services as needed; you can return to that article or the Apple Knowledge Base for more information on using Push Notification as it matures.

We covered installing the Push Notification and Mobile Access services earlier in the chapter. Once it's enabled, you can use the Push Notification service to push events from the server into a client application. For example, if you create an event in the web portal for the iCal service, then you should see it appear "automagically" into the iCal application.

Before configuring Push Notification, first you'll need to configure the services that you're going to use Push Notification to send events on behalf of, namely, Mail and iCal. To configure Mail to work with Push Notification, follow these steps:

1. Click the Mail service of your mail server, keeping in mind that the mail server isn't necessarily the same as the Push Notification server if you have a multiserver environment.

2. From the Mail service, click the Settings icon in the Server Admin toolbar. Then click the Add button, shown in Figure 13–10.

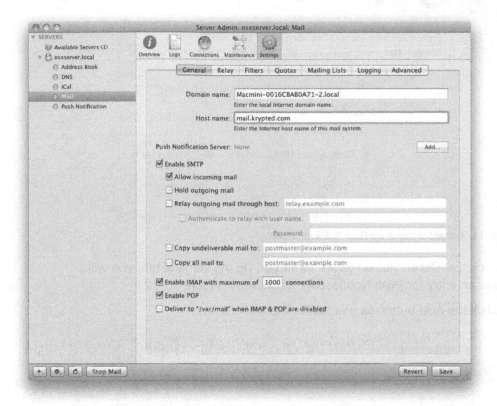

Figure 13–10. *Adding Push Notification*

3. Clicking the Add button opens a dialog box to provide a server that will handle notifications from the service.

4. If you are using the same server for Push Notification that you are using for mail, you can enter **127.0.0.1**; otherwise, enter the IP address or host name of the server that will be configured as the Push Notification server.

5. Provide an administrative username and password, and click the Connect button, as shown in Figure 13–11.

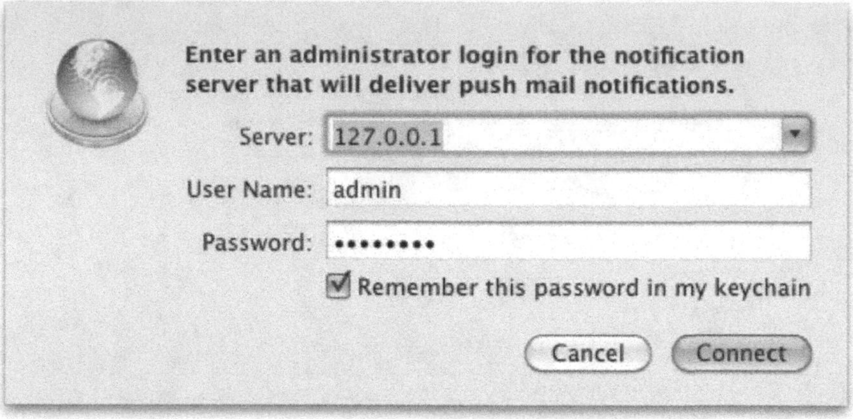

Enter an administrator login for the notification server that will deliver push mail notifications.

Server: 127.0.0.1

User Name: admin

Password: ••••••••

☑ Remember this password in my keychain

Cancel   Connect

Figure 13–11. *Authenticating to the Push Notification server*

6. Click the iCal service on your iCal server. On the General tab, you will see an entry for Push Notification, as shown in Figure 13–12.

7. Click the Add button as you did for the Mail service.

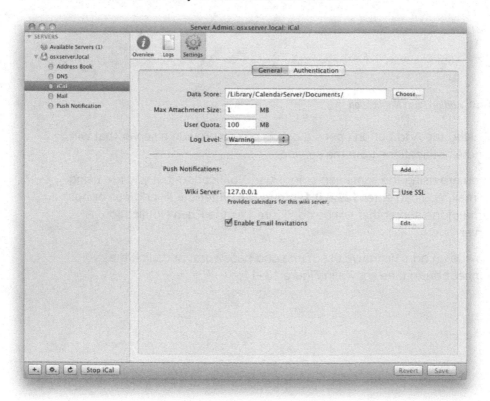

Figure 13–12. *Enabling Push Notification for iCal*

8. Clicking the Add button opens a dialog box to provide a server to handle notifications from the service.

9. If you are using the same server for Push Notification that you are using for iCal, you can enter **127.0.0.1**; otherwise, enter the IP address or host name of the server that will be configured as the Push Notification server.

10. Provide an administrative username and password, and click the Connect button.

Once you have configured the services in your environment that require Push Notification, click the Push Notification service in the SERVERS list of Server Admin (configured earlier in this chapter). Then click the Start Push Notifications button, and the Push Notification service should change its status to Running, as shown in Figure 13–13.

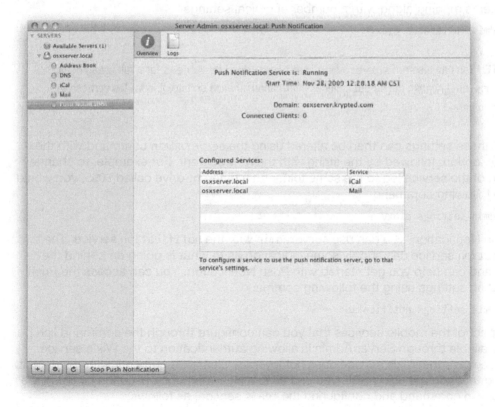

Figure 13–13. *Starting Push Notification*

You can then use the Overview button in Server Admin to view the status of the server, the number of clients, and the date that the service was started on an ongoing basis.

Using the Command Line to Manage Mobile Access and Push Notification

The command-line options for the Mobile Access and Push Notification services are fairly rudimentary compared to some of the other services in Mac OS X Server. The `serveradmin` command is capable of starting and stopping the services and of more granularly configuring settings. When running the `serveradmin` command, you will use the proxy and notification options to specify the service that you are working with as Mobile Access and Push Notification, respectively. A basic version of this would be to use the following command, which uses the `status` verb to determine whether the service is running:

`serveradmin status proxy`

In addition, you can use `serveradmin` to look at the critical settings for the service by running it with the `fullstatus` option. For example, the following command shows that the server is running along with a number of critical settings:

`serveradmin fullstatus proxy`

> **NOTE:** You can also run `serveradmin settings Mobile Access` for a full listing of all settings, but because the output includes information on each update, it is far too verbose to include here.

Each of these settings can then be altered using the `serveradmin` command with the `settings` option, followed by the string with the new content. For example, to change the path of the service log to the same folder on a different drive called `LOGS`, you would use the following command:

`serveradmin settings proxy`

For Push Notification, you can use `serveradmin` with the `notification` service. The `notification` service can supply some indication as to what is going on behind the scenes and can help you get started with Push Notification. You can access the Push Notification settings using the following command:

`serveradmin settings notification`

One aspect of the mobile services that you can configure through the command line but is not available through Server Admin is allowing authentication to the Wikis service. This is because the Wikis service does not leverage clear-text authentication by default. Provided that you are using SSL, you can enable clear-text authentication by using the `serveradmin` command and configuring the `teams` service, as follows:

`serveradmin settings teams:enableClearTextAuth = yes`

Another aspect of the server that can be configured from the command line, but not the graphical interface, is the blacklist and whitelist functionality in the proxy service.

Finally, not all certificates are friendly to the Keychain Access tool. Therefore, you can use the locations of the certificate files and call them directly from within the proxy settings for each service.

Summary

Many of the collaborative services included with Mac OS X, such as iChat, Mail, and iCal, need to be interfaced with securely. Apple has integrated server-side services in previous versions of Mac OS X Server, but in Snow Leopard, the enhancements of Push Notification and Mobile Access help take Mac OS X Server to the next level.

With Push Notification, you can interact with the server in a more immediate fashion, using the steps outlined in this chapter. Also using this chapter, you can substantially increase the security of your environment by leveraging Mobile Access to integrate a proxy for secure remote connectivity with your server.

In Chapter 14, we'll complete our discussion of collaboration and look at doing so online.

Web Servers

The web server in Mac OS X is as versatile, stable, and scalable as you are likely to find in any operating system. Apple built the web server using the highly modular Apache server that kick started the Web as we know it, now with more than 100 million web sites and serving up more than half the web sites in the world. The maturity of the product is unparalleled, and the care Apple takes to integrate it is painstaking to say the least. Because Mac OS X Server comes preloaded with Apache, this chapter will focus wholly on that product.

A Mac OS X Server–based web server has a number of uses above and beyond serving up the web pages of your favorite web site. Without needing to perform costly and custom programming, you can serve web-based mail, web-based calendars, wikis, and blogs all by checking a box. Each of these roles that the web server can fill are made easy to use but still require some explanation, which is where this chapter comes into play in your Mac OS X Server deployment.

In this chapter, we will start by covering what you need to know before you install the web server. This will involve a little bit of DNS and some Open Directory, so check out Chapters 6 and 4, respectively, if you have not already done so. We will then cover some ways to configure the web service and a number of pretty granular settings you can use when building out the location to serve web pages. And most importantly for those of you who will be using your web server as an internal web site (in other words, a site to house internal data rather than a publicly facing web site), we will cover how to configure the web service to communicate with the other services that it can leverage.

Your Company Site

As we mentioned, the web server in Mac OS X is based on the Apache web server. The server is extensible and comes with a number of tools and modifications that will help you serve up whatever kind of web pages you need to serve. But before we discuss the actual setup and management of the web service, first think about whether you want to host your web site yourself or whether you will just pay someone else to do so. Almost any modern Mac (which roughly means any Intel-based Mac) is going to make a good web server. Provided you have enough memory, then even a Mac mini is likely to be ample for an environment with a T1 or two worth of web traffic. (You can never have enough memory, but 2GB to 16GB should do the trick according to the size of what you are serving, how well the code is designed, and the amount of traffic you are going to get.)

But is the rest of your environment ready to host a web server? If you have a T1 that is only 1.544Mbps and no backup of that line, then if it goes out, your web site will be offline until you get the Internet circuit back up and running. If you have an even faster connection, then is it a residential-class Internet connection? What is the service level agreement of your Internet service provider to get the circuit back up and running? Do you have redundant power? Redundant servers? (By the way, did we mention clustering is built into the Apache web server?) Are you monitoring the server so that if it goes down you can proactively fix it before getting a call from someone attempting to access it? If any of these go out, then your web site will be down, and that can cause trust issues, be it with students, clients, or end users trusting your organization's ability to maintain a simple web server.

If you do not already have all the fault tolerance in place to effectively host a web site, then you may have a costly journey ahead of you if you want to try to account for every possible failure and a possible situation to remedy that failure. Ask yourself whether you really want to embark upon that journey when you can pay as little as a few dollars a month for someone else to deal with all of those headaches!

If you come back with a yes to all of these questions, then like many of us you have chosen to host your own web site. You can still choose to place it in someone else's network cabinets, like MacMiniColo.net, where they take care of all of the environmental concerns so that you can focus on your server. Or you can simply throw the thing down in the basement like some of us do. Either way, you have full control of your server. You are now going to have the versatility to do practically anything you want with that web server. Want to host 50 web sites? 500? Want to connect the server to Podcast Producer to publish video streams? Want to view your family, class, or company calendar? Want to teach it to make coffee? All of this is possible (although we're not going to cover the coffee part in this chapter because we're saving that for a *Stupid Mac OS X Server Tricks* book).

Once you are committed to hosting your own web site, you can then move on to planning to install the site. To maintain security and stability, it is important to measure twice and cut once. At a minimum, we recommend doing the following before you start to configure the web server:

- Although the IP address that you use for Mac OS X Server on your internal network may be static, it is not safe to assume that the IP address your ISP provides you with is static. So, make sure you have a static IP address from your ISP. Sure, you can use a service that provides dynamic DNS to your site, but that is a road fraught with peril. Instead, make the call, unless you already have one.

- Verify that the ISP is not blocking the port (likely either port 80 or port 443 for *incoming* traffic).

- We strongly recommend that all servers be placed behind a firewall or router. Therefore, you will also need to map out which ports will need to be forwarded to your web server and from what IP address you will forward them from (for more on routing, see Chapter 6).

- Work with the web developer to determine what is used in the site, including where possible the version of each Apache module that will be needed (more on modules later in this chapter) and the version of any third-party services such as MySQL that you will need.

- Read the whole chapter, and only then follow along with the steps outlined.

- Check your uninterruptable power supply (UPS), and find out how long your power can go out before it goes down.

- Consider any clustering you will want to do, and make sure you map out each aspect of the site that will need to be clustered.

- Get a monitoring service. Whether it's something as simple as an iPhone application or something like a dedicated Lithium server (a popular monitoring server for Mac OS X), create a plan for making sure that you know your site is down before your customers do.

- Consider any of the other services, such as calendar integration.

- If you have *any* forms that allow for an end user to enter content, then make sure to get an SSL certificate, which can be self-assigned or from a third-party vendor (for more on SSL certificates, see Chapter 3).

- Check with your DNS provider, and verify that your public DNS is pointing at the proper IP address that you will use (or that you can point the DNS to the site you will use and that you know the procedure to do so when you are ready).

> **TIP:** Keep in mind that DNS can take up to 72 hours for propagation. During that time, you can use a local DNS server or the /etc/hosts file to point DNS to your web server for testing until you are ready to repoint DNS. Given the potential latency for updates to public DNS records, you will not want to be changing them frequently.

Once you have all this information, a plan for integrating the server should start to prove self-evident. Now it's time to start the installation.

Setting Up Your First Site

There are two ways to set up the web service in Mac OS X. The first and by far simplest is to use the Server Preferences tool. This tool will provide you with a limited but common set of options. The second is to use Server Admin, which will provide you with a lot of options. If you require options that are not available in Server Admin, then there are still a number of configuration files that you can use to configure the web service. We'll start with using Server Preferences and then move on to Server Admin next.

The Easy Way to Set Up a Web Server

Server Preferences allows an administrator to set up a web server quickly and without much knowledge of what the underlying server is going to be doing. You can set the site up in Server Preferences and then move on to managing it in Server Admin once it is configured how you would like, and you can even alternate between the two for certain tasks.

To get started configuring your sites in Server Preferences, open the Server Preferences tool from the Dock of Mac OS X or from the `/Applications/Server` directory. The entry for Web will appear with a gray indicator light (Figure 14–1), meaning the service has yet to be started. Click the service to configure and start it.

Figure 14–1. *Server Preferences*

Once you have clicked the Web service, you will see the Web Server screen, as shown in Figure 14–2. Here, you can start and stop the web server, and you can also configure which of the web services the server will run, above and beyond the standard Apache web server and common Apache modules. These include the following:

- *Wikis*: This provides web sites that are easily editable by anyone with permission to do so within the browser, allowing users to dynamically generate content.

- *Calendar*: If you are running the iCal service, then users will be able to manage and view calendars using the web portal of Mac OS X Server.

- *Blogs*: This allows users to be able to create and manage their own weblogs.

- *Webmail*: This gives users the ability to check their mail using a web portal (requires that the Mail service also be running to do so).

You can also configure a page that the web server will point users to when they visit the site based on a wiki page that you have configured, an option that's useful when you are redirecting users to a specific landing page that you have prepared for just that purpose.

NOTE: By default, the server will assign the default landing page for the domain to the `index.html` or `index.php` file in the *webroot*, or top-level directory of your web site.

Figure 14–2. *Enabling the Web service*

By default, the web server will be installed for a single web site. That site will respond to any requests sent to a DNS name that resolves to the server or to the IP address of the server. The site files are stored in `/Library/WebServer/Documents`, and you can copy the contents of a web site that you have set up in iWeb or Dreamweaver or that you programmed manually to this page. You can also create other sites, and the web server will assign traffic to each site based on the DNS resolution to that site. To do so, click Custom Sites on the Web Server screen, and then click the plus (+) sign. Here, you will be greeted with a screen that allows you to enter text in the Domain Name field and choose a location for the new site to store its files in the Store Site Files In field, as shown in Figure 14–3.

First you will want to provide a name for the site in the Domain Name field. This will be the name of the site that you are forwarding to the IP address of the server. For example, if the name `seldom.krypted.com` were pointed to the external IP address of a server, then that name would be filled into the Domain Name field. Once you have provided the domain name and the location that the site will reference, click the Create button.

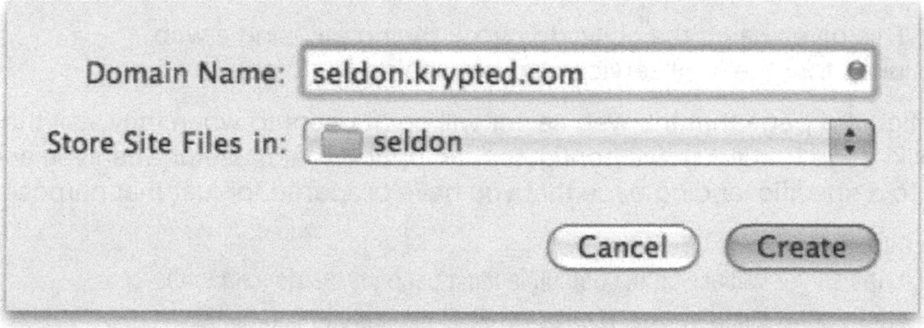

Figure 14–3. *Setting up a custom site*

At this time, if the domain name can be resolved for the site, it will simply be created. However, if the DNS cannot be resolved, which you will know to be the case because of the red sphere in the Domain Name field (Figure 14–4), you will be prompted to enter an IP address and a port for the site. If you have only one IP address and are not using SSL, then you can simply leave these fields at their defaults and click the Create button. However, if you have multiple IP addresses configured on your server, then you will want to choose the previously configured address and provide a port number for the traffic before hitting the Create button again, which will create the site. (See Chapter 3 for more on using multiple IP addresses on your server.)

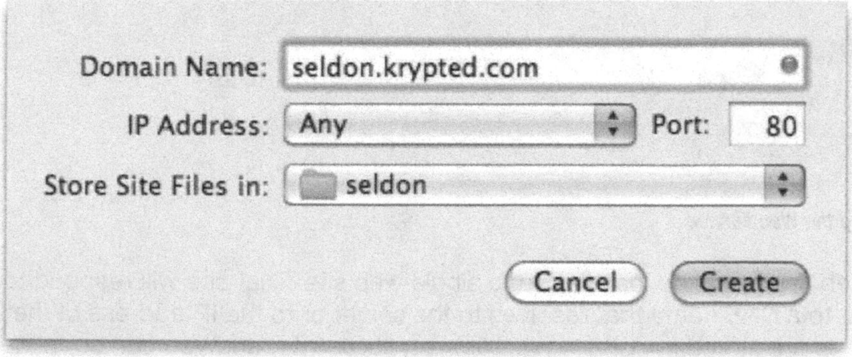

Figure 14–4. *When a custom site cannot resolve properly*

Once the site has been created, you will see it listed on the Custom Sites tab of the Web screen, as shown in Figure 14–5. This means that if a user's DNS points the user at that web server to access that site (or their `/etc/hosts` file points them at the site), then that user will see the data (the `index.html` or `index.php` file for starters) that you have placed in the `/seldon` directory.

Figure 14–5. *Your new custom site*

Your next task is to test the site by opening it in a web browser. If the site comes up once you've placed valid HTML or PHP pages into the directory, then you have successfully set up both a default site and a custom web site. And you likely were able to configure them to reside on the same IP address, a pretty advanced configuration on some other platforms. But wait, you're not done yet. Now we'll cover how to granularly configure a number of settings for your sites using the Server Admin tool!

Configuring Web Services from Server Admin

As we've mentioned, the Server Admin tool is far more powerful than the Web Server pane of Server Preferences. It has a little bit more of a learning curve, but you can grow into it. Or if you're ready, you can jump right in. To follow along with the upcoming examples, you'll want to turn off the Web Server component of Server Preferences. You will now start with a fresh installation and move through the steps to get the web server up and running.

The first step to setting up web services is to show the services in Server Admin. To do so, first open Server Admin from /Applications/Server. After authenticating, click the name of the server where you will be installing the service onto, and open the server's base settings. Here, click the Settings icon in the toolbar to open the services selection screen, where you can configure which services will run on the server (although simply enabling them in this screen will not start them), as shown in Figure 14–6.

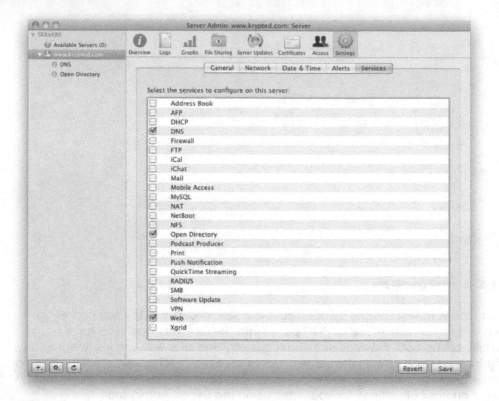

Figure 14–6. *Enabling the services*

Select the Web box, and then click the Save button. You should then see the service appear in the c when you click the disclosure triangle to display the active services on the server. This means that the service has been added to the view in Server Admin; however, it will not yet be started. Next, click the Settings icon in the Server Admin toolbar to open the settings that Apple has provided for that service, as shown in Figure 14–7.

At this point, you can start the web service by clicking the Start Web button. You'll notice the light next to the service turn green, similar to how the light turned green when you started the Web service in Server Preferences. You can continue configuring the web server while it is started or stopped, but keep in mind if you proceed with the service started that you will occasionally need to restart it (by clicking the Stop Web and then the Start Web button each time you go to restart the service).

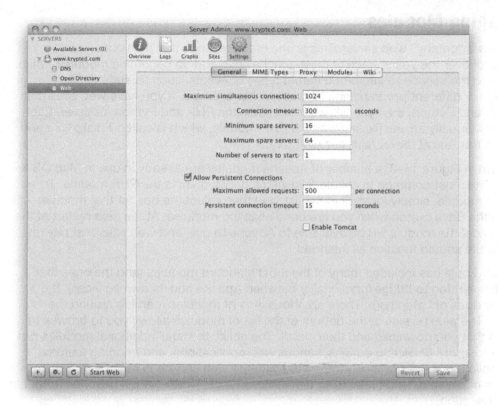

Figure 14–7. *General settings for the Web service*

NOTE: If you have both the Server Preferences and Server Admin tools open concurrently, then you can see inconsistent results between the two. We recommend working in one at a time. Then, when you open the other, it should have consistent results.

Global Configuration Options

Once you have the Web service enabled, then you will want to configure the server for the options that your web sites needed. It's not yet time to configure the web sites themselves, but given the extensibility of Apache, it is a good idea to enable the options you need while disabling the options that you don't need, which affords a much higher level of security than leaving everything with the default configuration. This isn't to say that Apple hasn't provided a secure solution for serving up your web pages; however, you can never be too careful when exposing a server to a workgroup—or the world, for that matter.

Managing Modules

Apache is a "patchy" web server. This is one of the reasons that it has been so successful over the years. Each of these patches can end up becoming *modules*, which will extend the service to interpret different types of events, such as authorization protocols or different programming languages. For example, if you have web sites that use PHP and Python, then you will want to enable the PHP and Python modules. Each module is actually an .so file, such as the PHP module, which is called libphp5.so and stored in the /usr/libexec/apache2 directory.

As shown in Figure 14–8, a number of Apache modules are already in use in Mac OS X Server. The most common to enable following a deployment is the PHP module. To enable a module, simply locate it in the list, and then select the box for that module, clicking the Save button when you are done enabling modules. At the next restart of the web service, the module will be available to Apache to use, and web sites that rely on that module should function as intended.

Although Apple has included many of the most standard modules (and the ones that Apple has written to bridge functionality between Apache and its own services), the flexibility does not stop here. There are thousands of modules roaming around the Internet. The plus (+) sign at the bottom of the list of modules allows you to browse to .so files that you download and then install. The ability to install additional modules can provide for more clustering options, various web applications, and bridging features from applications not previously integrated with the web service in Mac OS X Server. Modules can also extend to handling different file types, which we will describe further in the next section.

> **CAUTION:** Be very careful about extending Apache to include new modules. Know exactly why you are doing so, and work with web developers when needed to make sure that you are installing only the modules that are required.

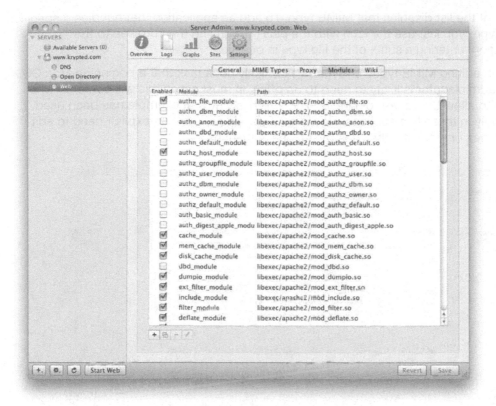

Figure 14–8. *Enabling modules for the Web service*

MIME Types

Modules allow for interpreting different data or code that the web server encounters in each file that is served up. MIME types allow the web server to understand each file type that is encountered and points the web server to an application that will handle the interpretation of each different type of page. This is similar to how you tell Mac OS X to open each file type with a different program, but it relies on file extensions as is common in Microsoft Windows. In order for your server to understand PHP files, Apple has built in the PHP MIME type. That entry in the MIME Types screen in Mac OS X Server points PHP files to the program that opens them (in this case x-httpd-php), which handles serving up PHP pages. Each type of file that the server understands how to interpret will have a MIME type that tells Apache which application is capable of handling that file type.

You can disable a file type to keep your server running securely. For example, if you are not using Atom feeds (for RSS) in your site, then you can disable the file type. To do so, open Server Admin, and go to the Web service in the SERVERS list. From here you would click the Settings button in the Server Admin toolbar and then click the MIME Types tab. There, you will be able to find the entry using Atom in the Suffix column, as shown in Figure 14–9. Clicking the entry and then clicking the minus (–) button at the bottom of the list disables that MIME type. To add an application that handles a specific MIME type, you just use the icon with the plus (+) sign and then browse to the application, entering a suffix of the file type in question.

Although editing MIME types and modules is likely not a task that a beginning Mac OS X Server administrator is likely to need to do often, in most cases this will come up when looking to allow the server to handle PHP, which is why that example has been used repeatedly in these two sections. However, if you do not have an explicit need to edit MIME types or modules, then it is best to leave them be.

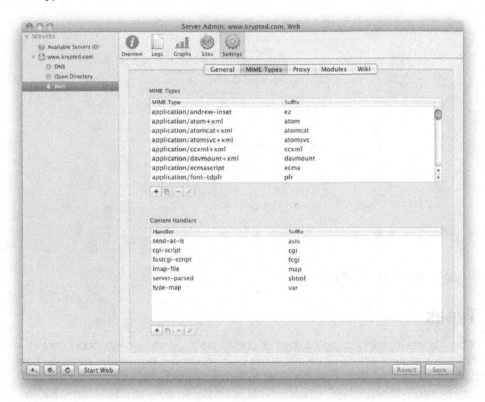

Figure 14–9. *Editing MIME types for the Web service*

Warning: Before you remove MIME types, make sure that you don't need the web server to handle each one. If you remove one that you need, then you can cause certain code to not function anymore.

Proxy Services

Now that you have configured MIME types and modules, you can move on to any environment aspects of server configuration. Much of this is going to be security related, and one way to both further secure your server and allow it to serve pages faster is to use what is known as a *proxy*. A proxy caches content, much like your web browser will cache web data in order to speed up access to that site the next time you visit it. A proxy can also mean anonymizing the server (which is one purpose of the Mobile Access service) and potentially acting as a load-balancing web cluster that actually stores content (the Mobile Access service in Mac OS X is described further in Chapter 13) and the Reverse Proxy option in each web site (which we will cover later in this chapter).

The proxy in Mac OS X Server caches pages of a web site that are visited so that as each additional user of your local network visits the site, they do not have to download images, movies, and other file types and graphics, speeding up access to the site for subsequent visits after the first visitor has downloaded the pages. This type of proxy is known as a *forward proxy*. The forward proxy is a little different from most other aspects of the Web service for Mac OS X Server because it actually provides a service to your client computers that is more network-oriented than most. The forward proxy can help reduce the total saturation of your Internet connection by using a shared cache for all your client computers.

To enable the forward proxy, open Server Admin, and then click the Settings for the Web service, clicking the Proxy tab of the global configuration settings. The Proxy screen will have a number of settings, which you can see in Figure 14–10. Here, select the Enable Forward Proxy check box, and then save the settings, restarting the service when you are finished.

The proxy will now cache files downloaded for clients. These clients will then not access the Web directly but do so through the web server. These files will by default download to the /var/run/proxy directory, although you can choose a different folder to store the files if you so choose (for example, if you want to use the solid-state drive on an Xserve so that the cache is faster than an internal drive). You can also set the size of the cache; the default is set to 1MB, but it can be increased to much higher (we often set it to 1024). You can also set an interval to empty the cache, which allows for redownloading data. By default this is set to 24 hours, which is typically a good setting to stick with. Finally, you can set sites that are blocked. In doing so, any site entered into this field will then not be accessible to client computers who use the proxy to access the Web through the proxy.

For a client computer to make use of the forward proxy, it will need to be configured to do so. To set the proxy settings in Mac OS X, open the Network pane of System Preferences. From here, click the adapter that you would like to enable the proxy for. (Proxies are dependent on the adapter for Safari but configured in the application for Firefox, so configure proxies within Firefox if you have users that use that browser rather than Safari.) Then click the Proxies tab. Next, select the Web Proxy box, and provide the name of your server that is running the proxy in the Web Proxy Server field, as shown in Figure 14–11. As you can see, you can also provide a port number in the field, but with Mac OS X clients leveraging Mac OS X Server as a proxy, there is no need to do so.

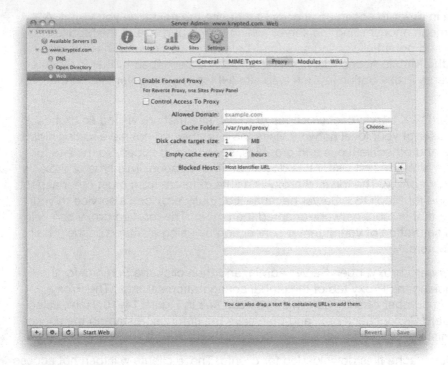

Figure 14–10. *Configuring proxy options for the Web service*

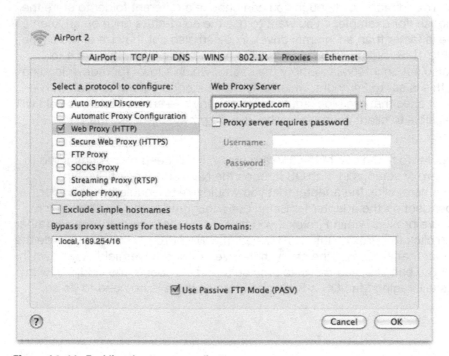

Figure 14–11. *Enabling the proxy on a client*

Now that you have configured the important global settings of your web service, it's time to move on to setting up your web sites that the service will host.

Creating a Site

Earlier in this chapter we covered using Server Preferences to create the default site and a custom site. When you do so in Server Preferences and then you move over to Server Admin to obtain more granular configuration options, you will see those sites listed if you click the Sites button in the Web service within Server Admin. Continuing from the previous example, Figure 14–12 indicates how those sites would appear.

Enabled	Host Name	IP Address	Port
☑		*	80
☑	seldon.krypted.com	*	80

Figure 14–12. *Web sites in Server Admin*

You can easily add and remove sites by clicking the plus (+) or minus (-) sign below the list, respectively. When you click the plus sign, you will then be allowed to provide the site-specific information for that site.

> **NOTE:** Deleting a site does not delete the data that the site was hosting, only the reference to the site in the web server itself.

Configuring Site-Specific Options

The site-specific options provide administrators with the ability to assign a number of different options. If you have only one site, then many of these options will not be required, although they can still be used. As you start to further secure sites, integrate sites into the Mac OS X Server services (that is, iCal Server, Wiki, and so on), and create more sites, then you will invariably look to more granularly configure sites than how you were able to do so in Server Preferences.

> **NOTE:** If you have only one site, then it will likely have a blank host name and an IP address of *. This means that all traffic destined for the IP address(es) hosted on the Mac OS X Server will be handled by this site.

Once you have added a site, then you will move on to configuring the various options for it. These allow you to configure each site a little bit differently, thus assigning a different folder for the contents of the site, a different template, or theme, if the site is a wiki and different security settings. Each site is then able to only have settings or features required by that site to function. As shown in Figure 14–13, there are a number of settings. In fact, as you will find through the progression of this section of the chapter, each site has a number of settings under each tab and a number of tabs. You can find the most basic settings, though, under the General tab:

- *Host Name*: The URL of the web site such as www.krypted.com or seldon.krypted.com. These can each represent a separate entry, as can wiki.krypted.com and calendar.krypted.com. All of these can be hosted using the same IP address and web site or using different sites.

- *Host Description*: A description of the site. This is solely for tracking sites for administrative purposes and has no impact on the performance of the site or how it is presented to visitors.

- *IP Address*: The IP address on the server that the site will be hosted on. Since each Mac OS X computer can have a number of IP addresses configured for each adapter, you can host each site on a dedicated IP address if you so choose. There is little need to do so, though, for most sites.

- *Port*: By default the port is 80, or 443 for SSL-enabled sites. The port can be changed, although if you do change it, then visitors will need to append a colon (:) followed by the port number to their address when accessing the site. For example, this could be http://www.krypted.com:8080 if you used 8080 as the port number for www.krypted.com.

- *Web Folder*: The folder where the web pages that comprise a site are stored. This can be changed as needed, and if you build multiple sites, then you will likely want to have a folder dedicated to each.

- *Default Index Files*: Divert the site to open a different index file (the default page to look for in a directory if no page is indicated in a request).

- *Error Document*: Web page loaded in the event that an error occurs.

- *Administrator Email*: An email for the administrator to be used in the case of an error accessing the site or to reach the site administrator.

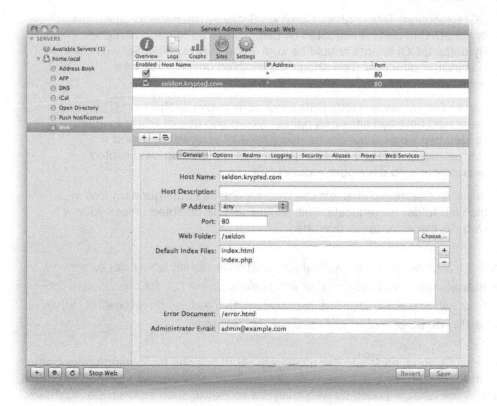

Figure 14–13. *General web site settings*

There are also a number of options for each site. On the General tab, you can configure where the site was stored, how the web service directed traffic to the sites, and the files that were called up in each scenario. By default, the features on the Options tab are all disabled for security purposes. However, to enable each one, simply select the box for the required option (Figure 14–14), click Save, and restart the service. The options include the following:

- *Folder Listing*: The web server will display a list of files in a folder if no default index file is found and if a file is not explicitly in the address that a browser is attempting to open. This should always be disabled unless you require that users be able to see a list of files rather than a collection of links.

- *WebDAV*: This enables a web-based disc for the site (more on WebDAV in the next section). This should be used only when using WebDAV for file sharing.

- *CGI Execution*: This enables Common Gateway Interface (CGI) scripts, or scripts that can be executed by being called up in pages on sites. By default, CGI scripts should be kept in the /Library/WebServer/CGI-Executable directory. This should be disabled unless your web developer requires CGI.

- *Server Side Includes (SSI)*: SSIs allow code (typically PHP or HTML) to be shared between sites and pages. A common use of SSI is to use a header.php file as a header for every page of your web site and a footer.php as a footer for each page. This should also be disabled unless your web developer requires SSI.

- *Allow All Overrides*: This lets the Web service use configuration files in the web folder for requests. This should also be disabled unless your web developer requires overrides.

> **NOTE:** It is important to keep in mind that you should not enable any options that are not otherwise required. It is not uncommon for web developers to use CGI, SSI, and overrides, but you do not want to enable them unless they're needed. The developer should be able to tell you whether they will be required for your site to function properly.

In addition to Options, each site has a different set of options for logging visitor traffic. Logs for the Web service are divided into two types of logs: access logs and error logs. *Access logs* are what are used by web analytics software, such as Urchin or AWStats, for showing the quantity of visitors you have. *Error logs* are more valuable for troubleshooting problems with sites and the Web service. In most environments, both should be enabled. If you enable error logs, you can set the level to higher or lower logging levels.

When you enable logs, according to how much traffic you get, the logs can become cumbersome. Both access logs and error logs should invariably be enabled. This allows you to view issues and traffic. In environments where you have analytics packages, you can likely rotate logs, which keeps the amount of space consumed by log files at a minimum. To set up rotating log files, select the "Archive every" box, as shown in Figure 14–15, and then indicate the number of days between log rotations.

You can also customize where log files are stored. This is often helpful when you are centralizing the location for log files or want to set up a share point to allow a centralized logging server to access the log files. You can also move logs to a separate drive if you do not want to archive logs or need faster logging for high-traffic sites.

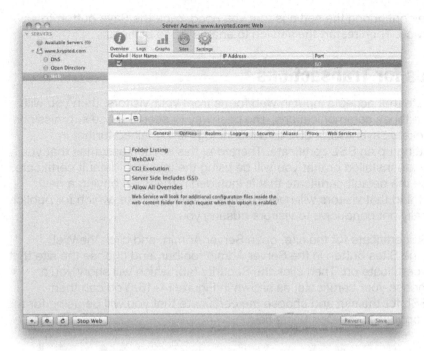

Figure 14–14. *Web site options*

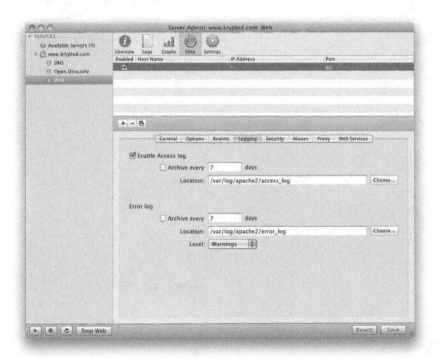

Figure 14–15. *Per-site logging*

When you are done configuring the settings that you need, click the Save button to save settings for the service. Then restart the service to enable those settings.

Securing Sites for Transactions

If you have a web site that accepts input in web forms from your visitors, then you will likely want to secure those communications. The best way to secure those submissions is using Secure Sockets Layer (SSL). SSL as a technology is explained further in Chapter 2, as is setting up an SSL certificate. Therefore, this section assumes that you have an SSL certificate installed or that you will be using the included default certificate. If you choose to use the default certificate that is included rather than buying a new certificate, keep in mind that visitors will need to accept the certificate, which for publicly facing sites is typically not conducive to visitors trusting you.

To configure an SSL certificate for the site, open Server Admin, and click the Web service. Then click the Sites button in the Server Admin toolbar, and choose the site that you will enable the certificate on. Then click the Security tab, which will show you a simple screen to choose your certificate, as shown in Figure 14–16. You can then choose to enable SSL for the site and choose the certificate that you will be using for the site from the list of options in the Certificate field.

NOTE: Certificates must be installed in Keychain Access prior to enabling the certificates for sites.

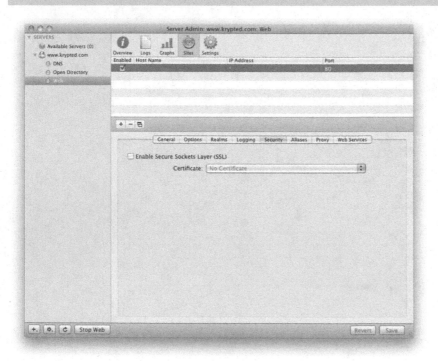

Figure 14–16. *Configuring certificates for web sites*

When all your settings are configured, click the Save button, and then restart the service. You will then be prompted to change the port number for the site. The port number will need to change from 80 to 443, because SSL-enabled web sites will require an HTTPS prefix to access the site rather than the HTTP prefix.

Password Protecting Sites

Each site can also have areas within the site that are accessible only to users who have been granted access. Access is controlled using a username and a password. This is made possible using *realms*. The .htaccess files that you may have created can still be used, but the realms option in Mac OS X Server also affords the ability to use users and groups from the local directory service or from Open Directory (more on Open Directory in Chapter 4) to access resources on the sites hosted on the server. Realms are managed using the Realms tab for each site. Each site can have multiple realms. These realms then become useful for administrators who want to share files, build test sites, or do any other task that requires authentication so that only a limited set of users are able to access the resources.

To configure realms, open Server Admin, click the Web service, and then click the site for which you want to set up controlled access. Then click the Realms tab for the site, as shown in Figure 14–17. Next, specify a directory using the plus sign in the realms field, indicating a path to the realm you want to create. Then, with the realm highlighted, use the plus sign for the Users & Groups field to specify a collection of users and/or groups to grant access and the permissions for the access.

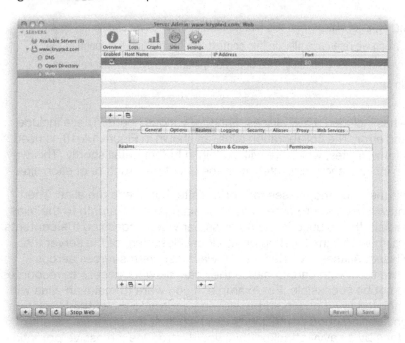

Figure 14–17. *Working with realms*

Once you have enabled realms, you can test access to the directory from a client by browsing to the directory that was created in the realm. Users will then see a dialog box similar to that when logging into a file server. The name of the realm becomes the path in the site that you use to access the resources protected by the realm. For example, if you create a realm called laws in a site called seldon.krypted.com, then you would access it using the path http://seldon.krypted.com/laws.

After users have authenticated, you can them at specified pages or have them access files through HTTP.

> **NOTE:** If you have also enabled WebDAV, then you can also now use your new realms to allow users to edit data in your realm.

Providing Access to Directories Outside the Site

The Web service will not allow access to resources that are outside the folder hierarchy defined for the site. Therefore, you have the option to create what is known as an *alias*. An alias gives access to resources in a directory that can then be shared by multiple sites. For example, if you have an image that you use in a few different sites, you would not want to have multiple copies of each image within the folder structure for each site. Therefore, you can create an alias to a folder within each site. This folder could then store the image, and each of the sites can access the image as needed.

> **NOTE:** There are other types of aliases, and this feature of Mac OS X Server should not be confused with them. When we reference alias in this context, we are limiting the scope of the term to aliases in Server Admin for web sites. This does not include file system-level aliases, symbolic links, and so on.

As an example, Apple has included a few aliases, each for various needs. These include *collaboration*, *icons*, and *error*. The collaboration alias, as shown in Figure 14–18, is used to access the themes for wiki sites, which we will explain in further detail shortly. This way, Apple does not have to include each template within the directory structure of each site.

To create your own aliases, click the Aliases tab for the site that needs the alias. Then click the plus sign. You will then be prompted to provide a name and a path to the alias. The pattern will be the path that is used in the address bar when accessing the contents of the folder, and the path will be the location on the local filesystem of the server that stores the contents aliased. Aliases provide an easy way to share resources across sites, but you should use them with care because they can allow for access to resources that potentially should not be accessible. For example, if you were to make an alias with a pattern of root that pointed to /, you would be allowing access to the entire filesystem of the server. Although keeping good permissions can help limit the potential extent of damage that can be done by a savvy attacker, this would introduce a massive potential for exploitation.

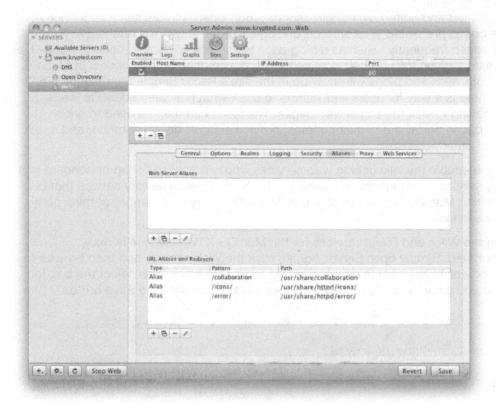

Figure 14–18. *Managing aliases*

Once you have configured the aliases you want to use to share resources between your sites, click the Save button, and test your configuration. Provided that the alias works as intended, you should be able to access directories that are not underneath the root directory for each site.

Now that you have configured the most commonly used settings for a web server, let's take a look at those that were introduced in Mac OS X Server by Apple for collaborative purposes.

Wikis and Blogs

The Mac OS X Server Web service has a number of services built in for collaboration. These include calendars, wikis, blogs, and mail integration. Although calendars and mail integration are described further in their respective chapters, wikis and blogs are specifically designed for user-generated content, and we will cover them in this chapter. But first it might help to explain what they are and what the difference between them is.

In the context of Mac OS X Server (and most other solutions as well), a *wiki* is a web site (or a collection of interlinked collaborative web sites) that can be edited by multiple users within the web site without opening a text or web editor. A *blog* is a web site that can be created and edited by a single user or group where visitors see a sequence of discrete posts, presented in reverse-chronological order. A wiki will often have pages that are edited frequently, whereas a blog page is not typically edited once the page has been created, given the chronological sequence the creation date provides. In Mac OS X Server, both wikis and blogs will show up in the site's Really Simple Syndication (RSS) feeds. A *feed* is a way for users and visitors to track what has been added to a site without having to visit the actual web pages. The feeds can then be used to show students pages pertaining to their courses, provide support documentation, and a number of other purposes.

Before you enable the wiki or blog web services, you will want to set up or connect to a directory service. Although this will often be the Apple Open Directory service that is included with Mac OS X, you can also use Active Directory or a number of third-party directory services.

Enabling the Wikis and Blogs services for the Mac OS X Web service is really straightforward. Simply open Server Admin, click the Web service, and then browse to the site for which you want to enable the wiki and/or the blog. Then select the box for each that you want to use (as shown in Figure 14–19), and click the Save button.

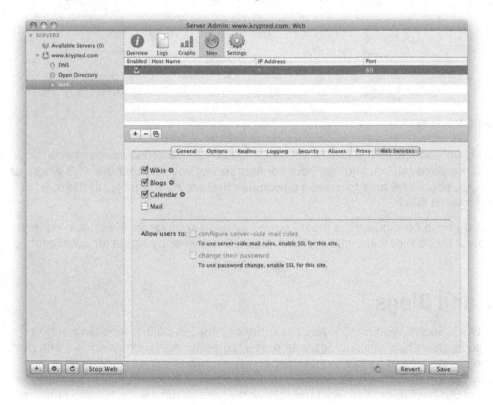

Figure 14–19. *Enabling wikis and blogs*

Once you have enabled the blog and/or the wiki, you will find the rest of the steps to use them a bit less obvious. Therefore, we'll cover each step in the remainder of this chapter, starting with wikis.

Using Wikis

As we mentioned, a wiki is a means for users to generate content. This can be an IT department setting up a site of how-tos, a shopping list, or a page dedicated to a lesson for a class. But a wiki is going to typically mean that more than one user can edit the content on the page. And each page is going to need to be linked together with other pages.

Once you have enabled the wiki, then it is time to configure the settings for the sites that will be hosted. Wiki settings are initially configured per server. To do so, open Server Admin, and click the Web service. Then click the Settings button in the Server Admin toolbar. From here, click the Wiki tab. As shown in Figure 14–20, you will have a number of settings that you can configure. These include the following:

- *Data Store:* Location to the wiki service's database (make sure you back this up).

- *Maximum Attachment Size:* The maximum size of files that can be added to wiki pages (keep in mind that although users will likely be able to download these attachments, QuickLook is able to preview the files, which is a very cool feature for most sites).

- *Default theme:* The default theme that is used for each wiki (there are a number to choose from, so we recommend checking out each one). As you create a wiki, you can use a different theme, so this is simply the default theme that will be used.

- *Wiki Creators:* Users and groups that can create new wiki pages.

- *SMTP Relay:* The mail server that will be used to announce new pages and updates to pages.

- *External Web Services:* To integrate with an iCal Server and a Mac OS X Server-based Mail server (which can be running on this server).

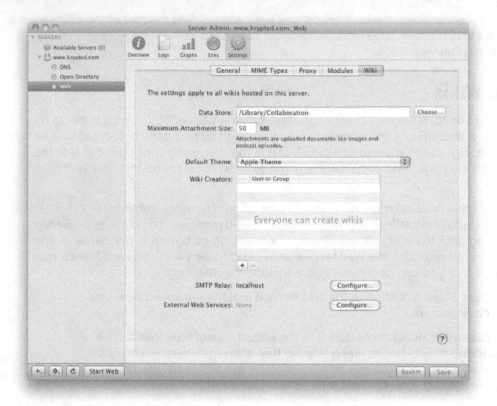

Figure 14–20. *Configuring the wiki*

When the settings match your desired settings, click the Save button, and then restart the service. Once you have configured the global settings for the wiki server and configured each site, then you can move on to setting up your first wiki. The setup and configuration of each wiki is done through the Web. To get started, open a web browser, and provide the name of the site that you will be using. In this example, the site will be home.local, but it could be any site that you have configured for your environment. The index.html file that is in each site by default is a splash page (Figure 14–21) that provides access to all the services you may be running. If you are using the site for another page, then you may want to rename the index.html file that is currently in the default web directory to something like services.html or, better yet, use a domain name that is dedicated to your collaboration services, such as blog.krypted.com or wiki.krypted.com. You can also build your own site using the three links on the web services page or whichever you consider most important.

Figure 14–21. *Accessing the web services page*

When you go to the site (be it from the server or a client), you will not initially be authenticated. Click the My Page icon, and you will be taken to a page where you can see information pertinent to your account. However, as you will note in Figure 14–22, if you haven't logged in, you won't yet see any pertinent information. Click the "Log in to" link to authenticate to the service. The administrator accounts will be able to authenticate and create the wikis and blogs, as will any accounts that were given the right to do so in Server Admin, so to follow along with our setup of a wiki, you will want to authenticate as one of those accounts.

Figure 14–22. *The wiki site before authenticating*

You will then have the ability to browse to updates, wikis, and blogs, and, if configured, calendar and mail. Updates will show you the aforementioned RSS feeds of information. The wikis and blogs pages will show you a splash page for managing and accessing content for each. But as shown in Figure 14–23, you will not be able to see any content until you begin to generate some.

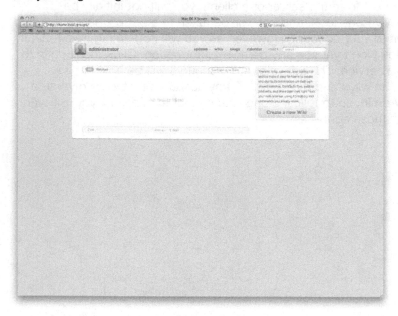

Figure 14–23. *The wiki site after authenticating*

To create a wiki, click Wikis; if there is preexisting content, it will be shown in the feeds, and if not, you will have a lonely but infinitely hopeful Create a new Wiki button. Click that button, and you can finally name your new wiki. As an example, we will show how to create a shopping list. So, let's enter groceries into the Name field, as shown in Figure 14–24. You can provide a description in the Description field as well if you so choose, but this is not required. Once you've entered information as needed, click the Next button.

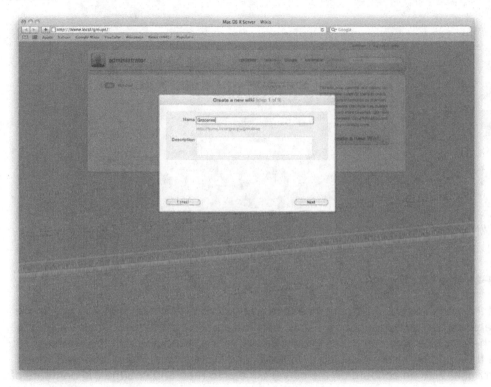

Figure 14–24. *Creating a new wiki site*

As we mentioned earlier, you can assign a different theme for each wiki you create. Here, you will see a list for each. Scroll through the available options, and pick one that best fits your purpose. For the groceries list example, choose Block Green Books, as shown in Figure 14–25. Once you have chosen a template that matches your use (or personality), click the Next button again.

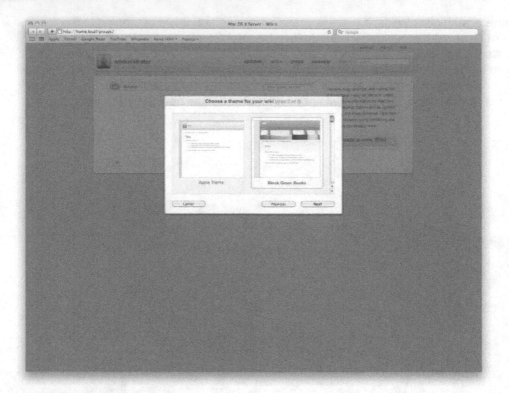

Figure 14–25. *Choosing a template*

You will then need to edit who can access and augment the content that you put on the site. There are two primary options: Public and Private. If you choose to make your wiki public, then anyone who can access your web server can read and edit the content. You can use the options "Users must log in to read" and "Users must log in to write," which allow any user with an account on the server access to read and change the contents of a page, respectively. If you choose Private, then you will enter users and groups that are allowed to access your content. Here, enter a name for a user or group from Open Directory (or a third-party directory service) into the "Type a user or group name here" field. If the name of the user or group is able to resolve, then you will be able to click that name to add them to the list of users and groups, as shown in Figure 14–26. Once added, you can then choose whether users should be able to read or also be able to write to the pages that comprise the wiki. Once all the users and groups have been added, then you can also use the Send Welcome Email to New Members check box to send email to users as they are added to the wiki, announcing the URL they can use to access content. When you are satisfied with your user and group configuration, click Create to generate the new wiki.

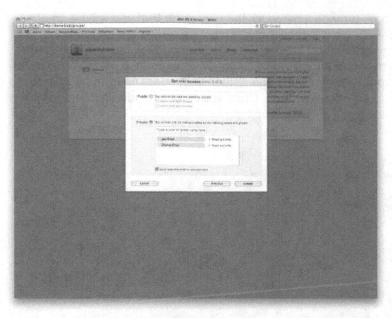

Figure 14–26. *Limiting access to wiki sites*

You will then be placed into the new wiki. Here, you will see a site full of promise and hope that quality content will be generated within it. This landing page for the wiki, as shown in Figure 14–27, can be edited using the icon of a pencil in the right side of the screen; however, since most will add links to pages they create, let's first look at creating a new page. To do so, click the plus (+) sign beside the icon for the pencil.

Figure 14–27. *Editing wiki sites*

In the New Page dialog box, provide a name for the new page that you will be creating. For example, in Figure 14–28, we will show how to create a new page for a grocery list for a specific trip to the grocery store: February 2008. Each page within the wiki can be accessed directly, circumventing the main wiki page, or you can take the address of the new page and link to it from the main wiki page. Either way, users need to be able to find content if it is going to be of use to them. Once you have provided a name for the page, click the Create button.

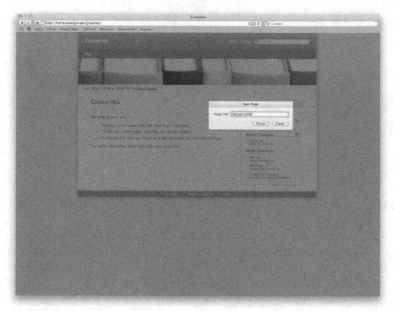

Figure 14–28. *Creating new wiki pages*

Next, you will be able to enter the content for the page. Here, you will see a toolbar, similar to those in a number of web sites and Office-like applications, that allows you to format the content that you enter. You will also be able to insert images, movies, documents, and other files into the page. Once you are done entering your content, think again about how users will access the content. As shown in Figure 14–29, there is a Tags field toward the top of the screen. Here, you can provide a number of descriptions for the page you are creating, each separated by a comma (,). These help users find your content by choosing tags appropriate to them on their landing page. You can also use the Add this to "What's Hot" check box to provide an easy way for users to see content they should make sure to see. As an example, you might choose to use the What's Hot tag to indicate pages that students will need to review before a test or to show new settings that your IT department is rolling out.

Once you have entered your content, proofread it. Then, provided it is satisfactory, click the Save button, and the first page of your wiki will be created.

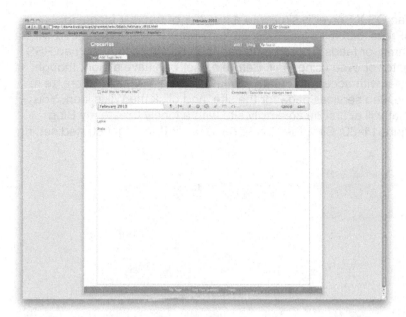

Figure 14–29. *Editing a wiki page*

As we mentioned, wikis are pages that are generated by users and are often for users. Because you end up with hundreds of pages, you will invariably find that the ability to leverage the tags in conjunction with the RSS feeds will allow you to guide users to appropriate content quickly and dynamically. Maintaining a list of each page, or of the important pages (that can then reference the less important pages) on the landing page of the wiki, is also a helpful mechanism for guiding users to appropriate information. You can also point users to the Recent Changes section in the box on the right side of the screen and even delete pages as time goes on.

Overall, wikis in Mac OS X can be powerful mechanisms to manage content. Although we have endeavored to show how to generate some content, it will ultimately be up to each administrator or set of users to guide how the content is generated, organized, and accessed. Although not technical, that pedagogical aspect of data is often the hardest hurdle to overcome with wikis as time goes on. But the trade-off is the infinite potential. Now that you've seen a wiki, we'll cover a similar feature of Mac OS X Server, the Blogs service.

Using Blogs

As we mentioned earlier, a blog is a stream of web pages created by a user, displayed in reverse-chronological order and accessible via tags. Each Open Directory user can have a blog, and each user's blog can have as many entries as they so choose (many bloggers tend to be verbose, while others will post content only occasionally). Blogs are often used so groups in an organization can provide content to other groups or so educators can have students comment on what they have learned.

The Blogs service in Mac OS X Server is similar to a number of popular blogging engines, such as WordPress, albeit it's less extensible by nature. Much like with a wiki, a blog will appear in streams, or feeds. These feeds can then be accessed using an RSS reader, such as Newsgator or even using Mail. Before a user can have a blog, though, an administrator (or a user with access to create a wiki or a blog) will need to create it. To do so, go back to the web services page for the site, and click the Wikis icon. You will then be taken to what will at first be an empty site with a lonely Create my Blog button, as shown in Figure 14–30. Click the Create my Blog button to get started setting up your first blog.

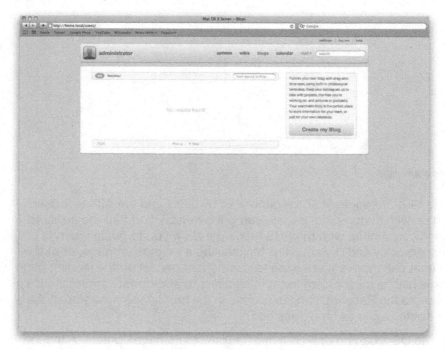

Figure 14–30. *Getting started with blogs*

You will then be prompted for a username in the Create Your Blog dialog box (Figure 14–31). Here, type a username from Open Directory (or another directory service that you're using (for example, Active Directory). It is typically best to give the user a short name (which can be obtained through Workgroup Manager if needed; learn more about Open Directory in Chapter 4). To create the blog, click the Create button.

> **NOTE:** If the user does not yet exist in Open Directory, then you will receive an error indicating that they cannot create an account.

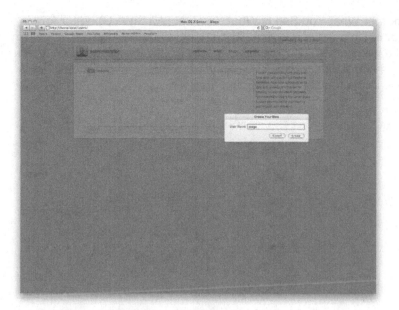

Figure 14–31. *Creating a blog*

Once the blog is created, then the administrator (or the user) can create new entries in much the same way that a wiki entry was created. Simply click the plus sign for the blog, and then you will be prompted by the New Entry dialog box to provide a name for the entry. Enter the title for the page you will be creating. In the example shown in Figure 14–32, we're creating an entry called Stardate 290110. When we click the Create button, the page will be created.

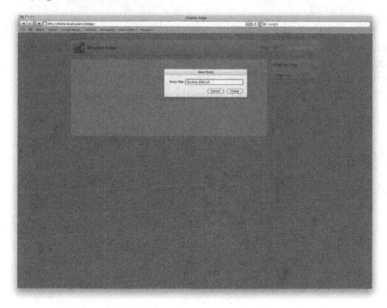

Figure 14–32. *Creating a blog entry*

Here, you will see yet another What You See Is What You Get (WYSIWYG) editor for typing in content, embedding images and videos, and attaching documents (as shown in Figure 14–33). As with the wiki entries, you will also be able to use the What's Hot check box and tags to help users find your content. You can then format the content just as you want it and click Save in the toolbar to finish the page.

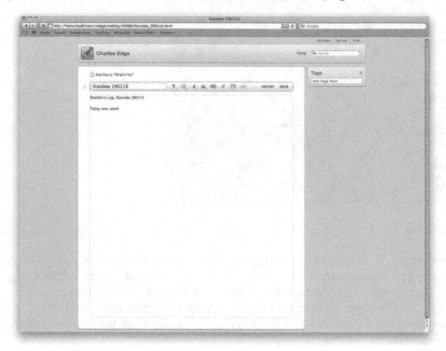

Figure 14–33. *Editing a blog entry*

Once you save the content, you will see a page showing you what other visitors will see when they visit your site, as shown in Figure 14–34. Along the sidebar, you will notice that you can tag content and comment on the pages. The comments are good ways to get feedback on your posts. Typically, any user can authenticate on content produced by any other user.

Figure 14–34. *Accessing the blog page*

As with a wiki, a blog will typically take on a life of its own, especially those that are used over a long period of time. System administrators often simply lay out the infrastructure for users to generate content and then watch how that content unfolds. One thing that we can do, though, to help our users and visitors is to show them how they can access the content that they need so they don't spend countless hours combing through thousands of entries.

Accessing Content

When you first start a wiki or a blog, it is pretty easy to find relevant content. However, as time goes on, you will likely find this to be more and more of a challenge. This becomes exponentially worse with each user you add. Apple realized what a chaotic mess that user-generated content could become when developing the web services in Mac OS X Server and so integrated a few features to make it easier to find data that is relevant to what your visitors need to find.

The first of these features is the updates page. As we mentioned previously in this chapter, the updates page becomes a one-stop location where you (or your users) can see when updates to each page that you have access to are made. As shown in Figure 14–35, the updates page shows each of the changes that we have made to both the blog and the wiki while writing this chapter. As more and more content is generated, you can limit the updates page to show you only updates made to wiki and blog pages that are tagged a certain way. This allows you to track updates based on subject or event.

Figure 14–35. *Your updates page*

You can also use Spotlight, the popular indexing service in Mac OS X. The pages that are generated in your sites are indexed by Spotlight, in much the same way that content on your computer is indexed by Spotlight. Once indexed, the content can then be searched for very quickly from any page on the site using the Search box. Simply click in the box, and type a string of characters. As you type, any matches that are found will be displayed in the QuickSearch box. For example, if you want to search for your groceries list, you could type **Groc**, and your matches would be displayed quickly, as shown in Figure 14–36.

NOTE: If your site is public facing and has been indexed by Google, then you can also use Google, although the results aren't typically as fast as with Spotlight.

Figure 14–36. *Spotlight for blogs and wikis*

Summary

As you likely noticed through this chapter, the web server in Mac OS X Server is a powerful tool for sharing content, accessing information stored in Mac OS X Server, and collaborating with other users within a team.

The web server can also be as complicated to manage as you need it to be (because some web sites have needs that are more complicated than others) because of the mature and extensible nature of Apache. If you have fairly straightforward needs, the web server can be quick and easy to set up, as can be done in Server Preferences. Or if your needs are more granular, then you can look to Server Admin. Beyond Server Admin, you can use the `serveradmin` command or even edit the configuration files for the service directly, as we've shown how to do in a number of other chapters. You can add new MIME types and modules, providing an almost infinite extensibility to your web server.

Although we do not want to discourage you from pushing the envelope, we have issued warning where certain aspects of managing the web server can get you into more trouble than most. This is because web servers, especially those with as much firepower as in Apple hardware, make for juicy targets to those looking to destabilize the security of a server for whatever purposes they have in doing so. You should allow only what is absolutely necessary in order to maintain a maximum level of security for your environment.

But do push the envelope. Leverage the Wikis and Blogs services as instructional, marketing, or communications tools where possible. Using the techniques that have been laid out in this chapter, you can get a site up and running with absolutely no web site design. You will more than likely want to further brand the pages that you see, but using a single Mac OS X Server, you can serve numerous sites, each providing different features and giving your organization the ability to take the next step forward, whether that step is getting your message out or enabling your people to be more effective through the smart use of collaborative tools.

Chapter 15

Managing MySQL

MySQL has more than 6 million installations worldwide, is one of the most mature relational database management systems in the world, and best of all is open source. Whether you are running a dedicated database server or a database server and a web server in one computer, Mac OS X Server makes it easy to set up both. The web server is covered further in Chapter 14, but the logical extension of the web server is the server (or service) that stores the back-end data that feeds that web server—or perhaps the back-end server that stores data accessible from a fat client used for a variety of purposes. Either way, MySQL can be a good, scalable, and clusterable fit for many organizations.

But managing MySQL isn't as seamless a transition as many of the other services we've discussed throughout this book. In fact, MySQL is probably one of the most complicated services to manage that is included with Mac OS X Server. Databases are meant to be highly specialized and optimized systems that vary widely between configurations based on their final intended configuration. Creating MySQL databases for a dynamic website system such as a WordPress blog is worlds apart from a database for a business account program. We will cover the steps it takes to get the MySQL service up and running, ready for configuration of a basic database. There are numerous other resources, everything from books to certified MySQL DBAs, that can provide more information specifically on optimizing the performance for your specific usage needs.

In this chapter, we'll start with some of the basics of what MySQL is. Then we'll cover how to set up MySQL and perform a number of basic tasks. As you'll notice quickly, the options included with graphical interfaces by default in Mac OS X are limited. Therefore, we'll look at working with the MySQL service both using the command line and using a third-party application that will ease the task of administration for even seasoned MySQL administrators.

What Is MySQL?

MySQL is a relational database management system. MySQL is a daemon, *mysqld*, that can listen for network traffic on port 3306. That daemon runs a database (or a number of databases in most cases) that stores data for other applications to utilize. That data is stored in tables.

Wikipedia provides a succinct definition of a *table*: "…a table is a set of data elements (values) that is organized using a model of vertical columns (which are identified by their name) and horizontal rows. A table has a specified number of columns but can have any number of rows. Each row is identified by the values appearing in a particular column subset that has been identified as a candidate key."

You can access your data via *queries*, which are statements that the MySQL clients use to store and retrieve information from the database. Instead of directly reading the file stored on the disk (such as an application opening a file over a network share), the *mysqld* process accepts queries from the clients and does the related computational work on the server side before sending the information back to the clients.

Setting Up MySQL

The first step to setting up MySQL is to show the service in Server Admin. To do so, first open Server Admin from /Applications/Server. After authenticating, click the name of the server where you will be installing the MySQL service to open the server's base settings. Here, click the Settings icon in the toolbar to open the services selection screen, where you can configure which services will run on the server (simply enabling them on this screen will not start them), as you can see in Figure 15–1.

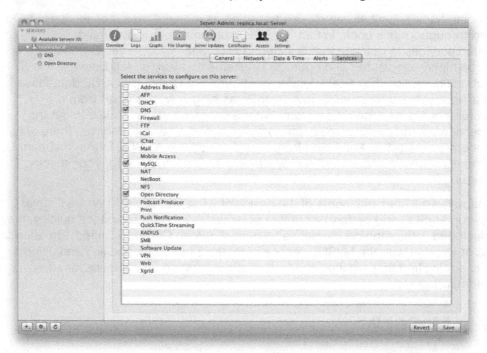

Figure 15–1. *Enabaling the MySQL service*

Select the MySQL box, and then click the Save button. You should then see the MySQL service appear in the SERVERS list when you click the disclosure triangle to show the active services on the server. Here, click the Settings icon in the Server Admin toolbar to open the settings that Apple has provided for MySQL. At this point, you can use the following options to configure the MySQL service, as shown in Figure 15–2:

- *Allow network connections*: Configure the server to allow connections from outside the computer that is running the service. Connections are established over TCP port 3306.

- *Database location*: Configure the filesystem path or use the Choose button to select a location for the MySQL databases to be stored.

- Set MySQL Root Password: MySQL does not use Open Directory or any other accounts natively used within Mac OS X Server. Instead, MySQL maintains its own repository of users and groups. You can use this button to set the root password for MySQL so that the server can effectively be administered.

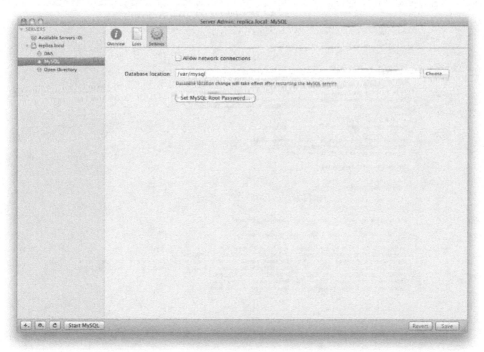

Figure 15–2. *Configuring MySQL*

Choose the settings that best match your environment, and then click the Save button. The service will then be configured to use the settings that were provided. If you chose to use the Set MySQL Root Password button, then you will be prompted with a dialog box for what that password should be. Otherwise, you can click Start MySQL in order to start the service, once you are satisfied with your settings.

NOTE: When setting the "root" password for MySQL, keep in mind that this is not the same account as the server's "root" account. Never use the same password for both accounts, because that would make a vulnerability in one system jeopardize the security of the other.

Once the service has been configured and started, you'll immediately want to look at the service logs. To do so, click the Logs icon in the Server Admin toolbar. In the Logs window, you can choose whether to view logs for the service or logs pertaining to the administration of the service. The service logs will indicate any errors encountered while trying to start the daemon, whereas administration logs are more granular and configure real-world use of the service itself. For an example of some common log entries found in the service log, see Figure 15–3.

Figure 15–3. *MySQL logs*

Tuning MySQL

MySQL is a command-line–heavy application. In this section, we'll cover how to tune it via the command line.

> **NOTE:** For some basic tasks, GUI administrative tools are available from MySQL, which you can find at http://dev.mysql.com/downloads/gui-tools/. Keep in mind that it is considered best to use one GUI tool to manage a service, so if you do use the MySQL tools, you may have inconsistent results trying to also manage the service in Server Admin.

The /etc/my.cnf file is the configuration file that is used for MySQL. In this file a number of settings are configured and impact how the MySQL daemon interacts with databases. This includes settings for items that are also included in Server Admin, such as whether the daemon listens on a TCP port, but it also covers a lot more information, such as how data is cached, flushed, and buffered, all of which have a massive impact on the performance of databases. A good, quick read is the manual page for /etc/my.cnf. But for true mastery and performance tuning, consider purchasing one of the following books from Apress to assist in your quest for MySQL guru-ness:

- *Pro MySQL* by Michael Kruckenberg
- *The Definitive Guide to MySQL* by Michael Kofler
- *Beginning MySQL: From Novice to Professional* by W. Jason Gilmore

One difference between the MySQL as covered in these books and the MySQL Apple gives you in Mac OS X Server is the serveradmin command. Using serveradmin, you can perform a number of basic tasks, which should always be performed within serveradmin rather than doing so in the my.cnf file. To see the status of the service, use the status option with serveradmin, followed by the word mysql. Here's an example:

```
serveradmin status mysql
```

This will result in output similar to the following, which will basically just indicate whether the service is started or stopped.

```
mysql:state = "STOPPED"
```

The fullstatus option will show a lot more information and is used in much the same fashion:

```
serveradmin fullstatus mysql
```

As you can see next, this shows the information included with status and also shows a number of other settings. Unlike settings for other services, many of the service settings can be changed from the command line and respected by the service and Server Admin GUI(as we will describe later in this chapter).

```
mysql:state = "STOPPED"
mysql:networkConnectAllowed = no
mysql:readWriteSettingsVersion = 1
mysql:servicePortsAreRestricted = "NO"
mysql:databaseLocation = "/var/mysql"
mysql:pluginVers = "10.6.22"
mysql:defaultFilesInstalled = no
mysql:logPaths:mysqlAdminLog = "/Library/Logs/MySQL.log"
mysql:logPaths:mysqlServiceLog = "/var/mysql/mysql_service.log"
```

```
mysql:setStateVersion = 1
mysql:startTime = ""
```

You can also use the settings option, which will show only the available settings that can be configured using serveradmin for a given service. For example:

```
serveradmin settings mysql
```

When run, the settings option will output the following information, which allows you to do a few basic tasks, including allowing network connections to the MySQL databases, setting a location for the databases, and configuring a root password. The output of the settings option is as follows:

```
mysql:allowNetwork = no
mysql:databaseLocation = "/var/mysql"
mysql:rootPassword = ""
mysql:mysqlrunning = no
mysql:installDefaultFiles = no
```

To make a change to one of these settings, include the serveradmin command followed by settings and then the information from the output of the settings option. For example, to change the location of the database to a folder called mysql on an internal drive (maybe one that is solid-state storage) called SSD, you would use the following command (assuming you have already stopped the service and relocated the database files):

```
serveradmin settings mysql:databaseLocation = "/Volumes/SSD/mysql"
```

Managing MySQL Databases

MySQL database management includes a number of complicated tasks. But the basic items that need to occur in most environments are connecting to a database, creating tables, creating fields within tables, running queries, and repairing databases when they have problems. Those tasks will be focus of the next few sections of this chapter. After covering MySQL-specific management of the databases, we'll cover related administrative tasks, such as ensuring the databases are being backed up properly.

You can use a number of tools to connect to databases. These range from web portals that allow on-the-fly modification to full clients developed for Mac OS X. Some of the more popular include the following:

- *phpMyAdmin*: http://www.phpmyadmin.net
- *MySQL GUI Tools*: http://dev.mysql.com/downloads/gui-tools/5.0.html
- *Navicat*: http://www.navicat.com/

Although all of these are great solutions, we're going to use Sequel Pro, which you can obtain at http://www.sequelpro.com/download.html. The reason is that in an incredibly "scientific" poll that we conducted on Twitter and Facebook, it seemed to be the choice of seven out of ten (yes, a total of ten respondents if you don't count the one guy who yelled "Play Freebird" from the back).

Connecting to a Database Server

Once you have downloaded Sequel Pro, drag it to your /Applications directory (on the server itself or onto your workstation if you have not blocked remote MySQL access on your firewall), and double-click it. If network access is allowed, then you can use the Standard tab to connect to the server. As you can see in Figure 15–4, you can then configure Sequel Pro to connect to your server over a standard network connection provided that either the MySQL service accepts network connections or the application is running directly on the server.

When connecting to the server, you will need the following settings:

- *Name*: A friendly name associated with the server so it is easily remembered.

- *Host*: The name or IP address of the server you are connecting to.

- *Username*: The user's short name that you will be connecting to the server as (if you don't otherwise know the name, just try *root* initially).

- *Password*: The password for the previously used username.

- *Database*: The name of the database (if any) that you will be connecting to for administration.

- *Port*: The TCP port number, which has a default of 3306, which can be customized in the my.cnf file using the port directive (usually configured between lines 15 to 19 in the my.cnf file). Only change this setting if you have customized the TCP port that MySQL runs on for your server environment.

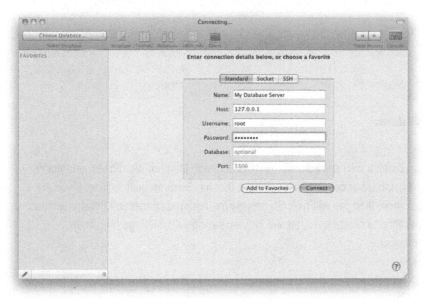

Figure 15–4. *Connecting to Mac OS X Server with Sequel Pro*

Once you have provided all the necessary information, click the Connect button to log in for the first time.

Setting Up a Database

Why have a database server if you don't have a database running on it? Once you have configured the service appropriately and configured your copy of Sequel Pro to connect to the server, now it's time to prepare the data environment for use.

Once you have logged in, one of the most typical first steps is to create a database. To do so, from the main Sequel Pro screen, which you can see in Figure 15–5, click the Select Database menu.

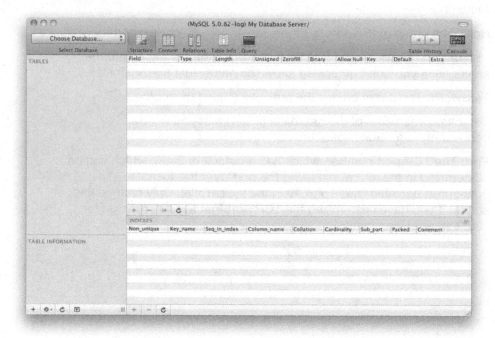

Figure 15–5. *Creating a database*

NOTE: A number of prebuilt web applications, such as Joomla!, Mambo, WordPress, and many others, will create a database or come with a database that has been prebuilt for use. If you are using such an application, then you will typically provide the required connection information and then allow the application to create the database for you, saving valuable time (and likely frustration) in the process.

The resultant menu will afford you the choices to perform one of the following (as you can see in Figure 15–6):

- *Choose Database*: Pick a database.

- *Add Database*: Create a new database.

- *Refresh Databases*: Refresh the list of databases.

- *Information_schema*: Make changes to how the database handles information on the records themselves (why type and structure). This is not something you want to modify unless you already know what you are doing.

- *Mysql*: Make changes to the MySQL configuration.

- *Test*: Work on a test database that has been preconfigured.

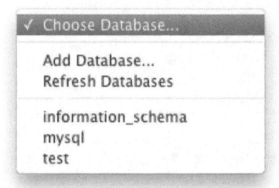

Figure 15–6. *Database options*

Click Add Database in the menu, which opens a screen to name the database, and choose an encoding type for the newly created database. In the example shown in Figure 15–7, we're called the database *krypted* and providing it with an encoding type of Default, which will work in a number of environments.

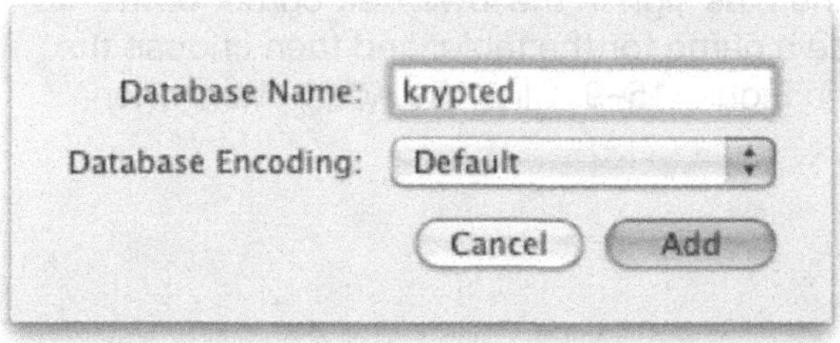

Figure 15–7. *Naming and encoding a new database*

NOTE: Check with your database architect or application vendor for which type of encoding to use on newly created databases. This option can have a long-term impact on the performance and scalability of your database solution.

Click the Add button, and the database will be created (usually this takes all of three seconds to do). Once created, the Select Database option should show the name of the newly generated database, as you can see in Figure 15–8.

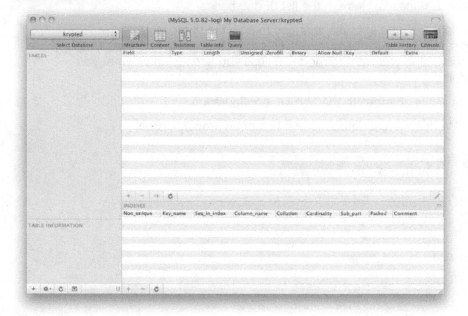

Figure 15–8. *Virgin databases*

Creating a Table

Now that you have a new database, you need at least one table. The table will be used to store the fields. Think of a table as similar to a worksheet in a Microsoft Excel document (this is far too basic an explanation but appropriate for our purposes right now).

To get started with your new table, click the plus sign in the lower-left corner of the screen. In the resultant dialog box, provide a name for the table, and then choose the table encoding and table type, as shown in Figure 15–9. Click the Add button when you're done.

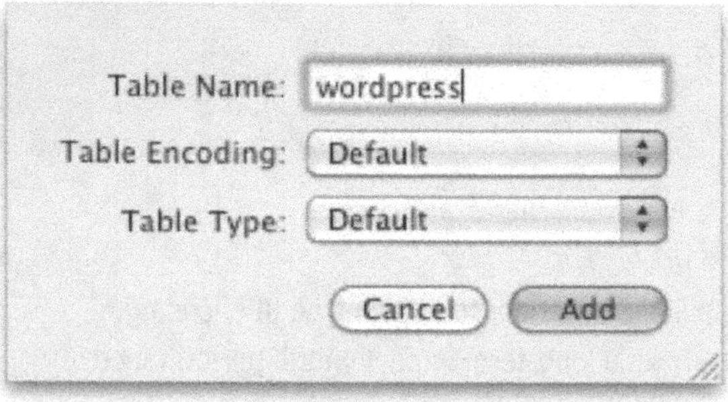

Figure 15–9. *Creating a table*

The three main choices that you will typically use for the type of a new table include the following (Figure 15–10):

- *MyISAM*: Provides fast nontransactional tables. This is the default table type.

- *MEMORY*: Provides built-in memory functions.

- *InnoDB*: Allows for transactional data.

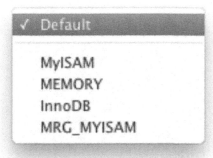

Figure 15–10. *Table types*

NOTE: When you are choosing a table type, consult with your database architects and/or application vendors.

Working with Fields

A *field* is where actual data is stored. Field can be anything from a date to a phone number to a placeholder. Fields can be configured in a variety of manners. Oftentimes the business logic behind the database will determine the types of data stored in a given field more than anything else. Continuing with the previous Microsoft Excel analogy, a field is akin to a column in a spreadsheet.

Creating a field is a pretty easy task, according to what type of data the field will hold. Simply use the plus sign in the middle bar of the SequalPro screen while you have the table highlighted, as shown in Figure 15–11.

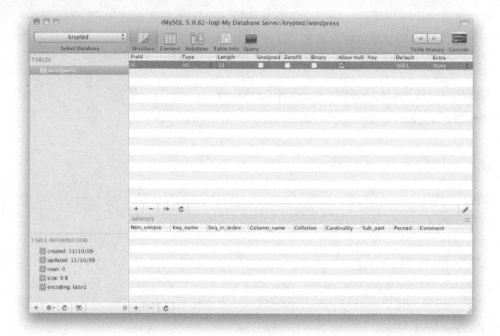

Figure 15-11. *Creating fields*

The new line will allow you to name the field and then select what type of data the field will allow to be inserted into it. Each field type will come with its own restrictions, both in terms of the types of characters that it can hold and in terms of the amount of characters that it can hold. You can also limit the length of a field further using the length column and configure a few other features including the following:

- Unsigned
- Zerofill (an option that pads the empty space with 0 for a numeric value, so a field with a length of 3 and the value 4 would be recorded as 004, for example)
- Binary
- Allow Null
- Key
- Default
- Extra (additional parameters that affect the behavior of this field can be stored here, such as auto-incrementing, and so on)

Writing a Query

Once you have created fields, you will want to populate them with some information. This could be something as simple as filling in some names in a database or something as complicated as hooking the database up to an application and testing connectivity and data entry.

Once you have data entered into the database, you can then query the database for that data or perform searches. Queries are in Structured Query Language (SQL), a standard among competitors to MySQL such as Transact-SQL, PostgreSQL, and Microsoft SQL. There are entire books dedicated to writing queries that accomplish as much as possible in as few characters (or cycles) as possible.

When you are considering what you would like to look up, a common strategy is to use the Console application for assistance. If you perform a search using the graphical tools in Sequel Pro, you can then use the output that is logged into the Console application (accessible by clicking the Console button in the upper-right corner of the screen) to run those same queries in a programmatic fashion or to make them more customized, constraining, or compounding searches. You can see some sample output of the Console tool in Sequel Pro in Figure 15–12.

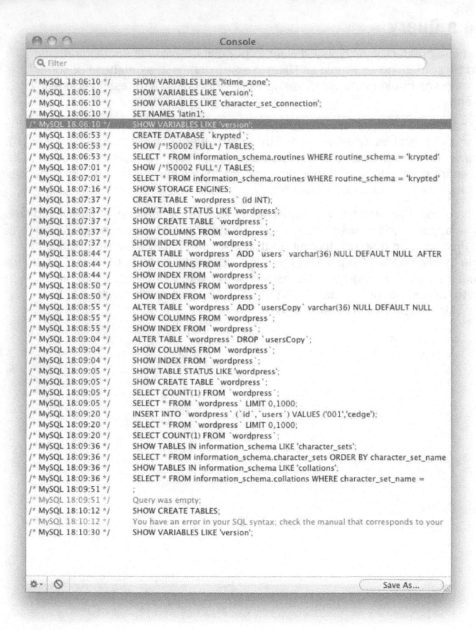

Figure 15–12. *The Console tool*

Once you have a query written and ready to use, you can use the Query button in the application toolbar to run the query. Simply click the appropriate table, click the Query button, and then paste the query in. When you're satisfied with the query, click Run all, and then you'll see the output in the bottom pane of the screen, as shown in Figure 15–13.

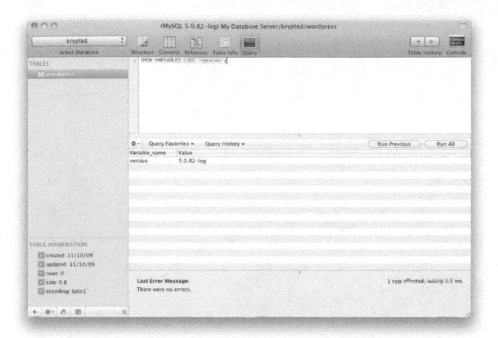

Figure 15-13. *Running a query*

Inspecting Existing Elements

Another aspect of Sequel Pro that we'll cover is the ability to look at what an existing table or other element is comprised of. This comes in handy when you have a tool that performs an automated installation of tables and fields into a MySQL database (or databases in many cases) and you later want to inspect what was created. Although there are limited abilities to change this data, doing so is often dangerous. But if you want to query for information and view data in other tools, then it can be helpful to understand what you are dealing with.

To view the information on a table, click the table in question, and then click the Table Info button in the application toolbar. From here, you will see all the necessary statistics including the number of rows (again, synonymous with an Excel spreadsheet), the length of rows, the amount of data consumed by the table, how the table is encoded, and any developer comments, as shown in Figure 15–14.

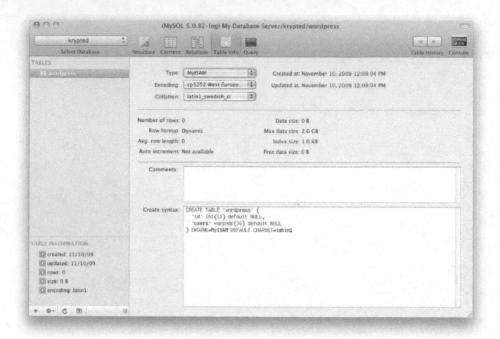

Figure 15–14. *Viewing a table*

Database Maintenance

The final aspect of Sequel Pro that we'll cover is how to do basic MySQL database management. Most of the other aspects of Sequel Pro are similar to features in other applications. However, the ease that Sequel Pro allows you to perform basic database administration (and maintenance more than anything) is the primary reason we decided to include it in this chapter.

To see the basic options available, click a table, and then click the Table menu. This will show you the following options, which you can see in Figure 15–15. You can find out what these options do from these locations:

- Copy Create Table Syntax:
  `http://dev.mysql.com/doc/refman/5.0/en/alter-table.html`

- Show Create Table Syntax:
  `http://dev.mysql.com/doc/refman/5.0/en/show-create-table.html`

- Check Table: `http://dev.mysql.com/doc/refman/5.1/en/check-table.html`

- Repair Table: `http://dev.mysql.com/doc/refman/5.1/en/repair-table.html`

- Analyze Table: `http://dev.mysql.com/doc/refman/5.0/en/analyze-table.html`

- Optimize Table: http://dev.mysql.com/doc/refman/5.1/en/optimize-table.html

- Flush Table: http://dev.mysql.com/doc/refman/5.0/en/flush.html

- Checksum Table: Creates a hash of the table to be able to later tell whether the table was altered (great for when you are doing backups)

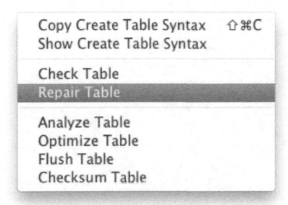

Figure 15–15. *Repairing tables*

These options give you the ability to quickly and easily do basic database management without having to learn how to use complicated command-line utilities to do so. But if you would like to learn those utilities, which is recommended, then read the "More on the Command Line" section later in this chapter.

Backing Up MySQL

Backing up MySQL is a bit different from backing up most other services. For starters, you need to back up the database files from within the daemon or you risk corrupting the database while backing it up and potentially having a garbage file that will not restore as your backup. In other words, you cannot simply copy the contents of the active database folder to another drive and be sure that you have a valid backup of your database.

One way to go about backing up your database is to continue using Sequel Pro, as we showed earlier. Here, you can click the name of a database and then use the File menu to select Export. From Export, click mysqldump, and then select the tables that should be backed up within the database and whether the template (or create) tables will be created, as shown in Figure 15–16.

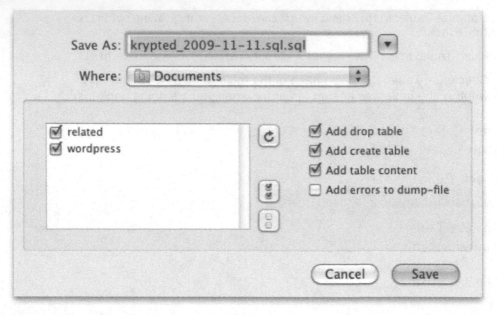

Figure 15–16. *Backing up MySQL*

As great as it is to be able to run a backup manually, you should automate it. No wait, don't argue with us on this point because you will lose! To back up, change directories into the /usr/local/mysql/bin folder. From here, you will find a command called mysqldump. In a basic form, you can use the mysqldump command to run a backup of the server to a file in the /backups directory called backup.sql:

```
./mysqldump --add-drop-table databasefilename > /backups/backup.sql
```

Once you have run a backup using mysqldump, you can then copy the backup elsewhere or back it up as a flat file using your standard backup software. This means that a script that can run prior to your backups could be as short as a file called mysqlbackup.sh, scheduled to run using cron or launchd. As long as you make sure that the destination folder (/backups in this example) is being backed up by your server backup system, the following script would provide the basic functionality you need:

```
#!/bin/bash
/usr/local/mysql/bin/mysqldump --add-drop-table databasefilename > /backups/backup.sql
```

More on the Command Line

You can also use the mysqladmin command to manage MySQL. Many of the features described previously in the "Database Maintenance" section of this chapter and features from other chapters are included with the mysqladmin command, although there is a bit more of a learning curve to become acquainted with its use.

mysqladmin comes with a number of commands. These include create, flush (there are actually multiple types of flush commands), kill, drop, debug, ping, process list, refresh, options for dealing with multiple servers (that is, a cluster), `status`, `shutdown`, `refresh`, `reload`, `processList`, `variables`, and others. If you would like to use the `mysqladmin`, then it is recommended that you fully read the entire manual page using the following command (run it from a Mac OS X Server computer):

```
man mysqladmin
```

Here are some common tasks you may be performing from the command line:

If the database server were called `db.krypted.com` and you were to set a password of *mysecretpassword*, then you could use the following command:

```
mysqladmin -u root -h db.krypted.com password "mysecretpassword"
```

To quit the database server, use this:

```
mysqladmin -u root -p shutdown
```

Summary

We have now gone through the steps needed to get the MySQL process up and running under Mac OS X Server. MySQL is a large and dynamic product, and we barely scratched the surface in this chapter; however, we have gotten you on your way toward setting up and running the needed business and web applications quickly on it. Most importantly, you will want to make sure that your databases are being backed up properly and reliably. In other words, make sure you are backing up your database before you close this book; entire websites have shut down because they assumed their MySQL database was being backed up, only to discover that one day all their content was gone and unrecoverable.

Chapter 16

Using Podcast Producer

Podcast Producer gives users the tools to create and publish professional-quality podcasts with simplicity and ease. This is accomplished by leveraging half a dozen built-in services and technologies within Mac OS X Server and making them all interact and work together to produce the kind of polished results that once required hours of manual effort and a myriad of high-end and expensive tools.

Podcast Producer builds on many of the services that we have described in other chapters, including DNS, Web/Wiki, Mail, and most notably Open Directory. Podcast Producer can also interact with other Mac OS X 10.6 services such as iChat, Xgrid, and Push Notification to encode, announce, and deliver podcasts to their intended recipients and the world. Because Podcast Producer has such a heavy dependency on these other services, it can make them all appear to be more advanced and complex than they otherwise might seem to be individually. However, as you will see in this chapter, it is actually quite simple and easy to set up a functioning Podcast Producer with relative ease once you understand how all of the components fit together.

Podcast Producer performs a variety of roles. The Podcast Producer service captures a stream of rich multimedia content, such as audio, video, or a montage of graphics and interwoven video streams. The Podcast Producer then publishes the media into an RSS feed or other repository depending on the customizable automation, or *workflow*, that you choose to use. Once the workflow has been run, you can then view the media using the built-in wiki, using iTunes, or even employing iTunes U for educational institutions that have iTunes U accounts. Because the streams are posted as standard RSS feeds, you can also then interface between popular blog engines such as WordPress or course management systems such as Moodle.

Because of how much Podcast Producer does behind the scenes, a number of tools are used to manage the service. The Podcast Producer service itself is managed and configured as a service within Server Admin. The Podcast Capture utility is used to run workflows using multimedia files, a camera connected to a computer, or the built-in camera. You can also use Podcast Capture to bind a camera to a server, thereby allowing workflows to be built in such a way that they do not require someone at the computer operating a camera manually. All of the podcast workflows are created within yet another utility called Podcast Composer. All of the workflows, cameras, Xgrid agents, and settings are then managed by Server Admin, where you can define who has access to the workflows and even cameras.

In this chapter, we will first cover what to do before you install Podcast Producer. Then we'll cover how to set up the Podcast Producer services. Once the services have been configured, we'll show how to create a basic workflow and how to control access to workflows. Then we'll cover how to set up cameras and run workflows. Finally, we'll give you a cursory overview of how to use the Podcast Producer command-line tools so that you can build powerful automations that might be useful even if you won't otherwise be using Podcast Producer!

Preparing for Podcast Producer

Despite the simplicity of the interface that your users will see when creating their podcasts, Podcast Producer is one of the most complicated processes in Mac OS X Server. This is largely because of the interdependencies that it requires of the different services running on Mac OS X Server. But don't fear—Apple understands the complexity and has provided an easy-to-use wizard that can do much of the more complicated heavy lifting for you. However, if you are going to be integrating certain other services with Podcast Producer, then it helps to have at least a cursory setup of them first. Depending on what kind of workflows you want to have, there are a number of different services that can interact with Podcast Producer. Over the course of the next few sections, we will look at each; Table 16–1 provides a summary.

Table 16–1. *Podcast Producer Dependencies*

Service Name	Required	Purpose
Mail	Optional	Provides mail services if messaging is needed as part of a workflow
Directory Services	Required	Provides authentication to the data as well as between components of Podcast Producer (Especially Xgrid)
Web	Optional	Shows the contents of a capture to end users in a wiki or blog

Preparing Directory Services

Podcast Producer needs a directory service. And Podcast Producer works best with Open Directory. In Chapter 3 we covered Open Directory and so won't bore you with the details yet again. But if you have a Microsoft-based Active Directory environment, then you can use this as well, although it's a bit more of an advanced topic. For the purposes of this chapter, we will be using the Open Directory setup that was configured in the earlier chapters.

Preparing Mail Services

To have Podcast Producer automatically send e-mail notifications, which is a common workflow element, you will need to first set up mail services on your Mac OS X Server. You can leverage an existing mail server, but if you do, then when you are building workflows, if an e-mail fails, it will also cause the workflow to fail. To set up basic mail services, see Chapter 12.

Preparing Web Services

To publish data from Podcast Producer to a web page, you'll want to enable the wiki and blog services in Mac OS X Server. To do so, follow these steps:

1. Open Server Admin.

2. From the Server Admin sidebar, click the disclosure triangle to see the services running on the Podcast Producer server.

3. Click the web service. You will then see the Sites icon in the Server Admin toolbar, unique to the web service.

4. Next, click Web Services.

5. Click the Default Wiki and Blog Theme option. You can also select the theme that most closely suits your environment.

6. Click the site you are configuring (if there is only one site, then just click it), and then click the Web Services tab provided for the site.

7. Select the Wiki and Blog box.

8. When you are finished, click the Save button to commit your changes.

9. Click the Start Web icon in the lower-left corner of the Server Admin screen.

Preparing Video Assets

Because we are working with video, you can also have a few creative assets available that will come in handy later in this chapter when you begin to develop your workflows. Podcast Producer is going to give you some options for augmenting video. This is going to include the ability to place a video clip in front of, and another behind, each of the videos that get uploaded to the server. You will also be able to watermark video using a graphics file. Video files should be in H.264, and graphics files are best in the PNG format.

> **NOTE:** Video clips should be an appropriate length compared to the average size of your movies. If they are too long, then users will not want to watch them.

Wizardly Podcasting

Once upon a time, Podcast Producer was a complicated beast. It was a dark art that many a solid engineer met their demise while trying to configure. Then Podcast Producer 2 came along. These days, you can quickly and easily set up Podcast Producer using the handy little wizard, which makes the process much easier—although it is still not simple. To get started, open Server Admin from /Applications/Server, and then click the name of the server you will be configuring Podcast Producer to run on. Then click the Settings icon in the Server Admin toolbar. Select the Podcast Producer box in the list of services, as shown in Figure 16–1.

Figure 16–1. *Adding the Podcast Producer service*

Once the service has been added, click the Podcast Producer entry underneath the server name in Server Admin. Next, click the Overview button. Here, you will see a number of statistics on the server. Most will show as Not Available until the service has been configured and started, as you can see in Figure 16–2.

Click the Configure Podcast Producer button to open the Podcast Producer Setup Assistant.

CAUTION: If your Podcast Producer has already been set up or configured, do not click this button or you risk wiping out the existing configuration and any customizations that were done to it!

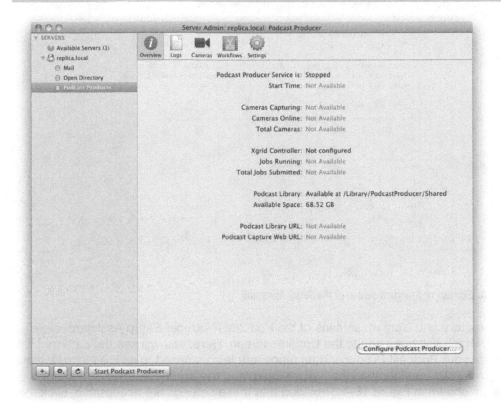

Figure 16–2. *Launching the Setup Wizard*

The first screen of the Podcast Producer Setup Assistant is an introduction. Simply click the Continue button to open the Express or Standard screen. Clicking Express will automatically configure the accounts that will be required in your directory service, the shared space that the Podcast Producer data repository will reside in (including the NFS share that can be used if you will have multiple Xgrid agents), and the Xgrid controller service. Clicking Standard will give you the option to use preconfigured accounts for intraprocess (Xgrid and Podcast Producer) communications, configuring a custom path for the library and customizing the Xgrid setup. For the purpose of this walk-through, simply click Continue with the "Express setup" option selected, as shown in Figure 16–3.

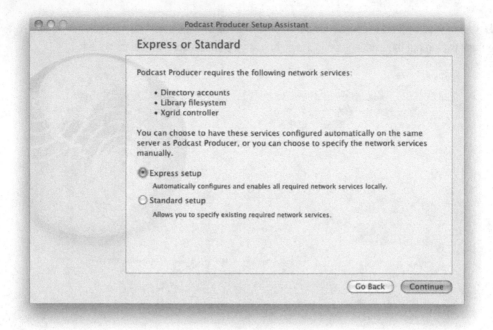

Figure 16–3. *Express or Standard screen of the Setup Assistant*

On the Directory and Confirm screens of the Podcast Producer Setup Assistant, click Continue, which will bring you to the Confirm screen. Here, you will see the path that will be used for your Podcast Producer data repository (also referred to as the *Library*), the directory services configuration that will be used, and the Xgrid controller and agent settings, as shown in Figure 16–4. Provided that these settings are acceptable, click the Continue button.

The Setup Assistant will then begin configuring the services. After a short time, a dialog box will appear asking you to provide the username and password for an administrative account to your directory service (in the case of Figure 16–5, Open Directory). The reason the account needs to be administrative is that it will be creating other accounts for intraprocess communication. Provide a directory administrator username and password, and then click Continue.

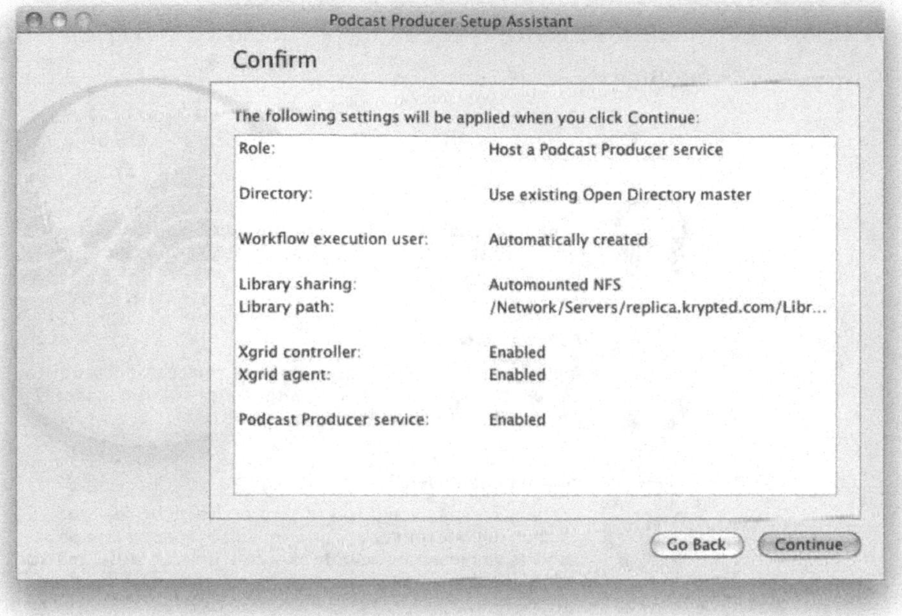

Figure 16–4. *Confirm screen of the Setup Assistant*

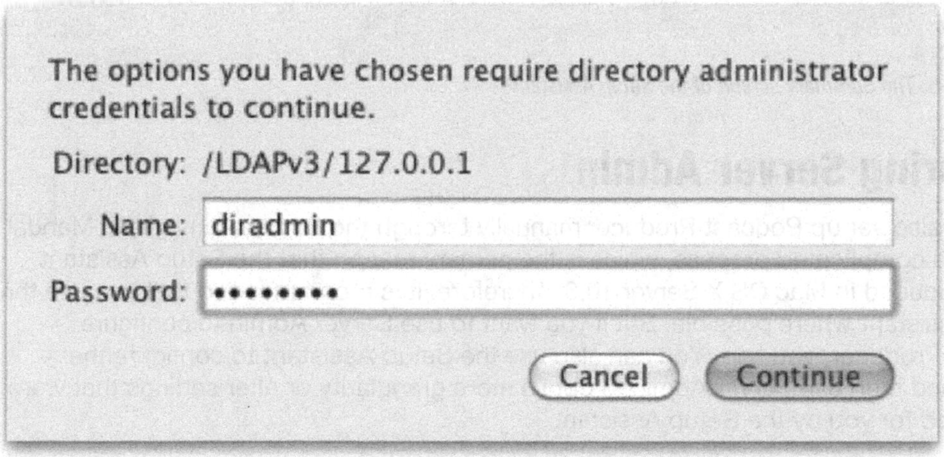

Figure 16–5. *Providing directory services credentials*

Once the service has been configured, you will see a Summary screen (as shown in Figure 16–6) where you can browse to any of the other services that will be explained later in this chapter. Here, click Done, and you will be finished with the base installation of Podcast Producer.

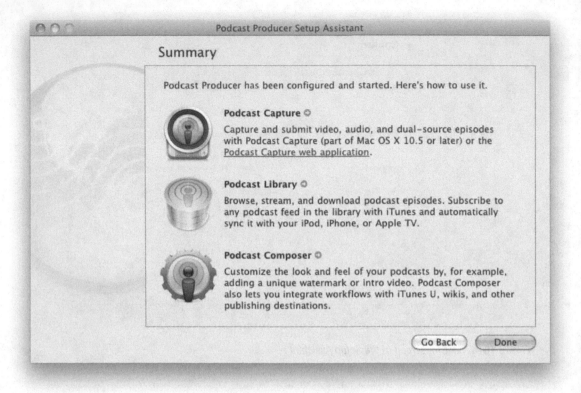

Figure 16–6. *The Summary screen of the Setup Assistant*

Exploring Server Admin

You can also set up Podcast Producer manually through the Server Admin tool. Manual setup is a complicated process, which is the primary reason that the Setup Assistant was introduced in Mac OS X Server 10.6. Therefore, it is recommended that you use the Setup Assistant where possible. But if you want to use Server Admin to configure Podcast Producer, you can. You can also use the Setup Assistant to configure the service and then use Server Admin to obtain more granularity or alter settings that were configured for you by the Setup Assistant.

To see settings for the Podcast Producer service, open Server Admin from /Applications/Server. Then click the Podcast Producer service listed under the server that it is running on. From here, click the Overview button in the Server Admin toolbar. Here you will see statistics on the service, as shown in Figure 16–7. These include the cameras currently available and/or in use, the Xgrid controller, the running jobs, the total jobs ever submitted, the location of the library, the space available on the server, the URL to access the Library, and the URL to access the Podcast Producer web portal, which we will cover later in this chapter.

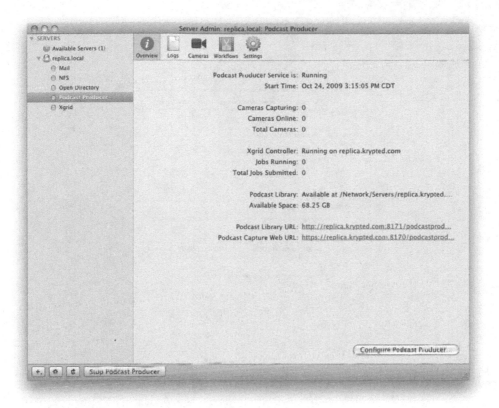

Figure 16–7. *The new Overview screen*

Although the statistics are nice, they don't allow you to change much. To see more granular settings and perhaps change them, click the Settings icon in the Server Admin toolbar. You will then be on the General tab of the Settings screen, as shown in Figure 16–8. Here, you can type in a location for the video that is captured by Podcast Producer (or browse using the Choose button), select an SSL certificate to use (the default certificate will be assigned by the Setup Assistant, but you can always select a different certificate if you have one), enable or disable the web application (which provides access for Windows clients and Mac OS X computers that don't otherwise have the appropriate tools available to them), assign a different Xgrid controller (by default the service will use the same computer that the service is running on, but you can use another controller if your organization has one), and assign the account information to communicate with the controller.

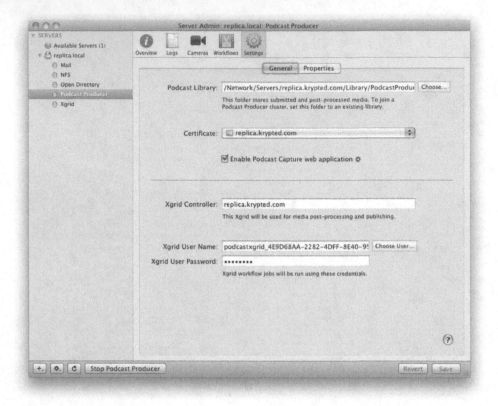

Figure 16–8. *General settings for Podcast Producer*

Next click the Properties tab shown in Figure 16–9. Here, you can change some of the more granular settings that Podcast Producer will use when generating podcasts, as shown in Figure 16–9. These include the short name of an administrative account for the service, the copyright information to be associated with each podcast (if you will be inserting copyright information), folder locations, script locations, language preferences, and the name of the organization to be used in podcasts where the name is applied.

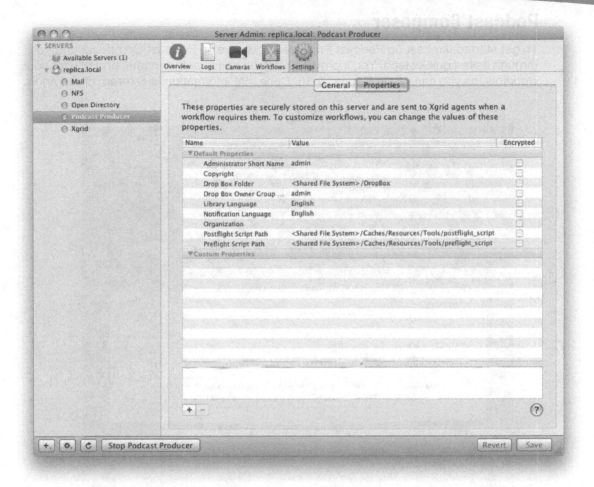

Figure 16–9. *Granular settings for Podcast Producer*

If you make any changes to any of the settings, click the Save button to commit the changes. However, unless you're sure you want to make any changes, it is never a bad idea to research the specifics as to what exactly each of these Podcast Producer options does (see http://support.apple.com/manuals/#serversandenterprisesoftware).

Setting Up Workflows

In Snow Leopard Server, Apple has introduced a whole new way to make podcast workflows. It's now simple to use but still has amazing and powerful new automations that give Podcast Producer administrators the ability to configure a host of new options quickly and easily.

Podcast Composer

To get started, first set up Podcast Producer. Then, fire up Podcast Composer and go through seven quick steps. You'll provide a default name, author name, and title for your workflow, as you can see in Figure 16–10. Once that information is entered, click Import.

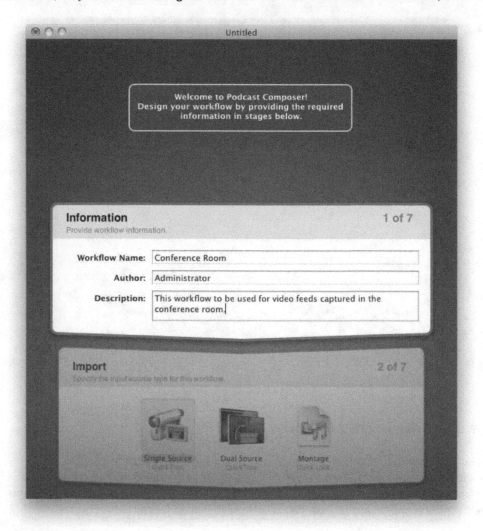

Figure 16–10. *Podcast Composer step 1: title and author information*

For step 2, configure the source of the video and audio, as shown in Figure 16–11. For each of the three options, Single Source, Dual Source, and Montage, you'll have an option to obtain more information about the source and configure settings more granularly. Single Source will perform much of the same functionality as Podcast Composer 1; you can select Audio, Video, or Screen Recording (aka screen capture).

There's a nice new feature for automatic chapter generation for longer videos now as well. Dual Source will allow users to use Keynote along with the video being captured, which is one of the coolest aspects of Podcast Composer 2 by far. With this option, you can select how the Keynote will interact with the video using some transitions familiar to users of both Keynote and iMovie. Finally, you can select Montage, which will use QuickLook to transition between various movies, images, documents (Word, Pages, PDF), and presentations (PowerPoint and Keynote). If QuickLook can interpret a media type, then you can drop it into the montage.

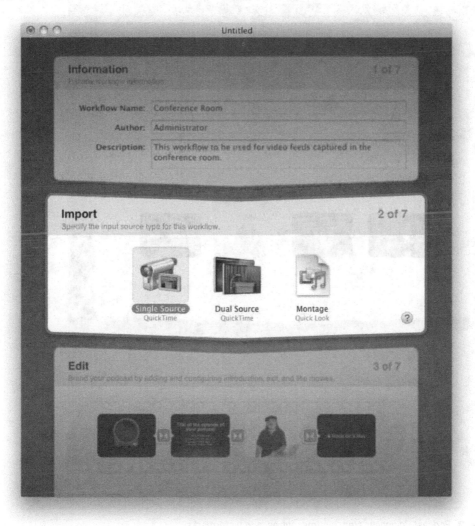

Figure 16–11. *Podcast Composer step 2: selecting a source*

Now that you've defined your source, let's move on to step 3, a very basic editorial workflow going from left to right on the screen, as shown in Figure 16–12. Use the information overlay (when you mouse over an item) to first define an introduction movie lead-in. Then you will define title sequence and effects for the title (which is user defined using your defaults). Next you can select a watermark, which you can now place anywhere on the screen, control the opacity, and place a bar along the bottom with information from your title bar. Finally, you define the exit credits. For all of these, Apple has provided some stock footage, but you can also define your own as well.

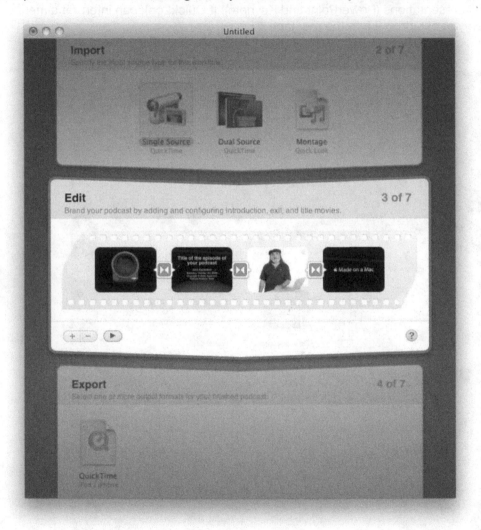

Figure 16–12. *Podcast Composer step 3: intros, outros, and watermarks*

In step 4, you'll define the output format (or formats, because you can output a number of different clips if you choose), as shown in Figure 16–13. Here, you can set the video and audio codecs that you want to use. You don't actually usually need to change anything in this step once it has been predefined in the workflow on the server.

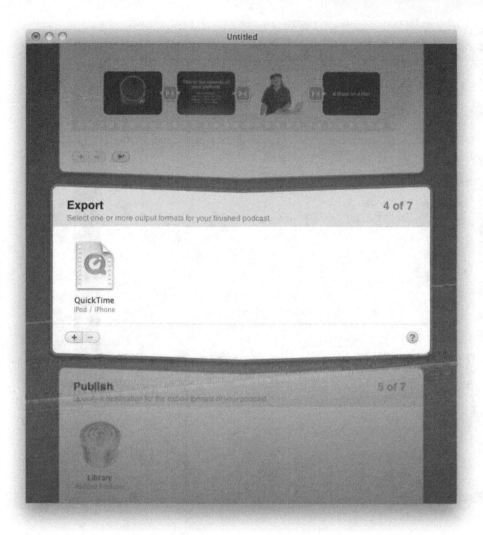

Figure 16–13. *Podcast Composer step 4: export settings*

In step 5, as shown in Figure 16–14, you will choose where the recorded podcast content will be published. Using this is really nice because you can simultaneously send your new podcast to a wiki, a Final Cut Server, and a workflow-defined directory. If sending to a directory or a Final Cut Server, then you have the option to perform further automations against the file.

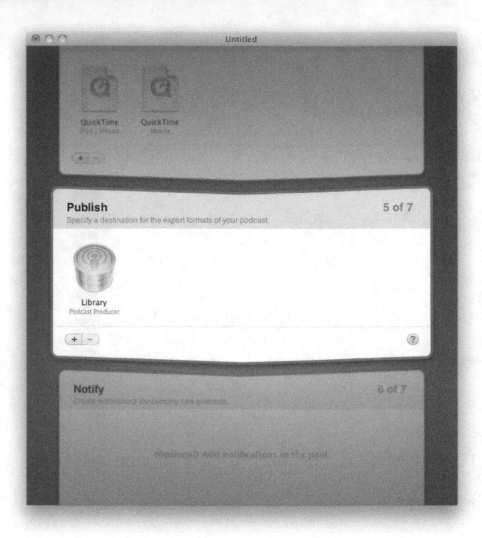

Figure 16–14. *Podcast Composer step 5: destinations*

In step 6, choose who to notify (if anyone) about the new podcast, as shown in Figure 16–15.

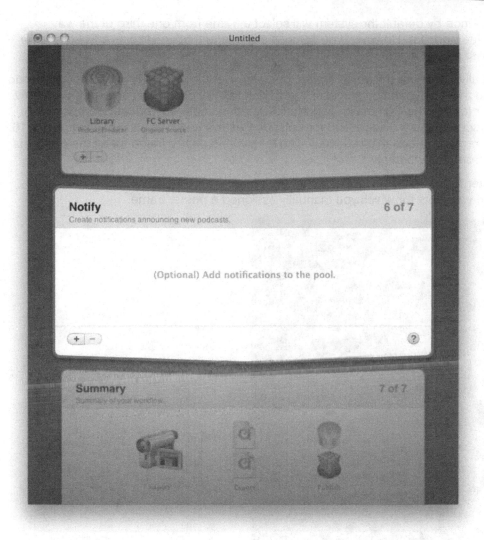

Figure 16–15. *Configuring notifications in step 6*

Step 7 is to deploy the podcast workflow to your server. Simply click Save to output a file, or click Deploy to actually add that workflow to a Podcast Producer server (plug in the host name, username, and password and hit Save). Now, when users go to use Podcast Capture, they'll be able to use the new workflow!

Setting a Poster Frame

Podcast Producer will automatically generate a *poster frame* for each video that is generated. A poster frame is a frame of the video that is automatically generated and then applied to the video. The poster frame that each video has can therefore be a bit random, since by default the system will select a frame from one third of the way through the podcast. However, you can use any image that you like as a Poster frame (also called *poster image* in Podcast Producer).

To manually configure the poster frame, open the workflow in Podcast Composer (or do so during the initial creation process). Then click the Window menu and click Workflow Inspector (or use the Command+I shortcut key when you're in Podcast Composer). At the next screen you will see a field for Episode Poster Image, as shown in Figure 16–16. Simply drag any image that you would like to use as a poster frame for all the podcasts created from this workflow.

The poster frame will then appear in the wiki or in iTunes for each podcast generated using the workflow for which you manually assigned a poster frame.

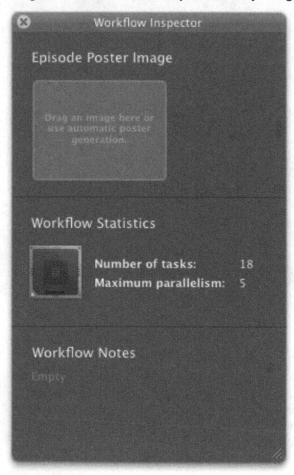

Figure 16–16. *Setting up poster frames*

Exporting Workflows

Once you have workflows configured, you can also share them with other servers or simply export them for backup purposes. This is also done in the Podcast Composer tool. While the workflow is open, simply click the File menu, and select Save As. This will result in a dialog box like the one shown in Figure 16–17. After selecting a filename and location, click Save to export the workflow.

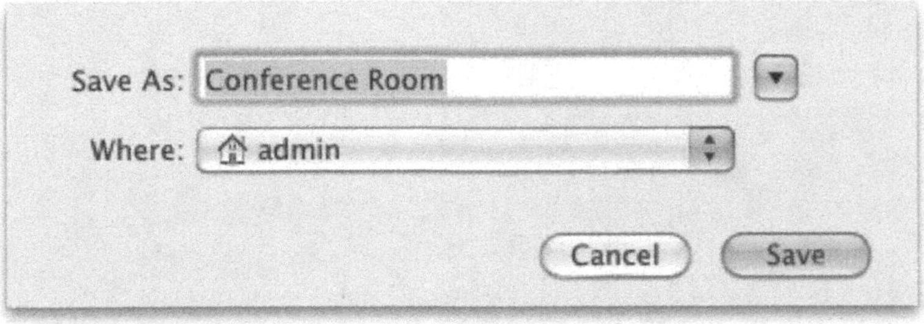

Figure 16–17. *Saving workflows*

The resultant file is actually not a single file at all. In Mac parlance, it is referred to as a *bundle*; within it is a number of files including an `Info.plist` file and a `Resources` directory. Within `Resources` are the images, intro and outro movies, any associated tools, and a collection of property lists that define things like sources. These allow you to customize a workflow simply by altering the files in a given location. For example, if you just wanted to change a watermark, you could `cd` into the workflow's `Images` folder and replace the file, therefore duplicating a workflow or altering it without even having to open Podcast Composer!

Controlling Access to Workflows

When using Podcast Producer, the Podcast Capture client application will ask each user for a username and password, which will determine what workflows and cameras that users can use for producing and publishing their podcasts within the server. Once a podcast has been captured, then the user will be provided with a list of workflows to which they have access. But where are these configured? They can be added and removed from Server Admin. And each can have a user, users, a group, or groups that have access to use them. By limiting access to each workflow, based on the workflow ACL, you can then limit who can access to different blogs, who can use various automations, and even who can publish to an iTunes U account, or a different third-party service if you've scripting against a given API.

To set these workflow ACLs, open Server Admin, and choose the Podcast Producer entry in the Server Admin sidebar, from the appropriate server. Then click the workflow to which you would like to limit access. By default, all users have access to all workflows, as you can see in Figure 16–18. Click the "Allow access to the following users and groups" radio button, and then click the plus sign (+). Then from the floating list of users and groups, choose the object you want to grant access to, and then drag it into the list. Then click the Save button to save your changes.

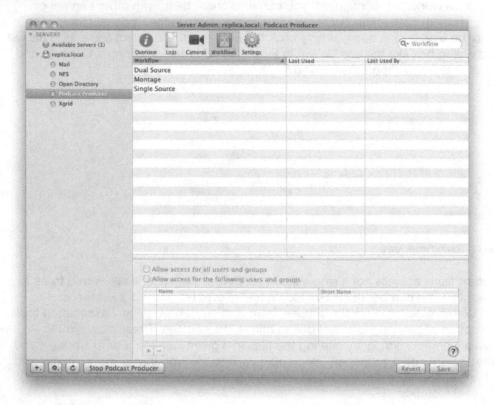

Figure 16–18. *Configuring the Podcast Producer access lists*

Using Workflows

Once a workflow has been created, you can use Podcast Capture to run it, provided that the appropriate permissions were granted earlier in this chapter.

When you open Podcast Capture for the first time, you are greeted with an account setup screen, as shown in Figure 16–19. This screen connects your local copy of Podcast Capture to the Podcast Producer services running on the server. Here, provide the name of the server as well as the username and the password that the client will use to authenticate into the server. Additionally, you can use the "Remember this password in my keychain" option from to add the information into the keychain, so future logins will not require entering the credentials again. When you are satisfied with your settings, click Continue.

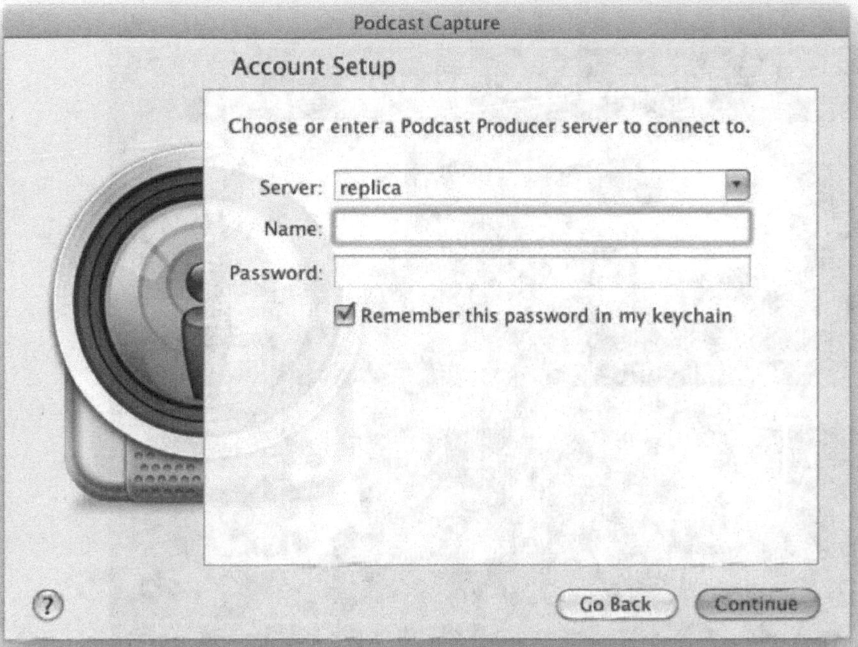

Figure 16–19. *Connecting Podcast Composer to a Podcast Producer server*

NOTE: The information that you place into the keychain will be accessible by the account that is being used when the checkbox is selected. Therefore, do not use administrative credentials at this time. Provided that you do save information into the keychain, though, you will see the Account Setup screen only the first time you open Podcast Capture.

Provided that the client can communicate with the server, you will then be placed into the Choose a Podcast Type screen. Here, you can select whether the podcast will use a camera, screen share, audio, or dual (which is a combination of the others). As you may have noticed in Figure 16–20, you will also have the Open an Existing File option, which can be used to import previously captured movies and run a defined workflow automation on them. For the purposes of this example, click Screen, which will prepare you for a screencast.

Figure 16–20. *Choosing a source in Podcast Capture*

You will then see a picture of the screen that you will be recording once you hit the
Record button. To begin recording, simply click the red button toward the bottom of the
screen, as shown in Figure 16–21. Once you are recording, you can use the
Command+F2 keystroke to pause or resume recording.

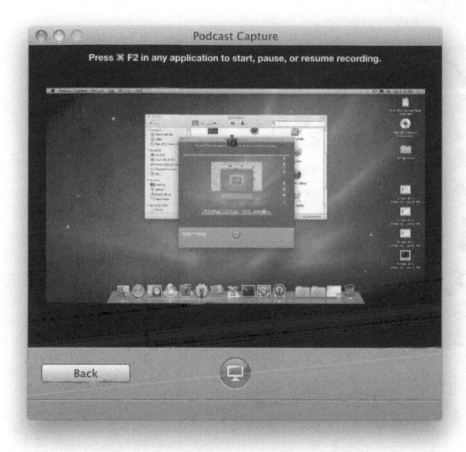

Figure 16–21. *Recording a screencast in Podcast Capture*

Once recording is underway, there are a number of things to keep in mind. First, as you can see in Figure 16–22, during recording, the recording screen and timer will be overlaid on the Podcast Producer's render of the screen being captured; the numbers overlay will not actually be part of the final video file. Also, when you pause a recording and later resume it, your video will be one contiguous file rather than a separate file per portion of the composition. Finally, you can click the Publish button to proceed or click the Start Over button if the video did not turn out quite as planned.

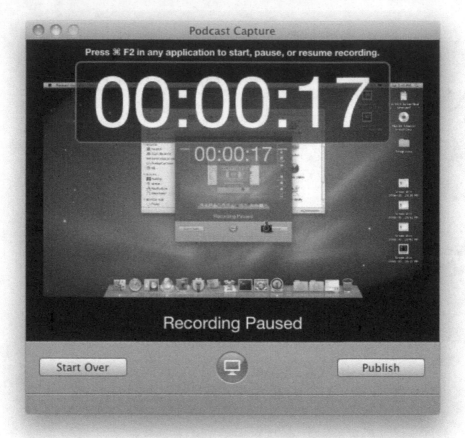

Figure 16–22. *Recording video*

NOTE: Keep in mind that recording is a science, and the technical quality of your podcasts will depend somewhat on the equipment you are using. Although the built-in microphone and iSight camera of a Mac OS X computer are better than the standard equipment built into most other computers today, they are still nothing like what you would get from purchasing dedicated professional gear for your podcast.

Once the podcast has been captured, you will need to provide some information so it can be easily identified when it is published. The Podcast Information screen, as shown in Figure 16–23, will capture a number of fields for this purpose. First is the date, which is why the date is shown in the upper-right corner of the screen. Because you do not possess a time machine, you cannot change the date. The second piece of information is a title field, which is the very first field. This title, if you included an automation to place a title in the beginning, end, or throughout a podcast, will determine the name of the podcast in iTunes and will be used to generate a number of automations. It will also provide a title for the corresponding wiki article that will be published if you are using one. And finally, there is the description, which is used in the body of the corresponding wiki article or as the description of the resultant video in iTunes.

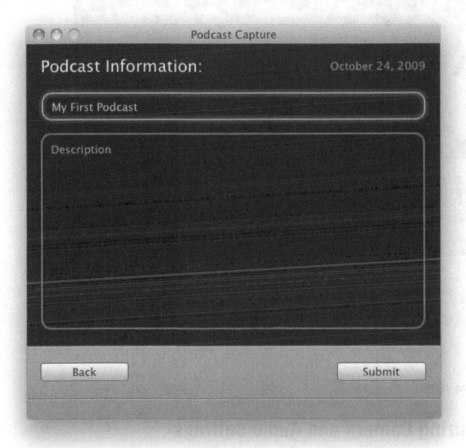

Figure 16–23. *Entering podcast information*

Finally, click the Submit button, and then select the appropriate workflow that your podcast will use, which is populated from the list of workflows that your account has access to in Server Admin. Once it's complete, you'll see the screen shown in Figure 16–24, which tells you that the podcast has been submitted for publication. The podcast will spend some time rendering the video. If you have a lot of effects or watermarks, you can track the status of these renders within Xgrid Admin.

Figure 16–24. *Podcast submitted screen*

Configuring Camera and Audio Settings

Although we recommend using third-party equipment where possible, you can use certain settings to help tune the quality, video source, and audio source. To access these settings, open the Podcast Capture tool, and then click the Podcast Producer menu. From here, click Preferences, and then click the Audio/Video icon in the Preferences toolbar.

Next, configure settings for your devices. First, click Video Source, and select a specific camera (Figure 16–25). Then, click Microphone, and select a specific device. Finally, select an option in the Quality menu: Good, Better, and Best. The quality should typically be set to as high as your environment allows. However, by reducing the quality, you also reduce file sizes and the required speed to stream content; therefore, in order to conserve resources, many environments will choose Good.

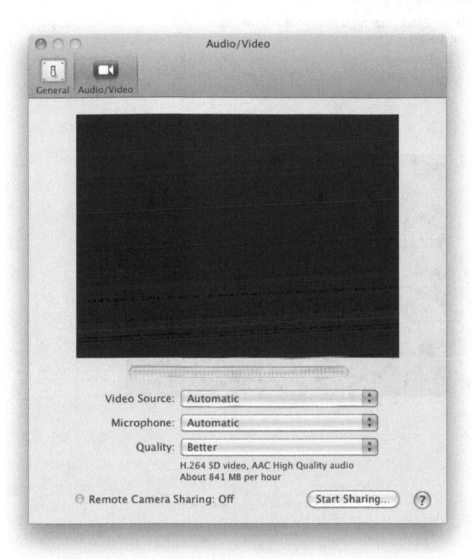

Figure 16–25. *Audio/video preferences*

Binding Cameras

When you are setting up workflows, you can configure Podcast Producer to automate connecting to specific cameras in each workflow. But to select a camera in a workflow, you must first be able to access it in Server Admin.

To share a camera to Server Admin, open Podcast Capture from /Applications/Utilities. Then click the Podcast Capture menu and select Preferences. From here, click the Audio/Video icon in the Preferences toolbar. From here you will see the Start Sharing button in the lower-right corner of the screen, as you can see in Figure 16–26.

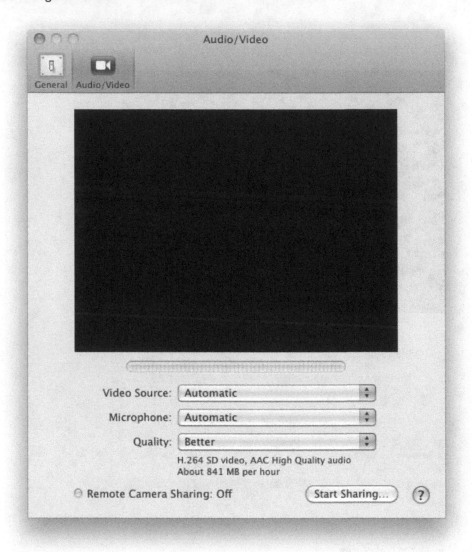

Figure 16–26. *Enabling camera sharing*

In the remote camera sharing dialog, shown in Figure 16–27, provide a name to be associated to the camera in the Camera Name field. Then, select a server from the Server list (or type the name into the field). Next, in the Name field, provide a username that has administrative rights over the Podcast Producer service. Finally, provide a password, and then click the Start Sharing button.

To start remote camera sharing, provide a camera name and an administrator login to a Podcast Producer server.

Camera Name: Room 401
Server: replica.krypted.com
Name: diradmin
Password: ••••••••

Cancel   Start Sharing

Figure 16–27. *Authenticating for camera sharing*

Next, open Server Admin from /Applications/Server and connect to the server that you configured earlier, as shown in Figure 16–28. Then, click the Podcast Producer service in the SERVERS list, and click the Camera icon in the Server Admin toolbar. Here, verify that you can see the camera that was just configured. You can then use the "Allow Access to" options at the bottom of the screen. Clicking the option to restrict access and then the plus sign (+) will open a list of users to provide access to the camera.

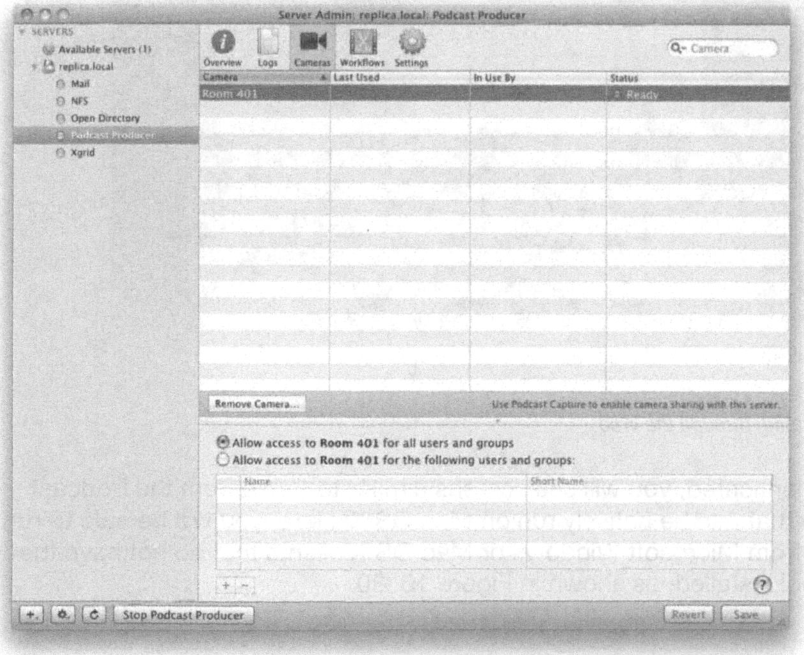

Figure 16–28. *Shared cameras in Server Admin*

> **NOTE:** If you select to restrict access and do not put a user or a group into the list of allowed users, then the camera will be inoperable.

Running Workflows from the Web

From the Overview page of the Podcast Producer service in Server Admin, you will see a URL that can be used to access the Podcast Capture web portal. Clicking this URL in a web browser will open a login screen, as you can see in Figure 16–29. Here, you can enter a username and password that has access to use the Podcast Producer service.

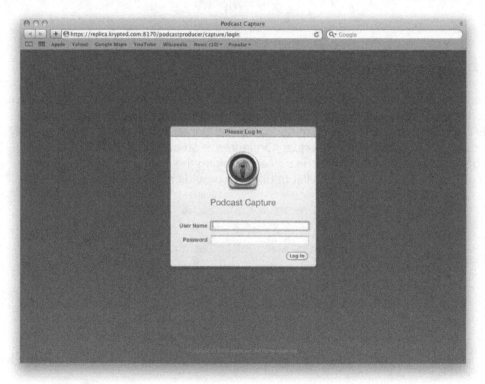

Figure 16–29. *Authenticating through the Web*

Once you have authenticated, you will see screens similar to those from the Podcast Capture application that can be natively run on Mac OS X. Here, you will be able to run podcast workflows from Microsoft Windows or Mac OS X clients that do not have the Podcast Capture tool installed, as shown in Figure 16–30.

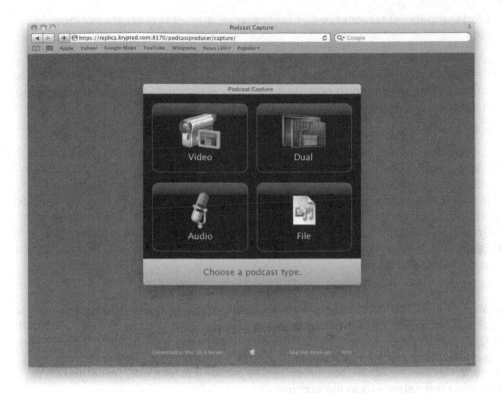

Figure 16–30. *Podcast Capture from the Web*

Using Podcast Producer from the Command Line

At the end of the day, Podcast Producer is a fairly straightforward solution. You have a nice little GUI application that users can use to publish audio, video, screencasts, or files to an RSS feed. Using that RSS feed, you can then integrate that data with a number of other solutions. You can also use Podcast Producer to remotely fire up bound cameras and begin Podcast Producer workflows, which means you don't even need to be at a conference, in a shareholder meeting, or in a classroom to capture video from cameras.

Podcasting

The real power and flexibility of Podcast Producer comes from the ability to programmatically interface with the sandbox that Apple has provided. Workflows are a collection of actions that run when you submit a podcast. This can include leveraging Ruby to integrate complicated workflows, or it might even be using the command-line interface on clients in your own applications. It all starts with a simple command, podcast. To get started with the podcast command, let's first just list the assets that your computer has at its disposal. These can include workflows, cameras, and servers. These can be listed using the -listworkflows, -listcameras, and -listservers options, respectively.

When you run the list commands, you'll need to authenticate into your Podcast Producer server in order to list the objects that are on the server. To do so, in addition to the list options, you'll also need to provide a -server, -user, and –pass option, following each with the correct value for the obvious setting, as you can see here:

```
podcast -server www.krypted.com -user charles -pass secretpassword -listcameras
```

The list options display objects that are housed on or connected to the Podcast Producer server. Each laptop that Apple distributes has a camera. You can also plug in most standard cameras and use them with Podcast Producer, assuming that your computer is able to see the video feed on the camera. Once you have a camera installed on the computer, you can then "bind" it to a Podcast Producer server, as we covered in the "Binding Camera" section earlier in this chapter. This gives users the ability to remotely stop and start captures. To bind a camera, first run the podcast command with the -devices option as follows:

```
podcast -devices
```

This will show you all the devices on your computer capable of being bound to a Podcast Producer server. This is similar to the drop-down lists displayed in the Podcast Capture GUI tool. Once you have the name of the camera that you'd like to bind to, you will use the podcast command with the appropriately named –bind option to, well, bind the camera to the server. Again, you'll include the server address and credentials that you are binding the camera to in the command:

```
podcast -server www.krypted.com -user charles -pass secretpassword -bind
'0xfd40000005ac8501'
```

Once you have your camera bound, run the list option again, and you can then start capturing a podcast from it by using the –start option followed by the name the server uses to reference that camera:

```
podcast -server www.krypted.com -user charles -pass secretpassword
-start "ConferenceRoom"
```

You could also have indicated a -delay value, in seconds, to specify how long before the camera would start the recording once the signal to do so has been received. You could also have specified an –audioonly option, which would record only audio. By default, podcast will use the default audio device indicated in your System Preferences, although you can specify the deviceID from the –devices output to indicate a different audio input source (for example, -microphone).

While you are recording, the file will be stored in the /var/pcast/agent/recordings directory. Once you have started a capture, you can then –pause, –resume, –cancel, and –stop the camera. When you –stop the recording, you will also want to include a –metadata option followed by the path to a property list that includes the available metadata for the podcast you are publishing and the –workflow to be assigned to the podcast.

```
podcast –server www.krypted.com –user charles –pass secretpassword –stop
"ConferenceRoom" –metadata ~/ConferenceRoomMeeting10012009_metadata.plist –workflow
"Meetings"
```

The –metadata option and the ability to stop, start, and publish into workflows allows for integration with a number of other solutions, including Final Cut Server and various third-party capture tools. These often have the ability to control quality, something you can easily feed back into Podcast Producer using the output from the other tool. Quality is applied per device connected to a device that is "bound." Run the podcast command using the –getconfig option to see the quality settings for each device connected to a specific computer:

```
podcast –getconfig
```

You can alter the quality for some devices. To start, run the podcast command with the –presets option as follows:

```
podcast –presets
```

This is going to list all the preset settings that you can easily use to configure the devices. You can then set the configuration using the –setconfig option to set the preset for a given device, following it with the appropriate key. For example, we're going to switch from the default format for videos, MPEG-4, to using uncompressed video by using the Best video preset instead of the Good video preset:

```
podcast –setconfig Capture=Video:Best
```

To then change it back, you would use the following command:

```
podcast –setconfig Capture=Video:Good
```

As the quality of recordings and their length increase, you may incur a backlog of recordings waiting to be processed by a server, so there may be a time when you want to check the status of an upload. To do so, use the –list_uploads option:

```
podcast –list_uploads
```

You can also submit files (common when bringing in assets from other solutions) instead of live video recordings:

```
podcast –server www.krypted.com –user charles –pass secretpassword –submit –file
~/Movies/file.mov –workflow 'Meetings' –metadata ~/Desktop/todaysmeetingmetadata.plist
```

Again, if you're leveraging podcast as a sort of API and you're going to be generating this programmatically, then you'll also likely push your metadata fields into the appropriate format in the property list that you had on the desktop, maybe storing it in a temp location instead. The metadata format is as follows:

```
<?xml version="1.0" encoding="UTF-8"?>
<!DOCTYPE plist PUBLIC "-//Apple//DTD PLIST 1.0//EN"
"http://www.apple.com/DTDs/PropertyList-1.0.dtd">
<plist version="1.0 >
<dict>
<key>Author</key>
<string>NAME OF AUTHOR</string>
<key>Comment</key>
<string>COMMENTS GO HERE.</string>
```

```
<key>Copyright</key>
<string>COPYRIGHT INFO GOES HERE</string>
<key>Description</key>
<string>DESCRIPTION GOES HERE
</string>
<key>Keywords</key>
<string>KEYWORDS OR TAGS GO HERE</string>
<key>Title</key>
<string>TITLE OF PODCAST GOES HERE</string>
</dict>
</plist>
```

Because the previous information is in a standardized format, then if you have another solution or a script, you can use a tool such as `plistbuddy` to programmatically generate the metadata files from other sources, thus trading metadata between solutions. For example, a very simplistic way to watch that feed would be using the `curl` command:

```
curl http://www.krypted.com/feed
```

If you'd rather use Podcast Producer's engine to work with files offline, then you can do so as well. In the `/usr/libexec/podcastproducer` directory, you can use a number of commands to work with video files, allowing you to do anything that you can do within a Podcast Producer workflow. Additionally, most of these are wrapped into the `pcastaction` command in `/usr/bin`.

Automations

You can use the `pcastaction` command to perform most of the automations that Podcast Producer performs on files as part of automations run from the Podcast Composer tool. This command comes with a number of verbs, each specific to a type of automation that can be used. These include the following:

- ▪ `unpack`: Extracts a folder archive before running the automation
- ▪ `shell`: Runs a command or shell script
- ▪ `preflight`: Runs a script before the automation
- ▪ `postflight`: Runs a script after an automation
- ▪ `encode`: Inputs a standard video file and then output a video file using a different codec
- ▪ `annotate`: Annotates a files metadata
- ▪ `qceffect`: Runs a custom Quartz Composer composition against a file
- ▪ `watermark`: Inserts a watermark into an indicated video file
- ▪ `title`: Provides a title for the resultant file
- ▪ `merge`: Merges two existing files
- ▪ `iTunes`: Indicates the video is to be included in an iTunes RSS feed

- iTunesU: Interfaces with iTunes U the same way that the iTunes verb can do

- mail: Sends an e-mail announcement about the new video

- archive: Archives files used in the automation

- publish: Publishes the required files into the root of the web server

- groupblog: Adds the item into the group's RSS feed

- template: Creates a new file from a template

- approval: Submits content for approval

As with many other commands, pcastaction has a man page if you need further help; however, the man page is not as informative as the help page for each verb. To obtain this help, run the pcastaction command, followed by an additional help verb and then the verb you would like more information on. Here's an example:

```
pcastaction help merge
```

Authentication Types

By default the /Library/Preferences/com.apple.pcastserverd.plist file allows basic, digest, and Kerberos authentication. Attempts to authenticate will be made in the reverse order, respectively. This is pulled from the http_auth_type array, which you can see using the following command:

```
serveradmin settings pcast
```

You can then remove an entry and edit existing entries to change the supported mechanisms using serveradmin if you cannot stop the Podcast Producer service. If you can stop the service, then the easiest way to edit the authentication mechanisms is to edit the /Library/Preferences/com.apple.pcastserverd.plist file directly. To do so, locate the http_auth_type key as you see it here:

```
<key>http_auth_type</key>
<array>
<string>basic</string>
<string>digest</string>
<string>kerberos</string>
</array>
```

Here, remove each string that you no longer want to support. Removing all except Kerberos will provide support for only Kerberos as an authentication mechanism.

Summary

As demonstrated in this chapter, the Podcast Producer system that is included with Mac OS X 10.6 Server can be a powerful tool that enables unprecedented collaboration and multimedia publishing for your users. We looked at some of the basic uses of Podcast Producer and walked you through setting up the typical types of workflow that can be done quickly and easily. At this point, you should be able to capture content from cameras, build screencasts, combine video, watermark video, and perform any combination of these tasks.

With a little patience and care, you can also develop advanced workflows to produce content and workflows that previously were not possible. For example, you can create workflows that house assets on multiple servers, allowing for an infinite number of people to access your content. You can also integrate Podcast Producer with Final Cut Server, QuickTime Streaming Server, and third-party solutions. But the first step is to get started, and after following along with this chapter, you should be ready to move on to more advanced topics!

Chapter 17

Streaming QuickTime Video

Streaming video is now commonplace. Practically every vendor with a server product has a solution that enables server administrators to stream video files to clients in one way or another. Two notable and widely adopted protocols are Microsoft's Silverlight and Apple's QuickTime Streaming Server. Obviously, this chapter is about Mac OS X Server's QuickTime Streaming Server.

Why stream content? One reason is so users will be able to download content easily. For example, you might not have distribution rights for content but you have permission to show it. In that case, you can choose to stream the content, which protects the streams. In addition to protecting streams, you may want the streams to start quickly rather than requiring users to download an entire video or audio file prior to watching or listening to content.

Why stream content on Mac OS X Server specifically? It's a great format because there are no per-user, per-stream, or per-file fees. Mac OS X Server is sold as a single-server license, and therefore you can stream as much as a single server can sustain. In other words, you can impose limitations in order to conserve bandwidth or hardware resources such as RAM and processor, but the service itself will impose no limitations if you so choose. Depending on the other services running on the server and the resources required, you can tune the maximum number of streams that the hardware and load will allow.

In this chapter, we'll first cover the protocols that Mac OS X Server supports for streaming video. Then we'll cover how to configure the servers to serve content for each and the strategies that go into doing so. Once you've learned how to configure a solid server environment, we'll show how to set up and manage client systems to access those streams.

Supported Protocols

A number of protocols are used for streaming media over the Internet. Many will use HyperText Transfer Protocol (HTTP) since that is the most native to the Web. However, Mac OS X Server uses an interesting interpretation of what HTTP means, which is basically to tunnel traffic for the QuickTime Streaming Server over port 80. Or, you can store files and provide access to them over HTTP and other file sharing protocols; however, these are not typically real-time streaming.

The main protocol to focus on in QuickTime Streaming Server is the Real Time Streaming Protocol (RTSP). In terms of functionality, RTSP is a bit like a VCR, where the client sends commands, such as play and pause, to streams of content, which are played or accessed by a client, which in most cases is QuickTime.

Implementation Strategies

As we've alluded to, there are a few different options for how to implement QuickTime Streaming Server. The strategy that you use will determine the complexity of your environment and the technical requirements.

The first and simplest strategy is to put a file on a web server and then summon it from a web page or manually through QuickTime (or another application capable of playing the format you will be using). This can be great for small files and files that you want to allow users to download.

Streaming video is another option that is common and optimal for files longer than 15 minutes. The reason that longer movies are better over streaming is that they are typically going to take a long time to download. QuickTime Streaming Server allows a user to start watching a movie while it is being downloaded, which is referred to as a *progressive download*. As we have mentioned, streaming video from the QuickTime Streaming Server perspective is done over RTSP. The most common way to stream video is to place a file into the directory that QuickTime Streaming Server uses to stream from and then use a different type of URL, which calls the video on-demand and begins to cache it while it begins to play. Another way to stream video, though, is to stream live video, which we will describe in the "QuickTime Broadcaster" section later in this chapter.

Finally, QuickTime Streaming Server can also stream live audio streams via looped MP3 tracks, similar to how a radio station would broadcast content. Visitors log into the server and listen to the stream as it's playing and do not have any control over the stream itself. However, this feature has not been updated for a few different versions of Mac OS X Server, and the tools for configuration on Server 10.6 are still not being distributed at the time of this book's printing; therefore, we will not be covering it in detail.

Bandwidth Considerations

One of the most important aspects before you begin installing your server is to determine how much load you can put it under. This is going to be different for every environment, but keep in mind that it's the lowest common denominator between a few different factors.

The first is bandwidth. How much bandwidth does your environment have? If you have a T1 (which is 1.544Mbps in the United States), that might not cut it anymore with modern streaming data rates rising as quickly as bandwidth. That brings up the second aspect of bandwidth; how fast is the streaming codec that you are using? Table 17–1 describes some popular streaming formats for video. You can take the amount of bandwidth you have and divide it by the speed of the codec you are planning to use, which will produce the number of potential streams you can have running concurrently.

Table 17–1. *Streaming Codec Speeds*

Video Type	Speed in Megabytes	Speed in Megabits
Standard Definition		
MiniDV, DVCAM, and DVCPRO	3.6MBps	28.8Mbps
DVCPRO 50	7.7MBps	61.6Mbps
Uncompressed SD (8-bit)	20MBps	160Mbps
Uncompressed SD (10-bit)	27MBps	216Mbps
Compressed High Definition		
DVCPRO HD	5.8MBps to 14MBps	46.4 to 112Mbps
Apple ProRes 422	5.25 to 27.5 MBps	42 to 220Mbps
Redcode RAW (24fps)	28 MBps	224Mbps
Uncompressed High Definition		
720p 24fps	46MBps	368Mbps
720p 30fps	50MBps	400Mbps
720p 60fps	100MBps	800Mbps
1080 24p (8-bit)	98MBps	784Mbps
1080i (8-bit)	120MBps	960Mbps
1080 24p (10-bit)	110MBps	880Mbps
1080i (10-bit)	165MBps	1,328Mbps
Redcode 4k	334MBps (and up)	2,672Mbps

In Table 17-1, we reference speed in megabytes or gigabytes per second. You may notice that your Internet service provider (ISP) or hosting/collocation facility references your speeds in megabits or gigabits per second, much more common outside of video. There are 8 bits (uses a small *b* as in bps, or Mbps for 1,024 kilobits per second) in a byte (notated using a big *B* as in Bps, or MBps for megabytes per second), so you can multiply the speed in the table by 8 to get the total megabits per second for streams. Let's take Apple ProRes 422 as an example, since it's a very popular codec to use these days. That can top out at 27.5MBps, but if your video editors export the QuickTime movies properly, then it can be as low as 5.25MBps; this translates to 42Mbps. Now let's say you have a 100Mb fiber line supplying Internet into your office and can use the entire pipe for serving video (rare but possible). In this case, you would be looking at being able to stream approximately two of your streams off that line concurrently.

Since having two streams isn't suitable for most streaming environments, let's actually look at the lower end. If you have a QuickTime movie at 320 by 240 pixels running at 30 frames per second, you can actually get bandwidth speeds down closer to 768Kbps, which is great for an iPhone, for example. If your 100Mbps line is actually 102,400Kbps, then you can have roughly 133 users streaming content concurrently, which is much more palatable. Further tuning of these streams can allow for even more streams. Here are some strategies for tuning:

- iTunes has a built-in converter, but there are no customized options for encoding into H.264.

- Handbrake can do more than just H.264 and can be further customized for encoding.

- Media Cleaner is an extremely customizable tool for converting files and provides an extensive set of transcoding options. It's not cheap, but it's one of the best.

- Squeeze, from Sorenson Media, has one of the best H.264 codec implementations on the market. You can automate conversions and perform a variety of other tasks.

- Final Cut Server, Compressor, Podcast Producer, and the various command-line tools surrounding each of the Apple product offerings can do almost anything that the other tools can, although it might require a little more thinking outside of the box, which we'll discuss later in this chapter.

Installing QuickTime Streaming Server

The first step to getting QuickTime Streaming Server in Mac OS X up and running is to show the service(s) in Server Admin. To do so, first open Server Admin from /Applications/Server. After authenticating, click the name of the server where you will be installing the service onto and bring up the server's base settings. Click the Settings icon in the toolbar to bring up the services selection screen, where you can configure which services will run on the server (although simply enabling them in this screen will not start them), as you can see in Figure 17–1.

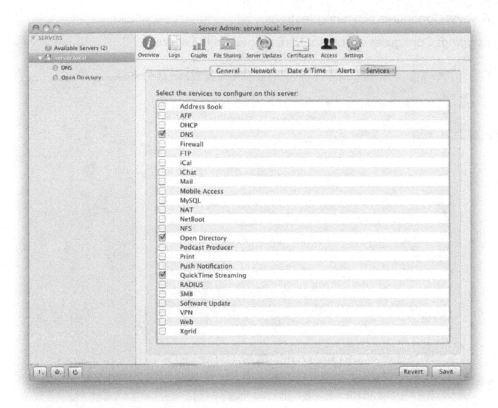

Figure 17–1. *Enabling the services*

Select the QuickTime Streaming box, and then click the Save button. You should then see the service appear in the SERVERS list when you click the disclosure triangle to show the active services on the server. Click the Settings icon in the Server Admin toolbar to bring up the settings that Apple has provided for configuring that service.

Configuring QuickTime Streaming Server

Now that you have enabled the service, you will want to configure and start it up. By default, the settings for the QuickTime Streaming Server are divvied up into five types, which you can see in Figure 17–2:

- *General*: Includes global settings, such as the location of movies to be served, maximum throughput, and maximum number of available connections.

- *Access*: Configures how users will access content, including security information regarding supported password types.

- *IP Bindings*: Allows you to configure which IP addresses users will utilize to access the server.

- *Relays*: Configures clustering features.

- *Logging*: Configures events that are logged on the server.

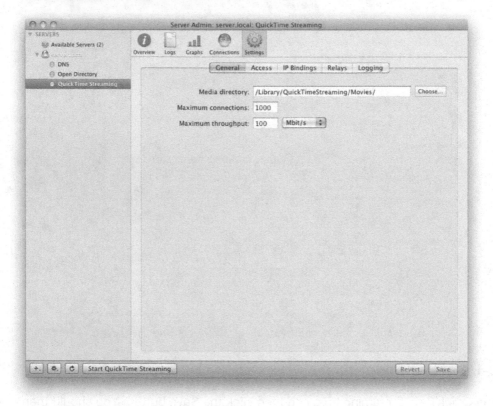

Figure 17–2. *QuickTime Streaming Server's settings*

For most administrators, the key settings available in Mac OS X Server will be the general settings. Here, click in the "Media directory" field, and type a path to the location of the files that you will be sharing over QuickTime Streaming Server. You can also click the Choose button to browse to the location that you will be using. You can use the "Maximum connections" setting to throttle the number of users who can access the QuickTime Streaming Server and view streams concurrently (keep in mind that a paused connection does not necessarily appear in the list of connections). Finally, the "Maximum throughput" field allows you to configure the maximum speed that the total connections are able to take up on the server. By configuring both the "Maximum connections" and "Maximum throughput" fields, you can limit the load that will be placed on the server.

When you are satisfied with your General settings, click the Access tab to begin more granularly defining how users will interact with the server. Under Access, you have a number of settings. These include the following, as you can see in Figure 17–3:

- *MP3 Broadcast Password*: If you will be using Mac OS X Server to serve up audio only, this is the password that will be used to listen to streams.

- *Authentication Scheme*: This controls what type of password to submit over the network. Basic passwords are akin to inserting the username and password into a connection string to a web server. For example, data is submitted in clear text as http://charles:mypassword@www.krypted.com. However, since network sniffers can easily pull this information, digest authentication was introduced, meaning that an MD5 hash of the password is sent to the server and therefore not easily enumerated by network sniffers. This is set to Digest by default and should likely stay there.

- *Authentication*: This includes options for acceptable repositories of authentication credentials (these are explained further later in this chapter):

- *User and password in Open Directory*: Allows for leveraging user accounts from Open Directory

- *User and password in file*: Allows using accounts and passwords stored in a flat file on the server

- *Accept Incoming Broadcasts*: Enables QuickTime Broadcaster use

- *Enable web-based administration*: Enables the web administration tool

- *Allow guest viewer*: Allows unauthenticated access to the server

- *Enable home folder streaming*: Allows users to stream files from their home directories

Next, click the IP Bindings tab of the server. Here you will configure which IP addresses clients will be able to use to access the servers. If you have only one IP address active on the server or you want to use more than one IP address, then the "Enable streaming on selected addresses only" setting may be irrelevant, but in many environments only a network interface that is connected to a demilitarized zone (DMZ) will be streaming content. If you want to stream content through only one interface, then click the "Enabled streaming on selected addresses only" option, and select the box for each listed IP address that you want to be accessible, as shown in Figure 17–4. If you want the QuickTime Streaming services to be accessible on all IP address, simply use the "Enable streaming on all IP addresses" option.

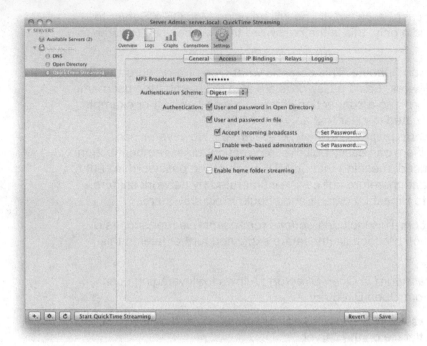

Figure 17–3. *QuickTime Streaming Server's access settings*

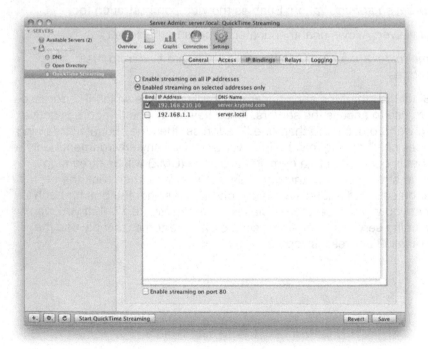

Figure 17–4. *QuickTime Streaming Server's IP bindings*

Another option on the IP Bindings tab is the option to enable streaming on port 80. By enabling this feature, streamed RTSP data will be routed through port 80. This process encapsulates the RTSP streams over port 80 but does not play data through HTTP. The encapsulation will slow down streams and increase processor load, and the reaction to this type of traffic by certain firewalls and proxies that perform deep packet inspection for traffic over port 80 may throw up a red flag and drop the traffic outright. For some environments, this can be an easy way to allow traffic for clients whose firewall doesn't allow traffic over RTSP; however, for most environments, this option should be left deselected.

When you are satisfied with your IP Bindings options, click the Relays tab. Here, you will configure servers that can relay connections to one another. For example, if you record a stream in your home office or at a school district office, you can then relay it to each of the remote locations where you have Mac OS X Servers, thus allowing users in each of those locations to access the services as though they were local to them. The list will initially be empty. To configure a relay, simply click the plus (+) sign, and then provide the required information. For more on relays, see http://www.apple.com/quicktime/streamingserver.

- *Relay Name*: A name for the relay

- *Relay Type*: The type of relay

- *Request Incoming Stream*: Use to relay live broadcasts from another server (perhaps one using Announced UDP with QuickTime Broadcaster) or request stored files to convert to outgoing live stream.

- *Unannounced UDP*: Use to relay streams on static IP addresses.

- *Announced UDP*: Use for QuickTime Broadcaster or other streaming encoders that support RTSP.

- *Source IP*: Name or IP of the host running the initial streams

- *Path*: Path on the host to the stream

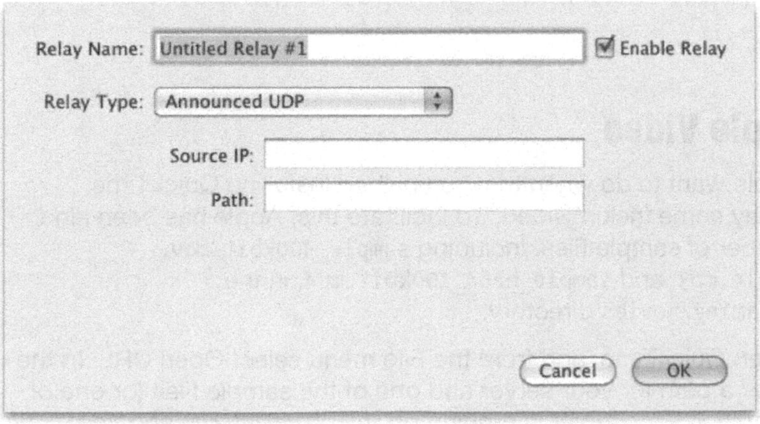

Figure 17–5. *Configuring a relay*

Finally, click the Logging tab. Here, you can enable error logging and access logs as well as customize the number of days that logs will be stored prior to being moved to archives, as you can see in Figure 17–6. Once you have configured all the settings to your satisfaction, click the Save button in the bottom-right corner of the screen, and then click the Start QuickTime Streaming icon to start the service. Provided that the service indicator light turns green, you have finished the initial configuration of the server and can move on to testing.

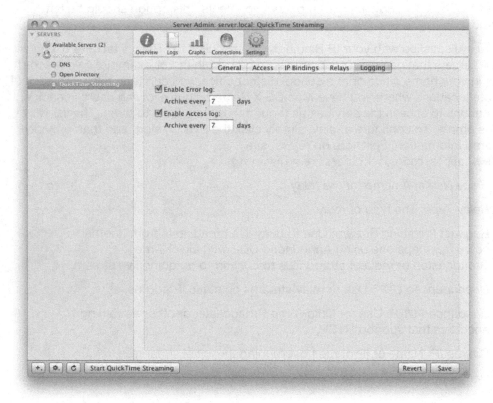

Figure 17–6. *Logging options*

Playing the Sample Video

The first thing most people want to do when they're finished installing QuickTime Streaming Server is to play some frickin' video. To facilitate this, Apple has been kind enough to include a number of sample files, including `sample_300kbit.mov`, `sample_50kbit.3gp`, `sample.mp3`, and `sample_h264_100kbit.mp4`, in the `/Library/QuickTimeStreaming/Movies` directory.

To play video, simply open QuickTime, and from the File menu select Open URL. In the resultant dialog box, enter a path for your server and one of the sample files (or one of your own files). For example, if your server is running on `www.krypted.com` and you wanted to look at the `sample_h264_100kbit.mp4`, then the path you would enter into the

URL would be `rtsp://www.krypted.com/sample_h264_100kbit.mp4`. You can also open multiple files to get an idea of the quality of each one and play them in QuickTime windows side by side, as shown in Figure 17–7. This can really help you get a perspective on the differences between the video types that were discussed in the section "Bandwidth Considerations."

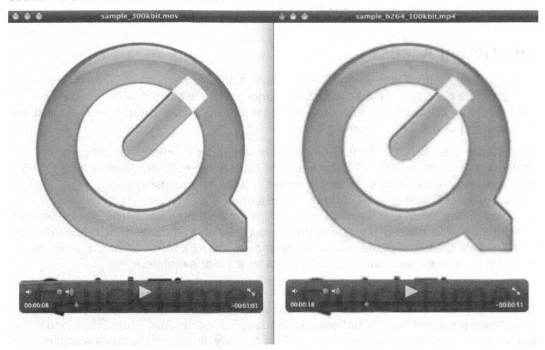

Figure 17–7. *Viewing files*

> **NOTE:** If you have customized the location of the media directory, then you will want to copy the sample files from the `/Library/QuickTimeStreaming/Movies` directory if you want to test with them.

Setting Up Home Directory Use

You may simply be looking to allow users to stream content to one another on your network. In these environments, the user is able to place hinted movie files (*hint tracks* specify how to package media for the network) in their own home directory, and the QuickTime Streaming Server will automatically share the files, making them accessible via RTSP for other users.

If you enabled the "Enable home directory streaming" option in the "Configuring QuickTime Streaming Server" section of this chapter, then users with home directories on the server (that is, Network Home folders, described further in Chapter 4) can place hinted QuickTime movies in the `/Sites/Streaming` folder that is in their home folder.

These can then be viewed using their private movie directory. For example, if a file called Emerald was placed into the /Users/cedge/Sites/Streaming directory on a server called video.krypted.com and the /Users/cedge directory was a user's home folder, then with this option a client could access that data by entering the following string in a browser (assuming authentication was not required to access the stream): **rtsp://video.krypted.com/~cedge/Emerald.mov**.

Restricting Access

One of the key elements to using RTSP to share data is to keep other users from easily capturing the content. One way to further restrict access is to control who can view it in the first place. The best way to control access is to password protect the assets that are shared using QuickTime Streaming Server.

Password protecting QuickTime Streaming Server is a bit different from password protecting most other Mac OS X services. For starters, you should define a local QTSS users file and a local groups file for the server. You can do so using /Library/QuickTimeStreaming/Config/qtusers and /Library/QuickTimeStreaming/Config/qtgroups, respectively. Each user can be defined in the qtusers file, and each group in the qtgroups file should contain the pertinent users on a line with the name of the group, followed by a colon (:), followed by the users who make up the group, with each separated by a space. For example:

```
AuthUsers:cedge cbarker eschwiebert
```

To password protect a stream served by Quick Time Streaming Server, you will then need to create a text file that defines an AuthUserFile and an AuthGroupFile, along with the required user and group permissions. This actually allows you to store your files outside the Config directory, which we don't really recommend. The file will need to specify an AuthName, which you can use to define a realm of "QTSS," a AuthUserFile (the URI to the qtusers file), the AuthGroupFile (the path to the qtgroups file), and require statements for users and groups. It sounds complicated, but it's just something similar to the following:

```
AuthName "QTSS"
AuthUserFile /Library/QuickTimeStreaming/Config/Users/qtusers
AuthGroupFile /Library/QuickTimeStreaming/Config/Users/qtgroups
require user viewer
require group viewer
```

The previous would require one of the passwords in order to open a stream. As of 10.5, you can also integrate streams with Open Directory (OD), using the users and groups from OD to tap into streams. In versions of the operating system subsequent to 10.5, you might have to go to a 10.5 box to get a copy of the template qtusers and qtgroups files because they might not be present by default.

Creating Movies

When you want to publish a movie in QuickTime Streaming Server, there are a few key aspects to those videos that you want to make sure to have taken care of. The first is the speed of the video, which is determined by the number of frames per second and the resolution of the video. Speeds are covered earlier in this chapter (see "Bandwidth Considerations"). In addition to speeds, you would need to hint each movie that will be served and then determine how end users will access them—either through an embedded RTSP stream in a web page or through using an RTSP-based URL to access them through QuickTime.

Adding a Hint Track to Movies

Hinting movies is similar to placing chapter markers in a DVD. Movies that will be streamed with QuickTime Streaming Server will need to be hinted. *Hinting* a movie means that you create a hint track for each streamable media track. The hint tracks tell the server (hint being for the server in this case) how to serve the QuickTime movie over the network. A number of applications can produce hinted movies including QuickTime Pro and iMovie, which is built into Mac OS X.

To hint a movie using iMovie, open the movie that you want to hint, click the Share menu, and then select Export Using QuickTime. In the Movie Settings dialog box (which you can see in Figure 17–8), you will notice the option toward the bottom of the screen under Prepare for Internet Streaming. Use the drop-down menu to select Hinted Streaming.

Each environment is different, and you can use a myriad of settings when preparing a movie for Internet sharing. If you click the Settings button, then you will get a glimpse into some of these settings. Here, as you may notice in Figure 17–9, you will want to leave the movie self-contained, or the server will not be able to serve them. You will, though, be able to customize the Optimize Hints for Server options, which will create a larger self-contained QuickTime file but which will perform better on the server.

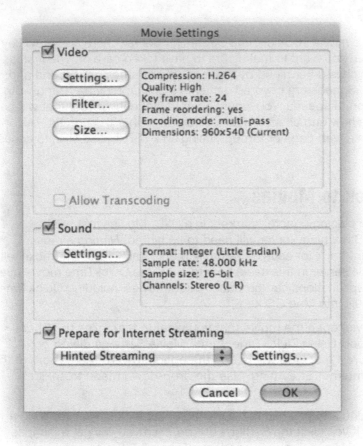

Figure 17–8. *The Movie Settings dialog box in iMovie*

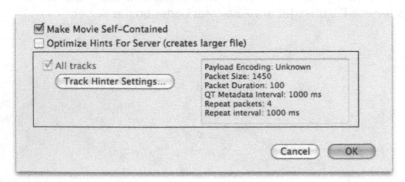

Figure 17–9. *Hinting tracks*

You can continue to get more granular with how you structure packets by clicking the Track Hinter Settings button, which opens the RTP Track Settings dialog box shown in Figure 17–10. Here, you can choose encoding options and packet options, although in most cases there is no need to customize any of these settings. Having said that, if you look at the MTU size for your network firewall (or the lowest common denominator between your firewall, switch, and server), then you can set that as the Packet Size Limit setting, which can help optimize the amount of data shoved into each packet and therefore network and video performance.

> **NOTE:** Check with your network administrator for the MTU size of your network firewall.

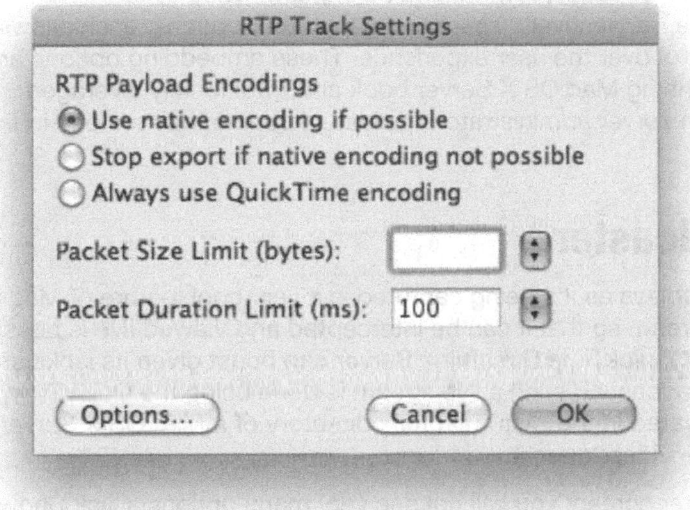

Figure 17–10. *RTP Track Settings dialog box*

Accessing Video Through a Browser

When you place a video into the media directory (by default this is set to /Library/QuickTimeStreaming/Movies), you can then access it using RTSP. To access video, you can simply call it in a web browser, in QuickTime, or by embedding a link into a web page. This link will start with rtsp (which defines the protocol), followed by the traditional URL identifier of ://, followed by the name of the server and finally the name of the file. For example, if you have a server called qtss.krypted.com and you place a file called Emerald.mov there, then the path to access that file would be rtsp://qtss.krypted.com/Emerald.mov.

> **NOTE:** Although you can enter a URL for a QuickTime movie into the address bar of Safari or your favorite browser, the movie will still open in QuickTime.

You can also embed video into a web page using JavaScript. Simply placing a video file into a web page is fairly straightforward, but in addition, Apple provides a number of options for embedding video that allow the video to appear or be controlled in different manners, thus customizing the end user experience. To get started with embedding video into your web pages, check out the Apple tutorials for doing so at http://www.apple.com/quicktime/tutorials/embed.html.

Toward the bottom of that page you'll notice the embed tags, which include items such as volume, starttime, controller, and autoplay. These can control the volume of the movie, where in the movie you start playing control, whether you give the end user a controller (used for fast-forward, pause, rewind, and so on), and whether to automatically start the movie, respectively. There are many other options, each allowing for even more granular control over the user experience. These embedding options are beyond the scope of a beginning Mac OS X Server book and traditionally leveraged more by web designers than server administrators (unless of course they are one in the same).

QuickTime Broadcaster

Streaming data so that it displays as it's being captured is a very cool feature of Mac OS X Server. Casting a video stream so that it can be intercepted and viewed live is possibly one of the best features that QuickTime Streaming Server can boast given its lackluster development as of late. Broadcasting such a live stream is done using the QuickTime Broadcaster application, located in the /Applications directory of a Mac OS X Server. To get started streaming live video, open it.

At the QuickTime Broadcaster screen, you will not see very many options. Click Show Details in the lower-right corner of the screen to see a number of the options you likely thought you'd have, as shown in Figure 17–11. Here, you'll see options for choosing the camera to use (selecting no camera will do a live audio-only broadcast), the audio input to use, network compression codecs, and frames per second, the filename, and a variety of other settings, including customizing packet sizes. But in the beginning, you can just use the audio, video, and network settings to get broadcasting quickly.

Once your broadcast is configured as you want, click the Broadcast button. Now you should be broadcasting. Go to your first client system, and open QuickTime. From here, click the File menu, and select the Open URL option. At the resultant dialog box, type **rtsp** followed by **://**, followed by the name of the server and then the name of the file you provided in the Network options in QuickTime Broadcaster (or mystream.sdp if you did not customize this setting), as shown in Figure 17–12. Click OK, and QuickTime should begin playing the stream as you see it in QuickTime Broadcaster. If you are going to watch yourself streaming, turn down your speakers to avoid feedback.

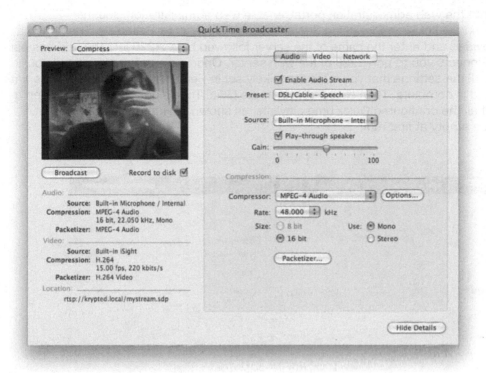

Figure 17-11. *QuickTime Broadcaster*

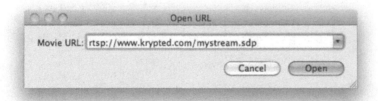

Figure 17-12. *Viewing broadcasts*

Finally, once you've had a chance to do a little testing, you can go back into the QuickTimeBroadcaster application and further refine and tune your streaming options.

Streaming Playlists

Almost any task that can be done for QuickTime Streaming Server through the web administration portal can be done through Server Admin. However, if you want to get started streaming looped MP3 tracks, you'll more than likely need to use the web administration tool.

To log into the web administration portal, enable web administration (see the "Configuring QuickTime Streaming Server" section earlier in this chapter). Then open a web browser, and enter the name of the server followed by a **:1220** into the address bar, which connects you to port 1220 of the web server. Once open, a wizard will run you through all the settings that you more than likely set in Server Admin; click Continue until the wizard is complete. Then click Playlists in the QuickTime sidebar, which will open a listing of all the configured QuickTime playlists, as shown in Figure 17–13 (a list that should be empty at first run).

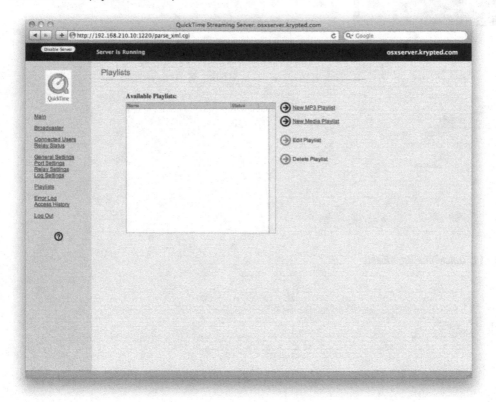

Figure 17–13. New QuickTime playlists

You will then click New MP3 Playlist or New Media Playlist. New MP3 Playlist will allow only audio files, whereas New Media Playlist will allow for any QuickTime files or Advanced Audio Coding (AAC) files to be streamed. Provide a name for the playlist, as you can see in Figure 17–14, and then provide the media files in the media directory.

Now that you have created your playlist, you'll likely want to watch or listen to it. To do so, open a web browser, and point it at the location of your server followed by a **:8000** (again, the colon defines the port number) and then the name of the playlist. For example, if your playlist is called *presentations* and your server is qtss.krypted.com, you would type the following URL: **http://rtsp.krypted.com:8000/presentations**.

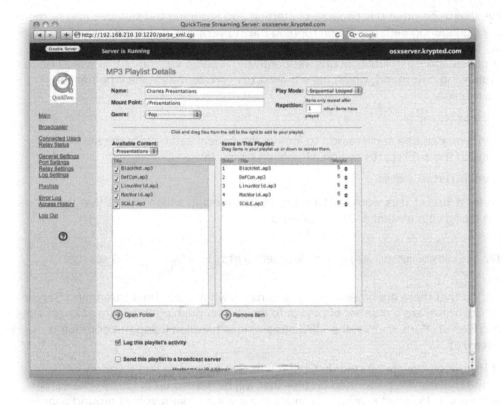

Figure 17–14. *Configuring the playlist*

> **NOTE:** You can also enter the same URL in iTunes to play streams there by using the Open Audio Stream option under the Advanced menu.

Using the Command Line

The command-line options for QuickTime Streaming services are fairly rudimentary compared to some of the other services in Mac OS X Server. However, you can also configure the QuickTime Streaming Server from the command line. Like many of the other services in Mac OS X Server, some of the underlying components are open source and therefore can be configured to go make you a pot of coffee (http://www.ietf.org/rfc/rfc2324.txt) if you're that good at such things (programming, not making coffee). Unlike many of the other services in Mac OS X Server, the underlying components are made open source by projects by Apple called Darwin Streaming Server. You can learn more about Darwin Streaming Server at http://dss.macosforge.org.

The serveradmin command is capable of starting and stopping the services and of more granularly configuring settings. When running the serveradmin command, you will use the proxy and notification options to specify the service that you are working with as Mobile Access and Push Notifications, respectively. A basic version of this would be to use the following command, which uses the status verb to determine whether the service is running:

```
serveradmin status qtss
```

In addition, you can use serveradmin to look at the critical settings for the service by running it with the fullstatus option. Here's an example:

```
serveradmin fullstatus qtss
```

Querying for a fullstatus would net a more verbose result, which shows that the server is running along with a number of critical settings.

> **NOTE:** You can also just run the serveradmin setting qtss for a full listing of all settings.

You may find that there are times when you surpass what QuickTime Streaming Server itself can do. There are a number of places to look when pushing the limits of QuickTime Streaming Server. For example, the MP3 streaming is handled using the command mp3broadcaster.

Podcast Producer, covered further in Chapter 16, is a source to find a variety of automations that can be performed on files that will be served up in QuickTime Streaming Server. Podcast Producer is more of a solution that revolves around allowing users to download *and* view content. Podcast Producer also gives you the ability to place a file in a directory. Provided this directory is the media directory (by default set to /Library/QuickTimeStreaming/Movies), then you will be able to perform a whole host of automations shuffling data between Podcast Producer, Final Cut Server, and QuickTime Streaming Server, as needed.

Summary

QuickTime Streaming Server hasn't changed much in the past seven years. But that could be attributed to the fact that it doesn't need to change that much. QuickTime Streaming Server provides a number of options for providing streams of content. Content can be streamed live, played over files that can be cached to the client, protected, and played using files that can't be cached to the client and compressed in a number of ways. QuickTime streaming can also be a final destination for content generated using the Podcast Producer service, which is described in Chapter 16.

In this chapter, we covered many of the use cases for QuickTime Streaming Server and how to implement them. This completes our look at the various content generation and cataloging that can be done in Mac OS X Server. Next, we'll cover some of the more finely grained controls in file sharing in Chapter 18, looking at AFP and SMB.

Sharing Files

We covered file sharing a bit in Chapter 2, but that was just walking you through the steps to create a single share to be accessed solely by Macs in your own office. Mac OS X Server allows you to create multiple share points, with varying levels of access and the ability to communicate with just about every client computer in a network or Internet environment.

In this chapter, we will cover the four protocols that allow you to share files under OS X Server. These four protocols consist of Apple Filing Protocol (AFP), which is Apple's native file sharing protocol; Server Message Block (SMB), which is a file protocol with origins at IBM but is the most commonly used protocol for Windows networks (it also goes by the name CIFS); Network Filesystem (NFS), which is commonly found in Unix environments, because it allows near seamless integration at the filesystem level between folders stored on local disks and folders/files accessed over the network; and File Transfer Protocol (FTP), which is one of the most common ways to send files across the Internet. In terms of sharing protocols, FTP is one of the most loosely defined, because it meant more for sending and receiving files, not actively working off a remote volume mounted with FTP (there are utilities that allow you to edit files over FTP, but those work by caching the file locally and then uploading it when you save).

Configuration

The first step to setting up the NFS, SMB, AFP, or FTP services is to show the service in Server Admin. To do so, first open Server Admin from /Applications/Server. After authenticating, click the name of the server where you will be installing the service onto, and open the server's base settings. Here, click the Settings icon in the toolbar to open the services selection screen, where you can configure which services will run on the server (although simply enabling them in this screen will not start them), as shown in Figure 18–1.

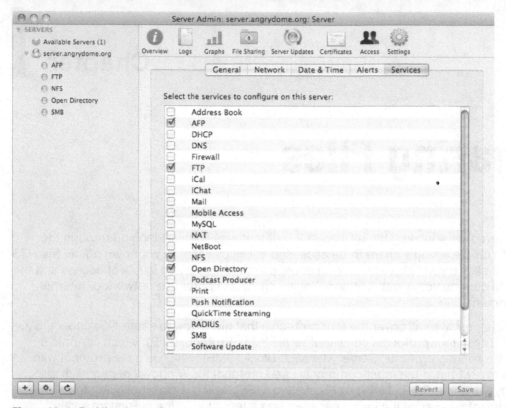

Figure 18–1. *Enabling the services*

Select the box for the appropriate service (AFP, SMB, NFS, and FTP), and then click the Save button. You should then see the service appear in the SERVERS list when you click the disclosure triangle to show the active services on the server. Click the Settings icon in the Server Admin toolbar to open the settings that Apple has provided for that service.

AFP

The Apple Filing Protocol is loved and hated by Mac admins. On one level, it has a ton of features and services that you still can't find in something such as SMB (such as resource forks and complex filesystem metadata), but it also has some drawbacks (such as you can have only a single authenticated session per computer, so you can't connect to the same server as two different users at the same time). For the most part, it is one of the simplest protocols to work with when it comes to configuration, and it will "just work" as a logical extension of the local filesystem with Mac OS X applications. In Snow Leopard, Apple has revised AFP to version 3.3.

Configuring AFP

The Apple Filing Protocol has only a few options, because for the most part it tries to be autotuning. It is still good to understand what those options are and how to best use them in your network, especially when it comes to troubleshooting and securing your environment.

The first screen you will see on the Settings tab is the area for creating the login greeting. Here you can enter your company-appropriate usage policy, and by selecting "Show this message only once per user," you will send it to users only the very first time they connect to this server. It is useful, but in many cases we have never configured the welcome screen at all and just gone on to the next tab, Access. See Figure 18–2 for the AFP Access screen.

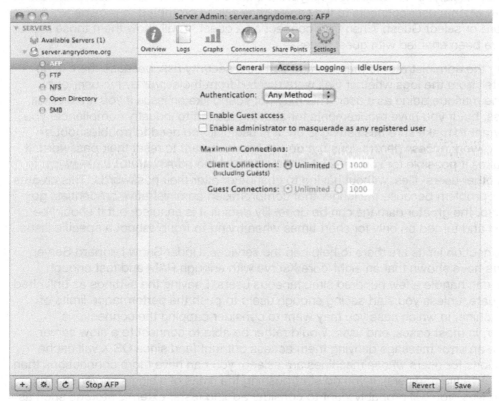

Figure 18–2. *AFP Access tab*

On the Access tab, you have a few more options. For authentication, you can pick between Any Method, Standard, and Kerberos. Any Method will allow a user to authenticate with a Kerberos ticket if they have it. And if their client is configured for Kerberos but does not have a Ticket Granting Ticket (TGT), the users will be prompted to get one when they connect. But if they don't, it will allow them to log in directly, using the less secure Standard method. By selecting Kerberos only, you are ensuring that only users who properly have a more secure Kerberos ticket are able to connect to the server; this will require more administrative oversight, because as discussed earlier, Kerberos is a complicated service, and some users may not understand why they can't log into their primary work server when their password is fine (but maybe their clock is out of sync). Standard authentication is just that; it uses a method that has no external verification, so it is technically not as secure as Kerberos (Kerberos also provides single sign-on access for workstations that are joined to your directory system). However, it is a fairly secure authentication method, and it's acceptable to configure if you want to have a fallback in cases when Kerberos is not an option (such as you have mobile users who have Kerberos access while in the office but not while remotely connecting over the VPN). Of those options, leaving it to Any Method is adequate in most circumstances.

Enable Guest Access does exactly that. This does not allow guests to connect to your server specifically, but it does allow for you to enable shares with guest access on them, and then when a user connects to the server, they will be prompted to provide a password or select Guest. When they connect as a guest, it will show them those shares that have been enabled with guest access.

Allowing the administrator to masquerade can be a security risk, because there is no way to tell from the logs whether files were deleted from the server by the user or by someone masquerading as a user. This may not sound like an issue if you are a small business, but if you have requirements for auditing related to industry compliance, you would want to make sure this setting is off. It is useful if you need to troubleshoot a user's network access permissions but do not know or want to reset their password. It also makes it possible for someone who has acquired the administrator's password to access other users' files, without having to change or alter their passwords. This creates a bigger problem because the longer that compromised administrative credentials go unnoticed, the greater damage can be done. By default it is enabled, but it should be disabled and turned on only for short times when trying to troubleshoot a specific issue.

The connection limits are there to help cap the services. Under Snow Leopard Server, the limits have shown that an eight-core Xserve with enough RAM and fast enough storage can handle a few hundred simultaneous users. Leaving the settings as unlimited is adequate, unless you start seeing enough users to push the performance limits of your machine, in which case you may want to consider capping the connections. However, in most cases, end users would rather be able to connect to a slow server than see an error message denying them access outright (and since OS X will cache connections for users whose machines are asleep, you can have more connections than actual active file transfers). If you do start pushing the limits of a single server sharing out your files, you will probably want to consider adding faster external storage such as a Promise RAID, adding more RAM, or moving one or two of the shares to another dedicated server in order to get faster access to each share (which is another reason for directory services—you don't have to re-create user accounts on the second server if it is tied into the directory services).

Moving on to Logging, you will see that the tab is fairly self-explanatory. The big thing to note is that in the AFP logging world, actions are logged by IP address, not by user. So although it is possible to correlate actions with a specific user (and this is one of the biggest reasons why you should always use individual user logins), you will have to do so by first finding the username of the person to last connect from that IP. A quick way of doing so is using the Console application (in /Applications/Utilities), finding the entry you are looking for (such as the name of a file that was deleted), and then filtering the view by that correlated IP address. Figure 18–3 shows the logging configuration pane.

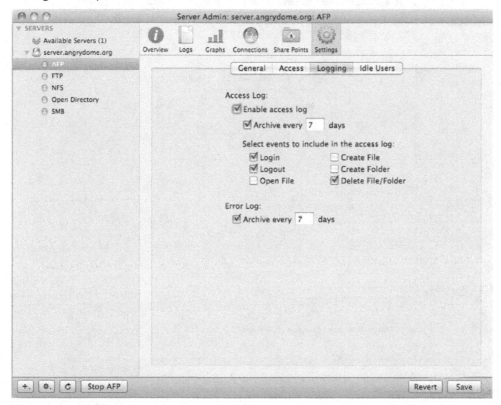

Figure 18–3. *Logging settings*

For Idle Users, shown in Figure 18–4, you can allow them to keep their AFP session key cached, which means they will be able to reconnect automatically if their workstation goes to sleep and reawakens in the set time frame. Another option is to disconnect idle users; if you are in an environment where server performance is critical, you may want to minimize the amount of passive, idling connections. In most environments, it is common practice for users to mount all their network shares the first thing in the morning and sometimes never access any files from them. This is in theory done because they can log into those shares all at once, but if you are using Kerberos, which gives them a login ticket when they log into their desktop in the morning, you may be able to get away with using aliases and entries in the users' Docks that reference these shares and then connecting only when the user actually needs to retrieve their files. If that is the workflow you want to enforce, you will want to enable it so that users who have tried to log in during the morning will be disconnected if they truly aren't using the network share for anything. You don't have to worry about them losing open documents, because the server will allow you to toggle those options and have it check to see whether they have a Word document open while they went to lunch before unmounting the share, for example. Below the idle options, you can specify what message the user will see when they are automatically disconnected.

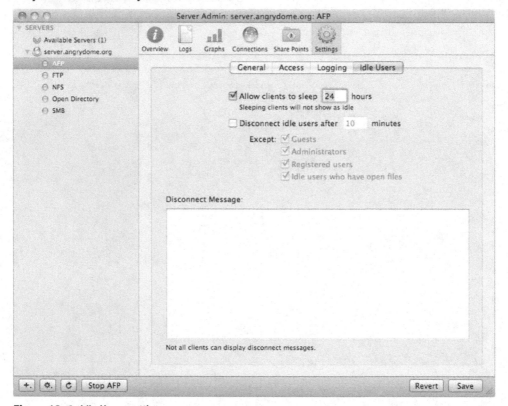

Figure 18–4. *Idle Users settings*

Connecting to AFP from Mac OS X

By default, a 10.6 client will show the available network servers that it can see in the local subnet on the left side of any Finder window. When you select the server, you can then connect and see all the share points available to connect to. It will not actually mount those share points until you select them. However, there is another method that is more akin to Apple's pre-Leopard ways of connecting to fileservers, which some find faster.

By selecting Connect to Servers from the Go menu, you are able to specify the domain name or IP address of the server you want to mount, and if you already know the share name, you can put that in as well. In fact, if you know the subfolder you want to open, you can also add that. The final entry you can use would look something like afp://server.angrydome.org/Users/ladmin/Desktop, which would mount the share Users on server.angrydome.org and then open the subfolder ladmin/Desktop. If you are just connecting to an AFP server and want to see a list of all the shares available to your user account, you can just put the server IP or FQDN in the To field, with no afp://, because it is assumed. Figure 18–5 shows the Connect to Server dialog box.

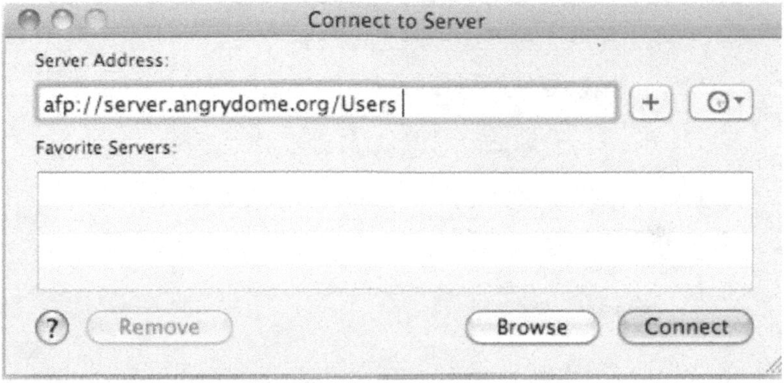

Figure 18–5. *Connect To Server dialog box*

SMB

The common mode of file access for Windows-based clients is using SMB. In the case of OS X, SMB file access is provided using the open source package of utilities called Samba. If you have any Windows machines that you want to provide access to, this is the service you will want to enable to make it possible.

Configure SMB

Once you have enabled SMB, you will want to start the configuration process. If you want to just allow a few Windows machines access to share points you have enabled using SMB, the default settings should be adequate. Figure 18–6 shows the initial settings window for the SMB service.

The role definition for the server in SMB determines how the server will act in accordance to other servers and other Windows clients. The options presented look like those of the Open Directory service, and in fact you could use your OS X Server to provide Open Directory–like unified logins and management to Windows clients. There are some limitations; managed settings and group policies are not easily implemented with an out-of-the-box Mac OS X server, and if your organization has a significant number of Windows clients, you will probably get more benefit from using a Microsoft Active Directory configuration and nesting the OS X Server/Open Directory inside of that to provide those Mac-specific services (such integration is covered in more depth in Chapter 4).

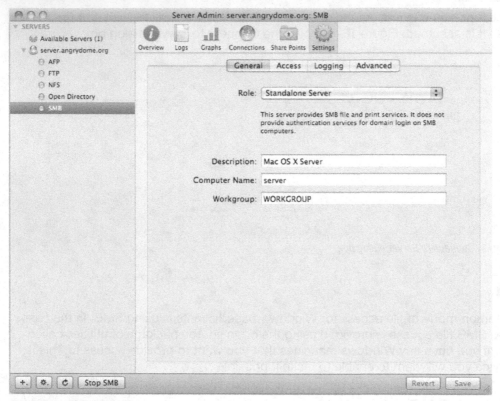

Figure 18–6. *SMB settings*

- *Standalone Server*: For a stand-alone server. Just as in Open Directory, clients can connect to the server and access files; they will be prompted for their password each time they connect (or their client machine can store that password for future use).

- *Domain Member*: For when your server is connected to an Open Directory or Active Directory server; it allows for Kerberos and other directory service–related connections to work, without the server acting as a replica or master for that domain.

- *Backup and Primary Domain Controllers*: For domain controllers, which are roles where the server acts as the replica/master for SMB-based directory service. If you were to configure your server as an Open Directory master and wanted to have shared logins for your Windows users, you would also configure SMB to be the primary domain controller. If you had an Open Directory replica on your network, you would then configure that replica as a backup domain controller.

If your server is bound to Active Directory, it will have already preconfigured some of the SMB options to match the Active Directory environment for you. Fields such as Computer Name and Workgroup will be prepopulated with information used in the bind process. Don't be alarmed that you can't change this information. If you were able to, you could lose connectivity to Active Directory.

If you are just configuring your server to allow a handful of Windows desktops to access the files stored on the server, Standalone Server is the simplest option, because it allows users to authenticate to the server with a username and a password and see file shares. If you want to automate some of the connections and possibly do more advanced integration (such as tying into your company's Active Directory infrastructure), that is what connected to a domain implies. This option would already be configured if you have previously bound the server to Active Directory.

The Access panel is where you set the types of passwords that your server will accept from clients when they connect. Again, the defaults are adequate, except in some cases where you have older clients, which would require you to enable the most basic, NTLM, authentication method.

NOTE: If you are using Windows 7, Vista, or Server 2008 machines in your environment, you will want to enable NTLM authentication negotiation on those machines, or else they will not able to log into your OS X server.

While configuring the logging settings for the server, keep in mind that the High setting for the log file also means the biggest in terms of file size. It will track and record all the network traffic related to SMB that is on your network, even if it is not directly related to your server. If an administrator leaves the log level on High to troubleshoot an issue, they may find out two weeks later that the boot drive of the server had become full, making the server nonresponsive. If you aren't specifically troubleshooting SMB (or have taken steps to modify the configuration files by hand to relocate the logs), try to keep the log settings at Medium or Low.

SMB has a few advanced options available in the SMB user interface. The following is a quick overview of what some of these options are and why you might need to change them. In most cases, you can leave the defaults alone unless you start running into problems.

- The code page is the character set that the server uses to communicate with clients (unlike AFP, which supports Unicode, so filenames with any character can be used).

- For services, having either checked will enroll your server in the election process to determine what machine is providing name resolution to clients at any one time (a shared dynamic system, almost like Bonjour in some ways).

- If you are running as a primary or backup domain controller, Domain Master Browser is mandatory. The WINS server is used so clients can again determine what your machine's IP address is from the NetBIOS name.

- If you need support for share names with longer characters or are seeing log entries about SMB not being able to find a server name that is similar to but not the same as a share you have configured (for example, it can't find *thisisashar* when you have a share named *thisisashare*), you will want to check that you have WINS set to register with your domain controller, or you should enable WINS server on your machine.

- The Virtual Sharepoints option is used to present SMB users with their home folder (if it has been configured, just as it would show up for a Mac user). This will be enabled by default if your machine is connected to a domain or directory service (or is running one itself).

The SMB Configuration File

SMB is the result of the Samba open source project. As a result, you can find multiple resources online to explain how to do more advanced configurations outside of what Apple has configured for you. You can edit some of those settings by hand in the /etc/smb.conf file. It is suggested you always make a backup of this file before doing any editing and that you have the SMB service disabled before editing the live file. Once you have saved the file, you can start the SMB service backup and verify that your settings are what you wanted. There is a file referenced in the .conf file at /var/db/smb.conf, which is an autogenerated file that synchronizes other system-wide settings (host name, share points) with the SMB instance.

> **NOTE:** The scripts that perform these synchronizations are stored in /usr/libexec/samba, in case you are interested in digging around more.

The primary reason for working in the /etc/smb.conf file as of the writing of this book is to ensure compatibility with SMB shares hosted on an Xsan volume. To ensure that permissions are respected and that users can connect, you will want to change the Darwin streams and support options to no.

SMB as a Domain Controller for Windows

If you want single sign-on functionality for your Windows clients in your office, you will want to enable one of your Open Directory master or replicas as a domain controller for your office. By configuring your OS X Server to act as a domain controller, you will now also be publishing and broadcasting your Open Directory infrastructure over the SMB system to Windows machines. This means that features such as login scripts determined in Workgroup Manager on the SMB tab will be executed by clients as they log in. Also, this saves you the task of having to manage and create accounts individually on each workstation. Instead, each workstation that is joined to the domain will allow any user in your Open Directory system to log into the workstation. If this unified login is not enough of a solution for your Windows users, you may want to investigate using an Active Directory system instead, which provides much more granular controls for Windows machines.

WINS

In the beginning there was NetBIOS, and it was adequate. And then TCP/IP matured, Ethernet became more popular (and cheaper), and managing multiple servers and services in a network environment became more complicated. NetBIOS allowed for the easy mapping of logical names (Bob's computer) to actual devices (Dell computer connected to port 17 of the switch with this IP address); however, the protocol was limited and made it difficult to scale. WINS was created to allow NetBIOS information to be stored in a central directory, similar to DNS, allowing for easier management. An important aspect of understanding the WINS system is that it allows service names longer than 15 characters and makes looking up services faster for clients, because they can register their own services with a central server and look up others more quickly.

Part of ensuring your clients are using WINS correctly is to make sure that your network's DHCP server is providing a proper WINS server that they can check into. By default, Windows machines (and OS X machines looking for WINS-based services) will look at the DHCP packet (for options 44 and 46 specifically) for that IP address. If your DHCP server does not support WINS or you cannot control those options, you can override those settings in your Windows clients' network interface configuration settings. Using `ipconfig getpacket en0` or `en1` (for Ethernet or wireless, respectively) will show you what WINS IP address is being propagated on your network, if one is at all. The DHCP server that is built into Mac OS X Server includes a WINS option, so you can also broadcast that information there if need be.

For your servers, if you are running your server as a domain controller with the master browser, it would make sense to also have your servers configured as the primary WINS server. For other machines on your network, you will want to specify "register this server with" and enter the IP address of your primary machine.

Samba Clients

Now that you've set up a server, you'll want to move on to setting up the client. Because not everyone is lucky enough to have a Mac on their desk, we will cover how to set up the client on the major platforms.

Connecting to SMB from Other Unix and Linux Clients

The SMB service used by OS X (server and client) is provided by the open source project Samba, and it is commonly used under Linux, but there are many different ways and techniques for attaching to an SMB share from various Linux distributions depending on what your intended goal is. In recent years, it has become as simple as entering **smb://servername/sharename** in your Linux window manager, with the rest being taken care of for you. Covering all those variances is beyond the scope of this book, but if you are interested in doing more things with SMB anyway, plenty of resources are available on the Internet, especially related to the SMB connection options for Linux clients; in that case, try Samba.org. We will discuss how to connect to the shares for Mac and Windows users.

Connecting to SMB with Windows

For a one-time connection, you can use Start ➤ Run and then enter the server name and share name, as in **\\servername\share**. Doing so will open a window asking you to authenticate (unless your OS X server and your Windows client are part of the same domain), and then you can mount and access the share.

If you want a more static mount, you can use the option to add a network location from your Computer/My Computer view in Windows. From there it will launch a wizard that will walk you through the steps to map a drive letter to your OS X Server. Remember that the slash (/) you are familiar with from OS X will need to be switched to \.

Connecting to SMB from Mac OS X

You will also want to connect to your SMB server from the Mac client, just so you can test its accessibility without having to use a Windows client (however, it should be noted that you will want to test from a Windows machine at some point also, because settings that affect a Windows client using SMB may not become apparent to a Mac client).

From the Go menu, select Connect to Server. For URL, just use `smb://` instead of `afp://` and then the server host name. You will then be prompted by a dialog box to authenticate. Once authenticated, you will see the shares you are authorized to mount and be able to selectively mount them.

FTP

FTP is a common method for transferring documents over the Internet. Every modern operating system includes an FTP client of some sort, making it easy to provide access to files to any client or user. However, FTP is a basic protocol, and for most practical purposes it should be used for delivering or receiving files, and not as some continual working environment that would be an active workspace (like AFP or SMB, which allows for you to actively edit and change documents stored on the shares). Common uses for FTP are for the final delivery of files to a print house for publishing or for a drop space for customers to send large documents that may not be easy to send over e-mail.

The important part to remember is that although FTP can be configured with a share point just as AFP and SMB can be configured, you should not consider it to be in the same class of file access and security as those options. Just because you configured a share to be accessed for AFP does not mean you should configure it for FTP access as well.

Security Concerns with FTP

Since FTP is a ubiquitous and old protocol, it has some limitations to how secure it can be made. In most environments, there is no security at all, and usernames, passwords, and files are transferred in the clear, making it possible for anyone to gain access to your FTP accounts if they are listening. There has been some movement to create more secure implementations of FTP, some of which includes wrapping FTP with SSL, the same way websites are secured by wrapping HTTP with SSL. However, not all clients support SSL, which can add to the troubleshooting and management overhead for FTP, especially if you are using it as a drop point for your customers or other third parties to retrieve files from your server.

One common practice for FTP accounts is to create a dedicated set of users, with very limited access, which are then configured to be just FTP accounts. This lets you isolate the FTP accounts from compromising the rest of your file access. In an implementation such as this, you would have specific folders configured as the only space that the FTP accounts can access, and then you'd map an AFP/SMB share to the same location, granting permission for more secure access by those who are part of your office. That way, it is easy for an office user to move files to the FTP space (they just mount the folder over the more secure AFP protocol), while preventing a compromised FTP account from opening access to your entire server.

Anonymous FTP access is almost never a good idea, and many hackers actively scan the Internet looking for FTP servers that grant it, because they can use those spaces as hidden caches to store files to be distributed to other people. As a result, if you enable anonymous FTP, you may find your Internet connection takes a large performance hit as you become an unsuspecting movie-sharing server.

Welcome Messages

Adjusted on the Messages tab of the FTP service settings, the welcome messages are a holdover from the time of command-line FTP. The first message that will greet users as they try to connect to your server is the banner message, which is displayed before the user is prompted for authentication (if their FTP client is configured to do so). After they successfully log in, the welcome message will greet them. The banner message is a good place to put simple information about the server, if you want to identify it at all; some companies choose to suppress the message entirely so they aren't advertising to anyone scanning the network what type of FTP server it is. Keep in mind that these messages will be sent every time a user connects, so you should keep them succinct and concise; in some cases, the clients will never see them because they have the console window closed. Also, if the message is too long (you've included your company's entire acceptable usage policy), it can cause problems some clients. You can see what a successful command-line FTP login looks like in Figure 18–7.

```
server:~ ladmin$ ftp server.angrydome.org
Connected to server.angrydome.org.
220------------------------------------------------------------------------
220-This is the "Banner" message for the Mac OS X Server's FTP server process.
220-
220-            FTP clients will receive this message immediately
220-            before being prompted for a name and password.
220-
220-PLEASE NOTE:
220-
220-      Some FTP clients may exhibit problems if you make this file too long.
220-
220------------------------------------------------------------------------
220-
220 server.angrydome.org FTP server ready.
Name (server.angrydome.org:ladmin): bender
331 Password required for bender.
Password:
230------------------------------------------------------------------------
230-This is the "Welcome" message for the Mac OS X Server's FTP server process.
230-
230-FTP clients will receive this message right after a successful log in.
230-
230------------------------------------------------------------------------
230-
230 User bender logged in.
Remote system type is UNIX.
Using binary mode to transfer files.
ftp>
```

Figure 18–7. *Successful login from the command line, with default banner and welcome messages*

FTP Roots and Presenting Data to Users

The FTP root is starting point (or the base) of the filesystem as it will appear to FTP clients. By default it is the folder located inside /Library/FTPServer/FTPRoot. OS X Server will populate that folder with symbolic links to share points that are configured for FTP access in their sharing properties. In a way, it acts as the share point selection screen that you see when you connect to a server over AFP or SMB (or browse to it in the Finder); from there you can navigate to all the configured share points that you have access to as a user logged in over FTP. The root itself can also contain files if you want to modify the permissions to allow users, but we choose to leave it be, so it acts simply as a place to navigate to other folders easily.

There are three options for what an authenticated user will see when they connect to the FTP server. They are not entirely clear from the wording, so here's an explanation:

- *FTP Root with Share Points*: This is the aforementioned FTP root folder, and when a user connects, they will see all the folders configured on the server that have the FTP Protocol option enabled. If the user's account is configured with a home folder (such as in the Workgroup Manager on the Home tab), the user will by default start in their configured home first. The home has to be in a folder configured as an FTP-accessible share point as well, or else the FTP server will not be able to access it, and the user will end up in the FTP root. To access other share points, the user will have to navigate through the parent directory to find them.

- *Home Folder with Share Points*: This option requires for the home folder to be configured properly for the accounts using FTP, but along with starting the user in their home folder, it adds a link to the FTP root so they can easily navigate to the other share points without having to traverse the parent directory.

- *Home Folder Only*: This option will have users dropped only into their designated home folder, and they will not have access to shares or any other share point on the FTP server, even if it is configured. This is a useful way for outside users to upload and download specific files to your server without giving them full access to the rest of the server. Since this is a global option, you would turn FTP solely into a limited-access system for outside users, which is not necessarily a bad thing. You would first want to create an *ftpuser* account and assign it to a home folder stored in the subdirectory of an existing share point (in Workgroup Manager, you can just manually enter the path), and then you will want to add an ACL ensuring that other users can read and write to that folder. With that in place (along with the Home Only FTP option enabled), when someone connects as the FTP account, they will only see the contents of that folder on the server; users connecting over AFP and SMB will have access to that folder as well.

Configuring FTP

You will first have to enable the service in the server's settings panel and then select the service button when it appears. Once you have enabled the service, you will want to either create or select a share point that you want to have enabled for FTP access and load the Protocol Options window. From here, you will select the FTP tab and enable the FTP access, as shown in Figure 18–8; you can also give this share point a simpler name for FTP users, such as replacing spaces with an underscore, and so on.

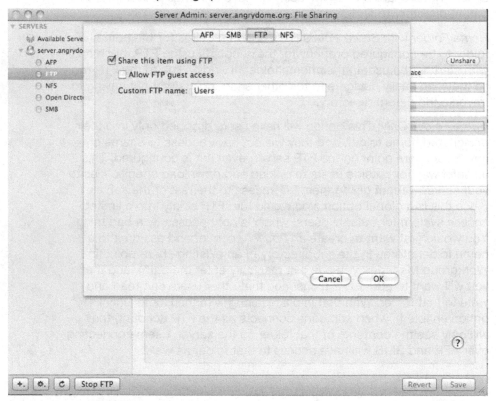

Figure 18–8. *Enabling an FTP share point*

Once you have enabled FTP for at least one share point, you can continue to the Settings tab. The options that you should really worry about for the General area are Error Notification Address (you may not actually want to set this, because you will get all the failed automated attempts to log into your server) and the Enable Anonymous Access check box (which, unless you are planning to share the contents of your server with the rest of the Internet, do not ever select this). The File Conversion option is a useful tool that will help preserve files with resource forks when they are being transferred. They will convert the files to MacBinary on the fly, so the clients will actually see File.indd.bin instead of File.indd, and since many Mac FTP clients automatically decompress the MacBinary format, it enables you to transfer files from client to server, preserving resource forks in the process.

The only other section we have not already covered is the Logging tab, which does not log the error messages as you would think but instead logs the actions taken by users, such as file uploads, downloads, removals, and attempts for them to navigate to directories they can't access. These options can be enabled for both anonymous and authenticated users. If your company requires auditing or similar, you may want to enable these options. By default the settings can be left as shown in Figure 18–9, but keep in mind on an FTP server with heavy FTP traffic, those logs can grow quickly.

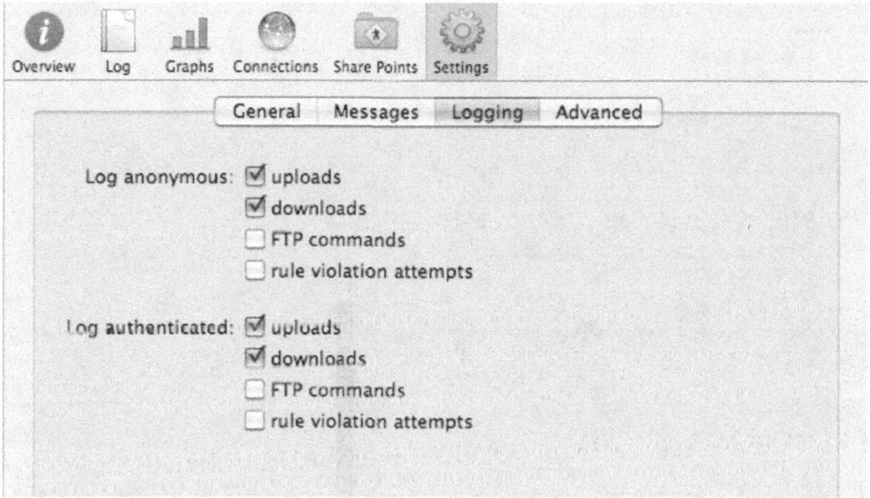

Figure 18–9. *FTP logging configuration*

Connecting to FTP Using Cyberduck

Cyberduck is a free FTP client for Mac OS X, and it makes accessing FTP servers easy. You can download it from http://cyberduck.ch/. Once you have it installed, all you need to do to connect to an FTP server is open the application and select Open Connection from the browser window. If the browser window is not present, you can select New Browser from the File menu.

When you are starting a new connection, you will see a window similar to Figure 18–10. All you should need to enter is the server name, the username, and the password associated with it, and you will be able to connect. As you can see in the figure, there are some other options you can configure, and the log window is exposed, allowing you to see any banner and welcome messages (Command+L). Once connected, the window looks very similar to a Finder window in list view, and you can drag files to it to upload and out of it to download.

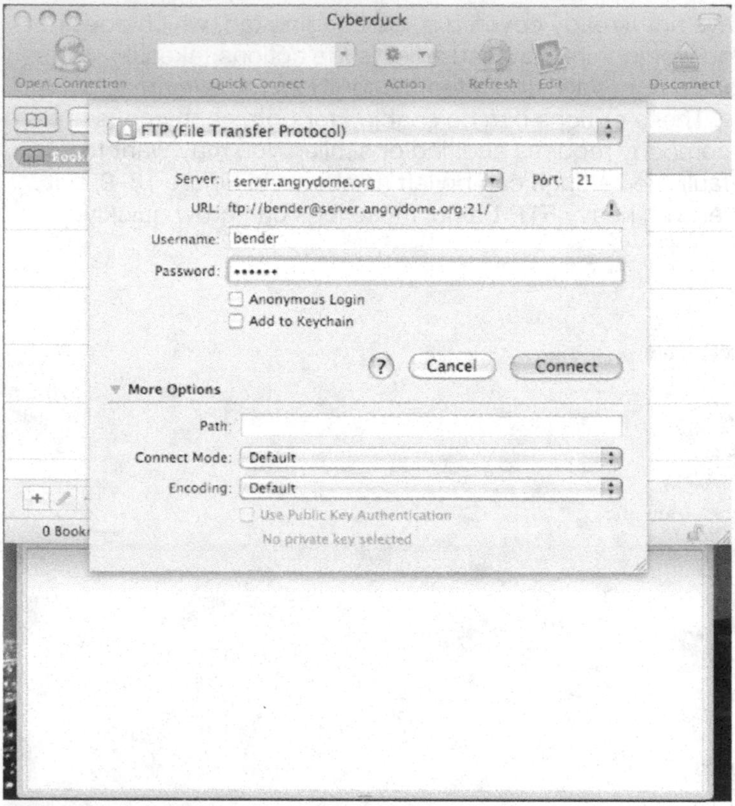

Figure 18–10. *Cyberduck login sheet and browser window*

Connecting to FTP Using ftp

The simplest and most widely available way to access your FTP server (and a useful way to troubleshoot it) is from the command line using the ftp command. This is as simple as loading the Terminal from the Utilities application and typing the following command:

```
ftp server.angrydome.org
```

This will open the login prompt for the session (after displaying the banner) and then the password prompt. If you have successfully authenticated, you will be at the FTP root, and you can navigate around using common commands (cd to change directory, ls to list, and so on). To download a file, you would type get filename, and to upload a file from your computer to the current directory you are in, you would type put pathtofile. If you are uncertain where you were when you ran ftp (and therefore what path to use to find the file and where files will be downloaded to when you get them), you can use the lcd command to list your local directory.

Configuring PASSV

Passive FTP (PASSV) should almost always be enabled on your FTP client. It allows for the server to connect to and work with clients that are behind firewalls (and if the server itself is behind a firewall). You will want to configure inbound access on your own firewall for port 21 as well. PASSV works by allowing the client to pull files down, instead of the server trying to push files directly to the client, which occurs in the case of an active transfer. Because most networks and computers do not allow random inbound connections, it is always best to keep PASSV enabled.

NFS

Although historically not as secure as other file sharing options, NFS has started to include advanced security options such as encryption and Kerberos authentication. One of the security issues (or features) is that an NFS mount can be configured globally for a workstation connection to the server, trusting that the connecting client will respect the filesystem permissions. This allows for one server to reshare files of another server as if it were a locally attached drive, but it also means that if a malicious host were able to attach to the NFS share, that host could have full access across all the files, regardless of what the permissions were (since NFS is trusting the client to honor permissions). AFP and SMB, on the other hand, require a user account before they allow a connection, and the actions allowed during the session are determined based on the account that authenticated. One benefit of NFS's "trust the client" behavior is that when used for network home folders, users with network accounts can "fast user switch" to other network user account, something not possible because of AFP's limitation of one trusted connection per computer, preventing the second user's home folder from mounting.

Since NFS's actual configuration is done on a per-share basis, the Server Admin pane of System Preferences is extremely barren. Here you can set the protocol types (leaving the TCP and UDP settings is adequate for most environments) and the number of connections available. If you have previously configured your server to provide NetBoot (for system imaging), NFS will be enabled already for that service.

Shares

In Mac OS X Server 10.6, one welcome change to the Server Admin interface has been the presence of the Share Points tab being available in every sharing-related service, allowing you to quickly view and manage those shares easily without having to go back to the broad server-level global settings view. Now from any service you can quickly check and see the settings of a specific share point and enable or disable access to it for those services.

Configuring Share Points

The first thing when working on a server is to ensure that you know where you want your share points to reside. Although OS X Server creates a folder called Shared Items at the root of your Boot drive, which contains a Public and Groups folder, we always remove the default shares because they may not be pertinent to a specific environment. Instead, set up a new folder containing all the share points on the disks set aside as dedicated storage space. Remember, you will want to create a folder such as Share Points or similar on the root of any disk; then try not to share out that disk directly because you can introduce needless security risks when doing so.

To enable a folder as a share point, you will need to get to the File Sharing tab in the server settings view by selecting the server in Server Admin (or the Share Points tab if you are already in the AFP, SMB, NFS, or FTP services). By default it will show you just the configured share points, but you will want to click Volumes and Browse so you can see the entire filesystem available to the server. Figure 18–11 shows the view of the default Shared Items folder. From this interface, you can also create a new folder (in the upper-right corner of the panel) and enable that folder as a share. Once you have done that, you can click the Save button in the bottom right and toggle back the view to Share Points to see your new share point with the default options enabled.

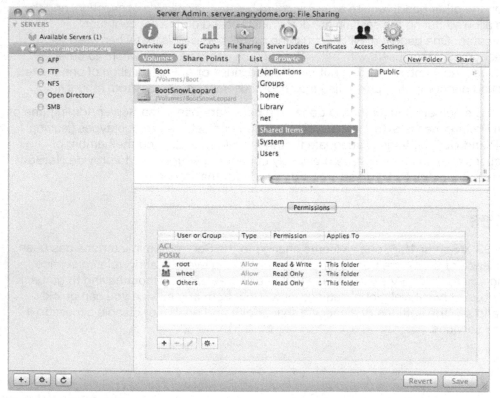

Figure 18–11. *File sharing view*

Share Point Options

By default a new share point is configured to be accessible by AFP and SMB; you will have to manually enable FTP and NFS settings on your own. There are some other options, such as to publish the share point in Open Directory (so clients in Open Directory can automatically mount it), enable Spotlight indexing, and allow users to use a specific share point as a Time Machine destination, as shown in Figure 18–12.

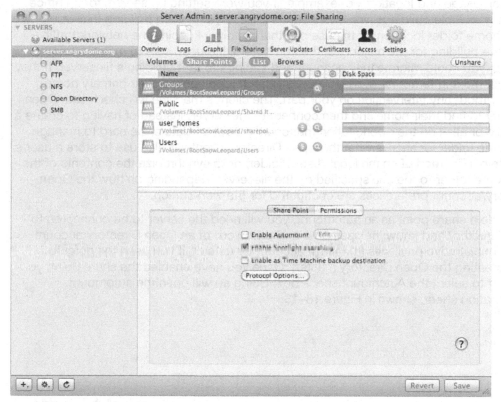

Figure 18–12. *Share point–specific settings*

Automounting

The Enable Automount option for a share point allows for that share to be published in your Open Directory system as a possible automount for a client. By default, you will want to enable whatever folder you use for home accounts as an automount, which will then allow you to designate network folders that users will see as their own "private" spaces only when they connect to the server. Also, this will be where mobile accounts pull down their templates when they connect (if it was created already) or where network machines will store the users' Library, Documents, and Desktop folders, instead of the local /Users folder on the machine. You can also map Applications and Group folders by default, allowing for applications to be stored on a server but launched by client machines. The Group folder, which provides a common share point that is mounted for users who are members of that group, then allows those members to interact with that shared group space.

To make a share point an automount, let's start with the most common one, the home folder location for Open Directory users. Since an Open Directory environment can consist of multiple servers, each fileserver in your Open Directory could provide a home folder location, and then you could assign different groups of users to different servers based on usage and location. For example, if you were setting up servers for an office spanning multiple buildings, you could set up a fileserver in each building that would act as the home folder location for the users in that building, keeping the network traffic within the building for the majority of the computers. If a user were to move to another building, you could migrate their account and settings to that building's fileserver. If they were just moving temporarily, they would still be able to contact their primary home server without any intervention on your part. The client's machine will check with Open Directory to find their home and then connect to the server, instead of having to create a static file or alias on their workstation that could go out-of-date or be hard to manage. This home folder location is what the Open Directory client will also use to store a user's home folder (instead of on the local /Users folder) or to synchronize the contents of the local home folder to the one specified on the fileserver, depending on how the Open Directory/account preferences are configured for the workstation.

To enable a share point as an automount, you will need the server to be connected to Open Directory and know the username and password of an Open Directory account with administrative privileges (diradmin account by default, if you used the defaults when creating the Open Directory master). Once you have enabled the share point, you will want to select the Automount check box. Doing so will open the automount configuration sheet, shown in Figure 18–13.

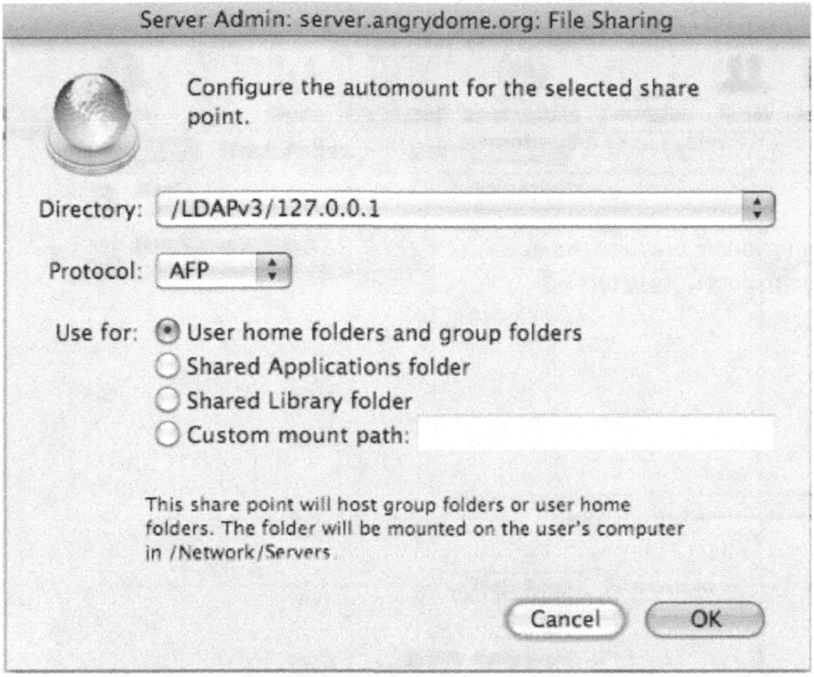

Figure 18-13. *Automount configuration sheet*

Here you will want to select AFP as the protocol and the radio button "User home folders and group folders." Once you click OK, you will be prompted for the directory administrator's username and password. After the window closes, click Save to ensure that the share point settings are updated, and you are done. To double-check that the automount was creating properly in Open Directory, open Workgroup Manager, make sure you are looking at your Open Directory view, and then select a user and that user's Home tab. There you will see all the share points configured as automounts for home folders in Open Directory, and your just-added share will be among them. (If the view does not show it, make sure you are looking at the same directory and that you have refreshed the window.) Figure 18–14 shows Workgroup Manager with two home folders configured as automounts.

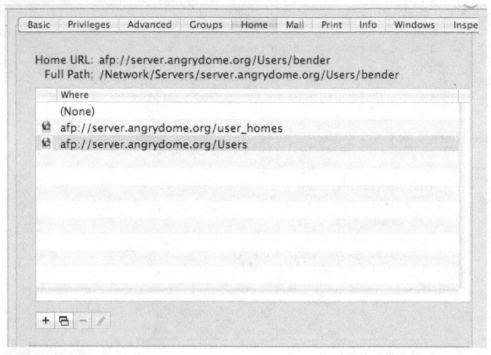

Figure 18–14. *Showing configured automounts*

Spotlight

Introduced in Mac OS X Server 10.5, the Spotlight option allows for a share to be searchable by the Finder easily, by having the server manage and keep an index of all files on the share, including their contents. By having the Spotlight option enabled, it lets users quickly find files based on a plethora of criteria, while also ensuring they are not seeing files they are not meant to be seeing.

In some cases, the indexes for Spotlight can get corrupted or out-of-date, and an easy way to force a rebuild is to just disable and then reenable the Spotlight option for a share point (saving those settings between steps).

SMB Share Options

SMB has some more advanced options compared to AFP, in part because you are configuring the Samba open source software, not a protocol or service developed in-house by Apple. SMB is used mostly by Windows clients, and there are implementations in the SMB protocol that do not have options or functions for AFP access. These two big options are the Strict and Op Locking settings, which change how SMB will lock a file, preventing two users from accessing it at the same time.

Strict locking allows for two users to access the file at the same time by isolating the byte ranges of the file from being modified (which is useful if you are storing a shared database file that's being edited by two different machines). Op Locking will flag the file as locked, and then the client will cache their changes locally before sending them back to the client. Both of these options should remain off unless you have isolated the share so only Windows clients are accessing it and so no server-side file operations are being performed on the file (Spotlight indexing is disabled for the share point). Otherwise, you can get file corruption issues when an AFP client requests a lock on a file that isn't compatible with the lock that the SMB (Windows) client thought it had on the file, making it lose the changes that the Windows user was doing once the Mac client opens the files.

Besides locking, there is also the option to override how permissions are assigned to the files when they are created or added to the share point from an SMB perspective. By deselecting the "Inherit permissions from parent" setting, you can make it so any file added by a SMB client will have group Read and Write permissions, instead of just allowing for the creator of the file permissions to edit it. If you are using ACLs to grant permissions to files but are still seeing some permissions issue (possibly because you have older SMB clients or are using an application that is not aware of ACLs), you also use this in conjunction to ensure files are created on the share with proper permissions. Figure 18–15 shows the protocol options for SMB.

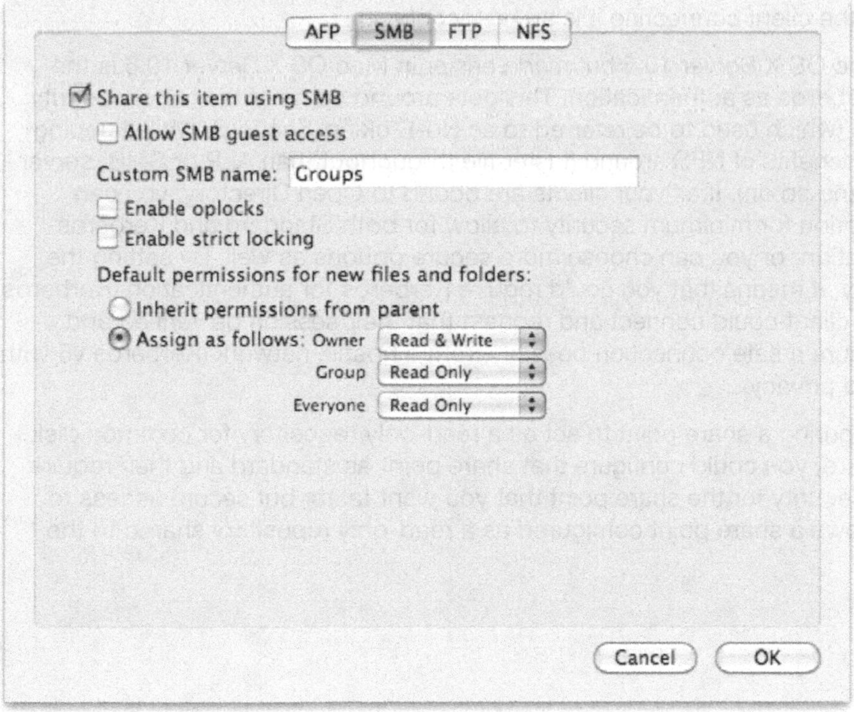

Figure 18–15. *SMB share point options*

NFS Shares

A share point can be implemented using the NFS protocol, which is useful if you want to provide a folder or share to be accessed at all times by another computer, as if it were a direct-attached storage device.

The protocol options for NFS are a bit different. Since the technology was based on server-to-server file sharing, you instead "export" the folder to other servers that can connect to it. Unless you know exactly what you are doing, you will never want to export a share to World, which would allow anyone who knows the mount path and IP of your server access to that share point. The other options are much more specific and provide a better layer of security. Specifically, you can provide the single IP address (or domain name) of a computer that has access to that share, allowing for you to specify only one other computer access (such as an internal web server that may use the NFS mount point as a place to store logs, backups, or large video files) or a range (subnet) of computers that can have access. For example, if this were the NFS home folder server for a group of computers, you could allow that groups subnet access to it. Because of how NFS implements permissions, you will probably want to keep root mapped to nobody, because any computer could in theory connect, and if that user had access to root on their local machine, they could have root access to that share point otherwise (NFS trusts that the client connecting it is an honest client).

Introduced in Mac OS X Server 10.5 but made easier in Mac OS X Server 10.6 is the option to use Kerberos as authentication. This gets around some of the major security concerns of NFS (which used to be referred to as No-F*cking-Security), while keeping some the major benefits of NFS around (faster file throughput than AFP or SMB, server-level mounting, and so on). If all your clients are bound to Open Directory, you can select the Any option for minimum security to allow for both Standard and Kerberos-based authentication, or you can choose more secure options as well. By setting the minimum security, it means that you could require Kerberos for authentication (Kerberos v5 option), but a client could connect and request that their session be verified and encrypted to ensure a safe connection possibly from a hostile network (Kerberos v5 with data integrity and privacy).

If you were configuring a share point to act as a read-only repository for common disk images or software, you could configure that share point as standard and then require encryption and security for the share point that you want faster but secure access to. Figure 18–16 shows a share point configured as a read-only repository shared to the local subnet.

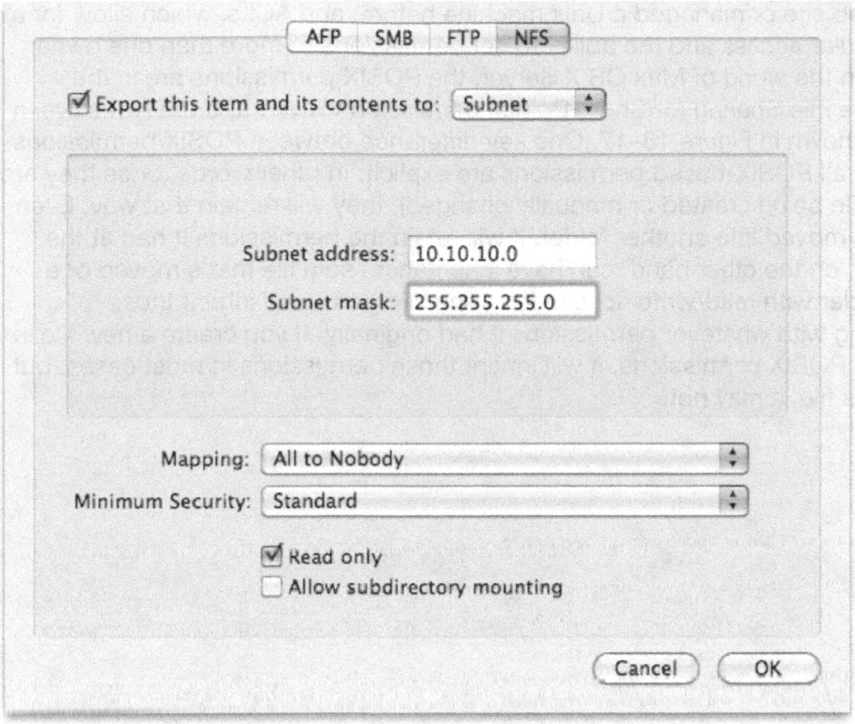

Figure 18–16. *NFS share point options*

Server-Side File Tracking

Server-side file tracking is an option enabled on the General tab for each server. This option allows the user to upload and change the contents of their home folder, without requiring their mobile account (which is synchronized with the home folder) to do a full scan the next time it connects. This is useful if you have users who use network homes while on their desktop machines but have their laptops use mobile versions of their home folder so they can work on it on the road. There is always a possibility of a sync going awry (or a user selecting an option to delete a file on their laptop that they really wanted uploaded to the server), so any syncing or management option should always be considered a convenience feature, not a major form of backup.

File Permissions

Permissions are one of the most critical aspects of managing a fileserver. As important as it is to make sure that your users are able to access the fileserver, it is equally as important in many environments to make sure that they can't access everything on the fileserver.

There two ways filesystem permissions are implemented in OS X: POSIX permissions, which are the old system User-Group-Everyone settings you may be familiar with if you have set up a web site or managed a Unix machine before, and ACLs, which allow for a much more granular access and the ability to set permissions to more than one owner and one group. In the world of Max OS X Server, the POSIX permissions are in the bottom half of the File Sharing (or Share Points) permission viewer, and the ACLs live in the top half, as shown in Figure 18–17. One key difference between POSIX permissions and ACLs is that all POSIX-based permissions are explicit. In other words, once they are set (by a folder/file being created or manually changed), they will remain that way. Even if the resource is moved into another folder, it will retain the permissions it had at the beginning. ACLs, on the other hand, can have inheritance, so a file that's moved or a copied into a folder with read/write access for a specific group will inherit those permissions along with whatever permissions it had originally. If you create a new file in a folder with just POSIX permissions, it will inherit those permissions in most cases, but if you just move a file, it may not.

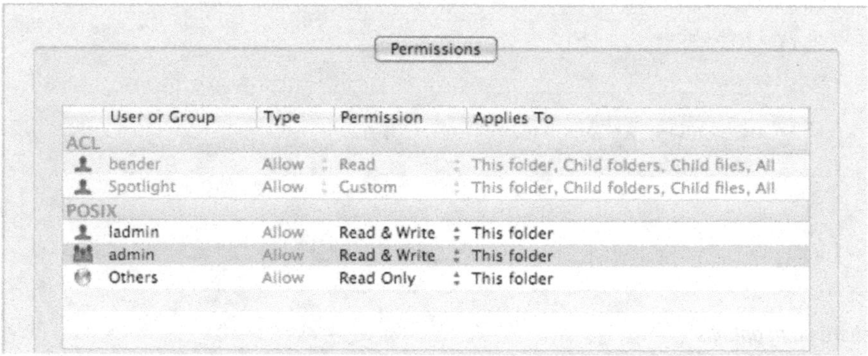

Figure 18–17. *POSIX and ACL views*

POSIX

POSIX permissions have three levels of access: Owner, Group, and Others. Only Owner and Group can be specified for any file; Others means any other user or group that does not match the specified Owner or Group. At each level you can grant the permission to read, write, and execute the file (in the case that it is an application or script, executable permissions on a folder means you can view or list the contents of the folder).

So, a file can be owned by Bob with his permissions set as Read/Write; the group can be set to Engineering, with its permission set as Read access and with Others set to None. Changing the group permission to Read/Write would allow for other people in the Engineering group to read/write. However, if you are changing the permissions on a folder, the files contained within that folder will still retain their old permissions.

To update the permissions of several files all at once, you can use Server Admin to propagate permissions for you. To do this, you would use the same pane you have been using to select and view the file, and instead of enabling sharing on the folder (or file), you can just review and edit the permissions for the file. Once you have set the permissions for the folder, near the bottom of the window is a gear icon that, when you click it, presents a selection of tools, including the option to propagate permissions (as shown in Figure 18–18). Once selected, a sheet will prompt you for the permissions you would like to propagate. By selecting the various options, you are telling Server Admin to take those specific values from the folder you have selected and apply them to all child files, folders, and their descendents (to use an ACL term). When you click OK, Server Admin will start a process on the server to change those permissions. Depending on the number of files in question, the process can take a while.

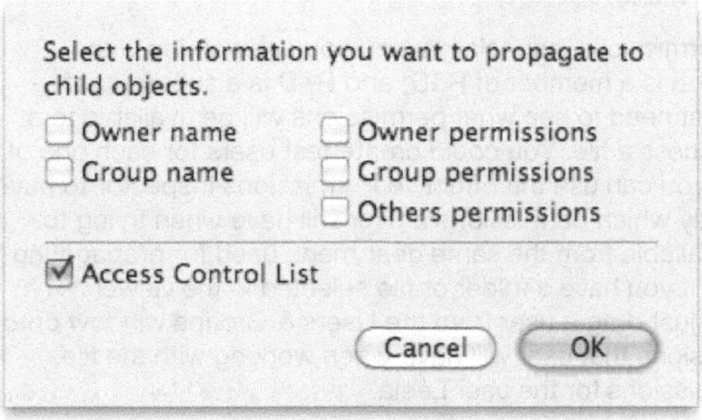

Figure 18–18. *Propagate permissions sheet*

ACLs

Files being able to have only one owner and one group can be a huge limitation for any organization requiring any kind of tiered access or complicated permission schemes. One big weakness is that the only way to be able to grant a user (such as a system administrator or an auditor) access to all your files under POSIX, without actually changing the file permissions, is to give them root (or super administrator) privileges to your server. You also can't grant multiple groups access to a shared folder space and have them be able to edit other people's files without running into some permissions headaches.

ACLs are a set of extended attributes that the server will use to determine additional permissions with more granular options that can even override the permissions declared by the POSIX settings of a file. Also, ACLs allow for inheritance, so a file dropped into the engineering department's folder by the accounting department will become editable by the engineers, even though it was not editable when it was sitting on the accounting department's server. Setting ACEs (a specific entry in a file's ACL) in Mac OS X Server 10.6 is as easy as dragging a user (or group) from the Users & Groups window to the ACL portion of the File Sharing window. By default this assigns them Read access to that folder and sets the ACE to be copied to any new files that are added to the folder. If you want to update the ACLs on the existing files, you will have to use the permissions tool discussed earlier.

Four predefined ACEs are ready for you: Full Control, Read & Write, Read, and Write. Full Control means that not only can a user read and write to a file, but they can also modify the permissions of the file, removing other users' access if they want. The other three options are actually a combination of specific elements of the ACL system that grant those privileges. To see all the combinations available by ACL, you can select the Custom option. You can define the different aspects of an ACE to the point of limiting users from deleting files and making it so the ACE is not inherited by new files (for a drop box, you can make it so the folder is Write only, add a Deny Read option to it, but prevent the Deny from being transferred to files dropped into the box). Figure 18–19 shows an example of the Custom menu.

When you are troubleshooting permissions, especially when you are working with nested groups (in other words, Bob is a member of R&D, and R&D is a subgroup of Engineering), sometimes you'll just need to see what permissions will be available to a user or group when they try to access a file. You could create test users for each one of those groups to access from, or you can use the Effective Permissions Inspector to have the server calculate for you exactly which permissions a user will have when trying to access a file. This inspector is available from the same gear menu used for propagating permissions and will be available if you have a folder or file selected in the viewer already. Once it is open, you can just drag a user from the Users & Groups window onto it, and you can see which permissions that user will have when working with the file. Figure 18–20 shows access permissions for the user Leela.

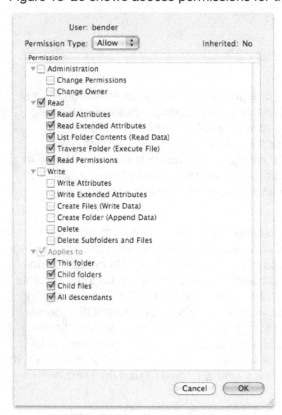

Figure 18–19. *Custom ACL sheet*

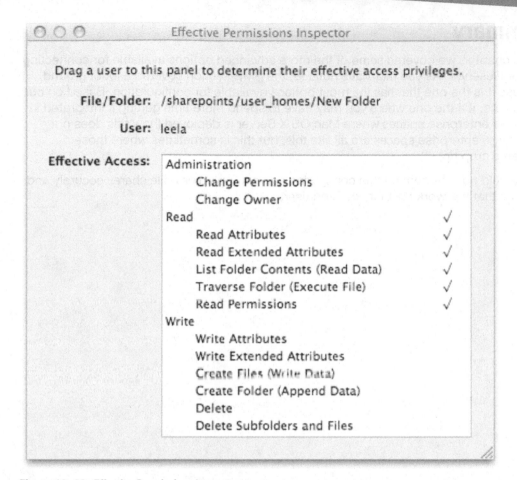

Figure 18–20. *Effective Permissions Inspector*

One problem with ACLs is that because of inheritance and nesting, you may find files that all of a sudden have 12 different ACEs that are conflicting with each other, and the server will have to descend the entire list of ACEs until it can determine the satisfactory permission access. You can find a more in-depth run-through of how ACLs are provided in the Fileserver Admin manual available from Apple. However, keep in mind that ACLs are additive for access (so a user may be granted write access and be a member of a group with read access, so the final actual access is Read & Write). Use the Effective Permissions Inspector to familiarize yourself with how those permissions can be combined to create a very powerful access system. And of course, if you have a specific folder that just is not behaving as expected, you can always remove the ACLs either using Server Admin or using the following command (the –R will remove the ACLs from any subfolder or file as well):

```
sudo chmod –N –R /Path/To/Folder
```

Summary

In this chapter, we covered some of the more advanced options available for connecting to your fileserver. As you may have noticed, the SMB section covered a lot of ground, because it is the one that has the most options available for configuration. Based on our experience, it's the one where you may have to spend more time getting it integrated in the larger enterprise spaces where Mac OS X Server is deployed (how this does not mean large enterprise spaces are all like this, but this is sometimes where those problems crop up).

You should now be comfortable configuring and setting up new file shares securely and in a way that will work best for your end users.

Chapter 19

Setting Up Printing Services

Smaller networks typically have a printer connected to each computer. Over time, as more computers are purchased, users will often start sharing larger printers that have more features than the simplistic printers that most organizations start with. A *print server* is a computer that shares printers for other computers and systems on the network to use. These printers each have queues that are usually centrally visible and controllable from a single location, the print server. Mac OS X and Mac OS X Server can both act as a print server.

You can also use printer spoolers built into most network printers, rather than sharing printers through a dedicated server. The distributed management of printers in this fashion, although initially convenient, can begin to cause headaches as the user base grows. For example, in larger environments, it helps to be able to allow users to manage print jobs. You also will encounter scenarios where you want to create a single queue for multiple physical printers and even assign a maximum number of print jobs to a given printer. Finally, the distribution of printer queues, or automated installation of printers on clients, can help you manage computers and the printers that they use en masse.

There are a number of reasons to use Mac OS X Server as opposed to the Mac OS X client for managing printers. Perhaps the biggest reason is the granularity that you can apply to configure printing services. Although it is possible to use the command-line options included with Mac OS X client to configure things such as printer pools and quotas (which we will explain in further detail later in this chapter), it is not exactly easy and is likely not worth the time to do so when compared to leveraging the built-in tools of Mac OS X Server. But in addition to features specific to managing print queues, Mac OS X Server is also tuned to serving data rather than being used, which is an aspect that should not be overlooked.

In this chapter, we will cover setting up and managing the Print service in Mac OS X Server. This includes setting up shared print queues, quotas, and printer pools; managing print jobs; and even getting started with leveraging CUPS, the back-end printing subsystem. But before you can leverage the Print service, you need to first have installed at least a printer to share to users. Therefore, we'll start the chapter by covering how to install a number of different types of printers.

Installing a Printer

Before you can share a printer, you must first install one. In this regard, Mac OS X Server is almost identical to the Mac OS X client. In this section, we'll cover how to configure your server to print to a printer.

Mac OS X 10.6 comes with a number of print drivers installed as part of the operating system installation. For a list of printer (and scanner) drivers that are available, see the Apple Knowledge Base article located at http://support.apple.com/kb/HT3669. Unlike previous versions of the operating system, Snow Leopard has the ability to install printer drivers automatically using the software update service. As you will see later in this section, if the operating system does not have the driver installed at the time that you install a printer, the installation wizard will check for the driver automatically and prompt you to download and install it.

However, Apple cannot support all printers. A number of printers will come with special software that should be used for installing the printer. Multifunction printers from a variety of vendors will commonly use custom installers rather than leverage supported standards because these printers often carry model-specific features that the OS cannot account for.

Basic Printer Management

As previously mentioned, installing printers in Mac OS X Server is identical to installing printers in the Mac OS X client. Unless your printer requires a special installation, for most environments you can install the printer using the Print & Fax System pane of System Preferences. To get started, click the Apple menu in the upper-left corner of the screen, and select System Preferences; the screen shown in Figure 19–1 will open.

From the System Preferences screen, you will click the Print & Fax icon. In the event that you have not yet configured any printers, this System Preferences pane will invoke an empty Print & Fax pane, as shown in Figure 19–2.

At any point in the management of Mac OS X or Mac OS X Server's printing services, you will use the Print & Fax System pane of System Preferences to add and remove printers. Simply click the plus (+) sign to get started.

> **NOTE:** You can also configure a new default printer in the Print & Fax pane of System Preferences, a common task when installing your shared printers on clients.

Figure 19–1. *System Preferences*

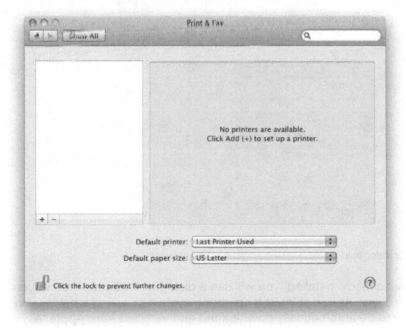

Figure 19–2. *Print & Fax pane of System Preferences*

USB or Bonjour Printing

In your experience with connecting printers to a Mac workstation, you probably have used either a direct-attached USB-based printer or a network-based printer using a protocol called Bonjour. Bonjour is Apple's name for a network discovery protocol, which allows nodes on a network to see each other and communicate, with very little configuration required. Bonjour and USB printers will install similarly. When you connect the device, nothing will happen initially. But when you click the plus (+) sign of the Print & Fax System pane, you will see the Add Printer dialog box. From here, the computer will poll the network and USB ports for new printers to connect. If the printer that you would like to install is listed, click it, and then click the Add button, as shown in Figure 19–3.

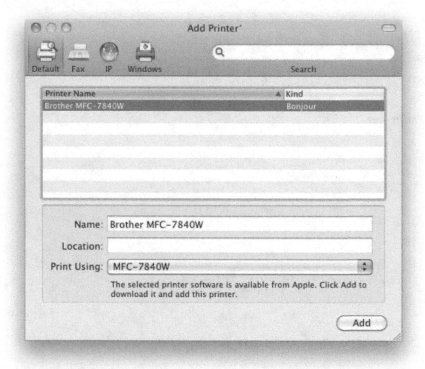

Figure 19–3. *The Add Printer dialog box*

If the printer driver is not already installed, you will see a dialog box asking whether you would like to install the driver. At this point, the operating system is asking whether you would like for the driver to be automatically downloaded and installed from Apple, as shown in Figure 19–4. Click Install to proceed with downloading and installing the driver. If you would rather install the printer driver manually, such as from a CD-ROM or an installer from a local or network location, click Not Now.

Figure 19–4. *Installing drivers from Apple*

When you click Install, the printer will then be installed, and the drivers, provided the printer is included in the printer list, will be downloaded and installed as well. This helps streamline the process for printer setup and make the process easier and smoother for end users.

Network Printing

Most readers will already know this, but Bonjour is not bulletproof for printing in larger environments. Therefore, when you are setting up printers that are connected to a network, it is best to set them up using IPP, LPD, or JetDirect (the three supported protocols for network printers in Mac OS X 10.6) where possible. From there, you can use your Mac OS X Server as a printer queue and get all the control that you would expect from a dedicated print server. But first you need to install the printer on the server. You can also print to these printers directly from client systems, but using a centralized server provides centralized management that will otherwise be unavailable. To ensure that your users are connecting through the network print server and not directly via Bonjour, you may need to take extra steps such as putting your printers on a subnet or VLAN that only your server can see. Otherwise, people can simply bypass your print server and all of the control it affords you!

Choosing the protocol that you will use is typically an easy choice: use the protocol that is most natively supported by the printer. If the printer is an IPP-based printer, then use IPP. But if you are setting up a networked HP printer, then you are more than likely going to be using JetDirect.

IPP

The first of these protocols that can be used to connect to printers is Internet Printing Protocol (IPP). IPP is a protocol written to print to network printers. IPP can work remotely and is a standard in Unix-based environments. IPP is widely implemented and supported by printing manufacturers. To get started with IPP, from the Add Printer dialog box referenced in the USB or Bonjour printing coverage earlier in this chapter, click the IP button in the dialog box's toolbar. From here, as you can see in Figure 19–5, you will be able to select the protocol that your printer supports using the Protocol field. Here, enter an address and a queue name in their respective fields. The address should include either a DNS host name or an IP address of the printer, and the queue name should match the queue that has been configured for that printer (although a queue is not always required if there is only one queue in use on the printer).

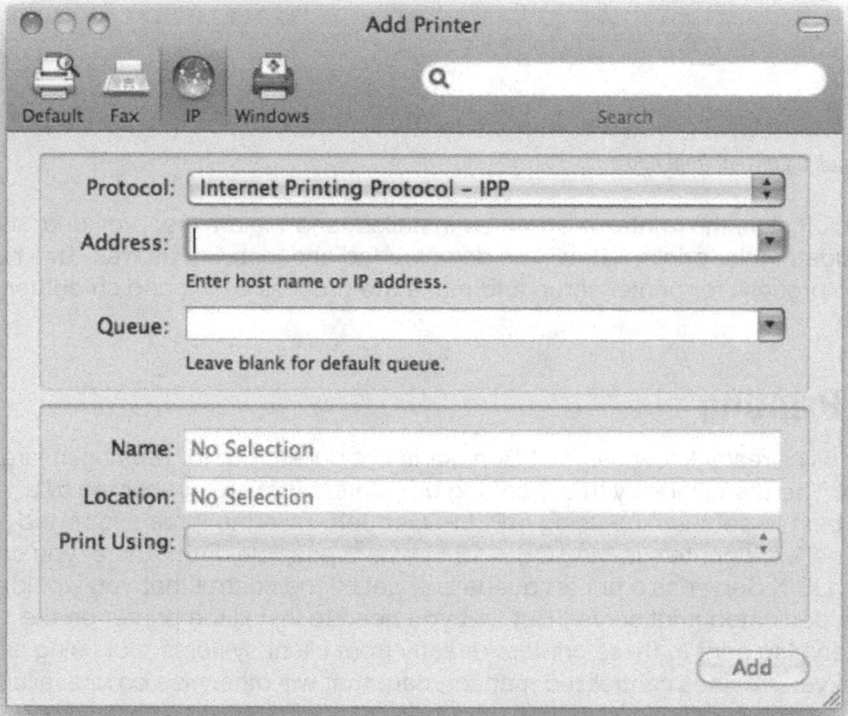

Figure 19–5. *Setting up an IPP printer*

Additionally, provide a name and a location, although these are not necessary to add. Finally, in the Print Using field, select the appropriate printer driver. The IPP print queue should then be installed and functional. Test printing a document to it just to make sure, and then you can move on to setting up the shared print queue.

LPD

The next protocol, LPD, is very similar to IPP. Line Printer Daemon (LPD) is a collection of tools in Mac OS X and other Unix-based operating systems that can be leveraged to provide network printing. LPD options are identical to IPP options, and for the most part the LPD configuration is identical as well, as shown in Figure 19–6.

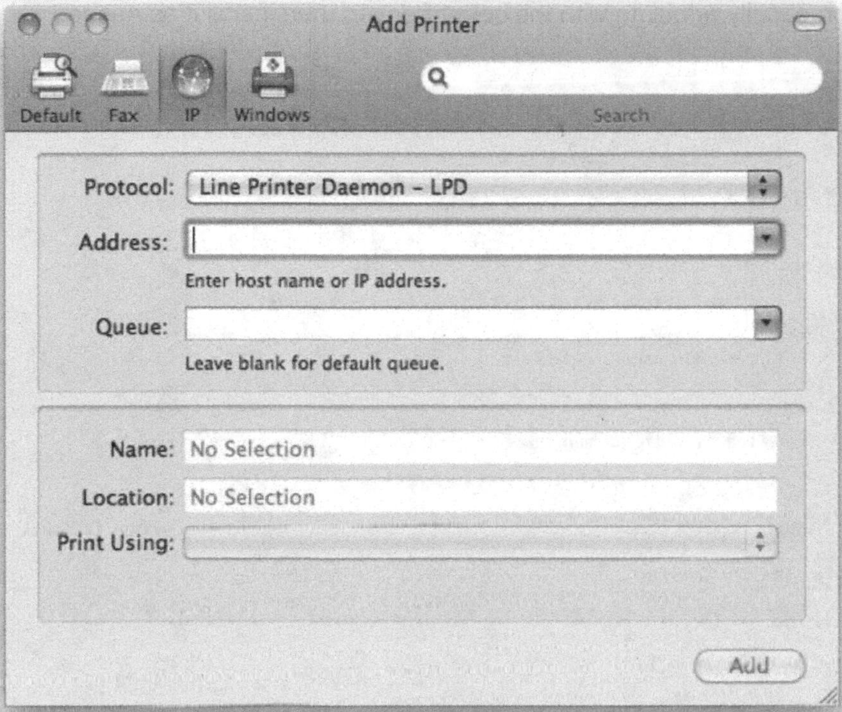

Figure 19–6. *Setting up an LPD printer*

Once the appropriate information has been provided, click Add, and the print queue should be created. Once created, test printing to it from the print server. If the print jobs that you send to the printer over the network print as intended, then you can move on to setting up the Print service in Mac OS X Server and setting up the shared print queue.

JetDirect

HP is the market leader in networked printers. In this capacity, HP has developed its own technology for communicating effectively with those printers, JetDirect. JetDirect also encompasses the cards that go into many HP printers that allow them to be networked. Although JetDirect is different in a number of ways from IPP and LPD, the options for JetDirect are again the same as they were with IPP and LPD.

To set up a Mac OS X Server as a JetDirect server and client, you will first need to install the printer on the server. Again, begin with the Add Printer dialog box. Here, select HP Jetdirect Socket from the Protocol menu. The other options will be the same as with LPD and IPP; provide a host name or IP address, provide a queue name from the printer (where applicable), and, if you like, enter a name and a location in the Address, Queue,

Name, and Location fields, respectively, as shown in Figure 19–7. If the Print Using field does not automatically populate with the correct driver, then install it as needed.

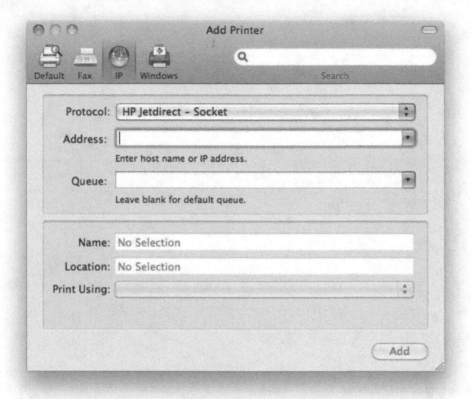

Figure 19–7. *Setting up a JetDirect printer*

Once the queue has been set up, you can move on to setting up the Print service so that the printer can be shared to client computers and then to setting up the print queue, as we will explain in further detail throughout this chapter.

TIP: The first step in troubleshooting issues with printing to these print queues typically will be to first attempt to print to the printer from the print server.

Setting Up the Print Service

Once you have installed the printers that you will be sharing, it is time to set up the printing service. To get started, open Server Admin from /Applications/Server. Then click the name of the server in the SERVERS list that you will be installing the Print service onto. Here, you will see a number of services, as shown in Figure 19–8. Click the check box for the Print service, and then click the Save button, which will result in the

Print service appearing in the list of services that opens when you click the disclosure triangle to the left of the name of the service.

Figure 19–8. *Enabling the Print service*

Next, click the Print service, and then use the check box to enable the service. Once enabled, click the Save button to commit your changes, and you should see the service appear in the list of available services under the SERVERS list, with a gray circle next to it. Click Print in the SERVERS list, and then click the Overview icon in the Server Admin toolbar. You will then see the number of print queues installed, the number of spooled jobs, whether the service is running, and, if running, when it was started. Although we have not yet shown how to configure the global configuration options for the Print service, you can click Start Print in the lower bar of the Print service screen in order to start the service. Once started, the service should appear as Running, as indicated in Figure 19–9.

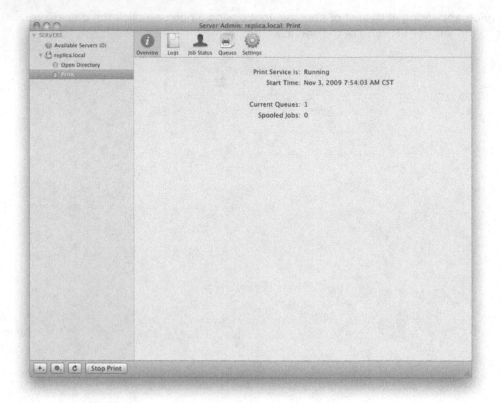

Figure 19–9. *The Overview screen for the Print service*

If you click Settings for the Print service in the Server Admin toolbar, you will see a number of global settings for the service, as shown in Figure 19–10. The maximum log size allows you to limit the amount of space taken up by logs on the server. The archive server log will compress logs and retain them. The log level allows you to set the level of logging that will be used on the server. Available logging levels include the following:

- *None*: No logging is performed.

- *Emergency*: Only items that prevent the services from functioning are logged.

- *Alert*: Only log items that need to be dealt with immediately are logged.

- *Critical*: This logs errors that are critical but that do not hamper the Print service from functioning.

- *Error*: This logs general errors.

- *Warn*: This logs errors and warnings.

- *Notice*: This logs temporary errors.

- *Information*: This logs all requests.

- *Debug*: This logs debugging information.

- *Debug 2*: This logs essentially all activity.

Finally, the "Require Single-Sign On authentication" check box will force users to connect to the server using Kerberos. This provides a much more secure printing solution, although it can be more complicated to configure on the client. Having said that, it can also be simpler to configure on the client if you require authentication in order to print, because there are fewer steps for clients to take in order to connect to the Kerberos printer. Kerberos is explained in further detail in Chapter 5.

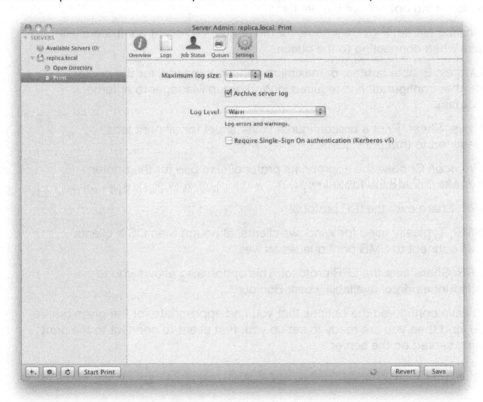

Figure 19-10. *Configuring the Print service*

Once configured to your preferences, click the Save button. The service will now be configured to your new specifications. Once complete, in order to start the service and begin sharing printers (if you have not already done so), click the Start Print button in Server Admin.

TIP: It is usually a good idea, once you have started a service, to click the Logs button and look for any errors. In some cases this will save a substantial amount of time.

Sharing a Printer

Once a printer has been installed and the Print service has been configured and started, you can start sharing printers to clients. Each printer, by default, will have a dedicated queue. Each printer can be shared with a different name than the name it was installed as and can have a number of basic options associated with it in Server Admin.

To get started, open Server Admin, and click the Print service for the server in question from the SERVERS list. Then click Queues to open a list of the installed printers on that server. Then click the printer that you would like to share to open the configurable options in Server Admin (shown in Figure 19–11). From here, you can choose to enable any of the following options for the printer:

- *Sharing Name*: Provide a name for the printer that client computers will use when connecting to the queue.

- *Quotas*: Enable quotas, or maximum printing capacity, for the printer (further configuration is required in Workgroup Manager to enforce quotas).

- *Cover Sheet*: Print a preconfigured cover sheet for all print jobs destined to that print queue.

- *Protocol*: Choose the appropriate protocol(s) to use for the printer; options include the following:

- *IPP*: Share over the IPP protocol.

- *SMB*: Typically used for Windows clients, although Mac OS X clients can connect to SMB print queues as well.

- *LPR*: Share over the LPR protocol. This option also allows you to announce printer availability over Bonjour.

Once you have configured the options that you find appropriate for the given queue, click Save, and then you are ready to set up your first client to connect to the print queue being served on the server.

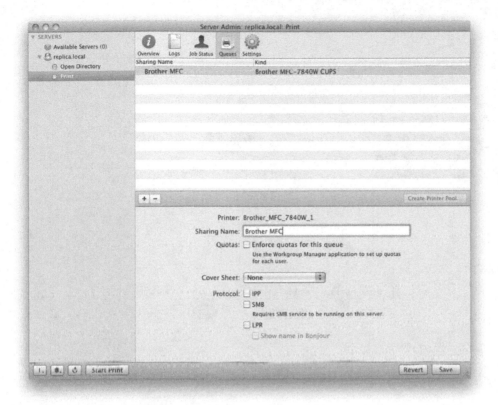

Figure 19–11. *Sharing a printer in Server Admin*

Creating a Printer Pool

As mentioned in the previous section, by default each printer has a dedicated queue. As the number of printers grows, you will often look to create a single queue that spans across multiple printers. In Mac OS X Server, this is known as a *printer pool*. Printer pools allow administrators to ease administrative burden in environments where a number of printers are heavily in use and typically when those printers are geographically similar.

> **NOTE:** Although you can pool printers that are not close to one another, it can cause a headache for end users who just want to find their print jobs.

Once you have installed multiple printers, then creating a printer pool will seem simple. One way to create a printer pool is in the Print & Fax pane. From here, click the two printers that you want to pool while holding down the Control or Shift key. Once they're highlighted, you will see a Create Printer Pool button, as shown in Figure 19–12. Click the Create Printer Pool button.

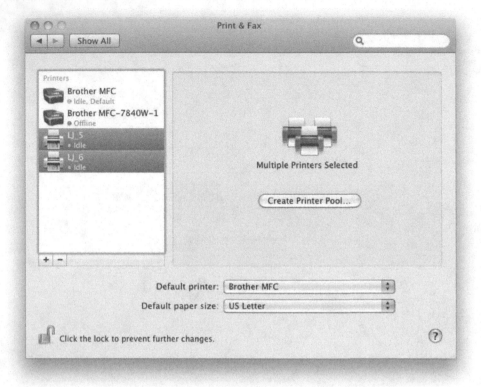

Figure 19–12. *Creating a printer pool in System Preferences*

When the pool has been created, you will see a screen similar to Figure 19–13. Here you can name the queue and manage it as though it were a standard print queue. You can also make it the default queue for a user or for the server itself. Once the queue has been created, you can then share it as you would a standard printer.

You can also create a printer pool in Server Admin. Here, click the Print service, and then highlight the printers that you would like to pool together, as shown in Figure 19–14. In this example, we are using only two printers, but you could use many more if needed. When all the printers that you would like to pool have been highlighted, click Create Printer Pool.

You will then be prompted for a name to give the printer pool. Enter the name, and then click the OK button, as shown in Figure 19–15. You should see the new pool listed in Server Admin, with a disclosure triangle so you can view the printers that comprise the pool. The pool itself can then be managed and shared as a standard printer.

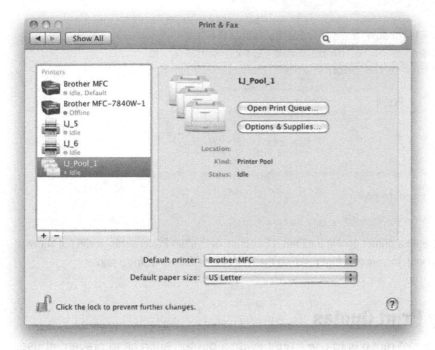

Figure 19-13. *Printer pools in System Preferences*

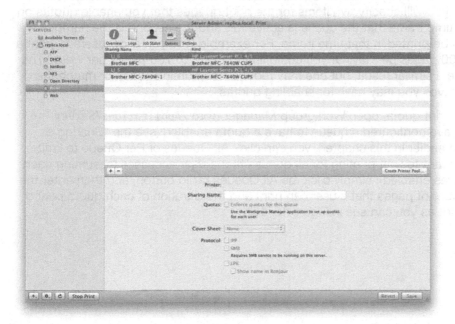

Figure 19-14. *Creating a printer pool in Server Admin*

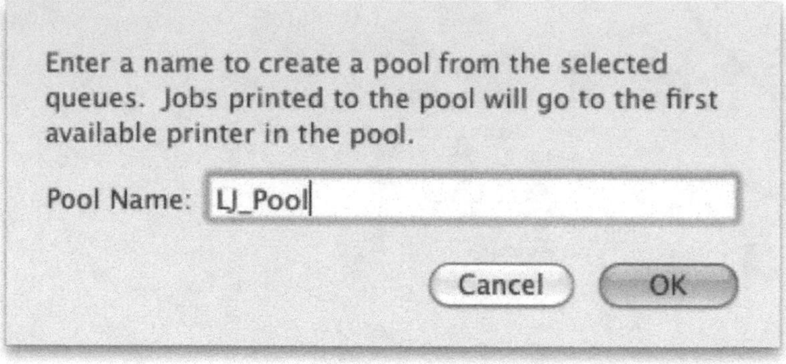

Enter a name to create a pool from the selected queues. Jobs printed to the pool will go to the first available printer in the pool.

Pool Name: LJ_Pool

Cancel   OK

Figure 19–15. *Naming a printer pool*

NOTE: If you create a printer pool in the Print & Fax pane of System Preferences, it will not show in Server Admin with the printers that make up the pool but instead as a single printer.

Configuring Print Quotas

There are a number of reasons to use a quota with a printer, such as to prevent abuse. But you can also use quotas as a rudimentary print job costing solution (although there are a number of third-party solutions that are much better at such a task). When you enable quotas, you will specify two items for the print queues that you enable quotas on. The first is the time frame that the queue is active for, and the second is the number of pages that can be printed in that time frame. For example, you can allow users to print a maximum of 100 pages per day. Or you could limit printing to 700 pages per week. The two would have a similar result, but one may require less administration or match the business objectives you may have for enabling quotas.

To configure a print quota, open Workgroup Manager from /Applications/Server. Provided you have configured a queue to have a quota enabled (see the "Sharing a Printer" section earlier in this chapter), you can click All Queues or Per Queue to limit printing. If you want to limit printing for all queues that a user accesses (assuming each queue has quotas enabled), simply click the All Queues radio button, and then enter the maximum number of pages that a user can print and the duration of each quota period in the Every field, as you can see in Figure 19–16.

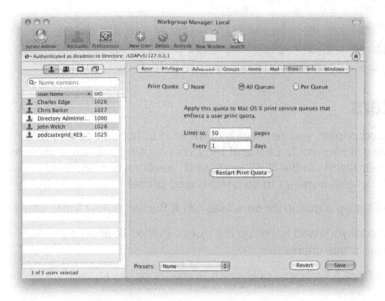

Figure 19–16. *Global quotas*

If you want to be more granular and to configure maximums on a per-queue basis, then instead of clicking All Queues, click Per Queue, as shown in Figure 19–17. A great example of Per Queue printing quotas is to allow users to print many more copies of print jobs on black-and-white printers but to limit the printing further on color printers. Here, you use the Queue Name field to select a shared printer and then the Print Server field for which computer that the shared printer is running on.

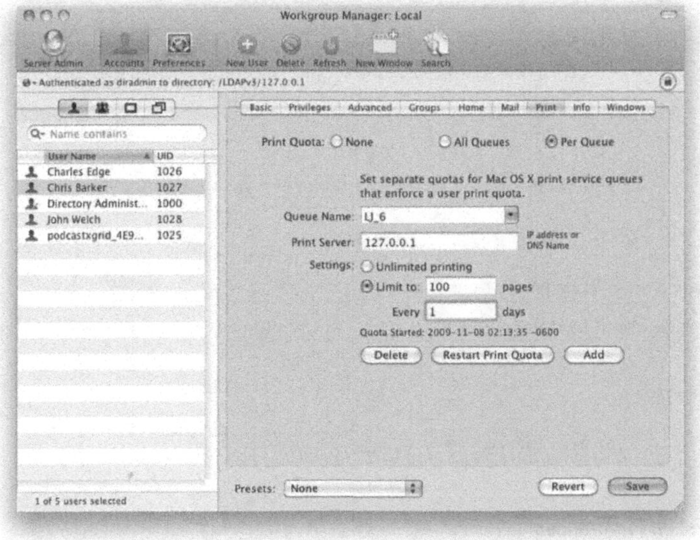

Figure 19–17. *Per-queue quotas*

NOTE: The Restart Print Quota button should be available and usable on a per-user basis in order to reset a user's quota, which is very helpful when it comes to troubleshooting!

Deploying Printers

Once you have built a shared printer, you will have a number of options to deploy it for Mac OS X. Because clients will connect to LPR and IPP printers using the same process that servers use, see the instructions in the "IPP" and "LPD" sections earlier for how to set up queues. Mac OS X can also connect to an SMB-based printer.

To install a printer that you set up a queue for on a Mac OS X Server, follow these steps:

1. First look at the protocol you used to set up the queue in the "Sharing a Printer" section earlier in this chapter.

2. From here, open the Print & Fax pane of System Preferences, as shown in Figure 19–18.

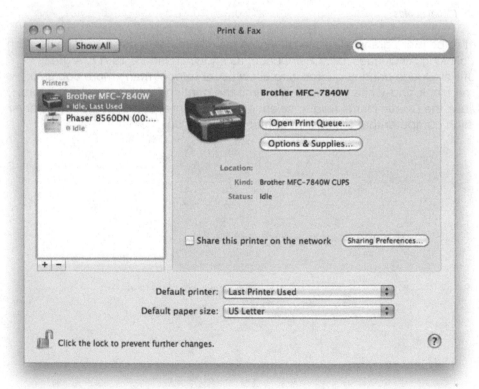

Figure 19–18. *Print & Fax pane of System Preferences*

3. From here, click the plus (+) sign. You will see the Add Printer dialog box.

4. In the Add Printer dialog box, select the protocol that you shared the printer using from the Protocol drop-down list.

5. Enter the address in the Address field.

6. Finally, either select the queue or manually enter the queue in the field name. The queue will be the name that you selected for the shared printer earlier. You can optionally enter a custom name for the printer in the Name field and a location in the Location field, although these will not impact whether you can print.

7. Finally, select a printer driver in the Print Using drop-down list, and then click the Add button to set up the print queue. Assuming a print server name of replica.krypted.com and a shared printer called LJ_5 using LPR, Figure 19–19 shows the appropriate settings used.

NOTE: Managing print jobs involves looking at a job that has been sent to a print queue, determining why that job may or may not have printed and other common tasks related to printing. When troubleshooting a print server, your first objective, though, is to typically try to determine whether the issue is with users sending print jobs to the shared queue or whether the issue is with print jobs getting from the queue to the actual printer. The easiest way to triangulate this is to look at the queue and attempt to print directly from the server.

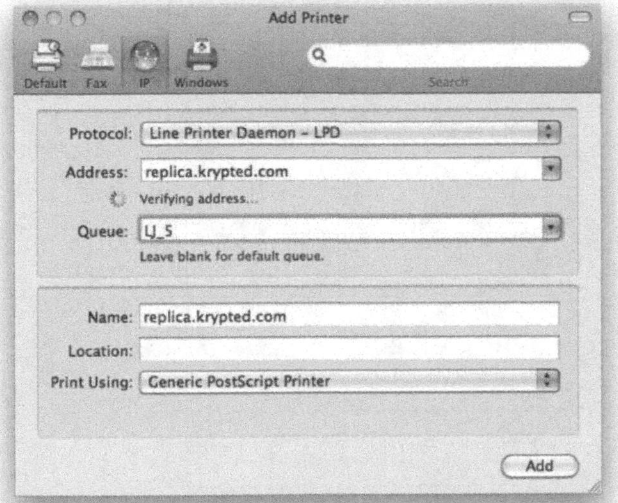

Figure 19–19. *Installing a shared printer*

Once you have set up the queue, test printing to it. Provided that the test prints correctly, then the printer setup process should be complete.

> **NOTE:** In some cases, the test print job will have the wrong fonts or not be in color. In most cases, this is an incompatibility with the printer driver, so you will want to download the latest drivers from your vendor and test printing again.

Deploying Printers to Large Groups of Users

If you have only a few computers, then deploying printers manually as we just described is a fairly simple task. However, when you have a lot of users and a lot of computers to deploy printers onto, then you will likely want to automate the process. Luckily, Apple has hooked you up. If you are running Open Directory, you can deploy printers en masse through managed preferences, which are described in further detail in Chapter 4.

To deploy the shared printer to Mac OS X clients that are logging in with Open Directory accounts, first open the Workgroup Manager application from /Applications/Server, and then click the user, computer, or group to which you want to deploy the printer. With the objects highlighted that you want to manage, click the Preferences button in the Workgroup Manager toolbar to bring up the Overview screen that shows all of the configurable managed preferences, as shown in Figure 19–20.

Figure 19–20. *Managed preferences in Workgroup Manager*

Next, click the Printing managed preference. As shown in Figure 19–21, you will then see a number of options for managing printing preferences for clients. The Available Printers list should show all printers that the server is able to communicate with. To the right you will see the User's Printer List. Simply click a printer from the Available Printers list, and click the Add button to move it to the User's Printer List. You can then click Apply Now, and the printer will be installed on the client at their subsequent login. You can also configure a few global settings for those clients. These include the following:

- *Allow user to modify the printer list*: Allows the user to add and remove printers once the printers have been initially deployed (saves the server administrator from a lot of headache for some environments).

- *Allow printers that connect directly to user's computer*: Allows the user to add USB and other types of printers that are physically connected to their workstation (saves the server administrator from a lot of headache for some environments).

- *Require an administrator password*: Forces a password when making changes to printer lists.

- *Only show managed printers*: Only shows the user printers that are managed from Open Directory.

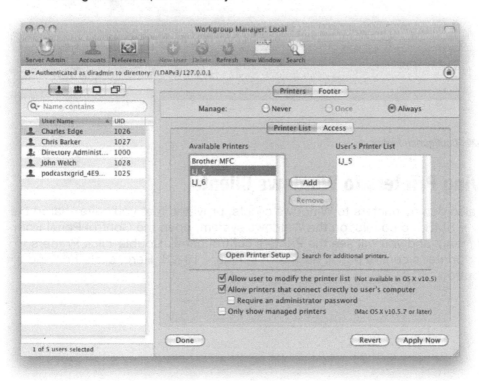

Figure 19–21. *Printers managed preference*

You can also configure each job to print with a footer. The footer will include the name of the user and the date that the job was submitted to the print queue. To do so, click the Footer tab, and then select the "Print page footer (user name and date)" box, which you can see in Figure 19–22.

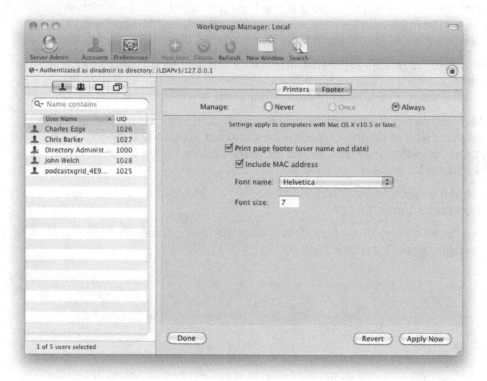

Figure 19–22. *Configuring footers*

Deploying Printers to Windows Clients

You can also deploy printers to Windows clients, provided that you have shared the printer over SMB. To do this, on the Windows system, open the Control Panel from the Start menu, and you will see the Printers control panel. Double-click Printers to open your printer's control panel, as shown in Figure 19–23. Here, click the "Add a printer" button.

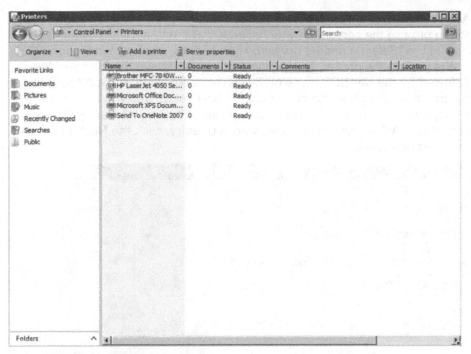

Figure 19-23. *The printer's control panel*

In the Add Printer dialog box, you may already see your printer. If not, then click "The printer that I want isn't listed," as shown in Figure 19–24.

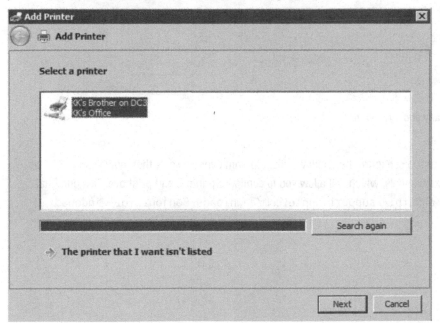

Figure 19-24. *Add Printer dialog box*

At the new Add Printer screen, you can use "Select a shared printer by name" or the Browse button to browse the servers on your network that the Windows system has access to. Click in the "Select a shared printer by name" field, as shown in Figure 19–25, and then type the path to the printer. This printer name should have the format of the standard \\ followed by the NetBIOS name of the server, followed by a \ and finally the SMB sharing name that was given the printer when it was set up (refer to Figure 19–19 earlier in this chapter). This process is similar to accessing SMB file shares using the Run dialog box as well. When you are satisfied with your entry, click the Next button to install the driver and test printing.

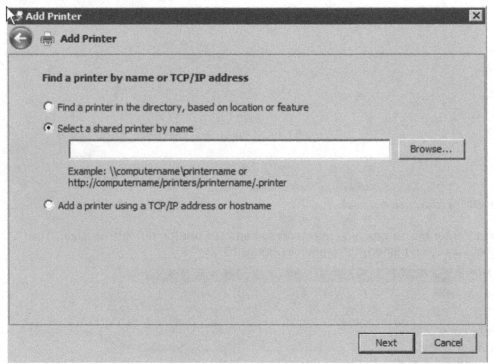

Figure 19–25. *Manually adding a printer*

NOTE: If you want to configure the Windows client to print over Bonjour, then download the Bonjour for Windows tools, which will allow you to configure printers and print over Bonjour. That tool is available at http://support.apple.com/downloads/Bonjour_for_Windows.

Managing Printing with Common Unix Printing System

You can configure printer sharing via the Terminal command line or through the CUPS web interface. The Common Unix Printing System (CUPS) is the Unix printing system at the core of the Mac's printing services and what you will be configuring whether you manage printers through the Print & Fax pane of System Preferences, through the command line, or through the CUPS web interface. CUPS can provide you with even more control over the printing experience for your end users when managed directly than you have through the Print & Fax pane. CUPS uses HTTP as its transport protocol to provide printing services to users and has a built-in web interface to allow configuration of the service. To access the web interface, type the address **http://127.0.0.1:631** into your web browser (see Figure 19–26).

Figure 19–26. *CUPS web interface*

Click the Administration tab at the top to perform basic printer configurations. If you'd like to get more refined (and you know what you're doing), the CUPS server has a configuration file that is editable from within the CUPS web interface. To access this file, under the Administration tab, click the Edit Configuration File button under the Server heading (Figure 19–27). Some settings that can be altered by editing this file include the following:

- MaxCopies
- Port

- BrowseAllow

- BrowseAddress

- SystemGroup

- The Location's directive's Allow option

- AuthType

- AuthClass

One example of a task that you may want to perform on this screen is to assign a preferred printer to a printer pool. To do so, add two or more printers as described earlier in the "Creating a Printer Pool" section. Then open the Administration screen, as shown in Figure 19–27. From here, click Add Class in the Classes section; provide a name for your class, choose the first printer that should be printed to, and add the class. Then click the class, Command+click each printer to add, and choose to modify the class. Once you have added all the printers to the pool, test the pool. When you set up printer pools using the web interface, printing to those printers should occur in the order that you added printers to the pool.

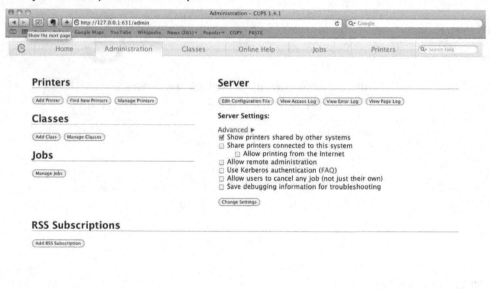

Figure 19–27. *CUPS web interface Administration tab*

Another task that you will occasionally want to be able to do is manage the print queues from the command line. When you are managing print jobs and network printing in Mac OS X Server, it's good to understand how Mac OS X, and more specifically, how CUPS, is interacting with those jobs. The following are some basic print job/queue management commands:

- `lpr`: Sends a print job to a print queue
- `lpq`: Shows the status of jobs sent to a print queue
- `lprm`: Deletes jobs from a print queue
- `lpc`: Controls print queues

Summary

Printing is one of the most basic tasks a computer can do, and it's one of the functions that has driven the personal computing boom over the past few decades. But as computers and printers have gained new capabilities and features, the need to manage who is printing to which devices has become more important than ever. Limiting the ability to print to certain printers can save organizations countless time and money. Thankfully, Mac OS X Server includes these capabilities, and it should now be clear to you how to use them.

Most environments are not homogenous. So, you also need to be able to print from computers that run different operating systems. In this chapter, we covered setting up shared printers, and we also covered installing those shared printers on both Mac and Windows computers.

Additionally, pushing out printers to users is a massive time saver as environments grow. In this chapter, we covered pushing out printers through managed preferences and then gaining even more control over printers with CUPS. Overall, the printing services in Mac OS X, as with other Unix variants, are a mature and stable solution. Now that you've seen what you can do with printing in Mac OS X Server, you will shift your attention to backing up your server in Chapter 20.

Backing Up Your Data

A well-architected backup scheme will plan for every possible failure, whether it's using a RAID so that you don't have to restore from backup or restoring from offsite tapes in the event of a disaster. A number of things can go wrong with your server, and planning for each one takes time, care, and sometimes creativity (as does any priceless piece of art).

There are two primary aspects to backing up Mac OS X Server: the first is the operating system and the second is the storage that is used by each service. Throughout this book, we have looked at setting up each service in Mac OS X Server. Some services, such as file sharing, typically require a lot of storage, whereas others will not (e.g., Address Book services). But each service should be looked at and reviewed independently. You should test data restores and routinely verify backups. In addition to backing up the services, you need to back up the actual operating system as well. Both aspects must be considered when looking at how long it takes to restore a machine back to working order in the event of a failure.

Like any art, backup is holistic. Therefore, the first part of this chapter will be theoretical and will try to provide some deep thoughts for you to mull over. In the second part of this chapter, we'll jump right into how to use some popular solutions for Mac OS X and even how to interconnect iSCSI (a network attached storage protocol) so that, for example, you can use a Drobo (a brand of storage device) over iSCSI to backup your data. If the theoretical parts of this chapter start to put you to sleep, please try to stick with it; a lot of logic needs to be applied to architecting a solid backup plan, as you cannot backup through software and hardware alone.

Managing Information *En Masse*

Information life cycle management (ILM) is a process for maximizing information availability and data protection while minimizing cost. It is a strategy for aligning your IT infrastructure with the needs of your business based on the value of data. Administrators must analyze the trade-offs between cost and availability of data in tiers by differentiating production or transactional data from reference or fixed-content data.

ILM includes the policies, practices, services, and tools used to align business practices with the most appropriate and cost-effective data structures. Once data has been classified into tiers, storage methods can be chosen that are in line with the business needs of each organization. The policies to govern these practices need to be clearly documented in order to keep everyone working towards the same goals.

Classifying Storage

ILM dictates that we classify our storage. Classifications typically start with online, offline, and near-line storage:

- *Online storage* is highly available and has fast and redundant drives, for example, Promise RAID and Xserve RAID before it. This type of storage is best used for production data, as it is dynamic in nature. It can include current projects and financial data, which must be backed up often and rapidly restored in the event of a loss. It is not uncommon to use one physical Promise RAID to backup another physical Promise RAID for (almost) immediate restoration of files and a tape library to maintain offsite backups of the Promise RAID.

- *Offline storage* is used for data retained for long periods of time and rarely accessed. Data often found on offline media includes old projects and archived e-mail. Media used for offline storage is often the same as media used for backup, such as tape drives and optical media. When talking about offline storage we refer to *archives*, not *backups*. Generally, archives are static, whereas backups are dynamically changed with each backup. Offline storage still needs to be redundant or backed up, but the schedules for backup are often more lax than with other classifications of storage. In a small- or medium-sized company, offline media is often backed up, or duplicated, to the same type of media that it is housed on. There may be two copies of a tape (one onsite and one offsite) or two copies of DVDs that the data has been burned onto, with each copy stored in a different physical location.

- *Near-line storage* bridges the gap between online and offline storage by providing faster data access than archival storage at a lower cost than primary storage. FireWire drives are often considered near-line storage, because they are slower and usually not redundant. *Near-line* can refer to recent projects, old financial data, office forms that are updated rarely, and backups of online storage to be made readily available for rapid recovery. Backup of near-line storage will probably be to tape.

As you can see in Figure 20–1, each of these tiers (your environment may have more or less than three tiers) will typically provide data to the next as the data ages.

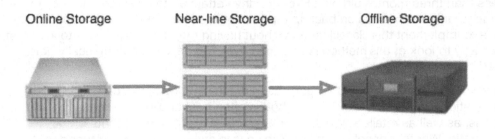

Online Storage   Near-line Storage   Offline Storage

Figure 20–1. *Online, offline, and near-line storage*

NOTE: Do not confuse the term *online storage* as you see it in this chapter with cloud-based storage, which we will get to later.

Classifying Data

Mission-critical data is typically stored in online storage. This data is the day-to-day production data that drives information-based businesses. It includes the jobs being worked on by graphic designers, the video being edited for commercials and movies, the accounting data that is needed by business units and current items within an organizations groupware system.

For the small business, vital and sensitive data are often one in the same. *Vital data* is used in normal business practices but can be down for minutes or longer. Similarly, a company can live without certain types *sensitive data* for a short period of time but will need that data to be quickly restored in the event of a loss. Small business will typically keep vital and sensitive data on the same type of media but may have different backup policies for each. For example, a company may choose to encrypt sensitive data and not vital data.

Noncritical data includes items such as digital records and personal data files of network users, or even a duplicate of mission-critical data from online storage. Noncritical data often resides on near-line or offline media (as is the case with e-mail archives). Noncritical data is primarily data kept as part of a company's risk management strategy or for regulatory compliance and includes financial records and similar data, as well as e-mail.

Understanding the Classification Methods

You have three options for classifying data: chronologically, characteristically, or hierarchically.

The chronological method for classifying data is often the easiest and most logical. For example, a design firm may keep mission-critical current jobs on a Promise RAID, vital jobs less than three months old on a FireWire drive attached to a server, and noncritical jobs older than three months on backup tapes or offline FireWire drives. It would not be possible to implement this classification without having the data organized into jobs first. Another way to look at this method is that data over 180 days old automatically gets archived.

The characteristic method of data organization means that data with certain characteristics can be archived. This method is often best applied to accounting and legal firms, as well as retailers. Whether or not a client is active represents a characteristic. Whether or not a type of clothing is in style represents another possible characteristic. Provided that data is arranged or labeled by characteristic, it is possible to archive using a certain characteristic as a variable or metadata. Many small- and medium-sized companies are not using metadata for files yet, so a good substitution can be using a filename to denote attributes of the files data.

In the hierarchical method of data organization, files or folders within certain areas of the filesystem can be archived. For example, if a company decides to close down its music supervision department, the data stored in the music supervision share point on the server could be archived.

Building Service Level Agreements

The final piece of the ILM puzzle is building a service level agreement (SLA) for data management within a company. In this agreement, the people who use each type of data within an organization sit down with IT staff and define how readily available that data needs to be and how often that data needs to be backed up.

In a small business, often the owners of the company make this decision, which in many ways makes drafting an SLA easier than in a larger organization. The owner of a small business is more likely to have a picture of what the data can cost the company. When given the cost difference between online and near-line storage, small business owners often more easily make concessions than managers of larger organizations.

Building a good SLA means asking and answering questions about the data for each classification. Some of the most important questions follow:

- How much data is there?
- How readily available does the data need to be?
- How much does data cost the company, including backups?
- Given the type of storage used to house this data, how much is the total cost of ownership of storage for your organization?
- If half the data can be moved to near-line storage, what will the savings be to the company?
- In the event of a loss, how long will a restoration take?
- How far back in time does your organization need to go for retrieval?

- Is the data required to be in an unalterable format for regulatory purposes?
- How fast must data be restored in the event of a loss?
- Will client systems be backed up? If so, what on each client system will be backed up?

Managing the Information Life Cycle

Most companies will use a combination of methods to determine their data classification. Each classification should be mapped to a type of storage by building an SLA. Once the SLA is done, software programs such as BRU or Retrospect can be configured for automated archival and backups. The backup and archival software chosen will be the component that implements the SLA, so it should fill the requirement of the ILM policies put into place.

The schedules for archival and backups should be set in accordance with the businesses needs. Some companies may choose to keep the same data in online storage for longer than other companies in the same business, because they have invested more in online storage or because they reference the data often for other projects. The business logic of the organization will drive the schedule using the SLA as a roadmap.

Setting schedules means having documentation for what information lives where and for how long. ILM brings the actual data locations in line with the ideal data locations. Once these are aligned, the cost to house and back up data becomes more quantifiable and reasonable. The SLA is meant to be a guideline and should be revisited at roadblocks and intervals along the way. Checks and balances should be put into place to ensure that the actual data management situation accurately reflects the SLA.

ILM and regulatory compliance are more about people and business process than about required technology changes, and understanding the life cycle of data is key to creating an effective SLA. As storage requirements spiral out of control, administrators of small- and medium-sized organizations can look to the methods of enterprise networking for handling storage requirements with scalability and flexibility.

Getting Redundant Before You Back Up

Redundancy is more important on servers than on desktop computers. Redundant hard drives are possible in the Mac mini Server, Apple Xserve, and Mac Pro with no additional hardware. Or, for server-class uses, you can use a RAID 5 card or dual power supplies in Xserve. Ultimately, the goal is to plan for disasters to happen to the hardware in your server, and in the event that a disaster happens, you will want to bring the server back into use as soon as is humanly (or *computerly*) possible. Why? Because multiple people are unable to access data when that server is not online!

Network attached storage (NAS) devices are a popular alternative to providing centralized file services to smaller environments and include devices such as the Seagate BlackArmor, the DroboShare NAS, and the Netgear ReadyNAS Pro. As compared to an actual server, these are inexpensive, require less management, and often come with some pretty compelling features. But one of the primary reasons to buy a NAS can end up being a potential pain point as well: they require less management than a server because they can't do as much.

For example, consider the ability to replicate data between two servers. Most have NAS-to-NAS replication built in. However, that replication ends up being dependent on having two servers. What if you just have a computer on the other side of the replication and want to remotely back up and compress it or want to back it up to a cloud environment? If the original and backup are not running a client-server combination specifically designed for backup, you're typically stuck using CIFS, NFS, HTTPS (WebDAV), or FTP. The devices don't typically give you the option to push directly from them or to run a daemon that a nonproprietary device can connect to directly, so you'd have to use a client to do the offsite sync. One example of how to do this would be to use JungleDisk and an Amazon S3 account. JungleDisk would mount the AmazonS3 storage and the NAS storage (all share points). You would then use a tool such as ChronoSync, Retrospect (which duplicates scripts instead of backing up scripts by the way), or even rsync to back up the device over CIFS. Using two tools like this is not pretty and causes extra latency and management, but it would work.

You can also synchronize data. If you need to back up (for example, using Retrospect backup scripts) and send big, monolithic files over the wire, the smaller the increments of data you can send over the network, the better. Another tool that can do that type of sync is File Replication Pro, which actually sends blocks instead of files, pushing an even smaller increment of data over the wire. You could even open up the firewall (for just the specific ports/IP addresses requiring connectivity) and have a remote backup service come in and pull the data sync over FTP, CIFS, or WebDAV (if you want to stick with a cloud backup solution). However, those types of services are a bit more difficult to find, and shutting down the firewall is always a potential security risk

The same is pretty much true for cloud-based storage—with the exception that instead of a built-in feature, you're looking for a built-in feature or an API that allows you to develop your own.

Here's the moral of the redundancy story: if you use a NAS or a cloud-based solution and you want to back your data up, your options are limited. Keep this in mind when you decide to purchase a NAS rather than, let's say, a Mac OS X Server running on a Mac mini with some direct attached storage (DAS) connected to it.

Using Backup Applications

A number of backup applications are available for Mac OS X. The first and often most desirable of these is Time Machine, which is built into Mac OS X. But it is not for everyone, so later in this section, we will also look at Retrospect, a backup tool that has been popular on the Mac platform for well over ten years. Not included in this chapter but certainly worth note are Atempo's Time Navigator, ArchiWare's PresSTORE, and Bakbone's NetVault.

Before you start to configure any of these solutions, consider what you are going to back up and why. To help with this, use a worksheet similar to the one shown in Figure 20–2 (available for download at `http://www.krypted.com/Scripts/bak.zip`).

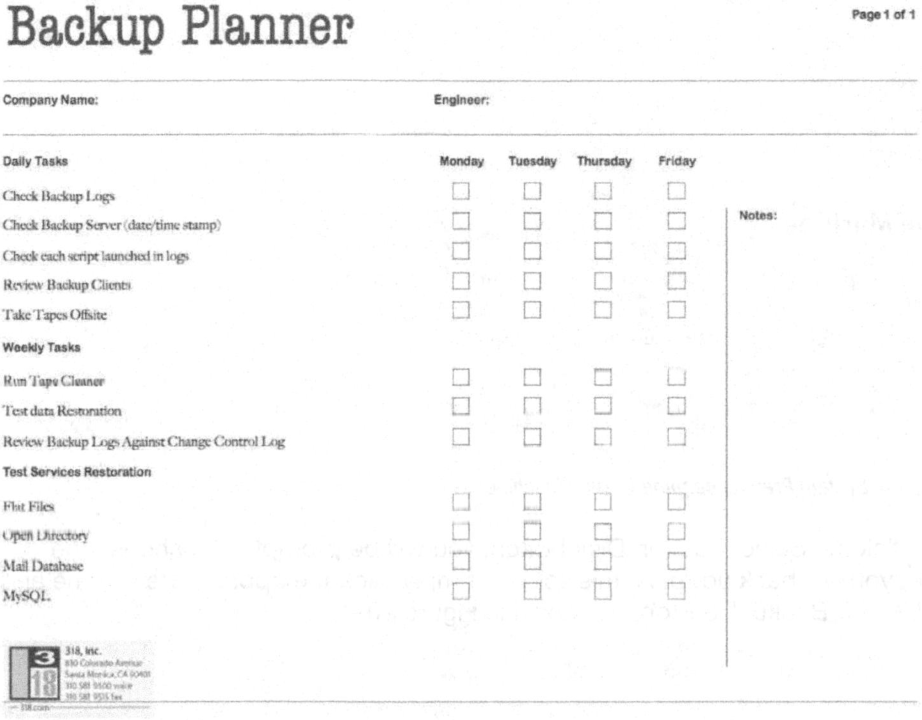

Backup Planner
Page 1 of 1

Company Name: _____   Engineer: _____

Daily Tasks	Monday	Tuesday	Thursday	Friday	
Check Backup Logs	☐	☐	☐	☐	
Check Backup Server (date/time stamp)	☐	☐	☐	☐	Notes:
Check each script launched in logs	☐	☐	☐	☐	
Review Backup Clients	☐	☐	☐	☐	
Take Tapes Offsite	☐	☐	☐	☐	
Weekly Tasks					
Run Tape Cleaner	☐	☐	☐	☐	
Test data Restoration	☐	☐	☐	☐	
Review Backup Logs Against Change Control Log	☐	☐	☐	☐	
Test Services Restoration					
Flat Files	☐	☐	☐	☐	
Open Directory	☐	☐	☐	☐	
Mail Database	☐	☐	☐	☐	
MySQL	☐	☐	☐	☐	

318, Inc.
830 Colorado Avenue
Santa Monica, CA 90401
310.581.9500 voice
310.581.9513 fax
— 318.com —

Figure 20–2. *A backup planning worksheet*

Backing Up with Time Machine

When you are planning your backup, it helps to have the operating system and the data separated. The operating system should rarely change. Because the operating system is so static, you can use a simplistic backup scheme for it. In this example, we're going to look at leveraging Time Machine for this very purpose.

Setting Up Time Machine

Time Machine is a fairly simple backup application, but it does come with the capability to back up a Mac OS X Server. To use Time Machine, first connect and format the storage that will be used with your Time Machine backups. When you connect new storage to Mac OS X Server (or a Mac OS X client for that matter) and Time Machine is enabled, you will initially be asked if you will be using that storage as a backup device. For now, ignore that prompt.

In Time Machine, open the System Preference pane. Here, you will see a button labeled Select Backup Disk (see Figure 20–3) that can be used to select your target backup volume.

Figure 20–3. *The System Preference pane in Time Machine*

When you click the Select Backup Disk button, you will be prompted to choose the volume that you will back up to. At this screen, simply click the appropriate volume and click the "Use for Backup" button, as shown in Figure 20–4.

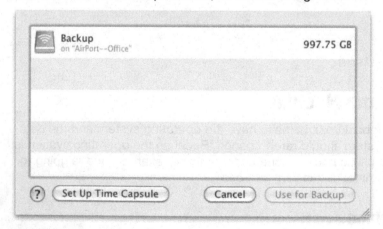

Figure 20–4. *Selecting a Time Machine target*

The "Use for Backup" button will take you back to the System Preference pane, where you will see the schedule that Time Machine will be using to back up your system (as shown in Figure 20–5). This schedule can be altered, although the alterations will need to be made through the command line or a third-party application such as

TimeMachineEditor, which can be found at
http://timesoftware.free.fr/timemachineeditor.

Figure 20–5. *Enabling Time Machine*

Simply select a destination for your backups to enable Time Machine. You can then configure any backup options that you see fit. The Options button will bring up the exclusion list for Time Machine. Here, you can do two things, as you will note in Figure 20–6: choose items to exclude from the Time Machine backups, and indicate whether or not you would like to be notified in the event that an old backup is deleted.

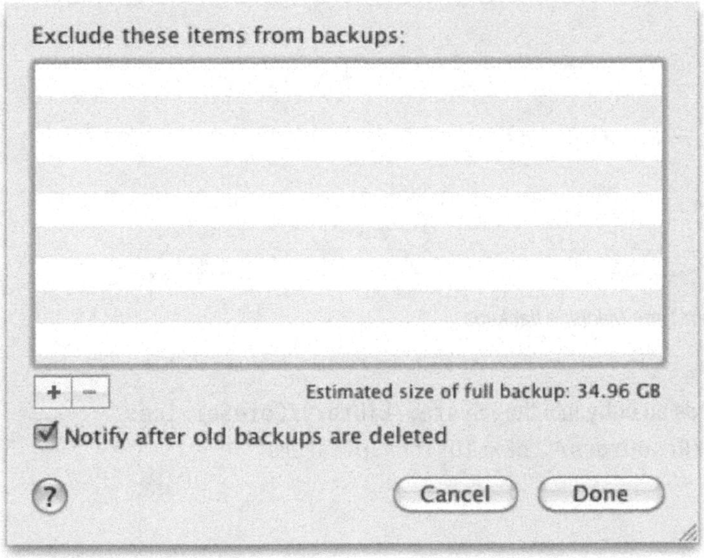

Exclude these items from backups:

Estimated size of full backup: 34.96 GB

☑ Notify after old backups are deleted

Cancel   Done

Figure 20–6. *Time Machine options*

Clicking the plus sign (+) will bring up a screen that you can use to exclude folders that you do not want to back up; select any of these, and click the Exclude button (see Figure 20–7). Some directories to consider skipping might include the mail directory for a user (~/Library/Mail) if you use IMAP mail, iTunes libraries for corporate scenarios, and temporary directories.

> **NOTE:** If you are in an environment that has a good imaging solution, such as those described in Chapter 8, you likely won't need to rely on your backup application for items stored in /Applications and other folders where the data will also be on your image. In those environments, focus on the data that must be backed up and is not present elsewhere, namely the data in each user's home folder and any user-generated content that might reside outside of that folder.

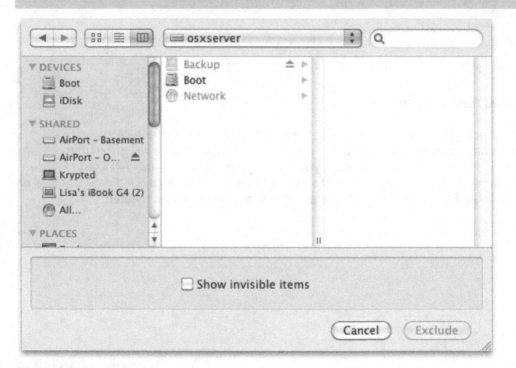

Figure 20–7. *Excluding directories from Time Machine backups*

> **NOTE:** Excluding directories adds an entry into the /System/Library/CoreServices/ backupd.bundle/Contents/Resources/StdExclusions.plist file.

Using Command Line Options for Time Machine

Time Machine is a simple application to set up and manage, but most backup environments are a little more complicated. This means that you will need to use more granular configuration to achieve your desired results in many cases. And for that, you will need to revert to the command line, assuming specific options are available there. Otherwise, you may need to look at a more robust tool for backing up your environment.

By default, when you are using Time Machine in Mac OS X, every time you insert a drive, the system will ask you if you would like to use that drive as a Time Machine backup destination. If you are like me and you swap drives around a lot, this question can get annoying. To stop it, you can actually just disable a launched system daemon, com.apple.backupd-attach. To do so, simply move the /System/Library/LaunchDaemons/com.apple.backupd-attach.plist to another location, and on the next restart when you attach a disk, Time Machine won't ask you if you wish to add the disk to your Time Machine destinations.

You could also achieve the same result by editing the /Library/Preferences/com.apple.TimeMachine.plist file, adding a DoNotOfferNewDisksForBackup key that is set to true, which can be done using the following command:

```
defaults write /Library/Preferences/com.apple.TimeMachine \
DoNotOfferNewDisksForBackup -bool true;
```

Next, let's look at how to change the frequency of backups. Backups are initiated by com.apple.backupd-auto.plist, stored in /System/Library/LaunchDaemons. The contents of this file are as follows by default:

```
<?xml version="1.0" encoding="UTF-8"?>
<!DOCTYPE plist PUBLIC "-//Apple Computer//DTD PLIST 1.0//EN"
"http://www.apple.com/DTDs/PropertyList-1.0.dtd">
<plist version="1.0">
<dict>
 <key>Label</key>
 <string>com.apple.backupd-auto</string>
 <key>ProgramArguments</key>
 <array> <string>/System/Library/CoreServices/backupd.bundle/
Contents/Resources/backupd-helper</string>
 <string>-auto</string>
 </array>
 <key>StartInterval</key>
 <integer>3600</integer>
 <key>RunAtLoad</key>
 <false/>
 <key>KeepAlive</key>
 <false/>
</dict>
</plist>
```

The StartInterval integer controls the frequency, in seconds, with which backups occur. You can customize this by altering the integer in the line below. For example, if you set StartInterval to 360, backups will occur every 6 minutes, or more likely, if you set the integer to 14400, your backups will occur every 4 hours.

Finally, only volumes that are directly connected to a Mac OS X computer or sitting on an Apple AirPort or Time Machine are supported for use with Time Machine by default. If you want to use an unsupported disk type for your Time Machine archives, such as an NFS or SMB volume, running the following command on workstations will allow you to do so:

```
defaults write com.apple.systempreferences TMShowUnsupportedNetworkVolumes 1
```

Backing Up with Retrospect

Historically, one of the most popular alternatives to Time Machine for Mac OS X is EMC's Retrospect, which is capable of doing many of the tasks that Time Machine can't. This includes performing scripted and uncompressed backups (timed file copies), backing up client computers, performing proactive and tape-based backup, and using a myriad of exclusion options and a number of other features. In this section, we're going to focus on getting Retrospect up and running and mirroring much of the same functionality that Time Machine was able to provide.

Installing Retrospect

To install Retrospect, download the latest version from the EMC web site at http://www.retrospect.com/supportupdates/updates. You will also need a serial number that's provided to you when you purchase it.

> **TIP:** Even if you purchase the software in a retail outlet such as the Apple Store, it is still best to use the latest version of the software from the web site for installation.

Once downloaded, the disk image will mount. Here, you will see a collection of directories and the Install Retrospect Engine package. Retrospect 8 introduces the ability to run your backups on a dedicated computer and to manage those backups from any system that is running the Management Console, so the Management Console can run on your laptop or on your backup server. For our example setup though, we're going to run the Management Console on the same system on which we install the Retrospect engine (the Management console manages this engine).

To put the Management Console on your system, simply drag the folder from the disk image to the Applications alias, as shown in Figure 20–8.

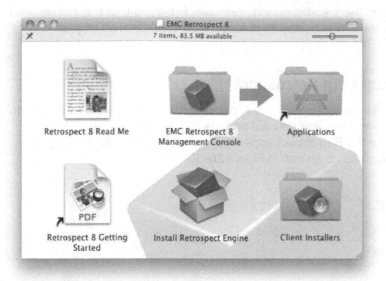

Figure 20–8. *The Retrospect disk image*

Once the copy is complete, you can double-click the Install Retrospect Engine package, also in the disk image, to be greeted with the "Welcome to the Retrospect Installer" screen. Here, click the Continue button to advance to the SLA. Again, click the Continue button to proceed to the Standard Install screen where you can click the Change Install Location button to select a different drive for installation, as shown in Figure 20–9.

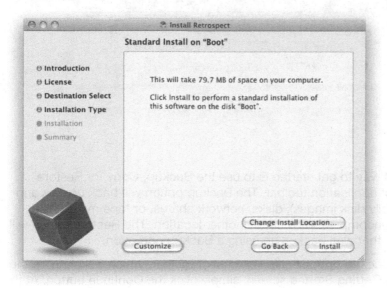

Figure 20–9. *Performing a standard installation*

Click the Install button, and the installation will complete. Provided that the installation is successful, you will click the Close button to proceed with configuration of your first backup.

Configuring a Backup with Retrospect

Once you have installed Retrospect, you'll want to connect to your server. To do so, go into your /Applications directory, and you will find the EMC Retrospect 8 directory. Within this directory will be the Retrospect application. Double-click it to bring up the main Retrospect window, which is shown in Figure 20–10.

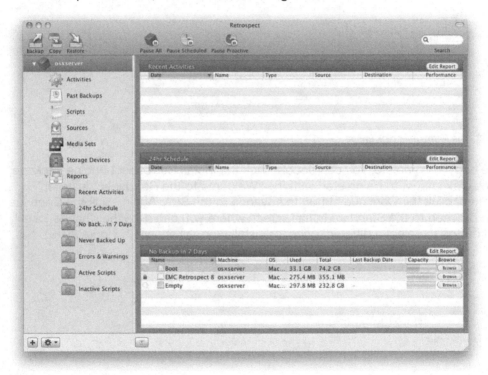

Figure 20–10. *Retrospect*

The quickest and easiest way to get started is to use the Backup, Copy, or Restore buttons in the Retrospect application toolbar. The Backup option will back up files and folders into files (essentially disk images), disks, network shares, or tape media. The Copy function will copy uncompressed data to another location. The Restore option will allow you to restore data that was backed up using a Backup operation.

Go ahead and click the Backup option in the Retrospect toolbar, which will bring up the Backup Assistant. At the Getting Started screen, simply click the Continue button. At the Select Sources screen, you will be able to choose which volumes and files on your system to back up. For the purpose of this example, we're going to back up all of the files on the server, but keep in mind that you have a plethora of options for skipping specific files and folders; you can skip certain folders, file types (such as MP3 or AAC files), and even directories based on the color codes of objects that have been labeled from the finder. Select the backup drive (as shown in Figure 20–11), and click the Continue button.

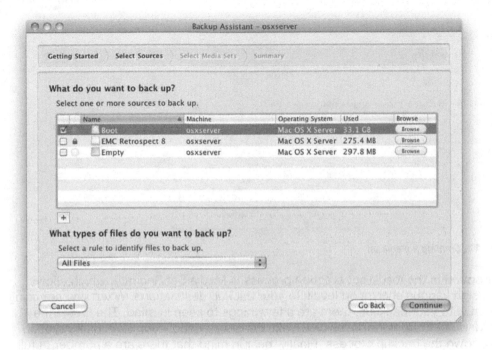

Figure 20–11. *Selecting sources in Retrospect's Backup Assistant*

The next screen will allow you to select a media set, but if there are no media sets on the system yet, you will immediately see the media set creation screen. Here, you can provide the specifics to the target of your backup. Remember that backups can have a variety of destination types in Retrospect. In the Media Set Type field, you will have the option to select from Tape, Tape WORM, Disk, Optical, and File. Of these, the most common will be Tape, Disk (which assumes control of an entire volume), and File (which creates a disk image or an encrypted disk image as a backup destination). In the Media Set Name field, provide a name for the device (e.g., type **weekly offsite**, **Set A**, or **daily recycle**) as shown in Figure 20–12. Then choose a location for the Catalog files using the Catalog Location field.

> **TIP:** Don't forget to back up the catalog location, as it will be needed during restores. Although it can be rebuilt if needed, doing so is not exactly a zippy process!

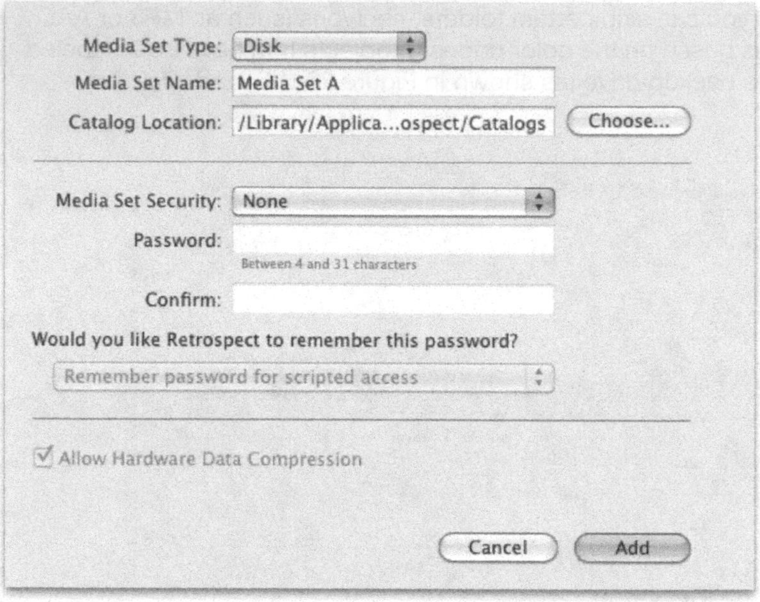

Figure 20–12. *Creating a media set*

Another option in the media set creation process is Media Set Security, which allows you to assign various encryption levels to your backup destinations. When you are using encryption with your backups, there are a few things to keep in mind. The first is the password: *do not forget the password*. Next, consider speed: each level of encryption will slow down the backup process. Finally, bear in mind that there are a number of full disk encryption products that can do a great job encrypting data without the need to encrypt in the software if you are backing up to a disk. By using full-disk encryption, rather than the encryption engine from within Retrospect, you can get great protection at a fraction of the performance cost.

Once you are satisfied with the choices for your media set, click the Add button. You will then see the "Add a new member" screen, which Figure 20–13 shows for a disk-based set. If you are using a tape-based set, you will be able to add tapes as members, and if you are using a file-based set, you will be able to add files sourced in multiple locations as members.

The great part about a set in Retrospect is that it represents a logical consolidation of media, so you can leverage multiple locations for a resultant set of storage that logically appears in Retrospect as a single repository. This virtualization of the destination storage layer allows you to have a massive amount of storage on relatively inexpensive media.

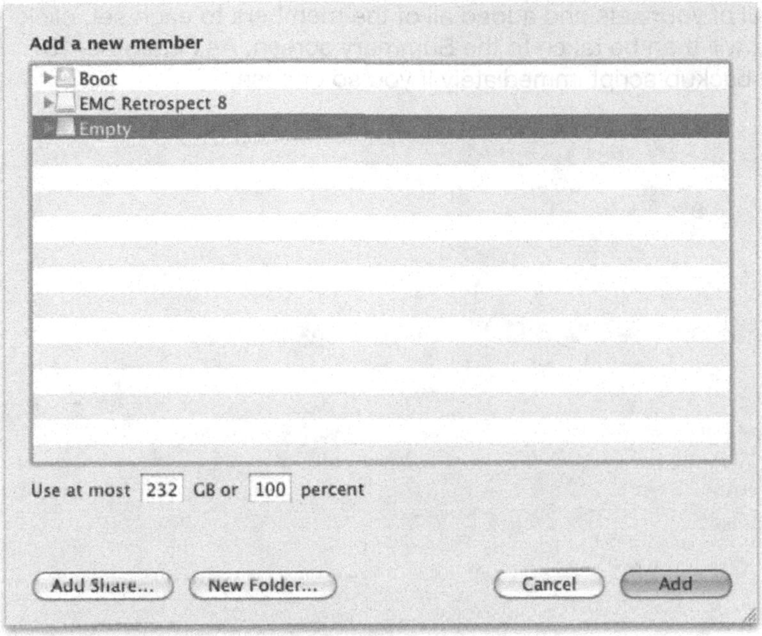

Figure 20–13. *Adding a member in Retrospect*

Once you have chosen the members of your set, click Add, and the assistant will allow you to choose the set that you will back up to. Here, you can use the plus sign (+) to add more sets or the Add Member button to add members to an existing set, as shown in Figure 20–14. By adding multiple sets, you can have a rotation of media, as you might do if one set of media were to always remain offsite as a backup component.

Figure 20–14. *Retrospect's Select Media Sets screen*

Once you have created all of your sets and added all of the members to each set, click the Continue button. You will then be taken to the Summary screen. As Figure 20–15 shows, you can start the backup script immediately if you so choose.

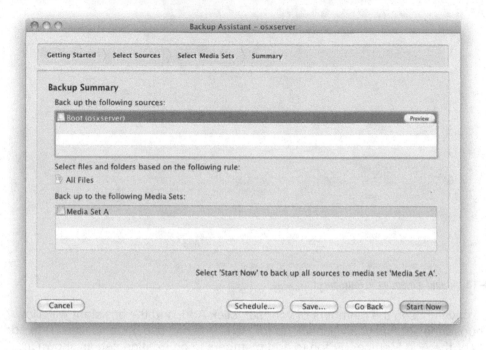

Figure 20–15. *The Backup Assistant summary screen*

Alternatively, you can also click the Schedule button to configure the script to run automatically on a daily, weekly, or monthly basis. You can also choose the time that the script will run and the set into which the script will back up data. As Figure 20–16 shows, there are a number of options in the schedules and strategies behind the use of each one. For example, when automating the weekly rotation of backup drives or tapes, you can use the "every" field to select that a scheduled instance of a script run every two weeks. You can then create another scheduled instance of the same script for the other weeks. Each would have a different set, which would allow you to routinely swap drives.

Figure 20–16. *Scheduling a script in Retrospect*

Once you have scheduled your backups, it's time to consider a grooming script, a type of utility script, to keep your backups running lean and mean.

Grooming Scripts

Retrospect backup scripts use snapshots. If you do a backup 20 times without a recycle, you will have 20 snapshots. If you then changed a 1-GB file every day, you'll have 20GB taken up by that one file. Now, let's say that you groom away ten of those backups by setting a grooming policy, so any file not required for the ten last backups will be removed from the disk-based backup set when the next grooming script runs. Now, that file requires only 10GB.

When would you use grooming? Anytime you have sets that grow and you don't want to recycle them. Why wouldn't you want to recycle them? Because right after the recycle event, you'll have a potential point of failure where you don't have a copy of your data, which you currently mitigate by having multiple sets with the same data.

One of the things consistent about Retrospect for Windows over the years is the ability to groom a backup set. *Grooming* is essentially taking the old data that doesn't need to be in the set and removing it, providing there's still a copy if the file is still resident on the source. We've always felt the lack of grooming left Retrospect for Mac clients at a serious disadvantage. In Retrospect 8, the Mac has this same feature. From within

Retrospect, you can click the Scripts menu to add a new utility script. In this case, we'll select Groom. You then check the box for each set you'd like to groom using this script and set a schedule.

Next, you'll want to go into your sets and configure a grooming policy. To do so, click Media Sets, click the set you'd like to set up a grooming policy for, and then click the Options tab. As Figure 20–17 shows, you'll see an option for "No grooming" (the default), or you can select the second radio button to specify the number of backups to keep. There is also an option to "Groom to Retrospect defined policy", which indicates that grooming will follow the policy that you set for all sets (unless a policy is otherwise specified for that set specifically).

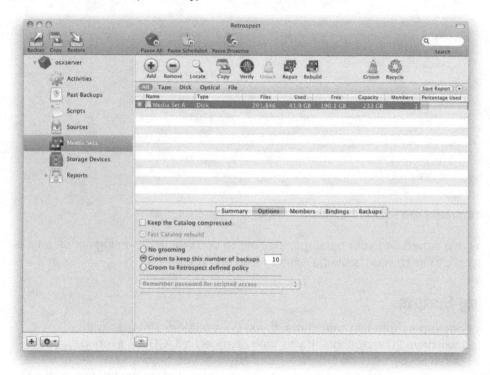

Figure 20–17. *Configuring Retrospect 8 grooming scripts*

Basically, by telling Retrospect to retain six or seven backups for a given set, you are eliminating the need to do an occasional recycle script, although you can also use the same script architecture as in previous versions. You can also tell a given set to use the global grooming policy.

But grooming isn't always the greatest thing ever. Keep in mind that it has a history of causing corrupt catalog files in the Windows version of the software. Make sure to back up your catalog files before grooming scripts are run. Also, be careful when stopping grooming scripts, as doing so has the potential to cause your catalogs to require a rebuild (stands to reason the catalogs might be corrupted if you stop a stream of data writing to them). Then too, Retrospect grooms disk-based sets only, so you'll have to avoid file-based ones. Finally, don't groom across disks; use grooming on sets that take up only one disk.

Another great utility script in Retrospect 8 for Mac is the ability to copy a media set or another backup, so you to skip a step in a number of offsite rotation scripts or disk-to-disk-to-tape setups. One immediate use might be to duplicate a recently groomed set of disk-based backups to tape before sending them off to Iron Mountain or some other offsite storage.

> **NOTE:** iWork 2008 applications (Keynote, Numbers, and Pages) and iLife 2008 components (iPhoto, iTunes, and Garage Band) have a slight issue with Retrospect—their data files are not considered documents using the Documents selector. Now, in the case of iLife application, this is probably a good thing. However, if you're using Keynote, Numbers, and Pages, you will likely want Retrospect to back up these files. If you are using selectors and the Documents selector, check out this Knowledge Base article from EMC: `http://kb.dantz.com/article.asp?article=9632&p=2`.

Creating Utility Scripts

As mentioned previously, an immediate use for a utility script might be to duplicate a recently groomed set of disk-based backups to tape in order to send them off to offsite storage. To set up a copy in this fashion, simply open Retrospect, and click the plus sign in the lower left corner of the window. In the new script dialog box, click Copy Media Set (see Figure 20–18). Click the Sources tab to select the source media Destinations to choose the target sets. Finally, click the Options tab to configure the appropriate options for you, which include these:

- *Copy backups*: Enables the copy of the backup set

- *Media verification*: Compares the source and target to verify they are the same

- *Data compression*: Enables compression in the software (disable when using tapes)

- *Recycle source Media Set after successful copy*: Good option for disk-to-disk-to-tape environments where the source is a disk-based staging area

- *Don't add duplicate files to the Media Set*: Provides a basic tool to avoid excess duplication

- *Eject tapes and discs when script is complete*: Eject the target media when the script has completed

Figure 20–18. *Retrospect 8 for Mac's Copy Media Set options*

iSCSI

iSCSI is a network storage protocol that allows sending and receiving of SCSI commands over a TCP/IP network. It allows you to leverage Ethernet, a low-cost network medium to get storage area network (SAN) performance and network-based storage. While you can use pretty much any Ethernet switch, we recommend dedicating a switch to iSCSI or using quality switches and building a dedicated virtual local area network (VLAN) for your iSCSI traffic.

Recently, we've heard a lot of discussion about whether you can use iSCSI with Mac OS X. The answer is yes. As with Apple's Xsan, to get started with iSCSI you'll need an initiator and a target. Studio Network Solutions (SNS) provides a software-based iSCSI initiator called globalSAN that can be downloaded and used free of charge from their site. Alternatively, you can look into the Atto Xtend SAN, which runs about $200 for one user with volume discounts slashing the prices to about $90 each for 100 users. Software-based initiators will use the CPU of your system and a built-in or third-party standard Ethernet port, but you can also buy a dedicated card for offloading the processing power, which in some cases may be required for performance reasons.

For the purpose of this chapter, we're going to use the SNS globalSAN software's free version called Starwind from RocketDivision. However, we've also tested OpenFiler, iSCSI Target from Microsoft, and many others with the Mac, and they all work similarly on the client side.

For starters, fire up your iSCSI storage, and share it out (you can use the instructions on the storage you own to do so). Next, extract the installer and then launch the Installer, and click the Continue button at the Welcome screen.

On the SLA screen, read the agreement, and click the Continue button if you agree to the terms. Then, at the uninstall screen, click Continue. If you later need to uninstall the software, rerun this installer, and click the Uninstall button.

At the Standard Install screen, you can click the Custom Install button to choose which packages within the metapackage to install. It is best to leave them all checked, and click the Continue button.

Provided everything installs properly, you will next be at the Installation Completed Successfully screen. Here, click Restart, log into the system when it comes back online, and open System Preferences. You'll see the new system preference for globalSAN iSCSI.

If you click the globalSAN system preference, you'll be able to add your first portal. Each share will have a unique IP address and be referenced as a portal. Click the plus icon (+) to add your first portal. At the dialog box, type the IP address and port number of your iSCSI target; the port defaults to 3260 for the majority of products.

If you require authentication to your target, click the Advanced button, and enter the pertinent information (Kerberos is not yet supported as an authentication method but the option for CHAP is). You can also click the IPSec tab if you use that for target authentication. Next, click OK to add your portal, and you will be taken back to the Portals tab of the globalSAN System Preferences, where you should see your portal listed. If you don't, click the Refresh button.

Now that you have your portal populated, click the Targets tab to see the storage listed. Click your storage, and then click the Log On button to initiate your session. At this point, the session will mount on the desktop (provided you have already given it a filesystem), and you will be able to use it as you would any other storage. You can check the Persistent box if you would like the volume always mounted on the system.

If you click the Sessions tab, you will be able to look at various statistics about your storage including the LUN identifier and disk name. If you don't yet have a filesystem on the storage device, you can open Disk Utility to see the storage listed there. Click it, and click the Partition tab, and you will then be able to assign a filesystem.

Using iSCSI with Time Machine

It's pretty easy to use iSCSI with Mac OS X. You don't have to open Terminal or do anything crazy. It just works, and while it's not going to be as fast as something like Fibre Channel, it also doesn't come with the costly infrastructure requirements that Fibre Channel comes with. The LUNs can be accessed by multiple hosts, provided the filesystem supports that. However, HFS+ does not support iSCSI, nor do any of the current filesystems for the Mac that we've tested other than acfs (Apple Clustered Filesystem) and cvfs, the filesystem for Xsan.

Mac OS X can leverage iSCSI targets and mounted filesystems from fileservers. Since they're often not your typical disks, you need to run a small command to make these foreign disks work:

```
defaults write com.apple.systempreferences TMShowUnsupportedNetworkVolumes 1
```

Essentially, once you've run this command, you'll be able to back up to anything that appears in /Volumes and more (for example, share points on your local network might appear even if you haven't yet authenticated to them). You'll also be able to back up to disks that are directly attached to an AirPort Extreme.

Summary

In this chapter, we looked at backing up Mac OS X Server using different strategies and methodologies. We also brought some logic and order to the chaos that stems from the fact that every environment is different. We cannot cover every possible service, but you need to plan for each of your services, whether or not they are built into Mac OS X Server. The items on the checklist that was provided (see Figure 20–1) in this chapter can be changed to each service in your environment. Each of those services should then be backed up as needed.

Remember that you need to check the logs when you run your backups. You need to test the restoration of each service and be aware of all of the moving parts. Software alone will not do the job of ensuring a comprehensive backup plan. The software that we looked at in this chapter is just the beginning. For example, version control of files, replication of data, and other features glossed over here are certainly requirements in many environments. While we can't cover everything that might come up when backing up Mac OS X Server, this chapter has provided some insight into the most common environments and how to bring order to them.

In the next chapter, we will discuss Software Update services, the last service of Mac OS X Server that is covered in this book.

Chapter 21

Configuring Software Update Server

Mac OS X Server can also run as a Software Update server and share updates with other Mac OS X clients. The Software Update service mirrors updates from the Apple Software Update service that you use by default when running Software Update. This helps keep larger Apple updates for operating systems and Apple software packages from taking up all of your Internet connection when 5 or 500 computers go to download that update all at the same time.

The server runs a modified version of Apache and is therefore basically just a web server. The updates are synchronized with Apple's updates, and as the administrator, you have the ability to simply mirror or freeze updates to certain time frames. That way, you can do more comprehensive testing than just reading up on MacFixIt or VersionTracker to see whether anyone else has had an issue.

Before you install Software Update services, first make sure that you have enough hard drive space available. The updates will be stored in the /var/db/swupd directory, along with a number of catalog files in property list format, that instruct the client as to where to find updates. Because this includes all the updates from Apple that might be needed to make a system current, you will want at least 20GB of free space, although as time goes on and updates grow, then chances are you'll want to future-proof your server by having at least 30GB or 40GB of free space.

Provided you have enough free space, your first step is to enable the service. To get started with Software Update services, first open Server Admin, and click the name of the server on which you will be installing Software Update services. Then, click the Settings button in the Server Admin toolbar and the Services tab just below that. You'll find the Software Update service in the list; select the box to enable it. Once it's selected, click Save.

Configuring the Software Update Service

Now that you have enabled the service, you will want to configure and start it. By default, the settings for Software Update are to automatically mirror all Apple updates and essentially act as a proxy for the Apple Software Update service. If this is what you want to do, then you will have little more to configure. Simply click the Software Update entry in the SERVERS list, under the server that you are configuring. Then click the Settings button to see the available settings, as shown in Figure 21-1.

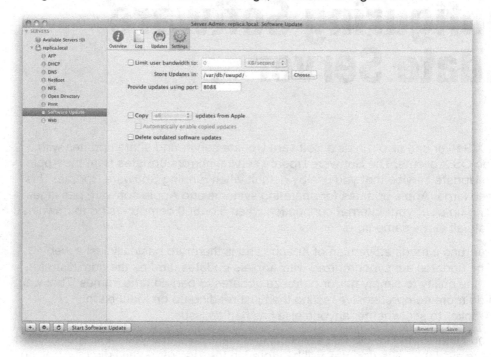

Figure 21-1. *Software Update settings*

For most environments, the default settings will suffice, but if you choose to customize the settings, they include the following:

- *Provide updates using port*: Defaults to 8088. This can be changed if 8088 is problematic for your environment.

- *Copy all updates from Apple*: Determines whether the server should automatically download updates from Apple.

- *Automatically enable copied updates*: Determines whether all files synchronized from Apple will be provided to clients (use this feature and the Copy all Updates from Apple feature together if you want to mirror all updates).

- *Delete outdated software updates*: Determines whether old software updates will be discarded.

■ *Limit user bandwidth for updates to*: Configures per-user bandwidth throttling for the Software Update service. As you can see, this check box is disabled by default, but if your server is bearing heavy bandwidth loads serving software updates, you can enable it to prevent multiple users' updates from bringing your server's network performance to a crawl. The number you select will depend on the number of systems on your network and the speed of your network, so you may need to play with the settings to find the right number.

Once you are satisfied with your settings, click the Start Software Update button toward the bottom of the Server Admin screen and wait. Keep in mind that the server is caching a large number of updates and will possibly take up to a few hours to refresh the updates that are available and be fully ready for client connectivity.

Managing Your Software Update Server

Now that you have installed the Software Update service, you'll want to get familiar with managing the server. Luckily, it's one of the easiest to manage, assuming everything is working as intended. The main thing that will need to be done is enabling and disabling updates. For example, if a Final Cut Pro update is released and renders half of your editing workstations useless, then you might want to deselect the Enable button for that update until you figure out a resolution.

To disable an update that may be problematic for your environment, you can click the Updates tab and deselect the Enable dialog box for the specified update. Or if you have chosen not to automatically enable copied updates, then you will be able to enable the updates using the check box shown in Figure 21–2 on a per-update basis. In our experience, the maturity of your imaging and patch management environment will dictate whether you decide to enable updates automatically.

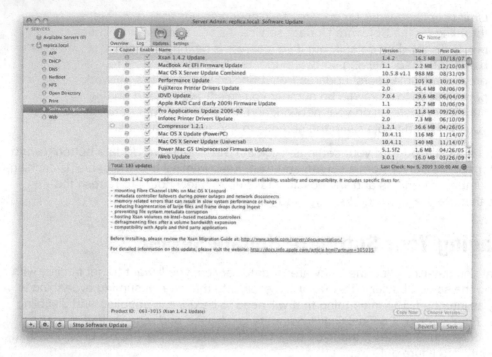

Figure 21–2. *Enabling and disabling software updates*

Configuring Updates for Clients

Once the server has been configured, you can move on to installing the clients. The easiest way to do this is to use Open Directory and configure Software Update as a managed preference. However, this is not a luxury everyone will have. As such, you can also manually configure each client to use the Software Update service that you have installed from the command line.

To deploy the Software Update services using Open Directory, open Workgroup Manager, and connect to an Open Directory server or the appropriate directory service; then click the user, computer, or computer group for which you would like to edit the Software Update information, and click Preferences in the Server Admin toolbar. On the preferences screen, you will see each of the items that you can configure for managed preferences, as shown in Figure 21–3.

Click the Software Update icon to open the managed preferences settings for Software Update, as shown in Figure 21–4. Here, type in the appropriate URL following the format below the box. Assuming that you have not customized the port you are using, this would be `http://server:8088/index.sucatalog,` where the server in the string is replaced with the name or IP address of your server. In the example in Figure 21–5, the server name is replica.krypted.com, and the port number has not been customized.

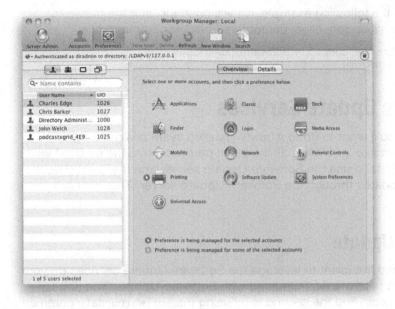

Figure 21-3. *Managed preferences*

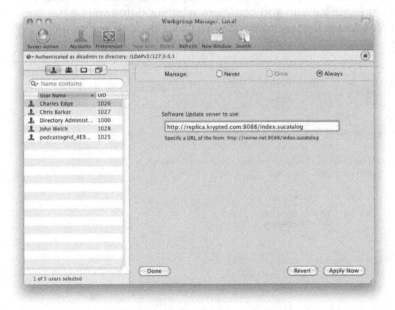

Figure 21-4. *Software Update managed preference settings*

Setting up a Software Update server if you are using Open Directory is a fairly simple task. But what if the system is not managed using Open Directory? That's when you would use a terminal command or use Apple Remote Desktop (ARD) to send out the command en masse. In the following example, we will continue with the previous example, but this time we'll update client computers from the command line:

defaults write /Library/Preferences/com.apple.SoftwareUpdate CatalogURL "http://replica.krypted.com:8088/";

Using Software Update Services

One of the first things you'll want to do to a newly installed system is run a fresh software update on it to make sure it has all the latest patches since the media it was installed from was created. To use the Software Update server, you first configure the client to run software updates through the Software Update server. Then you run software updates.

Using Software Update

Once you have configured the client to leverage the Software Update services on your Mac OS X Server, there are two ways to interact with Software Update. The first is through System Preferences, and the second is by using the softwareupdate command. To use System Preferences, open System Preferences from the Apple menu. Then click the Software Update pane, which will open the Software Update application. Here, you can see when the application was last run and configure when updates will be run and whether they will be downloaded in the background automatically for the client, as shown in Figure 21–5.

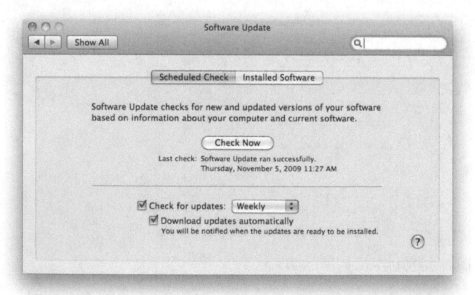

Figure 21–5. *Software Update pane*

When you click the Check Now button, Software Update will check for updates on the server. If updates are found, then you will be presented with a list on the client computer to install each update, as shown in Figure 21–6. Here, you can deselect updates to run them later or click the Install button toward the bottom of the screen to install them immediately. Additionally, you can select items and then use Ignore Update or Go to Apple Downloads Page in the Update menu to tell the system never to run the update or to go to the specific web page that explains the update in further, respectively.

NOTE: In the list, you will see an icon with a sideway triangle in it that indicates which updates require restarts.

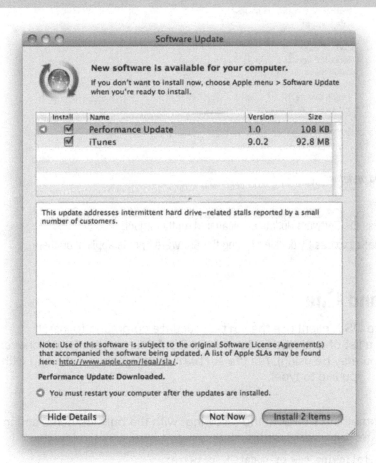

Figure 21–6. *Checking for updates*

Back on the Software Update screen, you can also click the Installed Software tab to see a listing of all the software updates that have run on that system, as shown in Figure

21–7. You can find each of these updates in /Library/Updates. Cached updates will be stored in the ~/Library/Caches/com.apple.SoftwareUpdate directory.

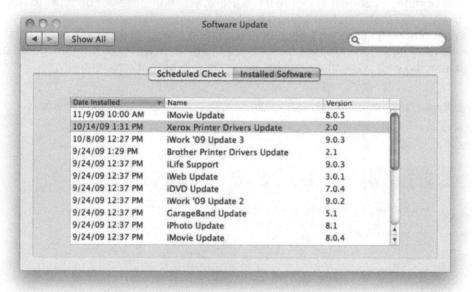

Figure 21–7. *Reviewing installed updates*

> **NOTE:** You can also access the Software Update application directly through /System/Library/CoreServices by double-clicking the Software Update application there.

Using the Command Line

Mac OS X Server and Mac OS X client use the softwareupdate command to install software updates. To get a list of available updates from the Apple servers (or whichever software update server you may be using), run the softwareupdate command along with the --l option (or --list if you like to type):

```
softwareupdate --l
```

The output should look something similar to the following, with the bulleted items acting as the label for each update:

```
Software Update found the following new or updated software:
   * iTunesX-9.0.2
        iTunes (9.0.2), 90630K [recommended]
   * HDDUpdate10-1.0
        Performance Update (1.0), 105K [recommended] [restart]
   * iMovie_805-8.0.5
        iMovie Update (8.0.5), 36076K [recommended]
```

To install the available updates, simply run the softwareupdate command along with the --all option:

```
softwareupdate --all
```

To install specific updates, you can use the softwareupdate command along with the --i option and the label for an update, which can be obtained using the --list option, as described previously:

```
softwareupdate --i <label>
```

For example, to install the iMovie update from earlier in this section, you would use the following command:

```
softwareupdate --i iMovie_805-8.0.5
```

Working with the Repository

You can also browse the update server directly by looking at the index.sucatalog file. This is a great step when troubleshooting service-related issues. If you are using the default port number of 8088, then the URL to do so would be http:// followed by the name or address of your Software Update server, followed by :8088/index.sucatalog. If the browser successfully opens the page, then it will appear as shown in Figure 21–8.

```
http://192.168.210.11:8088/index.sucatalog
```

Figure 21–8. *Viewing the catalog directly*

Using the Command Line

The command-line options for Software Update services are fairly rudimentary compared to some of the other services in Mac OS X Server. Nevertheless, sometimes you will want to use the command-line interface to control how the Software Update service operates.

Running the serveradmin Command

The serveradmin command is capable of starting and stopping the Software Update service and is capable of more granularly configuring settings. When running the serveradmin command, you will use the swupdate option to specify the service that you are working with as Software Update. A basic version of this would be to use the following command, which uses the status verb to determine whether the Software Update server is running:

```
serveradmin status swupdate
```

In addition, you can use serveradmin to look at the critical settings for the service by running it with the fullstatus option. For example, the following command will show the status of a server along with critical settings:

```
serveradmin fullstatus swupdate
```

As mentioned, querying for fullstatus indicates that the server is running along with a number of critical settings:

```
swupdate:state = "RUNNING"
swupdate:lastChecktime = 2009-11-09 03:00:00 -0600
swupdate:setStateVersion = 1
swupdate:syncServiceState = "RUNNING"
swupdate:readWriteSettingsVersion = 1
swupdate:logPaths:swupdateAccessLog = "/var/log/swupd/swupd_access_log"
swupdate:logPaths:swupdateErrorLog = "/var/log/swupd/swupd_error_log"
swupdate:logPaths:swupdateServiceLog = "/var/log/swupd/swupd_syncd_log"
swupdate:pluginVers = "10.6.58"
swupdate:checkError = no
swupdate:updatesDocRoot = "/var/db/swupd/"
swupdate:hostServiceState = "RUNNING"
swupdate:autoMirror = yes
swupdate:numOfEnabledPkg = 290
swupdate:servicePortsAreRestricted = "NO"
swupdate:numOfMirroredPkg = 290
swupdate:startTime = 2009-11-08 14:50:22 -0600
swupdate:autoMirrorOnlyNew = no
swupdate:autoEnable = yes
```

NOTE: You could also just run the serveradmin setting swupdate for a full listing of all settings, but because the output includes information on each update, it is far too verbose to include here.

Each of the previous settings can then be altered using the serveradmin command with the settings option, followed by the string with the new content. For example, to change the path of the service log to the same folder on a different drive called LOGS, you would use the following command:

```
serveradmin settings swupdate:logPaths:swupdateServiceLog =
"/volumes/LOGS/var/log/swupd/swupd_syncd_log"
```

The serveradmin command primarily gives you the ability to configure the service from the perspective of Mac OS X Server. However, keep in mind that the Software Update service is actually a vanilla implementation of Apache 1. Therefore, you can also edit the Apache configuration files directly or edit /etc/swupd/swupd.plist, as we will review in the next section of this chapter.

Multiple Software Update Servers

Software Update services allow your server to cache updates from Apple and then redistribute them to clients within your organization. This can greatly cut down on the amount of bandwidth consumed with new software patches. But if you have a very large distributed organization, you might want to have multiple Software Update servers daisy-chained together in a cascade to download updates from each other and provide updates to sets of clients (maybe they're geographically separated or you just have too many clients to provide updates to for just one server). Cascading the Software Update services would further conserve bandwidth in your environment if you have multiple Software Update servers.

Because Mac OS X Server 10.6 does not allow you to manage cascading software update servers in the GUI tools, you'll need to manually edit some configure files on the servers. Follow these steps:

1. Set up your first Software Update server. Let's say that you set it up as SUS1.krypted.com and set it to run on port 8080.

2. Set up your second server (let's call it SUS2.krypted.com) and edit the file /etc/swupd/swupd.plist with your favorite text editor or Terminal editor.

3. Locate the metaindexURL key (by default it's set to be swscan.apple.com). Change that key this value:

SUS1.krypted.com/content/meta/mirror-config-1.plist.

The second software update server will now pull its updates from the first one that you configured.

Summary

Distributing critical security and performance patches and updates to your systems is an important aspect of managing a network of Mac computers. It ensures that everybody is running the latest version of software. Mac OS X Server 10.6 lets you manage the distribution of these updates, preserving your bandwidth and allowing you to control which updates are distributed.

DHCP Option Numbers

DHCP uses what are referred to as *options* to extend the functionality. You can learn more about what the options can do for you in Chapter 6. They're identified numerically, and each number corresponds to the services that they provide.

0: Pad

1: Subnet Mask

3: Router

4: Time Server

5: Name Server

6: Domain Name Server

7: Log Server

8: Quotes Server

9: LPR Server

10: Impress Server

11: Resource Location Server

12: Host Name

13: Boot File Size

14: Merit Dump File

15: Domain Name

16: Swap Server

17: Root Path

18: Extensions Path

19: IP Forwarding

20: WAN Source Routing

21: Policy Filter

22: Maximum Datagram Reassembly Size

23: Default IP Time-to-Live

24: Path MTU Aging Timeout

25: Path MTU Plateau Table

26: Interface MTU Size

27: All Subnets are Local

28: Broadcast Address

29: Perform Mask Discovery

30: Mask Supplier

31: Perform Router Discovery

32: Router Solicitation Address

33: Static Routing Table

34: Trailer Encapsulation

35: ARP Cache Timeout

36: Ethernet Encapsulation

37: Default TCP TTL

38: TCP Keep-Alive Interval

39: TCP Keep-Alive Garbage

40: Network Information Service Domain

41: Network Information Servers

42: NTP Servers

43: Vendor-Specific Information

44: NetBIOS Over TCP/IP Name Server

45: NetBIOS Over TCP/IP Datagram Distribution Server

46: NetBIOS Over TCP/IP Node Type

47: NetBIOS Over TCP/IP Scope

48: X Window System Font Server

49: X Window System Display Manager

50: Requested IP Address

51: IP Address Lease Time

52: Option Overload

53: DHCP Message Type

54: Server Identifier

55: Parameter Request List

56: Error Message

57: Maximum DHCP Message Size

58: Renew Time Value

59: Rebinding Time Value

60: Class-Identifier

61: Client-Identifier

62: NetWare Over IP Domain Name

63: NetWare Over IP Information

64: Network Information Service Domain

65: Network Information Service Servers

66: TFTP Server Name

67: Bootfile Name

68: Mobile IP Home Agent

69: Simple Mail Transport Protocol Server

70: Post Office Protocol Server

71: Network News Transport Protocol Server

72: Default World Wide Web Server

73: Default Finger Server

74: Default Internet Relay Chat Server

77: User Class Information

78: SLP Directory Agent

79: SLP Service Scope

80: Rapid Commit

81: Fully Qualified Domain Name

82: Relay Agent Information

83: Internet Storage Name Service

85: NDS Servers

86: NDS Tree Name

87: NDS Context

88: BCMCS Controller Domain Name List

89: BCMCS Controller IPv4 Address List

90: Authentication

91: Client Last Transaction Time

92: Associated IP

93: Client System Architecture Type

94: Client Network Interface Identifier

95: LDAP, Lightweight Directory Access Protocol

97: Client Machine Identifier

98: Open Group User Authentication

100: IEEE 1003.1 TZ String

101 : Reference to the TZ Database

112 : NetInfo Parent Server Address

113 : NetInfo Parent Server Tag

114: URL

116: Autoconfigure

117: Name Service Search

118: Subnet Selection

119: DNS Domain Search List

120: SIP Servers DHCP Option

121: Classless Static Route Option

123: GeoConfiguration

124: Vendor-Identifying Vendor Class

125: Vendor-Identifying Vendor Specific

128: TFPT Server IP Address

129: Call Server IP Address

130: Discrimination String

131: Remote Statistics Server IP Address

132: 802.1P VLAN ID

133: 802.1Q L2 Priority

134: Diffserv Code Point

135: HTTP Proxy for Phone-Specific Applications

136: PANA Authentication Agent

139: IPv4 MoS

140: IPv4 Fully Qualified Domain Name MoS

150: TFTP Server Address

176: IP Telephone

220: Subnet Allocation

221: Virtual Subnet Selection

252: Proxy Autodiscovery

254: Private Use

255: End

Taking It to the Next Level

We hope that by the time you finish this book you're a first-class Mac OS X Server administrator. But it would be naïve of us to think that you won't need to know anything else. If you want to take your skills with Mac OS X Server to the next level, you'll be able to find a lot of resources that you can look to for assistance. Perhaps the most important resource is Apple. Apple has posted the documentation for Snow Leopard Server at http://www.apple.com/server/macosx/resources/documentation.html.

Books

The Apress enterprise Mac bookshelf begins with this book, but it also includes the following books:

- *Enterprise Mac Administrators Guide*

- *Foundations of Mac OS X Snow Leopard Security*

- *iPhone for Work: Increasing Productivity for Busy Professionals*

Courses

Apple courses are a more costly option than reading books, but many prefer instructor-led training to the self-paced style of learning of books. The official Apple courseware is designed for, and specific to, Mac OS X Server and Mac OS X–based technologies. You can find out more about Apple training options at http://training.apple.com.

These courses are developed in partnership with Peachpit Press. For those who do not have the resources to attend the courses, there are the Apple Authorized training guides:

- *Apple Training Series: Mac OS X Support Essentials v10.6: A Guide to Supporting and Troubleshooting Mac OS X v10.6 Snow Leopard*

- *Apple Training Series: Mac OS X Server Essentials v10.6: A Guide to Using and Supporting Mac OS X Server v10.6*

- *Apple Training Series: Mac OS X Directory Services v10.6: A Guide to Configuring Directory Services on Mac OS X and Mac OS X Server v10.6*

- *Apple Training Series: Mac OS X Security and Mobility v10.6*

- *Apple Training Series: Mac OS X Deployment v10.6: A Guide to Deploying and Maintaining Mac OS X and Mac OS X Software*

Mailing Lists

Mailing lists are another way of finding answers to technical questions that you encounter in your journey to becoming part of the Mac OS X Server elite. These include the following:

- MacEnterprise, found at `http://macenterprise.org`

- Apple lists, found at `http://lists.apple.com`

Web Sites

Finally, a number of web sites are dedicated to Mac OS X Server and Mac-centric networking issues. These include the following:

- `http://afp548.com`

- `http://macenterprise.org`

- `http://krypted.com`

- `http://bynkii.com`

- `http://318.com/techjournal`

Index

N

X